Health
Economics
and Policy

7TH EDITION

James W. Henderson

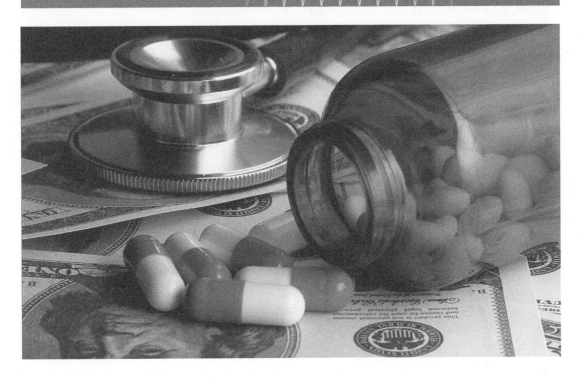

CENGAGE

Australia • Brazil • Mexico • Singapore • United Kingdom • United States

**Health Economics and Policy,
Seventh Edition**
James W. Henderson

Senior Vice President: Erin Joyner

Product Director: Jason Fremder

Product Manager: Christopher Rader

Senior Project Manager: Julie Dierig

Content Developer: Kayci Wyatt, MPS

Executive Assistant: Denisse
   Zavala-Rosales

Associate Marketing Manager:
   John Carey

Manufacturing Planner: Kevin Kluck

Production Management and
   Composition: Lumina Datamatics, Inc.

Sr. Art Director: Michelle Kunkler

Cover Image: lenetstan/Shutterstock.com

Intellectual Property

   Analyst: Jennifer Bowes

   Project Manager: Reba Frederics

For product information and technology assistance, contact us at
Cengage Learning Customer & Sales Support, 1-800-354-9706

For permission to use material from this text or product,
submit all requests online at **www.cengage.com/permissions**
Further permissions questions can be emailed to
permissionrequest@cengage.com

Library of Congress Control Number: 2017947973

ISBN-13: 978-1-337-10675-7

Cengage Learning
20 Channel Center Street
Boston, MA 02210
USA

Cengage Learning is a leading provider of customized learning solutions with employees residing in nearly 40 different countries and sales in more than 125 countries around the world. Find your local representative at **www.cengage.com.**

Cengage Learning products are represented in Canada by Nelson Education, Ltd.

To learn more about Cengage Learning Solutions, visit **www.cengage.com**

Purchase any of our products at your local college store or at our preferred online store **www.cengagebrain.com**

Printed in the United States of America
Print Number: 04   Print Year: 2019

Brief Contents

Contents

CHAPTER 10

PART 4   Public Policy in Medical Care Delivery

CHAPTER 16
Lessons for Public Policy 474

Preface

On January 20, 2017, Donald Trump took the oath of office and became the 45th president of the United States. One of his campaign promises was to repeal the Affordable Care Act and replace it with a plan more compatible with the market orientation of rest of the U.S. economy. Initial attempts to pass legislation failed to gain enough support in the House of Representatives to reach the floor for a vote. Undeterred, Republicans are confident they can pass a bill that will improve the way health care is delivered and financed.

A firm understanding of the impact of health care policy on the costs and consequences of health care delivery and finance is essential for a clear understanding of the impact of the proposed changes in health care policy. My purpose in writing this text is to provide the reader with the economic background to understand and analyze the national dialogue on health care issues. The text's primary goals are to enable readers to:

- recognize the relevance of economics to health care issues.
- apply economic reasoning to understand the challenges of delivering health care in a cost-effective way.
- understand the mechanisms of health care delivery in the United States within broad social, political, and economic contexts.
- explore the changing nature of health and medical care and its implications for medical practice, medical education and research, and health policy.
- analyze public policy in health and medical care from an economic perspective.

To accomplish these goals, the book's 16 chapters are organized into four parts.

Part One: The Relevance of Economics in Health and Medical Care

The text begins with a basic overview of the health care industry with emphasis on the economic issues that affect medical care delivery and finance. Chapter 1 examines the nature of the economic problem as it pertains to health care. Chapter 2 demonstrates the usefulness of economics in understanding medical care issues—including matters of life, death, disability, and suffering. Chapter 3 examines problems encountered in applying standard economic models to the study of health care markets. Chapter 4 introduces the readers to the tools of economic evaluation and their application to medical care with special emphasis on cost-effectiveness analysis, the preferred technique among most health economists.

Technical appendices, intended for use by more advanced students, appear at the end of each of the first three chapters. Appendix 1A provides an overview of the challenges of measuring medical price inflation using the medical care price index. Appendix 2A serves as a primer on graphing, while 2B introduces important statistical tools used in empirical studies. The two appendices at the end of Chapter 3 present the neoclassical models of consumer choice and production.

Part Two: Demand-Side Considerations

Part 2 examines the demand side of the market. Chapter 5 identifies and describes various factors that influence the demands for health and health care. It explores and explains observed patterns in the quality and price of medical care. Chapter 6 discusses the basic dimensions of population health and the risk factors leading the differences in health outcomes across demographic groups. Chapter 7 assesses the market for health insurance, comparing and contrasting the private and social insurance models. Chapter 8 evaluates the efficiency of alternative health care delivery systems in containing medical care costs. It also describes an increasingly popular coverage option, the consumer-directed health plan that combines a high-deductible health insurance policy accompanied by a health savings account to cover out-of-pocket expenses.

Part Three: Supply-Side Considerations

Part 3 addresses the supply side of the health care market. Chapter 9 describes the market for health care practitioners and the effect of recent changes in the health care sector on their behavior. Brief discussions of the markets for nurses and for dentists are also included. Chapter 10 summarizes major theories of hospital behavior and describes the role of not-for-profit hospitals in the U.S. health care industry. The U.S. pharmaceutical industry and the challenges facing drug and device innovators and their target markets are the focus of Chapter 11.

Part Four: Public Policy in Medical Care Delivery

The text's final chapters squarely address health policy and its economic implications. Chapter 12 formally introduces Medicare and examines its economic impact on medical care delivery. The appendix to that chapter addresses the implications of an aging population. Chapter 13 examines the other major health care entitlement program, Medicaid. The appendix to Chapter 13 provides a brief discussion of the challenges of making projections with economic data. Chapter 14 summarizes important characteristics of medical care delivery systems in six major developed nations—Canada, France, Germany, Japan, Switzerland, and the United Kingdom. Chapter 15 summarizes major features of the Affordable Care Act and describes the current health care reform initiatives being considered by Congress. Finally, Chapter 16 restates the major lessons we can learn from the economic approach to public policy.

Pedagogical Features

This text's ultimate focus is on public policy. The technical tools of economics are important, but they are not ends to themselves. Instead, the approach uses theory as a way of preparing students to address policy questions.

Each chapter begins with a brief policy issue related to the chapter's focus. Also included are a number of special features called "Issues in Medical Care Delivery." They summarize important studies in medical research, epidemiology, public health, and other fields as they relate to the economics of health care delivery. Another feature found at the conclusion of each chapter is a "Profile" of an individual who has made a significant contribution to the field of health economics. Many profiled individuals are economists; some are physicians; all have had a profound impact on how we view health, health economics, and health policy.

The "Back of the Envelope" features show the economic way of thinking, using graphs. These and similar graphical presentations are frequently used by economists in informal settings. They might represent scribbles on the back of an old envelope used to make a point during lunch with colleagues. Topics include: the valuation of a life, how to calculate a rate of return, the notion of elasticity, the welfare implications of subsidies, the impact of employer mandates, cost-benefit calculations, and the cost-effectiveness of disease prevention, among many others. Developing the ability to use models in this way is an important goal of this book.

Chapter 1 introduces 10 key economic concepts that serve as unifying themes throughout the book. As you read, you will notice the key icon in the margin reminding you that the adjacent material is related to that key concept. Other marginal notations include definitions of key words and phrases, recommended websites where you can go for additional information, and policy issues related to the reading.

New in the Seventh Edition

The most notable change to the seventh edition is the addition of Applied Micro Methods in each chapter. One of the major challenges in using observational data in social science and medical research is how to interpret empirical results. Are linkages between variables causal or merely correlational? It is important to know the difference when reading empirical research. Most chapters have at least one extended abstract of a paper that uses one of the identification strategies popular in the literature: propensity score matching, synthetic control, difference-in-differences, and instrumental variables.

New discussions on Arrow's critique of health care markets in Chapter 1 and a more formal presentation of Baumol's cost disease in Chapter 3 set the tone for future discussions of market relevance. Chapter 6 provides a new discussion of the basic dimensions of population health.

The chapters in Part 4 have been reorganized to focus on the environment as it exists under the Affordable Care Act and the uncertainty introduced by attempts to repeal and replace it. Medicare reform and Medicaid expansion are discussed more fully. The health systems discussion in Chapter 14 expands on the metrics used to distinguish the characteristics and quality indicators across countries.

The biggest challenge manifests itself in Chapter 15. Focusing on the features, costs, and consequences of the Affordable Care Act and the attempt to repeal and replace it is a daunting task—the target is constantly moving and evolving. By the time you read this chapter there will be additional changes. At some risk, I include my predictions on what the changes will look like. As you read the book, develop your own list of predictions. When it is all over, we can compare notes.

Level

Health Economics and Policy is written with the non-economics major in mind but contains enough economic content to challenge economics majors. My undergraduate class at Baylor University is composed of both economics majors and premedical students, most of whom have little or no economics background. There are usually a number of other business majors, many of whom are interested in studying health care administration in the future. I also use this text in a required graduate course for MBA students who are concentrating in health care administration. All these students are good thinkers and most have done well despite having had no previous economics coursework.

The text is appropriate for an introductory health economics course offered in an economics department, in a health care administration graduate program, or in a school of public health, college of medicine, or school of nursing or pharmacy.

Supplementary Items

An Instructor's Manual provides support to instructors who adopt *Health Economics and Policy*, 7th edition. The manual includes suggested answers to the end-of-chapter questions, lecture suggestions, and test questions. In my teachings of health economics I have improved student engagement and comprehension of concepts by providing television and movie clips to introduce discussion topics in my class. I've had great success with this and have included a chapter break out of what I use from both TV and movie clips in my classroom. These are only suggestions and we are NOT offering any video or movie clips to accompany the text. If you are interested in possibly implementing these in your class, I have provided clear instructions on using these clips.

The text's website contains resources for both students and instructors. You can access the website using www.cengagebrain.com. The site also provides access to Economic Applications, a feature that includes EconNews articles, EconData links, and EconDebates. Students may access MindTap, a platform that enables professors to use preloaded and organized MindTap materials or provide custom content. Additionally, imbedded content may include Open Educational Resources and YouTube.

Acknowledgments

As the sole author of this book, I take full responsibility for its contents. Nevertheless, a single individual could not complete a project of this magnitude. I owe a great deal to my Baylor University colleagues who have sharpened my focus and challenged my inconsistencies. A number of capable research assistants have contributed to my efforts. Most notably, I would like to thank past graduate assistants who have worked on this project in one of its editions. Most recently, Meiqing Ren has provided invaluable assistance in preparing tables and artwork for the PowerPoint slides that accompany the text.

Instructors from across the country have reviewed the manuscript for this and previous editions. Their comments and suggestions have been important to me, and the book is better because of their efforts.

I am also grateful to the hundreds of Baylor University students who used this book in its first six editions and even earlier in manuscript form. Their comments have proven invaluable in developing an integrated framework for discussing health care issues.

Of course, I could never have completed the project without the support of my wife and family. Thank you, Betsy for your support and understanding over the past 20 years since the publication of the first edition. As my extended family grows, it does not get easier. Three grandchildren and the promise of more to come merely increases the pressures on my time. However, they provide me with a renewed interest in reevaluating my position of health care policy. Thanks to you all.

James W. Henderson

CHAPTER 1

U.S. Medical Care: An Uncertain Future

ISSUES IN MEDICAL CARE DELIVERY

THE PATIENT PROTECTION AND AFFORDABLE CARE ACT OF 2010

If you are like many who follow the health care reform debate, you grow weary of the rhetoric and find yourself disillusioned by the acrimony it produces. Passed without a single Republican vote, President Barack Obama signed the Patient Protection and Affordable Care Act (ACA) into law by the United States on March 23, 2010. Despite predictions that support for the plan would increase as Americans became familiar with its details, the number favoring the bill steadily declined throughout the year. By the November 2010 midterm elections, tracking polls indicated that nearly 60 percent of voters opposed the measure and actually favored its repeal (Rasmussen, 2010). Since the 2010 elections, the ACA's popularity has not improved substantially—30 percent would like to see the legislation repealed entirely, 56 percent prefer marginal improvements be made, and only 12 percent say to leave it alone (Rasmussen, 2017).

The negative public perception is really quite puzzling because the act actually addresses many of the concerns of Americans—covering the uninsured, subsidizing the purchase of insurance to make it more affordable, and allowing those with preexisting conditions to purchase insurance at standard premiums. Nevertheless, the plan also has its unintended consequences. The new insurance pooling requirements resulted in significantly higher premiums for the young and healthy in an effort to subsidize the elderly and those with preexisting conditions. With the addition of 20 million newly insured, access to care, especially primary care, is more difficult for many.

American voters not only elected a Republican president in 2016 but also left the Grand Old Party (GOP) in control of both houses of Congress. Instead of talking about expanding the ACA, we are in the middle of a discussion on how to change it: repeal, replace, delay, and repair. What is it going to be? The Republicans have a clear path to repeal much of the ACA but must rally around a single plan for replacing it. With all the **uncertainty**, one thing is certain: The debate is just now heating up. There is still plenty of work to do.

POLICY ISSUE
How can we best deal with the trade-off between quality and access on the one hand and affordability on the other?

POLICY ISSUE
Most privately insured Americans receive health insurance coverage through their employer, while those without insurance rely on public assistance and charity care.

uncertainty A state where multiple outcomes are possible but the likelihood of any one outcome is not known.

Medicare Health insurance for the elderly provided under an amendment to the Social Security Act.

Medicaid Health insurance for the poor financed jointly by the federal government and the states.

Public concern over the future of health care has not changed with the passage of health care reform legislation. Americans still worry about three broad issues: quality, access, and affordability (what some call the "triple aim"). Limited access for the uninsured[1] and the uncertainty of continued access for those with insurance are key considerations as policymakers deliberate reform options. High and rising spending (with the associated increases in premiums) continues to challenge employers' ability to offer group insurance to their employees and focuses attention on the growing burden of the two major government health care programs—**Medicare** and **Medicaid**. An additional concern is whether the spending increases associated with expanded access will have a negative effect on the quality of care.

This chapter will first examine the historical development of the medical care delivery system in the United States: the reasons for high and rising spending and the major changes in medical care delivery since the end of the Second World War. We will then develop a framework for the study of health economics. Finally, we will introduce 10 key economic concepts that will serve as unifying themes for our study of health care.

Historical Developments in the Delivery of Medical Care

premium A periodic payment required to purchase an insurance policy.

gross domestic product (GDP) The monetary value of the goods and services produced in a country during a given time period, usually a year.

No matter where a health care discussion begins, the topic of conversation soon turns to the issue of affordability. Employees and employers complain about high **premiums**, patients and providers note high treatment costs, and policymakers lament high and rising spending. Each perspective presents a different aspect of the same problem. In 2016, the average cost of a health insurance policy was $18,142 for a family and $6,435 for an individual (Kaiser Family Foundation, 2016). The average cost per hospital stay was almost $10,000, and Americans spent over $3.2 trillion on health care—17.8 percent of the **gross domestic product (GDP)**.

The major concern over health care spending is not that it is high; the concern is that the steady upward spiral does not seem to have an end to it. Government projections estimate that medical care spending will continue its rise, topping $5.5 trillion by 2025—over 19.9 percent of GDP (Keehan et al., 2017). Although economic theory has yet to determine what the optimal percentage ought to be, the United States spends more on medical care by virtually every measure than any other country in the world. What does it mean then to spend 8, 10, or 16 percent of a country's GDP on medical care? More importantly, should the amount spent on medical care be a concern to policymakers?

★ **POLICY ISSUE**

How many years does it take to constitute a trend?

★ **POLICY ISSUE**

What is the optimal percentage of GDP that a country should spend on health care? Is a continuously growing percentage affordable?

Postwar Experience

HTTP://
The National Institutes of Health provides an overview of its programs and activities at http://www.nih.gov.

Table 1.1 summarizes medical care spending in the United States over the post-World War II period. The four summary measures provide evidence that medical care spending is high and growing. During the decade of the 1950s, total spending increased at a rate of 8 percent per year. Total spending at the beginning of the decade was $12.7 billion, doubling by its end. Medical care spending as a percent of GDP increased from 4.5 to 5.0 percent, and per capita medical care spending increased from $82 in 1950 to $146 ten years later.

The 1960s was the first of three decades characterized by rapid growth in medical care spending. The annual compound rate of growth was 11.5 percent between 1960 and 1990. At the beginning of that 30-year period, medical care spending was $27.2 billion, 5.0 percent of GDP, and $146 per capita. By 1990, it stood at $721.4 billion, 12.1 percent of GDP, and $2,854 per capita. The primary factors contributing to growth in spending during

---

[1]The Emergency Medical Treatment and Active Labor Act (EMTALA) passed in 1985 made it illegal for hospital emergency departments to deny care to anyone requesting care. Turning away patients because of lack of health insurance is not an option.

TABLE 1.1 U. S. HEALTH CARE SPENDING SUMMARY MEASURES, VARIOUS YEARS

Year	Total spending (in billions)	Percent change[1]	Percent of GDP	Per capita spending
1950	$ 12.7	–	4.5	$ 82
1960	27.2	7.9	5.0	146
1970	74.6	10.6	6.9	354
1980	255.3	13.1	8.9	1,108
1990	721.4	10.9	12.1	2,854
2000	1,369.7	6.6	13.3	4,857
2005	2,035.4	8.1	15.5	6,856
2010	2,595.7	5.0	17.3	8,402
2011	2,696.6	3.9	17.4	8,665
2012	2,799.0	3.8	17.4	8,927
2013	2,877.6	2.8	17.2	9,110
2014	3,029.3	5.3	17.4	9,515
2015	3,205.6	5.8	17.8	9,990
2018[2]	3,785.5	5.7	18.1	11,499
2024[2]	5,425.1	6.2	19.6	15,618

Source: Centers for Medicare and Medicaid Services (CMS) website, *http://www.cms.hhs.gov/NationalHealthExpendData/ 02_NationalHealthAccountsHistorical.asp#TopOfPage*. Accessed February 1, 2017; and Keehan et al., "National Health Expenditure Projections, 2015–2025," *Health Affairs* 35(8), August 2016, 1522–1531.
[1] Annual rate of change from the previous year listed.
[2] Projected.

cost shifting The practice of charging higher prices to one group of patients, usually those with health insurance, in order to provide free care to the uninsured or discounted care to those served by Medicare and Medicaid.

Employee Retirement Income Security Act (ERISA) Federal legislation that sets minimum standards on employee benefit plans, such as pension, health insurance, and disability. The law also protects employers from certain state regulations. For example, states are not allowed to regulate self-insured plans and cannot mandate that employers provide health insurance to their employees.

self-insurance A group practice of not buying health insurance but setting aside funds to cover the projected losses incurred by members of the group.

this period include the expansion of federal government involvement in the payment for medical care services for specific groups—Medicare for the elderly and Medicaid for the indigent—and **cost shifting** by providers to subsidize care for those without insurance.

Rapid advancement in medical technology and the subsequent cost-containment strategies that emphasized regulation and planning characterized the 1970s. The federal government became a major force in biomedical research and development with the expansion of the National Institutes of Health. Technological advances that included open-heart surgery, organ transplantation, various types of imaging, and the ability to preserve and prolong life in the intensive care unit increased public awareness of medicine and served as a major cost driver. While it all seemed justifiable, this emphasis on advanced technologies precipitated a growing concern over cost issues.

Federal legislation, specifically the National Health Planning Act of 1974, created a network of government planning agencies to control medical care costs. In addition, states passed certificate-of-need (CON) laws to limit the growth in hospital investment in capital improvements and technology. Even a brief national experiment with wage and price controls during the Nixon presidency did little to curb the growth in medical care costs and spending.

Possibly the most significant piece of legislation affecting health care was not viewed as particularly significant at the time. Passed to regulate the corporate use of pension funds, the **Employee Retirement Income Security Act (ERISA)** of 1974 exempted self-insured health plans from state-level health insurance regulations. The passage of ERISA provided an incentive for employers to switch to **self-insurance**. Today, companies who self-insure employ more than two-thirds all workers who participate in group health insurance plans.

entitlement program
Government assistance programs where eligibility is determined by a specified criterion, such as age, health status, and level of income. These programs include Social Security, Medicare, Medicaid, Temporary Assistance for Needy Families (TANF), and many more.

prospective payment
Payment determined prior to the provision of services. A feature of many managed care organizations that base payment on capitation.

capitation A payment method providing a fixed, per capita payment to providers for a specified medical benefits package. Providers are required to treat a well-defined population for a fixed sum of money, paid in advance, without regard to the number or nature of the services provided to each person.

diagnosis-related group A patient classification scheme based on certain demographic, diagnostic, and therapeutic characteristics developed by Medicare and used to compensate hospitals.

relative-value scale
An index that assigns weights to various medical services used to determine the relative fees assigned to them.

managed care A delivery system that originally integrated the financing and provision of medical care in one organization. Now the term encompasses different arrangements designed to coordinate services and control costs.

The 1980s ushered in a change in direction in health care policy, resulting in a shift away from regulation and planning and toward a greater reliance on market forces. A president who wanted to lower taxes and a Congress that refused to cut spending characterized the era. Federal budget deficits grew dramatically. By the end of the decade, those areas of the budget in which spending was mandated—the **entitlement programs** including Medicare and Medicaid—grew seemingly without limit and came under intense pressure to reduce their rate of growth. During this period, the introduction of alternative payment schemes and delivery systems was significant. **Prospective payment**, **capitation**, the use of **diagnosis-related groups** (DRGs) to pay hospitals, and the introduction of a **relative-value scale** (RVS) to pay physicians are all examples of these changes. Health maintenance organizations, preferred provider organizations, and other systems of **managed care** became more common.

The 1990s saw a moderation in the growth in spending. Most experts attribute at least part of the slowdown to the movement of patients into managed care. The annual percentage increase in nominal spending fell from 15.9 percent in 1981 to around 5.0 percent in the mid-1990s. A steady increase in growth rates resulted in an annual change of 9.1 percent in 2002. The expansion of medical care spending as a percentage of GDP remained between 13.0 and 14.0 percent until 2001, when it nudged above 14 percent for the first time.

The federal government has taken more of an activist role in health care policy in the past decade. Although an attempt to restructure the health care system failed in 1994, important legislation was enacted that was expected to improve access to care. At the federal level, Congress established the Health Insurance Portability and Accountability Act (HIPPA) of 1996 providing insurance portability to individuals with health insurance. In 1997, Congress passed the Children's Health Insurance Program (CHIP), the largest expansion of a federal medical program since its original enactment. Moreover, in late 2003, Congress voted to expand the coverage for outpatient prescription drugs within the Medicare program.

Over the last decade, spending growth has actually slowed from over 9 percent in 2002 to less than 3 percent in 2013. A Kaiser Family Foundation study (2013) attributed 77 percent of that decline to the overall slowdown in the economy resulting from the 2007–2009 recession. However, that does not explain the experience prior to the recession. Cutler and Sahni (2013) provide an alternative explanation in a study where they estimated that only 37 percent of the overall decline was due to the recession and 8 percent to the decline in private insurance coverage. Ryu et al. (2013) attribute 20 percent of the decline to changes in benefit design leading to increased cost sharing and more cost conscious decision-making for the insured. Other factors, such as the slower adoption of new technology and improvements in provider efficiency, contributed to the results. Continuation of these trends (all predating the full implementation of the ACA) could have a major impact on the economy in the next decade.

Concern over High and Rising Spending

There is widespread consensus that the current path of health care spending growth is unsustainable. Even with the changes resulting from passage of the ACA, success in achieving the triple aim of access, affordability, and quality will be elusive. What are the obstacles? Why is success so elusive?

Improvements in affordability and access will remain elusive until we accept certain realities about the problem. In a series of articles, Fuchs (2008, 2013, 2014) shared his insights into the scope of the challenge.

1. Growth in health care spending outpaces growth in the rest of the economy. In the past 40 years, health care spending has grown at an annual compound rate of

FIGURE 1.1

Growth in Health Care Expenditures and GDP (less heath care), in real terms, 1971–2016

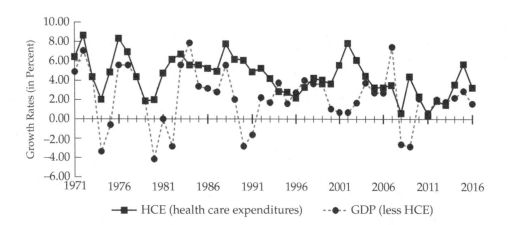

8.0 percent compared to GDP (less health care) that grew at only 5.7 percent per year (see Figure 1.1). Every year health care spending growth on average exceeded GDP growth by over 2 percentage points. It is no wonder that health care represents a larger share of the economy today than in 1976. If the trend continues, the health care sector will continue to absorb an ever-increasing share of GDP in the future.

2. A lot of the increased spending is the result of supply side advances in medicine and the appetite of Americans to consume a more expensive mix of health care services. More specialists, improved diagnostic tools, advances in surgical interventions, improved therapies, and pharmaceuticals that are more effective represent quality improvements that allow us to live longer and better. Newhouse (1993), Ginsburg (2004), and the Congressional Budget Office (2010) have examined the impact of technology growth on spending and conclude that about one-half of the increase in medical spending is due to the introduction of new technology. Few are suggesting that we forego these improvements to save money.

3. Another demand-side factor leading to more spending is the prevalence of health problems associated with obesity and other lifestyle conditions, and the onset of diseases related to an aging population. The prevalence of unhealthy lifestyles is another reason for increased health care spending. Poor nutrition, too many calories, and too much fat, along with a lack of exercise have led to an alarming increase in the proportion of the population that is overweight and obese. Obesity-related conditions may be responsible for as much as 27 percent of inflation adjusted per capita medical expenditures in the United States (Thorpe et al., 2004).

4. There is a link between high spending and relatively high input prices. Prices for prescription drugs are about 30 percent higher in the United States than the Organization for Economic Cooperation and Development (OECD) average; U.S. physicians earn considerably higher salaries that their foreign counterparts; and hospitals charge substantially more for their services than is typically charged abroad.

5. Changes in spending growth are often accompanied by developments in the macro economy (economic growth and job creation). Historically, downturns in the economy occur simultaneously with a slowing in the rate of growth in health care spending (evidenced by the decline in spending growth during downturns in the economy).

6. Insurance coverage has increased dramatically over the past four decades. Insurance, both public and private, covered 62.7 percent of all medical spending in 1970. By 2015, almost 90 percent of all medical care was purchased through third-party insurance. As a result, the percentage paid out of pocket has fallen from 37.3 percent

of total spending to 10.5 percent over that same period. To determine the extent that increased insurance coverage contributes to overall spending, Finkelstein (2007) examined how the introduction of Medicare in 1965 affected spending by the elderly. She calculated that the overall increase in insurance coverage might be responsible for as much as one-half of the increase in per capita spending from 1950 to 1990.

7. Attributing the growth in spending to waste, fraud, and abuse may be the political scapegoat, but undoubtedly, many of the commonly cited administrative problems result in wasteful spending (Fuchs, 2014). Two commonly cited problems that lead to wasteful spending are billing fraud and **defensive medicine**. The National Health Care Anti-Fraud Association estimates that each year about 3 percent of health care spending is lost to fraud (Iglehart, 2009). The improper payment rate in the government-run Medicaid program may be as high as 10.5 percent of total spending (federal share only). The Medicare fraud rate is around 8.5 percent.

defensive medicine
Medical services that have little or no medical benefit; their provision is simply to reduce the risk of being sued.

The fear of litigation creates an atmosphere where physicians may perform unnecessary tests and procedures to reduce the risk of a malpractice claim. Roberts and Hoch (2009) estimate that 2–10 percent of health care spending is due to physicians practicing defensive medicine.

Undoubtedly, all these factors contribute in one way or the other to the overall inefficiencies in health care delivery and finance. Debate over the relative contributions of these factors has contributed to the political divide on the necessary steps to address the spending problem. One thing is certain: To control spending, we must spend our health care dollars efficiently. Until everyone—patient, provider, and payer—has the incentive to spend money wisely, the problem will remain.

ISSUES IN MEDICAL CARE DELIVERY

SPENDING SOMEBODY ELSE'S MONEY

A *Wall Street Journal* article provides an interesting example of how spending someone else's money distorts the decision-making process. A 70-year-old man suffering from a ruptured abdominal aortic aneurysm was admitted to the hospital. After several weeks in the intensive care unit—with all the modern technology that goes with it—and a three-month stay in the hospital, the bill approached $275,000, none paid out of pocket by the patient. The man's physician determined that his poor eating habits, caused by poorly fitting dentures, were contributing to his slow recovery. He requested that the hospital dentist perform the necessary adjustments. Later, the doctor discovered that the man had not allowed the dentist to adjust the dentures. When asked the reason, the man replied, "$75 is a lot of money." It seems that Medicare would not pay for the adjustment, so it would have been an out-of-pocket expenditure for the patient.

third-party payers
A health insurance arrangement where the individual, or an agent of the individual, pays a set premium to a third party (an insurance company, managed care organization, or the government), which in turn pays for health care services.

When you are spending somebody else's money, $275,000 does not seem like a lot. Nevertheless, when you are spending your own money, $75 is a lot. Our reliance on a third-party payment system is the major institutional feature contributing to rising costs and increased spending. Cost-conscious consumers have little or no role in a system dominated by **third-party payers**.

Source: James P. Weaver, "The Best Care Other People's Money Can Buy," *Wall Street Journal*, November 19, 1992, A14.

Changes in Medical Care Delivery

The last 30 years have witnessed major changes that have affected medical care delivery and costs. The shift from private to public sector financing, the shift from out-of-pocket spending to third-party payment, the changes in hospital usage and pricing, and the growth in managed care have all had profound effects on medical care delivery and pricing.

Shift from Private to Public Financing   Quite possibly, the single most important change affecting medical care delivery has been the shift from private to public sector financing. Referring to Table 1.2, the private sector was responsible for $3 of every $4 spent in the industry in 1960. The government role in financing was modest, standing at less than 25 cents out of every medical care dollar. The introduction of Medicare and Medicaid in the mid-1960s resulted in an increase in the government's share of spending to almost 40 percent within 10 years. Since then government's total share has risen to about half of total spending, while the federal share has more than tripled, from 10 percent in 1960 to approximately 40 percent in 2015. This translates into a federal budgetary obligation that has grown from $2.9 billion to almost $1 trillion in five decades. As the federal share has exploded, the share of state and local governments has remained relatively stable at around 13 percent.

Shift to Third-Party Payment   Even as the private share of total spending has fallen, the role of private insurance has expanded. Private insurance paid a little more than 25 percent of the total cost of medical care in 1965, with that share rising to about one-third by 1990, where it has remained since that time. The major change in private spending has been the dramatic decline in private, out-of-pocket spending. Out-of-pocket spending was approximately half of total health care expenditures in 1960. By 2015, that total had fallen to 10.5 percent. With the increased importance of third-party payers such as government and private insurers, the insured patient has relatively little out-of-pocket spending at the point of purchase.

Payment by third parties provides little incentive to control spending on the part of either the provider or the patient. As long as insurance companies are willing to pay the bills, physicians will continue to provide all the care that patients request. Fully insured patients have no incentive to limit their utilization. Even when the expected benefit of a procedure is small, in most cases patients will demand it, because the patient's share of the cost is small.

It should come as no surprise that the cost of services covered by insurance—public and private—has risen at a faster rate than the cost of services that are not covered. Why? When consumers purchase goods and services at discount prices, they tend to buy more than when charged the full price. What other reasonable explanation would explain the crowds that flock to clearance sales and the enthusiastic consumer acceptance of outlet malls? Health economists refer to this phenomenon as **moral hazard**. Between 1970 and 2006, hospital spending for services usually covered by insurance increased 20 times, whereas spending on eyeglasses—something typically not covered by insurance—increased only 10 times. Insulating patients from the full cost of medical care has had the effect of desensitizing patients to the prices charged and at the same time has encouraged greater utilization.

Change in Hospital Usage and Pricing   Hospital usage has also changed dramatically. As seen in Table 1.3, almost every measure of inpatient hospital usage has fallen in the past 30 years, in some cases quite dramatically. The number of hospital beds is down, admissions are down, the average length of stay is down, and occupancy rates have fallen

moral hazard In the context of health care, the risk that individual behavior changes because of insurance coverage. By decreasing the out-of-pocket price of medical services, insurance increases the quantity demanded.

TABLE 1.2 FINANCING OF HEALTH CARE EXPENDITURES, VARIOUS YEARS IN BILLIONS OF DOLLARS AND PERCENTAGE OF TOTAL SPENDING

	1965 $	1965 %	1970 $	1970 %	1980 $	1980 %	1990 $	1990 %	2000 $	2000 %	2010 $	2010 %	2015 $	2015 %
Out-of-pocket	18.2	48.9	25.0	37.3	58.1	24.6	137.9	20.5	199.0	15.5	298.7	12.2	338.2	11.1
Private insurance	10.1	27.2	15.5	23.1	69.2	29.4	233.9	34.7	458.5	35.6	863.1	35.2	1,072.1	35.1
Medicare	0	–	7.7	11.5	37.4	15.9	110.2	16.3	224.8	17.5	519.3	21.1	646.2	21.2
Medicaid	0	–	5.3	7.9	26.0	11.0	73.7	10.9	200.3	15.6	397.2	16.2	545.1	17.9
Other programs[1]	2.0	5.4	3.3	4.9	9.7	4.1	21.4	3.2	35.8	2.8	95.6	3.9	121.1	4.0
Other third party[2]	6.3	16.9	9.0	13.4	28.6	12.1	77.1	11.4	124.9	9.7	204.3	8.3	247.2	8.1
Public health	0.6	1.6	1.4	2.1	6.4	2.7	20.0	3.0	43.1	3.4	75.5	3.1	80.9	2.7
Health care consumption	37.2	100.0	67.0	100.0	235.7	100.0	674.1	100.0	1,286.4	100.0	2,453.7	100.0	3,050.8	100.0
Investment[3]	4.7		7.8		19.9		47.3		83.3		142.7		154.7	
Total health care spending	41.9		74.6		255.3		721.4		1,369.7		2,596.4		3,205.6	

Source: Centers for Medicare and Medicaid Services (CMS) website, available at https://www.cms.gov/NationalHealthExpendData/03_NationalHealthAccountsProjected.asp#TopOfPage. Accessed January 8, 2016.

[1]Children's Health Insurance, Department of Defense, and Veterans' Affairs.

[2]Worksite health care other private revenues, Indian Health Service, Workers' Compensation, general assistance, maternal and child health, vocational rehabilitation, and other federal programs.

[3]Research, structures, and equipment.

TABLE 1.3 SHORT-STAY COMMUNITY HOSPITAL CHARACTERISTICS, UNITED STATES

Category	1970	1980	1990	2000	2005	2010	2014
Hospitals	5,859	5,904	5,420	4,915	4,936	4,985	4,926
Beds (per 1,000 population)	4.2	4.4	3.7	2.9	2.7	2.6	2.5
Admissions (per 1,000 population)	144.0	159.6	125.4	117.6	118.9	113.8	103.7
Average length of stay (days)	7.7	7.6	7.2	5.8	5.6	5.4	5.5
Outpatient visits (per 1,000 population)	657	893	1,212	1,846	2,198	2,125	2,173
Outpatient visits /admissions	4.6	5.6	9.7	15.8	16.6	18.5	21.0
Outpatient surgeries (% total)	–	16.3	50.5	62.7	63.3	63.6	65.9
Percent occupancy	78.0	75.4	66.8	63.9	67.3	64.5	62.9

Source: *Health United States*, various years.

significantly. Some would go so far as to say that hospitals have gone from overcrowded to underused. Another important trend is the shift from inpatient to outpatient care. The number of per capita outpatient visits has tripled since 1970, and outpatient visits per hospital admission are almost four times higher.

Cost plus was the standard approach for hospital pricing from the inception of Medicare until 1983, when pricing shifted to prospective payment using DRGs. Under DRG pricing, payment is fixed in advance and based on the principal diagnosis at the time of hospital admission. In contrast, private insurance pays hospitals negotiated prices based on discounts from billed charges. As a result, the financial risk of treating patients has shifted from the payer to the provider, creating an incentive for providers to limit access to care. Many providers participate in provider networks that offer discounts to group members. Because all must abide by the fee limits placed on them by Medicare and Medicaid, actual transaction prices are deeply discounted from actual billed prices.

The Growth in Managed Care   The managed care approach became the prevailing form of insurance in the U.S. market during the decade of the 1990s. By 1999, employer-based **group insurance** covered nine out of ten employees in a managed care plan (a health maintenance organization, a preferred provider organization, or a point-of-service plan). The rest were still in traditional **indemnity insurance** plans. The increased popularity of managed care has begun to change the incentive structure within the industry, forcing providers to consider costs more carefully. No longer are physicians' fees constrained by a pricing model that limits fees to usual, customary, and reasonable (UCR) levels.

In 1986, the federal government established a pricing model for Medicare based on an RVS. The Medicare RVS is an index of resource use for every medical procedure across all specialty areas. It translates into a fee schedule by adjusting resource use by a monetary conversion factor. Most fees charged by physicians are in some way tied to this index.

Many physicians participate in at least one risk-sharing contract with a health plan, in which they receive payment under a capitation arrangement. *Capitation* is a fixed fee, paid in advance, for all necessary care provided to a well-defined group. Providing care for a

group insurance A plan whereby an entire group receives insurance under a single policy. The insurance is actually issued to the plan holder, usually an employer or association.

indemnity insurance Insurance based on the principle that someone suffering an economic loss receives a payment approximately equal to the size of the loss.

fixed fee changes the nature of the physician–patient relationship. With cost increasingly an issue, the provider has a stake in eliminating all unnecessary care, which increases the risk that plans may deny potentially beneficial care in the name of cost savings.

The Current Framework and Its Consequences   The current medical care delivery system has been shaped by the passage of the ACA. Now that the key components of the law are in place, we have some reckoning of the consequences of the legislation, intended and unintended. The key elements of the ACA are summarized as follows.

1. *Medicaid expansion.* States are provided federal subsidies (100 percent of the cost of the expansion initially and falling to 90 percent by 2020) to set a national eligibility standard for Medicaid qualification. Individuals making less than 138 percent of the federal poverty income level can receive free care through this state-administered and federally funded expansion. (The original intent was that all states would be required to participate in the expansion, but the 2012 Supreme Court decision made the expansion voluntary for the states.)

2. *Premium subsidies in the insurance exchanges.* Electronic marketplaces were established where insurance companies offer qualified health plans to individuals who do not have access to affordable plans through an employer. Premium subsidies are available to individuals earning between 100 and 400 percent of the federal poverty level income making the plans more affordable. States may set up their own marketplaces or use the federal marketplace, Healthcare.gov.

3. *Individual mandate.* Individuals are required to purchase qualified insurance. Failure to comply will result in penalties (labeled a tax in the 2012 Supreme Court decision declaring the law constitutional).

4. *Employer mandate.* Firms employing more than 50 full-time workers are required to provide a qualified insurance plan or pay a penalty tax.

5. *Expanded insurance regulations.* The new law requires guaranteed issue, **guaranteed renewability**, and eliminates preexisting condition exclusions from all health insurance. Adult children can receive coverage on their parents' plan until they are 26 years old, and there can be no lifetime maximums on spending.

6. *Medicare-related changes.* As part of the financing package, Medicare spending will be cut by $741 billion over the next decade. One-third of these cuts will be from Medicare Advantage, the premium support program that allows seniors to purchase subsidized private insurance. Further, the Medicare payroll tax increased from 2.9 percent to 3.8 percent on families earning more than $250,000. Medicare benefits were expanded to mirror the features of qualified plans in the rest of the system (free preventive services and expanded prescription drug benefits).

7. *New federal taxes.* An increase in federal taxes will raise over $1 trillion in additional revenue over the next decade. Taxes will include fees on health insurance premiums, caps on the maximum contribution individuals can make to their tax-exempt flexible-spending accounts, an excise tax on comprehensive health insurance plans (Cadillac tax), an additional Medicare tax on family incomes above $250,000, a surtax on investment income (dividends and capital gains), and of course the penalty tax on individuals and firms that do not comply with the insurance mandate.

8. *Co-op health plans.* Consumer groups used over $2 billion in federal loans to establish 23 nonprofit cooperative health plans in 22 states to compete directly with the plans available from private insurance companies.

Proponents of the ACA point out the increased insurance coverage as the major accomplishment of the reform. Frean, Gruber, and Sommers (2016) estimate that approximately

20 million Americans who were previously uninsured now have insurance, reducing the percentage of the population uninsured from 16 to 9 percent. Critics point to this same research as proof that the ACA was essentially the Medicaid Expansion Act. Approximately, 63 percent of the newly insured received insurance coverage through Medicaid. Furthermore, of the 12.6 million new Medicaid enrollees, almost 70 percent (8.8 million) were eligible for the program under eligibility standards that existed prior to the passage of the ACA. Less than one-third (3.8 million) received coverage under the expanded eligibility standards.

The remaining 7.4 million newly insured gained coverage because of the premium subsidies available in the exchanges. Most of these individuals earn less than 250 percent of the federal poverty level (FPL) and are eligible for cost-sharing subsidies, covering a substantial portion of their out-of-pocket spending on deductibles and copayments.

Surprisingly, the individual mandate has had little impact on coverage. The penalty is still relatively modest, exemptions common, and enforcement difficult. Over time if the penalty remains in place and increases in size, the mandate may play a larger role in expanding coverage.

Two of the most popular features of the law are the coverage provision for adult children and the exclusion of preexisting conditions from the insurance underwriting process. Together these two features have worked against the creation of workable risk pools in the insurance exchanges. The dependent coverage provision is keeping healthy young people out of the exchanges, and the preexisting conditions exclusion is populating the risk pools with older and sicker individuals. As a result, insurance premiums for the young and healthy who remain are twice as high as they would be otherwise, further discouraging this important demographic cohort from participating in the exchange pools.

Finally, the co-op health plans have not served their intended purpose to provide a reliable alternative to the for-profit plans in the exchanges. What seemed like a good idea was actually doomed from the outset. Underfunded and staffed with inexperienced administrators, only five of the original 23 were still active by the end of 2016. The other 18 have failed and lost over $2.5 billion in taxpayer funds. Most of the remaining five are losing money and likely to fail. In many ways, the exchange experience of the co-ops is similar to the other insurers. Most insurance companies are losing money on their exchange plans and no longer participate. Over one-third of all counties in the country had only one insurance choice in 2017.

Looking Ahead: An Uncertain Future　　The 2016 election reopened the health care reform debate. It is difficult to speculate what the Republican reform plan will look like, but if President Trump's early actions are an indication of his intentions, it is reasonable to expect that he will make every effort to fulfill his campaign promise to repeal and replace Obamacare. Simultaneous action is the most likely approach. Even though repeal is possible (under Senate reconciliation rules), repeal and delay has too many obstacles, namely 48 Senate Democrats, to be a viable option. Moreover, it is unlikely that Senate will change its filibuster rules to accommodate a repeal-now-and-replace-later strategy.

The majority of Americans want to see an incremental approach to reforming the health care system. Moreover, early indications from Republican leadership in the Congress make it clear that incremental change is their preferred strategy. What will the reform plan look like? What follows is my best guess.

- *A partial repeal of the ACA: Keep most of the insurance regulations and taxes.*
- *Deregulate the insurance exchanges.*

- *Simplify the premium subsidy calculation: Age-adjusted tax credits that are advance-able and refundable will replace income-based subsidies. (Expect four age categories, 0–17, 18–34, 35–49, and 50–64.)*
- *Allow individuals who work for small firms (with fewer than 50 employees) to purchase non-group insurance using the tax credits.*
- *The tax exclusion for employer-sponsored insurance will remain in place but with a cap on the maximum exemption. (This will replace the unpopular 40 percent marginal tax on high-premium plans.)*
- *Expand the use of health savings accounts (HSAs) to support high-deductible health plans (HDHP) by providing new enrollees with a one-time tax credit to set up their HSA. Require HDHPs to cover preventive services and maintenance drugs at zero copay.*
- *Provide a one-year window with guaranteed issue for individuals experiencing certain life transitions (newborns, 18 year olds, and 19–25 year olds who had insurance on their parents' plans).*
- *Coverage provisions for individuals with preexisting conditions during the start-up period. This may be a federally subsidized, high-risk pool or premium tax credits adjusted by health status in addition to the age categories.*
- *Congress will be forced to address Medicaid because of the significant role it has played in expanding coverage to low-income Americans. They will likely allow states to apply for a per-capita allotment (modified block grant) instead of the current matching payment and encourage states to seek waivers to experiment with different coverage options. Enrollees will be free to use the tax credit to purchase private insurance and set up HSAs (similar to the Healthy Indiana Plan or HIP 2.0).*
- *Eventually, Medicare will become part of the conversation: Changes may include adjusting the eligibility age, combining hospital and physicians' coverage to simplify the administration, providing catastrophic coverage, and replacing the current financial arrangement with premium support.*

Recommending changes to Medicare and Medicaid is the well-known third rail of national politics. Go there at your own risk. As we move through the next 15 chapters, we will examine what economics has to say about developing a viable health care system and the specific characteristics of the different reform options will become clearer.

Health Economics Defined

Health economics emerged as a subdiscipline of economics in the 1960s with the publication of two important papers by Kenneth Arrow (1963) and Mark V. Pauly (1968), both published in the *American Economic Review* (AER). Many consider Arrow's paper the seminal contribution to the field of health economics and health policy. Recognizing its importance, the *Journal of Health Politics, Policy, and Law* (Peterson, 2001) devoted a special issue to the paper's important contributions, including a foreword written by Pauly.

Health economists examine a wide range of issues, extending from the nature and production of health to the market for health and medical care to the microeconomic evaluation of health care interventions and strategies. Figure 1.2 provides a diagrammatic overview of the structure of health economics. Beginning with the box labeled "Nature of Health," we can ask ourselves a number of questions: What does it mean to be healthy? How do we measure health? What is the best possible way to measure

FIGURE 1.2 The Structure of Health Economics

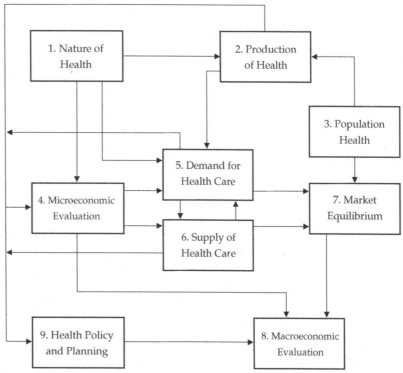

Source: Adapted from Alan Maynard and Panos Kanavos, "Health Economics: An Evolving Paradigm," *Health Economics* 9, 2000, 183–90.

quality of life? Because of the nature of the questions, research on this topic is interdisciplinary. Even though economists are not the only ones studying these questions, their contributions have been significant. The development of the quality of life measure, called the *quality-adjusted life year* (QALY), was in part a result of the participation of economists.

Grossman (1972) developed an economic framework for the study of medical care demand in which medical care is simply one of many factors used to produce good health. In this framework, "Production of Health" looks at the determinants of health, including income, wealth, education, genetics, and public health. Our ability to maintain a desired level of health depends largely on the lifestyle choices we make. The topic "Population Health" examines challenges in health care delivery across different groups in a diverse population. For example, differences in tobacco, alcohol, and drug use and differences in obesity rates and rates of sexually transmitted diseases affect our ability to produce similar health outcomes across different populations.

The principle activity of health economists outside the United States is microeconomic evaluation or the evaluation of alternative ways to treat a specific medical condition. Policymakers within fixed-budget systems find it necessary to conduct studies comparing the costs and consequences of diagnosis and treatment options in order to make informed decisions on the optimal allocation of scarce resources. Cost-benefit analysis, with its welfare economics framework, provides the foundation for most of the research in economic evaluation, and health economists have adapted that framework in developing cost-effectiveness analysis, the evaluation method of choice in medical care decision-making.

The primary focus of U.S. health economists is the market for health care. The boxes in Figure 1.2 numbered 5 through 7, and the topics covered in them, summarize this emphasis. The "Demand for Health Care" is affected by the elements discussed in boxes 1 and 2, the nature and production of health. The early contribution of economics to the study of health care demand considered improving health to be one way to increase future productivity (Mushkin, 1962). Thus, the demand for health care is not only influenced by a desire to feel better when ill, it is also viewed as investment in human capital. Factors affecting the demand for medical care include the socioeconomic characteristics of the population, patient demographics, access barriers (including cost-sharing arrangements), and the role of providers in determining the type and level of care prescribed.

The "Supply of Health Care" encompasses a broad spectrum of economics on such topics as production theory, input markets, and industrial organization. Specific issues examined include the cost of production, input substitution, and the nature and role of incentives. Demand and supply interact with one another to establish "Market Equilibrium." Markets are able to allocate scarce resources effectively where they are most productive by establishing a price for everything.

Analysis of the overall goals and objectives of the health care system is the subject of "Macroeconomic Evaluation." How well is the system performing? Is it accessible? Is it affordable? Is quality at the desired level? How does our system compare to those of our neighbors? Finally, "Health Policy and Planning" involves the interaction of private sector, government, and nongovernmental organizations (NGOs) in setting national goals, determining the strategies for reaching those goals, and establishing the rules of the game that regulate how medical care markets work.

Health care systems are constantly changing. Policymakers and planners are always looking for better ways to produce, deliver, and pay for a growing menu of medical care services demanded by an insatiable public. The goal of this book is to provide you with the tools to understand the role of economics in this important task.

Ten Key Economic Concepts

Given the complexity of economic theory, it may come as a surprise that a relatively small number of key concepts guide economic thought. These concepts will serve as unifying themes throughout the book.

1. *Scarcity and choice* address the problem of limited resources and the need to economize. Not enough resources are available to meet all the desires of all the people, making rationing in some form unavoidable. We are forced to make choices among competing objectives—an inescapable result of **scarcity**.
2. *Opportunity cost* recognizes that everything and everyone has alternatives. Time and resources used to satisfy one set of desires cannot be used to satisfy another set. The cost of any decision or action is measured in terms of the value placed on the opportunity foregone.
3. *Marginal analysis* is the economic way of thinking about the optimal allocation of resources. Choices are seldom an all-or-nothing proposition—decisions are made at "the margin." Decision makers weigh the trade-offs, a little more of one thing and a little less of another. In this environment, the incremental benefits and incremental costs of a decision are considered.

scarcity A situation that exists when the amount of a good or service demanded in the aggregate exceeds the amount available at a zero price.

4. *Self-interest* is the primary motivator of economic decision makers. Driven by the power of self-interest, people are motivated to pursue efficiency in the production and consumption decisions they make. According to the well-known eighteenth-century economist Adam Smith, this pursuit of self-interest, moderated by market competition, causes each individual to pursue a course of action that promotes the general goals of society.

5. *Markets and pricing* serve as the most efficient way to allocate scarce resources. The market accomplishes its tasks through a system of prices, what Smith called the "invisible hand." The invisible hand can allocate resources because everyone and everything has a price. When they desire more, prices increase. When they desire less, prices decrease. Firms base their production decisions on relative prices and relative price movements. The price mechanism becomes a way to bring a firm's output decisions into balance with consumer desires—something that we refer to as **equilibrium**.

6. *Supply and demand* serve as the foundation for all economic analysis. Pricing and output decisions are based on the forces underlying these two economic concepts. Goods and services are allocated among competing uses by striking a balance, or attaining equilibrium, between consumers' willingness to pay and suppliers' willingness to provide. This is rationing via prices.

7. *Competition* forces resource owners to use their resources to promote the highest possible satisfaction of society, including consumers, producers, and investors. If resource owners do this well, they are rewarded. If they are inept or inefficient, they are penalized. Competition takes production out of the hands of the less competent and places it into the hands of the more efficient, constantly promoting more efficient methods of production.

8. *Efficiency* in economics measures how well resource use promotes social welfare. Inefficient outcomes waste resources, but the efficient use of scarce resources enhances social welfare. The fascinating aspect of competitive markets is how the more-or-less independent behavior on the part of thousands of decision makers serves to promote social welfare. Consumers attempt to make themselves better off by allocating limited budgets. Producers seek maximum profits by using cost-minimizing methods.

9. *Market failure* arises when the free market fails to promote the efficient use of resources by either producing more or less than the optimal level of output. Sources of market failure include natural monopoly, externalities in production and consumption, and **public goods**. Other market imperfections, such as incomplete information and immobile resources, also contribute to this problem.

10. *Comparative advantage* explains how people benefit from voluntary exchange when production decisions are based on **opportunity cost**. The individual or entity that has the lowest opportunity cost of production has the comparative advantage.

equilibrium The market-clearing price at which every consumer wanting to purchase the good finds a willing seller.

HTTP://
"Health Economics— Places to Go" provides links to sites related to health economics, health policy, managed care, and more. http:// www.healtheconomics .com/resource/health- economics-places-to-go/.

public good A good that is nonrival in distribution and nonexclusive in consumption.

opportunity cost The cost of a decision based on the value of the foregone opportunity.

Summary and Conclusions

The medical care industry in the United States is large and growing in relative size. Medical care is one of the largest industries in the vast U.S. economy. At more than $3.2 trillion, it was four-and-one-half times larger than the domestic auto industry and four times larger than the total defense budget in 2015. In addition, medical care employed more people and exported more goods and services than either defense or automobiles. It may be difficult to imagine, but the economic output of the U.S. medical care industry was larger than the entire French economy.

As shown in Figure 1.3, a potpourri of public and private sources finances U.S. medical care. The public sector directly finances over 45 percent of total

FIGURE 1.3 Where the Money Comes From…

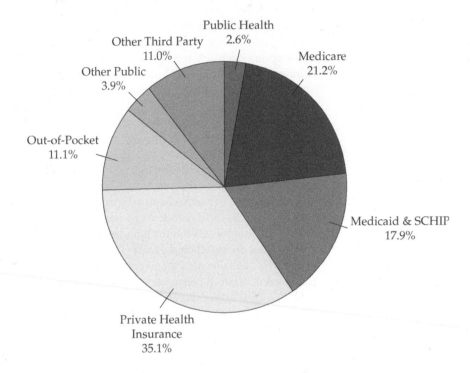

spending. Private health insurance and private philanthropy finance 43 percent, leaving about 11 percent to come from direct, out-of-pocket payments from individuals.

Most of the money Americans spend on medical care covers either hospital or physicians' services (see Figure 1.4). The percentage of total spending in these two areas has remained at around 55 percent. Pharmaceutical spending amounts to 10.6 percent of total spending. Other personal and professional services, home health, medical products, and nursing home care combine for approximately one-fourth of the total spending. The other 10 percent is due to administration and public health spending.

The U.S. system of medical care delivery is far from perfect. Critics claim there are too few primary care physicians and too many specialists, leading to greater reliance on acute and specialty care and underutilization of **primary and preventive care**. Policymakers designed the ACA to close some of the gaps in health insurance coverage that limit reliable access for many

Americans. The legislation has introduced a modest measure of **portability** in the market for group health insurance, and denying coverage to individuals with preexisting health conditions is no longer possible.

The system also has its strengths, and its defenders argue that quality is unquestionably high. Citing evidence from polls, they note that around 70 percent of Americans are happy with the quality of the medical care they receive personally. Over one-third of the same individuals would give the overall health care system a failing grade (Kleckley et al., 2010). The U.S. system has progressed much faster than its European counterparts in developing quality assessment and output measures. The United States is still the world leader in innovation, research, and the development of state-of-the-art technology.

The growth in medical care spending has moderated somewhat since 1990. It could be that the aggressive action by employers and state governments to reverse the escalation in spending is finally paying off or possibly that the threat of government intervention at the

---

primary and preventive care Routine medical care and screening generally provided by physicians specializing in family practice, general internal medicine, and pediatrics.
portability The ability to easily transfer insurance coverage from one plan to another as a covered employee changes jobs.

FIGURE 1.4 How
the Money's Spent

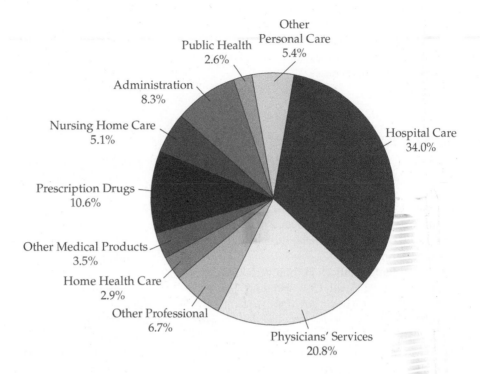

federal level has served to intimidate providers, who now fear public backlash and political reprisals. Whatever the reason, spending growth has moderated without significant legislative action.

In general, spending growth in the public sector has outpaced spending growth in the private sector. Over the past decade, overall spending has increased 4.04 percent per year, private spending has grown at an annual rate of 3.34 percent, while public medical spending has risen at an annual rate of 5.34 percent. Over that time, Medicare spending has increased 4.82 percent per year and Medicaid 5.94 percent. Regardless of the measures used, health care expenditures continue their upward trend, and policymakers continue to debate ways to address the problem.

Questions and Problems

1. Thomas Sowell, a senior fellow at the Hoover Institution, has stated that we "have difficulty understanding the strange way words are used by politicians and the media." We often think of a crisis in terms of an emergency, a situation of utmost urgency, maybe even life or death. According to Sowell, politicians use the term differently. They define a crisis as any situation they want to change. How do you define the term *crisis*? Does the United States have a health care crisis?

2. Discuss the magnitude of the financing problem in medical care. What are the major reasons that medical spending is absorbing an increasing share of national output?

3. How important is cost containment in establishing a national health care policy? In addition to controlling costs, what are the alternative goals for a national medical care system?

4. What do economists mean by *scarcity*? Why is the concept so important in economic analysis?

5. Paul Krugman recently opined in the *New York Times* that "ever since Kenneth Arrow's seminal paper, [economists have known] that the standard competitive market model just doesn't work for health care … to act all wide-eyed and innocent about these problems at this late date is either remarkably ignorant or simply disingenuous." The paper that Krugman refers to is the 1963 *AER* article where Arrow catalogues five health care market distortions: unpredictability, entry barriers, the importance of trust, asymmetric information, and payment idiosyncrasies.

a. Explain how each of these distortions is true of the health care market.
b. Are these five distortions that unusual for markets in general? Explain.

References

Arrow, Kenneth, "Uncertainty and the Welfare Economics of Medical Care," *American Economic Review* 53(5), December 1963, 941–973.

Centers for Medicare and Medicaid Services (CMS), National Health Expenditure Data, available at http://www.cms.gov/NationalHealthExpendData/. Accessed February 3, 2017.

Congressional Budget Office, "Technological Change and the Growth of Health Care Spending," January 2008, available at www.cbo.gov/ftpdocs/89xx /doc8947/01-31-TechHealth.pdf. Accessed September 2, 2010.

Cutler, David M. and Nikhil R. Sahni, "If Slow Rate of Health Care Spending Growth Persists, Projections May Be off by $770 Billion," *Health Affairs* 32(3), May 2013, 841–850.

Finkelstein, Amy, "The Aggregate Effects of Health Insurance: Evidence from the Introduction of Medicare," *The Quarterly Journal of Economics* 122(1), February 2007, 1–37.

Frean, Molly, Jonathan Gruber, and Benjamin D. Sommers, "Disentangling the ACA's Coverage Effects—Lessons for Policymakers," *New England Journal of Medicine* 375(17), October 27, 2016, 1605–1608.

Fuchs, Victor R., "The Gross Domestic Product and Health Care Spending," *New England Journal of Medicine*, May 22, 2013 [Online First].

Fuchs, Victor R., "Three 'Inconvenient Truths' about Health Care," *New England Journal of Medicine* 359(17), October 23, 2008, 1749–1751.

Fuchs, Victor R., "Why Do Other Rich Nations Spend So Much Less on Healthcare?" *The Atlantic*, July 23, 2014.

Ginsburg, Paul B., "Controlling Health Care Costs," *New England Journal of Medicine* 351(16), October 14, 2004, 1591–1593.

Grossman, Michael, "On the Concept of Health Capital and the Demand for Health," *Journal of Political Economy* 80(2), March/April 1972, 223–255.

Iglehart, John K., "Finding Money for Health Care Reform—Rooting Out Waste, Fraud, and Abuse," *New England Journal of Medicine* 361(3), July 16, 2009, 229–231.

Kaiser Family Foundation, "Assessing the Effects of the Economy on the Recent Slowdown in Health Spending," April 22, 2013, available at http://kff.org/ health-costs/issue-brief/assessing-the-effects-of-the-economy-on-the-recent-slowdown-in-health-spending-2/. Accessed April 7, 2017.

Kaiser Family Foundation, "Employer Health Benefits: 2016 Annual Survey," 2016, available at http://kff .org/health-costs/report/2016-employer-health-benefits-survey/. Accessed April 6, 2017.

Keehan, Sean P., et al., "National Health Expenditure Projections, 2016–25: Price Increases, Aging Push Sector to 20 Percent of Economy," *Health Affairs* 36(3), 2017, 553–563.

Kleckley, Paul H., et al., "2010 Global Survey of Health Care Consumers," Deloitte Center for Health Solutions, April 20, 2010, available at https://www.imtj.com/news /deloitte-2010-survey-global-health-care-consumers/.

Mushkin, Selma J., "Health as an Investment," *Journal of Political Economy* 70(5, part 2), October 1962, 129–157.

Newhouse, Joseph, "An Iconoclastic View of Health Cost Containment," *Health Affairs* 12(Suppl), January 1993, 152–171.

Pauly, Mark V., "The Economics of Moral Hazard: Comment," *American Economic Review* 58(2), June 1968, 531–538.

Peterson, Mark A., ed., "Kenneth Arrow and the Changing Economics of Health Care," *Journal of Health Politics, Policy and Law* 26(5), October 2001.

Rasmussen Reports, "Health Care Law," March 8–9, 2017, available at http://www.rasmussenreports .com/public_content/politics/current_events /healthcare/health_care_law. Accessed April 7, 2017.

Roberts, Brandon, and Irving Hoch, "Malpractice Litigation and Medical Costs in the United States," *Health Economics* 18(12), December 2009, 1394–1419.

Ryu, Alexander J., et al., "The Slowdown in Health Care Spending in 2009–11 Reflected Factors Other than the Weak Economy and Thus May Persist," *Health Affairs* 32(5), May 2013, 835–840.

Thorpe, Kenneth E., et al., "The Impact of Obesity on Rising Medical Spending," *Health Affairs Web Exclusive*, October 20, 2004, W4-480–W4-486, available at http://content.healthaffairs.org/content /early/2004/10/20/hlthaff.w4.480.full.pdf+html?sid= 4642c39b-6152-4ea2-a7ac-df258fe71692. Accessed April, 2017.

The Medical Care Price Index

The conventional wisdom in many policy circles embraces the notion that medical care inflation is out of control. How much of the increase in medical spending is due to inflation, and how much is due to improved services and changing demographic patterns? The way we answer this question will ultimately determine the type of medical care reform we will get. It is important, therefore, to understand how price indexes are used to measure medical care price inflation.

Measuring Price Changes with Index Numbers

The principal measure of inflation used by business and government policymakers is the year-to-year change in the consumer price index (CPI). The index plays an important role in determining cost of living adjustments (COLAs) for everything from union wages to social security and pension benefits to federal income tax brackets. The CPI is a fixed-weight or Laspeyres index that measures price changes for a market basket of items defined for a base period. In other indexes, such as the GDP price deflator, the composition of the market basket changes every year to reflect different spending patterns.

A fixed-weight index has become the index of choice used to measure inflation. Because the weights do not change, movements in a fixed-weight index are due solely to changes in the prices of the goods included in the market basket. In contrast, a movement in a deflator reflects changes in prices of goods and the composition of the market basket. In reality, consumers adjust their spending away from goods whose prices increase, making it necessary to change the composition of the fixed-weight market basket periodically to reflect more accurately consumer-spending patterns. The weights

for the CPI are based on a survey of consumer spending patterns and are changed approximately every 10 years. The current CPI weighting scheme was revised in 1987 based on results from the 1982–1984 Consumer Expenditure Survey.

Table A1.1 presents data for the CPI from 1970 through 2012. Overall, the index is broken down into seven major spending categories: food (18 percent), housing (42 percent), apparel (6 percent), transportation (18 percent), medical care (6 percent), entertainment (4 percent), and other (6 percent). The index in each case equals 100 for the 1982 to 1984 period. When interpreting these indexes, note that the inflation rate from one-time period to the next is calculated by dividing the change in the index by its previous value. For example, the CPI changed from 237.0 to 240.0 between 2015 and 2016. This change of 3.0 percentage points divided by 237.0 results in an estimated annual inflation rate of 1.27 percent. Over the period shown, the medical care component increased at a faster rate than any other component of the CPI—over 13 times from 1970 to 2016.

Medical Care Price Index

Table A1.2 shows the major index of medical care prices, the medical care price index (MCPI). Medical care is divided into commodities and services. Medical commodities are subdivided into seven categories: prescription drugs, nonprescription drugs, first aid and dressings, general medical equipment, convalescent equipment, hearing aids, and unpriced items. Medical services are divided into nine categories: physician, dental, optometry, other professional, hospital room, other inpatient, outpatient, nursing home, and unpriced. Health insurance is priced using a separate category.

TABLE A1.1 CONSUMER PRICE INDEXES FOR MAJOR EXPENDITURE CLASSES SELECT YEARS, 1960 TO 2016 (1982 TO 1984 = 100)

Year	All items (CPI-U)	All services	Apparel	Food and beverage	Housing	Energy	Medical care	All items excluding medical care
1960	29.6	24.1	45.7	30.0	–	22.4	22.3	30.2
1970	38.8	35.0	59.2	40.1	36.4	25.5	34.0	39.2
1980	82.4	77.9	90.9	86.7	81.1	86.0	74.9	82.8
1990	130.7	139.2	124.1	132.1	128.5	102.1	162.8	128.8
1995	152.4	168.7	132.0	148.9	148.5	105.2	220.5	148.6
2000	172.2	195.3	129.6	168.4	169.6	124.6	260.8	167.3
2005	195.3	230.1	119.5	191.2	195.7	177.1	323.2	188.7
2010	218.1	261.3	119.5	220.0	216.3	211.4	392.0	210.7
2015	237.0	291.7	125.9	246.8	238.1	202.9	446.8	226.9
2016	240.0	299.9	126.0	247.7	244.0	189.5	463.7	229.3

Source: Bureau of Labor Statistics, CPI Detailed Reports, various years.

TABLE A1.2 THE MEDICAL CARE PRICE INDEX AND ITS MAJOR COMPONENTS SELECT YEARS, 1950 TO 2016 (1982 TO 1984 = 100)

Year	Total medical care	Compound rate of change from previous year listed	Medical care commodities	Medical care services
1950	15.1	–	39.7	12.8
1960	22.3	4.0	46.9	19.5
1970	34.0	4.3	46.5	32.3
1980	74.9	8.2	75.4	74.8
1990	162.8	7.4	163.4	162.7
1995	220.5	6.3	206.6	227.8
2000	260.8	3.4	241.1	270.4
2005	323.2	4.2	280.8	342.0
2010	392.0	3.9	317.2	415.1
2015	446.8	2.7	354.6	476.2
2016	463.7	3.8	366.8	494.8

Source: Bureau of Labor Statistics, CPI Detailed Reports, various years.

Typically cited as the measure of medical care inflation, the MCPI has steadily increased over time. Interpreting the index as a measure of inflation suggests that medical care prices have risen at a compounded rate of over 5.56 percent since 1980, over two-thirds faster than prices in general. If this is true, we have a real problem on our hands. Can we believe what the statistics seem to tell us? Is the MCPI a good measure of medical care price inflation?

Problems with Using a Fixed-Weight Index as a Measure of Inflation

In reality, changes in a fixed-weight index do not accurately reflect changes in the cost of living. Using a fixed-weight index, such as the MCPI, to measure medical care price inflation introduces a substantial upward bias to the estimate. It is important that we understand the problems associated with using indexes to measure inflation and take appropriate steps when interpreting indexes to minimize the bias.

Measuring Inputs Instead of Outcomes

The MCPI measures the wrong thing. The price index measures the cost of inputs: an office visit, a day in the hospital, a surgical procedure, or a prescription drug. Sick patients do not desire the inputs; they are interested in the restoration of their health. Nevertheless, as we will see in Chapter 5, health is difficult to define, let alone measure.

Given the difficulty in measuring health, one possible solution would be to measure the cost of curing a particular illness. For example, the average length of stay in the hospital has steadily fallen over the course of the past several decades. Reduced stays have dampened the hospital-cost escalation measured in terms of average cost per day (what the CPI measures). Even more dramatic has been the increased use of outpatient procedures to treat illnesses that formerly required extensive hospital stays. Repair of an inguinal hernia, one of the most common surgical procedures, formerly required several days in the hospital and several months of limited activity. Today the procedure is performed on an outpatient basis and requires only a few hours in an outpatient surgical center and minimal rehabilitation time. In fact, most patients are encouraged to resume their normal daily activities as soon as possible.

The shift to outpatient surgery has greatly reduced the cost of treating many common problems, but the cost savings has largely been lost on the MCPI. As outpatient procedures grow in popularity, two things happen: First, patients who continue to be treated in the hospital are, on average, sicker than before. They require more resources on average and thus drive up the average cost of their hospital stays. Second, when an outpatient procedure actually replaces a conventional hospital procedure, as is the case with cataract surgery and lens replacement and many orthopedic surgeries, it drops out of the hospital component of the price index and is included later in the outpatient component. The result of both of these factors is an increase in the MCPI, even though the cost of treating the illness has decreased.

Measuring Quality Changes

Technological progress typically results in improvements in the products and services available to consumers. Price increases due to quality improvements are mistakenly identified as inflation in a fixed-weight index. This is not a severe problem in industries where innovation takes place slowly. However, technological progress takes place at different rates in different industries. This is especially true in the medical industry, in which quality of care has improved dramatically over the past 50 years. Treatments for once untreatable diseases offer new hope. Inexpensive prevention of diseases such as polio and smallpox has led to near eradication of these once-costly illnesses, and improved surgical techniques allow patients to leave the hospital sooner and recuperate faster.

If price indexes are to be an accurate measure of changes in the cost of living, price changes due to quality improvements must have no impact on the value of the index. The Bureau of Labor Statistics (BLS) attempts to factor in quality improvements, but once again, infrequent changes in the composition of the index fail to keep up with the rapid advance of technology. As a result, quality improvements are mistakenly interpreted as pure price movements.

Accounting for New Products

The CPI, as a fixed-weight index, relies on the assumption that the product and service mix of the market basket remains unchanged. The use of this assumption makes it difficult to incorporate new products into the calculation. In some industries, this poses only minor problems. For gasoline and other components of the energy price index, this assumption works reasonably well. The medical care industry is different. The rapid introduction of new medicines and new technologies over the past several decades poses problems for the fixed-weight MCPI.

Infrequent revisions in the index mean that the price index fails to account for significant reductions in the price of newly discovered products. Penicillin, for example, did not enter into the index until its price had fallen to about 1 percent of its original level. A more common problem deals with the introduction of generic drugs. Generics are chemically identical to their name-brand alternatives and are usually much cheaper. They do not enter into the calculation of the index until weights are revised and only then as an entirely new product. By that time, they may have captured a significant portion of the market and lowered costs to users substantially. Their addition to the index, however, does not reflect the price decline.

The introduction of the laparoscope has revolutionized many forms of surgery, from knee reconstruction for damaged ligaments to the removal of the gall bladder. In most cases, the new surgical method costs considerably less than the traditional alternative because of shorter hospital stays. Gall bladder removal using laparoscopic techniques requires a 1- to 2-day hospital stay compared with 3 to 7 days using traditional surgical techniques. Repairing a damaged anterior cruciate ligament using the new technique costs 75 percent less for the same medical result.

The BLS incorporates new products and procedures into the index by price linking, replacing the old product with a new one at some arbitrary point in time. This adjustment is made in such a way that the price index remains unchanged; price increases are considered an improvement in quality, but price decreases are simply lost to the index.

Other Problems

In addition to the problems already addressed, several other factors play an important role in creating biased indexes. These include statistical sampling problems, a substitution bias, and the use of list prices instead of transaction prices.

Use of List Prices   All published indexes from the BLS use list prices in their calculations rather than transaction prices. The list price is the billed price that originates from each provider's charge list. Information on list prices is easier to collect but bears little resemblance to the amount that providers actually receive. The actual transaction prices are discounted from the listed prices. In reality, very few patients actually pay list prices for services.

Suppose a hospital charges $12,500 for a particular procedure. Furthermore, the patient is covered by an insurance plan that contracts with the hospital and agrees to pay $4,000 for this procedure. In this case, $4,000 should be the price that enters into the price index. However, more often than not, the discounted price differs across payers and is more difficult to determine, so the list price of $12,500 is used.

If list prices and transaction prices change at roughly the same rate, the use of list prices does not create a problem for our index. Medical discounting, however, has become an increasingly important phenomenon in recent years, so the use of list prices produces an upward bias on the MCPI. In fact, the CMS have developed a transaction price index for hospital services. Not surprisingly, the transaction price index has increased at a more moderate rate than the hospital index based on list prices.

Sampling   The high cost of collecting price data dictates that only a limited number of transactions are included in the price index. Sampling can introduce several types of biases into the price index. Prices paid in the sampled locales may not represent prices paid by most consumers. Discounts for bulk purchases and the increased popularity of generic and store brands are lost in the sampling procedure used.

Substitution Bias   Economists have observed that when the price of a good increases relative to other goods, consumers tend to buy less of it. Therefore, as the prices of goods change relative to one another, spending patterns change. Consumers substitute lower-priced items for higher-priced items. Fixed-weight indexes like the CPI completely miss this changing pattern of spending, called the *substitution effect*. As long as the prices of all items in the index rise at roughly the same rate, this phenomenon causes few measurement problems. Over time, however, small differences can add up and result in the statistical phenomenon called *substitution bias*. This bias does not pose a problem with a deflator, because the market basket changes annually to reflect changing spending patterns. In a fixed-weight index, the weights are changed infrequently (every 10 years or so with the CPI), placing too much emphasis on goods whose prices rise the fastest.

Alternative Methods to Measure Medical Care Inflation

Researchers have suggested alternative measures that might better reflect changes in the price of medical care. Wilensky and Rossiter (1986) advanced the case that a change in the measure of medical output would more accurately reflect changes in medical care prices. The most commonly used measure of output is the procedure (e.g., one dose of chemotherapy for the treatment of cancer). Alternatively, output could be defined by the case, such as treatment of cancer from diagnosis to outcome; the episode, using a particular phase of the illness; or on a per capita basis, measuring the total cost per patient for all medical care.

Another suggested method involves defining a good by a set of characteristics demanded by consumers. This so-called hedonic approach prices those individual characteristics and recombines them to determine the quality-constant price of the good. Trajtenberg (1990) used the hedonic approach to estimate the change in the cost of computerized tomographic X-rays or CT scans. Defining a CT scan as a set of characteristics, the hedonic index actually declined from 100 to 27.3 from 1973 to 1982. In contrast, the standard index with no quality adjustment showed an increase from 100 to 259.4.

The use of these alternative approaches, though promising in some cases, is not appropriate in others. Even when appropriate, the cost of data collection rises dramatically.

Summary and Conclusions

Measuring price changes with the indexes we have available is somewhat problematic. Outputs are difficult to measure, new products are included arbitrarily, and the methods for dealing with quality improvements are inadequate at best. Depending on how we interpret the evidence, medical care may be the fastest-rising component of the CPI or using a quality-adjusted notion, medical care prices may be actually falling. Papers by Graboyes (1994) and Newhouse (1989) provide additional insight into understanding and interpreting medical care price indices.

References

Graboyes, Robert F., "Medical Care Price Indexes," *Federal Reserve Bank of Richmond Economic Quarterly* 80(4), Fall 1994, 69–89.

Newhouse, Joseph P., "Measuring Medical Prices and Understanding Their Effects," *The Journal of Health Administration Education* 7(1), Winter 1989, 19–26.

Trajtenberg, M., "Economic Analysis of Product Innovation: The Case of the CT Scanners," *Harvard Economic Studies* 160, Cambridge, MA: Harvard University Press, 1990.

Wilensky, Gail R. and Louis F. Rossiter, "Alternative Units of Payment for Physician Services: An Overview of the Issues," *Medical Care Review* 43, Spring 1986, 133–156.

CHAPTER 2

Using Economics to Study Health Issues

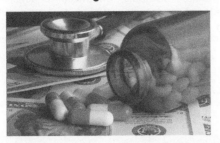

IS "SAFE" SEX REALLY SAFE?

One of the costs of risky sexual behavior is an increased likelihood of contracting a sexually transmitted infection (STI) such as syphilis, gonorrhea, or AIDS. As with any activity involving human choice, as the perceived cost of engaging in risky behavior increases, the number of risky sexual encounters decreases. This suggests that by making sex "safer" through free condom distribution—in effect lowering the cost of risky behavior—public health officials may be increasing the incidence of that behavior and in turn the incidence of STIs.

The logic of this possibility is because there is a demand for sex. It is difficult to know the exact shape of the demand curve, but most economists would agree that it is likely downward sloping. As the perceived cost of a sexual encounter (the risk of contracting an STI) falls, the number of sexual encounters will increase. The "risk elasticity of demand for sex" determines the size of the increase.

The risk elasticity of demand for sex is defined as the percentage change in the number of sexual encounters relative to the percentage change in the risk of each encounter. If the risk elasticity is less than one, then free condom distribution will reduce the incidence of disease. If it is greater than one, the incidence of disease will increase.

Consider a closed community, where condoms must be purchased and no one uses them. According to research (Rosenberg et al., 1992), the risk of contracting three common STIs—gonorrhea, trichomoniasis, and chlamydia—during unprotected sexual activity is 23.4 in 100. If the number of risky sexual encounters is 250 per week, there will be 58 new infections every week (250 × 0.234). Assume that condoms are now distributed free of charge, and their use is widely encouraged through a sex education program. The use of condoms will result in a reduction in the incidence of STI to 18.8 per 100 risky sexual encounters—a 20 percent reduction.

If the demand for sex is inelastic, and the risk elasticity of demand is, say, −0.5, the incidence of sexual intercourse will increase by 10 percent, from 250 per week to 275. In that case, there will be only 52 new cases of STI every week (275 × 0.188), a 10 percent decrease. On the other hand, if the demand for sex is elastic and the risk elasticity of demand for sex is, say, −1.5, sexual intercourse increases by 30 percent—from 250 incidents per week to 325. In that case, there will be 61 new cases of STI reported every week (325 × 0.188), a 5 percent increase.

Does the policy of making condoms available increase or decrease the number of cases of STI? While the value of risk elasticity of demand for sex is an empirical matter, there is some evidence that sexual activity is higher in those situations in which condoms are widely available. According to Planned Parenthood, in schools with formal sex education programs and free condom distribution, the percentage of males engaging in sex increased from 60 to 84 percent and the use of condoms actually decreased (Family Planning Perspectives, 1994). Kasun's review (1994) of seven sex education programs with easy access to condoms revealed that six of the programs resulted in an increase in sexual activity.

Any attempt by policy makers to make sex safer could actually exacerbate the problem by encouraging sexual activity. Economists call this principle "moral hazard." When policy makers try to insulate individuals from the consequences of their own behavior (by providing free condoms), the incentives to reduce those negative outcomes on their own (by avoiding risky behavior) are also reduced. By trying to soften the impact of bad outcomes (STIs), we actually increase the likelihood of those outcomes.

Sources: Dwight Lee, "Will Condoms Mean Less AIDS? It's a Question of Elasticity," The Margin, September/October 1989, 28; "As Adolescent Males Age, Risky Behavior Rises but Condom Use Decreases," Family Planning Perspectives, January/February 1994, 45–46; Jacqueline R. Kasun, "Condom Nation: Government Sex Education Programs Promote Teen Pregnancy," Policy Review, Spring 1994, 79; and Michael J. Rosenberg, et al., "Barrier Contraceptives and Sexually Transmitted Diseases in Women: A Comparison of Female-Dependent Methods and Condoms," American Journal of Public Health 82(5), May 1992, 669–674.

Economics offers a framework to study the implications of individual decision-making, and it can help define the alternative mechanisms available to improve resource allocation. Understanding what economics can and cannot do is the first and possibly most important step in using economics as a tool of public policy. It cannot provide solutions to all the problems of medical care access and delivery. When using economics to study medical care, it is important to avoid extremes. Arguing that economics does not matter, or at least should not matter, when it comes to medical care issues is as ill advised as arguing that economics is all that matters. We cannot avoid the economic implications of our actions any more than we can avoid their moral implications. Sound policymaking is based on sound economic principles applied in a compassionate and consistent manner. The premise of this book is that policymaking based on sound economics is better than policymaking in an economic vacuum. Basic economics teaches us many lessons: about human behavior and the way individuals make decisions and respond to incentives, about the way people interact with each other, and about the efficient allocation of scarce resources. Economists do not claim to have the final word about how to organize and run a health care system, but they do have something relevant to add to the discussion.

> **POLICY ISSUE**
> *Does sound policymaking require an understanding of economic principles?*

The goals of this chapter are somewhat ambitious. Those of you who have been exposed to an economics course may be tempted to skip this chapter completely: *Avoid that temptation.* At a minimum, use the chapter to refresh your memory of the important concepts that will come into play in analyzing medical markets and the policies that affect them. Those of you who have never had the privilege of taking a course in economics will find this chapter useful in setting the tone for the rest of the book. The principal focus here will be the examination of the basic principles of supply and demand.

The Relevance of Economics in Health Care

Economics is a way of organizing our thinking about problems that confront us in our daily lives. To think like an economist requires a disciplined approach to problem solving, and sound reasoning within a systematic framework is essential. The value of economics stems from its usefulness in making sense out of complex economic and social issues, including issues in medical care delivery. Future health care decision makers will need training and knowledge in many areas: not only biology and chemistry but statistics, epidemiology, behavioral science, ethics, decision analysis, and, of course, economics.

Economics is one of the several social sciences that attempt to explain and predict human behavior. It is unique among the social sciences in establishing a context of scarcity and uncertainty. More specifically, economics is concerned with the way scarce resources are allocated among alternative uses to satisfy unlimited human wants.

economic efficiency
Producing at a point at which average product is maximized and average variable cost is minimized.

The quest for **economic efficiency** stems from the fact that there are never enough resources to provide all the goods and services desired by a society. Economists call this concept *scarcity*. Using resources in one activity precludes the use of those same resources in a different activity. When resources are used in medical care delivery, those same resources are not available for use in other beneficial activities, for example, food distribution, education, housing, and national defense.

The economic concept of cost stems from the notion that resources have alternative uses. The term *opportunity cost* is defined as the potential benefit that could have been received if the resources had been used in their next-best alternative. Tax dollars used to purchase medical care for the elderly cannot be used to buy education for the young. Money spent in a rehabilitation program for drug addicts is not available to spend on prenatal care for indigent women. Pursuing economic efficiency implies that choices are made in a way that maximizes the total benefit from the available resources. In the practice of medical care delivery, this involves the evaluation of health care alternatives by calculating the benefits and costs of each and allocating resources in a way that maximizes the net benefits to the community.

Critical Assumptions in Economics

rational behavior
A key behavioral assumption in neoclassical economics that decision makers act in a purposeful manner. In other words, their actions are directed toward achieving an objective.

All scientific models start with assumptions. Economic models start by assuming **rational behavior** on the part of decision makers, meaning everyone involved in a decision behaves in a purposeful manner.[1] Economics is different from other social sciences in its emphasis on rational decision-making under conditions of scarcity.

In **microeconomics**, the assumption of rational behavior establishes a consistent framework for evaluating individual decision-making. We assume that individuals, in an attempt to reach certain objectives, must choose among competing alternatives. The problem becomes one of allocating scarce resources among these competing ends. In other words, we cannot satisfy every desire we have; we must make choices.

microeconomics
The study of individual decision-making, pricing behavior, and market organization.

Decision makers, motivated by self-interest, respond to incentives. In fact, decision-making is dominated by the pursuit of self-interest. Individuals use their resources to advance their own economic well-being. When confronted with alternative actions, they choose the one that makes them better off.[2]

rational ignorance
A state in which consumers stop seeking information on a prospective purchase because the expected cost of the additional search exceeds the expected benefits.

People look for the best way to achieve their goals. This does not rule out impulsive behavior or mistakes. In fact, because information is costly to gather and process, decision makers often practice **rational ignorance**: They decide between alternative actions with incomplete information. From the decision maker's perspective, the information left to be gathered costs more to gather than it is worth.

Scarcity is the reason we study economics. In a world of superabundance, there would be no compelling reason to make choices. All people could have all that they wanted without concern for alternative uses. On the other hand, if all individuals had the divine nature of saints, then our attitude would be one of relative indifference toward material goals, and

---

[1] Note that it is possible to study human behavior without assuming rationality, but that would not be economics.

[2] Altruistic behavior is not ruled out; it is merely interpreted as self-interested behavior.

scarcity would not be an issue. However, we do not live in a world of superabundance, and the world is not populated by saints, so decision-making must take into consideration forgone opportunities.

The Scientific Method

The challenge at hand is to understand economic relationships without the luxury of controlled experiments. Economic inquiry utilizes the scientific method in much the same way that physics and chemistry do. There are five basic steps in the scientific method:

1. Every scientist starts with a premise, or *postulate*, that serves as a foundation for the inquiry. Some may call it an *ideology* or even a *vision*. Either way it represents the scientist's understanding of the way the world works. The culture around us, the way our parents raised us, and years of scientific training and inquiry, all affect the way we view the world around us. Even the most unbiased among us are affected by some bias; at minimum, our biases affect the nature of our inquiry.
2. The world arouses our curiosity. Scientists are careful observers of real-world phenomena and events. These observations concerning the real world are organized and catalogued.
3. A theory is developed to explain the observed behavior or predict future behavior. Model building captures the essential features of the observed behavior. It is a meaningful abstraction, decomposing the problem into its elemental parts.
4. The scientist then formulates a hypothesis to test the predictions of the theory. This requires gathering of facts and data.
5. In the final step, hypothesis testing, we use quantitative techniques (econometrics) to improve our understanding of the issue and promote predictions that are more accurate.

In practice, an economist might approach a problem using the scientific method as follows: One vision of the way the world works might be that people who are truly motivated by self-interest will respond in measurable ways to changes in incentives. From this vision, a theory is developed that people will respond to higher out-of-pocket payments for health care by demanding fewer elective procedures. The RAND insurance experiment conducted controlled trials that randomly placed individuals into different types of health plans (Manning et al., 1987). By varying the out-of-pocket payments required of individuals, their demand for medical care was analyzed. Empirical results supported the hypothesis that higher out-of-pocket payments would lead to lower utilization, measured as fewer physician visits. The RAND experiment has spawned many additional studies, testing numerous different hypotheses. The way we think about health insurance pricing and payment policies has been significantly affected by this important research.

These are the steps involved in the scientific method: an ideological base, observation of events, development of a theory, hypothesis testing, and, finally, rethinking. Empirical results that run counter to expectations may cause the scientist to rethink the theory or develop a different hypothesis.

Model Building

One of the main goals of economics is to understand, explain, and predict the behavior of decision makers. To this end, economists find it necessary to simplify that behavior; this simplification is accomplished through generalization, often through the construction of models.

APPLIED MICRO METHODS

SELECTION BIAS IN OBSERVATIONAL STUDIES: THE CASE FOR RANDOMIZATION

Can observational studies answer the important questions in social science? Alternatively, do we need to rely solely on randomized controlled trials? R. A. Fisher (1928) argued that the only way to ensure equivalence between a treatment group and a control group is through random selection into each group. The feasibility and ethics of such assignment via social experimentation are open to considerable debate.

The advantage of randomized experimental research over nonrandomized observational studies is made clear using a simple model of a treatment effect (T). Suppose the behavioral outcome of interest is $Y = \alpha + \beta T + \gamma X + \varepsilon$, where X represents an observed characteristic of each individual in the study sample; α, β, and γ are parameters; and ε captures the random error or measurement error in Y.

Let's say, for example, that Y represents health care spending and T the degree of cost sharing (out-of-pocket spending) required by an individual's health plan. X might be certain demographic characteristic such as age, sex, or race, or it might be the existence of a preexisting health condition such as diabetes or coronary heart disease (CHD). Under the condition that ε is uncorrelated with both T and Y, least-squares regression provides an unbiased estimate of the treatment effect, β.

If, however, there is a characteristic, D, which is not observed for some reason (a hidden characteristic, unmeasured or simply unavailable) and D is correlated with T, then β will be a biased estimate of the treatment effect. This easily happens if D affects the type of plan that a person chooses. This might materialize if generous insurance coverage causes an increase in health care spending or if anticipated health care spending results in purchasing a more generous health plan. The true model is

$$Y = \alpha + \beta T + \gamma X + \delta D + \varepsilon$$

Moreover, because D is unobserved, its effect shows up in the new error term $u = \delta D + \varepsilon$. Due to data limitations, the observational model becomes

$$Y = \alpha + \beta T + \gamma X + u$$

where T is correlated with U (through D), causing the bias in β.

To summarize, the estimation bias in this case exists in observational studies because of the endogeneity between the treatment effect (T) and any unobserved covariates (D). The estimation problem may be avoided if the study can take advantage of randomized selection into the two groups, which in this case is unlikely.

One of the most recent large-scale randomized social experiments in health economics examined health plan generosity and its impact on health care spending and health status. The RAND Health Insurance Experiment randomly placed individuals into plans that varied along two dimensions: maximum out-of-pocket expenses and coinsurance rates that varied from 0 percent (completely free care) to 95 percent. The experiment ran from 1974 to 1982 and spawned a number of peer-reviewed studies. Two in particular (Brook et al., 1983; Manning et al., 1987) provided details on the impact of health plan generosity on medical care consumption and unbiased estimates of the price elasticity of demand for medical care (the RAND experiment will be discussed more thoroughly in later chapters).

However, randomization in social science research is seldom used on a large scale. Even though it is a common feature of medical research and is often required before medical treatments or procedures are approved for widespread use, its use in shaping social policy is often criticized. Experimentation on human subjects carries a high cost, starting with the ethical issues of subjecting humans to experiments. Rather than deal with these issues, economists use a variety of tools that we will address in the following chapters, applied micro techniques including difference-in-difference, instrumental variables, propensity score matching, regression discontinuity, and synthetic control.

Sources: Robert H. Brook et al., "Does Free Care Improve Adults' Health?" *New England Journal of Medicine* 309(23), December 8, 1983, 1426–1434; R. A. Fisher, *Statistical Methods for Research Workers*, 2nd ed., London: Oliver and Boyd, 1928; Willard G. Manning et al., "Health Insurance and the Demand for Medical Care: Evidence from a Randomized Experiment," *American Economic Review* 77(3), June 1987, 251–277.

A model is nothing more than a way of organizing knowledge on a particular issue so that it becomes more than a set of random observations. An economic model explains how the economy, or part of the economy, works. Economists often use the terms *model* and *theory* interchangeably. By their very nature, models are simplifications of the real-world phenomena they attempt to explain, and model building is an exercise in abstract thinking.

Microeconomic models examine the behavior of decision makers—individuals, households, firms, and government agents—and the behavior of specific markets. We use microeconomic models to study how a patient's demand for a particular diagnostic test varies, depending on the out-of-pocket cost of the test. We can examine how a shortage of qualified nurses affects nurses' salaries, or how the relative income of specialists affects the demand for residency-training positions in all specialties.

Problem Solving

Economics emerged as a science in the late eighteenth century with the publication of Adam Smith's *The Wealth of Nations*. Since that time, a wealth of theory has accumulated to help us understand and describe **economizing behavior**. Most microeconomic theory can be classified under the framework of **neoclassical economics**. Relying heavily on the rationality assumption, the neoclassical framework classifies all decision makers as optimizers—those who attempt to maximize their well-being. **Optimizing behavior,** or **optimization**, is nothing more than a decision maker pursuing certain objectives: maximize sales or profit, minimize cost, or maximize income. Economists often talk of decision-making calculus, which refers to the notion that individuals make mental calculations before arriving upon a decision. Optimization fits the calculus model well in that it evaluates a mathematical function for its maximum or minimum value.

Economic Optimization

When more than one alternative is available, the optimal choice produces an outcome that is most consistent with the decision maker's stated objectives. Optimization is nothing more than discovering the best course of action given the decision maker's goals and objectives. Constrained optimization takes into consideration the cost and availability of resources. Would it be better for the hospital to enter into a contract for housekeeping services with an outside firm, or perform the activity in-house? Following an increase in patient volume, should physicians in a small group practice hire an office manager, an additional nurse, or both?

Choices in health care delivery must be made at two levels: Individual physicians must decide on a particular course of treatment for a particular patient, and policy makers must decide on a course of action in planning the availability of health services for an entire community. The delivery of health care in any form must cover the following areas: whom

economizing behavior When individuals choose to limit their demand for goods and services voluntarily to save money.

neoclassical economics A branch of economic thought that uses microeconomic principles to defend the efficacy of perfectly competitive markets in resource allocation.

optimizing behavior, or **optimization** A technique used to determine the best or most favorable outcome in a particular situation.

KEY CONCEPT 1
Scarcity and Choice

ISSUES IN MEDICAL CARE DELIVERY

POSITIVE AND NORMATIVE ANALYSIS

positive analysis
A factually based statement whose validity can be tested empirically.

normative analysis
An economic statement based on opinion or ideology.

To a great extent, we will mix positive and normative analysis in our discussions. **Positive analysis** is the testing of hypotheses against facts; it examines the way things are. **Normative analysis** prescribes policies and actions to achieve certain goals; it purports to examine the way things ought to be.

The differences between positive and normative statements are easy to spot. "The United States spends more money per capita on medical care than any other country" is an example of a positive statement. "Congress should guarantee universal insurance coverage by requiring all employers to provide health insurance to their workers" is a normative statement.

Positive statements are either true or false. It is the task of science to determine which they are. Normative statements are matters of opinion, so science is of little help in determining their legitimacy. Fuchs (1996), in a survey of 90 economists concerning issues in health economics and health policy, found that over 90 percent disagreed with the positive statement, "In the long run, employers bear the primary burden of their contributions to employees' health insurance." In contrast, opinion was divided almost equally on the normative statement: "National standardized health insurance benefit packages should be established." Disputes over facts can be settled through careful observation and analysis. Settling disputes over differences of opinion, on the other hand, is almost never easy. In fact, disagreements among economists are typically disputes over normative issues, and these disagreements represent differences of opinion based on differences in ideology.

☆ **KEY CONCEPT 8**
Efficiency

to treat, when to begin treatment, where to treat, and how much treatment to offer. Of the many ways to go about choosing the best alternatives, economic efficiency will be the criterion examined in this section.

In a sense, optimal decision-making is nothing more than the classic "economic problem." Resource allocation demands that we answer three basic questions:

1. *What do we produce?*
2. *How do we produce it?*
3. *Who gets it?*

Regardless of our perspective, whether we are examining economic systems, health care systems, business firms, individuals, or decision makers of any kind, something must drive the system to produce and distribute what people want. Just remember: what, how, and for whom? This is the economic problem that must be solved to promote growth and welfare in any modern society.

To resolve the economic problem, firms attempt to maximize profit, given the production technology and the cost of available resources; consumers attempt to maximize satisfaction, subject to limited money income and the prices of goods consumed; and workers supply labor services in an attempt to maximize satisfaction derived from goods and services consumed and leisure time available subject to current wages. Together, this more or less independent behavior results in markets that tend toward equilibrium as represented by the familiar, or soon to be familiar, supply-and-demand framework.

☆ **KEY CONCEPT 3**
Marginal Analysis

marginal benefit
The change in total benefits resulting from a one-unit change in the level of output.

Within this framework, *optimal* means that individuals will continue to purchase a good or service as long as the **marginal benefits** (MB) from consumption exceed the

FIGURE 2.1
Economic Optimization

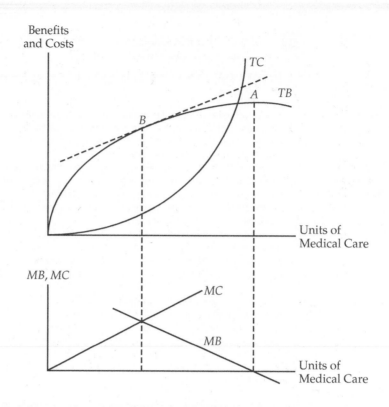

marginal cost The
change in total cost
resulting from a one-
unit change in the level
of output.

☆ **KEY CONCEPT 2**
Opportunity Cost

marginal costs (MC). Given that marginal benefits are declining and marginal costs are increasing as more of the good is consumed, eventually the two will be equal. As soon as MB = MC, equilibrium is reached, and the individual will consume no more. In Figure 2.1, the total benefits (TB) received from a medical procedure increase as more care is provided, but at a decreasing rate. For reasons both ethical and practical, medical practitioners tend to provide additional care as long as the treatment results in positive benefits. Beyond point *A*, additional medical care is equivocal or wasteful—the marginal benefits are not worth the medical risk.

From the perspective of economics, exhausting all possible medical benefits wastes scarce resources. In fact, any care provided beyond point *B* is wasteful, because the marginal benefits received from the additional care are less than the marginal costs.[3] The resources used in providing the excess care could be better used somewhere else. Money wasted in the provision of unnecessary care cannot be used to further other important goals, such as improving education, repairing the interstate highway system, or cleaning up the environment.

When consumption is subsidized, the cost to the consumer is less than the total resource cost, as in the case of medical care purchased with insurance. In other words, the cost of an extra unit of care to the individual is close to zero (on average 12 cents on the dollar), providing an incentive to consume medical care with low marginal benefits. When the marginal cost to the consumer is artificially low, resources are treated as if they had little or no value—a prescription for overconsumption. This tendency to overconsume means that medical care consumption is likely to be closer to point *A*, where the marginal benefit

---

[3]In this discussion, cost is measured in terms of total resource cost, the actual opportunity cost of the resources consumed in the production of medical care, not merely the out-of-pocket cost to the consumer.

KEY CONCEPT 9
Market Failure

KEY CONCEPT 6
Supply and Demand

is close to zero, than point *B*, where the marginal benefit is equal to marginal cost. This phenomenon is called *flat-of-the-curve medicine.*[4]

Supply and Demand

Many consider supply and demand the two most useful concepts in economics. Regardless of the issue, the analysis often hinges on some aspect of supply and demand. The theory of supply and demand is also a powerful tool in predicting future behavior. How does a change in price affect the consumer's willingness or ability to purchase a commodity? How does a change in the price of a key input affect the producer's decision about the optimal input combination to use in the production process?

In modeling behavior, economists attempt to simplify relationships. The amount of a particular commodity that a consumer plans to purchase depends on several factors. Instead of looking at the large number of variables that would affect demand, we focus on the most important ones: the price of the commodity; the price of related commodities; the number of people desiring the commodity; and consumer income, preferences, and expectations.

The Law of Demand

The theory of demand occupies such an important place in economic analysis that economists have given it the status of a law. The law of demand states:

> *There is an inverse relationship between the amount of a commodity that a person will purchase and the sacrifice required to obtain it.*

When the price of an item is high, you purchase less, and when price is lower, you purchase more. It is important to understand that this inverse, or negative, relationship holds as long as the circumstances of the consumer do not change materially. Remember, other things affect the demand relationship: prices of related items, the consumer's income, and preferences. As long as there are no changes in these other factors, the inverse relationship holds. When prices rise, consumers desire less. When prices fall, they desire more.

Changes in price affect the demand relationship in two very important ways. First, consumers have alternative ways to spend their money. If the price of a name-brand drug goes up, they substitute an alternative drug or even a generic version for the name brand. Alternatively, if money is tight and no insurance coverage is available, the patient can choose to skip the treatment and let the disease go untreated. In any case, when price rises, the quantity demanded goes down. Economists refer to this phenomenon as the *substitution effect.*

A change in price affects the consumer in another important way. Paying higher prices for a desired commodity reduces the consumer's overall level of satisfaction. Spending more for one item leaves you with less to spend on everything else. With less money to spend, the consumer is unable to buy as much of everything else as before and thus feels worse off. This aspect of a price change on quantity demanded is called the *income effect.*

Part (a) of Figure 2.2 illustrates how an increase in price affects demand. Suppose that the demand curve labeled D_1 represents the demand for a particular commodity. Assuming no other changes, an increase in the price from P_0 to P_1 will reduce the quantity demanded from Q_0 to Q_1. A movement along the stationary demand curve from point *A* to point *B*.

---

[4]The phrase "flat of the curve" is attributed to Alain Enthoven (1980).

FIGURE 2.2

A Change in Quantity
Demanded and a
Change in the Level of
Demand

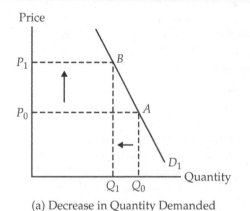

(a) Decrease in Quantity Demanded

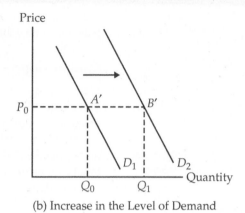

(b) Increase in the Level of Demand

depicts this change in quantity demanded. A change in price, holding everything else constant, changes the quantity demanded.

Many factors other than price influence our purchasing decisions. These factors are held constant in the analysis and are sometimes referred to as *ceteris paribus* conditions. These conditions are factors that are held constant when examining the relationship between price and quantity demanded. They include:

- *The price of related commodities*
- *The number and type of people desiring the commodity*
- *Consumer income*
- *Consumer preferences*
- *Consumer expectations about future prices and product availability*

A change in the price of a related commodity changes the demand for the commodity in question. Related commodities are either substitutes or complements. An increase in the price of a substitute increases the demand for a commodity. Coronary artery bypass graft (CABG) surgery and cardiac angioplasty are two procedures used to accomplish the desired outcome. If the price of a CABG increases, heart patients—or rather whoever is paying for the procedure—may view cardiac angioplasty as a more viable alternative. The demand for cardiac angioplasty will increase.

When the price of a complement goes down, demand goes up, because complementary goods are consumed together. Dentists often recommend that full-mouth X-rays accompany the annual dental exam; X-rays complement the annual exam. If the price of the X-ray goes down, more patients will make appointments for dental exams.

An increase in the size of the population or its composition affects demand. More consumers result in a higher demand for all goods and services, including medical care. The addition of an infant to a family increases the demand for visits to the pediatrician. An increase in the birth rate raises the demand for disposable diapers, even if the average baby still uses the same number of diapers per day. An older population has a higher demand for treatments for chronic illnesses, such as arthritis and emphysema.[5]

A change in income affects the consumer's ability to purchase goods and services. In situations where higher income leads to increased demand, the good in question is referred to as a *normal good*. In some cases, an increase in income leads to a decrease in

---

[5]The examples point out the importance of distinguishing between individual demand and market demand. Clearly, the market demand curve is determined by combining the demand curves of all the individuals actively participating in the market.

demand. In those situations, the good is called an *inferior good*. Medical care is usually considered a normal good. For individuals with comparable levels of health, higher income means a higher demand for medical care. Good health improves a person's ability to earn income. Higher income in turn increases the return to good health and increases the demand for medical care.

Consumer preferences play a key role in determining an individual's demand for goods and services. Some flu sufferers will consider a visit to the physician only as a last resort. They prefer to treat their ailment with over-the-counter medications. Some people hold religious beliefs (e.g., Christian Scientists) that strongly discourage the use of medical care. Others are convinced of the efficacy of chiropractors, herbalists, acupuncturists, midwives, and other alternative providers. They prefer these alternatives to the more traditional health care providers, and this shift in preferences can have a powerful impact on demand.

Consumer expectations play a key role in determining the level of demand. If consumers expect prices to increase steeply and suddenly, or if they are afraid, the product will be difficult to obtain in the near future, demand will rise sharply.

Finally, it is important to note that the demand for resources is a derived demand. Whenever a resource is used to produce a final product, the demand for that resource is ultimately determined by the demand for the final product. If medical care is considered an essential element in promoting the health of an individual or a group of people, an increase in the demand for health will increase the demand for medical care.

A change in one of these other factors changes the level of demand and causes a shift in the demand curve. Refer once again to Figure 2.2. Part (b) depicts a change that increases the level of demand caused by an increase in the price of a substitute commodity, a decrease in the price of a complement, an increase in consumer income, a positive shift in preferences, the expectation of a price increase, or a decline in availability in the future. Suppose the level of demand is originally D_1 in part (b). At the price P_0, the quantity demanded is Q_0. With the price held constant, an increase in consumer income will cause a rightward shift in the demand curve to D_2. This shift in the demand curve depicts an increased demand for the commodity. The consumer will now desire Q_1 at the price P_0.

To summarize, a change in the price of a commodity or service, holding everything else constant, will result in a change in quantity demanded, shown as a movement along a stationary demand curve. A change in any of the factors that affect the level of demand results in a shift in the demand curve—consumers demand more or less of the commodity or service at every price level.

Price Elasticity of Demand

An important corollary to the law of demand is the concept of price elasticity of demand. The law of demand answers the question, "When price changes, what is the effect on the quantity demanded?" Taking this notion one step further, price elasticity of demand is a technical concept used to answer the question, "When price changes, how much does quantity demanded change?" The inverse relationship between price and quantity is relatively easy to comprehend. In most cases, it is important to include not only the direction of the change but also the magnitude of the change.

Price elasticity of demand measures consumer responsiveness to a change in price, holding the other variables that affect demand constant. Slope also measures the relationship between quantity demanded and price, but slope is not elasticity; slope measures the change in quantity demanded that results from a price change in absolute terms. Elasticity measures the change in relative (percentage) terms.

TABLE 2.1 PRICE ELASTICITY OF DEMAND

Coefficient value	Nature of demand	Impact of a 10 percent price increase on quantity demanded	Impact of a 10 percent price increase on total expenditures
$|\varepsilon| = \infty$	Perfectly elastic	Falls to 0	Falls to 0
$1 < |\varepsilon| < \infty$	Elastic	Decreases by more than 10 percent	Decreases
$|\varepsilon| = 1$	Unit elastic	Decreases exactly 10 percent	No change
$0 < |\varepsilon| < 1$	Inelastic	Decreases by less than 10 percent	Increases by less than 10 percent
$|\varepsilon| = 0$	Perfectly inelastic	No change	Increases by 10 percent

Price elasticity of demand is defined as the percentage change in quantity demanded divided by the percentage change in price. Formally, price elasticity (ε_p) is calculated as

$$\varepsilon_p = \frac{percentage\ change\ in\ Q}{percentage\ change\ in\ P}$$

where Q is quantity demanded, and P is the unit price.

If consumer demand increases 10 percent because of a 5 percent price decrease, price elasticity of demand is 10 percent divided by 5 percent, or 2.0.[6] Values for the elasticity coefficient range from zero (0) to infinity (∞).

A summary of all possible values for the price elasticity coefficient is provided in Table 2.1. In the case in which price elasticity equals zero, consumers are completely unresponsive to changes in price. Their consumption patterns are fixed, and a higher price does not affect quantity demanded. Under these circumstances, demand is said to be *perfectly inelastic* or *totally unresponsive*. The demand for addictive substances may come about as close to perfectly inelastic demand as anything. The demand for life-saving procedures, such as kidney dialysis and organ transplants, may also fall into this category.

A more likely scenario would be the case in which a price change has an impact on quantity demanded, but the consumer response is less than proportional. In other words, we consider consumer demand somewhat unresponsive when the percentage change in quantity demanded is less than the percentage change in price. In this case, the elasticity coefficient is less than one, and demand is inelastic. Even addicts and terminally ill patients have their limits on how much they are willing or able to pay for a desired commodity.

An elasticity that is greater than 1 represents a change in quantity demanded that is proportionately greater than the change in price. Consumers are said to be *relatively responsive*, and in this case, demand is elastic. In the rare case where the elasticity coefficient is equal to infinity, demand is *perfectly elastic*; consumers are intolerant of even small changes in price and refuse to buy the item if its price goes up at all.

An important use of the concept of price elasticity is illustrated in the right-hand column of Table 2.1. When price changes, it is important to know how much quantity demanded changes. It is also important to realize that this same information enables us to predict what will happen to consumer expenditures. With perfectly elastic demand, any price increase causes quantity demanded to fall to zero. In this case, it may be obvious that consumer

---

[6]The actual calculation is $[(+0.10)/(-0.05) = -2.0]$. While the price elasticity coefficient is always negative, for simplicity, we usually ignore the negative sign, or more precisely, we consider its absolute value.

expenditures also fall to zero. The case of unit elasticity may not be so obvious. When price elasticity equals one, a 10 percent price increase causes quantity demanded to fall by 10 percent, and consumer expenditures do not change. Likewise, price increases cause consumer expenditures to fall when demand is elastic and to increase when demand is inelastic.

What determines the price elasticity of demand? Why are consumers more tolerant of price changes for some items but not others? Price elasticity depends primarily on the consumer's ability to find suitable substitutes for a good or service. The easier it is to substitute, the more elastic the consumer's demand. If the consumer perceives a number of good alternatives to the item, demand is likely to be more responsive to changes in price. Patients with no established preference for a general practitioner (GP) might view a 20 percent increase in the price of an office visit as intolerable in light of the number of suitable alternative GPs in practice. However, if there are relatively few GP practices open to new patients, individuals may be willing to remain a loyal patient in spite of the price increase. In this case, the GP will lose some business but not all of it.

Other factors that influence the degree of consumer responsiveness are the proportion of a person's income spent on the item and the urgency of the purchase. If the cost of the item comprises a substantial portion of a consumer's total income, demand will likely be elastic. Consumers are more sensitive to a price change on the purchase of big-ticket items. Insulin-dependent diabetics are more sensitive to a change in the price of syringes than the typical nondiabetic patient is. The diabetic patient buys a lot more syringes per year than the nondiabetic. Finally, demand for nonurgent procedures will be more elastic than demand for emergency procedures. The more time a patient has to make a decision, the more price sensitive he or she will likely be. A patient entering the emergency room with a compound fracture does not have much time to shop around for an orthopedic surgeon. Patients desiring elective rhinoplasty, however, have the opportunity and the luxury to shop around for the best plastic surgeon, the best price, the best financing, or whatever else they consider important. A patient who shops around is more likely to find suitable alternatives.

Demand curves are typically drawn as straight lines for the sake of simplicity. There are three possibilities, as shown in Figure 2.3. Perfectly inelastic demand curves are drawn as vertical lines indicating zero response, and perfectly elastic demand curves are depicted by horizontal lines, indicating infinite response. The typical downward-sloping demand curve is shown at the right. Although slope is the same at every point, elasticity is not. The relationship between slope and elasticity at any point on the demand curve is

$$\varepsilon_p = \frac{\Delta Q/Q}{\Delta P/P} = \frac{P\Delta Q}{Q\Delta P} = \frac{P/Q}{slope}$$

where Q is the quantity demanded, P is the unit price, and Δ is used to represent a change in the variable.

FIGURE 2.3
Elasticity of Demand along Straight-Line Demand Curves

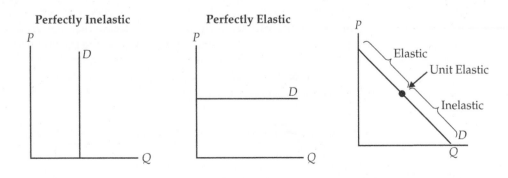

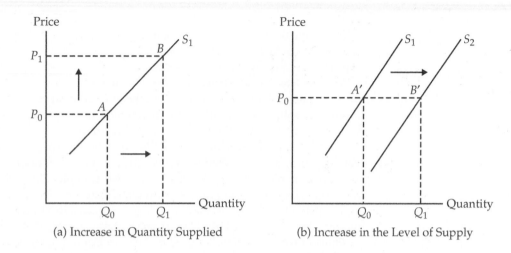

FIGURE 2.4
A Change in Quantity Supplied and a Change in the Level of Supply

(a) Increase in Quantity Supplied

(b) Increase in the Level of Supply

A demand curve with a constant slope has a continuously declining elasticity. Moving from the upper left to the lower right on a downward-sloping demand curve, the P/Q ratio is declining: As price falls, quantity demanded increases. It follows that the demand curve goes from elastic to inelastic as you move down a straight-line demand curve.[7]

The Law of Supply

The theory of supply assumes that decision makers, producers in this case, are faced with scarce resources and must choose among alternative uses. Supply decisions involve the allocation of resources among competing uses. The law of supply states:

> *There is a direct relationship between the amount of a commodity that a producer will make available and the reward for making it available.*

KEY CONCEPT 8
Efficiency

Higher prices increase the availability of an item. At lower prices, less will be available. Suppliers practice economizing behavior much as consumers do. The market rewards efficiency and punishes wastefulness.

Producers are concerned with cost. This concern is more than an accounting of the value of inputs; it involves establishing the opportunity cost of those inputs. In economics, cost reflects the value of resources in their next-best alternative use. In other words, forgone opportunities are an important element in determining value. Resources used in the production of one commodity are not available to produce another. Economizing behavior guarantees that resources are used where they have the highest value. Therefore, cost is determined by the value of what is being given up to produce any item.

Part (a) of Figure 2.4 illustrates how a change in the price of a commodity affects quantity supplied. Suppose that the curve labeled S_1 depicts supply. Assuming no other changes, an increase in price from P_0 to P_1 will increase the quantity supplied from Q_0 to Q_1. At higher prices, suppliers will transfer resources to the production of the higher-priced commodity, making more of it available to the market. A change in price, holding everything else constant, results in a change in quantity supplied, depicted by a movement along the stationary supply curve.

---

[7]Economists sometimes refer to an entire demand curve as inelastic if it is generally steep and elastic if it is generally flat. While technically incorrect, as a matter of convenience, we often think in these terms.

Many other factors affect the availability of goods and services in a market. A change in any one of these factors, the ceteris paribus conditions, will change the level of supply. Other factors that affect the level of supply include:

- *The prices of resources used to produce the commodity*
- *The number of firms supplying the commodity*
- *The state of technology*
- *Producer expectations about future prices and availability*

In general, anything that changes the costs of producing a commodity will affect the level of supply. Resources have alternative uses. In order to use resources to produce a particular commodity, producers must bid them away from their next-best alternative use. An increase in the price of a resource decreases the supply of the commodity that uses the resource as an input in the production process, and it raises its price. Technicians trained to operate the new magnetic resonance imaging (MRI) machines are in short supply. As competition bids up their wages, the cost of providing MRI services increases, shifting the supply curve for MRIs to the left and raising the price of the service in the market.

An increase in the number of suppliers increases access to a product or service. More suppliers mean that consumers have more choices. The construction of a new 250-bed hospital in a community will increase the availability of inpatient hospital services to local residents. At any given price per day, there are now more beds available to serve the patient population.

New technology that reduces the cost of producing a commodity or service increases the level of supply. In the case of medical technology, certain analytical problems make it difficult to evaluate the different supply responses of cost-reducing and quality-enhancing technology. Arthroscopic surgery provides a clear example of a technological advance that represents both a cost-reducing and a quality-enhancing change. The repair of a damaged anterior cruciate ligament was once a major ordeal for both surgeon and patient. Before the introduction of the laparoscope, an athlete who suffered this knee injury endured a four-hour surgery requiring a six-inch incision, several days in the hospital, and six weeks on crutches. Today, the same procedure is a routine outpatient procedure. It requires three small incisions and a much shorter recovery period.

If suppliers expect the price of a commodity or service to fall in the future, they have an incentive to make it immediately available. If for some reason suppliers expect an increase in future availability, current supply will increase. As the medical marketplace moves systematically toward the managed care model, physicians scramble to join provider networks. Expectations create powerful incentives. As more physicians join networks, fueling expectations, others feel an urgency to join them.

An increase in the level of supply is illustrated graphically in part (b) of Figure 2.4. Anything that enhances a producer's ability to bring a product to the market increases the level of supply and results in a rightward shift in the supply curve. A decrease in resource costs, an increase in the number of providers, a technological advance that increases production efficiency, and the expectation of downward-price movements, all increase the level of supply and cause the supply curve to shift to the right. Suppose that the supply curve shifts from S_1 to S_2. At any given price level, say P_0, providers will be willing to increase the quantity supplied from Q_0 to Q_1.

To summarize, a change in the price of a commodity or service, holding everything else constant, will result in a change in the quantity supplied. This change is shown as a movement along a stationary supply curve. A change in any of the factors that affect the level of supply results in a shift in the supply curve and a change in the availability of the commodity or service at any given price.

ISSUES IN MEDICAL CARE DELIVERY

HOW TO SURVIVE SUPPLY AND DEMAND?

Succeeding in any economics course, especially a course in health economics depends on your mastery of the twin concepts of supply and demand. Listen carefully to economic commentators when they are queried on a complex issue in economic theory or public policy, and their answer is frequently preceded by "It's because of supply and demand." The introduction of supply and demand into the economics vocabulary is soon followed by adding supply and demand curves to the lexicon. Your success depends on your ability to keep your wits about you while others around you fail. To ensure your success, follow these simple rules of survival (Ripsin et al., 1992):

- *Use common sense.* Most students already know a great deal about supply and demand. The key is to use what you know. Remember, economics is a way of thinking. For the most part, it is intuitive. Think about the market for oatmeal. Scientific evidence has suggested that consuming large quantities of oat products every day reduces the level of cholesterol in the bloodstream and thus the risk of heart attack. What do you suppose happened to the demand for oatmeal, and its price, immediately after this information was made public? If you said that demand for oatmeal increased and its price also went up, then you already have some intuitive notion of the workings of supply and demand.
- *Learn the language.* After a few weeks in Econ 101, many students feel the professor is speaking a foreign language. Mastery of economics requires that you learn the language of economists. When it comes to supply and demand, economists speak in graphs. Understand graphs and you understand supply and demand. If freshman literature were taught in Greek, it would be extremely difficult for the typical student. The subject matter is not particularly hard; it is the language. Introductory economics is taught in graphs. Learning to use graphs makes learning economics much easier.
- *Practice.* The rules of graphing are simple. Unlike a foreign language, there are no irregular verbs. However, like a foreign language, it takes practice to master the subject matter. Practice whenever you can; economics is not a spectator sport. Watching your professor manipulate graphs is not enough: You have to do it yourself. Remember, demand curves are downward sloping, and supply curves are upward sloping. Economists place price on the vertical axis and quantity on the horizontal axis. The intersection of the supply and demand curves determines equilibrium price and quantity.
- *Shift the appropriate curve.* The discovery that oat products have health benefits affected the market for oats. Did it affect supply, demand, or both? Remember what causes shifts in each of the two curves. For the supply curve to shift, a change in the cost or profitability of making a product available to the market is required. Anything that changes the willingness or ability of consumers to buy something causes a shift in the demand curve. The discovery that oatmeal works like drain cleaner to clean out your arteries affected consumers' willingness to buy the product. Therefore, the demand curve shifted. Did it shift to the right or to the left? If in doubt at this point, go back to rule number one: An increase in demand will increase price. The only way to get this result is to shift the demand curve to the right. Shifting the demand curve to the left, or shifting the supply curve, is counterintuitive.

It is now time to test your mastery of supply and demand. Consider the market for hospital services. Use a graph similar to the one in Figure 2.5. Label the vertical axis "Price of Hospital Services" and the horizontal axis "Quantity of Hospital Services." Draw the supply and demand curves, and identify the equilibrium price and the quantity of hospital services. Now suppose that due to a nursing shortage, the average nurse's salary increases 10 percent. What effect will this increased cost have on the market for hospital services?

Source: Cynthia M. Ripsin et al., "Oat Products and Lipid Lowering: A Meta-Analysis," *Journal of the American Medical Association* 267(24), June 24, 1992, 3317–3325.

Equilibrium

Price changes affect buyers and sellers differently. An increase in price reduces the consumer's willingness to buy and at the same time increases the producer's willingness to provide. The most fascinating aspect of the marketplace is how the more or less independent behavior of buyers and sellers results in an allocation of resources that guarantees that all consumers willing to pay the market price will find willing sellers, and all sellers willing to accept the price will find buyers. Smith observed that it is as if an "invisible hand" were responsible for the price adjustments that promote the best use of resources.

We define the equilibrium price as the market price that exists when the quantity demanded equals the quantity supplied. Suppose that the price of the commodity depicted in Figure 2.5 is P_1. At that price, producers would like to sell more than consumers are willing to buy. There is a surplus, because the quantity supplied is greater than the quantity demanded. When prices are too high in the medical marketplace, hospitals, for example, will have unused capacity. This excess capacity takes the form of idle resources, empty beds, and unused operating rooms. Physicians find their appointment books unfilled and their waiting rooms empty. A surplus serves to increase competition among providers. The competition may manifest itself in many ways, but one sure way to eliminate the surplus and increase quantity demanded is to lower prices.

At the price P_2, quantity demanded exceeds quantity supplied, resulting in a shortage. Patients experience significant delays in getting appointments. When they do get an appointment, the waiting room is crowded and delays are frequent. Nonemergency surgeries have to be scheduled far in advance. Access to diagnostic imaging equipment is limited. Under these conditions, prices have a tendency to adjust upward. Competition among consumers bids prices up and reduces quantity demanded. Coupled with an increase in quantity supplied, the shortage is eliminated.

Only one price does not result in either a surplus or a shortage. That price, P_0, the equilibrium price, clears the market. At P_0, the behavior of buyers and sellers coincide. Buyers are willing to pay the price that providers are willing to accept. Everyone who wants to buy at P_0 is able to buy, and everyone who wants to sell at that price is able to sell. In a market economy, people are free to make transactions: They are free to bid for goods and services at any price and free to offer those same goods and services at any price. When buyers seek the lowest price that producers are willing to accept, and sellers seek the highest price that consumers are willing to pay, the transaction price that clears the market is the equilibrium price.

FIGURE 2.5
Equilibrium

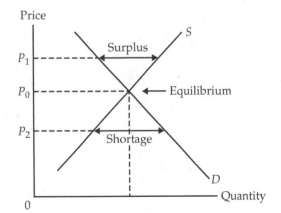

The Competitive Model

Free markets play a crucial role in the free enterprise system. The market system is grounded in the concept of consumer sovereignty: What is produced is determined by what people want and are able to buy. No one individual or group dictates what is produced or purchased. No one limits the range of choice.

The market accomplishes its task of resource allocation through a system of prices, again, what Smith called the "invisible hand." In a market system, this invisible hand allocates resources because everyone and everything has a price. There is a tendency for prices to increase if more is desired and to decrease if less is desired.

Firms base their production decisions on relative prices and relative price movements. The price mechanism becomes a way of bringing a firm's output decisions into balance with consumer desires, something that we refer to as *equilibrium*.

Prices serve not only as a signal to producers but as a means of rewarding popular decisions. Producers who invest in appropriate technology are able to produce goods and services desired by consumers. Their rewards come in the form of profits. The market punishes poor decisions, and the producer suffers losses. This market discipline, accompanied by the freedom to compete within a system that allows private property ownership, is largely responsible for the efficient use of resources.

The Theory of Firm Behavior

One desirable outcome of a perfectly competitive marketplace is the efficient use of resources. The characteristics of the model of perfect competition are many buyers and sellers, a standardized product, mobile resources, and perfect information. These four characteristics guarantee that risk-adjusted rates of return will be equal to the normal rate of return for the economy, that prices are equal to minimum average cost of production, and that all transactions beneficial to both buyer and seller will take place.

Every firm must decide how much to produce and what price to charge. The firm's costs ultimately determine the choice of an output level and a pricing strategy. In a perfectly competitive market, the pricing decision is easy, because the product is standardized and firms must follow the dictates of the market. Firms that charge more than the market price lose customers. Firms have no incentive to charge a price lower than the market price, because they find all the willing customers they desire at that price. Firms are called *price takers*.

Figure 2.6 provides an illustration of the perfectly competitive market. The interaction of supply and demand in part (a) determines price. At the price P_0, the representative firm

FIGURE 2.6 Perfect Competition

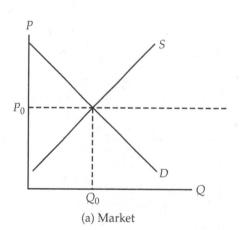

(a) Market

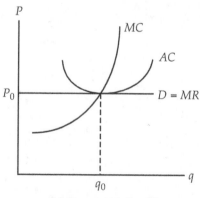

(b) Representative Firm

can sell all it can produce. A profit maximizer will produce every unit of output when the selling price is greater than the marginal cost of production—that is, as long as P_0 is greater than MC. Because the competitive firm is a price taker, its demand curve is perfectly elastic at the market price. In the case of a horizontal demand curve, the firm's marginal revenue (MR) curve is equal to price. Profit is maximized where MR = MC, or at q_0 units of output.

Competitive forces will lead to prices equilibrating at minimum average costs. At a price above P_0, price is greater than the average cost of production. Firms enjoy excess profits, or higher than normal rates of return, which encourages the entry of new firms into the market. As these new entrants establish their presence, supply increases and prices fall, until all excess profits are eliminated.

KEY CONCEPT 7
Competition

The Economics of Price Controls

The impact of government-imposed price controls depends on the competitive nature of the market in which they exist. In a competitive market, a binding **price ceiling**—one where the legal price is below the equilibrium price—will cause a shortage.

price ceiling
A maximum price established by law, contract, or agreement.

The left-hand side of Figure 2.7 depicts the demand curve (D) and supply curve (S) for a product sold in a competitive market. With no market interference, the equilibrium is established at the intersection of supply and demand, yielding the market-clearing price (P_0) and quantity (Q_0). If government uses its authority to set a binding price ceiling (P_1), producers will choose to produce at a lower level of output (Q_1). At the lower price, however, consumers will want more (Q_2). The resulting discrepancy between the quantity demanded and the quantity supplied, Q_2-Q_1, is the shortage.

Ironically, the unintended consequence of this action to lower the price of the product has actually raised its effective price to consumers. How? In their quest to secure desired quantities of the product at a lower price, consumers will compete in other ways. If price does not serve to ration the product, another mechanism will emerge. Consumers will get up early, stay up late, become friends with producers, resort to bribes, and buy in large quantities when the product is available, all of which add to the nonpecuniary cost of the product. Added to these costs is the anxiety created by the increased uncertainty of not knowing whether you will ever have as much of the product as you want.

Referring back to Figure 2.7, the nonpecuniary costs grow until their combined effects shift the consumers' demand curve down to D'. At the new equilibrium, consumers are paying less in money terms (P_1) but more when you combine both monetary costs and nonmonetary costs (P_2).

FIGURE 2.7 Price Ceiling

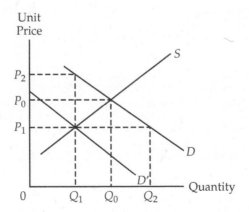
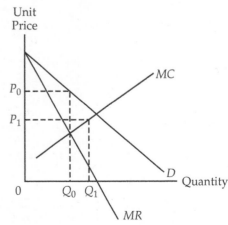

Price controls can be effective in a market controlled by a monopolist. The right-hand side of Figure 2.7 shows a monopolist, as sole seller, facing the market demand curve and producing where marginal revenue (MR) equals marginal cost (MC). The profit-maximizing equilibrium price and quantity are established at P_0 and Q_0. In this case, the government can set a price below P_0 and actually increase the quantity produced. A price ceiling set at P_1 will change the effective shape of the demand and marginal revenue curves. They both become a horizontal line at the ceiling price. Thus, marginal revenue (now P_1) equals marginal cost at the quantity Q_1.

Do price controls produce shortages, black markets, and reduced quality? It depends on the nature of competition in the market. How do price controls affect medical markets? It depends, once again, on which segment of the medical market you are considering. The market for patented drugs probably fits the classical case of monopoly better than any other aspect of the medical market. A suitably chosen price could improve the efficiency in this market, assuming that regulators are clever enough to choose the right price. Failure to choose the right price will lead, however, to reduced research and development, fewer discoveries, and the loss of consumer welfare (decreasing quality of life). The markets for physician and hospital services are much closer to the competitive model in many health services markets, and price controls are likely to have undesirable effects.

At least one former government policy analyst seems to agree that price controls could lead to restrictions on the rate of technological development and ultimately the rationing of health care (Wagner, 1993). As director of the Congressional Budget Office (CBO), Robert Reischauer testified before the House Ways and Means health subcommittee on the possible effects of price controls on medical care. Research by the CBO, which conducts financial analysis for Congress, concluded that price controls could severely limit the quality and quantity of medical care in the United States. Reischauer went on to argue that the only way to control medical care spending is by imposing global health care budgets at the national level. Thus, Reischauer exhibits the irony of government policy makers—arguing for and against price controls at the same time.

Policy makers are desperate to control medical care spending. Many feel that desperate times call for desperate measures. Some even think that their ability to write laws also applies to the laws of supply and demand. Governments have been trying for centuries to rewrite the laws of supply and demand and have always failed miserably.[8]

BACK-OF-THE-ENVELOPE

Why a Price Ceiling May Not Lower Spending

It is easy to understand why the casual observer could expect price controls to slow spending growth. Using the following diagram, the demand for medical care is depicted by the downward-sloping demand curve, labeled D_0. For purposes of this discussion, assume that providers are accommodating to the wishes of the patient population and supply all the medical care desired at the prevailing price. If equilibrium is at point A, quantity demanded is Q_0, and price is P_0. Total spending will be P_0 times Q_0, depicted by the area $0P_0 AQ_0$. If regulators enact a price ceiling at P_1, the new equilibrium will be at point B, and quantity will be Q_1. Since demand for medical care is relatively price

---

[8]For a history of government price controls, see Robert L. Schuettinger and Eamonn F. Butler, *Forty Centuries of Wage and Price Controls: How Not to Fight Inflation,* Washington, DC: Heritage Foundation, 1978.

inelastic, the new level of spending, $0P_1BQ_1$, is less than before (if the demand were relatively elastic, the new level of spending would be greater).

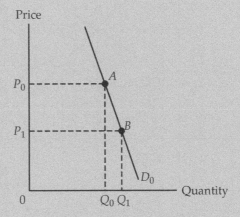

It would be great for policy makers if things worked out this way. Controlling the growth in medical care spending would be simple. Mandate lower prices in a market characterized by inelastic demand, and spending levels will fall. Several problems are inherent in this approach. Providers will only accommodate patient desires up to a point. Drive the price down below cost, and quantity supplied will go down. Even with accommodating providers, spending is likely to rise. The following diagram shows how.

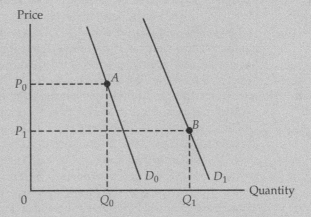

Begin with the same demand curve D_0, price P_0, quantity Q_0, and spending $0P_0AQ_0$. A price ceiling at P_1 creates an incentive for providers to increase service intensity and maybe even influence demand (remember the concept of supplier-induced demand). Expanding the size of the eligible population and incorporating advances in technology created for the uncontrolled segment of the market—which is three to four times larger than the controlled segment—work together to shift demand to the right, to D_1. The resulting level of spending, $0P_1BQ_1$, is actually higher than before the drop in price.

The Impact of an Excise Tax

The excise tax is becoming an increasingly popular way of imposing user fees on the consumption of specific items, such as gasoline, tobacco, and alcohol. Excise taxes may be set at a fixed dollar amount or at a percentage of selling price, called either a *specific tax* or an *ad valorem tax*.

FIGURE 2.8 Excise
Taxes

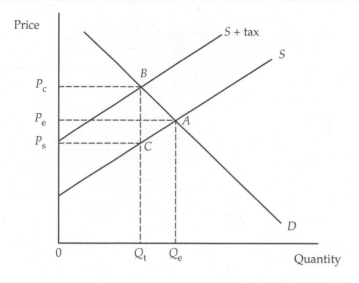

KEY CONCEPT 9
Market Failure

In a competitive market, depicted in Figure 2.8, price and output are determined by the interaction of supply and demand. The commodity will sell for the price P_e, and quantity purchased will be Q_e. An excise tax of a fixed amount will raise the cost of providing the commodity to the market and shift the supply curve leftward to the curve labeled S + tax. The dollar magnitude of the shift, measured by the vertical distance between the two supply curves, will be exactly equal to the specific tax.

The new equilibrium price will be P_c. Because producers are legally responsible for paying the tax, they only net P_s from the transaction. The difference between the price consumers pay and the price producers receive is the amount of the excise tax. At the higher price, consumers buy less of the commodity, or Q_t instead of Q_e. The excise tax generates revenues for the government equal to the area bounded by P_sP_cBC. The higher price and lower output cause a loss in surplus value—a deadweight loss from the tax equal to ABC.

The impact of this loss is minimized when the lost output is small; that is, when the demand curve is inelastic. It should come as no surprise that excise taxes on cigarettes, alcohol, health insurance, and hospital stays have been proposed as financing alternatives for the various health care reform options. A tax on alcohol, cigarettes, and fast foods is often called a *sin tax*. Now that health insurance and hospital stays are in the mix of taxable items, proponents will have to come up with a new label.

BACK-OF-THE-ENVELOPE

Using Game Theory to Study Economic Behavior

Game theory is a branch of applied mathematics used by economists to study strategic behavior. As individuals, we interact with parents, children, siblings, spouses, friends, rivals, and colleagues, and we often find it useful to behave strategically. Strategic behavior is practiced in business, policymaking, international diplomacy, and anywhere else interactive decision-making takes place. The study of game theory attempts to build on strategic ability to develop a systematic approach to strategic behavior and improve strategic skills. Game theory is not a game. It involves important issues in economics, adding another dimension to the foundational assumption of rational behavior—the interaction of two or more rational decision makers.

When considering strategic games, we frequently think of head-to-head interaction between two rivals. The prevailing wisdom in economics is that competition improves all outcomes. Competitive markets are more efficient, prices are lower, and everyone is better off. Game theory goes beyond the simple interaction of supply and demand in the standard competitive model. No longer are we dealing with the impersonal market but with interpersonal strategic interaction between two decision makers.

Interaction can be either sequential or simultaneous. Players can take turns, each waiting to see what the other does before responding or they can choose without prior knowledge of the other's decisions. Gambling is a zero-sum game; one person's winnings are the other person's losses. International trade is not zero-sum, because both trading nations generally benefit from increased economic activity. Some games are played one time; some are repeated. Sometimes information is equally available to all players. Often it is asymmetrically distributed. Game theory is used to explain past events, predict future events, and advise players on the appropriate strategies under different circumstances.

The classic case of the simultaneous game is the prisoner's dilemma. The payoff structure of the prisoner's dilemma is important, because it arises in many strategic situations and thus has a wide range of applicability. The following payoff matrix depicts the predicament that two bank robbers, Bonnie and Clyde, find themselves in once captured. Placed in separate interrogation rooms, they are given an opportunity to provide evidence against the other for a reduced prison sentence.

		BONNIE	
		CONFESS	DENY
CLYDE	CONFESS	20, 20	1, 30
	DENY	30, 1	5, 5

First, examine the situation from Bonnie's perspective. The payoff matrix represents the length of her prison sentence if both confess (20 years), if Clyde confesses and she does not (30 years), if she confesses and Clyde does not (1 year), and if they both choose not to confess (5 years). Even if they agreed prior to their arrest to never confess their crimes, what should she do now that they are both confronted with the opportunity to limit their sentences by confessing? Does she really trust Clyde not to confess when confronted with the same payoffs?

The prudent strategy in this situation, and Bonnie's best response, is to base her decision on what is best for her regardless of Clyde's choice. If Clyde confesses, Bonnie will spend 20 years in prison if she confesses, 30 if she does not. It is better to confess. If Clyde does not confess, Bonnie will spend 1 year in prison if she confesses and 5 if she does not. It is better to confess. Bonnie has a dominant strategy; regardless of Clyde's decision, she spends less time in prison if she confesses. With this payoff structure, Clyde's situation is the same, so his dominant strategy is to confess. When both follow their dominant strategy, we reach a Nash equilibrium in which both confess and go to prison for 20 years.*

Regardless of the circumstances, the pursuit of the dominant strategy in a prisoner's dilemma results in lower payoff. Even though cooperative behavior would result in a higher payoff, the consequences of the other's defection are too great to take the risk. How do you avoid the consequences of opportunistic behavior? What can you do to guarantee a better outcome?

*John Nash won a Nobel Prize in Economics in 1994 for his contribution to economics in game theory.

Welfare Implications

Consider another way to look at demand and supply curves. Instead of viewing the demand curve as the amount demanded at various prices, it can be interpreted as the maximum price that consumers are willing to pay for each unit of a product. Likewise, the supply curve can be interpreted as the minimum price that providers are willing to accept for each unit of a product. From this perspective, demand curves are "willingness-to-pay" curves and supply curves as "willingness-to-provide" curves.

★ **KEY CONCEPT 6**
Supply and Demand

Consumer Surplus   Value depends on the consumer's willingness to pay. Items are valued for the utility they provide when purchased and consumed. In free markets, consumers do not pay more for a good than the subjective value they place on it. In fact, much of the time the value placed on an item exceeds its price. In those instances in which value exceeds price, consumers enjoy surplus value, called *consumer surplus*.

In Figure 2.9, the demand curve labeled DD' represents the maximum price that consumers are willing to pay to obtain a good, which is its subjective value. At the equilibrium price P_0, consumer surplus is the difference between the subjective value consumers place on the good, shown by the demand curve itself, and the price they must pay (P_0). All Q_0 units of output sold have surplus value. The triangular area between the demand curve and the price, P_0AD, shows total consumer surplus.

Producer Surplus   In the case of voluntary exchange, surplus value is created for both consumers and producers. A producer's willingness to provide goods and services is determined largely by the opportunity cost of the resources used in production. Supply curves reflect these forgone opportunities. Producer surplus is defined as the difference between the price that is received (P_0 in this case) and the minimum price that producers are willing to accept (represented by the supply curve SS'). Graphically, producer surplus is the area below the equilibrium price (P_0) and above the supply curve (SS').[9] Total producer surplus is the triangular area P_0AS.

Any output level other than P_0 results in a loss of surplus value and represents lost social welfare. In other words, given the demand and supply curves, DD' and SS', any price other than the perfectly competitive equilibrium price P_0 represents an inefficient outcome.

FIGURE 2.9
Consumer and Producer
Surplus

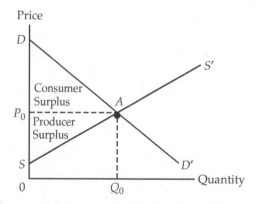

---

[9]Remember, the supply curve represents the subjective value providers place on the resources used to produce the good or service—its opportunity cost.

Imperfect Competition

In the case of the medical marketplace, violations of the assumptions of perfect competition are common. Although the incidence of monopoly is rare, the number of providers often falls far short of the perfectly competitive ideal. For example, many communities around the United States are served by a single hospital. Many factors determine the strength of this monopoly status; among them are the relative ease of access to other hospitals and the urgency of the services provided. Monopoly power leads to monopoly returns or excess payments.

Other violations of the assumptions of the perfectly competitive model include entry restrictions that limit the number of providers that can practice in a particular area. These restrictions come in the form of certification requirements, such as compulsory licensure for physicians, and by limiting hospital privileges to certain providers. Information costs— in particular, unequal distribution of information between patient and provider—also present impediments to the market.

Supply-Side Imperfections   Imperfections on the supply side of the market allow providers to enjoy monopoly returns. These imperfections usually deal with the nature of the rivalry, or the lack of rivalry, among firms. Too few firms, a non-standardized product, barriers to entry, and information problems manifest themselves in the medical marketplace.

The presence of a single firm in a market is referred to as *monopoly*. As the sole provider in a market, monopolists have market power—the ability to set a price. This market power is inversely related to the elasticity of demand for whatever the monopolist is selling. Demand that is more inelastic results in greater market power.

Monopolists enjoy their special position in the market because, for various reasons, rivals are unable to compete effectively. Barriers to entry may be the result of cost advantages due to size, something economists call *economies of scale*. Barriers may exist because of the sole ownership of an essential input in the production process or the franchise rights to a particular geographic region. These barriers can arise naturally or can result from legal restrictions on competitors. Whatever the source of the monopoly power, the result is a single provider serving a given market.

Monopoly is really quite rare in the U.S. economy, even in the medical marketplace. A more likely scenario is oligopoly, or the presence of a few firms in a market. The most important aspect of oligopolistic markets is the nature of the rivalry among firms. The pricing and output decisions of one firm depend on those of its rivals. The recent wave of consolidations in the hospital industry is bringing this form of market organization into the spotlight.

It is unusual to find markets where a single firm dominates, especially in those markets that deal in services. Often small firms attempt to differentiate themselves from their competitors in various ways: higher quality, advanced technology, and more choice. Successful differentiation sets a firm apart from its competitors and leads to market power. A market with a large number of suppliers selling a variety of similar products is classified as monopolistic competition.

In all cases of imperfect competition, the firms share a common characteristic: They face downward-sloping demand curves. Firms in perfectly competitive markets, facing horizontal demand curves, have no market power; they are price takers. Pricing strategy changes whenever a demand curve is downward sloping. Market power allows firms to set a higher price, one that potentially increases profit. Firms that find themselves in this situation are called *price searchers*.

Figure 2.10 illustrates the pricing and output strategy of a price searcher.[10] Faced with a downward-sloping demand curve, the firm must choose the profit-maximizing price and

⭐ **KEY CONCEPT 9**
Market Failure

⭐ **KEY CONCEPT 5**
Markets and Pricing

⭐ **KEY CONCEPT 3**
Marginal Analysis

---

[10]The model discussed here is that of the single-price monopolist, one that sells to each customer at the same price. Other pricing strategies include price discrimination, in which different consumers are charged different prices depending on their price elasticity of demand.

FIGURE 2.10
Pricing and Output
under Imperfect
Competition

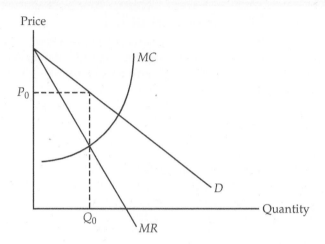

quantity. The price searcher is confronted with a marginal revenue curve that is situated below the downward-sloping demand curve. When the demand curve is downward sloping, the firm must lower the price to sell more of the product. As a result, the extra revenue from the sale of one more unit of output is less than its price. To sell the extra unit of output, the provider must lower the price on all the output that could have been sold at a higher price. In other words, the marginal revenue curve is below the demand curve. It has the same intercept on the price axis and twice the slope.[11] Although the rule of thumb for profit maximization is the same, MR = MC, the intersection takes place below the demand curve. So the profit-maximizing output is lower than in the case of perfect competition, and the resulting price is higher.

Whether the price searcher makes a profit depends a great deal on the existence of the entry barriers. Because of entry barriers, a monopolist can expect to maintain profits as long as the level of demand is maintained. In contrast, without entry barriers, firms in monopolistic competition will see profits eliminated, because profits attract competitors, and competition for market share results in lower prices, higher costs, and lower profits.

Demand-Side Imperfections   On the demand side of the market, imperfections manifest themselves in a number of ways; a limited number of buyers and imperfect information are two possibilities. *Monopsony*, or a single buyer, is the classic case of a demand-side imperfection. This situation emerges in medical care when consumers form into groups to consolidate their purchasing power and get lower prices from insurers and providers. The Canadian single-payer system is an example of a monopsony.

As sole purchaser in the market, the monopsonist faces an upward-sloping supply curve and a marginal cost curve that is above the supply curve. Figure 2.11 illustrates the operation of a market with a single buyer. Faced with an upward-sloping supply curve, the monopsonist must pay increasingly higher prices to obtain more output, even on those items that could have been purchased at lower prices if less had been bought. The relevant purchasing decision takes into consideration the marginal cost of purchasing one more unit of output, not the opportunity cost of that last unit of output. Instead of equilibrium occurring where supply and demand are equal, the monopsonist equates marginal cost with demand.

KEY CONCEPT 9
Market Failure

---

[11]A mathematical proof of this proposition is as follows:

Demand curve: $P = a + bQ$

Total revenue: $TR = P \times Q = (a + bQ) \times Q = aQ + bQ^2$

Marginal revenue: $MR = \dfrac{dTR}{dQ} = a + 2bQ$

FIGURE 2.11
Monopsony

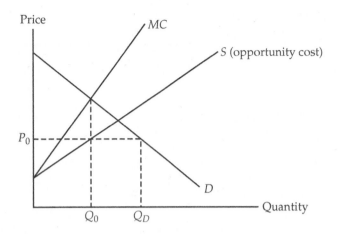

Monopsony equilibrium occurs at a lower level of output and a lower price than in the case of perfect competition. Society is worse off because fewer services are provided. At the lower price, quantity demanded (Q_D) exceeds quantity supplied (Q_0). The monopsonist exercises market power and creates a shortage that competition with other purchasers does not eliminate, because no other purchasers exist.

Summary and Conclusions

Economists seldom hesitate in applying economic tools in a variety of circumstances to evaluate individual choice and behavior. Do not misinterpret this tendency. Few members of the economics profession believe that economics provides all the answers. As you progress through the book, it will become obvious that the health care marketplace fails to achieve its theoretical optimum in many cases, making the strict application of the neoclassical model problematic. The goal of this book, however, is to show that economics can provide insights into the study of human decision-making that few other disciplines offer.

The central message of economics presented in this chapter is simple:

■ *Resources are scarce relative to unlimited human wants. Inevitably, we must face the fact that resources used in the delivery of medical care have alternative beneficial uses. To strike a balance between scarce resources and unlimited wants involves making choices. We cannot have everything we want. Trade-offs are inevitable.*

■ *Medical care decisions involve costs as well as benefits. For many clinicians, allowing cost considerations into treatment decisions is morally repugnant. To counter this feeling, it is essential that practitioners have knowledge of the fundamentals of economics to provide a foundation for understanding the issues that affect medical care delivery and policy.*

■ *It is important to strike a balance between incremental benefits and incremental costs. Most choices in medical care involve determining the level of an activity, not its existence. The issue is not whether it is beneficial to perform widespread screenings for colon cancer, but whether it is cost effective to perform a sixth test, when five have already been done (Neuhauser and Lewicki, 1975). Decision-making is seldom an all-or-nothing proposition. It usually involves a trade-off. If we are to spend a little more on one thing, we must be willing to spend a little less on something else.*

■ *Human behavior is responsive to incentives and constraints. If you want people to practice economizing behavior, they must benefit individually from their own economizing. People spending other people's money show little concern over how it is spent. People spending their own money spend it more wisely.*

As concern over escalating costs grows, economics takes on an increasingly important role in the study of medical care issues. Future clinicians must be well grounded in economic theory. Only then can they help shape the debate on the future direction of medical care delivery.

Questions and Problems

1. What are the likely consequences on the U.S. market for tobacco products for each of the events listed below? Which curve shifts, supply or demand? Please indicate the direction of shift. State whether the equilibrium price and quantity would increase, decrease, or stay the same. Show the changes using a standard diagram with an upward-sloping supply curve and a downward-sloping demand curve.
   a. The Food and Drug Administration classifies tobacco as an "addictive substance."
   b. The Congress votes to raise the excise tax on all tobacco products.
   c. Hurricane Fran dumps 15 inches of rain on North Carolina and destroys 80 percent of that state's tobacco crop.
   d. Sixteen states sue the major tobacco companies for billions of dollars because of tobacco-related costs in their Medicaid programs.
   e. Medical evidence that more than two cups of coffee a day, considered by many to be a substitute for smoking, greatly increases the risk of stomach cancer.

2. What is the proper role of economics in the study of health and medical care? What does economics have to offer? What are its limitations?

3. "The laws of supply and demand are immutable. No one, including government, can affect a commodity's demand curve or supply curve." Answer true or false. Please comment.

4. Indicate whether the following statements are positive or normative.
   a. Smokers should pay higher health insurance premiums than nonsmokers.
   b. The United States should enact a comprehensive health care plan that provides universal coverage for all Americans regardless of their ability to pay.
   c. The primary reason for the escalation in health care spending over the past 30 years has been the rapid development of expensive medical technology.
   d. The high cost of providing health care for employees is a major reason U.S. firms are not competitive with their foreign counterparts.
   e. Individuals born with certain genetic defects that predispose them to higher medical care spending over their lifetimes should be charged higher health insurance premiums than people without those defects.

5. [This problem is based on material discussed in Appendix 2B.] The relationship between health care spending (E) and per capita national income (Y) was estimated using cross-section data from 31 developed countries. The resulting equation (HCE = −538.3 + 0.11 GDP) relates spending and GDP.
   a. Interpret the coefficient on the national income variable.
   b. Complete the table.

INCOME IN $	HEALTH CARE SPENDING
10,000	
20,000	
30,000	
40,000	
50,000	

   c. Graph the relationship.

PROFILE   Kenneth J. Arrow

Kenneth J. Arrow, known primarily for his work on general equilibrium and welfare economics, wrote what many consider to be one of the classic articles in the field of health economics. "Uncertainty and the Welfare Economics of Medical Care" (*American Economic Review*, 1963) has had as much impact on economic thinking as any single paper written in the modern era. Members of the International Health Economics Association considered his contribution so important that they named their annual award for the outstanding published paper in health economics after him.

    Born of immigrant parents in 1921, Arrow spent his early childhood in relatively comfortable surroundings. His father's business, however, fared poorly during the Great Depression, forcing Arrow to attend City College, which was free at that time to the residents of New York. After graduating at the age of 19 and unable to get a job, he decided to pursue graduate studies in statistics at Columbia. Even though his interests were in mathematical statistics, he switched to economics to receive financial aid. He soon discovered his interest in economics surpassed his love for statistics.

Arrow's early work completely revolutionized the way economists think about general equilibrium and social choice. Winner of the 1972 Nobel Prize in Economics at the age of 51, he is widely considered one of the most important figures in general economic equilibrium theory and welfare theory.

In his own words, he describes his contribution to health economics as "not so much a specific and well-defined technical accomplishment as a point of view that has served to reorient economic theory" (Breit and Spencer, 1995). Arrow's work to integrate uncertainty into economic models led to his 1963 paper on the economics of medical care. In it, he was able to show that the key element in insurance markets was the difference in information between the buyers and the sellers of insurance. The very existence of health insurance causes individuals to spend more on medical care than they would otherwise. His emphasis on moral hazard and adverse selection served to focus research in health economics on these important issues.

Arrow joined the U.S. Air Force during the Second World War and served as a weather officer. His wartime contribution included important work on long-distance flight planning. At the time, the important all theoretical work was based on the assumption of a flat earth. Arrow's reformulation took into consideration the true nature of flight in a spherical world and helped determine optimal flight paths. After almost five years in the military, and still in his mid-twenties, he returned to Columbia University to finish his graduate studies. Before receiving his Ph.D., Arrow joined the Cowles Commission at the University of Chicago but soon moved to Stanford University, where he became a full professor at age 32. By the end of his first decade in academics, he was named president of the Econometric Society and winner of the John Bates Clark medal, given by the American Economic Association for the most distinguished work by an economist under the age of 40.

Most of his academic career has been spent at Stanford, except for 11 years at Harvard. He returned to Stanford in 1979, where he is currently emeritus Professor of Economics. In 1981, Arrow was named Senior Fellow at the Hoover Institution. In addition to his many honors and affiliations, he has been president of the American Economic Association, the Institute of Management Sciences, the Western Economic Association, the American Association for the Advancement of Science, and the International Economic Association. Often quoted and frequently criticized, his work has been so far reaching that we may never fully appreciate the extent of his contribution to economic and political thought.

Source: "Kenneth J. Arrow," in *Lives of the Laureates*, 3rd ed., edited by William Breit and Roger W. Spencer, Cambridge, MA: MIT Press, 1995, 43–58 and "Interview with Kenneth Arrow," *The Region, Review of the Federal Reserve Bank of Minneapolis*, December 1995.

References

Fuchs, Victor R., "Economics, Values, and Health Care Reform," *American Economic Review* 86(1), March 1996, 1–24.

Manning, Willard G., et al., "Health Insurance and the Demand for Medical Care: Evidence from a Randomized Experiment," *American Economic Review* 77(3), June 1987, 251–277.

Neuhauser, Duncan and Ann M. Lewicki, "What Do We Gain from the Sixth Stool Guaiac?" *New England Journal of Medicine* 293(5), July 31, 1975, 226–228.

Wagner, Lynn, "CBO Head Warns Price Controls Could Severely Limit Quality, Quantity of Medical Care in the U.S.," *Modern Healthcare* 23(3), March 8, 1993, 22.

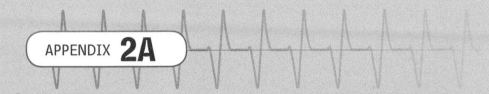

Graphing Data

Someone once said that a picture is worth a thousand words. Economists must take this axiom to heart. Seldom will an economist get far into a discussion without reaching for a pencil and paper. The picture often takes the form of a **graph**, one of several ways that economists use to convey ideas.

Some Basics of Graphing

Most graphs that we use in economics are two-variable graphs. The relationship between the two variables is illustrated by drawing two axes perpendicular to each other. The dependent variable is usually plotted on the vertical or y-axis; the independent variable on the horizontal or x-axis. Point a in Figure 2A.1 represents a combination of the variables x and y equal to x_0 and y_0, respectively. The x–y values for point a are called the **coordinates** of point a.

Graphs are used to describe relationships between variables. Scatter diagrams are often used for this purpose. The scatter diagram in Figure 2A.1 suggests that variable x and variable y are associated with one another; as the value of x increases, the corresponding values of y are also larger. Economists use scatter diagrams to get a feel for the relationship between two variables, looking for linkages, a correlation, or simply a random pattern.

When a relationship between variables is hypothesized, it is often depicted by a linear function or curve. Straight-line relationships can be expressed by the familiar equation $y = mx + b$, where m is the slope of

FIGURE 2A.1 Graphing Two Variables Using a Scatter Diagram

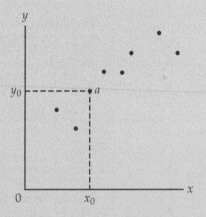

the line and b is its y intercept. Graphically, this relationship is shown in part (a) of Figure 2A.2. The slope of a straight line is calculated by dividing the change in the variable on the y-axis (Δy) by the change in the variable on the x-axis (Δx). The slope of the curve in part (b) of Figure 2A.2 is determined by the slope of its tangent, a straight line that touches the curve at only one point.

The slope of a function or curve is a convenient way to describe the relationship between two variables. A slope of $+3.0$ indicates that for every one unit increase in the variable measured on the x axis, the variable on the y-axis increases by 3. The intercept represents the value of the variable measured on the y-axis when the variable on the x-axis has a value of zero.

---

graph Chart or diagram depicting the relationship between two or more variables.
coordinates A system of uniquely determining the position of a point in a number space.

FIGURE 2A.2 Slope and Intercept

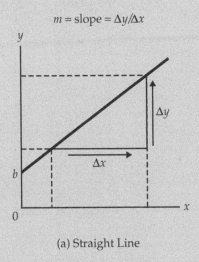

(a) Straight Line

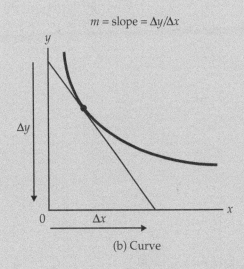

(b) Curve

Functional Relationships

Graphs are an efficient means of expressing relationships between variables. Often the relationship between two variables is functional in nature, implying dependence or causation. A causal relationship has a **dependent variable** and an **independent variable**. The value of the dependent variable is determined by the value of the independent variable. Suppose that we want to examine the relationship between the amount of money spent on medical care and the health of a person or a group of people. Instead of spending one or two pages of valuable paper describing this relationship, I can simply use a graph to convey the main idea.

Figure 2A.3 indicates that there is a direct (positive) relationship between the level of health and the amount spent on medical care. The higher the level of spending, the healthier the person or population. The shape of the line indicates that there is a limit to how much health you can buy with increased medical care spending. Additional medical spending buys progressively smaller increments of health. Genetics and lifestyle choices are other variables that affect the relationship between health and medical spending. Smokers as a group experience more respiratory and circulatory problems than nonsmokers. Figure 2A.4 depicts the relationship between the level of health and medical spending for smokers and nonsmokers. The graph indicates that at

FIGURE 2A.3 The Functional Relationship between Health and Medical Care Spending

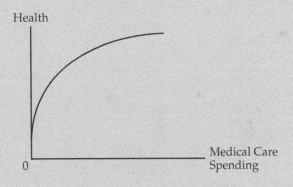

FIGURE 2A.4 The Functional Relationship of More than Two Variables

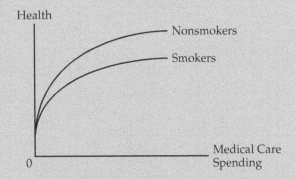

---

dependent variable Response variable.
independent variable Causal variable.

FIGURE 2A.5 Infant Mortality by Birth-Weight Category

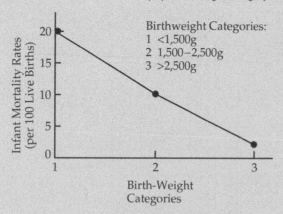

any given level of spending, nonsmokers are healthier on average than smokers.

Sometimes two variables are indirectly (negatively) related to one another. The relationship between infant mortality rates and birth weights is a good example of this phenomenon. Empirical data suggest that as birth weight increases, mortality rates decline. Figure 2A.5 illustrates the negative relationship between infant mortality and birth-weight category. Some hypotheses question whether high mortality rates are due to low birth weights or some other factor, such as prematurity.

As we discussed earlier, one of the important concepts in economics is optimization. Efficient production techniques promote the goals of average cost minimization. Optimal pricing strategies enable firms to maximize profits. Graphs showing a minimum or a maximum are illustrated in Figure 2A.6.

Part (a) illustrates the hypothetical relationship between the average cost of services and the number of beds in a typical community hospital. This U-shaped relationship is typical of average costs in producing a product or service. As the size of the operation increases, average costs decrease. If the operation expands beyond a certain level, average costs begin to increase. The most efficient level of operation for the hospital, the optimal level, is B_0.

A functional relationship with a maximum is shown in part (b). Here the relationship between the total revenues of a physician's practice and the number of patient visits is illustrated. To generate more patient visits, a physician must offer discount prices to some groups—a practice that is typical for physicians who participate in many insurance networks. What is the optimal pricing policy? A physician trying to maximize total revenue will charge a price that will result in a volume of business equal to V_0.

Time-Series Graphs

On occasion, it is important to examine how variables change over time. The use of longitudinal, or time-series, graphs often illustrates trends in a data series. Time-series graphs typically use daily, weekly, monthly, quarterly, or annual data to track changes in an economic variable. Figure 2A.7 graphs the changes in U.S. health care spending over the three plus decades since 1970. Health care spending has shown a long-term upward trend since 1970. Starting at less than $100 billion, it has risen dramatically to over 20 times that amount in just over three decades.

FIGURE 2A.6 Minimum and Maximum Values

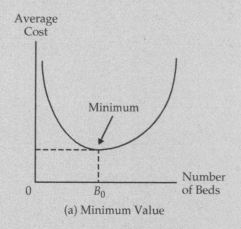

(a) Minimum Value

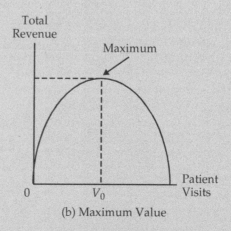

(b) Maximum Value

FIGURE 2A.7 U.S. Health Care Spending 1970–2008

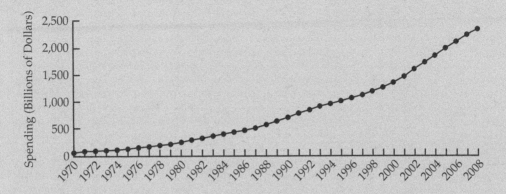

FIGURE 2A.8 Per Capita Health Care Spending and Per Capita GDP (United States, 1980–2008)

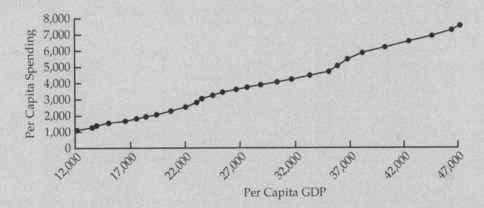

If we were interested in examining the relationship between health care spending and income, we could collect data on spending and income in a single country over a number of years. While a time series on two variables provides insight into the relationship, so many other factors change over time that we may not be sure of our results. Figure 2A.8 illustrates a time-series relationship between per capita health care spending and per capita GDP in the United States between 1970 and 2006.

Cross-Section Graphs

Another approach to graphing the same relationship is the use of cross-section data. A cross-section graph provides a number of observations on two variables at a given point in time across different entities: individuals, firms, states, or countries. Figure 2A.9 illustrates the same relationship for the year 2009 using data from the Organization for Economic Cooperation and Development (OECD). The two graphs depict the relationship between income and spending. Each point on the time-series graph shows U.S. spending compared to income over a number of years. The cross-section graph shows the same two variables for 31 different countries during a single year (2009). Each point represents income and spending (in U.S. dollars) for a given country.

FIGURE 2A.9 Relationship between Health Care Spending and GDP in OECD Countries, (2009 Per Capita Amounts)

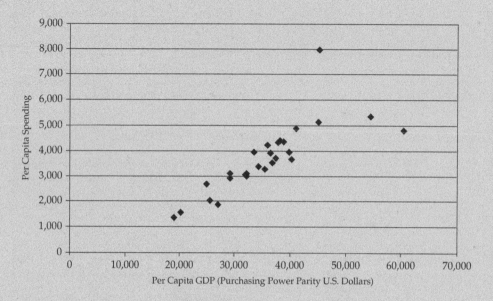

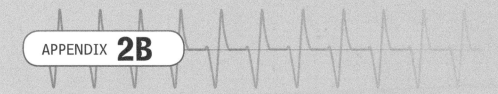

Statistical Tools

Descriptive Statistics

Whenever confronted with a body of data, the challenge is how to summarize the relevant information to make it useful to the reader. Economic researchers are often confronted with large amounts of data, hundreds and sometimes thousands of observations on a number of variables. A useful way of summarizing large amounts of data is by way of a graph, sometimes called a **histogram**.

Figure 2B.1 shows the distribution of maternity patients by age at Hillcrest Baptist Memorial Hospital in Waco, Texas, for 1991. A simple viewing of the histogram tells us much about the ages of the 2,476 mothers who delivered that year. The youngest was 12 years old, the oldest 44—a spread of 32 years. The most frequent age was 25 years, the approximate center of the distribution.

Histograms can be summarized by statistical measures. These statistical measures help define the center of the distribution and the spread around the center. These concepts are formally called *central tendency* and *dispersion*.

Measures of Central Tendency

Measures of central tendency are often used to describe the typical value in a data set. The most commonly used measure of central tendency is the **mean**. Often referred to as the *average*, the mean of a distribution is the sum of the individual values divided by the total number of cases. Summing the ages for the maternity patients comes to 64,137 years. Dividing by the total number of patients (2,476) gives a mean value of 25.9 years.

FIGURE 2B.1 Histrogram Showing the Distribution of Obstetrics Patients by Age, Hillcrest Baptist Memorial Hospital, Waco, Texas, 1991

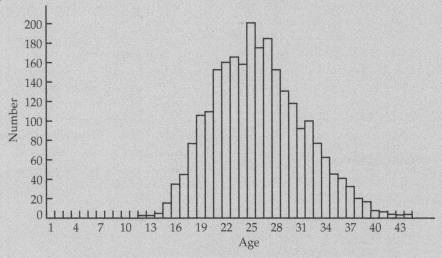

histogram Graphical presentation in the form of a bar graph of the probability distribution of a continuous variable.
mean The average of a set of numbers.

Reporting the mean value as the typical value can be misleading, because it may place too much weight on extreme values. Suppose five infants were born on a given day, and their mothers were 42, 27, 25, 23, and 22 years old. The average age of these five women is

$$\frac{42 + 27 + 25 + 23 + 23}{5} = 28 \text{ years}$$

By weighting the observations equally, the 42-year-old causes the measure of central tendency, or mean in this case, to be inflated and not very typical of the rest of the data.

When dealing with data that has a relatively small number of unusually large or small numbers, many researchers use an alternative measure of central tendency known as the **median**. The median is a popular summary statistic for demographic data with extreme values or outliers. To calculate the median, the values of a group of numbers are ranked from largest to smallest. In the case of an odd number of observations, the median is the middle number. In the case of an even number of observations, the median is the average of the middle two values. Its position at the fiftieth percentile implies that exactly half of the distribution falls above the median and half falls below it. The median age of the five new mothers listed earlier is 25 years, a much better indication of the typical age of that sample of patients. The median for all 2,476 maternity patients is 26 years.

Another measure of central tendency is the **mode**. The mode is the value occurring most frequently in the distribution. The most common age of the five maternity patients listed earlier is 23. For the entire group it is 25. The mode is used primarily on those occasions where the distribution has more than one mode. Under these circumstances, take care to understand what is truly typical of the data values. Confounding factors may cause measures of central tendency to convey quite different results concerning the overall data set. Without controlling for these confounding factors, reliance on a single measure of central tendency may produce spurious results.

Measures of Dispersion

Focusing on the central tendency can obscure other interesting features of a collection of numbers.

Concentrating on averages would lead us to conclude that a person standing with one foot in a bucket of scalding hot water and the other foot in a bucket of ice water is, on average, comfortable. Instead of simply looking at the central tendency of the data, it is useful to examine the way the numbers spread out around the center or average. Deviations around the average are typically indexed by statistical measures termed the *variance* and the *standard deviation*.

The **variance** is a measure of the dispersion of the data around the mean (average) value. It is one way of describing how closely individual observations in a data set cluster around the mean. The sample variance, denoted s^2, is calculated as follows:

$$s^2 = \frac{\sum_{i=1}^{N}(x_i - \overline{X})^2}{N}$$

where x_i is the "ith" observation of the variable x, $\overline{X}$ is the sample mean, and N is the number of observations in the sample. The deviations from the mean $x_i - \overline{X}$ are squared to take into consideration all values above or below the mean. Otherwise, deviations for values below the mean would enter the numerator as negative numbers and result in an artificially low measure of dispersion. Whenever the values of a variable are similar, the variance will be small. Variance, or the variability in the observed values, is a key concept in statistics and plays an important role in the calculation of many statistical tests and procedures. In fact, one of the goals in empirical research is to explain as much of the variance as is practicable.

A related measure of dispersion around the mean is the **standard deviation**. Even though the variance is computed in terms of squared values of the deviations, the standard deviation measures the average deviation; it is an estimate of how far on average the values are from the mean value. Mathematically, the standard deviation is the square root of the variance. This measure of deviation has more intuitive appeal, because it is measured in the same units as the original variable. If the variable being considered is years, variance is measured in square years and standard deviation in years. For our sample of maternity patients, the variance is 28.6 square years, and the standard deviation is 5.3 years.

---

median The middle value of a finite set of numbers arranged from lowest to highest.
mode The most frequently occurring number in a set of numbers.
variance A measure of dispersion of a set of numbers around their mean.
standard deviation A measure of dispersion equal to the square root of the variance.

FIGURE 2B.2 Skewed and Normal Distributions

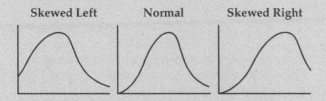

Another common issue concerning a distribution is its shape. A symmetrical distribution is often called a **normal distribution**. A distribution that has a long tail is called a **skewed distribution** (see Figure 2B.2). A normal distribution is bell-shaped and can be reconstructed rather well from its summary statistics, mean, and standard deviation. For a normal distribution, roughly 70 percent of the observations fall within plus-or-minus one standard deviation of the mean, and about 95 percent fall within two. For our maternity patients, over 72 percent fall within one standard deviation (+5.3 years) of the mean, 25.9 years. In other words, 1,787 of the 2,476 patients are between the ages of 20 and 31 years. Additionally, over 96 percent (2,386 out of 2,476) are between the ages of 15 and 36 years, or two standard deviations from the mean.

Correlation

Descriptive statistics are useful when dealing with one variable at a time. However, a study of the relationship between two or more variables is more interesting and requires other techniques. The scatter diagram described in Appendix 2A is one way of examining the relationship between two variables (see Figure 2A.1). Consider the points on a scatter diagram: A tight clustering around a straight line indicates a strong linear association between the two variables. A loose clustering indicates a weak linear association.

The strength of the association can be measured by a summary statistic commonly called the **correlation coefficient**. The correlation coefficient may be visualized as an expression of how two variables are "co-related." It is calculated using the respective standard deviations and means of the variables. Practically speaking, a perfect correlation between two variables indicates that all the observations lie on a straight line that is either positively sloped or negatively sloped. In these two cases, the correlation coefficient will have the value of either +1 or −1. If the two variables show no tendency to increase or decrease together, the points on a scatter diagram will show no clustering. In such cases, the correlation coefficient will have the value of zero.

It is important to understand that a correlation coefficient indicates an association between two variables. Association, however, does not imply causation. Suppose researchers found a strong negative correlation between the number of cases of influenza and the amount of ice cream consumed. Could we say that eating ice cream reduces the incidence of influenza? As popular as this would be with the children of the world, we cannot honestly make the statement. If it were true, physicians would encourage the consumption of ice cream to reduce the chances of contracting an influenza virus.

Correlation may be telling us that there is a third factor at work in the influenza–ice cream connection: namely, the season of the year. Coincidentally, the flu is most prevalent during the winter months, when ice cream sales are low and least prevalent during the summer months, when ice cream sales are high. Correlation says nothing about these confounding factors. If it were possible to control for all of these confounding factors, correlation would provide a much stronger argument for causation. What we need is a way of controlling for these other factors.

Regression

Simple measures of central tendency and dispersion reveal little about the way two or more variables are "co-related." An empirical technique used to determine the nature of the **statistical relationship** among a dependent variable and one or more independent variables is called *regression analysis*. Regression analysis not only allows us to identify systematic relationships among variables, it provides estimates of the relative magnitude of the various relationships. The

---

normal distribution The distribution of a set of numbers around the mean that takes on a symmetrical bell shape.
skewed distribution An asymmetric distribution with a majority of the data points lying on one side of the mean, resulting in a tail on the other.
correlation coefficient A measure of the linear association between two variables.
statistical relationship Association between two or more random variables indicating correlation or association.

relationships may be discussed in terms of independent and dependent variables, stimuli and response, explanatory and explained variables, or cause and effect. Because it is one of the most frequently used empirical techniques in economic research, it is important to have a clear understanding of this powerful tool.

Least Squares Methodology

Regression analysis is used to identify a dependent relation of one variable or a set of variables to another. Most regression models use the least squares method for estimating parameters. The least squares method provides a means of fitting a curve to a set of data points. This technique is not without its methodological problems. Moving the line closer to some points moves it farther away from other points. Solving the problem is simple. First, find the average distance from the line to all points. Second, minimize the average distance. The least squares method uses this approach with one difference: Instead of using the average distance, it uses the average of the squared distance. This approach avoids the problem of positive and negative differences canceling each other out, hence the name *ordinary least squares*.

Suppose we are interested in examining the causes of increased health care spending. The first step in our analysis is to specify the variables to include in the model. The variables that influence health care spending are numerous and may include income, age, and sex among other things. To simplify our discussion, we will specify a simple regression model with one dependent variable and one independent variable. The dependent variable is health care spending and the independent variable is income.

Step two in the analysis involves collecting reliable estimates for the two variables. Two approaches are possible: time series and cross section. A time-series approach would require the collection of data over time, locating data from a published source that looks at spending and income over time for a single entity, such as a state, region, or country. A cross-section approach requires data from a number of entities during a single time period.

Data for a cross-section analysis of the effect of income on spending is provided in Table 2B.1. The data come from the OECD for 31 developed nations. *Income* is defined as per capita GDP, and *spending* is defined in per capita terms. All values are translated into U.S. dollars using purchasing power parity exchange rates.

TABLE 2B.1   PER CAPITA GDP AND PER CAPITA HEALTH CARE EXPENDITURES (HCE) IN OECD COUNTRIES, 2006 (PURCHASING POWER PARITY U.S. DOLLARS)

Country	GDP	HCE	Country	GDP	HCE
Turkey	11,973	696	Germany	32,900	3,471
Chile	13,004	772	Belgium	33,349	3,174
Mexico	13,383	761	United Kingdom	34,084	2,884
Poland	14,715	912	Sweden	34,330	3,113
Hungary	17,920	1,450	Iceland	34,971	3,193
Slovak Republic	17,955	1,318	Denmark	35,199	3,381
Portugal	21,662	2,151	Austria	35,252	3,629
Czech Republic	21,827	1,520	Canada	36,821	3,690
Korea	24,661	1,501	Netherlands	37,162	3,613
New Zealand	26,068	2,418	Australia	37,460	3,168
Greece	26,356	2,547	Switzerland	38,577	4,150
Italy	29,517	2,662	Ireland	41,425	3,094
Spain	29,638	2,477	United States	44,639	6,931
France	30,893	3,425	Norway	52,045	4,501
Japan	31,936	2,580	Luxembourg	58,409	4,210
Finland	32,321	2,710			

Source: *OECD Health Data 2010,* Organization for Economic Cooperation and Development, Paris, 2010.

FIGURE 2B.3 Relationship between HCE and GDP, OECD Countries (2006)

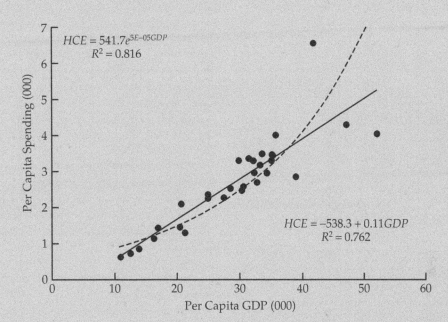

After collecting the data, the third step is to decide on the functional form of the relationship, or the regression equation. Choosing the simple linear model, the regression model that relates per capita health care spending to per capita GDP for these 31 OECD countries can be written as $HCE_i = a + bGDP_i + u_i$. HCE is per capita health care expenditures, GDP is per capita gross domestic product, u represents the random elements in the relationship, and the subscript i represents each observation (countries numbered 1 through 31).

Figure 2B.3 plots the actual data on spending and income provided in Table 2B.1. The regression results in the lower right-hand corner of the diagram report the ordinary least squares equation; depicted by the solid line. The constant term represents the intersection of the regression line with the y-axis, and the coefficient on income represents its slope. Using the least squares technique, the regression estimate predicts that, on average, for every one-dollar increase in per capita GDP, HCE increases by 11 cents.

Although the linear model is simpler, other models have their advantages. The multiplicative form can be written $HCE_i = ae^{bGDP_i}$, where e is the base of logarithms. In this form, the equation is estimating the relationship between HCE and GDP as an exponential relationship, where HCE increases at an increasing rate with rising GDP. The regression results in the upper left-hand corner of Figure 2B.3 report the logarithmic least squares equation depicted by the dashed line.

A third specification is to estimate the relationship using logarithms of both HCE and GDP. The advantage of this specification is that the coefficient b in a log transformation of the equation ($\log HCE_i = \log a + b \log GDP_i + u_i$) has a simple economic interpretation—it is an estimate of "income elasticity." An interesting result is the estimate of the income elasticity: $+1.37$ using this specification. The interpretation is straightforward. Increase per capita GDP by 1 percent and per capita health care spending increases by 1.37 percent. Higher income countries spend a greater portion of their GDP on health care.

In social science and demographic research, often more than one causal variable is identified. The technique used in this situation is *multiple regression analysis*. Researchers use multiple regression analysis to control for confounding variables; that is, other variables associated with changes in the dependent variable. For example, health care spending may also depend on other factors, such as the percentage of population covered by insurance or the number of active physicians per capita. A multiple regression equation adding these two regressors is written in linear form as

$$HCE_i = a + bGDP_i + cI_i + dP_i + u_i$$

where I is the percentage of the population with health insurance coverage, and P is the number of active physicians per 100 population. The coefficient on the income variable would now show the independent effect of income on expenditures, free from the influence of insurance coverage and the availability of providers.

Measures of Significance

Foremost on the minds of researchers is the reliability of the estimated coefficients. A number of significance tests can determine the accuracy of a regression equation. The *standard error of the estimate (SEE)* is the standard deviation of the dependent variable after controlling for the influence of all the independent variables. When data points are widely dispersed about the estimated regression line, standard error is large. If all the data points were to fall on the regression line, the standard error would be zero.

One of the objectives of regression analysis is prediction. Standard error provides an estimate of the accuracy of a prediction based on a particular regression equation. Based on statistical probabilities, when there are roughly 30 or more observations, there is a 95 percent probability that the dependent variable will lie within two standard errors of its estimated value. A smaller standard error provides greater confidence in the accuracy of the estimate.

Often the SEE is used to estimate confidence intervals around a given estimated equation. The 95 percent confidence interval has a range of roughly two standard errors around the estimate.

A second measure of accuracy is the *coefficient of determination*, or R^2. The coefficient of determination is an estimate of the percentage of variation in the dependent variable explained by the independent variables, sometimes called *goodness* of fit. R^2 ranges between zero and one. The higher its value, the greater the overall explanatory power of the regression equation. Referring back to the regressions depicted in Figure 2B.3 again, the linear relationship has an R^2 of 0.762 while that of the exponential relationship is 0.816, indicating a better "fit." In other words, the observations deviate less from the fitted regression line using the exponential model.

Standard error and R^2 are both important significance measures, but neither addresses the question of whether the independent variables as a whole explain a significant proportion of the variation of the dependent variable. The *F statistic* fills this void. Values range from zero upward. At the extreme, when R^2 equals zero, F equals zero. Whether a particular value of the statistic indicates a significant set of regressors depends not only on its value, but also on the number of regressors and the number of observations on which the estimated equation is based. In general, the larger F is, the greater the likelihood that the set of independent variables explains a significant proportion of the variance in the dependent variable.

Critical values of F are provided in statistical tables that are readily available in most introductory statistics textbooks. Roughly speaking, with five or fewer independent variables and 25 or more observations, values of F that are greater than 3 or 4 indicate a statistically significant proportion of the variance explained by the set of independent variables. Smaller sample sizes and a larger number of independent variables require larger values of significance.

In addition to the significance of the overall equation, often the researcher is interested in the significance of each independent variable. The standard deviation, or standard error, of the coefficient for each independent variable provides a means of creating a test statistic expressly for this purpose. The most commonly used *t statistic* in regression analysis is calculated to determine if an individual coefficient is statistically different from zero. The t value is calculated by dividing the coefficient estimate by its standard error. Values of t greater than 2 are usually associated with coefficients that are statistically different from zero. The critical values of the statistic are found in tables in most introductory statistics textbooks.

Summary and Conclusions

With the development of the microcomputer, data analysis is no longer the exclusive purview of statisticians. A standard personal computer equipped with a statistical software package gives the user a powerful set of tools for analyzing information.

The analytical techniques discussed in this appendix are among the most commonly used in the social sciences. Many of the referenced articles use them extensively. A thorough understanding of these tools will go a long way in making the study of health economics easier and more enjoyable.

CHAPTER 3

Analyzing Medical Care Markets

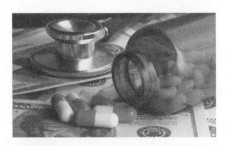

BACK-OF-THE-ENVELOPE

Monopsony: When Buyers Have Market Power

Market power on the buyers' side, called *monopsony*, gives buyers more leverage in determining the prices they pay for goods and services. If buyers are able to consolidate their demand within a cooperative arrangement, they may function as a buyers' club. In today's language, call it an *alliance* or an *exchange*. The larger the cooperative, the more control the group can assert over the prices charged to its members. As already discussed, equilibrium for the monopsonist occurs at a price and output level that is below the level that would exist in perfectly competitive markets, representing lost economic welfare.

Even with the lost productivity, some still argue that monopsony provides a net benefit to society. Proponents of market power for buyers agree that the unilateral exercise of market power on either side of the market should be illegal. They contend, however, that providers in medical markets already exercise a significant degree of market power on the sellers' side of the market. The use of power on the buyers' side represents a countervailing force that encourages competitive behavior among sellers and promotes the efficient use of resources.

Most intermediate microeconomics textbooks provide a formal explanation of this phenomenon under the heading **"bilateral monopoly."** A bilateral monopoly exists in a market when a single buyer seeks the output of a single seller. In other words, bilateral monopoly is characterized by monopsony on the demand side and monopoly on the supply side. In the following graph, D, MR, and MC depict the demand, marginal revenue, and marginal cost curves confronting the monopolist seller. Profit-maximizing price and output, P_2 and Q_2, are determined by MC = MR at point A.

A monopsonist with absolute control over demand could force the monopolist to behave like a firm in a perfectly competitive market. Under these conditions, MC is the firm's supply curve. Likewise, MC_B becomes the relevant marginal cost of buying an additional unit of the output. The monopsonist attempts to equate the marginal cost of buying with its own marginal valuation of the output (MV_P) at point B. At the optimal level of output, Q_1, the monopsonist pays the lowest price the provider is willing to accept and still cover marginal cost, in this case P_1.

KEY CONCEPT 9
Market Failure

bilateral monopoly
When there is monopoly on the seller's side of the market and monopsony on the buyer's side.

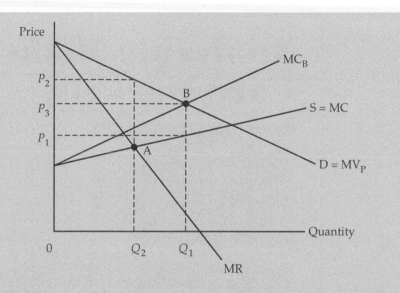

KEY CONCEPT 5
Markets and Pricing

In terms of the final price, the negotiated outcome will fall somewhere between the two extremes, P_1 and P_2. The exact solution depends on the relative bargaining strengths of the two sides. The monopoly seller enters the negotiations wanting a higher price and lower output than the monopsony buyer. To avoid an impasse, the seller will likely offer somewhat lower prices and slightly more output. The single buyer will agree to pay more than P_1 if the seller provides more than Q_2. As long as price does not fall below P_3, the final output level will fall between Q_1 and Q_2. Thus, for bilateral monopoly to benefit society, bargaining strengths of buyers and sellers must be approximately equal. If either side has a disproportionate share of the bargaining power, it will be able to tilt the balance in its favor to the detriment of society. (Technical note: Relative bargaining strengths and the final outcome will be different if the supply curve is so steeply sloped that $Q_2 > Q_1$. In this case, the monopolist wants to provide more output than the monopsonist wants to buy, weakening the monopolist's bargaining position.)

Source: Michael L. Ile, "When Health Care Payers Have Market Power," *Journal of the American Medical Association* 263(14), April 11, 1990, 1981–1982, 1986.

POLICY ISSUE
Government policy actions, no matter how carefully developed, always have their unintended consequences.

A compelling argument can be made that medical care delivery is far more complex and dynamic than is typically the case in the standard treatment of the market process. The trade-off between equity and efficiency is quite acute, calling for active regulatory oversight to ensure that the process works. Critics of government involvement offer an equally compelling argument. Even well meaning government policy has its unintended consequences. Oversight is costly and serves to impede growth and productivity in the private sector.

In this chapter, we will examine the competitive market model and its applicability to the medical market. We begin with an overview of the medical marketplace: justification for its existence and examination of its overall performance in recent years. We next consider the breakdown in the traditional market model and then examine how governments intervene to address the problems that arise. A general discussion of the causes and consequences of **market failure** will be followed by a more specific examination of market failure in medical markets. A discussion of government intervention in the form of regulation, public provision, and licensing follows. Finally, the question of how to deal with government failure is addressed.

market failure A situation in which a market fails to produce the socially optimal level of output.

Should Medical Care Markets Exist?

Before studying medical care using economics, it is important to accept the premise that a market in medical care can function effectively. In other words, the differences between medical care and other commodities are not so great to totally preclude the production and allocation of medical resources within markets.

Just how similar (or different) is medical care to other commodities? The pioneering work of Kenneth Arrow (1963) can provide us with some insight on how many of today's policy makers (especially those whose politics lean left of center) view medical care. Arguing that medical care delivery differs in fundamental ways from normal markets, Arrow contends "the *laissez-faire* solution for medicine is intolerable" and calls for government intervention to address the shortcomings.

Arrow's thesis is based on a number of distinguishing characteristics that contribute to the uniqueness of medical care as a commodity. The differences may be categorized as follows:

1. *Unpredictability*: Unlike other commodities, the demand for medical care is irregular. Except for the small percentage of care that may be defined as preventive, medical care demand follows an accidental injury or the onset of an illness. We can rarely predict the onset of an injury or illness, and thus cannot predict an individual's demand for medical care.

2. *Asymmetric information*: The medical care transaction is characterized by information problems that disproportionately affect patients. All consumers are frequently confronted with difficulties in collecting information about a product, but the problem is particularly acute for medical care consumers due to the complexity of medical knowledge. The typical consumer of medical care is poorly informed and finds it difficult to become well informed.

3. *Trust*: Because of this information imbalance, patients rely on their physicians to diagnose their illnesses and prescribe treatments, and they expect the physician to behave as perfect agents and proceed without consideration for his or her own personal gain. Thus, the medical transaction carries with it ethical overtones unlike any other transaction.

4. *Barriers to entry*: To protect the interests of the uninformed public, government has established licensing requirements and educational standards to ensure a minimum level of quality among providers, and provider organizations have adopted codes of conduct to guard against unethical behavior. Medical facilities must measure up to strict accreditation standards established by the industry.

5. *Payment practices*: Patients seldom pay directly for the care they receive. The vast majority of the care is a nonrefundable service and payment is facilitated through third-party insurance, insulating patients from the full price of the goods and services they consume. That they see no reason to have price information is why reliable *ex ante* price data are hard to find. Patients are not aware of the full cost of the care they receive until after it is consumed, too late for any meaningful comparison shopping.

Another interesting feature of the market for medical care is the widespread reliance on **not-for-profit** providers, especially in the provision of hospital services. The conventional wisdom would have us believe that the absence of the profit motive will mean decision-making without the influence of **self-interest** on the part of providers. Even with over 80 percent of the nation's hospitals are either government owned or otherwise not-for-profit, the profit motive has not been totally eliminated from the medical care sector. In fact, there are few operating differences between private not-for-profit hospitals and their

☆ **KEY CONCEPT 9**
Market Failure

not-for-profit An organizational form where the distribution of a surplus (revenue − cost) must be invested back into the operation. These tax-exempt firms are organized to promote community interest.

self-interest A behavioral characteristic where individuals act to promote their own interests.

for-profit counterparts. Moreover, most physicians' practices are for profit, as are virtually all pharmaceutical companies, retail drug stores, and long-term care facilities.

Arrow's viewpoint lacks our insight into the modern state of today's financial arrangements and regulatory framework. Pertinent to our understanding of the viability of markets in health care delivery is whether Arrow's criticism is still valid, some 50 years later. Are the market distortions Arrow addresses unique to the medical care industry? Or do they exist in other markets?

1. *Unpredictability* is hardly a phenomenon unique to medical care. Providers of nonmedical goods and services are faced with the same uncertainty in predicting demand for their products and services as medical providers do. Although it is difficult to predict the onset of illness for any one individual, it is possible to predict the number of people who will suffer from a particular medical condition within a large group of individuals. That task falls to actuaries who practice insurance underwriting. The market handles aspects of this uncertainty with extended warranties and insurance products of all kinds.

2. *Asymmetric information* is a common problem for buyers of most goods and services, medical and nonmedical. In fact, almost every economic transaction involves asymmetry. Ever heard the Latin phrase "caveat emptor" (let the buyer beware)? In any case, modern technology has emerged in the past 50 years to address the information asymmetries in all markets. Few of us know a lot about electronics, computers, automobile repair, or hip replacements. We get our information from many sources: advice of friends and family, print media, and the Internet. In fact, the Internet has done a lot to inform patients of disease symptoms and their treatments. Websites such as Good Rx, WebMD, Mayo Clinic, and many more have narrowed the information gap between patients and their providers. Often patients know as much or more about treatment options than their providers do.

3. Admittedly, we *trust* our medical providers with our lives and health, but we also place our well-being in the hands of bus drivers, airline pilots and mechanics, food handlers, financial advisers, and the makers of the thousands of other products we consume. We even have a way of valuing our life and health in the tort liability system, which works in all sorts of markets.

4. *Barriers to entry* resulting from licensing and accreditation are not unique to medical care. Many occupations require extensive training and credentialing, including hairdressers and manicurists, public accountants, financial analysts, lawyers, and airline pilots. Very few industries exist that approach the entry and exit requirements of the perfectly competitive industry.

5. Arrow's criticism about *payment practices* in medical care is his best point and one where there is still lots of agreement. It strikes at the heart of the third-party insurance system. Granted, the proliferation of generous insurance coverage has distorted medical markets. However, Arrow's solution is a government-run insurance model that does not address the problems of third-party insurance and actually takes us further away any discipline proffered by patient involvement. If insurance functions as insurance (whether provided publicly or privately), the market distortions would be minimized. The purpose of insurance is to protect against catastrophic losses that occur infrequently. The more frequent maintenance costs associated with home and automobile ownership, for example, are usually covered out-of-pocket. If we did the same for medical care with high deductible, catastrophic insurance policies backed by health savings accounts for routine care, medical markets would suffer fewer distortions.

Medical care markets are not that different from other markets. There is every reason to believe that we can use economic theory to help us understand resource allocation and pricing decisions in this critical industry. The challenge we face is not whether the theory is applicable but how to apply it.

The Medical Care Marketplace

http://
HealthWorld Online is a 24-hour resource center for health care information for journalists, researchers, those with health problems, and those who want to avoid health problems. http://www.healthy.net/.

Proponents of more government involvement in medical care claim that medical care is far too complicated for the market. Because medicine is difficult to understand, patients must rely on their physicians' recommendations. Others add that medical care is a social good and too important to leave to the workings of the impersonal marketplace. Some argue that the externalities involved in medicine, particularly in the area of infectious diseases, require collective action to maximize the benefits to society. Many base their support for government intervention on ethical grounds, claiming that the provision of medical care based on the ability to pay is morally repugnant. Together these arguments are responsible, in varying degrees, for the development of government-financed medical care in most developed countries throughout the world.

☆**POLICY ISSUE**
There are two opposing views on the best way to improve access to health care for those Americans without health insurance: more government involvement or market-based reforms.

Those who oppose more government involvement argue that the U.S. system has remained, for the most part, market based, which is in part evidence of the deep American distrust of federal government involvement in health care matters.[1] Experience has taught that government-run programs are costly. For example, when originally proposed in the mid-1960s, Medicare spending was projected to reach $9 billion in 1990; the actual cost in 1990 was $109 billion. The preamble to the original Medicare bill actually prohibited any federal "supervision or control over the practice of medicine or the manner in which medical services are provided." Anyone familiar with medical care delivery is well aware of how the federal government has violated the original intent of this legislation.

Regardless of how the system is organized, its aims are the same: Provide good access to high-quality medical care at affordable prices. Thus, spending, access, and quality are often called the "triple aim" of a health care system (Berwick et al., 2008).

Health Care Spending

http://
National Center for Health Statistics (NCHS) is the principal health statistics agency in the United States. Its goal is to provide accurate, relevant, and timely statistical information that will guide actions and policies to improve the health of the American people. http://www.cdc.gov/nchs/.

One of the major factors driving the health care reform debate is spending, including total spending, spending per person, and spending as a share of total economic output. Referring to Table 3.1, national health expenditures were $3,206 billion in 2015, 17.8 percent of the gross domestic product (GDP). Of this amount, 85 percent was spent for personal health care. This category of spending includes the purchase of all goods and services associated with individual health care, such as hospital care, the services of physicians and dentists, prescription drugs, vision care, home health care, and nursing home care.

Hospital Care   Spending on hospital services reached $1,036 billion in 2015. Hospital costs, valued as actual revenues received, experienced a decade of accelerated growth in the 1980s. The growth in hospital spending moderated in the 1990s due primarily to aggressive cost-control efforts on the part of private payers. From 2000 to 2005, hospital spending grew at a compound rate of 7.96 percent, increasing concerns that spending would continue to accelerate. In the second half of the decade, spending growth moderated

---

[1]Blendon et al. (1995) note that only 7 percent of Americans express a "great deal of confidence" in federal health care agencies, compared with 19 percent of Canadians and 41 percent of Germans.

TABLE 3.1 NATIONAL HEALTH EXPENDITURES, SELECT YEARS, IN BILLIONS OF DOLLARS (UNLESS OTHERWISE STATED)

Category	1960	1970	1980	1990	2000	2005	2010	2013	2014	2015
Hospital care	$9.0	$27.2	$100.5	$250.4	$415.5	$609.4	$822.4	$937.9	$981.0	$1,036.1
Physician and clinical services	5.6	14.3	47.7	158.9	290.9	417.2	513.1	569.5	597.1	634.9
Dental services	2.0	4.7	13.4	31.7	62.3	87.0	105.0	110.1	112.8	117.5
Other professional services	0.4	0.7	3.5	17.4	37.0	52.7	69.8	78.8	82.8	87.7
Home health care	0.1	0.2	2.4	12.6	32.4	48.7	71.0	80.0	83.6	88.8
Nursing home care	0.8	4.0	15.3	44.9	85.1	112.5	140.0	149.2	152.6	156.8
Prescription drugs	2.7	5.5	12.0	40.3	121.2	205.3	253.0	265.1	297.9	324.6
Other medical products	2.3	5.0	13.9	36.2	56.8	71.7	91.1	100.8	103.5	107.5
Other personal care	0.5	1.3	8.5	24.3	64.5	96.5	129.1	144.3	151.5	163.3
Personal health care	$23.3	$63.19	$217.2	$616.8	$1,165.7	$1,700.9	$2,196.6	$2,435.6	$2,562.8	$2,717.2
Government administration	0.1	0.3	2.8	7.2	17.1	28.3	30.1	37.2	41.2	42.6
Net cost of health insurance	1.0	2.0	9.3	31.6	64.2	122.5	153.5	173.8	195.3	210.1
Public health activities	0.4	1.4	6.4	20.0	43.0	57.2	75.5	77.9	79.0	80.9
Research	0.7	2.0	5.4	12.7	25.5	40.3	49.2	46.7	45.9	46.7
Structures and equipment	1.9	5.8	14.7	36.0	62.5	86.5	93.5	106.4	105.0	108.0
National health expenditures	$27.3	$74.8	$255.8	$724.3	$1,378.0	$2,034.8	$2,596.4	$2,877.6	$3,029.3	$3,205.6
Per capita personal Spending (dollars)	$125	$300	$942	$2,430	$4,129	$5,757	$7,109	$7,710	$8,049	$8,467
Per capita national Spending (dollars)	$147	$356	$1,110	$2,855	$4,881	$6,887	$8,404	$9,110	$9,515	$9,990.0
National spending Percent of GDP (%)	5.0	7.0	8.7	12.1	13.4	15.5	17.4	17.2	17.4	17.8

Source: Centers for Medicare and Medicaid Services (CMS) website, http://www.cms.hhs.gov/NationalHealthExpendData/02_NationalHealthAccountsHistorical.asp#TopOfPage (Accessed January 11, 2017).

somewhat to 6 percent per year. Hospital care accounted for 38 percent of personal health care spending, and patients paid for approximately 3 percent of hospital care out-of-pocket.

Physicians' Services   Spending on physicians' services amounted to 23 percent of the total spent on personal health care in 2015. The total of $634.9 billion tends to mask the importance of physicians in the health care sector. Even though only 23 cents of every medical care dollar flows directly to physicians, they are indirectly responsible for most of the rest. Physicians admit patients to hospitals, recommend surgeries, prescribe drugs and eyeglasses, and in general oversee the entire health care delivery system. Roughly, 10 percent of physicians' services are financed by patient out-of-pocket payments.

Prescription Drugs and Other Medical Products   Consumers spent $325 billion on pharmaceuticals and $108 billion on other medical products in 2015. This absorbed 11.9 and 4 percent of personal health care spending, respectively. Patients pay only 17 percent of all prescription drug costs out-of-pocket.

Other Personal Health Care Spending   Other spending includes payments for dentists' services and other professional services, nursing home care, and home health services. When combined, these categories of care account for approximately 23 percent of all personal health care spending. Nursing home care amounted to $156.8 billion of total personal health care spending in 2015, making it the fourth largest spending category. Dental services accounted for $117.5 billion and other professional services $87.7 billion. Home health spending at $88.8 billion has increased over six times since 1990.

Prospects for the Future   Total per capita medical care spending reached $9,990 in 2015. At this level, U.S. per capita spending on medical care is anywhere from 40 to 300 percent higher than in other developed countries. Much of the difference is predictable: Countries with higher living standards, measured by per capita income, spend more on promoting health.

Even within the United States, variations in spending across the country are dramatic (Radnofsky, 2013). Per capita personal spending was $6,815 in 2009; it varied from a low of $5,031 in Utah to a high of $9,278 in Massachusetts ($10,349 in the District of Columbia). If per capita spending nationwide had mimicked Utah, personal health care spending would have been $1,547 billion in 2012, a 35 percent decrease. Likewise, spending would have been 13.8 percent of GDP (instead of 17.3).

Although high per capita spending paints a dramatic picture of spending disparities, the share of output devoted to medical care is more reflective of shifts in priorities. The percentage of GDP devoted to medical care spending has risen dramatically in the United States since the late 1960s, from less than 6 to 18 percent. In comparison, in most developed countries worldwide, the percentage ranges from 9 to 12 percent. Increasing health care expenditures as a percent of GDP may reflect a conscious choice on the part of the consuming public to spend more for health care. Alternatively, it may reflect an inefficient approach to health care financing that the United States experienced in its attempt to reform the system through the Affordable Care Act (ACA).

Clearly, the United States spends more on medical care and devotes a larger percentage of economic output to medical care, than any other country in the world. Although interesting, these facts ignore three important questions: What is a reasonable percentage of output to devote to medical care spending? Are we getting our money's worth? How much can we afford?

First, no one knows the ideal percentage of GDP that medical care spending should consume. We do know, however, that spending on all services, including health care, increases

POLICY ISSUE
The United States spends significantly more on health care than any other country in the world. Are we getting our money's worth?

POLICY ISSUE
What is the ideal percentage of GDP to spend on medical care?

as income increases. Wealthy countries spend proportionately more on medical care than poor countries. Because the United States is among the leaders in per capita income in the industrialized world, it should come as no surprise that U.S. medical care spending is the highest.

Second, empirical evidence indicates that the increase in health care spending witnessed over the past 40 years provides substantial benefits to society that far outweigh the associated costs. Lichtenberg's (2002) analysis strongly supports the hypothesis that medical innovation in the form of new drugs and overall health care spending contributed positively to increased longevity between 1960 and 1997. In fact, he concluded that the most cost-effective way to increase life expectancy is through increased spending on new drug development. Cutler and McClellan (2001) examined the benefits of technological change in five common conditions: heart attacks, low-birth-weight infants, depression, breast cancer, and cataracts. They concluded that health care spending on these conditions was worth the cost of care.

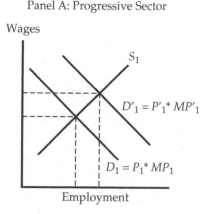

KEY CONCEPT 8
Efficiency

Finally, a growing economy allows more resources to be devoted to those areas of the service sector where productivity may lag, including medical care, education, police protection, and the performing arts. In an economy where productivity is growing in most sectors and declining in none, consumers can have more of everything. It is merely a matter of devoting a different proportion of income to the production of the various sectors (Baumol, 1967). This reapportionment is accomplished by transferring resources from those sectors where productivity is increasing to those where it is stagnant. Figure 3.1 is a graphical depiction of Baumol's model. We expect regular productivity growth in the progressive sector. Cost-saving, technological innovation results in economies of scale and lower per-unit costs of production. In Panel A, this phenomenon is depicted by a shift in the labor demand curve from D_1 to D'_1, caused by an increase in the marginal productivity of labor ($MP_1 > MP'_1$). Wages increase even as the price level stays the same at P_1.

Production in the non-progressive sector is highly labor intensive and enjoys only sporadic increases in labor productivity. Nominal wages are related in the two sectors because each represents alternative employment opportunities for the other. As labor productivity rises in the progressive sector resulting in higher wages there, if employers in the non-progressive sector wish to keep their workforce intact (preclude them from migrating to jobs in the progressive sector), wages must also increase in the non-progressive sector. The only way for that to happen is for prices to rise in the non-progressive sector (depicted by a change in the price level P_2 to P'_2). When prices rise, the demand for labor in the

FIGURE 3.1
Unbalanced Growth
across Sectors

Panel A: Progressive Sector

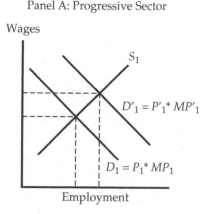

Panel B: Non-Progressive Sector

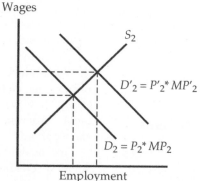

non-progressive sector increases from D_2 to D'_2 and wages go up. Moreover, because product demand is price inelastic in the non-progressive sector, quantity demanded is not impacted negatively. Over time, spending growth in the non-progressive sector outpaces spending in the progressive sector and larger and larger shares of total output are shifted to the non-progressive sector.

Baumol (1993) refers to the phenomenon of lagging productivity in the non-progressive sector, the service sector, as the cost disease of personal services. Applying his reasoning to medical care, the lag in productivity may be traced to two main factors: First, medical services are hard to standardize, making it difficult to automate. Before you can cure someone, it is necessary to diagnose the problem. Diagnosis and cure are done on a case-by-case basis. Thus, productivity tends to lag behind the rest of the economy. Second, most people perceive that quality of care is positively correlated with the amount of time the physician spends with the patient. Thus, it is difficult to reduce the labor content of medical services. Physicians who speed up the examination process are often accused of shortchanging their patients. This same reasoning may also be applied to education, the performing arts, legal services, and insurance.

Access to Care

According to recent census estimates, approximately 29 million Americans were without health insurance in 2015, creating mounting pressure on policy makers to come up with a plan to ensure access to medical care for all Americans. It is interesting to note that over 38 percent of the uninsured are between the ages of 18 and 34, age categories that use relatively less medical care.

Having no health insurance is not the same thing as having no access to medical care. In fact, the uninsured in this country receive about 60 percent of the medical care per capita of those with insurance. Nonelderly Americans who were privately insured spent $4,876 per capita on medical care in 2013 compared to $2,443 for those who were uninsured the entire year and $3,439 for those uninsured part of the year. In contrast, per capita spending in Canada that year was $4,502. While uninsured Americans are not going without care, they do receive less care than insured Americans do (Coughlin et al., 2014).

The ideological struggle surrounding medical care reform has focused on two competing visions of universality. One vision argues for **universal coverage** in a system that requires mandatory participation, and the other supports **universal access** in a voluntary system in which everyone can buy health insurance if they desire to do so.

Medical Outcomes

The third area of concern is the quality of care, often measured by health outcomes. Those critical of the U.S. delivery system cite the relatively poor health outcomes experienced in this country. The typical indicators used to evaluate the effectiveness of a health care delivery system include life expectancy (or one of its variants) and infant mortality. It is true that the United States lags behind many countries in the developed world in these two categories. Nevertheless, both are crude measures, at best, and ignore the contribution of the underlying demographic and social factors affecting health entirely. Life expectancy and infant mortality say a lot about environment, lifestyle choices, and social problems. The U.S. system must deal with a higher incidence of most of these problems than other industrialized countries—drug abuse, violence, reckless behavior, sexual promiscuity, and illegitimacy. These problems complicate the delivery of medical care and are, in part, responsible for the poor health indicators. A more detailed discussion of population health issues follows in Chapter 6.

POLICY ISSUE

What is the best way to ensure access to medical care for those Americans who do not have health insurance?

POLICY ISSUE

Is access to medical care an individual right? Does society have a responsibility to provide care to those who cannot afford it?

universal coverage
A guarantee that all citizens will have health insurance coverage regardless of income or health status. Coverage usually requires mandatory participation.

universal access
A guarantee that all citizens who desire health insurance will have access to health insurance regardless of income or health status. Participation is voluntary.

POLICY ISSUE

Is the U.S. health care system delivering high-quality medical care to Americans?

Underlying Factors that Drive Spending

Our concerns over health care spending ignore the fact that national spending has slowed considerably over the past decade. U.S. spending grew at an annual rate of 7.5 percent for the six years 2001–2007 and slowed to 3.8 percent for the years 2008–2013. Referring to Figure 3.2, it is clear that the annual growth in spending over the past 25 years peaked in 2002 at just under 10 percent. That rate fell almost continually until 2014, the first year of implementation of the ACA.

Any discussion of the role of the ACA in this slowdown in the growth of health care spending is overly emotional and always controversial. Advocates point to the structural changes made to the delivery system as the main reason for slowdown in spending growth. Others focus on the Great Recession as the main determinant of slow growth.

Other possible factors contributing to the slowdown point to a temporary decline in the introduction of new medical technologies and increase in patient cost sharing in the form of higher deductibles and copays (Chandra, Holmes, and Skinner, 2013). In addition, because Medicare and Medicaid represent over 40 percent of all spending, aggressive action on the part of the federal government (shift to managed care and reduction in payment rates to providers) has led to action by private insurers to make cost-saving adjustments of their own.

KEY CONCEPT 4
Self-Interest

The Competitive Market Model

Adam Smith asserted in his famous treatise, *The Wealth of Nations*, that individual decision making is motivated by self-interest. Guided by the "invisible hand" of the market, this self-serving behavior, in turn, serves to promote the interests of others. In other words, when markets exhibit certain ideal conditions, or perfectly competitive conditions, optimizing behavior on the part of individuals and firms leads to efficient outcomes.

Following the traditions that were established by Smith and the classical school of economics, modern-day economists evaluate markets according to the twin criteria

FIGURE 3.2 Health Care Spending Growth, 1990–2015

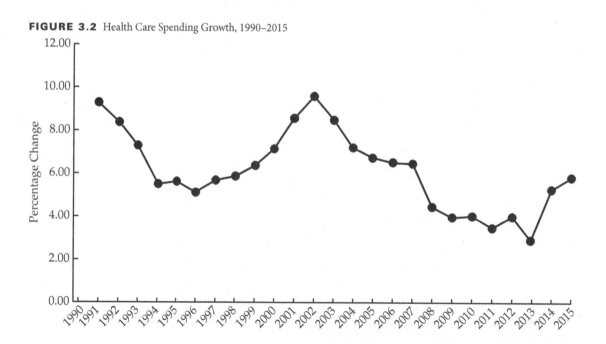

technical efficiency
Efficiency in production, or cost efficiency.

allocative efficiency
The situation in which producers make the goods and services that consumers' desire. For every item, the marginal cost of production is less than or equal to the marginal benefit received by consumers.

★ **KEY CONCEPT 8**
Efficiency

★ **POLICY ISSUE**
How important is equity in determining the effectiveness of a health care delivery system?

★ **KEY CONCEPT 7**
Competition

of efficiency and equity. There are two aspects of efficiency—**technical efficiency** and **allocative efficiency**. Technical efficiency may be thought of as efficiency in production or cost efficiency. In perfectly competitive markets, producers must minimize costs to maximize profits. When all producers pay the same input prices, goods and services that are produced will have marginal valuations that are higher than goods and services that could have been produced with the same resources. In summary, perfect competition guarantees both allocative and technical efficiency.

Allocative efficiency may be viewed as efficiency in the final distribution of consumption. Consumers buy a good until the benefits received from the last unit purchased equals the price.[2] Thus, everyone purchasing a good places a marginal value on the good at least equal to its market price. When everyone pays the same price for the good, there is no way to reallocate consumption from consumers to nonconsumers without lowering overall consumer welfare.

Equity considerations are also important when evaluating economic systems. Even though the issue of equity is based on some standard of fairness, ideological differences dictate whether that standard is defined either in terms of outcomes or in terms of opportunities. For example, one economist might define equity in terms of outcomes. In this case, any differences in infant mortality rates between, say, whites and African Americans would be viewed as inequitable and obviously the result of unequal access to the medical care system. How else could you possibly explain the significant difference between the 5.5 deaths per 1,000 live births among white Americans and 12.7 among African Americans (in 2011)?

Another economist defining equity in terms of opportunities rather than outcomes might interpret the same disparities in mortality rates another way. Even in a world of equal opportunities, there will be varied outcomes. Blaming the differences on unequal access ignores demographic differences such as age, education, and marital status between the two population cohorts. Additionally, differences in lifestyle choices are also important, including the decision to smoke cigarettes, drink alcohol, or take drugs during pregnancy. Whether defined in terms of outcomes or opportunities, equity has become an important component in the evaluation of markets, especially medical markets.

Few people will argue against the importance of an equitable distribution of health care availability. Nevertheless, health care is like any other desirable commodity: It is subject to an equity-efficiency trade-off. Access to medical care differs according to individual circumstances, such as age, sex, income, geographic location, and insurance coverage. No matter how much we may desire equity, it comes at a price; mandating equity may be desirable, but it is costly.

The formal argument for competitive markets is based on the notions of economic efficiency and social equity, but some favor competition simply because it guards against the concentration of market power and promotes consumer sovereignty. Competition among providers and their desire to satisfy consumer preferences ensures against consumer exploitation. Consumers always have alternative sources of supply in competitive markets. Cost-conscious behavior on the part of consumers increases their sensitivity to price changes. Individual providers face perfectly elastic demand curves when cost-conscious consumers have alternative sources of supply. Consequently, prices of goods and services equal the marginal cost of production.

When markets work, prices reflect the valuation of forgone opportunities. As equilibrium is reached, marginal values and prices converge, and the value of the goods and

---

[2] Downward-sloping demand curves are implied from the law of diminishing returns, indicating that the last unit of a good purchased has a marginal value equal to its market price.

APPLIED MICRO METHODS

EMPIRICAL STRATEGIES TO REDUCE SELECTION BIAS

When randomized sampling is unavailable or unfeasible, researchers turn to one of the several identification strategies to make comparison groups more similar with respect to the known covariates. The following note introduces four strategies that are regularly used to mimic the study design of a randomized control trial.

Difference in Differences Approach

Health policy researchers typically use observational data to study the impact of a change in health policy, or other intervention, on average health outcomes of different groups (Dimick and Ryan, 2014). One of the well-known limitations in observational studies is the need to control for underlying trends affecting the outcome of interest that are unrelated to the policy change. In situations where health outcomes were already improving, a pre–post comparison would provide a biased estimate of the improvement associated with the policy change.

The difference-in-differences (DiD) approach is a hybrid between a time-series approach (estimating outcome differences within a group over time) and a cross-section approach (estimating differences between two groups at a point in time). DiD uses panel data to measure differences, between a treatment group and a control group, in the changes in outcomes over time. The simplest DiD framework requires observations on outcomes for the two groups over two or more time periods (at least one before treatment and one after). One of the groups is exposed to the treatment and the other is not. The impact of the policy change is the average change in the health outcome in the control group (before and after the policy change) subtracted from the average change in the health outcome in the treatment group.

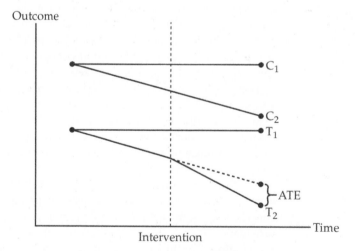

Suppose that the outcome variable under study is mortality rate or some other clinical outcome where smaller values denote a health improvement. Using the figure below, the treatment group (T) is exposed to a health policy change that does not affect the control group (C). In both groups, estimate the difference in outcome before and after the policy change, $T_2 - T_1$ for group T and $C_2 - C_1$ for the control group. The outcome change of interest is the difference of these two differences. In other words, the average treatment effect (ATE) is:

$$ATE = (T_2 - T_1) - (C_2 - C_1)$$

The design of the DiD approach is valid if two key assumptions hold: parallel trends and common shocks. The parallel trends assumption requires that the pretreatment outcome trends are the same within the two groups. In the absence of the treatment, the health outcomes for the two groups would have followed the same trend over time. The common shocks assumption requires that any events (unrelated to the policy change) that occur during the post treatment phase affect both groups equally.

Source: Justin B. Dimick and Andrew M. Ryan, "Methods for Evaluating Changes in Health Care Policy: The Difference-in-Differences Approach," *Journal of the American Medical Association* 312(22), December 10, 2014, 2401–2402.

Propensity Score Matching

Propensity score matching (PSM) is one of the several important techniques in non-experimental causal inference methodology used in medical, biostatistical, and epidemiological research. In observational studies, selection into treatment and control groups is not randomly assigned. Rather individuals are sorted into groups based largely on individual preferences. Thus, standard empirical methods may lead to biased estimates of the treatment effect because of this selection bias. Rosenbaum and Rubin (1983) to correct for this bias first introduced propensity score methods into the literature.

The reason for the bias stems from the fact that individuals in the treatment and control groups may differ from each other in unobserved ways that are correlated with both the clinical outcome and the actual treatment. For example, individuals who are prescribed statins (for high cholesterol) may be at greater risk for acute myocardial infarction (AMI) than those who are not. The degree to which the drug improves clinical outcomes (reduction in cardiac death rates) may be overstated due to "regression to the mean" or understated due to pre-treatment health status. PSM corrects this bias when all relevant characteristics (or covariates) are observed and measured without error.

PSM simulates randomization by identifying a control group that is comparable to the treatment group on the basis of observed characteristics (covariates). The basic framework for PSM is easy to understand and implement empirically (Luo and Gardiner, 2010). Each individual j with a vector of observed characteristics (x_j) either receives the treatment ($D_j = 1$) or does not ($D_j = 0$). The propensity score (p_j) for individual j may be written as follows:

$$p_j = Pr(D_j = 1 \mid x_j).$$

The first step in the empirical approach utilizes a logit regression (or other discrete choice model) to estimate the probability of receiving treatment as a function of the observed covariates. The estimate for p_j is valid only if the decision to receive treatment is independent of its potential benefit. This assumption balances the distribution of observed covariates across treatment and control groups.

Second, check the propensity scores across the two groups to make sure that the two distributions overlap sufficiently (defining the region of common support).

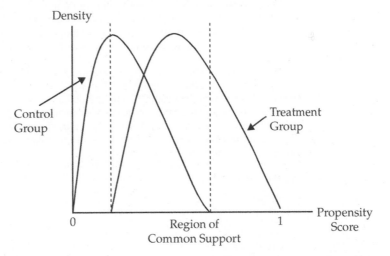

Third, match each individual in the treatment group with an individual in the control group that has a similar propensity score. Use a matching strategy that makes the most sense, the simplest being "nearest neighbor." The goal is to match as many in the treatment group with controls as possible. Sort the data by propensity score and block the observations by similar scores. Within each, block test whether the mean values of the covariates in the two groups are equal. If they are equal, stop and proceed to the next step. If not, divide the blocks where covariate means are unequal into finer blocks and repeat the test. Repeat until all means are equal. If some remain unequal, re-estimate the propensity scores using the original logit but include higher order terms or interactions between covariates. Repeat data blocking and covariate testing on the new matched sample until all covariate means are equal.

Finally, using regression analysis on the matched sample, estimate the effect of the treatment variable and other covariates on the outcome variable. Perform sensitivity analysis to measure the robustness of the estimated average treatment effect and to ensure that the approach mimics conditions present in a randomized control trial.

Sources: P. R. Rosenbaum and D. B. Rubin, "The Central Role of the Propensity Score in Observational Studies for Causal Effects," *Biometrika* 70, 1983, 41–55 and Zhejui Luo and Joseph C. Gardiner, "Applying Propensity Score Methods in Medical Research: Pitfalls and Prospects," *Medical Care Research and Review* 67(5), October 2010, 528–554.

Instrumental Variables

The instrumental variable (IV) approach has been an integral part of applied econometrics for decades. Successful implementation of this approach requires the availability of an IV (Z) that affects the likelihood of treatment (T) but has no direct, independent effect on the outcome variable (Y). The desired relationship between Z and T and Y may be depicted using the following diagram.

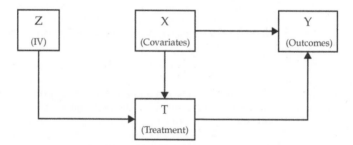

The relationship between the treatment variable and the outcome is confounded by the other covariates (X) that affect both T and Y, making T endogenous and estimates of the average treatment effect biased. The existence of the IV (Z) provides a way to estimate the effect of T on Y by first estimating the effect of Z on T. In other words, individuals in the treatment group are not analyzed on the basis of the treatment received but on the basis of the IV.

The estimation is carried out in two stages. First, the endogenous treatment effect (T) is regressed on all other covariates (X) and the IV (Z). Second, T is replaced by its predicted value from the first stage ($\hat{T}$) and the outcome variable (Y) is regressed on the predicted value of T and the other covariates. This approach provides a way to estimate how much of the variation in the treatment induced by the instrument affects the outcome.

IV is yet another way to correct for endogeneity in observational studies where randomization is impractical, impossible, or unethical. In practice, good instruments that satisfy the stated assumptions are difficult to find making the use of IV somewhat limited.

Source: Joseph P. Newhouse and Mark McClellan, "Econometrics in Outcomes Research: The Use of Instrumental Variables," *Annual Review of Public Health* 19, 1998, 17–34.

Synthetic Control

Economists regularly study events or interventions that affect aggregate entities, such as cities, counties, states, or entire countries. One popular method used in this research is the comparative case study. The approach compares the change in aggregate outcomes (mortality rate, the percentage of a population uninsured, and the level of premiums) for the entities affected by an event or intervention with the same outcome in a control group of unaffected entities. An application of this methodology might explore the change in marketplace premiums (the aggregate outcome) in (treatment group) states that expanded Medicaid (the intervention) compared to premiums in (control group) states that did not.

The primary objective in assembling a valid control group is to produce a counterfactual that accurately reproduces the treatment group's outcome that would have been observed in the absence of the treatment. This data-driven approach constructs a (synthetic) control group, a weighted combination of the available (donor) pool of potential control units that is approximately equal to the treatment group in terms of pretreatment characteristics and outcomes. (Weights are restricted to positive numbers and sum to one.)

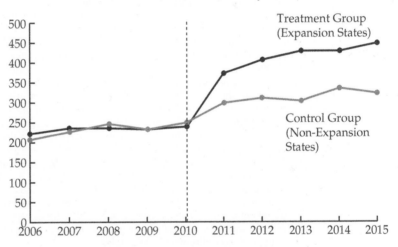

Outcome Trends: Treatment versus Synthetic Control

The critical assumption in this approach is that the synthetic control group (similar to the treatment group in the pretreatment period) is also similar to the treatment group in the posttreatment period. If this assumption holds, the treatment effect is the difference in the outcome variable between the treatment group and the synthetic control group (the synthetic treatment group without the treatment).

Source: Alberto Abadie, Alexis Diamond, and Jens Hainmueller, "Synthetic Control Methods for Comparative Case Studies: Estimating the Effect of California's Tobacco Control Program," *Journal of the American Statistical Association* 105(490), June 2010, 493–505.

services that are produced is greater than the value of the goods and services that could have been produced with the same resources. In other words, if individuals in society placed a higher value on the last dollar spent on medical care than on the last dollar spent on, say, education, then they would demand that more be spent on medical care and less on education, until the marginal valuations were equal.

> ## ISSUES IN MEDICAL CARE DELIVERY
>
> ## A NEW FORM OF COMPETITION IN MEDICAL MARKETS: MEDICAL TRAVEL
>
> As medical care prices and spending continue to escalate in much of the developed world, payers continue to look for innovative ways to reduce their costs. Patients, especially those without insurance coverage, have shown a willingness to travel to places such as Thailand, Singapore, India, and Costa Rica in search of affordable care.
>
> The search for lower prices is not the only reason that patients travel to receive their medical care. Large segments of all medical travelers seek the most advanced technologies and the high-quality medical care that follows. Many patients with this objective travel to the United States. Those on waiting lists simply desire quicker access to medical procedures. Unusually long waiting times for orthopedics, general surgery, and cardiology find residents in Canada and the United Kingdom traveling abroad for care.
>
> Medical travel companies have sprung up to provide all-inclusive arrangements that cover the medical procedure and include air and ground transportation, translation services, luxury hotel accommodations, and sightseeing excursions for family members—all for a price that is 15–25 percent of the U.S. price. Planet Hospital, a southern California company, provides Americans with overseas options. Société d' Assistance Médicale in Paris caters primarily to eastern Europeans seeking care in France.
>
> The number of individuals seeking overseas treatment is difficult to determine. Ehrbeck, Guevara, and Mango (2008) estimate the market for inpatient hospital procedures numbered 60,000 to 85,000 in 2007. However, the estimate from Deloitte Center for Health Solutions (2009) was quite different, reporting that 750,000 Americans alone had traveled abroad for medical care in 2007. Regardless of which estimate is closer to the truth, it is certain that the market will experience future growth of 30–35 percent per annum. Even McKinsey admits that the market will grow significantly, to as much as 700,000 patients annually, if payers begin to offer coverage to medical travelers.
>
> Health insurers including Aetna, WellPoint, Cigna, and UnitedHealth have established pilot programs experimenting with the concept. As other insurers begin to see that potential for savings, it is likely that all accredited hospitals abroad will be included in the travel options for medical tourists. As of 2016, there were over 400 medical organizations in 80 countries accredited by the Joint Commission International, an affiliate of the same entity that accredits all U.S. hospitals.
>
> Medical tourism has the potential to foster competition among health care providers in the United States. Where it is offered, selective contracting with specific providers, requiring patients to travel to other countries or even other regions within the United States, has already resulted in price competition in the affected markets.
>
> Sources: "Medical Tourism: Update and Implications," Deloitte Center for Health Solutions, 2009, available online at https://www2.deloitte.com/content/dam/Deloitte/us/Documents/public-sector/us-fed-risk-benefit-approach-to-translational-medicine-03242015.pdf and Tilman Ehrbeck, Ceani Guevara, and Paul D. Mango, "Mapping the Market for Medical Travel," McKinsey & Company, May 2008, available at https://www.scribd.com/document/276958378/Medical-Tourism-Market-Mapping.

optimal output level
A market equilibrium in which the marginal benefit received from every unit of output is greater than or equal to the marginal cost of producing each unit. The social optimum is that output level at which the marginal benefit of the last unit produced is equal to its marginal cost.

Market Failure

Various imperfections in medical markets increase the difficulty of delivering a product equitably and efficiently. When the underlying assumptions of competitive markets are not met, markets fail to deliver the **optimal output levels** (Rice, 1998). Markets fail to allocate resources optimally when firms have market power, when there are externalities in consumption and production, and when the good produced is a public good.

Market Power

Any departure from perfect competition—whether it be monopoly, oligopoly, cartel, monopolistic competition, monopsony, or any other market structure imperfection— violates the optimality considerations discussed earlier. A profit-maximizing firm with market power sets prices at levels that exceed marginal costs. To maintain those prices, the firm must restrict output to levels that are less than optimum. Prices will be too high, costs will be too high, resources will be underutilized, and society will suffer an economic loss.

Market power is depicted graphically by any departure from perfectly elastic demand curves. Figure 3.3 points out the differences in pricing and output between firms in perfectly competitive markets and those with market power. When demand curves are perfectly elastic, they are drawn as horizontal lines. Profit maximizers set marginal revenue (MR) equal to marginal cost (MC). With price equal to marginal revenue, MR = MC at the same output level (Q_0) where P_0 = MC (the condition for allocative efficiency).

Market power gives a firm some control over its pricing decisions. Raising price reduces quantity sold without the complete loss of customers. With a downward-sloping demand curve, the firm's marginal revenue is less than the price it charges. Setting MR equal to MC results in a lower output level (Q_1) and the ability to charge a higher price (P_1). Higher prices, lower output, and underutilization of resources result in a loss in welfare as measured by the loss in consumer and producer surplus.

In spite of these problems, monopoly may still be the most effective way to organize production in a market. When production is subject to economies of scale, the long-run average cost curve declines continuously as production increases. Competition will result in the exit of all but one firm. That remaining firm, the **natural monopoly**, will not set price competitively, and since P > MC, output is not provided at its optimal level. To correct this misallocation of resources, the most effective option may be regulation.[3]

We can use Figure 3.4 to illustrate this point. Suppose the firm has a long-run average cost curve that is downward sloping as it crosses the market demand curve. Under these circumstances, a single firm can supply enough output to satisfy consumer demand and can do so at progressively lower unit costs.[4] Shielded from competition from rival firms, the monopolist has no compelling reason to be efficient. Focusing solely on profit maximization, the firm will produce where MR = MC, where output (Q_0) is less than optimal, and price will be higher than if the market were competitive (P_0). To correct this problem, government price controllers often try to establish a maximum price the monopolist can

KEY CONCEPT 9
Market Failure

KEY CONCEPT 3
Marginal Analysis

natural monopoly
A firm becomes a natural monopoly based on its ability to provide a good or service at a lower cost than anyone else and satisfy consumer demand completely.

FIGURE 3.3
The Consequences of Market Power on Price and Output

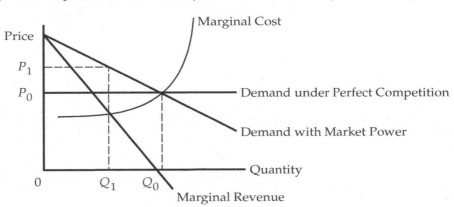

[3]Certain tax and subsidy schemes might actually be more efficient, but discussion of these alternatives is beyond the scope of this presentation.

[4]Because price, represented by the demand curve, is above the average cost curve at every point, the firm can increase sales by lowering price and still make an economic profit.

charge that more closely approximates the perfectly competitive solution. Setting a price at P_1, for example, enables the firm to earn a normal return on its investment and produce at a higher output level (Q_1).

Market power in an input market also causes an inefficient allocation of resources. A monopsonist, as the sole buyer of a particular resource, faces an upward-sloping supply curve instead of a perfectly elastic supply curve. As a result, the firm has some discretion over the price it pays for the resource. When consumers desire more, then the firm must pay a higher price. If they desire less, then prices fall accordingly. Figure 3.5 depicts the results, where the monopsonist faces a situation in which the marginal cost of the resource is greater than the price of the resource. Instead of setting demand equal to supply and paying P_0 to employ Q_0 units of the resource, the monopsonist equates demand—its assessment of the marginal value of the resource used in production—with the marginal cost of the resource and employs Q_1 units of the output. At this level of utilization, the monopsonist has only to pay P_1 to attract sufficient resources to satisfy the firm's demand.

Market power in the resource market enables firms to employ fewer resources and pay lower prices for their use than if the market were perfectly competitive. The result of lost output is lost income to resource owners and fewer goods and services available to consumers. In summary, market power insulates a firm from the competitive forces that ensure allocative and technical efficiency, resulting in a loss to society.

KEY CONCEPT 9
Market Failure

FIGURE 3.4
Regulating the Natural
Monopoly

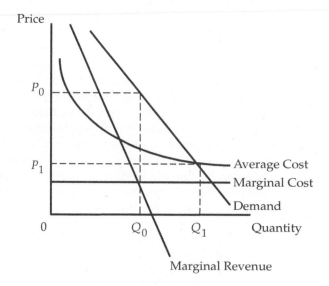

FIGURE 3.5
The Consequences of
Market Power on Price
and Output in Resource
Markets

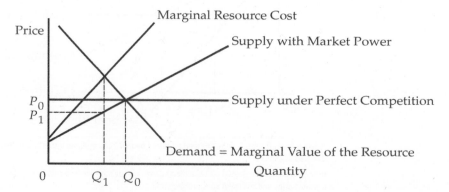

Externalities

externality A cost or benefit that spills over to parties not directly involved in the actual transaction and is thus ignored by the buyer and seller.

Sometimes the actions taken by individuals in the process of producing or consuming will have an effect on the welfare of others. An **externality** may be either positive or negative, depending on whether it benefits or harms other people. By maintaining his or her property, a homeowner generates a positive externality for all his or her neighbors. Not only is it pleasing to look at a freshly painted house and well-kept garden, but the market values of surrounding properties are enhanced at the same time.

Examples of negative externalities abound. Anyone smoking a cigar in a crowded room imposes costs on everyone else in the room. Everyone has less fresh air to breathe than if the smoker were forced to internalize all the costs of his or her smoking. A factory that dumps toxic waste into a nearby river shifts some of the cost of production (i.e., waste disposal) onto those people who live downstream from the plant. The same can be said about acid rain, traffic congestion, and the many other examples of negative externalities that could be listed.

Externalities affect economic efficiency, and normal market mechanisms have no way of accounting for them. Decision makers are not required to absorb the costs of negative externalities and have no way to capture the benefits of positive externalities. The result is a level of output that is nonoptimal.

Externalities exist as by-products of the decision to produce and consume. Because formal markets do not exist for these by-products, they are produced in nonoptimal quantities. Take, for example, the case of automobile emissions in a crowded metropolitan area. By choosing to drive your own car to work, you impose costs on others in the form of carbon monoxide emissions from the exhaust. A large percentage of the costs of commuting are internalized. You pay for the car, the gasoline, and the insurance. However, your fellow commuters pay the costs that you do not internalize, namely the costs of the by-products of your commute: traffic congestion and air pollution.

⭐ **KEY CONCEPT 3**
Marginal Analysis

Figure 3.6 illustrates the impact of an externality in a private market, the daily commute to work or school. Externalities arise because the driver does not internalize the full cost of the commute. Graphically, the vertical distance between the marginal social cost (MSC) curve and the marginal private cost (MPC) curve represents the external costs that the driver forces others to pay. Individual decision makers determine their own commuter miles by equating marginal benefit (MB) with MPC. Given the additional costs that society

FIGURE 3.6
The External Costs of a Daily Commute

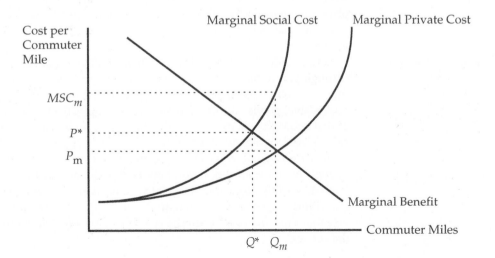

must pay, the number of commuter miles actually driven (Q_m) is greater than the optimal number (Q^*). To incorporate these externalities into individual decision-making requires some form of collective action to force commuters to pay the full costs of their actions. For example, through their elected representatives, voters may decide to reduce the number of commuter miles driven by private automobiles by erecting tollbooths on all major freeways or simply forcing everyone who drives into the city to pay a commuter tax. In either case, the goal is to force private decision makers to take into account the external costs of their actions. By moving the MPC closer to the MSC, the number of commuter miles driven will approach its optimal level, Q^*.

In the case of positive externalities, the competitive output rate will be too small if the decision maker cannot capture the external benefits generated. The problem emerges because the marginal private benefit is less than the marginal social benefit. When marginal cost and marginal private benefit are equated, the resulting output is less than optimal.

Public Goods

Markets distribute goods efficiently when people spend their own money to enjoy the benefits of consumption. The market for Nike shoes works because those unwilling to pay the price for Nike shoes do not own Nike shoes. The market mechanism provides purchasers with the benefits of consumption and excludes nonpurchasers from receiving those benefits. Additionally, the benefits flow to specific individuals. Consumption of a crispy taco by one person does not satisfy the hunger of another.

In certain situations, these two characteristics do not hold. In fact, many important goods, such as national defense and air traffic control, do not exhibit them fully. Nonexcludable and **nonrival goods** are called *public goods*. Nonexcludability in the distribution of a good results when the costs of preventing nonpayers from consuming are high, making it difficult to impose prices on these individuals. Once a strategic national defense system is operational, there is no way to exclude individuals from its protective umbrella simply because they refuse to pay their share of the costs.

Nonrivalry in consumption means that more than one person can enjoy the benefits of consuming a commodity without affecting the enjoyment of the other. One person's consumption does not reduce the benefit received by someone else. In technical terms, the marginal cost of providing the good to additional consumers is zero. For example, after the Army Corps of Engineers builds a levy, any number of houses may be built in the flood plain without increasing the marginal cost of flood control. If an air-traffic control system is in place, the marginal cost of monitoring the flight path of an additional aircraft is close to zero.

Serious efficiency problems arise when we attempt to provide **nonexcludable goods** through private markets. To understand the problem, note the difference between the provision of excludable and nonexcludable goods. Transactions involving private (excludable) goods take place in markets as long as the individual's marginal valuation of that good exceeds its price. Individuals have no incentive to lie about the marginal value placed on a good. Because of excludability, if you understate the marginal value you place on a good, you run the risk of not getting the good and missing the marginal benefits of consumption. If you have ever witnessed an auction of any kind, you are familiar with this concept. Marginal valuations are reflected in the prices individuals are willing to pay for items that are being auctioned. You must make those marginal valuations known, or you run the risk of finding yourself empty handed at the end of the auction.

nonrival goods
A good or service that does not, when consumed by one individual, limit the amount available to anyone else.

nonexcludable goods
A good or service that is difficult to limit to a specific group of consumers. In other words, if the item is available to anyone, it becomes available to everyone.

In contrast, when goods are nonexcludable, there is an incentive for individuals to understate their true marginal valuations. If I can enjoy all the benefits of consumption without paying for that privilege, why pay? Those individuals who refuse to pay for a good while still enjoying the benefits of consumption are called *free riders* (some might even call them *freeloaders*). Public television provides a good example of the free-rider problem. The number of people who watch public television far exceeds the number who subscribe. Of course, some ride free, but others have to pay, or no one rides at all. And that's the point. Private markets tend to undersupply nonexcludable goods.

The case of public goods is simply a special kind of positive externality. So to ensure its availability at optimal levels, public provision of the good may be required. Governments can require individuals to participate in paying for goods through the power to tax. Clearly, all goods publicly provided are not public goods. Whether the good is provided by a public or private entity is not the issue. Governments often engage in the provision of private goods, for example, by staging concerts in the park and collecting garbage. In both cases, it costs very little to exclude nonpayers from consumption, eliminating the problem of the free rider.

Even strong defenders of the market admit that private markets do not always provide goods and services at efficient levels. However, those critical of market outcomes must address the issue of whether the government can do a better job. Is government provision any more efficient than private provision? Does it result in a more equitable distribution of resources? Is a more equitable distribution of resources worth the cost? We will focus on these questions later in the chapter.

free rider
An individual who does not buy insurance, knowing that in the event of a serious illness, medical care will be provided free of charge.

POLICY ISSUE
Is government provision of medical care more efficient than provision through the private market?

merit good A good whose benefits are not fully appreciated by the average consumer and thus should be provided collectively.

ISSUES IN MEDICAL CARE DELIVERY

MEDICAL CARE AS A "MERIT GOOD"

Economic models predicting consumer behavior usually assume, among other things, that individuals know what they want and are able to rank their preferences. But often people avoid what is good for them and choose items that are actually harmful. Recognizing this fact, Musgrave (1959) classified certain goods as **merit goods** to describe commodities that ought to be provided even if private demand is lacking. Since merit goods have benefits that are not fully appreciated by the average consumer, their consumption should be encouraged through collective action.

Many would place medical care in the merit-good category. Individuals lacking the ability to fully appreciate the importance of primary and preventive care will under consume when it comes to this valuable commodity. Whether this classification is merely a case of imposing preferences on society, or whether it is a genuine merit-good situation, is open to debate.

The usual arguments used to justify government involvement in medical care delivery and finance include market failure, information problems, third-party financing, and even merit goods. These arguments are often compelling, if not always convincing. Nevertheless, when using the merit-goods argument, we must be careful that we are not merely replacing a personal value judgment—that everyone is entitled to medical care—with formal terminology to justify our personal preferences (Baumol and Baumol, 1981).

Sources: Richard A. Musgrave, *The Theory of Public Finance*, New York: McGraw-Hill, 1959 and William J. Baumol and Hilda Baumol, "Book Review," *Journal of Political Economy* 89(2), April 1981, 425–428.

POLICY ISSUE

Should everyone be required to participate in an immunization program designed to protect the entire population against a communicable disease?

Market Failure in Medical Markets

The obvious starting point in analyzing market failure in medical markets begins with the three causes of market failure discussed earlier. How prevalent are monopolies in medical markets? Are there significant externalities in consumption and production? Is medical care a public good, nonexcludable in distribution and nonrival in consumption?

APPLIED MICRO METHODS

CAN FINANCIAL INCENTIVES INCREASE ORGAN DONATIONS?

Background

The 1984 National Organ Transplantation Act (NOTA) established a network of organ procurement organizations tasked with the responsibility of securing a sufficient supply of organs. In a market where trade is prohibited, strict reliance on altruism has resulted in a shortage of most transplantable organs. NOTA was amended in 2000 allowing payment to donors for related expenses including lost wages, travel, and medical expenses. A number of states now allow a tax deduction for these costs that amount to a reduction in state income tax payments.

No reliable evidence supports the conclusion that these incentives increase organ donations. In fact, a consensus of four such studies using DiD methods indicates that the incentive may actually crowd out altruistic motives from unrelated donors. The reasons for the failure of previous research to identify a positive effect of incentives on donations fall into two categories: First, there is enough variation in impact of the covariates between treatment states (T, those that adopted financial incentives) and control states (C, those that did not) that the common trend assumption fails. In fact, Boulware et al. (2008) provide evidence that donation rates cross prior to the passage of legislation. Second, incentives tend to follow heightened public interest in the organ donation crisis, indicating that donation rates may regress to the mean in T and not in C, biasing estimates of the treatment effect downward.

Data and Methods

State-level panel data on organ transplantation between 1988 and 2012 were retrieved from the Organ Procurement and Transplantation Network. Demographic and disease-related data were gathered from other sources. Due to data limitations, the final estimates identify only one T state (New York) along with 13 C states.

This paper examines living kidney donation rates from both related and unrelated donors. The initial specification is shown as follows:

$$y_{it} = \mu_i + \delta_t + \alpha_i \tau_{it} + \gamma D_{it} + X_{it}\beta + \varepsilon_{it}$$

where y_{it} denotes living kidney donation rates, μ_i, δ_t, and α_i are state and year fixed effects and state linear time trends, D_{it} is the treatment variable (initially the tax legislation is treated as a binary variable and later the real value of the tax incentive is estimated), X_{it} is the vector of covariates consisting of the prevalence of end stage renal disease (ESRD) patients (all rates per million adult persons), real per capita GDP, the number of transplant centers in the state, number on the kidney waiting lists, and the cadaveric donation rate.

Results

Initial estimates using the binary treatment variable (D) check for endogeneity of cadaveric donations using DiD via limited information maximum likelihood (LIML) methods (instrumenting for cadaveric donations using motor vehicle fatalities and cerebrovascular deaths). Regardless of estimation strategy, tax incentives do not seem to have a statistically significant causal effect on living kidney donation rates. A second approach used the value of each state's tax incentive as the treatment variable (T). Two different instruments were employed for T (using the average federal marginal tax rates for itemizers and the share of federal Medicaid expenditures provided the states) resulting in the same outcome.

This paper then employs synthetic control in an attempt to reveal the causal effect of the tax incentives on living kidney donation rates. The empirical approach constructs the missing counterfactual (donation rate in the T states in the absence of the legislation) by estimating a vector of weights assigned to each of the C states that together replicate kidney donation rates of T state(s) prior to enacting legislation. The effect of the law is defined by $\alpha_{it} = Y_{1it} - Y_{Nit}$, where Y_{1it} is the donation rate of the state(s) enacting the legislation and Y_{Nit} is the donation rate in the states not enacting the legislation. First, estimate the missing counterfactual Y_{Nit} for states not affected by the legislation. The approach estimates a vector of weights attached to the covariates of control group members such that the trend in C state donation rates is the same as the trend in T state rates during the pre-treatment period. Synthetic control allows for existence of unobservable state heterogeneity to vary over time.

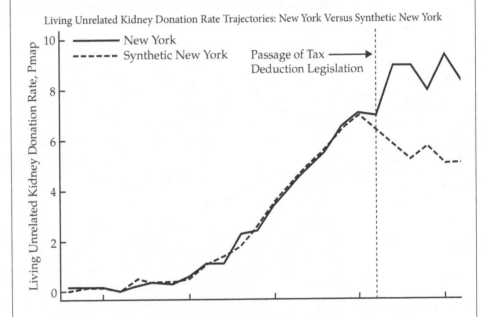

Living Unrelated Kidney Donation Rate Trajectories: New York Versus Synthetic New York

As seen in earlier figure, the estimated pretreatment period donation rates for synthetic New York (using the C state weights) are almost a perfect match for actual rates in New York. After the passage of the legislation in New York, the donation rate continues to increase and that of synthetic New York (in absence of the legislation) falls noticeably. The only difference between the two groups is the presence and absence of the tax incentive. The findings suggest that the unrelated kidney donation rate in New York increased 52 percent (during the post-legislation period, 2006–2012) relative to synthetic New York (modeled by the weighted comparison group).

The results of the synthetic control estimate reflecting the impact of tax incentive legislation on unrelated living-kidney donation rates were subjected to several falsification tests and found to be robust to the exclusion of any state as well as the use of different combinations of states as controls.

Discussion and Conclusions

Previous approaches using DiD do not find a positive causal effect of tax incentives on the living kidney donor rate. Failure of the common trends assumption may not allow the approach to remove the bias in the estimated coefficients caused by endogeneity. Likewise, the IV approach may fall short due to the failure to identify strong instruments for the treatment effect.

The synthetic control results potentially solve these problems and provide evidence that seems to indicate that tax incentives may result in higher rates of living kidney donation rates. An expanded pool of donors can have substantial benefits. Barnieh et al. (2013) estimate that even a 5 percent increase in living donations would add as much as 11,000 **quality-adjusted life years (QALYs)** for those suffering from ESRD. Further consideration of similar incentives seems warranted.

Sources: Firat Bilgel and Brian Galle, "Financial Incentives for Kidney Donation: A Comparative Case Study Using Synthetic Controls," *Journal of Health Economics* 43, 2015, 103–117; L. E. Boulware et al., "The Association of State and National Legislation with Living Kidney Donation Rates in the United States: A National Study," *American Journal of Transplantation* 8(7), 2008, 1451–1470; and Lianne Barnieh et al., "The Cost Effectiveness of Using Payment to Increase Living Donor Kidneys for Transplantation," *Clinical Journal of the American Society of Nephrology* 8(12), 2013, 1–9.

quality-adjusted life years (QALY) A measure of the effectiveness of a medical treatment that captures improvements in the quality of life, as well as extensions in the length of life.

Traditional Sources of Market Failure

POLICY ISSUE

Are subsidies to private providers better than direct government provision when the goal is to improve economic welfare?

Even though absolute market power in medical markets may be hard to find, lack of competition can still be a significant problem. Most metropolitan areas are served by more than one hospital due to the simple fact that economies of scale in the hospital industry are exhausted at relatively low levels of capacity. Even in communities as small as 180,000 people, two or three hospitals providing most general services could coexist. In smaller communities, the lack of competition presents a greater challenge for market proponents. In these small markets, some inpatient services must be shared to avoid substantial inefficiencies (Chronic et al., 1993).

Even in larger communities with multiple facilities, some providers may have a degree of market power. Some services and procedures exhibit significant economies of scale, such as organ transplantation and various imaging technologies that include CT scans (computerized tomography) and MRIs (magnetic resonance imaging).

KEY CONCEPT 7
Competition

http://
Many philanthropic organizations are using the Internet to advance their messages. The United Way of America has an extensive network of activities funded largely through payroll deductions. It may be found at http://www.unitedway.org

Although a pure monopoly may be difficult to find, firms often engage in collusive behavior to avoid competition. Recognizing that it is in their collective interest to avoid price competition, providers differentiate their products to make direct price comparisons difficult. There is competition along the lines of quality and the number of services offered but typically not price. Differentiation is often accomplished when providers agree to specialize, for example, with one hospital offering cardiac care and another obstetric care. This type of market segmentation is relatively easy, because most medical care is provided locally.

http://
Research for the prevention, detection, and treatment of cancer is the goal of the American Cancer Society at http://www.cancer.org

Externalities arise in medical care in a number of circumstances. The most obvious type of externality is associated with public health programs. Modern society can be a breeding ground for all sorts of communicable diseases. The ability of the public health service to enforce health regulations and monitor contagious diseases serves to improve public health. Related activities include the provision of clean water, clean air, and adequate sewage disposal, which greatly reduce the incidence of diseases such as cholera and dysentery. In addition, immunization against mumps, measles, small pox, polio, and whooping cough offers protection for more than one individual. The benefits extend to the entire population by eliminating potential carriers of the diseases. In other words, the incremental

http://
Raising funds to benefit children and the network's affiliated hospitals is the mission of the Children's Miracle Network at http://www.cmn.org/

http://
Volunteer opportunities and fund-raising information may be found at the website for the Ronald McDonald Houses. Ronald McDonald House Charities may be found at http://www.rmhc.com/

in-kind transfer
Welfare subsidies provided in the form of vouchers for specific goods and services, such as food stamps and Medicaid.

☆ **POLICY ISSUE**
Should medical care subsidies take the form of direct cash payments or in-kind transfers?

value to society is greater than the value to the individual alone. In a private market, fewer vaccinations would occur than is socially optimal and may call for collective action in the form of mandates or subsidies or both.

Many argue that social or philanthropic externalities are associated with the consumption of medical care. These consumption externalities arise because the healthy and economically well-to-do derive satisfaction, a type of social solidarity, from knowing that the sick and indigent also receive medical care. Individuals who share this philanthropic desire can and do combine resources to fund private foundations and medical organizations. With more than 1.5 million participants in over 150 separate events, the Susan G. Komen Race for the Cure provides individuals around the world with the opportunity to unite in the fight against breast cancer. Personal contributions to the United Way, the Ronald McDonald House, the Children's Miracle Network, the American Cancer Society, and numerous other national and local organizations advance the fight against specific diseases and provide access to medical treatments that might otherwise be prohibitively expensive.

Given the nature of the externality, even those who refuse to contribute enjoy the benefits of knowing that medical research is finding cures for certain diseases and that certain medical services are available for those who cannot afford to pay for them. If this consumption externality exists and is significant, then collective action through government can be used to provide medical care to that segment of the population that cannot afford to buy it privately. Those who would not contribute privately would then share the responsibility through mandatory taxation. Collective action determines the nature of the subsidy, the level of taxation, and the method of distribution.

The medical subsidy is usually an **in-kind transfer** rather than a cash payment. Beneficiaries prefer cash rather than services. They usually find themselves better off with the cash. Donors generally prefer in-kind benefits because of the lack of guarantees that cash would be used for medical care. In fact, Waldo et al. (1989) indicate that a cash transfer to the elderly equivalent to their per capita share of Medicare would do more to improve their welfare than the direct subsidy for medical services. It seems that donors—in this case, taxpayers—care about health differently than other aspects of the recipient's well-being, whether it is the food they eat or a house to live in.

Externalities may also be associated with exceptionally large medical expenditures. Frequently, those with incomplete or no health insurance coverage have medical bills that exceed their ability to pay. Faced with this event, they default on their obligation, and the community must pick up the tab. In other words, providers are forced to write off the expenses as bad debts and taxpayers and donors are called upon to subsidize the provision of indigent care.[5] The fact that we are unable or at least unwilling to exclude anyone from access to medical care for financial reasons creates free riders. For this reason, many advocate mandatory health insurance covering catastrophic (high cost) episodes of illness. In this way, everyone would be forced to participate in the cost of providing medical care, and the free-rider problem would be moderated.

Pure medical research that has no easily captured commercial value fits the definition of a public good. This is the type of medical research that is packaged and published primarily in medical journals. Much of the information that is shared in this manner shows other medical practitioners the ways to combine activities and procedures into a particular mode of treatment. Unless patentable medical devices are included in the procedures, it is difficult

---

[5]Medical care providers usually report the delinquent debtor to the appropriate credit bureau. This has become so common that many lenders, such as commercial banks and consumer credit companies, regularly ignore a default on a would-be borrower's credit history if the debt was associated with medical care (private conversation with Bart Cooper, General Motors Acceptance Corporation).

⭐ **POLICY ISSUE**
*Is medical research
a public good, thus
strengthening the
argument in favor of
government financing of
basic medical research?*

⭐ **POLICY ISSUE**
*Should physicians and
other health care providers
be allowed to advertise?*

for those responsible for the discovery to capture the benefits of their research. Good examples include radial keratotomy and the use of lasers in ophthalmological surgery.

Many will argue that medical research should be treated as a public good and financed collectively through government. In this way, basic advances financed by the taxpayer would belong in the public domain, freely available to potential users. The other side of the argument recognizes that academicians conduct much of our medical research. Working within the university and medical school setting, they are able to capture the benefits of their discoveries through the rules of promotion and tenure, so at least a portion of the benefit is translated into career enhancement opportunities and personal prestige. Some may choose to keep their findings out of the public domain in order to earn royalties or other payments.

To the extent that medical care has characteristics associated with market power among providers, externalities in production and consumption, and public goods, the level of services provided will fall short of the optimal level as defined by competitive markets.

Imperfections in Medical Markets

Other imperfections contribute to the failure of medical markets to provide the socially optimal level of service (Pauly, 1988). These imperfections include imperfect information, barriers to entry, and the prevalence of third-party payers.

Imperfect Information

Lack of information presents serious problems in a market economy. In medical markets, the problems that arise may be even more serious. Most patients are poorly informed about virtually every aspect of the medical transaction. They are usually aware of their symptoms and syndromes, but seldom do they understand the underlying causes of their medical conditions. They have scarcely an opportunity to form a learned opinion about the physician's diagnosis or the prescribed treatment. In most cases, nothing other than a complete recovery is the expected outcome.

The overall lack of information available to patients is compounded by the difficulty in securing the information, measured in terms of time and expense. As a result, most patients rely almost exclusively on their provider to keep them informed on matters dealing with their medical condition, its diagnosis, and treatment alternatives. Patients also have little knowledge about price and quality differences among alternative providers. This imbalance of information between patient and provider, referred to as **asymmetric information**, has led to two important market defects.

asymmetric information A situation in which information is unequally distributed between the individuals in a transaction. The person with more information will have an unfair advantage in determining the terms of any agreement.

First, patients are not able to judge price and quality differences among providers. As a result, providers can charge prices that are higher than the prevailing prices in the market for a given level of quality, or they may choose to offer a lower level of quality for a given price. The impact of this phenomenon can be seen in the variation in prices paid and the quantities of medical care provided to similar groups of patients. Evidence for these variations has been compiled by examining, for example, surgery rates for common procedures. In cases where alternative intervention strategies are not available—such as appendectomy, hernia repair, and hysterectomy—the variation in surgery rates is relatively low. But in cases where alternative treatments are available—such as tonsillectomy, disc surgery, and coronary artery bypass grafts—variation is high: up to four times the rate of the low-variance surgeries (Phelps, 1992).

The second problem is an agency problem. The physician serves as the agent of the patient and the patient delegates most of the decision-making authority to the physician. The expectation, in turn, is that the patient's best interests will be the top priority. The dual role of provider of services on the one hand and the agent in charge of information on the other creates a dilemma: The physician is in a position to induce the patient to purchase more medical care than is actually needed. Physicians can recommend not only medical care with little marginal value, medical care on the flat of the curve, but also medical care that may actually harm the patient. At the other extreme, enrollees in managed care organizations may find themselves denied care that offers positive net benefits, because it is not in the financial interest of the provider to offer that care.

This information problem does not mean that medical markets are hopelessly uncompetitive. Market mechanisms have arisen to minimize the impact of these information differences. The medical community has created licensing, certification, and accreditation requirements for physicians, specialists, hospitals, and medical schools to assure minimum quality standards. Professional organizations establish ethical standards. Moreover, if this is not enough, the threat of a malpractice lawsuit is always a reminder of the importance of promoting the best interests of the patient.

Keep in mind that other markets also exhibit this information problem and are relatively competitive. The market for personal computers is a good example. Except for a small segment of the market, the public is woefully ignorant of the differences between RAM and ROM, the number of Megs in a Gig, and the merits of Pentium and Celeron processors. Are there good reasons to buy a Mac instead of a PC? Do I want a zip drive or an external hard drive? Even with all this consumer ignorance, the market for personal computers is extremely competitive. Why? Because an informed minority provided the initial market discipline. They wrote the newsletters, contributed to the magazines, and spent endless hours on the Internet participating in forums and posting on bulletin boards. The demand for information fostered by this group created awareness among all consumers.

When consumers perceive that acquiring and using information best serves their own interests, there will be a demand for information. All but a minority of consumers in medical markets have little interest in spending time and money to acquire information. The third-party payer—the insurance company or the government—expropriates any savings from the search. Change that aspect of the medical marketplace, and consumers will have an incentive to become informed. Virtually all types of medical care, except emergency care, would be purchased in markets with enough informed consumers to ensure economic discipline. The demand for information is evident in the managed care marketplace, where many organizations and networks are reporting to their constituencies on how well they perform in certain critical areas, including primary and preventive care, surgical outcomes, and cost (Kenkel, 1994).

★ **KEY CONCEPT 4**
Self-Interest

Price Transparency   In order for markets to function properly, consumers must be able to rank order their preferences. The first step in this process requires the valuation of the expected outcome of a transaction. More specifically, value in health care is measured in terms of health outcomes relative to the price of services provided (Kaplan and Porter, 2011). To play a role in rational decision-making, prices must be known in advance.

Meaningful price information is difficult to obtain and rarely available prior to receiving care. Prices when available are centered on discrete medical services: an office visit, immunization, or diagnostic test. Patients do not want to know the prices of individual components of the treatment they desire. They want to know the price of an episode of care, such as a colonoscopy, hip replacement surgery, or a visit to the cardiac catheterization lab for stenting. Lack of good price information shields providers from any meaningful competition.

Reinhardt (2006) refers to the pricing practices of the hospital industry as "chaos behind a veil of secrecy." The difficulty in obtaining meaningful price information obscures one of the essential elements in determining the value of medical services.

Explaining, much less justifying, medical pricing practices is challenging. Each episode of care is unique, making it difficult to predict in advance all the services that will be included in the treatment. Multiple providers (e.g., a hospital, surgeon, and anesthesiologist), each billing separately, are often involved in a patient's treatment. Because of price discrimination, prices differ by the type of coverage (Medicare, Medicaid, and the various private insurance plans), making it difficult to quote a single price. Moreover, providers treat their prices like trade secrets, often placing "gag clauses" in their contracts with insurance plans.

Over 30 states have enacted price transparency initiatives to help medical consumers make informed decision. Rules vary by state, but the most common provision is the development of Internet websites with price information. The ACA also requires hospitals to provide information annually on standard charges for the items they provide.

Because patients with insurance pay such a small percentage of their medical bills, the demand for price information is almost nonexistent. Inelastic demand together with a lack of price transparency create an environment where insured patients have little use for price information, and the prices they know have little effect on the medical decisions they make.

Barriers to Entry   An important characteristic found in competitive markets is easy entry and easy exit of suppliers. Profits serve as a signal to prospective providers. If profits are greater than normal for a given level of risk, firms will enter the market and drive down prices, and profits will adjust to normal levels. Lower-than-normal profits will result in the opposite response, with marginally profitable firms leaving the market and driving up prices and profits for those who remain.

Entry barriers restrict resource movements and result in imperfect competition. Examples of barriers in medical markets are found in numerous restrictions on tasks performed and investments made. The licensing and certification of practitioners are two of the most common ways to restrict entry into the medical profession. The stated purpose of this policy is consumer protection, and its aim is to keep uninformed patients from seeking services from incompetent providers. **Certificate-of-need (CON)** laws require hospitals to secure approval from government planning agencies before adding new capacity or investing in expensive equipment. CON legislation seeks to eliminate the duplication of costly programs within a service area. Restrictions may sound good in theory, but one of the unintended consequences of any limits placed on a market is the elimination of competition. Reduced competition leads to market power, and market power leads to market failure.

Third-Party Payers   In traditional markets, individuals spending their own money provide the discipline that culminates in the efficient provision of goods and services. One of the main reasons medical markets are not efficient is that consumers do not spend their own money. Only about 3 cents of every dollar spent on hospital services, 9 cents out of every dollar spent on physicians' services, and 14 cents on pharmaceuticals come directly from patients' out-of-pocket spending. Third parties, primarily health insurance companies and the government, pay the rest. Therein lays the major problem in medical markets. Typically, pricing reflects the interaction of consumers' willingness to pay for goods and services and their ability to buy them. Medical markets virtually ignore the desires of those without insurance and those without the ability to pay for care out-of-pocket. The desires of those who have insurance are distorted by the subsidy provided by their insurance.

A system financed primarily through retrospective **fee-for-service** insurance reimbursement is open ended. Providers are able to pass through all their costs, no matter how inefficient the production of services. The system can be described as a **cost-plus pricing**

☆ **KEY CONCEPT 7**
Competition

certificate-of-need (CON) Regulations that attempt to avoid the costly duplication of services in the hospital industry. Providers are required to secure a certificate of need before undertaking a major expansion of facilities or services.

☆ **KEY CONCEPT 5**
Markets and Pricing

fee-for-service The traditional payment method for medical care in which a provider bills for each service provided.

cost-plus pricing A pricing scheme in which a percentage profit is added to average cost.

system (Goodman and Musgrave, 1992). In a cost-plus environment, there is no incentive for providers to search for more efficient methods of production, and patients have no incentive to search for providers who offer lower prices. In competitive markets, providers are rewarded for offering quality products at the lowest price. In cost-plus markets, providers are rewarded by offering more services at higher prices, passing on the additional costs to the third-party payers.

Several factors led to the growth and expansion of the cost-plus system from the end of the Second World War through the 1980s. The American Medical Association (AMA) controlled medical licensing. This not-for-profit institution effectively limited competition in the medical profession by requiring that anyone wishing to practice medicine must graduate from an AMA-approved medical school. Not-for-profit and government-run institutions dominated the hospital sector. Without the economic discipline provided by the profit motive, hospitals competed for physicians. Operating surpluses were directed toward investment in new services and expensive equipment by physician-dominated boards. As a result, excess capacity in beds, nursing staffs, and allied personnel were used to maximize the ability of physicians to generate income for themselves. Finally, Blue Cross and Blue Shield dominated the health insurance industry, and the addition of Medicare and Medicaid in the 1960s meant that not-for-profit payers were financing one-half of all medical care provided. This dominance created an atmosphere in which cost was a secondary consideration. Without a cost constraint, the only thing that mattered was the patient's health. Whether the procedure provided a net benefit was not an issue.

Restraint was not present on the demand side either, because insurance was paying the bills. Conventional health insurance distorts the decision-making process by making it appear that medical care is cheap at the point of purchase. Medical care, of course, is not cheap. However, cost-plus reimbursement by third-party payers provides an incentive for people to demand interventions that provide little benefit.

The cost-plus system began to run into problems during the 1980s. No matter how prosperous a nation is, there is a limit to how much its people are willing to spend on any single item. As health care spending approached and exceeded 10 percent of GDP, showing no signs of slowing down, policy makers and planners began to address concerns about the "health care crisis." Thus began the bureaucratic struggle to slow the growth in health care spending.

In its early stages, this struggle focused on reimbursement strategies and restrictions on access to services. Medicare and Medicaid placed restrictions on providers by creating fee schedules and changing the method of reimbursement from **retrospective payment** to prospective payment. Private payers did the same, using the strategy of managed care. In both cases, the focus was not on changing buyer behavior but on limiting unnecessary procedures and services.

The move to prospective payment created incentives on the supply side to limit care. The desires of patients become a secondary consideration, subordinated to the desire to control costs. The stage was set for the next phase of the cost-plus cycle. Either the system would evolve into one in which individuals were motivated by the economic discipline of the market or into one dominated by the bureaucratic discipline of the government.

Government Intervention in Medical Markets

Government involvement in the medical marketplace is extensive. This involvement includes financing, direct provision, regulation, and subsidization. Almost 50 percent of all health care spending comes directly from government sources, including

POLICY ISSUE
Conventional health insurance virtually eliminates any cost-conscious behavior on the part of the parties involved in the medical care transaction.

KEY CONCEPT 3
Marginal Analysis

retrospective payment Payment determined after delivery of the good or service. Traditional fee-for-service medicine determines payment retrospectively.

Medicare, Medicaid, and the various health plans covering government employees and their dependents, both civilian and military. Government regulators are responsible for licensing, occupational health and safety, the administration of food and drugs, environmental protection, public health, and other oversight functions. Finally, the government uses features of the tax code to subsidize and encourage the provision of group insurance in employer-sponsored plans.

Regulation

The health care industry is one of the most heavily regulated industries in the U.S. economy. Price controls, entry restrictions covering both providers and hospitals, and regulations on the development and introduction of new drugs and medical devices are the major areas of regulatory control affecting the health care economy.

Price Controls   The United States has a long history of placing restrictions on markets in the form of wage and price controls. World War II, the Korean War, and the wage-price freeze that was part of the stabilization program enacted during the Nixon administration are a few of the instances in which government has attempted to fight inflation by freezing prices. Since the inception of Medicare and Medicaid, medical markets have been subject to price controls of one variety or another. In the beginning, physicians' fees were limited to **usual, customary, and reasonable (UCR) charges**. Under UCR, physicians could charge the minimum of the doctor's *usual fee*, defined by the median fee during the past year, and the *customary fee*, defined by the fees charged by other doctors in the area. The use of UCR resulted in a steady escalation of physicians' fees. The formula left no reason for a physician's usual fee to be lower than the customary fee charged in the area. If the usual fee was the minimum in the formula, Medicare paid the usual fee. As individual fees escalated, area fees escalated. The underlying incentive was always to make sure that your usual fee was not the minimum.

Medical prices continued to rise faster than the rate of overall inflation. As prices increased, spending increased. Efforts to limit spending growth shifted to the hospital sector in the early 1980s with the introduction of prospective payment. This new approach paid hospitals for an episode of treatment instead of using the usual cost-plus method. Under prospective payment, hospitals were paid according to the expected cost of treating a particular patient based on the principal diagnosis.[6] If the actual cost of treatment was less than the payment, the hospital kept the surplus. If actual costs were greater, the hospital absorbed the loss. Prospective payment changed the incentive structure completely. Hospitals were no longer rewarded for providing more services at a higher cost, and it was actually in their best interest to limit the amount and quality of services offered and discharge patients as quickly as possible. Although hospital admissions moderated and average length of stay fell dramatically, the use of outpatient services increased dramatically, leading some to question whether the potential for savings has been exhausted (Schwartz, 1987).

Attributing the spending restraint to the method of paying hospitals, the focus shifted back to physicians' fees. The 1990s saw the advent of the relative-value scale for determining allowable physician fees. Basing fees on resource use, the relative-value scale is an attempt by bureaucrats to mimic markets. If the value scale is set correctly, prices will be set at levels that would exist in a competitive market.

usual, customary, and reasonable (UCR) charges A price ceiling set to limit fees to the minimum of the billed charge, the price customarily charged by the provider, and the prevailing charge in the geographic region.

---

[6]Other factors included in the reimbursement formula are the percentage of free care provided to indigents, whether the institution is a teaching hospital, and whether it is located in an urban area.

Entry Restrictions   The government has a long history of licensing, certifying, and accrediting medical care providers. Although the stated purpose of these restrictions is consumer protection, some evidence exists that the self-interest of the providers may be the driving force behind the practice (Kessel, 1958; Moore, 1961). Licensing attempts to limit the likelihood that incompetent providers will treat uninformed patients. Originally, licensing merely placed restrictions on who was allowed to open a medical practice. As time passed, restrictions were expanded to cover a wide range of activities deemed unethical by practicing physicians. These activities included advertising, price-cutting, and other conduct considered unprofessional. Clearly, licensing laws serve not only to protect patients but also to limit the number of practitioners, thus protecting physicians from would-be competitors.

Food and Drug Administration (FDA) A public health agency charged with protecting American consumers by enforcing federal public health laws. Food, medicine, medical devices, and cosmetics are under the jurisdiction of the FDA.

Limits on New Product Development   Congress established the **Food and Drug Administration (FDA)** in 1938 to oversee the entry of new drugs and medical devices into the medical market. The FDA does not allow new drugs on the market until they have been thoroughly tested and ultimately proved safe and effective.[7] Even though the FDA has had several major successes in the past (the most notable was keeping the tranquilizer, thalidomide, off the U.S. market), the FDA approval process is the reason the time from the discovery of a promising chemical compound to drug approval averages 12 years.

The welfare effects of overly restrictive policies regarding new drug introduction are not always clear. Eliminating all risk is impractical, because using and consuming any drug carries with it some level of risk. The optimal level of risk is not zero, but the potential costs and benefits of introducing a new drug must be weighed. Regulators must consider the two types of statistical errors, referred to as Type I and Type II errors, when evaluating the safety and efficacy of a new drug. For simplicity, assume that a drug is either safe or unsafe and that the FDA either approves the drug for use or rejects it.

Type I error occurs when an otherwise safe drug is rejected; in other words, the review process results in a false negative. Type II error occurs when an unsafe drug is approved, a false positive. Regulators are much more concerned about avoiding Type II errors, approving drugs that harm patients. The consequences of approving an unsafe drug are obvious; patients suffer complications, get sicker, and die. The consequences of rejecting a safe drug are hidden; patients do not have access to a drug that might improve their health. Critics argue that the bias inherent in the regulatory process is harmful to the most vulnerable patients, those who are critically ill and have few alternative treatments available to them. Clearly, the FDA serves an essential function in the new-drug approval process. Allowing the market to be the sole determinant in drug availability would result in market failure by subjecting poorly informed patients to undue levels of risk.

Tax Policy

Policy makers and planners often use tax subsidies to encourage certain types of behavior (those who do not qualify for them call these subsidies "loopholes"). Federal and state income tax provisions subsidize the purchase of health insurance. A key ruling by the Tax Court after the Second World War exempted certain nonwage benefits from being included in an employee's taxable income. It was during this period of wage and price controls that

---

[7]In 1971, proof of efficacy was added as a requirement for new drug approval. In other words, the drug not only had to be safe, it had to work as claimed.

ISSUES IN MEDICAL CARE DELIVERY

FDA REGULATION: THE CASE OF THE CARDIOPUMP

How can a patient who has no pulse give informed consent? Developers of the cardiopump, a cardiopulmonary resuscitation (CPR) device for heart-attack victims, must find a satisfactory answer to this question before the FDA will allow further testing. Manual CPR exerts downward pressure on the chest and must rely on the chest to re-expand naturally. The cardiopump, which looks like a modified toilet plunger, exerts pressure in both directions, pulling blood back into the heart and oxygen back into the lungs.*

The product is available elsewhere around the world, including England, Germany, Sweden, Canada, Australia, Japan, and Chile. In fact, it is a standard device in ambulances in Austria and France. Nevertheless, the FDA considers it a "significant risk device" that requires informed consent before it can be used on anyone in a medical trial. For the developers of the device, this designation represents a catch-22. Before the device can be used in a trial, the patient must give informed consent. But how can a patient with no pulse give informed consent?

The FDA is literally protecting patients to death. Approximately one million Americans have heart attacks every year. Of the 700,000 who are given CPR, only 20,000 survive to leave the hospital. Based on a limited sample in St. Paul, Minnesota, survival rates could increase by as much as 35 percent with the use of the cardiopump. That estimate fits comfortably within the range of a 10–50 percent improvement in expected survival rates. Extrapolating that number nationally implies that the device could save 7,000 lives annually.

The caution of the FDA is understandable. Regulators are sensitive to the criticisms that resound in the halls of Congress when a drug or medical device harms a single person during its testing. In contrast, the 7,000 people whose lives could be saved every year with the approval of the cardiopump are silent in their protest. When we are talking about life-or-death situations, would it not be wise to reconsider the requirement for informed consent?

Source: Alexander Volokh, "Feel a Heart Attack Coming On—Go to France," *Wall Street Journal*, August 2, 1994, A14.

*Cardiopump shown from Alcor Life Extension Foundation, http://www.alcor.org/AtWork/p1field.html.

government policy makers chose to use the power to tax—or in this case, the power not to tax—to encourage employers to offer group health insurance to their workers. Since that time, group health insurance has been a nontaxable benefit for employees and, at the same time, a tax-deductible expense for employers.

Current estimates of the subsidy in terms of forgone federal tax revenues have it approaching $550 billion 2017. Add to that foregone state taxes and the total is well over $600 billion (Joint Committee on Taxation, 2007). The value of the subsidy to the individual is equal to the annual insurance premium paid by the employer multiplied by the individual's marginal tax bracket. The benefits of the tax subsidy increase as a person's income increases. If the annual premium paid by the employer is $4,000, a person in the 15 percent marginal tax bracket saves $600 a year in taxes by receiving the benefit instead of the income. In contrast, a person in the 42 percent tax bracket saves $1,680 on the same policy.[8]

One of the major consequences of this tax subsidy is that individuals demand more health insurance when it is purchased by their employers than if they had received the income and bought it themselves. Most economists will agree that paying insurance premiums with before-tax dollars leads to overconsumption of medical care. Paying for expensive insurance with before-tax dollars makes more sense than paying for expensive medical care with after-tax dollars. As a result, insurance policies traditionally have had low deductible and copayment requirements.

Government Failure

KEY CONCEPT 7
Competition

Even markets that work perfectly offer no guarantee that the efficient allocation of resources will satisfy the public's desires for equity in the distribution of goods and services. On the other hand, no credible evidence supports government remedies as the answer for the perceived inequities either. It is debatable whether government solutions will always improve welfare. Markets may fail, but government is just as prone to failure. Moreover, correcting government failure is inherently more difficult than correcting market failure.

Few will question the intentions of government involvement in medical care. Everyone is in favor of improved access and lower costs. Nevertheless, careful consideration of the unintended consequences of government intervention is equally important. Choosing a health care strategy for yourself and your family is a difficult task. Choosing some other agent to make that decision for you is not only difficult, but it can also be dangerous. Transferring decision-making from the private sector to the public sector substitutes bureaucratic discipline (or lack thereof) for economic discipline.

Goodman and Porter (2004) have shown that when we have competing public policies (e.g., government versus markets), optimal decision-making on the part of government will almost never occur. Government failure is not a rare occurrence. It is normal.

POLICY ISSUE
Does imperfect government address the issues of equity and efficiency in health care delivery better than imperfect markets?

The notion of perfect democracy in political science is just as rare as the notion of perfect competition in markets (Becker, 1958). Criticism directed at market failure—without at least admitting the possibility of government failure—is dishonest or at minimum naive. Voters face considerable obstacles in getting their collective voices heard. The interval

---

[8]The self-employed did not always enjoy the same tax preference. The Tax Reform Act of 1996 allowed the self-employed to deduct only 25 percent of the cost of personal health insurance (up to a maximum of total self-employment income). The percentage increased over time and reached 100 percent in 2003.

cost containment
Strategies used to control the total spending on health care services.

between elections is long: two to six years. The viable choices are limited, usually to the two major-party candidates, and agreement with every aspect of a candidate's platform is highly unlikely. Special interest groups, through subsidized lobbying efforts, have disproportionate influence on the decision-making process. And at the same time, protecting minority desires when government is by majority rule poses a problem.

These cautions should not discourage us from using government intervention as a strategy to ensure efficient market performance and equitable outcomes. However, they should stand as a warning against relying too heavily on government to solve all our problems. Frequently, solutions proposed by well-meaning government policy makers ignore the realities of the real world. We may not be able to create heaven on earth, but we may be able to improve the circumstances of millions of Americans with the right mix of market discipline and bureaucratic oversight.

☆ **KEY CONCEPT 5**
Markets and Pricing

The appropriate perspective in this debate is not whether the proposed system is efficient or fair (Pauly, 1997). No matter which alternative approach is chosen, it will be imperfect in its implementation. The appropriate perspective is whether efficiency and fairness are best addressed by imperfect government or imperfect markets.

☆ **KEY CONCEPT 4**
Self-Interest

Summary and Conclusions

Traditional microeconomics views the price mechanism as the invisible hand that leads to economic welfare maximization in a perfectly competitive market. In this chapter, we have examined the requirements necessary for competitive markets to result in equitable and efficient outcomes. Sources of market failure—including market power, externalities, and public goods—were described and discussed. Other sources of failure were applied to medical markets, including information problems, barriers to entry, and third-party payers.

The invisible hand is not able to perform its usual function in a system dominated by government decision makers. When government oversees production and consumption, it is the visible, tangible hand, or its equivalent, that determines prices. With complete knowledge of consumer preferences and producer capabilities, the efficiency problems could be solved. Following the reasoning of Lerner (1944), the planning agency must obtain the prices of all inputs and outputs, publish and distribute a list containing this information, and instruct all decision makers to act as if they were maximizers in a perfectly competitive market. In other words, substitute the superior wisdom of the planners for the collective wisdom of the masses.

Markets sometimes fail to produce the optimal level of output. The challenge facing policy makers is to intervene only in those situations in which government action can improve welfare. Substituting government failure for market failure is not welfare enhancing. We need policy makers who understand this important lesson and intervene, not when they see market failure, but whenever government actions will actually take us closer to the social optimum.

If medical markets are to work, that is, if they are to produce acceptable levels of efficiency and equity, the following conditions must be present (Enthoven, 1988):

■ *Well-informed, cost-conscious consumers must make decisions. Motivated by self-interest, adequately informed about treatment alternatives, and knowledgeable about all prices, cost-conscious consumers will have the ability to place a value on treatment alternatives and will practice economizing behavior because they will personally benefit. The patient/buyer must be an active participant in the decision-making process if **cost containment** is to be achieved.*

■ *Competition among providers is essential. Competition guards against undue concentration, because substitutes are readily available. Coupled with the first condition, consumer demand is sensitive to price changes.*

■ *Cost-conscious decisions are possible only if consumers who desire to enter the market have money to spend. Often phrased in terms of equity, the real issue is economic self-sufficiency. As such, medical care markets require either universal insurance coverage or universal access to insurance. The choice depends on whether the majority of the populace is concerned with equal outcomes or equal opportunities.*

PROFILE Mark V. Pauly

If one journal article can launch a career, Mark Pauly has shown us how. His 1968 article in the *American Economic Review*, entitled "The Economics of Moral Hazard," has become essential reading for anyone desiring to understand the effects of health insurance on health care utilization and cost. After receiving his Ph.D. in 1967, Pauly catapulted himself into the epicenter of health economics with his classic treatise.

After brief academic appointments at Northwestern University and his alma mater, the University of Virginia, Pauly moved to the University of Pennsylvania's Wharton School, where he became the executive director of the Leonard Davis Institute of Health Economics. Founded in 1967, the Leonard Davis Institute (LDI) has maintained a commitment to health services research and education in an interdisciplinary setting. Pauly named Bendheim Professor in 1990 is currently Professor of Health Care Management at the Wharton School.

One article can launch a career, but the reputation of a scholar is based on continuous research output. *Continuous* may not be the appropriate term to describe Pauly's contribution to the health economics literature—*unbelievable* is probably better. Along with numerous books, articles, and monographs, his research interests encompass medical economics and the role of markets in medical care, national health care policy, and health insurance. In addition, he is co-editor in chief of the *International Journal of Health Care Finance and Economics* and the advisory editor of the *Journal of Risk and Uncertainty*. He has received numerous awards and honors over his career. Most recently, he was awarded the Victor R. Fuchs Lifetime Achievement Award from the American Society of Health Economists in 2012. That same year the Association of University Programs in Health Administration awarded him the William B. Graham Prize for Health Services Research from the Baxter Foundation.

Pauly is one of a handful of health economists worldwide who argue that competition, when appropriately defined and understood, can work effectively in medical markets. Contrast this belief with the mainstream thought that gives little consideration to market solutions for the problems of medical care delivery and finance, and you begin to understand why many of his colleagues consider him an anomaly within the profession.

His belief that the incentive structure can shape both the behavior of patients and providers has resulted in his teaming with John C. Goodman, director of the National Center for Policy Analysis, in publishing the article "Tax Credits for Insurance and Medical Savings Accounts" in the Spring 1995 issue of *Health Affairs*. This innovative approach to health care reform recommends the use of tax credits, **medical savings accounts**, and high-deductible health insurance to improve both efficiency and equity in the health care sector. A colleague who does not share Pauly's faith in market solutions referred to his belief in markets as a "disease." If Pauly's insistence on a place for markets in health care delivery and finance is a disease, he is not likely to accept the cure without a struggle, especially when the proposed cure is a government-run system.

On more than one occasion, after a previous speaker had stirred the audience into a feeding frenzy on the various evils of the U.S. medical care delivery system, Pauly has stepped to the podium only to quiet the crowd with his clear analytical approach and keen insight into the underlying issues, providing balance to a discussion in which balance is often lacking. If the essential ingredients for making enlightened choices are knowledge and academic inquiry, Pauly has advanced our ability to make enlightened choices through his outstanding contribution to the field of health economics and the economics of insurance.

Source: Mark V. Pauly, curriculum vitae and personal communication.

medical savings account A tax-exempt savings account used in conjunction with high-deductible health insurance. Individuals pay their own medical expenses using funds from the savings account up to the amount of the deductible. Once the deductible is met, the insurance policy pays all or most of the covered expenses.

Questions and Problems

1. What is market failure? What are the major reasons that a free, unregulated market in medical care might not be optimal?

2. Proponents of a government-run health care system argue that the market does not work well in the medical care industry. What evidence do they use to support this claim?

3. Explain how market failure can be used to justify government intervention in medical care markets.

4. How do price controls affect the workings of a perfectly competitive market? Use a supply–demand diagram as part of your answer.

5. What assumptions of the perfectly competitive marketplace are violated in medical markets? How does each affect equilibrium price and quantity?

References

Arrow, Kenneth J., "Uncertainty and the Welfare Economics of Medical Care," *American Economic Review* 53(5), December 1963, 941–973.

Baumol, William J., "Do Health Care Costs Matter?" *The New Republic* 209(21), November 22, 1993, 16–18.

_____, "Macroeconomics of Unbalanced Growth: The Anatomy of Urban Crisis," *American Economic Review*, 57(3), June 1967, 415–426.

Becker, Gary S., "Competition and Democracy," *Journal of Law and Economics* 1, October 1958, 105–109.

Berwick, Donald M., et al., "The Triple Aim: Care, Health, and Cost," *Health Affairs* 27(3), May 2008, 759–769.

Blendon, Robert J., et al., "Who Has the Best Health System? A Second Look," *Health Affairs* 14(4), Winter 1995, 220–230.

Chandra, Amitabh, Jonathan Holmes, and Jonathan Skinner, "Is This Time Different? The Slowdown in Health Care Spending," *Brookings Papers on Economic Activity*, Fall 2013, 261–323.

Chronic, Richard, David C. Goodman, John Wennberg, and Edward Wagner, "The Marketplace in Health Care Reform: The Demographic Limitations of Managed Competition," *The New England Journal of Medicine* 328(2), January 14, 1993, 148–152.

Coughlin, Teresa A., et al., "Uncompensated Care for the Uninsured in 2013: A Detailed Examination," Kaiser Family Foundation, May 30, 2014.

Cutler, David M. and Mark McClellan, "Is Technological Change in Medicine Worth It?" *Health Affairs* 20(5), September/October 2001, 11–29.

Enthoven, Alain C., "Managed Competition: An Agenda for Action," *Health Affairs* 7(3), Summer 1988, 25–47.

Goodman, John C. and Gerald L. Musgrave, *Patient Power: Solving America's Health Care Crisis*, Washington, DC: Cato Institute, 1992.

Goodman, John C. and Philip K. Porter, "Political Equilibrium and the Provision of Public Goods," *Public Choice* 120, 2004, 247–266.

Joint Committee on Taxation, Estimating the Revenue Effects of the Administration's Fiscal Year 2008 Proposal Providing a Standard Deduction for Health Insurance: Modeling the Assumptions (JCT-17-07), March 20, 2007, found at www.jct.gov.

Kaplan, Robert S. and Michael E. Porter, "The Big Idea: How to Solve the Cost Crisis in Health Care," *Harvard Business Review*, September 2011, 47–64.

Kenkel, Paul J., "Health Plans Face Pressure to Find 'Report Card' Criteria that Will Make the Grade," *Modern Healthcare*, January 10, 1994, 41.

Kessel, Reuben A., "Price Discrimination in Medicine," *Journal of Law and Economics* 1, October 1958, 20–53.

Lerner, Abba, *The Economics of Control*, New York: Macmillan, 1944.

Lichtenberg, Frank R., "Sources of U.S. Longevity Increase, 1960–1997," NBER Working Paper No. 8755, Cambridge, MA: National Bureau of Economic Research, February 2002.

Moore, Thomas G., "The Purpose of Licensing," *Journal of Law and Economics* 4, October 1961, 93–117.

Pauly, Mark V., "A Primer on Competition in Medical Markets," in *Health Care in America: The Political Economy of Hospitals and Health Insurance*, edited by H. E. Frech III, San Francisco: Pacific Research Institute for Public Policy, 1988, 27–71.

Pauly, Mark V., "Who Was That Straw Man Anyway? A Comment on Evans and Rice," *Journal of Health Politics, Policy, and Law*, April 1997, 467–473.

Phelps, Charles E., "Diffusion of Information in Medical Care," *Journal of Economic Perspectives* 6(3), Summer 1992, 23–42.

Radnofsky, Louise, "Health-Care Costs: A State-by-State Comparison," *Wall Street Journal*, April 8, 2013.

Reinhardt, Uwe, "The Price of U.S. Hospital Services: Chaos Behind a Veil of Secrecy," *Health Affairs* 25(1), January/February 2006, 57–69.

Rice, Thomas, *The Economics of Health Reconsidered*, Chicago, IL: Health Administration Press, 1998.

Schwartz, William B., "The Inevitable Failure of Current Cost-Containment Strategies: Why They Can Provide Only Temporary Relief," *Journal of the American Medical Association* 257(2), January 9, 1987, 220–224.

Waldo, Daniel, et al., "Health Expenditures by Age Group, 1977–1987," *Health Care Financing Review* 10(4), Summer 1989, 111–120.

APPENDIX 3A

The Economics of Consumer Choice

To explain consumer behavior, economists use a simple model based on the concept of utility. The theory posits that individuals derive satisfaction, or utility, from consuming goods and services. The more goods and services consumed, the higher the level of satisfaction achieved. A consumer's ability to satisfy his or her desire for goods is limited by the amount of money to spend and the prices of the goods available for purchase. The three prerequisites for the development of a theory of consumer choice are: (1) There must be goods to buy, (2) consumers must have money to spend, and (3) they must be able to rank their preferences.[9]

As in all neoclassical economics, consumers are assumed to be maximizers. In the case where there are two goods available for consumption, consumers are interested in maximizing utility subject to a budget constraint, or

Maximize $U = U(X, Y)$

subject to $M = P_X X + P_Y Y$

where U is the level of utility, X and Y are the two goods in question, M is the money income available for spending on the two goods, and P_X and P_Y are their respective prices.

Consumer Preferences: Indifference Curves

Economists depict consumer preferences graphically with indifference curves. An indifference curve illustrates the various combinations of goods that are equally satisfying to the consumer. In Figure 3A.1, having X_0 of good X and Y_0 of good Y places the consumer at point R

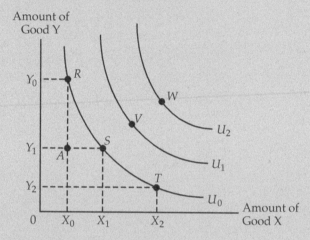

FIGURE 3A.1 Indifference Curves

on the indifference curve labeled U_0. Points S (X_1 and Y_1) and T (X_2 and Y_2) are likewise on U_0, indicating that these three combinations of X and Y provide the same level of satisfaction. The consumer is said to be indifferent as far as these three alternatives are concerned.

Higher levels of satisfaction are depicted by higher indifference curves. A combination of goods on indifference curve U_1 such as V is preferred to R, S, and T. Similarly, W on indifference curve U_2 is preferred to V. Because W is preferred to V and V is preferred to R, S, and T, the transitive nature of preferences implies that W is also preferred to R, S, and T.

When the consumer is able to rank all available alternatives, the set of indifference curves represents a preference map. Indifference curves serve the same purpose on this preference map that contour lines serve on a topographical map. As you move along an indifference

---

[9]The model does not require that consumers have the ability to attach numerical values to the utility levels. The requirement is that they be able to rank their preferences in an ordinal sense; for example, most preferred to least preferred.

curve, the level of utility stays the same. As you move along a contour line, the elevation stays the same. Move from one indifference curve to another and the level of utility changes. Move from one contour line to another and you move to a different elevation.

Indifference curves have certain properties that are important in the development of the theory of consumer choice. They are all negatively sloped, indicating that combinations of goods that have more of one good and the same or more of the other good are preferred. This property indicates that the goods in question are desirable. The consumer prefers more to less.

Indifference curves are typically drawn convex to the origin (they bow in, as shown in Figure 3A.1). Convexity implies that consumers are more willing to give up good Y for some amount of X when Y is plentiful. If the consumer has only a small amount of Y, it will take more X in the exchange to keep the consumer at the same level of satisfaction. The marginal rate of substitution (MRS) is defined as the amount of Y that the consumer would be willing to give up for a small increase in X and maintain the same level of utility. In other words, MRS is the importance attached to an additional unit of good X in terms of the amount of Y given up.

Movement from R to S on indifference curve U_0 results in a different combination of X and Y. Point S has more X but less Y than point R. The slope of U_0, defined as the change in the amount of Y relative to the change in the amount of X, is also the MRS. The movement from R to S may be broken down into two distinct moves. A move from R to A lowers the level of utility by reducing the amount of good Y. For small movements along U_0, this change in utility is equal to the marginal utility of Y (the change in utility resulting from a unit change in Y) multiplied by the total change in Y or $(MU_Y) \times (\Delta Y)$. Similarly, a move from A to S restores utility to its previous level due to the increase in the amount of good X. Using the same logic, that change is equal to $(MU_X) \times (\Delta X)$. These two changes offset each other and are thus equal in magnitude, so $\Delta Y/\Delta X =$

MU_X/MU_Y. In other words, the slope of the indifference curve ($\Delta Y/\Delta X$), the MRS good X for good Y, equals the ratio of the marginal utilities of the two goods (MU_X/MU_Y).[10]

Indifference curves do not intersect one another. Intersecting curves would present a logical inconsistency. Points on any one indifference curve provide the consumer with the same level of utility. Points on a separate indifference curve are equally satisfying to the consumer but at a different level of utility. If two indifference curves intersect, the point of intersection would be on both curves simultaneously. The implication is that points on the two indifference curves represent the same and different levels of utility simultaneously.

Consumer Constraints: The Budget Line

Consumers have a limited capacity to satisfy their preferences. Because of limited money income and positive prices for the goods and services, the ability to achieve the desired level of consumption is constrained. The consumer's money income constraint may be written as $M = P_X X + P_Y Y$. By rearranging terms, the constraint may be written in the form of an equation, or budget line, as follows

$$Y = (M/P_Y) - (P_X/P_Y)X$$

M/P_Y is the value of Y when $X = 0$ and is equal to the Y intercept. The corresponding X intercept, M/P_X, is the value of X when $Y = 0$. The slope of the budget line, P_X/P_Y, is the relative prices of the two goods. The budget line represents all combinations of goods X and Y the consumer is able to buy. Any combination of X and Y that is on or below the budget line is attainable. Given the prices of the two goods, the consumer does not have enough money to reach points above the budget line. In our model, we assume the consumer spends all

---

[10]This derivation may be shown more formally using the Lagrangian multiplier method. The consumer's effort to maximize utility $U = U(X, Y)$ is constrained by limited money income, $M = P_X X + P_Y Y$. The problem becomes one of maximizing $L = U(X, Y) + \lambda(M - P_X X - P_Y Y)$. Setting the partial derivatives of L with respect to X, Y, and λ equal to zero gives.

$$\partial L/\partial X = \partial U/\partial X - \lambda P_X = 0$$
$$\partial L/\partial Y = \partial U/\partial Y - \lambda P_Y = 0$$
$$\partial L/\partial \lambda = M - P_X X - P_Y Y = 0$$

Solving the first two equations for λ and setting them equal to each other yields

$$\lambda = (\partial U/\partial X)P_X = (\partial U/\partial Y)P_Y$$

In other words,

$$\lambda = MU_X/P_X = MU_Y/P_Y$$

FIGURE 3A.2 Income and Price Changes with Budget Lines

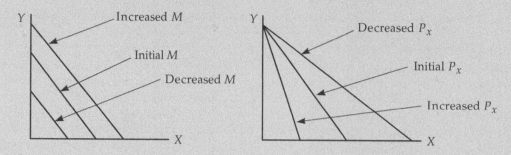

budgeted money for the two goods, and thus ends up on the budget line, not below it.

Holding prices constant, changes in income will shift the budget line. Using Figure 3A.2, it can be seen that increases in income shift the curve to the right and decreases in income shift it to the left. Changes in relative prices will cause the curve to rotate. Holding P_Y constant, if P_X increases, the curve will rotate to the left. If P_X decreases, it will rotate to the right.

Consumer Choice: The Concept of Equilibrium

Consumer preferences, graphically depicted by indifference curves, represent what the consumer is willing to buy. The money income constraint, depicted by the budget line, represents what the consumer is able to buy. Determining consumer choice is a matter of bringing together these two concepts—willingness to buy and ability to buy. The consumer's decision on how to allocate scarce money income between the two goods is an attempt to match preferences with spending power—wants with affordability, willingness to buy with ability to buy—and in the process attain maximum satisfaction.

Individuals adjust their consumption behavior to the point where they cannot increase total utility without increasing their budget. Graphically, the choice may be shown as one of finding a point of tangency between the consumer's budget line and the highest attainable indifference curve. This point is identified by superimposing the preference map over the budget line and determining the unique point of tangency. This point of tangency represents an equilibrium because it is the only point where the slope of the indifference curve equals the slope of the budget line.

The consumer maximizes utility at point B in Figure 3A.3. Points like A do not represent equilibrium since the consumer can reach a higher level of utility simply by moving down the budget line toward point B, spending the same amount of money, purchasing a different combination of X and Y, and reaching a higher level of utility. Likewise, the consumer could move down indifference curve U_1, maintain a constant level of utility, and spend less money. At point B, the slope of the indifference curve, MU_X/MU_Y, is equal to the slope of the budget line, P_X/P_Y. Thus, the equilibrium condition as already stated is satisfied. In equilibrium, $MU_X/MU_Y = P_X/P_Y$. This condition may be rewritten $MU_X/P_X = MU_Y/P_Y$. In the case where the number of goods the consumer may choose from is equal to n instead of two, this condition is

$$MU_X = P_X MU_Y/P_Y = 1/4 = MU_n = P_n$$

It may be said the consumer maximizes utility when the last dollar spent on each good consumed provides

FIGURE 3A.3 Consumer Equilibrium

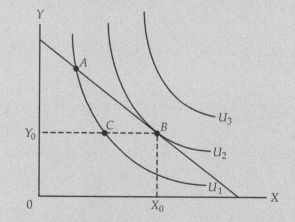

the same increment to utility as the last dollar spent on every other good.[11] This equilibrium condition provides one point on the individual's demand curve for each good consumed, X_0 at price P_X. Changing the price of the good and finding the new level of consumption identifies additional points on the demand curve. Connecting all these price-quantity pairs in a separate graph traces out the actual demand curve.

Implications of the Model

The shapes of indifference curves depend on the consumer's own assessment of the desirability of the available alternatives. Consumers with a strong preference for X will have relatively steep indifference curves. Those with strong preferences for Y will have relatively flat indifference curves. One possible extension of the model might be to examine the consequences of preference switching. The left-hand side of Figure 3A.4 shows the equilibrium between physicians' office visits (V) and other uses of income (Y). The healthy consumer will have a relatively flat preference map, indicating a strong desire to spend money on goods other than visits to the physician. With equilibrium at point A, this

consumer will spend Y_1 income on all other goods and visit the physician V_1 times per year, resulting in a utility level of U_1.

The onset of an illness results in a preference switch, depicted by a steeper preference map on the right. The consumer now places more importance on visits to the physician relative to other spending. The result is a new equilibrium at point B, spending Y_2 on other goods, V_2 visits to the physician, and utility on indifference curve U_1. If the consumer cannot afford to reduce spending on other goods below Y_1, the preferred equilibrium cannot be attained. Instead, the consumer will remain at point A, spending Y_1 on other goods, visiting the physician V_1 times, and attaining a lower level of utility, U_0.

Conclusion

The model of consumer choice discussed in this appendix is used to explain and predict consumer behavior. Even though consumers may not consciously apply this decision calculus in every situation, this does not mean that the model serves no useful purpose. Remember the model was developed to explain and predict. If it helps us accomplish these tasks, it serves us well.

FIGURE 3A.4 Changes in Consumer Preferences with Health Status

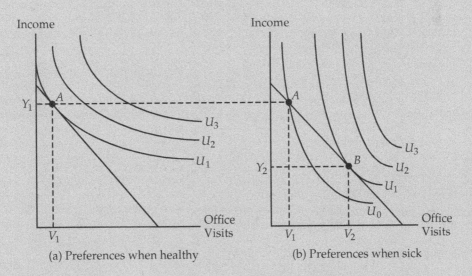

(a) Preferences when healthy   (b) Preferences when sick

---

[11]The marginal utility of the last dollar spent on every good is equal to the A in the previous footnote.

Production and Cost in the For-Profit Sector

In a world of competitive markets, firms that are successful in minimizing costs will earn a normal profit. Cost minimization is accomplished by the efficient use of resources. In this appendix, we will examine production and cost in a competitive market where firms attempt to maximize profits.

Production with Two Variable Inputs

Economists describe the production process as a functional relationship between inputs and outputs. The so-called **production function** shows the maximum output that can be produced from a given level of inputs using the available technology. Unlike utility, output is a measurable concept—bushels of grain, tons of steel, barrels of oil, or number of appendectomies performed. The inputs include land, natural resources, machinery, labor, and the entrepreneurial energies used to combine them and produce a product or service that people wish to buy. The production process with two variable inputs, labor (L) and capital (K), may be depicted in its generalized form as

$$Q = Q(L, K)$$

where Q represents the amount of the good produced and $Q(\ldots)$ the mathematical relationship describing the production process. Production functions are usually presented in one of the three forms: a table, an equation, or a graph.

Figure 3B.1 summarizes the output levels that may be attained when labor and capital are combined according to the production function $Q = 100\sqrt{LK}$. The amount of labor used in the production process is listed across the bottom of the table, and the amount of capital is listed along the left-hand side. Interpreting the data in the table is straightforward. For example, when five units of capital are combined with six workers, the firm is able to produce 548 units of output. Different combinations of labor and capital will result in different levels of output. As long as the inputs are used efficiently, the firm will produce exactly the level of output shown in the table.

Production Isoquants

It is possible to produce the same level of output using different combinations of the two inputs. For example, the firm may produce 316 units of output using 10 units of capital and 1 unit of labor. The same level of output can be produced using five units of capital and two units of labor, two units of capital and five units of labor, or one unit of capital and ten units of labor. A similar observation may be made about 200 units of output, or 400 units, or any one of many different levels of output. The curves drawn in the body of the table represent the different combinations of L and K that produce the same level of output. These equal quantity curves are called **isoquants** and serve the same purpose in production theory as indifference curves in consumer theory.

Plotting the isoquants in Figure 3B.2 provides a clear picture of the production levels that are attainable using the various combinations of labor and capital. The firm

---

production function A way to depict the relationship between the inputs in a production process and the resulting output.
isoquants Literally "equal quantity." A contour line that shows the different combinations of two inputs that produce the same level of output.

FIGURE 3B.1 Changes in Consumer Preferences with Health Status

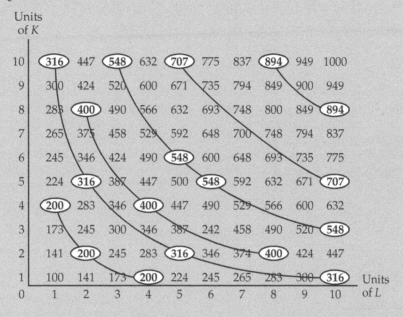

FIGURE 3B.2 Changes in Consumer Preferences with Health Status

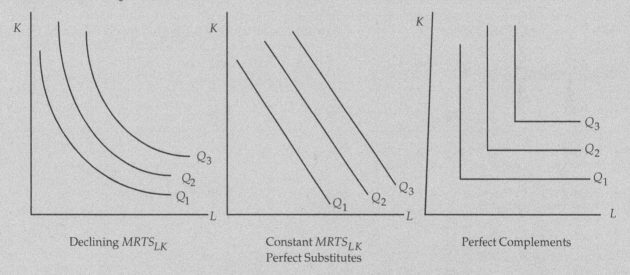

Declining $MRTS_{LK}$

Constant $MRTS_{LK}$
Perfect Substitutes

Perfect Complements

may use a number of different combinations of labor and capital to produce Q_1 units of output. Although only three are shown below, an infinite number of isoquants exist, one for every possible level of output. Because isoquants farther from the origin represent higher levels of output, $Q_3 > Q_2 > Q_1$.

Isoquants are usually drawn convex to the origin. The slope of the isoquant measures the ability to substitute one input for the other while maintaining the same level of output. As the firm adjusts its input mix, the ability to substitute, called the **marginal rate of technical substitution (MRTS)**, changes. When the

marginal rate of technical substitution (MRTS) As the amount of one input in a production process increases, the amount in the other input can be decreased without changing the level of output.

production process uses a large amount of capital relative to labor, the marginal productivity of labor is high relative to that of capital. One additional worker can easily make up for the reduction of capital. Substitution of labor for capital is relatively easy and the MRTS labor for capital ($MRTS_{LK}$) is relatively high.

When the amount of capital employed is low relative to the number of workers, the marginal productivity of labor is low relative to that of capital. It takes many more workers to make up for a reduction in capital. In other words, substitution of labor for capital is more difficult when capital is scarce relative to the number of workers competing for its use. Thus, as we move down an isoquant, using more labor and less capital, the $MRTS_{LK}$ declines.

All along the isoquant, the MRTS is the slope of the isoquant. It can be shown that $MRTS_{LK}$ is the ratio of the marginal product of labor to the marginal product of capital (MP_L/MP_K).[12] If labor and capital are perfect substitutes, $MRTS_{LK}$ will be the same regardless of the amount of labor and capital used in the production process. In this case, the isoquant will be a downward-sloping straight line. If instead labor and capital are perfect complements, always used in fixed proportions, the isoquants are L-shaped.

Production in the Short Run

When a firm uses its resources efficiently, the only way to increase output is to increase the amount of inputs used. In most cases, it is easier to increase the workforce than it is to add capital equipment. Inputs whose levels can be adjusted quickly, such as labor, are called **variable inputs**. Inputs that take more time to increase, such as machinery, are called **fixed inputs**. The time lags required for these adjustments further define the production process as either short run or long run. In the case of a two-input production function, the **long run** is defined as the time period where both inputs are variable. The **short run** is the time period where one of the inputs, usually capital, is fixed.

In the short run, the only way to change output is to change the amount of the variable input used. The amount of the fixed input cannot be changed. In other words, the size or scale of the operation is fixed in the short run. From Figure 3B.1, short-run production may be shown by fixing the capital input at, say, five units and varying the amount of labor used from one to ten units. This information is shown in Table 3B.1.

From the first two columns, production increases as the number of workers hired increases. The **average product** of labor (AP_L) and the **marginal product** of labor (MP_L) may also be derived from the data on the **total product** of labor (TP_L). The average product, a measure of technical efficiency, is calculated by dividing the total product of labor by the number of workers, or $AP_L = TP_L/L$. The marginal product is the change in total product when one additional worker is hired. It is calculated by dividing the change in the total product by the change in the number of workers used in the production process or $MP_L = \Delta TP_L/\Delta L$.

The production function utilized in this discussion illustrates an important empirical observation in short-run production, the **law of diminishing returns**.

---

variable inputs Inputs in the production process that are easily incremented.
fixed inputs Inputs in the production process that are difficult to increment.
long run The period of time where all inputs are variable.
short run The increment of time where at least one input is fixed.
average product Output per unit of input.
marginal product The change in total product resulting from a unit change in input.
total product Total output that results from using different levels of an input.
law of diminishing returns The empirical observation that expanding the use of one input (holding all others constant) will eventually result in a decreasing rate of change in productivity.

---

[12]The *MRTS* at any point on an isoquant may be derived by taking the total differential of the production function $Q = Q(L, K)$ and setting it equal to zero.

$$dQ = (\partial Q/\partial K)dL + (\partial Q/\partial K)dK = 0$$

As the amount of L and K change along an isoquant, the level of output does not change, or $dQ = 0$. Solving this equality for the slope of the isoquant, $dK/dL = (\partial Q/\partial L)/(\partial Q/\partial K)$. Since $(\partial Q/\partial L)$ equals MP_L and $(\partial Q/\partial K)$ equals MP_K,

$$dK/dL = MP_L/MP_K = MRTS_{LK}.$$

TABLE 3B.1   SHORT-RUN PRODUCTION WITH $K = 5$

Units of Labor	Total Product	Capital-Labor ratio	Average Product	Marginal Product
0	0	∞	—	—
1	224	5.00	224	224
2	316	2.50	158	92
3	387	1.67	129	71
4	447	1.25	112	60
5	500	1.00	100	83
6	548	0.83	91	48
7	592	0.72	85	44
8	632	0.63	79	40
9	671	0.56	75	39
10	707	0.50	71	36

Holding the amount of capital constant, each added worker has less capital on average to work with, as evidenced by a constantly declining capital-labor ratio (K/L). So each additional worker contributes less to output than the previous worker. The law of diminishing returns is not based on an economic theory; it is physical law that holds true for production in general.

Although the law of diminishing returns characterizes every short-run production process, marginal and product average do not always decline from the outset. Some production processes display increasing marginal and average product initially due to the benefits derived from specialization and the division of labor. Figure 3B.3 presents a generalized short-run production function. As the number of workers increases, total product increases at an increasing rate up to point A. Beyond point A, production continues to increase as more workers are used but at a decreasing rate. The rate of increase in output slows until a maximum output is reached at point B. Beyond point B, given the amount of capital available per worker, further increases in output are not possible. Adding workers actually decreases output.

Firms do not operate where the marginal product of an input is negative. Doing so would imply the firm could increase its output by decreasing the amount of the input used, increasing revenue and lowering cost. Thus, efficient production occurs when the marginal products of all inputs are positive.

Optimal Input Use

The profit-maximizing firm will attempt to maximize output from the resources committed to production. The firm faces a resource constraint determined by the cost of inputs and the amount of money it is willing to spend. When two inputs, labor (L) and capital (K), are used in production, the constraint may be written $C = wL + rK$, where C is the total cost, w is the wage rate paid labor, and r is the unit cost of capital. This cost constraint may be rewritten as an **isocost curve** or $K = (C/r) - (w/r)L$. The isocost curve is shown in Figure 3B.4 and may be interpreted as all possible combinations of L and K that can be hired for a total cost equal to Q when input prices equal w and r. The more money the firm is willing to commit to production, the farther the isocost curve is from the origin and the greater the output that can be produced.

The slope of the isocost curve is the relative price of the inputs or $-(w/r)$. Combining the isoquant map with the relevant isocost curve allows us to determine the combination of inputs the profit-maximizing firm will choose. Maximizing output at a given level of cost requires that the firm use the optimal or least-cost combination of the inputs. This is shown in Figure 3B.5 at point E where the isocost curve is just tangent to the isoquant Q_1. At the point where the isoquant is tangent to the isocost curve, their slopes are equal. In

---

isocost curve A locus of points that shows the various combinations of inputs that have the same cost.

FIGURE 3B.3 Generalized Production in the Short Run

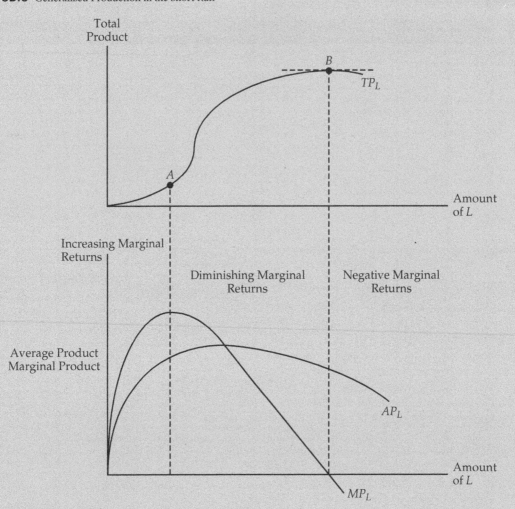

other words, the slope of the isoquant, or the $MRTS_{LK}$ ($= MP_L/MP_K$), equals the slope of the isocost curve, or w/r, when the firm is using the least-cost combination of inputs L and K. Formally, this equilibrium condition may be written as $MRTS_{LK} = MP_L/MP_K = w/r$.[13]

The equilibrium condition may also be written $MP_L/w = MP_K/r$. In this form it is easily seen that firms adjust the amounts of labor and capital used until the marginal product from the last dollar spent on labor is equal to the marginal product from the last dollar spent on capital.

---

[13]The mathematical derivation of the equilibrium condition in production mirrors that of the equilibrium condition in consumer theory. Using the Lagrangian multiplier method, it can be shown that the firm's effort to maximize output $Q = Q(L, K)$ is limited by a total cost constraint, $C = wL + rK$. The problem becomes one of maximizing $L = Q(L, K) + X(C − wL − rK)$. Setting the partial derivatives of L with respect to L, K, and λ equal to zero gives

$$\partial £/\partial L = \partial Q/\partial L − \lambda w = 0$$
$$\partial £/\partial K = \partial Q/\partial K − \lambda r = 0$$
$$\partial £/\partial \lambda = C − wL − rK = 0$$

Solving the first two equations for A and setting them equal to each other yields

$$\lambda = (\partial Q/\partial L)/w = (\partial Q/\partial K)/r$$

In other words,

$$\lambda = MP_L/w = MP_K/r$$

FIGURE 3B.4 Isocost Curves

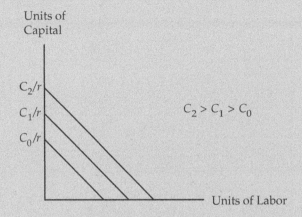

FIGURE 3B.5 Optimal Input Use

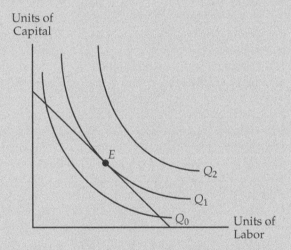

Extensions of the Model

The optimal input mix for producing a given level of output will change as the relative prices of the inputs change. Figure 3B.6 illustrates the least-cost method of producing Q* medical care at two different prices

for physicians' services. When the price of physicians' services is high (P_H), equilibrium will be at point H, using S_H. If physicians are paid less, holding the price of other medical inputs (P_O) constant, the same level of medical care will be provided using a different mix of physicians' services and other medical inputs. At low physicians' prices (P_L), equilibrium will be at point L, using S_L physicians' services.

The model provides several interesting implications. When the fees paid physicians are relatively high, the physician-population ratio will be relatively low and patients will visit their doctors less often. Additionally, higher physicians' prices encourage the use of other medical inputs. Thus, when physicians' prices are higher, we expect medical care to be produced using more capital per patient.

Estimating Production Functions

The simplest and most widely used production function in empirical work is of the Cobb-Douglas variety. The Cobb-Douglas production function may be written as $Q = AL^{\alpha}K^{\beta}$ where α and β are positive parameters estimated from the empirical data. Using this functional form, the exponents represent output elasticities, or the percentage change in output for every 1 percent change in the quantity of the input used. In the case of the labor input, a 1 percent increase in L will result in an α percent increase in Q. Likewise for capital, a 1 percent increase in K will result in a β percent increase in Q.[14] If $\alpha + \beta = 1$, the production function exhibits constant returns to scale. In this case a 1 percent increase in the amount of both inputs used yields a 1 percent increase in output. If $\alpha + \beta > 1$, say 1.2, then a 1 percent increase in L and K results in a 1.2 percent increase in Q and the production function exhibits increasing returns to scale.

The Cobb-Douglas production function is estimated empirically by first taking the logarithm of both sides, resulting in

$$\log Q = A + \alpha \log L + \beta \log K$$

---

[14]The marginal products of labor and capital for a Cobb-Douglas production function are determined as follows:

$$MP_L = \partial Q/\partial L = \alpha AL^{\alpha-1}K^{\beta} = \alpha(Q/L)$$
$$MP_K = \partial Q/\partial K = \beta AL^{\alpha-1}K^{\beta-1} = \beta(Q/K)$$

The output elasticities E_L and E_K are

$$E_L = (L/\partial Q)/(Q/\partial L) = (L/Q)/(\alpha Q/L) = \alpha$$
$$E_K = (K/\partial Q)/(Q/\partial K) = (K/Q)/(\beta Q/L) = \beta$$

FIGURE 3B.6 Producing Medical Care When the Price of Physicians' Services Varies

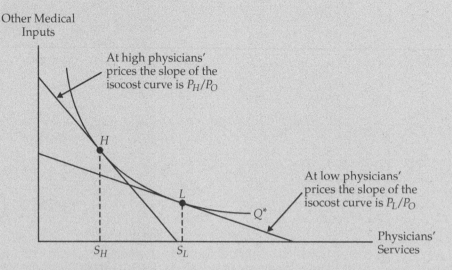

Regressing log Q on log L and log K provides estimates of the output elasticities from the estimated coefficients (refer back to the statistical appendix to Chapter 2 for the discussion on regression analysis).

Production to Cost

Cost may be divided into two categories: fixed and variable. Costs associated with the fixed inputs, costs that do not change as the level of production changes, are **fixed costs**. Costs associated with the variable inputs, costs that change as the level of production changes, are **variable costs**. Using the two-input production function introduced above, with capital representing the fixed input and labor the variable input, capital costs are fixed costs and labor costs are variable costs.

Total cost is the amount that must be spent on all inputs to produce a given level of output, including all applicable opportunity costs.[15] Total cost comprises fixed costs and variable costs, all the costs associated with the capital inputs and all the costs associated with the variable inputs. Using the same notation developed earlier, the total cost function may be written $C = rK + wL$. In other words, the production function

and the prices of inputs determine the firm's total cost function. The production function determines how much capital and labor are used in the production process, and the respective input prices determine the total amount spent on each input.

In practice, the short-run total cost curve may be derived from the short-run production function. With the amount of capital available fixed in the short run, rK is constant and represents fixed costs. In order to increase the level of output, the amount of labor used must increase. The production function determines the amount of labor needed to produce any given level of output. The short-run variable cost associated with each level of output (Q) is determined by the amount of labor required (L) multiplied by the cost of labor (w). Figure 3B.7 depicts the short-run total cost function associated with the production function shown in Figure 3B.3. Note the symmetry. In the range of output where production increases at an increasing rate (up to point A in Figure 3B.3), cost increases at a decreasing rate. When production increases at a decreasing rate, cost increases at an increasing rate.

This relationship is much clearer when viewed from the perspective of the short-run average and marginal

---

fixed cost The total cost of the fixed inputs.
variable cost The total cost of the variable inputs.

---

[15]Opportunity costs include both the explicit costs associated with actual payments to resources used in production and the implicit costs associated with the owners' time and investment. Explicit costs are all those costs recorded by the firm for accounting purposes, including rent paid on buildings, salaries paid to workers, and interest paid on loans. Implicit costs are the opportunity costs of using resources owned by the firm, including forgone earnings on money invested in the business.

FIGURE 3B.7 Short-Run Total Cost Curves

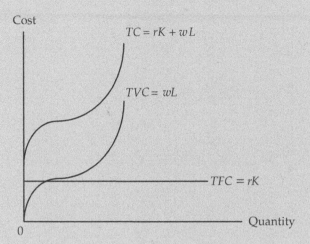

FIGURE 3B.8 Short-Run Average and Marginal Cost Curves

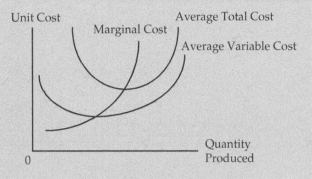

cost curves. By definition, average variable cost (AVC) is the total variable cost (TVC) divided by the level of output produced (Q), or $AVC = TVC/Q$. Since $TVC = wL$, $AVC = wL/Q$ or $w(L/Q)$. Remembering that Q/L is the average product of labor (AP_L), we note $AVC = w/AP_L$. As the average product of labor increases, average variable cost decreases. When AP_L reaches its maximum, AVC reaches its minimum. As AP_L decreases, AVC increases.

Likewise, the relationship between marginal cost (MC) and the marginal product of labor (MP_L) can be determined: $MC = ATVC/\Delta Q$. Substituting wL for TVC yields $MC = \Delta wL/\Delta Q$. In competitive labor markets, the firm is a price taker, so the only way to change wL is to change L, implying $MC = w(\Delta L/\Delta Q)$. Because $\Delta Q/\Delta L$ is the marginal product of labor, $MC = w/MP_L$. As marginal product increases, marginal cost decreases. When MP_L reaches its maximum, MC reaches its

minimum. As MP_L decreases, MC increases. Thus, we expect short-run average costs and short-run marginal costs to be U-shaped, initially decreasing, then reaching a minimum, and finally increasing.

The relationship between average costs and marginal costs is shown in Figure 3B.8. Average total cost is the sum of average fixed cost and average variable cost. As long as marginal cost is below average cost, notice that average cost decreases. When marginal cost rises above average cost, average cost begins to increase. Thus, marginal cost intersects each average cost curve at its respective minimum.[16]

Long-Run Costs

Long-run costs are also U-shaped but for different reasons. In the long run the firm has the option of increasing the size of its physical plant. Doing so often means the use of more efficient equipment, specialized labor, and lower average costs. The economic principle is called economies of scale. The long-run average cost

---

[16]For those with a little knowledge of calculus, the intersection of average and marginal cost at minimum average cost may be shown by noting that the slope of the average cost curve is equal to zero at its minimum; that is, its first derivative is equal to zero at its minimum. For the average variable cost curve

$$\frac{dAVC}{dQ} = \frac{d(TVC/Q)}{dQ} = 0$$

$$= \frac{Q(dTVC/dQ) - TVC(dQ/dQ)}{Q^2} = 0$$

Dividing both terms in the numerator and factoring out $1/Q$ results in

$$\frac{1}{Q}[MC - AVC] = 0$$

For the right side of the expression to equal zero, $MC - AVC$, or marginal cost equals average variable cost when the slope of average variable cost equals zero (when AVC has reached its minimum).

FIGURE 3B.9 Long-Run Average Cost

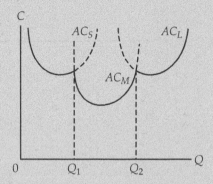 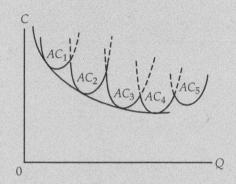

curve may be thought of as an envelope curve, depicting the least-cost option for producing each level of output. Figure 3B.9 shows the long-run average costs associated with three different plant sizes: small (AC_S), medium (AC_M), and large (AC_L). The minimum cost of producing each level of output depends on the size of the physical plant. If the desired level of output is less than Q_1, the firm will minimize cost if it uses the small plant. For output levels between Q_1 and Q_2, costs are minimized using the medium-sized plant. For output levels greater than Q_2, the large plant minimizes costs.

The envelope curve in the diagram on the right-hand side depicts all possible plant sizes. Competition will force the firm to use the plant whose costs are given by AC_4, the optimal plant. Firms that do not use this sized plant will find themselves with higher costs than their competitors, and they will lose money.

Conclusion

The theory discussed in this appendix provides a summary of the economic theory of the firm. The material is not intended to cover the full range of topics presented in a microeconomics course, but it should be sufficient to give the reader a broad overview of the standard neoclassical theory of the firm.

CHAPTER 4

Economic Evaluation in Health Care[1]

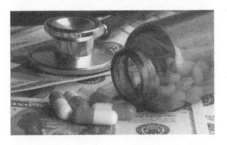

ISSUES IN MEDICAL CARE DELIVERY

RATIONING IS ALREADY HERE

The debate over rising costs in health care has fueled a growing concern that many treatment decisions are based on financial pressures, not clinical evidence. The Society for Critical Care Medicine distributed the *SCCM Healthcare Resource Utilization Opinion Poll* to more than 5,000 of its members in 2002. One of the 11 questions asked was: "Have you rationed any of the following medications or procedures in the last 12 months?" In addition to high-cost drugs, the list included MRI scans, PET scans, and coronary angiograms. Maybe even more interesting than what the respondents said they were rationing was the fact that less than one-third said that they never rationed.

Even though U.S. spending on medical care exceeds that of any other country (using virtually any metric imaginable), there is not enough money or resources to provide everybody with all the medical care they desire. In a world characterized by scarcity, how do we determine who gets care and who does not? Increasingly we seem unwilling to let the market price ration scarce resources, relying instead on the expert opinion of individual physicians across the country as they go about their daily practice of providing care to their patients (see the four-part series in the *Wall Street Journal*, September 2003). Certain aspects of the Affordable Care Act (ACA) have moved the United States closer to a more formal rationing mechanism, similar to those used in many European countries, where formal guidelines determine who receives care and who does not. A drug treatment that is appropriate for a young and otherwise healthy patient may be considered inappropriate for an elderly patient with a history of heart disease or stroke. Individuals whose illnesses are lifestyle-related can find themselves ineligible for certain procedures. In the United Kingdom, smokers and obese people can be refused treatment because research suggests that the probability of success is lower due to their unhealthy habits (Artz, 2011).

Is it ethical to withhold treatment from critically ill patients? Clearly most medical providers consider it unethical to withhold treatment if the primary reason is financial.

[1]Much of the content and examples used in the presentation of this chapter can be traced, either directly or indirectly, to the 2003 training program "Health Economics of Pharmaceuticals and Other Medical Interventions." I would like to thank Gisela Kobelt, director of the European School of Health Economics, and all the presenters and participants for their efforts in making the program worthwhile.

However, most do not consider it unethical when basing decisions on clinical evidence. The problem with the current ad hoc system of rationing is that decisions that stem from it are usually made under conditions of medical urgency. To some extent, all providers base their decisions on clinical evidence, and many take costs and benefits into consideration, but few want a rigid set of guidelines telling them how to practice medicine.

The U.S. health care system rations medical resources, a statement that is also true for every government-run system throughout the world. The difference is that most of our foreign neighbors have more formalized rationing mechanisms. The constant factor in all the health care systems that have adopted formal guidelines is cost control. Policies establishing medical guidelines are usually the result of financial constraints. Systems that promise access to everyone with no concern for ability to pay eventually discover that a growing demand on national budgets requires a formal rationing mechanism. Even though clinicians and policy makers resist the idea of including cost into the decision-making process, as the U.S. delivery system moves closer to its European counterparts, the reality of a formal rationing mechanism becomes more likely.

Sources: Kenneth Artz, "UK's NHS Seeks to Limit Care for Smokers, Obese," *Health Care News*, May 2011 and "Who Gets Health Care? Rationing in an Age of Rising Costs," four-part series in the *Wall Street Journal*; Geeta Anand, "The Big Secret in Health Care: Rationing Is Here," September 12, 2003; Laurie McGinley, "Health Club: Behind Medicare's Decisions, an Invisible Web of Gatekeepers," September 16, 2003; Antonio Regalado, "To Sell Pricey Drug, Eli Lilly Fuels a Debate over Rationing," September 18, 2003; and Bernard Wysocki, Jr., "At One Hospital, a Stark Solution for Allocating Care," September 23, 2003.

As we have seen, the existence of trade-offs is an inevitable consequence of scarcity. Eventually every physician must decide if the improvement in a patient's health is worth the additional spending for a particular intervention. Even those physicians who ignore costs will weigh the benefits in terms of clinical considerations.

In society at large, health plans must decide whether to cover a specific intervention or treatment. The formulary committee for a health maintenance organization (HMO) must decide which drugs in a particular category will be available to its members. The administrator of a hospital must decide where to invest the hospital's capital budget. Government agencies must determine which drugs will be eligible for reimbursement through public programs. By considering costs and benefits, these decision makers are actually applying economic analysis to their particular situations. In other words, they are looking for ways to improve how resources are used in pursuit of better health for individual patients, groups of patients, or their community as a whole.

★ **KEY CONCEPT 1**
Scarcity and Choice

Some may consider valuing life in monetary terms immoral or unethical, but the consequences of ignoring valuation are substantial. Too often, we ignore health effects when we focus on cost. However, when our focus is solely on health, we ignore cost issues. With no clear guidelines, decisions are made on a case-by-case basis, and rules are applied arbitrarily.

This chapter discusses the use of economic evaluation in health care decision-making. The first two sections explore the importance and meaning of economic evaluation. The third section provides a detailed discussion of the types of economic evaluation, including cost-of-illness studies, cost-benefit analysis, and cost-effectiveness (CE) analysis. Because CE analysis is currently the preferred method for analyzing treatment options in health care, this technique is the primary focus of this chapter. Details are provided for calculating the incremental cost-effectiveness ratio (ICER), issues in measuring costs and benefits (including a discussion of the quality-adjusted life year [QALY]), and the steps in performing a CE analysis. Section four is a discussion on the use of modeling in economic evaluation, looking specifically at decision analysis and Markov modeling. Section five examines how economic evaluation works in practice, particularly in Europe. Section six summarizes several case studies using the techniques discussed in the chapter. The final section provides a summary and conclusions.

ISSUES IN MEDICAL CARE DELIVERY

THE LIVERPOOL CARE PATHWAY

The National Health Service (NHS) that provides medical care to citizens of the United Kingdom relies on formal methods of economic evaluation to allocate scarce medical resources. One approach is the development and use of "clinical pathways." A clinical pathway is a structured medical intervention plan that translates clinical guidelines into a systematic course of treatment intending to standardize care for a specific medical problem. As long as the treatment objectives are aligned with patient interests, clinical pathways make a lot of sense.

The use of clinical pathways is not unique to the United Kingdom. Almost all government-dominated medical care systems emphasize clinical pathways as a resource allocation tool. If you do not allocate resources using some sort of pricing mechanism, you must use something else.

A growing debate has emerged over a particular clinical pathway that is in use in the United Kingdom, the Liverpool Care Pathway for the Dying Patient (LCP). Recognized in 2001 as a "best practice" model, the LCP, adopted for nationwide use in 2008, it became the recommended end-of-life strategy. The stated aim of the program is to ensure that dying patients receive the highest standard of care as they near death. As a sidebar we might also note that it is much cheaper for patients to die within 33 hours (the average for patients submitted to LCP) than to linger for weeks and even months using valuable medical resources that could be spent elsewhere.

Even with the increased emphasis on using the LCP, hospitals were slow to implement. A study found that only 16 percent of terminal cancer patients and 5 percent of noncancer patients would receive this care. Hospitals needed an added incentive to implement the LCP. There is no better motivator than cash money. So the NHS established targets for hospitals and provided bonuses for those hospitals that met or exceeded their targets.

As hospital providers assigned more and more dying patients to the LCP, more and more hospitals received bonus payments (Doughty, 2012). British media outlets including BBC News, the *Daily Mail*, the *Observer*, the *Standard*, and the *Telegraph* uncovered alleged abuses and ran with stories on almost daily basis. Even the *Huffington Post* opined "the UK's 'death pathway' may be a little too deadly."

An anonymous British physician challenged the sensitivity of the readers of the *British Medical Journal* (BMJ) with a letter published in the November 1, 2012, issue describing the emotional burden of working with parents who must witness the slow demise of a severely ill child. The situation as described in the letter was more than merely dealing with a dying child. It involved the ethical challenge of issuing the order to withdraw nutrition and hydration to speed up the process. Palliative care is supposed to ease a person's way into the final stage of life, not hasten death to save money.

An independent review of the NHS end-of-life policy, published in July 2013, made 44 recommendations that included a phase-out of the LCP, replacing it with a personal end-of-life care plan for all terminally ill patients. Critics continue to be unhappy with the policy, calling the new guidelines the same protocol under a different name.

The lessons are simple. When the government dominates a health care system, health care spending becomes another budget item. As a line on the budget, it becomes a target for cuts when spending exceeds targeted levels. Budget cutters look for the low-hanging fruit first. In medical care, the low-hanging fruit is end-of-life care. Deciding not to prolong the life of someone who has lived a "complete life" is one thing. Refusing nourishment and hydration to a new-born child for 10 days borders on cruel and unusual treatment, not compassionate care by any definition of the term.

Sources: Anonymous, "How It Feels to Withdraw Feeding from Newborn Babies," *BMJ* 345, 2012 and Steve Doughty, "Hospitals Bribed to Put Patients on Pathway to Death," *Daily Mail*, October 25, 2012.

Importance of Economic Evaluation

Because we live in a world of scarce resources, we do not have the ability to satisfy the desires of all the people all of the time. Different people have different objectives. We must make choices, and often these choices are difficult, if not downright unpleasant. Beneficial projects compete for the same resources: Expanding the mammography-screening program to include the routine use of magnetic resonance imaging may preclude the local hospital from investing in a neonatal intensive care unit. Providing preventive care with no patient cost sharing may mean that the health plan must restrict the use of expensive oncological drugs in the treatment of cancer.

⭐ **KEY CONCEPT 1**
Scarcity and Choice

Every day we must make choices among competing alternatives. We do not have unlimited resources, so programs compete for the same funds, and some worthwhile programs go unfunded. How we make these decisions is critically important. In most cases, the way we address these issues is a matter of quality of life; but in some cases, it is a matter of life and death. In either case, it is important that we approach resource allocation decisions in health care in a clear and systematic way.

⭐ **KEY CONCEPT 2**
Opportunity Cost

Meaning of Economic Efficiency

Before we get too far into our discussion, it may be helpful if we define what we mean by *economic efficiency*. The term as applied to health policy decision-making requires the consideration of both health benefits and resource costs. Health benefits are an important part of the evaluation process, but resource costs must take into consideration the value of the alternative uses of those resources. Economic evaluation itself is a comparative analysis. There must be at least two alternatives, or interventions, under consideration to perform a comparative analysis. We typically do not compare an intervention or procedure to doing nothing, unless doing nothing is a reasonable option. The economic evaluation must be viewed in sharp contrast to the clinical trial. The clinical trial, where one group of patients, the experimental group, is given the treatment under consideration, and a second, the control group is given a placebo (a sugar pill). Remember, this is a clinical setting. It is a test, the scientific equivalent of the gold standard; at the end of the test, no one suggests that the sugar pill, the do-nothing strategy, is a reasonable option.

As stated above, an economic evaluation examines alternative courses of action. We do not examine a treatment option in isolation from all other treatment options. Economic evaluation compares options that are reasonable alternatives to treating a well-defined medical condition.

⭐ **KEY CONCEPT 3**
Marginal Analysis

The comparisons in an economic evaluation are made in terms of costs and consequences. The specific costs to be included in the analysis are largely determined by the perspective taken; the view differs among an individual patient, a health insurance company, a health plan, a government agency, or society as a whole. The calculation must use the perspective of all relevant stakeholders—including those who are paying for the services. There is no assumption that costs must be minimized or benefits maximized, but that costs be measured against benefits, and the difference maximized. Costs include direct and indirect costs, both tangible and intangible. The consequences of an action are the benefits that accrue primarily to individuals, unless, of course, significant externalities are associated with the treatment, such as benefits that result from a vaccination program. The primary tasks required to successfully conduct an economic evaluation are to identify, measure, value, and compare all the relevant costs and consequences. All of these issues will be explored in more detail.

Types of Economic Evaluation

Three types of economic evaluation are used frequently in health care decision-making: cost-of-illness studies, cost-benefit analysis, and CE analysis (Garber, 2001). Each in its own unique way is an attempt to weigh the costs and consequences of alternative medical actions.

Cost-of-Illness Studies

Cost-of-illness studies merely look at the question, "What is the cost?" The quantification of the economic burden of a specific disease provides information on the cost structure related to that disease for a specific population in a well-defined geographic area. Because benefits are not considered formally, a cost-of-illness study is not an economic evaluation in the strictest sense of the term. It does provide important information to policy makers and health economists on the economic burden of a disease. In that sense, a cost-of-illness study may be a first, important step in cost identification leading to an economic evaluation.

Providers can use this type of analysis to guide medical decision-making when the clinical effectiveness of treatment options is equivalent. Under these circumstances, a better description might be cost-minimization analysis, a study to determine the low-cost treatment option to bring about a defined health outcome (e.g., the low-cost option to treat acute otitis media or middle-ear infection).

POLICY ISSUE

A large percentage of health care spending is attributable to lifestyle factors.

Druss et al. (2001) examined the economic burden of five chronic conditions affecting the U.S. population in 1996: mood disorders, diabetes, heart disease, asthma, and hypertension. Medical care costs to treat these five conditions amounted to $62.3 billion, with heart disease and hypertension making up over half of the total. Additionally, the cost of treating coexisting medical conditions totaled $207.7 billion. Adding to the total health costs of $270 billion, the estimated $36.2 billion in lost earnings due to missed work brings the total societal costs for those who suffer from these five conditions to over $306 billion.

Finkelstein et al. (2003) estimated the national medical spending attributable to overweight and obesity to be $92.6 billion (in 2002 dollars). Even though the estimated obesity-related expenditures is less than 6 percent of total health care spending, the research indicates that over one-third of the annual increase in health care spending is associated with conditions attributable to obesity: type 2 diabetes, cardiovascular disease, musculoskeletal disorders, sleep apnea, gallbladder disease, and several types of cancer, including endometrial and postmenopausal breast, kidney, and colon cancer. Other cost-of-illness studies have examined the societal costs of AIDS (Scitovsky and Rice, 1987), alcohol, drug abuse, mental illness (Rice et al., 1990), and cocaine-exposed infants (Henderson, 1991).

Even though the results of cost-of-illness studies are interesting, they do not answer questions related to the most effective options for treating the disorders. To answer questions concerning optimal resource allocation, we must try a different approach to economic evaluation—either cost-benefit analysis or CE analysis.

Cost-Benefit Analysis

Managers of for-profit firms must make decisions on how to allocate their firms' scarce resources among alternative investment projects. If a firm is to maximize profits and remain competitive in the marketplace, the net gain from a project (benefits minus costs) must be maximized. The financial analysis of alternative investment projects is known as *capital budgeting.*[2] However, private sector managers are not the only decision makers who have to make these capital budgeting decisions. Public sector managers must make decisions on how to spend scarce tax dollars to maximize the public welfare. The use of capital budgeting, a technique developed for and applied to decision-making in a market environment, is not applicable in a not-for-profit environment. Public sector managers make these decisions, in most cases, insulated from the full discipline of the market that directs private sector managers.

A simple extension of the capital budgeting process avoiding the limitation is cost-benefit analysis. First developed to assist government agencies in making decisions about the provision of public goods, cost-benefit analysis is an analytical technique that compares all the costs and all the benefits arising from a program or project. Thus, cost-benefit analysis is to the public, not-for-profit sector what capital budgeting is to the private, for-profit sector.

KEY CONCEPT 3
Marginal Analysis

As we saw in Chapter 2, the optimal use of resources requires that every program or project undertaken by the public sector have a marginal social benefit (MSB) that exceeds its marginal social cost (MSC). The problem for public sector decision makers is that the information required to construct MSB and MSC curves is unavailable, making it difficult to determine the social optimum. Cost-benefit analysis is a practical attempt to ensure optimal choice in the absence of markets, while remaining true to the traditional welfare economics approach (Sen, 1977).

Elements of a Cost-Benefit Analysis   Given the budgetary constraints on most public policy decisions, cost-benefit analysis is often used to justify expenditures on specific public sector projects. By forcing decision makers to determine whether the benefits from the project are worth the associated costs, measuring both in monetary terms, only those projects that show a positive net benefit are warranted on economic grounds. Alternatively, the ratio of benefits to costs can be calculated, and only those projects with a benefit-cost ratio greater than or equal to one are accepted.

In practice, benefits and costs accumulate over time, requiring the adjustment for the time value of money by using present value discounting. The concept of time preference simply recognizes that a dollar today is worth more than a dollar in the future. The inherent uncertainty of the future and the forgone opportunities of not having the dollar today are the two biggest reasons that people place a higher value on today's dollar. Because most people have a positive time preference, future costs and benefits must be discounted to make them comparable with current costs and benefits.

KEY CONCEPT 2
Opportunity Cost

Most people are familiar with the concept of compounding or earning interest on interest. Suppose that you could invest $1,000 in a 12-month certificate of deposit (CD) with a guaranteed 10 percent annual return. One year from now, that initial $1,000 investment would be worth $1,100. The general formula is stated as follows:

$$FV_1 = PV(1 + r)$$

where

FV_1 = the future value of the initial investment in one year
PV = the present value of the initial investment
r = the annual return on the initial investment or interest rate

---

[2]Any good managerial economics textbook will have a chapter analyzing long-term investment decisions, and many will have a chapter on public sector decision-making; see, for example, McGuigan, Moyer, and Harris (2002).

Compounding would require that you expand the number of time periods that you leave the money in the CD. At the end of the second year, you would have $1,210.[3] Continuing this logic through n periods, the formula for compounding is as follows:

$$FV_n = PV (1 + r)^n$$

In other words, an investment of PV today will grow to FV_n in n years at an annual interest rate of r percent.

Discounting takes the opposite perspective. If an individual wishes to have FV_n in n years, then PV would have to be invested at an interest rate of r percent. To solve this problem, we simply solve the earlier equation for PV and get:

$$PV = FV_n/(1 + r)^n$$

The present value of a stream of earnings, Y_i, may be estimated per year for n years using the same fundamental relationship and may be written as follows:

$$PV = \frac{Y_1}{(1 + r)^1} + \frac{Y_2}{(1 + r)^2} + \ldots + \frac{Y_n}{(1 + r)^n}$$

Assuming a constant discount rate (r) over time, this expression may be written more simply as:

$$PV = \sum_{t=1}^{n} \frac{Y_t}{(1 + r)^t}$$

This relationship may be adapted to depict the present value of a net benefits stream over time (NB) by defining the stream of earnings (Y_t) in the earlier equation as the difference between the annual benefits (B_t) and the annual costs (C_t) of the project:

$$NB = \sum_{t=1}^{n} \frac{B_t - C_t}{(1 + r)^t}$$

Projects are accepted only if the present value of the net benefits stream is positive. Alternatively, the relationship may be presented as a benefit-cost ratio. In this case, the ratio of benefits to costs must be greater than one before a project is accepted.

$$B/C = \sum_{t=1}^{n} \frac{B_t}{(1 + r)^t} / \sum_{t=1}^{n} \frac{C_t}{(1 + r)^t}$$

Valuing Benefits   Cost-benefit analysis requires that all benefits and costs be valued in monetary terms. Valuing benefits is usually not a concern when the project involves the construction of a dam or an interstate highway. However, when the technique

---

[3]This calculation would be [$1,000 × (1 + 0.1)] × (1 + 0.1).

is applied to medical care, the practice is equivalent to placing a monetary value on human life.

POLICY ISSUE
What is the value of human life?

Placing a dollar value on life may be unsettling to many, but the monetization of benefits is necessary to calculate a benefit-cost ratio. The technique rests entirely on the premise that the values used in social decision-making are simply the sum of all individual values. As we saw earlier, the prices individuals are willing to pay for items are determined by the values they place on them. Benefits are typically valued using the willingness-to-pay approach. An individual's willingness to pay for an improvement in health depends on four factors: wealth, life expectancy, current health status, and the possibility of substituting current consumption for future consumption (Bleichrodt and Quiggin, 1999). To the extent that the results of a cost-benefit analysis applied to a medical care decision reflect the willingness and ability to pay of the individuals who stand to benefit, the subsequent allocation of medical resources based on that analysis may be viewed suspiciously, because it will likely favor certain groups: the wealthy, the young, and those with serious health problems.

It is the task of decision makers to ensure that spending and investment decisions reflect stakeholder values. Individual providers make decisions with the values of their patients as the primary consideration and those of the hospital, health plan, and community of secondary importance. On the other hand, government policy makers are more likely to take the perspective of society as a whole and be as concerned with equity and other welfare considerations as they are with economic efficiency.

Choosing a Discount Rate   The choice of the discount rate is one of the most critical factors in determining the net present value of a project or program. In fact, the present value of a net-benefits stream is inversely related to the discount rate. Higher discount rates place more importance on costs and benefits realized early in the life of the investment. Future costs and benefits are not as relevant for current decision-making as those closer in time to the decision.

In theory the appropriate discount rate used to evaluate an investment depends on the opportunity cost of funds or, to be more specific, the risk-adjusted rate of return on the next-best investment alternative. For many private investment opportunities, the appropriate discount rate is the interest rate that must be paid on funds borrowed to undertake the project.

KEY CONCEPT 2
Opportunity Cost

In the final analysis, the choice of discount rate depends critically on the perspective taken in the analysis. From the perspective of society, the appropriate discount rate should be reflective of society's collective time preference, or the rate at which future consumption is collectively discounted. In practice, there are a number of interest rates that might be used, ranging from the prime lending rate charged by large money-center banks to their best customers, to the interest rate on U.S. government treasury bonds. In those countries that require an economic evaluation before a medical device or new drug is approved for reimbursement, the typical discount rate is between 1.5 and 6 percent.[4]

Applying Cost-Benefit Analysis   A number of studies have used the cost-benefit approach to examine the effectiveness of medical care programs. One of the early

---

[4]Australian and Canadian guidelines require a mandatory 5 percent discount rate; the United Kingdom calls for costs to be discounted at 6 percent and benefits at 1.5 percent; and the Netherlands mandates 4 percent (Hjelmgren et al., 2001).

applications of cost-benefit analysis in medical care is the classic study of poliomyelitis (Weisbrod, 1971). The study compared the costs and benefits of the medical research program that led to the development of the Salk and Sabin vaccines used against polio. The analysis included only a subset of benefits, focusing on reduced treatment costs and increased productivity. Per capita benefits were estimated as the sum of the market value of work lost due to premature mortality, the market value of work lost to morbidity, and the savings from resources used to treat and rehabilitate. Work-loss estimates were defined as the present value of expected future earnings lost due to the effects of the disease. Research costs were estimated as the sum of the awards for polio research. Weisbrod used several estimates for the vaccination costs to determine rates of return on the research. Rates of return on the basic research program ranged from 4 percent for the high-cost estimate to 14 percent for the low-cost estimate, with the most likely rate of return about 11 to 12 percent. Weisbrod's analysis showed that the methodology could be applied to a wide range of programs in the medical research field.

☆ **KEY CONCEPT 1**
Scarcity and Choice

The use of cost-benefit analysis in medical care prior to 1980 was reviewed by Hellinger (1980). More recent examples include the study by Goddeeris and Bronken (1985) on gonorrheal screening in asymptomatic women and the examination of a vaccination program by Jackson et al. (1995). Clarke (1998) examined the costs and benefits of a mobile mammographic screening program for rural Australia. Ginsberg and Lev (1997) studied the treatment of amyotrophic lateral sclerosis.

ISSUES IN MEDICAL CARE DELIVERY

TREATMENT ALTERNATIVES FOR PEPTIC ULCERS

What is the best way to treat duodenal ulcers? Until recently, most members of the medical profession felt that the overproduction of stomach acid due to stress, diet, or environmental factors was the major cause of this common peptic ulcer. If excess acid is the source, then the best treatment is the use of an acid blocker such as Tagamet, Zantac, Prilosec, or Nexium. It is widely known that a common bacterium causes most duodenal ulcers, opening up a new treatment pattern that includes acid blockers and antibiotics.

Research by Imperiale et al. (1995) examined the costs of three different treatments: (1) treat with acid blockers initially, and if the problem recurs, verify the presence of bacteria by endoscopy and treat with antibiotics; (2) prescribe routine endoscopy followed by acid blockers and antibiotics if bacteria are present; otherwise use acid blockers alone; and (3) use acid blockers and antibiotics, and resort to endoscopy only if the problem recurs within a year.

All three methods are proven means of treating this common form of peptic ulcer. Nevertheless, recurrence rates are extremely high with acid blockers alone, and endoscopy is an expensive diagnostic test, costing as much as $3,000. Because research confirms that a high percentage of ulcer patients are also infected with the bacterium, avoiding the invasive test can save money. Thus, the most cost-effective treatment may be an aggressive regimen of acid blockers and antibiotics without the expensive diagnostic testing.

Source: Thomas F. Imperiale, Theodore Speroff, Randall D. Cebul, and Arthur J. McCullough, "A Cost Analysis of Alternative Treatments of Duodenal Ulcers," *Annals of Internal Medicine* 123(9), November 1, 1995, 665–672.

Cost-Effectiveness Analysis

If improving the health of a given population is the primary goal of health policy, then the preferred measure of health benefits may be the health outcomes themselves and not their dollar value. CE analysis, developed outside the welfare economics framework, is a way to quantify trade-offs between resources used and health outcomes achieved without having to value health outcomes in monetary terms—a prospect that appeals to many policy makers.

The intuitive appeal of CE analysis is based on its pragmatic approach to resource allocation, sometimes referred to as a decision-makers' approach. The entire framework of CE analysis sounds like an economic problem: maximize the level of health for a given population subject to a budget constraint. Thus, CE analysis provides a practical guide for choosing between programs when limited budgets do not allow decision makers to implement every program that might improve the health of the population.

KEY CONCEPT 1
Scarcity and Choice

Elements of a Cost-Effectiveness Analysis   CE analysis relates the cost of two or more treatment options to a single, common consequence that differs among options (e.g., blood pressure reduction, hip fractures avoided, or increased life expectancy). The treatment options may be different treatments for the same condition, such as kidney dialysis compared with kidney transplantation, or unrelated treatments with a common effect, such as the life-saving treatment for heart disease compared to end stage renal failure.

The usefulness of CE analysis is more limited when the effectiveness of treatment options is measured differently or when there are multiple measures of effectiveness. If one treatment option prevents premature death and the other reduces disability days, comparing the two is questionable. One way around this dilemma, other than placing monetary values on outcomes and using cost-benefit analysis, is to use utility measures—actual measures of health preferences—for health outcomes. Cost-utility analysis, a special case of CE analysis, addresses quality of life concerns through the use of QALYs determined by the presence of intangibles such as pain, suffering, and disability. More will be said about QALYs later.

Incremental Cost-Effectiveness Ratio   When decision makers are faced with limited budgets, CE analysis provides a systematic methodology to achieve the best overall health benefit for a given population. When the most effective treatment option for a medical condition is also the least expensive, the choice is easy. The difficulty arises when the most effective treatment option is more expensive. Policy makers need an objective measure to help determine the preferred treatment option.

The measure provided by CE analysis is the ICER. The ICER provides a way to compare the differences in costs and effectiveness of two treatment options using the following formula:

$$\text{ICER} = \frac{C_B - C_A}{E_B - E_A}$$

where

$C_{A,B}$ = costs of treatment options A and B
$E_{A,B}$ = clinical effectiveness of treatment options A and B

When CE analysis is used in clinical decision-making, the usual approach is to define the treatment option being studied (treatment B) and an alternative treatment option for comparison (treatment A). If $C_A > C_B$ and $E_A < E_B$, option A is both more costly and less effective. In this case, we say that treatment option B dominates. If $C_A < C_B$ and $E_A > E_B$, option B is both costlier and less effective. In this case, we say that treatment option A dominates. In both of these cases, further analysis is unnecessary; the most

FIGURE 4.1
Incremental CE
Comparing Two
Treatment Options

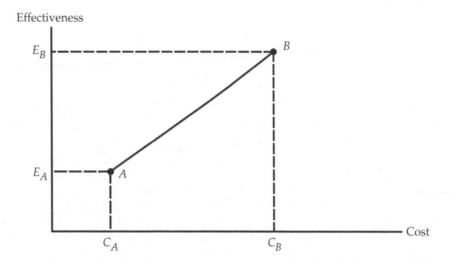

effective treatment option costs less, and the choice is simple. If, however, $C_B > C_A$ and $E_B > E_A$, the choice is not as obvious, and a CE analysis can provide additional insight in the decision-making process.

The ICER may be clearly depicted graphically as seen in Figure 4.1. The gain in effectiveness is plotted on the y-axis and the net present value of the total costs on the x-axis. With each treatment option represented by a point on the graph, it is easy to see that the higher the point, the more effective the treatment; the farther to the right, the more expensive the treatment.

Using this graphical presentation, the ICER comparing the two treatment options is the inverse of the slope of the line between points A and B. A steeply sloped line indicates a low ICER, or a substantial improvement in health effects for a relatively small cost. As the slope gets flatter, the ICER increases, which is indicative of higher cost interventions relative to their effectiveness.

If a number of treatment options are being considered for the same medical problem, the graphical presentation clearly depicts the relative values of the alternative strategies (Mark, 2002). Points A through G in Figure 4.2 represent the costs and effects of seven options for the screening or treatment of a disease. The options that form the solid line $ABDFG$ represent the economically efficient subset of treatment options. Points that lie below the line, such as points C and E, represent treatment options that are dominated by those that are on

FIGURE 4.2
Incremental CE
Comparing Multiple
Treatment Options

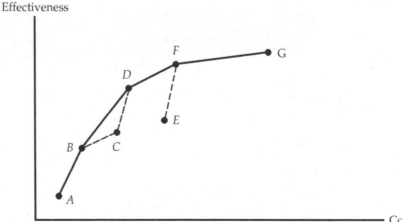

the line.[5] As the slope of the line gets flatter, the ICER increases, providing a clear depiction of the theoretical construct that Enthoven (1980) called the *flat of the curve* (indicative of high marginal resource use for a small marginal gain in health outcomes).

Measuring Cost and Effectiveness All types of economic evaluation require the measurement of cost and effectiveness, the inputs and outputs associated with the treatment. The costs of the treatment are the opportunity costs of the resources used in providing the treatment minus the value of any resources saved due to the treatment. Table 4.1 provides a summary of how cost and effectiveness are categorized. Costs may be classified as direct, indirect, or intangible. Direct costs are typically divided into direct medical and direct nonmedical costs. Direct medical costs include the cost associated with the use of medical resources. This includes hospitalization, outpatient visits, medical procedures, laboratory testing, pharmaceutical drugs, medical devices, and other medical services, such as home care and nursing care. Direct nonmedical costs are those costs typically borne by patients and their families. These costs include transportation expenses; home services such as cleaning, cooking, shopping, and other personal maintenance services; and other nonmedical investments, such as home remodeling to accommodate a physical handicap.

KEY CONCEPT 2
Opportunity Cost

TABLE 4.1 MEASURING COST AND EFFECTIVENESS

Cost measures		
Direct	**Indirect**	**Intangible**
Medical	Sick leave	Quality of life issues
■ Hospitalization	Lost income due to:	■ Pain and suffering
■ Outpatient visits	■ Disability	■ Grief
■ Procedures	■ Early retirement	■ Lost companionship
■ Lab testing	■ Premature death	■ Anxiety
■ Pharmaceuticals		■ Disfigurement
■ Devices		
■ Home care		
Nonmedical		
■ Transportation		
■ Home services (cooking, cleaning, etc.)		
■ Home remodeling		

Effectiveness measures		
Surrogate	**Intermediate**	**Final**
Blood pressure	Heart attack	Events avoided
Bone-mass density	Stroke	Disease-free days
Cholesterol levels	Hip fracture	Life years saved
Tumor size	Hospital readmission	QALYs
	Recurrence of disease	
	Death	
	Scores on evaluative exams	

---

[5]Note that the treatment option represented by point *E* is less effective than the one represented by point *D* and it is more expensive. Thus, treatment option *E* is strictly dominated by treatment option *D*. The treatment option represented by point *C* is dominated due to the logic of extended dominance. Because there are points on the line between *B* and *D* that represent combinations of options *B* and *D* that are more effective and cheaper, *C* is dominated by a combination of treatment options *B* and *D*.

Indirect costs are the costs related to lost productivity. This includes sick leave, reduced productivity at work, and other productivity losses due to early retirement or premature death. Intangible costs are those costs associated with a diminished quality of life. These costs include pain and suffering, grief and anxiety, and disfigurement. Because they are difficult to measure, these costs are often ignored.[6]

The effectiveness of a treatment is measured in terms of the improvement in health associated with it, which may be expressed in terms of surrogate, intermediate, or final measures. Surrogate measures examine the clinical effect of a treatment option or its clinical efficacy; these may be stated in terms of blood pressure, cholesterol level, bone-mass density (BMD), or tumor size. Intermediate measures include clinical effectiveness or outcome measures, and may be stated in terms of events, such as heart attack, stroke, hip fracture, remission/recurrence of cancer, or death. Scores on standard evaluative exams, such as the EuroQol, SF36, or Mini Mental State Exam (MMSE), are also intermediate measures. Final outcomes measure economic effectiveness and may be stated in terms of events avoided, infections cured, disease-free days, life years saved, or QALYs gained.

Generally speaking, the clinical endpoints—both the surrogate and intermediate measures—should be linked to final economic outcomes, or endpoints, in order to calculate the cost effectiveness of the various treatment options. Representing these linkages usually requires some type of modeling using epidemiological data to estimate the transition probabilities from one stage in the course of a treatment or disease progression to another. It is possible to determine the probability of a hip fracture using BMD scores at various ages, and the probability of heart attack or stroke at different blood pressure and cholesterol levels by age and sex. Ideally, we are interested in avoiding the consequences of an event rather than the clinical event itself. Thus, outcomes are measured in terms of improvements in survival and quality of life.

Survival Measures   Even though survival may be stated in a number of different ways, for the purpose of economic evaluation it is typically measured in terms of the number of years of life. When comparing the effects of two treatment options, the difference in life expectancy between the two is the preferred survival measure. Evidence of differences in survival is usually determined from the results of a clinical trial. Seldom do clinical trials last long enough to provide complete information to calculate differences in life expectancy between the treatment and nontreatment groups.[7]

Using the approach in Kobelt (2002), the problem with calculating the survival benefit of a particular treatment is illustrated in Figure 4.3. The two simplified survival functions in the graph represent the percentage of each group that survives over time. The area under the survival function is a measure of life expectancy. Thus, the area between the two survival functions represents the difference in life expectancy between the two groups. Suppose that the two groups have been chosen to test the effects of a new pharmaceutical drug for the treatment of heart disease. At the end of the 18-month trial, 90 percent of the treatment group is still alive, but only 77 percent of the control group is alive. For simplicity, assume that 20 percent of each group dies each year after the trial, implying that all are dead five years after the trial is over.[8]

---

[6]One line of economic research, highlighted by the work of Kip Viscusi, attempts to develop a measure of utility in monetary terms. This approach, when used to value health benefits, values an individual's or society's willingness to pay for improvements in health. See Viscusi and Aldy (2003) for an extensive literature review on the topic.

[7]Clinical trials usually last one to three years, much less than the life expectancy of the typical participant.

[8]The typical survival function is not linear but is drawn convex to the origin or decreasing at a decreasing rate. The usual function may be written $S(t) = e^{\lambda t}$. In this functional form, life expectancy is $1/\lambda$.

FIGURE 4.3
Improved Life Expectancy Due to Clinical Treatment

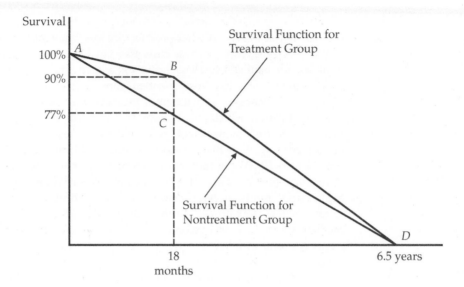

The gain in life expectancy during the trial due to the treatment is the area of the triangle ABC. The calculation is $1/2(0.90 - 0.77) \times 1.5$ or 0.0975 years.[9] Even if the treatment does not increase the overall longevity of the group receiving the drug, there is still a gain in life expectancy after the trial ends, represented in the graph by the triangle BCD. The post-trial gain in life expectancy for the treatment group is $1/2(0.90 - 0.77) \times 5$ or 0.325 years. Thus, the total gain in life expectancy for the group receiving the new drug is 0.4225 years, with over three-fourths of that gain coming after the trial is over. At the beginning of the trial, life expectancy without the treatment was 3.25 years. Because of the treatment, life expectancy increased to 3.6725 years or 13 percent.

Quality of Life Measures   Quite often improvements in life expectancy do not fully capture the benefits of a medical intervention. Extending life can result in a decrease in the quality of life. Furthermore, an intervention may result in quality-of-life improvements without actually extending life. What is needed is a measure of effectiveness that captures improvements in the quality of life, as well as extensions in the length of life. The quality-adjusted life year, or QALY (pronounced *kwa-lee*), serves this purpose.

The concept of the QALY was first introduced in the study of chronic renal failure (Klarman, Francis, and Rosenthal, 1968). The actual term was used for the first time a decade later (Weinstein and Stason, 1977) and has since become the quality of life measure of choice in cost-utility analysis. The measure simultaneously captures the value of reduced morbidity (improved quality of life) and reduced mortality (increased quantity of life).

The QALY may be viewed as life expectancy with a preference weight or quality weight attached to each year. Life is affected by functional limitations, pain and suffering, and the daily burden of a disease; all have an impact on the utility attached to each additional year of living. Normally, an additional year of life while suffering the effects of a particular disease will have less weight associated with it than an additional year of life in a healthy state. To use the QALY concept to represent quality of life for the health states under consideration, quality weights must be attached to the various health states. These quality weights are based on individual preferences for the various health states, measured on an interval scale anchored by death (equal to zero) and perfect health (equal to one).

---

[6]Remember that the area of a triangle is ½ base × height.

A QALY is a probability-weighted average of the expected quality of life estimates for a group of individuals associated with each possible health state. A QALY converts the number of years spent in a given health state to a smaller number of years spent in perfect health, which, according to the individual's preferences, is equally satisfying.

Consider a 55-year-old male with type 2 (non-insulin dependent) diabetes. Complications from type 2 diabetes include kidney disease, retinopathy, and damage to the nervous system that results in more than half of all lower-limb amputations in the United States. The risk of heart disease and stroke is two to four times greater for someone with diabetes. Normally, a 55-year-old male could expect to live an additional 25 years; however, diabetes shortens life expectancy by an average of 10 years. Thus, a 55-year-old male with diabetes can expect to live to age 70. Based on individual preferences, suppose our subject places a utility value of 0.4 on each of his 15 remaining years. His 15 remaining years have a QALY value of 6 (15 $\times$ 0.4). Based on individual preferences, the total utility of living an additional 15 years with type 2 diabetes is the same as the total utility of living an additional 6 years in perfect health. Thus, this man would equate living 15 years with diabetes to living 6 years in perfect health.

Using Figure 4.4, the utility of living one year with diabetes, $U(h_i)$, is 40 percent of the utility of living one year in perfect health, $U(h_1)$. The total utility over the 15 remaining years of life, $15U(h_i)$, is equal to the total utility of living 6 years in perfect health, $6U(h_1)$.

Some disagree on whose preferences should be measured in determining QALY weights—people currently with the specific disease or the general population. If people with the disease (in this case, those with type 2 diabetes) were surveyed, they would be asked to compare their current health to their ideal health. If the general population were surveyed, they would be asked to rate a described, hypothetical health state relative to their ideal health state.

A second major issue is how to measure quality of life. The World Health Organization (WHO) defines quality of life along three dimensions of well-being: physical, mental, and social. Using a quality of well-being approach, Kaplan et al. (1998) developed a classification system using four patient attributes: mobility, physical activity, social activity, and a symptom-problem complex. Dolan et al. (1996) used a time trade-off technique to measure preferences. This so-called EuroQol includes five health state attributes—mobility, self-care, usual activities, pain/discomfort, and anxiety/depression—to define 245 possible health states. Both approaches have been linked with the QALY to serve as a measure of the level of utility associated with the various health states.

FIGURE 4.4
Using Preferences for Health States to Calculate QALY

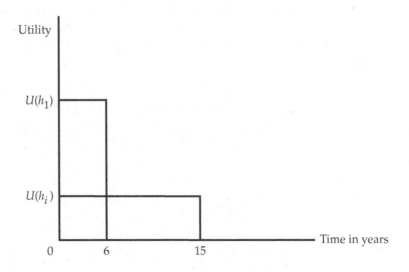

Another option is to calculate the QALY using the standard time trade-off method, in which the individual is offered the following two alternatives:

- *The chronic health state* i *for* t *years, followed immediately by death*
- *Perfect health for* x *years* (*where* x *is less than* t), *followed immediately by death*

Time (x) is varied until the individual is indifferent to the two alternatives. The utility of the chronic health state is determined by the individual's preferences for perfect health. Thus, the value of one year in the chronic health state (h_i) is x/t. Consider the 55-year-old male with type 2 diabetes. He can expect to live an additional 15 years ($i = 15$) with the disease. If he would be willing to sacrifice 6 years of his life with the disease to live in perfect health, $x = 9$. Based on personal preferences, he has placed a QALY value of 0.6 on one year in the disease state ($x/t = 9/15$).

An alternative approach to calculating QALYs uses the standard gamble. Used to measure the utility that a person attaches to a particular health state, the standard gamble is a direct application of one of the fundamental axioms of classical utility theory (von Neumann and Morgenstern, 1944). Intuitively, the premise behind the standard gamble is simple:

- *A treatment is available for individuals in the chronic disease state.*
- *When it works, the treatment provides a permanent cure. When it does not work, the result is immediate death.*
- *How high does the risk of dying have to be before the patient refuses treatment?*
- *The utility value of each year in the chronic disease state is equal to the associated probability that the treatment works.*

More formally, the axiom is based on the continuity of preferences and states that if there are three outcomes (x_1, x_2, and x_3), some probability p exists whereby the individual is indifferent to the certain outcome x_1, and the risky prospect that comprises outcome x_2 with probability equal to p and outcome x_3 with probability equal to $1 - p$.

Consider a situation where an individual in the chronic disease state x_1 (preferred to death) has two choices, either to reject treatment and remain in x_1 for the remainder of her life (t years) or to accept a treatment that has two possible outcomes, perfect health, x_2, for t years with a probability equal to p, or sudden death, x_3, with a probability equal to $1 - p$. Based on the continuity of preferences axiom, the probability p can be adjusted until the individual is indifferent to the two alternatives: either rejecting treatment and living in the chronic disease state for t years or accepting the risk of treatment and living t years in perfect health with a probability equal to p, or dying immediately. Under these conditions, the health preference weight for each year of living in chronic disease state x_1 is equal to p, the probability that the treatment will be fatal.

Steps in Performing a Cost-Effectiveness Analysis

The pieces involved in actually conducting a CE analysis are all in place. All that is left now is to actually set one up. The following steps summarize the process:

1. Rank the alternative treatment options by health benefit (beginning with the one with the lowest benefit).
2. Eliminate strictly dominated treatment alternatives that are more costly and less effective.
3. Calculate the ICER between each treatment option and the next most expensive option.
4. Eliminate treatment options that display extended dominance.
5. Determine which treatment options have an ICER that is below the threshold ICER.

Nothing in the exercise provides information on what society is willing to pay for a particular health benefit; in other words, we do not know what the threshold ICER should be. This step is somewhat problematic for those wanting to avoid valuing health benefits, which is implicit in choosing a cutoff value. One suggested approach is to construct league tables.

The concept of the league table originated from European football rankings (soccer for Americans). In a health care application, these so-called league tables compare the ICER for various interventions. The usual practice is to compile ICERs for a number of common medical interventions from a literature search and to place the intervention under study in the mix. In this context, a case for or against a particular intervention can be made through comparison with other interventions. Garber and Phelps (1997) provide a good example of a league table listing the cost per life year gained for a number of commonly used medical interventions. The usual practice is to discard interventions with high ICERs indicative of poor value in favor of interventions with low ICERs indicative of good value. In the United Kingdom, a commonly used rule of thumb places the cutoff at £30,000 (about $40,000) per QALY or roughly annual per capita income in the United Kingdom.

ISSUES IN MEDICAL CARE DELIVERY

THE COST-SAVING POTENTIAL OF PREVENTIVE CARE

My grandmother used to say "an ounce of prevention is worth a pound of cure." I am sure that she is not the original source (she likely heard it from Ben Franklin personally), but the American proverb seems reasonable. At least today's politicians seem to believe it and have used it as a cornerstone of the newly reformed U.S. health care system. We are told to focus on prevention because it will save countless lives and money in the long run. The Patient Protection and ACA require health plans to cover certain preventive care services at zero out-of-pocket cost to patients.

Evidence suggests that better preventive care can improve health. The health impact of tobacco, alcohol, and obesity in terms of mortality is estimated at 900,000 deaths annually with millions more suffering from the diseases associated with their impact. But can we expect that a new emphasis on preventive care will lower health care spending?

Using data from the Tufts Medical Center Cost-Effectiveness Registry, Cohen et al. (2008) examined almost 300 studies where the CE of preventive services was estimated. Their analysis indicated that only one in five preventive measures saves money, while the rest do not.

How can we explain these results? They do not make sense. If my gastroenterologist discovers a benign cyst during my colonoscopy and removes it, I have avoided the prospects of a colon cancer operation in the future and its associated treatment. Will that save money? In this one case, the answer is yes. However, screening thousands of patients to find one benign cyst may not save money.

These results do not mean that preventive care is not worthwhile. A formalized screening program makes sense when the risk of the underlying disease is significant and effective treatment is available. Preventive measures may even save money if they are applied to high-risk population groups. An aspirin a day will lower the cost of treating heart disease in men over age 45 that are high risk (Pignone et al., 2006).

Even though most preventive measures do not save money, that does not mean they are not good investments. Some treatments are good investments no matter how they are applied, while others are good investments when applied to targeted populations (Russell, 2007). Using $50,000 as the cutoff for cost-effective treatments, almost one-half of those examined by Cohen et al. (2008) were cost effective. In other words, some preventive measures add to medical cost, but they improve health at a reasonable cost.

Sources: Joshua T. Cohen, Peter J. Neumann, and Milton C. Weinstein, "Does Preventive Care Save Money? Health Economics and the Presidential Candidates," *New England Journal of Medicine* 358(7), February 14, 2008, 661–663; Louise B. Russell, "Prevention's Potential for Slowing the Growth of Medical Spending," Washington, DC: National Coalition on Health Care, October 2007; and M. Pignone et al., "Aspirin, Statins, or Both Drugs for the Primary Prevention of Coronary Heart Disease Events in Men: A Cost-Utility Analysis," *Annals of Internal Medicine* 144, 2006, 326–336.

Approaches to Modeling in Economic Evaluation

The biggest technical challenge in conducting a CE analysis is the availability of quality data. The proverbial gold standard for data on the costs and effectiveness of various treatment options is the randomized trial. In practice, however, randomized trial data are not always available. As we discussed earlier, trial periods are typically too short to capture all the costs and consequences of the treatment options. Additionally, randomized trials are costly to undertake and are driven by the requirements to prove safety and efficacy. Under the controlled conditions of randomized trials, many of the variables that would determine effectiveness and efficiency in the course of normal clinical practice are not present, limiting the researcher's ability to generalize from the trial results. These limitations highlight the importance of using sound modeling techniques as a framework for economic evaluation. The two modeling frameworks frequently used in economic evaluation are decision trees and Markov models (Kuntz and Weinstein, 2001).[10]

Decision Trees

Decision trees provide a logical framework for decision analysis, clearly illustrating the sequential nature of the decision-making process and capturing the uncertain nature of the environment in which people make decisions. Decision trees are designed to analyze problems that involve a series of choices that are in turn constrained by previous decisions. They provide a convenient way to show the effects of choices and the impact of the probabilities of subsequent events on outcomes.

The elements of a decision tree flow logically from an initial decision point or decision node. Branches from a decision node represent courses of action taken by the decision maker. Chance events, shown as chance nodes in the decision tree, are all possible outcomes that stem from each decision. Branches from chance nodes represent the events that result from each decision and their associated probabilities. A terminal node represents the outcome or stopping point in the decision analysis.

Figure 4.5 represents the elements of a simple decision tree with one decision node: whether to choose treatment *A* or treatment *B*. The decision to choose either treatment is followed by a chance node: live or die. In this simple decision tree, the only difference in the sequence of events is the probabilities associated with life or death after the choice

---

[10]TreeAge Software developed the decision analysis software used in developing the figures in this section. TreeAge has been producing decision analysis tools used in the medical care industry since 1988. In addition to CE analysis and Markov modeling, the software can be used for Monte Carlo simulation in clinical decision-making, epidemiological modeling, and pharmaceutical outcomes research. A student version of their DATA™ software is available on their website www.treeage.com/.

FIGURE 4.5
Simple Decision Tree

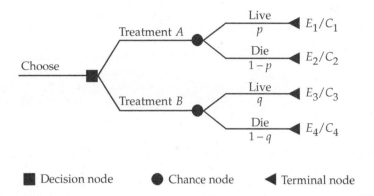

of treatments is made. The probabilities of life and death are p and $1 - p$ if treatment A is chosen and q and $1 - q$ if treatment B is chosen. This simple model has four possible terminal nodes, each with an associated cost (C_i) and effect (E_i).

When using decision trees in the economic evaluation of health care decisions, the model is solved using a technique called *roll back*. In other words, the tree is solved working from right to left, as if there were no uncertainty involved in the process. The expected cost of each possible action is calculated by summing the costs of each branch multiplied by the probability of reaching the terminal point of that branch. Each treatment option is ranked by expected cost, and then ICERs are calculated.

The data required to evaluate treatment options using decision analysis are typically gathered from different sources. Because clinical trials are usually protocol driven, they seldom collect all the information required to complete an economic evaluation. The usual practice in gathering data for the analysis involves integrating information from different sources, including disease data from epidemiological studies, patient management data from clinical practice, and resource utilization data from accounting sources.

	Treatment A	Treatment B
Mortality rate	5%	10%
Life expectancy for survivors	20 years	10 years
Initial treatment cost	$50,000	$20,000
Follow-up costs, year 1	$20,000	$10,000
Follow-up costs, subsequent years	$2,000/year	$2,000/year

Suppose the information above has been gathered on the costs and effectiveness of the two treatments described above.[11] Total cost for survivors receiving treatment A is $108,000; for decedents, it is $50,000. Survivors live an additional 20 years, and decedents experience sudden death. For the group receiving treatment B, the cost for survivors is $48,000; for decedents, it is $20,000. Survivors of treatment B live an additional 10 years.

At each decision node, the expected cost and consequences of each treatment option is calculated. For treatment A, the expected cost is $105,100 (0.95 [$108,000] + 0.05 [$50,000])

---

[11]In this simple example, costs and consequences are not discounted.

and the expected benefit is 19 life years saved (0.95 [20 years] + 0.05 [0 years]).[12] For treatment *B*, the expected cost is $45,200 (0.90 [$48,000] + 0.10 [$20,000]) and the expected benefit is 9 life years saved (0.90 [10 years] + 0.10 [0 years]).

Treatment	Expected cost	Expected benefit	Incremental cost	Incremental benefit	ICER
B	$45,200	9 years	—	—	—
A	$105,100	19 years	$59,900	10 years	$5,990

The treatment options are then ranked by expected cost, from lowest to highest. After calculating the incremental cost and incremental benefit of the treatment options, the ICER is calculated. In this example, treatment *A* results in an additional 10 years of life expectancy at a cost of $59,900 or $5,990 per life year gained.

⭐ **KEY CONCEPT 3**
Marginal Analysis

Markov Models

Decision trees can be as simple or as complex as the decisions they model. However, when there are numerous health states, including the possibility of transitions from one health state to another and back again, the decision tree may become far too complex to handle the problem efficiently. This problem of complex and recurring disease states is particularly challenging when modeling the progression of a chronic condition, such as loss of bone density, breast cancer, and the many forms of dementia. A Markov model is the appropriate choice for modeling such recurring health states.

Disease states and disease transitions may be modeled effectively with a Markov cycle tree, depicted in Figure 4.6.[13] This simple model shows two mutually exclusive health states, or Markov states, corresponding to all possible health states. The health states, alive or dead in this example, are shown at the Markov node. Transition subtrees, constructed at the transition node, depict the progression of the disease from one state to another. Transitions between disease states are based on probabilities that certain events occur—probabilities determined using data from epidemiological studies or clinical trials. In this example, there are only two events: live and die. The probability of living is p, and the probability of dying is $1 - p$.

The branches of the transition subtree end with a terminal node, indicating the end of a cycle, not the termination of the process. Transition subtrees are recursive and continue

FIGURE 4.6
Simple Markov Cycle Tree

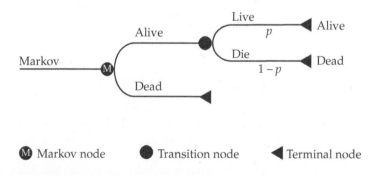

🅜 Markov node   ⬤ Transition node   ◀ Terminal node

---

[12]The calculation for expected cost for either treatment is the sum of the cost for survivors multiplied by the probability of surviving, and the cost for decedents multiplied by the probability of dying.

[13]The simple Markov model described in Figure 4.6 is actually a life-expectancy model. Age memory can be programmed into the Markov process, changing the transition probabilities from cycle to cycle.

for a predetermined number of time periods, called *Markov cycles*, or until everyone who began the process ends up in the absorbing state; in this case, dead.[14] The length of each Markov cycle is fixed and should represent an interval that has clinical meaning for the disease being studied. If cycles are too short, disease transitions are infrequent. If they are too long, individuals transition from one health state to another and back again during the same cycle, diminishing the explanatory power of the model.

Markov Decision Models

One of the most practical ways to take advantage of the power of the decision tree and the Markov model is to combine the two, creating a Markov decision model. In this format, the model starts at the initial decision node of a decision tree, where two treatment options are available. Instead of attaching a chance node to each option, a Markov node is attached. Now the decision model has two Markov processes, each associated with a treatment option, and we have a valuable tool for economic evaluation.

Each Markov process has costs and utilities associated with it. As the Markov process proceeds and participants transition from one health state to another, costs and utilities accumulate for each treatment group. The economic evaluation must keep track of these costs and utilities, so expected costs and expected utilities (usually QALYs) can be calculated. The expected values are calculated on a per capita basis and compared across treatment options to determine ICERs.

Figure 4.7 provides an example of a Markov decision model used to estimate the cost effectiveness of a new drug treatment for Alzheimer's disease, a form of dementia. In this example, data on the clinical effectiveness of the new drug, call it treatment *A*, are collected from a clinical trial in which the control group is given a placebo (no treatment). There are three health states for patients suffering from the disease—mild, moderate, and severe—and one absorbing state: death. The underlying disease progression is shown by transitions from one health state to another. For example, there are three possible transitions for someone beginning a cycle with a diagnosis of mild Alzheimer's: mild-to-mild, mild-to-moderate, or mild-to-dead. Those with severe Alzheimer's have only two transition possibilities: severe-to-severe or severe-to-dead.

The development of Alzheimer's is slow and difficult to confirm. Even though the actual diagnosis of Alzheimer's is not possible without a postmortem analysis of brain tissue, the patient's mental ability may be measured by using one of several cognitive tests. One popular instrument is the MMSE. The MMSE is a short 30-point questionnaire.[15] Mild Alzheimer's is linked to scores ranging from 21 to 26, moderate Alzheimer's to scores between 10 and 20, and severe Alzheimer's to scores below 10.

This Markov decision model was used to estimate the expected costs and expected utilities (measured in QALYs) resulting from four years of treatment with donezepil (Neumann et al., 1999). The data used in estimating the incremental cost effectiveness of the drug therapy came primarily from a 24-week clinical trial (Clegg et al., 2000).

It is beyond the scope of this chapter to go into much more detail on the use of Markov models in economic evaluation. For those interested in more information on the subject, there is a rich literature on the process. The interested reader might begin with Briggs and Sculpher (1998).

---

[14]Transition states are temporary, tunnel, or absorbing. Individuals move in and out of temporary states. The progression through a tunnel state follows a predetermined path, for example, the progression of a pregnancy. No one escapes an absorbing state once it has been entered.

[15]The questionnaire is divided into six sections testing orientation (what is today's date?), immediate recall (repeat three named objects in order), attention and calculation (count and spell backwards), recall (name the three objects from the earlier section), identification (name simple objects), and reading, writing, and copying.

FIGURE 4.7
Markov Decision Model
with Two Markov
Processes

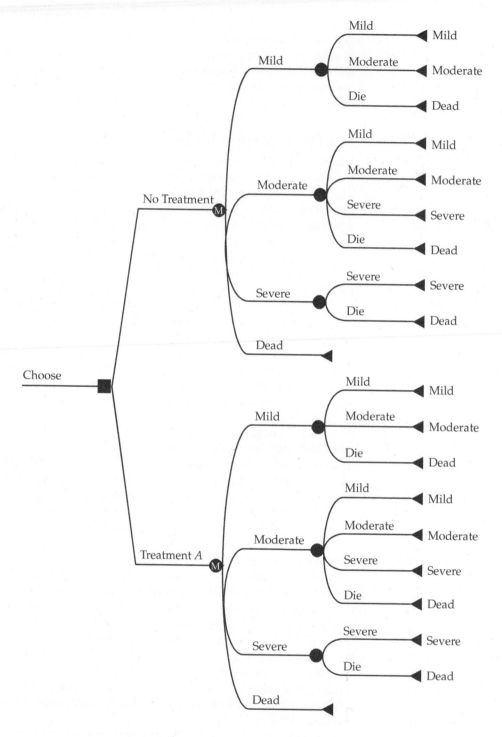

Sensitivity Analysis

The reliability of the results of any economic evaluation depends on the quality of the data used in the study. Due to uncertainty, economic evaluations may be sensitive to changes in key assumptions and parameters. One way to determine whether this uncertainty influences the results is to conduct a sensitivity analysis. A sensitivity analysis is a way of systematically exploring the variability of the results due to uncertainty. A basic sensitivity analysis entails changing the model's parameters or assumptions one at a time. A one-way sensitivity analysis might test the variability of the results to a change in the transition probability from one health state to another, or the initial cost of a treatment option, or the utility associated with a particular health state. Two-way or multiway sensitivity analysis is also quite common.

The typical sensitivity analysis described earlier is called a *cohort* analysis. Conducted with one of the decision models described earlier, a hypothetical cohort of individuals is followed through every event and cycle, expected costs and utilities are estimated, and treatment options are compared using calculated ICERs. This process is repeated for every parameter/assumption change, and the impacts on results are compared. Other approaches to sensitivity analyses include Monte Carlo simulations, in which a large patient cohort is tracked through the model individually. The simulations are repeated over and over to estimate the variance in results associated with the parameters.

KEY CONCEPT 3
Efficiency

ISSUES IN MEDICAL CARE DELIVERY

EFFICACY VERSUS EFFECTIVENESS

The "gold standard" in medical research is the randomized clinical trial (RCT), representing the best evidence in determining if a particular treatment has significant effect on outcomes. However, it matters more if a particular treatment works in practice than if it can work under controlled conditions. Too often, there is a substantial difference between the average treatment effect estimated from a randomized trial and the actual impact on patients receiving the treatment in a real-world setting.

Cochrane (1972) clarified the differences when he introduced his "hierarchy of evidence" asking three questions: Can it work? Does it work? Is it worth the cost? Understanding the implications of how each of these three simple questions is answered will help patients, providers, and policy makers improve the efficiency of medical care delivery.

The first step in understanding the implications of medical research is assessing the efficacy of a medical intervention: Can it work? Does it demonstrate the desired results under optimal conditions? Patients chosen to participate in an RTC are carefully screened and evaluated before being accepted into the trial. Research closely follows a well-defined protocol and participants are closely monitored to ensure compliance. However, efficacy does not necessarily apply to clinical practice.

The next level of evidence is effectiveness: Does it work? Does it demonstrate the desired results under normal conditions? There are many reasons that a treatment that works in a controlled trial may not work in actual practice, but the most likely confounding factor is patient compliance with the treatment. In the real world, patients do what they want to do. The medication causes nausea, incontinence, or sexual dysfunction. Some patients may stop taking the prescribed medication.

An even higher level of evidence, important for policy purposes, is cost effectiveness: Is it worth the cost? Rarely are treatments cost saving or cost neutral. So the cost effectiveness of a treatment is most often estimated in terms of the value of improvements in outcomes relative to the value of the resources consumed in its provision.

As economic evaluation becomes more integrated in the medical decision model, it is vital that all stakeholders work together to demand that effectiveness studies strictly adhere to accepted methodological guidelines, beginning with the collection of the epidemiological and outcomes data used in them. The problem with most CE studies as they are currently organized is that they are based on Markov models that use RTC data on the efficacy of treatment options. It is imperative that we extend these models to take into consideration the disease incidence and effectiveness of the treatment in a real-world setting.

Sources: Archie Cochrane, *Effectiveness and Efficiency: Random Reflections of Health Services*, Leeds: Nuffield Provincial Hospitals Trust, 1972 and Teppo L. N. Järvinen, et al. "The True Cost of Pharmacological Disease Prevention," *BMJ* 342, 2011, 2175.

Economic Evaluation in Practice

As part of the ACA (Section 6301 [c]), Congress created the Patient-Centered Outcomes Research Institute (PCORI). This quasi-governmental organization is charged with advancing comparative effectiveness research and its use. PCORI is responsible for identifying national research priorities, funding patient-centered outcomes research, and communicating research findings to patients, providers, and policy makers.

The use of comparative effectiveness research (formerly called health technology assessment) is not a new phenomenon. Its origin may be traced to "arithmetic medicine" practiced at the Edinburgh (Scotland) medical school in the eighteenth century (Evens, 2009). The twentieth-century expansion of government involvement in paying for medical services made it increasingly difficult for individuals to place a value on medical care, giving rise to the need for a more bureaucratic determination of the costs and benefits and the use of the ICER as a proxy for value.

Given the origins of comparative effectiveness research, it is no surprise that member countries in the European community have taken the assessment of health services technology beyond the narrative treatment of outcomes differences to a more systematic analysis. The National Institute for Health and Clinical Excellence (NICE) in the United Kingdom and the Institute for Quality and Efficiency in the Healthcare Sector (IQWiG) in Germany are two such organizations charged with conducting these assessments.

NICE has a well-defined regulatory role in determining the availability of drug treatments and medical procedures. The UK's NHS must adhere to rigid formal guidelines established by NICE. Without market pressures to guide resource allocation, this top-down process provides a way to justify the subjective budget decisions of politicians.

Germany has managed to avoid many of the shortages and resultant waiting lists so prevalent in the United Kingdom. Established more recently than NICE, the role of IQWiG is somewhat different. Faced with a popular private alternative to state-sponsored health insurance, the agency's primary charge is to hold down costs by improving the efficiency of the state system. Otherwise, differences in the availability of medical care between the public and private sectors could lead to an exodus of high-income consumers from the public system and undermine its popularity.

Other countries use these evaluative bodies in some fashion, either in an advisory role or in a more explicit regulatory role (Clement et al., 2009). As the United States moves toward a more formal reliance on comparative effectiveness research results, this tool to test unproven medical technology and curb spending growth has the potential to advance political and budgetary objectives. It will take diligence to make sure that cost-effectiveness analysis (CEA) does not become a tool for central planning, used to cast a veneer of objectivity on a methodology that is inherently subjective.

ISSUES IN MEDICAL CARE DELIVERY

WHAT IS A "COMPLETE LIFE"?

In a world of superabundance, we would never worry about how to effectively use our available resources to satisfy our many competing desires. However, scarcity is a fact of life; resources are not superabundant. Rich or poor, we are faced with difficult decisions on how to allocate our available resources among competing alternatives. Nowhere is this reality more critical than in those situations where our health is concerned.

Persad et al. (2009) evaluate eight allocation principles to develop a "morally justified" allocation criterion for scarce medical interventions. Arguing that no single principle encompasses all the ethical requirements for a just allocation system, the authors combine four of the individual principles into their proposed allocation system. The outcome is a "complete lives system" that allocates scarce medical resources based on youngest first, lottery, maximization of total lives saved, prognosis, and in the case of public health emergencies, social usefulness.

KEY CONCEPT 1
Scarcity and Choice

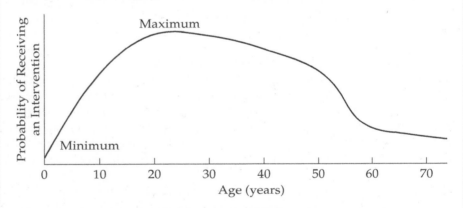

The allocation system generates a "priority curve" that gives preference to individuals between the ages of 15 and 40. Acceptance of this method of allocating scarce medical resources requires that society recognize a complete life as an important commodity and that fairness dictates that those whose lives are not yet complete should have priority. (In a separate publication, one of the authors offered 75 years as a reasonable measure of a complete life, Emanuel, 2014.) When resources are scarce, the youngest and the oldest receive less care. What is your reaction? Does your response have anything to do with your age? Ask your grandmother what she thinks about it.

Sources: Govind Persad et al., "Principles for Allocation of Scarce Medical Interventions," *Lancet* 373, January 31, 2009 and Ezekiel J. Emanuel, "Why I Hope to Die at 75," *The Atlantic*, September 17, 2014.

Case Studies

There are literally thousands of studies, using the techniques discussed in this chapter.[16] The following section highlights five studies that clearly illustrate the use of these techniques in lung cancer screening, cervical cancer screening, human papillomavirus (HPV) immunization, the drug treatment of Alzheimer's disease, and breast cancer screening.

Lung Cancer Screening

Approximately 50 million adult Americans between the ages of 45 and 75 are current, quitting, or former heavy smokers. Over 170,000 Americans are diagnosed annually with lung cancer—and only 15.7 percent survive five years after diagnosis.[17] In contrast, the U.S. five-year survival rate for breast cancer is 90.1 percent and that of prostate cancer is 99.3 percent (Verdecchia et al., 2007).

Mahadevia et al. (2003) examined the cost effectiveness of regular lung cancer screening using helical computed tomography (CT) using a Markov decision model. The study began with three hypothetical cohorts of 100,000 adults in each of the three smoking categories. If annual screening began at age 60, the program would prevent 553 lung cancer deaths over a 20-year period for every 100,000 screened—a 13 percent reduction in the death rate from lung cancer. At a cost of $500 per CT scan, if one half of all adult smokers received an annual screening, the program cost, discounted over 20 years, would be over $115 billion. The risk profile of the screened population affects the cost effectiveness of the program. If only former smokers are screened, the cost per QALY is $2.3 million. If screening is limited to current smokers, the cost per QALY is $116,300. Even with the prospective life-saving consequences of CT screening, age and smoking status may not represent high enough risk factors to make population-based screening cost effective.

Cervical Cancer Screening

At one time, cervical cancer was the leading cause of death among women in the United States. With the introduction of widespread screening, the death rate has declined to less than 8 per 100,000. Even with relatively low incidence rates in both Europe and the United States, deaths from cervical cancer number in the thousands annually, a relatively large number for an otherwise preventable disease (Henderson, 2004).

Mandelblatt et al. (2002) examined the social costs and quality-adjusted life expectancy of a number of different testing strategies for cervical cancer. With a model simulating the natural progression of the disease, they compared 18 different screening strategies using a combination of testing for the HPV, the traditional Papanicolaou (Pap) test, and a combination of the two at two- to three-year intervals, beginning at age 20 and continuing to 65 years, 75 years, or death. Direct costs for screening, diagnosis, and treatment were included in the analysis, along with the indirect costs of the patients' time associated with the process. Eliminating the dominated screening options, either strictly or via extended dominance, the six strategies listed comprised the frontier of economically rational strategies.

---

[16]The Center for the Evaluation of Value and Risk in Health at Tufts Medical Center has developed a comprehensive registry of CE studies, the CEA Registry. It can be found at http://healtheconomics.tuftsmedicalcenter.org/cear4/Home.aspx.

[17]The same is true in Europe, where the five-year survival rate is 10.9 percent (Verdecchia et al., 2007).

Strategy	Expected cost	Expected QALYs saved	ICER $/QALY
No screening	$5,018	26.8666	—
Pap every 3 years to age 75	6,833	27.0200	11,830
Pap every 2 years to age 75	7,280	27.0350	29,781
Pap every 2 years to death	7,308	27.0355	56,440
Pap plus HPV every 2 years to age 75	7,934	27.0444	70,347
Pap plus HPV every 2 years to death	7,980	27.0450	76,183

Source: Mandelblatt et al. (2002).

Maximum benefit in terms of QALYs saved results from Pap plus HPV testing every two years until death with an incremental cost of $76,183. Stopping the screening at age 75 captures approximately 98 percent of the benefits of lifetime screening at an incremental cost that is about $6,000 lower. Combining Pap plus HPV testing in a population-screening program consistently saves more lives but at higher costs. Sensitivity analysis revealed that if the cost of the HPV test fell from $30 to $5, the use of the HPV test every two years until death would become the cost-effective strategy, with an ICER of $50,100.

HPV Vaccination for Preadolescent Girls

HPV types 16 (HPV-16) and 18 (HPV-18) are linked to 100 percent of cervical cancers among women in the United States. Eliminating the transmission of these two types of HPV through a widespread vaccination program would seem to eliminate this cause of a cancer that kills almost 4,000 women in the United States every year.

Kim and Goldie (2008) analyze the cost effectiveness of vaccinating preadolescent girls (at age 12) when compared with the current cytologic screening practices.[18] Temporary catch-up programs to vaccinate women up to age 26 were also evaluated.

The cost effectiveness of a population-based screening program is sensitive to several important assumptions, the duration of the immunity, the successful implementation of a booster program if lifetime immunity is not achieved, and the future screening practices of the population. With lifetime immunity, the cost of screening preadolescent girls at age 12 is $43,600 per QALY. However, if immunity wanes in 10 years, the cost per QALY jumps to $144,100. Implementing an effective booster program causes the ICER to fall to $83,300. In general, vaccination catch-up programs cost over $100,000 per QALY gained.

Another factor to be considered is the assumption concerning future screening practices. By changing the screening interval to every year, the ICER for vaccinating all 12 year olds rises to $118,200.

Drug Treatment for Alzheimer's Disease

Alzheimer's disease usually strikes individuals over the age of 65. The most common type of dementia, over 15 million people worldwide suffer from this progressively degenerative disease, a number that is expected to rise to 81 million by 2040. One in three seniors die with Alzheimer's each year, and it was the sixth leading cause of death in 2012. Annual spending topped $200 billion and is expected to approach $1.2 billion in 2050.

Wimo et al. (2003) examined the costs and consequences of donepezil treatment in patients with mild to moderate Alzheimer's disease. Patients were evaluated as part of

---

[18]For modeling purposes the authors assumed that 53 percent of women received annual screening, 17 percent biennial screening, 11 percent screening every 3 years, 14 percent every 5 years, and 5 percent never screened.

a one-year clinical trial in which patients were randomized into a treatment group that received the therapy and a placebo control group. Mean annual total costs for the treatment group were $24,969; those for the control group were $26,066. Patients receiving the treatment showed cognitive and functional benefits as evidenced by scores on two cognitive tests.

Jönsson et al. (2000) reviewed several studies on the effectiveness of donepezil (including Neumann et al., 1999) and found that patients who received the drug had better outcomes in terms of both less time spent in more severe states and improved quality of life. In three of the five studies reviewed, donepezil was the dominant strategy (better outcome with a slight cost saving). It was a cost-effective treatment when prescribed to patients with mild to moderate Alzheimer's disease.

Mammography Screening

In November 2009, the U.S. Preventive Services Task Force published new guidelines for breast cancer screening (U.S. Preventive Services Task Force, 2009). The new recommendations turned the preventive screening world upside down. Reviewing several different screening modalities, the task force recommended against routine mammography screening for women between the ages of 40 and 49 years. Regular biennial screening should commence at age 50 and continue until age 74. The task force also recommended against clinicians teaching women how to perform breast self-exams. Even though the recommendations apply to women without a family history of breast cancer and to those without genetic mutations associated with breast cancer, patient advocacy groups including the American Cancer Society (ACS) and the Society for Breast Imaging were quick to criticize the recommendations.

The current ACS guidelines recommend that women in their 40s should be screened annually. While mammography screening saves lives, how many women must be screened to save one life? The task force provides evidence that shows over 1,900 women from 40 to 49 years old must be screened to save one life. For women between 50 and 59 years old, the number is 1,300. For women in their 60s, the number drops to 377. Thus, a decade of screening will add an average of 5 days to the lifespan of a woman in her 40s. Nevertheless, for the one woman whose cancer is detected with those 1,900 scans, the difference is literally life and death. What strategy makes sense? What is the cost per life year saved of the different screening strategies?

Ahern and Shen (2009) examined the cost effectiveness of the various breast screening strategies compared to no asymptomatic screening at all. The results of their analysis are shown in the following table.

Strategy	Mammography interval	Clinical breast exam interval	ICER $/QALY
No Screening			—
Strategy 1	Biennial (40–79)	Biennial (41–79)	35,500
Strategy 2	Biennial (40–79)	Annual (40–79)	90,100
Strategy 3	Annual (40–59)		
	Biennial (60–79)	Annual (40–79)	169,500
Strategy 4	Annual (40–79)	Annual (40–79)	367,100
Strategy 5	Annual (40–79)	Triennial (20–39)	
		Annual (40–79)	3,939,000

Note: Age intervals in parentheses.

Source: Ahern and Shen (2009).

When measured by its cost effectiveness, breast cancer screening is increasingly more expensive as the screening intervals fall from every two years to annually. Strategies 1 and 2 are both cost effective using standard guidelines. Strategy number 5 is the current ACS guideline, annual screening beginning at age 40 with clinical breast exams beginning at age 20. The ICER for the ACS strategy is almost $4 million per QALY gained (when compared to strategy number 4). If compared to strategy number 1, the cost per added QALY is still very high, more than $680,000.

If health care is rationed according to ability to pay, then individual women with the advice of their physicians will decide whether the benefit is worth the added cost. The alternative would consider fairness and efficiency and might substitute a collective decision that would not pay for the procedure.

Summary and Conclusions

This chapter provided an overview of economic evaluation in health care decision-making. Techniques that have become standard practice in Europe over the past decade are not as well integrated in the decision-making process in the United States. Of the three types of economic evaluation discussed, CE analysis is by far the most widely used technique for evaluating the economic efficiency of medical treatment options. The use of modeling in economic evaluation was also emphasized, highlighting the importance of strong quantitative skills for anyone interested in using this valuable analytical tool.

Even though economic evaluation as a tool has the potential to bring cost-conscious behavior back into the decision-making process, it is not the only thing that matters when judging health care alternatives. Equity in the distribution of care and the quality of care are also important considerations. The quantitative value of an ICER should never be the sole consideration in the decision to fund or not to fund a treatment program. The fact that one treatment option has a higher or a lower ICER means very little by itself. The number of patients who are affected by the program, the number and quality of treatment alternatives, and the final impact on overall spending are also critically important.

CE considerations are more formally integrated into health policy making in Canada, Australia, and Europe. Health economists abroad are more familiar with the methodology and receive substantially more formal training in the concepts and techniques that define the discipline. In fact, if you use the term "health economics" in Europe, it is assumed you mean "economic evaluation."

With only a few minor exceptions, economic evaluation is not used extensively in the appraisal of medical technology in the United States (Eddy, 1991). With the passage of the ACA, medical providers in the United States will no longer be able to ignore CE issues. U.S. citizens want comprehensive coverage. They are concerned with issues of affordability and accessibility and are obsessed with freedom of choice. Federal officials in charge of Medicare and Medicaid, the medical programs for the elderly and indigent, are looking carefully at cost as a factor in deciding whether to pay for certain pharmaceuticals. Pressure to hold down spending will only increase now that Congress expanded eligibility to the Medicaid program to include an additional 16 million Americans. It may be just a matter of time before these government-run programs begin to ask for formal CE studies to accompany all applications for approval of new medical technologies, creating what the Europeans call "the fourth hurdle" in the medical technology approval process.

PROFILE   Bengt Jönsson

Bengt Jönsson is part of what could arguably be called Sweden's first family of health economics. He and his wife, Gisela Kobelt, regularly collaborate on research projects and are assisted by Bengt's son, Linus, when additional analytical brainpower is needed. Born into a family without academic traditions, Jönsson managed to challenge the Swedish academic system that rewards a pedigree to become one of the most respected health economists in all of Europe.

Jönsson was born in the port city of Helsingborg, located at the narrowest point of the Oresund (one of the world's most frequented sounds and the gateway to the North Sea). He was raised in the small industrial town of Höganös, 10 miles to the north. Jönsson received his academic training at nearby Lund University, just across the sound from Copenhagen. His undergraduate degree in economics and statistics allowed him to combine his interest in social issues with his training in math and science. His interest in health economics was driven in part by Swedish national politics. Given the significant growth in Sweden's welfare state at the time, there was surprisingly little academic interest in the subject.

His masters' thesis in 1972 was a study of the rationale for subsidized childcare. Although these services were interesting and important, the study of the childcare industry did not lend itself to his vast technical expertise. While visiting a bookstore at the University of York that summer, Jönsson came across a book on health economics coauthored by Anthony J. Culyer and Michael H. Cooper. Subsequent conversations with Culyer and Alan Williams provided the inspiration for the dissertation that followed.

While a lecturer in the economics department at Lund, Jönsson completed his Ph.D. in 1976. After a short tenure as director of the Swedish Institute for Health Economics at Lund, he became Sweden's first professor of health economics and director of the Center for Medical Technology Assessment at Linköping University. In 1991, he moved to the Stockholm School of Economics, where he is currently Professor of Health Economics. Jönsson also serves as a member of the Scientific Advisory Board of the National Board of Health and Welfare, and is a member of the board of the Swedish Institute for Health Economics. He is associate editor of the *Journal of Health Economics* and a member of the editorial boards of both *PharmacoEconomics* and the *European Journal of Health Economics*.

Being one of the pioneers of a field and living in a small country has its advantages. Jönsson has had a stimulating research agenda with interests in technological change, health care financing and organization, and health care policy. But his most important contribution to the field has been his application of the methods of economic evaluation in health care. He has served as a consultant and policy adviser, not only in Sweden but also for the WHO, the World Bank, and the Organization of Economic Cooperation and Development. These opportunities have "taught [him] modesty in terms of what you can expect to achieve in the short term" and a greater appreciation for the long-term impact of economic fundamentals. Agreeing with his younger colleagues that an academician can have only limited influence in policymaking, Jönsson, with the perspective of 40 years in the discipline, "is more surprised about what has been achieved than disappointed about what is left to do."

Jönsson is an excellent cook, something you would expect from a person who lives in southern France part of the year. A better gardener than golfer, one might question how he finds the time for any of his extra-scholarly pursuits. Nevertheless, if you are around him long enough, you realize that he will not let his work get in the way of what is important. His wife, Gisela, summarizes it best: "He is unique and best in motivating, forming, and coaching bright, young people. I never met a teacher like him: rough, challenging, provocative—yet patient, indulgent, and kind."

Source: Bengt Jönsson, curriculum vitae and personal correspondence.

Questions and Problems

1. The health authorities are considering the treatment alternatives for three types of diseases: heart disease, cancer, and infectious disease. Each year there are 10,000 new cases of heart disease, 10,000 new cases of cancer, and 5,000 new cases of infectious disease. For each diagnosis, there are a number of mutually independent treatment alternatives (including no treatment) as shown in the following table.

Treatment	Cost per treatment	QALYs gained
Heart Disease		
A	0	0
B	100	2
C	300	8
D	400	8
E	600	12
F	800	15
Cancer		
G	0	0
H	200	8
I	400	10
J	500	12
K	600	9
L	700	14
M	800	15
Infectious Disease		
N	0	0
O	100	2
P	350	4
R	650	6

a. Identify all dominant treatment alternatives. Explain why each is dominant.

b. Calculate the incremental cost, incremental QALYs, and ICERs for all economically rational strategies (ICER = incremental cost/incremental QALYs). Why are these considered economically rational?

c. Using separate graphs for heart disease, cancer, and infectious disease, show the alternative treatment options, label the dominant options, and show the economically feasible alternatives. (Place QALYs on the vertical axis and cost per treatment on the horizontal axis.)

d. The local health district has asked your opinion on the "best" strategy from a public health perspective (disease covered, treatment strategy). What do you tell them? How much will it cost?

2. A recent article in *Journal of American Medical Association* (*JAMA*) by Mandelblatt et al. (2002) compared the societal costs and benefits of HPV testing, Pap testing, and their combination to screen for cervical cancer. The paper studied 18 different population-screening strategies—Pap testing alone, HPV testing alone, and Pap plus HPV testing every 2 or 3 years for women beginning at age 20 and continuing to 65 years, 75 years, and death. The following table summarizes some of the results (low cost to high cost). Costs include screening and treatment costs, discounted over the individual's expected lifetime.

Strategy	Cost ($)	QALYs saved	Incremental cost	Incremental QALY	Incremental CE ratio
0. No screening	5,000	26.87	—	—	—
1. Pap every 3 years to age 75	6,825	27.02			
2. HPV every 3 years to age 75	6,950	27.02			
3. Pap every 2 years to age 75	7,275	27.04			
4. Pap + HPV every 3 years to age 75	7,400	27.04			
5. HPV every 2 years to age 75	7,450	27.04			
6. Pap + HPV every 2 years to age 75	7,925	27.05			

a. Identify all dominant screening strategies. Explain why each is dominant.
b. Calculate the incremental cost, incremental QALYs, and ICERs for all economically rational strategies (Incremental CE = incremental cost /incremental QALYs). Why are these considered economically rational?
c. The local health district has asked your opinion on the "best" strategy from a public health perspective. What do you tell them?

3. The following information has been gathered on the costs and effectiveness of the two treatments, A and B. In this problem, costs and consequences are not discounted.
a. What is the total cost for the survivors receiving treatment A? For decedents (assuming sudden death)?
b. What is the total cost for survivors receiving treatment B? For decedents?
c. What is the expected cost for those patients receiving treatment A? And treatment B?
d. Draw a simple decision tree showing the costs and consequences of each treatment option.
e. Calculate the incremental cost and incremental benefit of the treatment alternatives.
f. What is the ICER?

	Treatment A	Treatment B
Mortality rate	2%	5%
Life expectancy for survivors	20 years	10 years
Initial treatment cost	$10,000	$3,000
Follow-up costs, year 1	$5,000	$1,000
Annual follow-up costs, all subsequent years	$1,000	$500

4. A new treatment is discovered that improves survival probability from 85 to 95 percent. Discuss the different ways a researcher might look at these results versus the way that the marketing department might discuss them. What is the difference in the way you would view a new treatment that improves survival probability by the same absolute magnitude, say, from 5 to 15 percent?

5. How does cost-benefit analysis differ from CE analysis? Why has CE analysis become the method of choice for health economists around the world?

6. In what sense is a cost-of-illness study a technique of economic evaluation? In what sense is it not? What is the primary motivation for doing a cost-of-illness study?

7. Calculating costs in an economic evaluation is very important. Classify the following costs as direct (D), indirect (ID), or intangible (IT).

Cost	Classification
Transportation (ambulance or personal auto)	
Sick leave	
Informal care performed by spouse	
Visit to private practitioner	
Inpatient hospital stay	
Nursing home stay	
Reduced productivity at work	
Pain and suffering	
Home health care services	
Diagnostic test	
Surgical intervention	
Grief and anxiety	

8. How would you explain the concept of a QALY? When is it appropriate to use QALYs instead of simply improved life expectancy as the outcome measure in an economic evaluation?

9. The following table represents the costs and benefits of four alternative clinical programs designed to treat a single disease. Benefits are measured in terms of the number of lives saved.
a. Finish the table. Which is the best program in terms of the number of lives saved? In terms of the ICER per life saved?
b. How does the CE ratio, defined as the average cost per life saved, differ from the ICER?
c. Which program would an economist favor? What would your argument be?

Program	Cost ($)	Lives saved	ICER
A	100,000	10	
B	100,000	12	
C	200,000	12	
D	200,000	15	

10. A controversial new device, the implantable cardiac defibrillator (ICD), was used in a clinical trial to determine if it improved survival for heart-attack patients over the standard drug treatment. The trial provided the following information: Two years after the first heart attack, 85 percent of the ICD patients were still alive, compared to 70 percent of the drug treatment group. No additional data were available after the 24-month trial.

a. What is your best guess on survival probability after the trial is over?

b. Calculate the improvement in life expectancy during the trial. What is your best estimate of improved life expectancy after the trial?

c. Graph the mortality function for both the ICD group and the drug-therapy group.

d. What is the difference in life expectancy between the two groups?

11. Choices in health care delivery must be made at two levels: (1) the individual physician prescribing a course of treatment for an individual patient and (2) the policy maker determining the availability of medical care to an entire group of patients or a community. One way to choose among alternative treatment regimes and community programs is by using the criterion of economic efficiency. Briefly describe the three types of appraisal that enter into medical economics. Discuss the unique features of each, and describe their basic strengths and weaknesses.

References

Ahern, Charlotte and Yu Shen, "Cost-Effectiveness Analysis of Mammography and Clinical Breast Examination Strategies: A Comparison with Current Guidelines," *Cancer Epidemiology, Biomarkers and Prevention* 18(3), March 2009, 718–725.

Bleichrodt, H. and J. Quiggin, "Life-Cycle Preferences, Overconsumption, and Health: When Is Cost-Effectiveness Analysis Equivalent to Cost-Benefit Analysis?" *Journal of Health Economics* 18, 1999, 681–708.

Briggs, Andrew and M. J. Sculpher, "An Introduction to Markov Modeling for Economic Evaluation," *PharmacoEconomics* 13(4), April 1998, 397–409.

Clarke, Philip M., "Cost-Benefit Analysis and Mammographic Screening: A Travel Cost Approach," *Journal of Health Economics* 17(6), December 1998, 767–787.

Clegg, A., et al., "Clinical and Cost-Effectiveness of Donepezil, Rivastigmine, and Galantamine for Alzheimer's Disease: A Rapid and Systematic Review," *Health Technology Assessment* 5, 2000, 1–137.

Clement, Fiona M., et al., "Using Effectiveness and Cost-Effectiveness to Make Drug Coverage Decisions: A Comparison of Britain, Australia, and Germany," *Journal of the American Medical Association* 302(13), October 7, 2009, 1438–1443.

Dolan, Paul, et al., "The Time Trade-Off Method: Results from a General Population Study," *Health Economics* 5(2), March 1996, 141–154.

Druss, Benjamin G., et al., "Comparing the National Economic Burden of Five Chronic Conditions," *Health Affairs* 20(6), November/December 2001, 233–241.

Eddy, David M., "Oregon Methods: Did Cost-Effectiveness Analysis Fail?" *Journal of the American Medical Association* 266(15), October 16, 1991, 2135–2141.

Enthoven, Alain, *Consumer Choice Health Plan: The Only Practical Solution to the Soaring Cost of Medical Care*, Reading, MA: Addison-Wesley, 1980.

Evens, Helen, *Comparative Effectiveness in Health Care Reform: Lessons from Abroad*, Backgrounder No. 2239, Washington, DC: The Heritage Foundation, February 4, 2009.

Finkelstein, Eric A., Ian C. Fiebelkorn, and Guijing Wang, "National Medical Spending Attributable to Overweight and Obesity: How Much, and Who's Paying?" *Health Affairs—Web Exclusive* W3, May 14, 2003, 219–226.

Garber, Alan M., "Recent Developments in CBA/CEA," in *Handbook of Health Economics*, Volume 1A, edited by Anthony J. Culyer and Joseph Newhouse, Amsterdam: North Holland, 2001.

Garber, Alan M. and Charles E. Phelps, "Economic Foundations of Cost-Effectiveness Analysis," *Journal of Health Economics* 16(1), 1997, 1–31.

Ginsberg, Gary M. and Boaz Lev, "Cost-Benefit Analysis of Riluzole for the Treatment of Amyotrophic Lateral Sclerosis," *PharmacoEconomics* 12(5), November 1997, 578–584.

Goddeeris, John H. and Thomas P. Bronken, "Benefit-Cost Analysis of Screening," *Medical Care* 23, 1985, 1242–1255.

Hellinger, Fred J., "Cost-Benefit Analysis of Health Care: Past Applications and Future Prospects," *Inquiry* 17(3), Fall 1980, 204–215.

Henderson, James W., "Cost Effectiveness of Cervical Cancer Screening Strategies," *Expert Review of Pharmacoeconomics and Outcomes Research* 4(3), 2004, 89–100.

Henderson, James W., "Economic Impact of Cocaine and Crack Abuse: Private and Social Issues," in Glen E. Lich, ed., *Doing Drugs and Dropping Out: Assessing the Costs to Society of Substance Abuse and Dropping Out of School.* A report prepared for the Subcommittee on Economic Growth, Trade, and Taxes of the Joint Economic Committee, Congress of the United States, Washington, DC: U.S. Government Printing Office, August 1991.

Hjelmgren, Jonas, et al., "Health Economic Guidelines: Similarities, Differences, and Some Implications," *Value in Health* 4(3), May 2001, 225–250.

Jackson, Lisa A., et al., "Should College Students Be Vaccinated against Meningococcal Disease? A Cost-Benefit Analysis," *American Journal of Public Health* 85, June 1995, 843–846.

Jönsson, Bengt, Linus Jönsson, and Anders Wimo, "Cost of Dementia: A Review," in *Dementia*, edited by Mario Maj and Norman Sartorius, Chichester, UK: John Wiley and Sons Ltd., 2000, 335–363.

Kaplan, Robert M., et al., "The Quality of Well-Being Scale: Critical Similarities and Differences with SF-36," *International Journal for Quality in Health Care* 10(6), December 1998, 509–520.

Kim, Jane, J. and Sue J. Goldie, "Health and Economic Implications of HPV Vaccination in the United States," *New England Journal of Medicine* 359(8), August 21, 2008, 821–832.

Klarman, H., J. Francis, and G. Rosenthal, "Cost-Effectiveness Analysis Applied to the Treatment of Chronic Renal Disease," *Medical Care* 6(1), 1968, 48–54.

Kobelt, Gisela, *Health Economics: An Introduction to Economic Evaluation*, London: Office of Health Economics, 2002.

Kuntz, Karen M. and Milton C. Weinstein, "Modeling in Economic Evaluation," in *Economic Evaluation in Health Care: Merging Theory with Practice*, edited by Michael Drummond and Alistair McGuire, Oxford: Oxford University Press, 2001.

Mahadevia, Parthiv J., et al., "Lung Cancer Screening with Helical Computed Tomography in Older Adult Smokers: A Decision and Cost-Effectiveness Analysis," *Journal of the American Medical Association* 289(3), January 15, 2003, 313–322.

Mandelblatt, Jeanne S., et al., "Benefits and Costs of Using HPV Testing to Screen for Cervical Cancer," *Journal of the American Medical Association* 287(18), May 8, 2002, 2372–2381.

Mark, David H., "Visualizing Cost-Effectiveness Analysis," *Journal of the American Medical Association* 287(18), May 8, 2002, 2428–2429.

McGuigan, James R., R. Charles Moyer, and Frederick H. deB. Harris, *Managerial Economics: Applications, Strategy, and Tactics*, 9th ed., South-Western College Publishing, 2002.

Neumann, P. J., R. C. Hermann, and K. M. Kuntz, "Cost-Effectiveness of Donepezil in the Treatment of Mild or Moderate Alzheimer's Disease," *Neurology* 52, 1999, 1138–1145.

Rice, Dorothy P., Sandler Kelman, Leonard S. Miller, and Sarah Dunmeyer, *The Economic Costs of Alcohol and Drug Abuse and Mental Illness: 1985*, San Francisco, CA: Institute for Health and Aging, University of California at San Francisco, 1990.

Scitovsky, Anne A. and Dorothy P. Rice, "Estimates of the Direct and Indirect Costs of Acquired Immunodeficiency Syndrome in the United States, 1985, 1986, and 1991," *Public Health Reports* 102, 1987, 5–17.

Sen, Amartya, "Social Choice Theory: A Re-examination," *Econometrica* 45(1), January 1977, 53–89.

U.S. Preventive Services Task Force (USPSTF), "Screening for Breast Cancer: U.S. Preventive Services Task Force Recommendation Statement," *Annals of Internal Medicine* 151(10), November 2009, 718–726.

Verdecchia, Arduino, et al., "Recent Cancer Survival in Europe: A 2000–02 Period Analysis of EUROCARE-4 Data," *Lancet Oncology* 8, September 2007, 784–796.

Viscusi, W. Kip and Joseph E. Aldy, "The Value of a Statistical Life: A Critical Review of Market Estimates Throughout the World," NBER Working Paper No. 9487, February 2003.

von Neumann, John and Oskar Morgenstern, *Theory of Games and Economic Behavior*, Princeton, NJ: Princeton University Press, 1944.

Weinstein, M. and W. Stason, "Foundations of Cost-Effectiveness Analysis for Health and Medical Practices," *New England Journal of Medicine* 296(13), March 31, 1977, 716–721.

Weisbrod, Burton A., "Costs and Benefits of Medical Research: A Case Study of Poliomyelitis," *Journal of Political Economy* 79(3), May/June 1971, 527–544.

Wimo, Anders, et al., "An Economic Evaluation of Donepezil in Mild to Moderate Alzheimer's Disease: Results of a 1-Year, Double-Blind, Randomized Trial," *Dementia and Geriatric Cognitive Disorders* 15, 2003, 44–54.

Checklist for Assessing Economic Evaluations

As the interest in the economic evaluation of health care interventions has grown, so has the interest in publishing the results of those studies in peer-reviewed journals. In an attempt to promote the quality of the economic evaluations published in the BMJ, the editors established a working group to clarify the components of an acceptable article. The guidelines are grouped under three major headings: study design, data collection, and analysis and interpretation of results.

I. Study design addresses the following seven issues:
1. Is the research question clearly stated?
2. Is the economic importance of the research question clearly stated?
3. Is the perspective of the analysis clearly stated and justified?
4. Is the rationale for the choice of comparison alternatives stated?
5. Are alternative treatment options clearly described?
6. Is the type of economic evaluation clearly stated?
7. Is the type of economic evaluation justified given the question addressed?

II. Data collection addresses the following 14 issues:
8. Are the sources of the effectiveness data clearly stated?
9. Is a systematic overview of the studies used as data sources provided?
10. Are details on the method of data synthesis provided, if based on several studies?
11. Are the outcome (utility) measures clearly stated?
12. Are valuation methods clearly stated?
13. Are details provided identifying the individuals making the valuations?
14. Are productivity changes (indirect) reported separately?
15. Is the relevance of productivity changes discussed?
16. Are resource prices and quantities reported separately?
17. Is the methodology for estimating prices and quantities described?
18. Are all currency and pricing data clearly recorded?
19. Are all inflation adjustments and currency conversions clearly stated?
20. Is the model clearly explained?
21. Is the choice of model and key parameters justified?

III. Analysis and interpretation of results addresses the following 14 issues:
22. Is the time horizon for costs and benefits stated?
23. Is the discount rate used stated?
24. Is the choice of discount rate justified?
25. Is rationale stated, if costs and benefits are not discounted?
26. Are confidence intervals and statistical tests discussed, if stochastic data are used?
27. Is the sensitivity analysis explained?
28. Is the choice of variables for the sensitivity analysis justified?
29. Is the range over which the parameters are varied stated?
30. Are all relevant alternatives compared?
31. Is the incremental analysis reported?
32. Are all major outcomes presented in both disaggregated and aggregated forms?
33. Is the original study question answered?

34. Does the reported data support the conclusions?
35. Are conclusions accompanied by the appropriate caveats?

Even though the guidelines are not intended to stifle innovative approaches, they are meant to improve the quality of economic evaluations that are eventually published in the BMJ. Many of you who read these guidelines may never submit an economic evaluation to the BMJ, but knowing what goes into a publishable economic evaluation will help you read, understand, and critique those you read from other sources.

Source: Michael F. Drummond and T. O. Jefferson, "Guidelines for Authors and Peer Reviewers of Economic Submissions to the BMJ," *British Medical Journal* 313, August 3, 1969, 275–283.

CHAPTER 5

Demand for Health and Medical Care

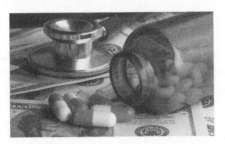

ISSUES IN MEDICAL CARE DELIVERY

FORECASTING MEDICAL CARE DEMAND

If reforming the health care system were not a daunting enough challenge in itself, the task increased in complexity with the promise that the changes would not add to the federal budget deficit. What impact will an additional 30 million newly insured individuals along with the promise of eventually covering everyone have on the demand for medical care over the next 20 or 30 years? Using the estimates of the Congressional Budget Office, by the time the program is fully implemented the 10-year cost of the plan will be an additional $2 trillion to national health care spending.

Will this budget scenario actually materialize itself over the next 15 years or will we somehow avoid a fiscal meltdown? To answer this question, we must understand the principal factors that drive the growth in health care demand. Students of economic principles learn that the principal factor driving the demand for most commodities is income. In this context, as people get more income, they spend more of that income improving their health.

Evidence from Fogel (2000) examines the changing structure of overall U.S. consumption between 1875 and 1995. The share of income spent on food, clothing, and shelter fell from 74 percent to 13 percent. In contrast, the share of income spent on health care rose from 1 percent to 9 percent. The United States is not unique among developed countries; what we see is a common trend worldwide.

What does this reveal about health care demand, you ask? The implied long-term income elasticity for health care is well above unity, 1.6 using Fogel's approach. An income elasticity that is greater than 1 means that as income rises, a larger percentage of that income will be spent on health care. Gross domestic product (GDP) is expected to double over the next 30 years to almost $30 trillion. If health care spending increases 2.6 times during the same period, as implied by the long-term income elasticity, it will grow to over $6.7 trillion or 23 percent of GDP from its current level of 18 percent. For those concerned about the percentage of income spent on health care, this observation borders on the cataclysmic.

Should we try to suppress the demand for health care? Our concern over health care spending stems from the way we pay for health care. Changing the way we finance health care spending, requiring more personal responsibility for the luxury components of this heterogeneous good, might change the way we view overall spending and relieve some of the pressure on the government budget.

Source: Robert W. Fogel, *The Fourth Great Awakening and the Future of Egalitarianism,* Chicago: University of Chicago Press, 2000.

Most people place a high priority on their health and consider access to quality medical care essential to achieving their health goals. Michael Grossman (1972) first introduced economic researchers to the notion that the demand for medical care is derived from the more fundamental demand for good health. Grossman's work established the theoretical framework examining health capital accumulation for the individual and from that the derived demand for health services.

Using his approach, medical care is one of the several factors that may be used to improve the health status of an individual or population. Other factors may be even more important in producing good health, including improvements in living standards, advances in medical research, changes in lifestyle, reductions in environmental pollution, and better nutrition.

The production of health with medical care as an input is the subject of the first section of this chapter. Alternatively, the process may be viewed as one in which various inputs are combined to produce the final product we call health. The remainder of the chapter examines how the desire for good health plays a role in determining the demand for medical care. The chapter concludes with a discussion on measuring medical care demand.

The Demand for Health

Americans value health, as evidenced by the fact that the pursuit of good health is a multi-billion-dollar business. In addition to the money spent on medical care, consumers spend countless dollars on health foods, fitness videos, and weight-loss programs. As important as good health is to our overall well-being, it would be a mistake to conclude that every person considers good health the primary goal in life. Our day-to-day behavior undermines this notion. Otherwise, how do you explain our overconsumption of food, alcohol, and drugs?[1] How can you explain the popularity of such risky behavior as motocross, skydiving, and bungee jumping? Why do many people refuse to wear seat belts? Why all the fuss about motorcycle helmets? Why do so many people still smoke cigarettes? With the recent resurgence of sexually transmitted infections, why do so many still practice risky sexual behavior?

As we begin to think about the demand for health, our starting point will be the relationship between health and the factors that contribute to it. Within this framework, medical care is but one of many inputs that contribute to improving the health of the population. Two important questions will be addressed: What is the most efficient way to produce and distribute health? And what is the incremental contribution of medical care to the production of health?

KEY CONCEPT 8
Efficiency

KEY CONCEPT 3
Marginal Analysis

---

[1]According to the government's technical definition of obesity, over 60 percent of American males and 50 percent of American females are either overweight or obese (Cutler et al., 2003). Almost 40 percent of Americans are classified as obese, or at least 35 pounds overweight (Wessel, 2003), and an estimated 300,000 to 582,000 deaths annually are associated with diseases related to obesity (Allison et al., 1999).

The Production of Health

In economics, production is depicted as a functional relationship that shows how inputs are combined to produce output. Specifically, the health-production function summarizes the relationship between health status and the various factors that may be used to produce good health. In order to derive the health production function, a good starting place is the individual's demand for health. For individual j in time period t, the initial health stock is H_{jt} and gross investment in health is I_{jt}. Net investment in health for individual j (ΔH_j) is the difference between health stock across time periods, t and t + 1. Adding to your stock of health requires that you invest more in your health (I_{jt}) than it depreciates ($\Delta_{jt} H_{jt}$), where Δ_{jt} is the annual rate of depreciation in individual j's health stock. This can be written as follows:

$$\Delta H_j = H_{j, t+1} - H_{jt} = I_{jt} - \Delta_{jt} H_{jt}$$

Grossman assumes that gross health investment during period t is directly related to the consumption of medical services (M_{jt}), the time devoted to the production of health (T_{jt}), and the human capital stock (C_{jt}). Individuals with more human capital are more efficient at improving and maintaining their health. He further assumes that the rate of depreciation in health is directly correlated with age (A_{jt}) and that certain behavioral factors (B_{jt}), such as smoking, alcohol consumption, exercise, and obesity, are associated with the rate of change in health stock.

In other words, gross investment in health in period j may be written as follows:

$$I_{jt} = I_{jt} (M_{jt}, T_{jt}, C_{jt}, A_{jt}, B_{jt})$$

In other words, people use medical care in combination with other inputs and their own time to improve their health.[2] An individual with more human capital puts that capital to use more efficiently in the overall health production process. Older people must invest more in medical care to maintain a given level of health than younger people. Moreover, lifestyle choices that people make have a significant impact on their health. Many of the predictions of the Grossman model have been supported by the empirical research that followed.

The hypothesized relationship between health status and medical care spending is shown in Figure 5.1. Stated in terms of the health status of an individual or a population, it is expressed graphically as a positively sloped function that increases at a decreasing rate. As the amount of medical care spending increases, health status improves. The incremental change in health status declines, however, as more is spent on medical care. In other words, at low levels of overall medical spending, additional spending improves health status substantially. At higher levels of medical spending, the same increase in spending buys a smaller improvement in health status. The economic principle is the law of eventually diminishing marginal returns, or more simply, the law of diminishing returns.[3] Graphically, the law of diminishing returns may be depicted in the top half of the diagram by a total product curve flattening out as medical care spending increases.

The relationship between the change in medical care spending and the change in health status is shown in the lower part of Figure 5.1. The marginal product of medical spending is inversely related to overall spending, indicating that the process of improving health is

KEY CONCEPT 3
Marginal Analysis

---

[2] Formally, $I_{jt} (\ldots)$ is the shorthand way of describing the process whereby inputs are combined to produce health.

[3] The production function in Figure 5.1 has the parabolic form $HS = a + bM - cM^2$, where *HS* denotes health status and *M* medical care spending. The constant term, a, represents the level of health realized with no medical care spending.

FIGURE 5.1 The Relationship between Health Status and Medical Care Spending

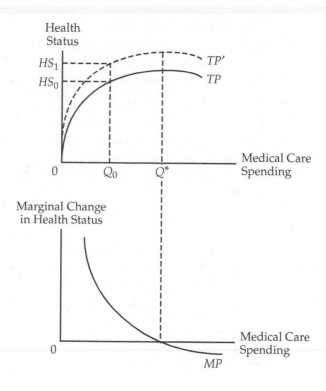

http://

The Institute of Medicine, chartered as a component of the National Academy of Sciences, provides information related to health and welfare issues. Recently released reports on such issues as schools and medicine, telemedicine, and medical outcomes research may be found at http://www.national academies.org/hmd/.

POLICY ISSUE

In addition to increases in medical care spending, other factors affect the health of the population, including lifestyle choices, environmental factors, and developments in technology.

subject to the law of diminishing returns. In economics, decisions are seldom made on an all-or-none basis. It is usually an issue of adjusting priorities, a little less of one thing in return for a little more of something else. The use of the marginal product graph shows how much extra health can be produced by increasing the amount spent on medical care.[4] Understanding this relationship is critical, because most issues in health care relate to changes in the level of medical care provided. The relevant issues deal with marginal changes in utilization and spending, not overall utilization and spending.

Economists and policy makers use the information provided by the marginal product curve to make decisions on the allocation of scarce resources among competing alternatives, such as education, police protection, and economic infrastructure projects. The marginal product curve makes a clear distinction between the impact of medical care on total health status and its marginal contribution to health status.

Medical care spending is not the only thing that improves health. Other factors that affect health status, such as lifestyle, environmental pollution, and technological developments, will shift the total product curve. For example, the presence and severity of respiratory problems are associated with high levels of air pollution. In many major metropolitan areas, automobile emissions are the single largest contributor to air pollution. The incidence of respiratory problems will likely fall with reductions in automotive emissions. Better eating habits and increased exercise will also improve health status. These improvements are depicted graphically by shifting the health status production function from *TP* to *TP'*. At every level of medical care spending, improving these other factors will result in better health.

---

[4]The difficulty in measuring health status makes the practical application of this relationship somewhat tenuous.

Another way to look at the relationship is to view the production function as the maximum health status that can be achieved at a given level of medical care spending. If an individual is spending Q_0 on medical care, holding the other factors that affect health status constant, the maximum health status achievable is HS_0. There are two obvious ways to improve health status: Spend more on medical care and move to a higher point on a stationary health production function (TP), or make better lifestyle decisions and shift the entire curve upward (TP'). At high levels of spending, even more spending on medical care does not buy much of an improvement in health status. The curve has already flattened out. Without spending any more money on medical care, however, HS_1 can be achieved with changes in lifestyle, such as losing weight, getting more exercise, and reducing stress.

One additional clarification may be in order before proceeding further: The health status production function is drawn with a negative slope at spending levels greater than Q^*. Beyond that point, more spending does not result in improvements in health. While it may be unlikely that we will ever reach that point as a society, in individual cases it may be a possibility. The graphical depiction recognizes the possibility of **iatrogenic disease**, net harm caused to a patient because of too much medical care. Prolonging death for a terminally ill patient with no chance of survival may be considered too much if the interventions are painful and the extra life gained is negligible. Quality of life is important. In another sense, as we saw in the last chapter, excessive medical care may be defined as intervention with little benefit relative to cost, because money spent on patients who do not benefit is money that cannot be spent on those it can help.

Every year thousands of patients are harmed, some permanently, by unnecessary procedures and overmedication. After comparing the results of a Harvard Medical School Study of New York hospital records and a similar study from California, Brennan (1992) concluded that adverse events occurred in approximately 4 percent of all hospitalizations. In addition, more than one-fourth of the adverse events can be attributed to substandard care, often the result of overtreatment or improper treatment. A 1999 study conducted by the Institute of Medicine estimated that medical errors are responsible for the deaths of at least 44,000 Americans annually, possibly as many as 98,000 (Kohn, Corrigan, and Donaldson, 1999).

A given level of health may be achieved using different combinations of the inputs. Of interest to economists and policy analysts is the most efficient way to combine the inputs to generate the maximum output possible. In this context, efficiency refers to technical efficiency, or that combination of inputs that minimizes the cost of producing a given level of health. To determine the efficiency of resource allocation in health care, we begin by estimating the production function for health.

Measures of Health Status

The first step in determining the production function for health is to choose an appropriate measure of health. Everyone has his or her own opinion on what constitutes good health. Health is more than the absence of disease. The preamble to the Constitution of the World Health Organization adopted in 1946 defines health as "a state of complete physical, mental, and social well-being and not merely the absence of disease or infirmity." The drawback in using such a definition is that in its broadest sense, health and well-being depend on everything. Health policy becomes all policy. If we are to give our discussion on the relationship between health status and medical spending practical importance, it is critical that we develop a quantifiable measure of health status. No single measure can capture all of the aspects relating to life and the quality of life that are considered important. Studies in the production of health have used such quantifiable measures of health as life

iatrogenic disease An injury or illness resulting from medical treatment.

KEY CONCEPT 2
Opportunity Cost

http://
The website for the National Library of Medicine provides information on every significant program for the world's largest biomedical library. Access to databases, upcoming events, research programs, and publications may be found at http://www.nlm.nih.gov/.

KEY CONCEPT 8
Efficiency

mortality The probability of death at different ages, usually expressed as the number of deaths for a given population, either 1,000 or 100,000, or the expected number of years of life remaining at a given age.

morbidity The incidence and probability of illness or disability.

expectancy and **mortality** rates. Disability statistics, lost days due to illness, the incidence of high blood pressure, and other measures of **morbidity** have also been used as measures of health status, including the quality-adjusted life year discussed in Chapter 4.

Mortality   One of the most common aggregate measures of health status is the crude death rate for a given population, measured as the number of deaths per 100,000 population. Often this measure is adjusted for age, sex, and race to make comparisons among subgroups across geographic regions or countries more meaningful. Table 5.1 lists the most common causes of death in the United States in 1980, 2010, and 2014. Historically, heart disease and cancer have been responsible for over half of the deaths in this country annually. However, progress in diagnosis and treatment has seen that number slip to 45 percent. After these two, no single cause is responsible for more than 6 percent of the total deaths. In fact, after the top 10, no single cause is responsible for more than 1 percent of the total.[5] Not shown in the table is the fact that the leading causes of death vary considerably by age. Overall, unintentional injuries were the leading cause of death for all groups up to age 44 years. HIV infection, once among the leading causes of death overall, was the ninth leading cause of death for Americans between the ages of 25 and 44. Cancer was the leading cause of death for those between 45 and 64 years of age, and for those over age 65, heart disease was the leading cause.

Other commonly used measures include male and female life expectancies at birth and infant mortality rates. Even so, mortality rates tend to be poor indicators of the quality of life. A low crude death rate does not always indicate a healthy population.

TABLE 5.1 MOST COMMON CAUSES OF DEATH (RATE PER 100,000); 1980, 2000, AND 2014

Cause of death	1980	2000	2014
All causes	1,039.1	869.0	724.6
Heart disease	412.1	257.6	167.0
Cancer	207.9	199.6	161.2
Stroke	96.2	60.9	36.5
Unintentional injuries	46.4	34.9	40.5
Influenza and pneumonia	31.4	23.7	15.1
Chronic lower respiratory disease	28.3	44.2	40.5
Suicide and homicide	22.6	16.3	18.1
Diabetes	18.1	25.0	20.9
Nephritis, nephritic syndromes, and nephrosis	9.1	13.5	13.2
Alzheimer's disease	NA	18.1	25.4

Source: *Health, United States 2015.*

---

[5]Only three of the top 10 causes of death in the United States make the worldwide top 10 list. In addition to diseases of the heart, cerebrovascular disease, and chronic obstructive pulmonary disease, the top 10 killers worldwide include tuberculosis, malaria, measles, and lower respiratory infections and diarrhea in children under five years of age (World Health Organization, *World Health Report* 110(4), July–August 1995, 509).

APPLIED MICRO METHODS

DOES BED REST IMPROVE BIRTH OUTCOMES?

Background

Pregnancy problems pose a significant threat to infant health, including premature delivery and low birth weight (LBW). Extreme prematurity (less than 32 weeks gestation) comprises only 2 percent of births but over 50 percent of infant deaths. Medical interventions prior to birth are important in improving short-term outcomes and long-term development. Durrance and Guldi (2015) explore the impact of maternal bed rest (BR) during pregnancy on birth outcomes at two margins: less severe outcomes, premature (<37 weeks gestation) and LBW (<2,500 grams) and extreme outcomes, and very premature (<33 weeks gestation) and very LBW (<1,500 grams).

Data and Methods

Information from three national surveys, including the National Maternal and Infant Health Survey, the National Health Interview Survey, and the Pregnancy Risk Assessment Monitoring Survey (PRAMS), suggests that BR during problem pregnancies is as prevalent today as it was in the 1980s. The paper goes on to use the PRAMS data to compare birth outcomes of women who experience BR to observationally equivalent women who do not receive bed rest (NBR).

   The study estimates the probability of BR as a function of individual maternal factors suggested by prior literature, including age, education, marital status, race, insurance status, prior pregnancy problems, and prior outcomes, to produce propensity scores for matching. Next, the authors use standard ordinary least squares (OLS) to estimate an outcome model (assuming random assignment of BR). Results from standard observational methods will be biased if there are any unobserved (or unmeasured) covariates that are correlated with both birth outcomes and BR, creating ambiguity in the estimated effectiveness of the treatment on outcomes. Finally, they estimate an outcomes model where observations are matched by propensity score (using one of the three approaches: nearest neighbor, inverse propensity weighting with regression adjustment, and entropy balancing).

Results

OLS results on the unmatched data set are statistically significant and indicate that BR increases the likelihood of premature delivery and LBW (+1.74 pp [percentage points] and +0.78 pp, respectively). The results also indicate that BR slightly decreases the likelihood of extreme outcomes (−0.25 pp for very premature delivery and −0.24 pp for very LBW).

   When the BR cohort is matched with the NBR cohort, reducing statistical bias, the results are consistent with the standard OLS, but show differences in magnitude. BR is still positively correlated with less severe outcomes. Depending on matching strategy used, the impact on prematurity ranges from +1.1 to +2.7 pp and the impact on LBW ranges from +1.6 to +3.2 pp (significantly higher impact in the case of LBW). BR has a significantly greater impact on extreme outcomes, lowering the probability of very premature delivery between 1.4 and 2.3 pp and the probability of very LBW between 1.0 and 1.9 pp.

Discussion and Conclusions

Clearly, the standard observational approach to estimating the relationship between BR and poor birth outcomes is biased. Using demographic information alone (without reference to pregnancy problems) assumes random assignment of BR and results in estimates that indicate that BR increases the probability of premature delivery and LBW (usual and extreme cases). Incorporating pregnancy problems and matching BR cohorts and NBR cohorts removes the statistical bias and suggests that BR is marginally effective in shifting birth results from more severe outcomes to less severe outcomes.

Source: Christine Piette Durrance and Melanie Guldi, "Maternal Bed Rest and Infant Health," *American Journal of Health Economics* 1(3), 2015, 345–373.

Morbidity   An alternative way to measure health status is to consider the prevalence of certain diseases or medical conditions. Typical morbidity measures include restricted-activity days due to illness, the incidence rate of certain chronic conditions, and a self-assessment of health status. Table 5.2 ranks the top 15 health conditions in terms of workdays lost and restricted activity days.

Although the rank ordering differs, the number of workdays lost and the number of restricted-activity days have the same causes. Arthropathies or other orthopedic impairments are responsible for the most activity impairments; and, more specifically, back problems result in the most workdays lost. Chronic conditions with the highest overall prevalence, but not necessarily the highest number of restricted-activity days, include chronic sinusitis, arthritis, asthma, chronic bronchitis, and diabetes.

Newhouse and Friedlander (1980) used six physiological measures to analyze the health status in a particular geographic region in relation to the level of medical resources available. The measures they used were diastolic blood pressure, serum cholesterol concentration, electrocardiogram abnormalities, abnormal chest X-rays, presence of varicose veins, and a periodontal index. The first three measures were chosen because of their association with cardiovascular disease, the number one cause of death. The latter three were included for the following reasons: Abnormal chest X-rays are associated with cancer, the presence of varicose veins reflects the general status of the body's connective tissues, and periodontal disease reflects overall preventive-care practices.

Using morbidity measures presents a serious challenge: Because the observed relationship between medical care spending and the incidence of high blood pressure, for example, is negative, more medical care reduces the incidence of hypertension. Care should be taken when graphing the relationship as we did in Figure 5.1. Because of the negative relationship, health status must be defined as the absence of the specific condition.

KEY CONCEPT 1
Scarcity and Choice

TABLE 5.2 WORKDAYS LOST AND ACTIVITY IMPAIRMENTS

Condition	Workdays lost (millions)	Rank	Activity impairments (thousands)	Rank
Acute respiratory infection	69.2	4	1,949.6	3
Arthropathies	67.2	5	3,070.5	1
Asthma	31.4	7	690.4	9
Back problems	83.0	1	1,380.9	5
Cardiac dysrhythmias	7.2	12	528.7	13
Cerebrovascular disease	8.2	13	1,084.1	6
Chronic obstructive pulmonary disease	57.5	6	889.3	7
Congestive heart failure	1.1	15	494.6	14
Diabetes	27.5	8	1,954.0	2
Hypertension	12.0	11	544.3	12
Ischemic heart disease	21.8	9	638.3	10
Mood disorders	78.2	2	1,400.9	4
Motor vehicle accidents	70.0	3	808.6	8
Peripheral vascular disorders	12.8	10	591.4	11
Respiratory malignancies	2.5	14	121.5	15

Source: Druss et al., 2002.

Quality of Life   Some may view measuring health status as a nice academic exercise, but it is a deadly serious proposition for health policy planners. In a world of scarce resources, some means of resource allocation is inevitable. Responsible planning requires the actual scheme to be clearly stated and easily understood, and those responsible for its implementation should be accountable for their decisions. Effective resource allocation requires establishing a measurable output. Otherwise, it is based on intuition without regard to explicit information on costs and benefits.

Recall from the previous chapter a measure of quality of life popular among European policy makers, called the quality-adjusted life year, or QALY. This measure of health status combines quality of life and survival duration into an index that is frequently used to evaluate programs and analyze clinical decisions, especially in countries with government-run systems on fixed budgets. The QALY provides a common unit of measurement that allows valid comparisons across alternative programs.

Possibly the most appropriate use of QALY analysis is the consideration of resource allocation within a single program. Setting priorities within the waiting list for kidney transplants provides a useful example. Members of the relevant population suffer from the same condition, end-stage renal disease (ESRD), and share the same disease-specific outcome measure. The use of the QALY approach arouses strong opinions among both supporters and critics. Those interested in more information about QALYs are directed to the vast British literature on the subject (Broome, 1988; Culyer, 1990; Lockwood, 1988; Loomes and McKenzie, 1990).

Determinants of Health Status

Medical care is not the only factor that contributes to the production of health. Others include income and education, environmental and lifestyle factors, and genetics. Research on the relationship between health status and medical care frequently has found that the marginal contribution of medical care to health status is relatively small. Some argue that at the current level of overall medical care spending, we are at the flat of the curve (Enthoven, 1980). Referring back to Figure 5.1, the flat of the curve would correspond to a level of medical care utilization at which spending approaches the point where *TP* is maximized. As spending approaches Q^*, the marginal productivity of additional spending approaches zero, and we are on the flat of the curve. Further spending will buy only small improvements in health. Even though this generalization may be true for overall spending, it is arguable that we are not on the flat of the curve for some services, including primary, prenatal, and preventive care. In either case, any significant improvements in health status are more likely to originate from factors other than medical care. The easiest way to improve health may be to shift the production function for health.

⭐ **POLICY ISSUE**
*At current levels of
spending, additional
resources devoted to
medical care may not
improve the health status
of the population significantly. We may be on the
flat of the curve.*

Income and Education   The link between an individual's state of health and socioeconomic status may not be direct, but the theoretical underpinnings are obvious. Income, education, and employment represent a level of social advancement that, largely, determines access to medical care. (In the U.S. system, employment determines insurance coverage to a great degree.) In turn, those with better access to care enjoy better health.[6]

---

[6]There is a glaring weakness with this line of reasoning. Countries with universal medical coverage experience the same correlation between socioeconomic status and health. For example, age-standardized mortality rates in the United Kingdom are twice as high for men in the lowest occupational classification. England's lowest socioeconomic group has infant mortality rates that are double those of the highest socioeconomic group, a difference that has persisted since the late 1940s. In Scandinavia, with its relatively homogeneous population, age-standardized mortality rates vary significantly across occupational categories. Certain low-income occupations, such as restaurant workers, have mortality rates that are twice as high as some high-income occupations, such as schoolteachers.

This association does not prove that low socioeconomic status causes poor health. It may be that low status is merely associated with the actual determinants of poor health. Other factors associated with socioeconomic status that may provide a more direct link include nutrition, housing, environment, and even individual time preference. Although the issue provides a wealth of data to examine, no real consensus has emerged.

Pappas and colleagues (1993) examined mortality rates for Americans at various income levels. Their research shows that the 1986 death rates for Americans with incomes less than $9,000 were significantly higher the death rates for Americans earning more than $25,000. More importantly, these differences have widened since 1960. They concluded that socioeconomic status is a strong indicator of health status.

Guralnik and colleagues (1993) have shown that one of the most important factors influencing good health and life expectancy is education (independent of income levels). The research still begs the relevant question: Is there a causal effect between more schooling and better health, or are the two variables related in some other way?

Research represented by Grossman (1972) and others assumes that individuals with more education are more efficient producers of good health. Education increases the ability to understand the importance of avoiding unhealthy behavior, the ability to communicate with health practitioners and understand instructions, and the ability to take advantage of the services available in the medical marketplace. By improving long-term opportunities, education increases the return on investing in health improvements.

Examining the relationship between income and health at the national level requires a completely different perspective. In comparisons of modern industrial nations, little correlation emerges between the level of national income and the various measures of health. When countries from the less-developed world are included, however, a connection between income and health can be made. This connection is probably due to better **public health** measures as the level of development increases, including sanitary water and sewage systems and immunization programs that reduce the spread of disease.

Environmental and Lifestyle Factors

Our discussion on market failure due to externalities in Chapter 3 emphasized the economic costs associated with environmental problems such as air and water pollution. In addition to the high economic costs, the toll on human life and the quality of life is also significant. For example, the American Cancer Society estimates that 65 percent of all cancer in the United States can be linked to lifestyle and environmental factors, including the air we breathe and the food we eat. Exposure to environmental toxins, especially during infancy and childhood, can be linked to illness in children. Harmful chemicals, such as lead, mercury, and polychlorinated biphenyls (PCBs), are associated with poor fetal growth, poor growth during childhood, reduced intelligence (measured by IQ), small head circumference (associated with mental retardation), and decreased lung capacity (Needleman and Bellinger, 1990; Rogan et al., 1986; Shannon and Graef, 1992).

Regardless of the level of income and education, health status depends to a large degree on personal behavior. Lifestyle factors that include diet, exercise, sexual behavior, cigarette smoking, substance abuse, and brushes with violence are important determinants of health status. The observed relationship between health status and socioeconomic status is interesting. However, insufficient evidence prevents a determination of whether we are actually witnessing a link between socioeconomic status and health, lifestyle behavior and health, or possibly socioeconomic status and lifestyle behavior, or all three.

Genetic Factors

Two factors play a critical role in determining the health of an individual: the risk of exposure to a particular disease and the ability of the individual to resist the disease and recover from its consequences once exposed. The former is the purview of

POLICY ISSUE
Does additional medical care spending on the poor significantly improve their health status?

public health
Collective action undertaken by government agencies to ensure the health of the community. These efforts include the prevention of disease, identification of health problems, and the assurance of sanitary conditions, especially in the areas of water treatment and waste disposal.

POLICY ISSUE
Much of the illness experienced by residents of industrialized countries is due to lifestyle and environmental factors, including the food we eat and the air we breathe.

POLICY ISSUE
Should the results of genetic tests be made available to all stakeholders: patients and their families, medical providers, and health insurance payers?

http://

The National Cancer Institute is the largest of the 17 biomedical institutes that comprise the National Institutes of Health (NIH). It serves to coordinate all research on the causes, prevention, detection, diagnosis, and treatment of cancer. Check it out at http://www.cancer.gov.

public health; the latter depends largely on genetics. Thinking about the etiology of certain inherited diseases, sickle cell anemia, for example, differs from thinking about causation in infectious diseases. If a critical number of bacteria enter the system, you get sick. If the bacteria are *Vibrio cholerae*, you get cholera. With certain cancers, the process is different. Cells mutate and multiply, and sometimes a single cell can become cancerous through a series of events. Inherited traits may predispose individuals to certain diseases.

Our genetic makeup is determined directly by our parents. You receive 50 percent of your genes from your father and 50 percent from your mother. You share 50 percent of your genes with your siblings or 100 percent if you happen to be an identical twin. These are all referred to as your first-degree relatives. You get 25 percent of your genes from each grandparent, and you share that same percentage with each aunt and uncle. These are called second-degree relatives. You also get 12.5 percent of your genes from each great-grandparent, so there is a chance that their genetic defects could surface in you.

Attempts to understand the hereditary factor in determining the predisposition to certain diseases have received a great deal of attention. Genetic research has focused on the mapping of the more than 100,000 genes in the human body, with one of the goals being to determine the genes that cause certain forms of inherited diseases. The inheritance of a particular gene greatly increases the risk of acquiring certain diseases. For example, women with a family history of ovarian cancer have a lifetime risk of developing the disease of about 40 percent, compared with the general population's risk of about 7 percent. Other genes are associated with an increased incidence of colon, breast, uterine, and prostate cancers. Genetic factors may account for as much as 10 to 15 percent of all colorectal cancers and 5 to 10 percent of breast cancers (Marra and Boland, 1995).

A hereditary component is suspected in many different disorders. A strong family predisposition is a significant factor in allergies, hypertension, obesity, cystic fibrosis, sickle cell anemia, and even snoring. Heredity may also be linked to pancreatic cancer, certain melanomas, and even kidney and lung cancer. Nevertheless, scientists are still trying to understand the biological basis for many diseases. A mere clustering of a common disease in certain families is not enough to prove a genetic link. The cause may be environmental, or it may be lifestyle related instead of genetic. But as the genetic components of many diseases are being discovered, a complete family medical history is becoming an important tool in the early diagnosis and treatment of certain diseases.

The Role of Public Health and Nutrition

Research by Thomas McKeown (1976) has served as the basis for most of our understanding concerning the improvement in mortality. Ranked in order of importance, McKeown attributed the secular decline in mortality rates in Europe and North America to four major sources:

POLICY ISSUE

Improvements in public health programs are responsible for much of the improvement in human life span experienced over the past century.

- *Living standards, primarily better nutrition and housing, advanced dramatically.*
- *Intervention of public health authorities improved sanitary conditions in the growing urban centers. Water purification and the treatment and disposal of sewage vastly improved the water supplies.*
- *Certain diseases declined in importance because of reduced exposure and increased natural immunity.*
- *Advances in medical science increased the ability to treat certain conditions. Improvements in surgery enabled physicians to treat accidents and digestive disorders, especially appendicitis; obstetric and pediatric care improved treatment of pregnant women and infants; and immunizations contributed to the control of certain diseases.*

The result was a decline in waterborne diseases responsible for intestinal infections, including cholera, dysentery, diphtheria, and other diarrheal diseases. Food hygiene, especially with respect to milk, improved significantly leading to a reduction in the number of infant deaths. The spread of airborne diseases resulting in upper-respiratory problems, such as bronchitis, pneumonia, influenza, and smallpox, became less of a problem because of reduced exposure due, in part, to the diligence of health officials in controlling the spread of these diseases.

Most of the reduction in mortality occurred before effective medical interventions were discovered. When considering the reasons for increased longevity, the role of public health intervention should not be overlooked. The U.S. Public Health Service was formed in 1912, emerging from the Marine Hospital Service. The purview of public health includes the control of communicable diseases, epidemics, and environmental hazards. Public health activities promote health through immunization programs, quarantines, and standards for clean air, clean water, sewage disposal, and the safe handling of food.

Although few critics argue with McKeown's list of reasons for the decline in mortality and morbidity, they do question his rankings and the relative importance he places on each. In particular, Woods and Hinde (1987) question McKeown's conclusion that up to half of the decrease in mortality was due to improved nutrition. They agree that nutrition played a significant role in determining the health of a population by increasing the resistance to disease. Obviously, the overt types of malnutrition, including rickets and beriberi, contribute to poor health. More importantly, an undernourished population lends itself to more frequent infections and infections that are more serious. Woods and Hinde, however, placed more weight on the importance of improvements in environmental conditions and less on nutrition. Neither attributed much of the decline in the incidence of disease to improvements in medical care.

The relationship between nutrition, mortality, and morbidity is complicated. Better nutrition played a significant role in the reduction in mortality from infectious disease, in particular, childhood diseases related to respiratory and intestinal infections. But McKeown's (1976) research, based on national data, did not include data on infant mortality, an important cause of death until well into the twentieth century. The debate rages among demographers and is likely to continue for some time regarding whether environmental or nutritional improvements had the most impact on health. It is important to note that the increased availability of medical care is only one way to improve the health status of an individual or population. In the developed world at least, better lifestyle decisions and a cleaner environment may do more to improve health than increased availability of medical care. In the less-developed world, better sanitation, potable water, and improved living conditions top the list.

> ☆ **POLICY ISSUE**
> *Improvements in public health may do as much to improve life expectancy in the less-developed world than increases in medical care spending.*

▣ ISSUES IN MEDICAL CARE DELIVERY

JOHN SNOW AND THE BEGINNING OF EPIDEMIOLOGY

Public health as a modern-day science can trace its roots back to nineteenth century England and the pioneering work of young British surgeon, John Snow. Responsible for advances in anesthetic surgery, Snow is best known for his work in epidemiology during London's worst outbreaks of cholera between 1848 and 1854.

The first cholera outbreak in Britain in the modern era occurred in 1831, killing over 23,000 inhabitants. The government response was minimal, but the aftermath did see an increase in public awareness on improving sanitary conditions of the poor and working class. Ultimately, a white paper was published in 1842 providing momentum for the passage of the first public health bill in 1848, known unofficially as the Cholera Bill.

A second cholera outbreak occurred in 1848, followed by a third one year later, resulting in 250,000 cases and 53,000 deaths. During these two outbreaks, Snow observed particularly high death rates in the Soho area of London. The commonly held scientific belief of the day assumed that cholera was an airborne disease. Nevertheless, Snow did not accept any of the many miasma, or bad air, theories of transmission. He argued that because the symptoms were intestinal, it was likely that cholera was a waterborne disease and entered the body through the mouth.

At the time of the second and third epidemics, there were two water companies serving the Soho district, Southwark and Vauxhall Waterworks and Lambeth Water Company. Both had their water intake source in the tidal basins of the Thames River, downstream from the major population areas. Using basic spatial analysis to prove his hypothesis, Snow mapped the cholera deaths and identified patterns associated with the water sources available in the neighborhoods.

In 1854 another cholera outbreak occurred, providing Snow with another opportunity to advance his theory. This time, however, circumstances provided him with a perfect natural experiment to test his hypothesis. In 1852, Lambeth moved its water source upstream in an area of the Thames that was not affected by the tidal waters and was thus much less polluted. Moving house to house, he spent several months mapping the occurrence of the disease and noted the difference in the death rates between the customers of the two water companies. Lambeth customers had a death rate of 180 per 100,000 customers while the death rate for Southwark and Vauxhall customers was 916 per 100,000, over five times as high.

Snow was able to convince the local water authorities to take the handle off the water pump on Broad Street (now Broadwick Street) that was the source of contaminated water for many of the local residents, and cholera cases diminished immediately. He documented his research in a book entitled *On the Mode of Transmission of Cholera* in 1855. However, the cholera problem did not end there. Unfortunately, most of the scientific community continued to hold to the miasma theory of cholera transmission for several decades. It was not until Koch and Pasteur developed the germ theory of disease long after Snow's death that his theory of transmission was substantiated.

Source: Simon Rogers, "John Snow's Data Journalism: The Cholera Map that Changed the World," *The Guardian*, Data Blog, March 15, 2013.

The Demand for Medical Care

KEY CONCEPT 4
Self-Interest

POLICY ISSUE
The most powerful force for controlling medical spending is the cost-conscious consumer.

As medical care spending continues to escalate, the search for alternatives to slow its growth has focused on the supply side of the market. Modifying provider behavior is seen by some as the only way to control runaway spending. By ignoring the demand side of the market, we may be forgoing one of the most powerful forces available for cost control: individual self-interest. A basic understanding of the demand side of the market is an important step toward fiscal responsibility in medical care. In this section, we will identify and examine the factors that determine the demand for medical care.

Medical Care as an Investment

One demand-side approach treats medical care the same as any other investment that enhances future productivity. Stated in economic terms, medical care increases human capital (Fuchs, 1982; Mushkin, 1962). Resources used to improve health reduce current consumption, resulting in a decrease in the amount of money available to spend on items other than health care, with the expectation that future consumption will increase because of the ability to work longer and earn more money. Individual willingness to invest in health improvements is determined by several factors: the current cost of medical care, the size of the future payoff, the time span over which the payoff is realized, and individual time preference. It is irrelevant whether the human capital investment is spending on medical care or spending for a college education. Individuals who are willing to invest in a college education are the same individuals who are willing to spend time and money on improving their health. Thus, the association between health and educational attainment is significant.

KEY CONCEPT 3
Opportunity Cost

Demand for medical care is not based solely on the desire to feel better but also on the desire to increase productivity. Within this framework, the demand for medical care has a consumption component and an investment component. People who invest in their health desire to have more healthy days available to produce income and leisure. This view incorporates the concept of the depreciation of health capital as one ages and the use of medical care to slow the process.

The model of derived demand provides the basis for our study of the determinants of medical care demand. The demand for medical care is derived from the demand for good health. Using this framework, the demand for medical care is inversely related to its price. Other relevant factors affecting the level of demand will now be examined.[7]

Factors Influencing Demand

The demand for medical care is determined to a great extent by patient need. Admittedly, need is a difficult concept to define, but one thing is certain: *need* and *demand* are not synonymous. Needs tend to be self-defined and thus represent unconstrained desires. Defining medical care demand in terms of self-defined need is a prescription for wasting medical care resources. As a society, we can never fully satisfy unconstrained desires. In economics, demand is defined in terms of the sacrifice an individual is willing to make to obtain a given amount of a particular good or service. In this context, to restrain medical care spending, we simply modify the incentive structure.

KEY CONCEPT 6
Supply and Demand

Following Intriligator (1981), an individual's demand for medical care may be depicted by the demand curves in Figure 5.2, where Q_M represents some minimum level of medical

FIGURE 5.2
Demand Based on Need versus Willingness to Pay

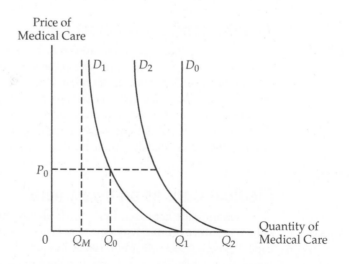

[7]Further discussion of the human capital model may be found in Chapter 8.

care required to maintain health. Society is unwilling to allow anyone to fall below this minimum threshold, and this minimum level will vary depending on the individual's current health status. Individuals with acute or chronic health problems will require more medical care. The demand curve D_0 represents the level of care established by the medical community as the clinical standard. It is the level of care that should be provided without consideration for cost. Medical planners often use D_0 to determine future requirements for medical facilities and personnel. Planning based solely on clinical standards (medically defined need) ignores the price of medical care completely. Under these circumstances, demand is treated as if it were perfectly inelastic. Consumers desire the same level of medical care (Q_1) regardless of its price.

Demand based on willingness to pay does not ignore need completely. Clinical need is merely considered one of several determinants of demand. In this case, demand is shown by the downward-sloping demand curve D_1. As the price of care changes, quantity demanded changes. When medical care is free to the patient ($P = 0$), the quantity demanded will be Q_1. As patients are required to pay more out of pocket, they demand less. When price rises to P_0, quantity demanded falls to Q_0. In this framework, health status becomes a demand shifter that changes the level of demand. If health deteriorates, the level of demand increases, and the demand curve shifts to the right to D_2. If health improves, the demand curve shifts to the left. Note that when demand shifts to D_2, clinical need also increases to Q_2.

The following discussion examines the major factors that influence medical care demand. Factors can be categorized as patient factors and physician factors. Patient factors include health status, demographic characteristics, and economic standing. Physicians affect demand through their dual role as providers of medical services and advisers to, or agents of, their patients. Because physicians also serve as agents, they are in a unique position to create demand for their own services. Medical care demand may be viewed as a functional relationship between medical care and its determinants.

$$M_{jt} = M_{jt}\,(H_{jt}, D_{jt}, E_{jt}, P_t)$$

Continuing with the same notation used earlier, patient factors include individual health stock (H_{jt}), demographic characteristics (D_{jt}), and socioeconomic standing (E_{jt}). Physician factors are denoted by P_t and $M_{jt}(\ldots)$ is a shorthand depiction of how these factors interact to generate a demand for medical care.

Patient Factors   With medical care, as with any other commodity or service, consumers must decide among the available alternatives designed to satisfy their desires. For the demand relationship to have any economic meaning, patients must have money to spend on treatment alternatives and the ability to rank them in order of preference. Otherwise, patients are merely pawns in the game of medical resource allocation.

Substitutes in medical care are the alternative methods of treatment that lead to the same outcome. Natural childbirth results in a newborn infant but so does cesarean delivery. Balloon angioplasty, along with stainless-steel stents, is one way to treat blocked coronary arteries; bypass graft surgery is another. Tennis elbow will improve in time with RICE (rest, ice, compression, and elevation); for those less patient, steroidal injections will also do the trick. Other examples include surgery performed on an outpatient instead of an inpatient basis, the use of the laparoscope for abdominal and knee surgeries, and lithotripsy instead of abdominal surgery to treat kidney stones. In most cases, the choice of treatment alternative is not solely a physician decision. The patient's desires are also considered.

Health Status   A patient seeking treatment for a medical condition typically initiates medical treatment. The patient's desire for treatment is often a response to an accident, injury, or other episode of illness. Thus, an individual's demand for medical care is usually triggered by the onset of an episode of illness. The desire to remain healthy will increase the demand for preventive care. For example, many people visit the local clinic annually for a flu shot to avoid the onset of the illness, women are encouraged to visit their gynecologists regularly for preventive tests, and some people see their dentists twice a year for checkups and cleanings.

The acute care model of medical treatment follows an expected pattern: A patient develops a medical condition (illness, injury, pregnancy, etc.), seeks out a physician, receives treatment, and either recovers or dies. Increasingly, a significant percentage of patients do not fit the pattern. Their medical conditions do not go away. Instead of recovering or dying, they simply live on with a chronic medical problem.

ISSUES IN MEDICAL CARE DELIVERY

WHAT CAN WE LEARN FROM CIVIL WAR VETERANS ABOUT CHRONIC CONDITIONS?

Have you ever heard of the theory of technophysio evolution? Well, I never had until reading about a line of research from Nobel Laureate economist Robert Fogel (2004). He argues that the advances in human physiology experienced in the past 300 years are not the result of a genetic shift but the result of environmentally induced changes. In other words, advances in life expectancy and morbidity are due to improvements in nutrition, public health, medical care, labor-saving technologies, and higher incomes. His research using data from developed and less-developed countries creates an image of the changing nature of human biology. Having largely defeated the scourge of malnutrition, the western world has seen a doubling of life expectancies and a 50 percent increase in average body size. Today, even developing countries are beginning to experience similar gains.

The empirical evidence for Fogel's theory came from the examination of detailed health and demographic records from 45,000 Civil War veterans who fought in the Union Army. The most dramatic discovery was the sheer number of chronic health conditions that the typical veteran suffered. One in four was sent home because of a physical disability, either a hernia, arthritis, tuberculosis, or heart problems. By 1910, approximately 70 percent suffered from arthritis and 75 percent had heart disease. The comparable numbers for World War II veterans at age 65 were 48 and 39 percent.

The commonly held belief had always been that survivors who reached old age in the early nineteenth century were likely to be relatively healthy. Fogel shattered that misconception with the fact that the Civil War veterans had an average of 6.2 chronic conditions. Today, white males who reach age 65 have an average of two chronic conditions.

The reasons for the significant improvements in health begin early in life. Infant and adolescent health and along with it survivability have improved substantially. Undernourishment and infectious diseases, particularly early in life, have been virtually eradicated. What does this tell us about the future in terms of life expectancy and morbidity? How will further improvements affect medical care, public health, and retirement? Many of you reading this book were born around the year 2000. According to Fogel's forecasts, you have a 50 percent chance of living to celebrate your 100th birthday. Plan accordingly.

Sources: Robert W. Fogel, *The Escape from Hunger and Premature Death, 1700–2100: Europe, America, and the Third World*, New York: Cambridge University Press, 2004; and Robert W. Fogel and Dora L. Costa, "A Theory of Technophysio Evolution, with Some Implications for Forecasting Population, Health Care Costs, and Pension Costs," *Demography* 34(1), February 1997, 49–66.

Chronic illness, defined as a condition where a complete cure is not possible, has become a major factor in U.S. health care spending. In fact, chronic conditions begin to dominate medical care demand as a person ages. The incidence of Parkinson's, Alzheimer's, and other dementias increases as we age. Individuals who once died of heart attack or stroke in their sixties are living into their eighties only to experience the effects of a chronic illness. Arthritis, diabetes, hypertension, and heart disease are growing problems among the elderly. A 65-year-old suffering from a chronic illness spends thousands of dollars more annually on medical care than a similar person without the chronic condition. Chronic conditions are responsible for a majority of the health care spending in the United States, and the top five—heart disease, cancer, stroke, emphysema, and diabetes—are responsible for over two-thirds of all deaths (Joyce et al., 2005). Using Medical Expenditure Panel Survey data, Druss and colleagues (2001) estimated that treatment costs for five chronic conditions—mood disorders, diabetes, heart disease, hypertension, and asthma—and the comorbidities associated with them accounted for over half of the total cost of health care in 1996.

Demographic Characteristics   Individual and population demographics are also important determinants of medical care demand. First, a growing population will increase the demand for medical care. Even as the population grows, the family structure is changing dramatically, increasing the demands on the medical care sector. More single parents, more women in the labor force, later marriages, fewer children per family, and greater mobility translate into fewer opportunities for direct family care and a greater reliance on medical providers.

An aging population is another factor contributing to increased demand for medical care. Using the terminology of the Grossman model (1972), as a person grows older, the stock of health capital begins to depreciate. Over the life cycle, people attempt to offset their depreciating stocks by increasing their spending on medical care. In addition to the increased frequency of chronic conditions discussed earlier, the elderly are more likely to suffer from cancer, heart attack, stroke, osteoporosis, poor eyesight, and hearing loss. All of these conditions are costly and contribute to the increased per capita spending for medical care.

http://
Links to over 100 sites with health information for women are available at the NIH at http://health.nih.gov.

Substantial differences are noted in medical care demand by sex (Sindelar, 1982). Early in the life cycle, men and women spend approximately the same amounts on medical care. Later in life, especially during the childbearing years, women spend approximately 50 percent more than men do. Women are hospitalized more often (primarily due to 1.9 childbirths per fertile female), but when men are hospitalized, they remain in the hospital 50 percent longer. Men are more able to substitute home health care for hospital care, especially older men, because they frequently have a wife at home to take care of them. Older women, because they live longer than their husbands, are more likely to be living alone with no one at home to take care of them. Single individuals, regardless of age, are hospitalized more often than married people are.

Men suffer more frequent health losses due to lifestyle choices, such as drinking, smoking, and overeating. With more women in the labor force, patterning themselves after their male counterparts, these differences in lifestyle factors are beginning to narrow. As women continue to act more like men, with higher rates of smoking, drinking, and stress, some medical experts suggest that they may one day start dying like men.

POLICY ISSUE
When spending someone else's money, consumers have little incentive to limit their demand.

Economic Standing   In the United States, education, income, and medical care spending have always been closely associated. Historically, individuals with higher incomes have demanded more medical care. More recently, the importance of income in determining medical care demand has diminished with the increase in third-party insurance coverage.[8] The availability of insurance increases demand for medical care by lowering direct out-of-pocket payment requirements. When someone else is paying the bills, there is no incentive to limit demand. Beginning in the early 1980s, individuals with higher incomes actually had fewer physicians' visits than those with lower incomes (reported in Somers, 1986). In spite of the importance of third-party coverage, direct out-of-pocket payments still account for about 10 percent of all personal health care expenditures, keeping income high on the list of important economic factors.

Income levels are highly correlated with educational levels. The association between income and education has fostered a huge body of economic research on the economic rewards of education, called *human capital theory*. Formal recognition of human capital research as a legitimate area of study may be attributed to the work of Nobel laureates Gary Becker (1964) and Jacob Mincer (1974).[9]

The role of education as a determinant in the demand for medical care goes beyond its association with higher incomes. It is hypothesized that higher levels of education make a person a better consumer of medical care services. Education improves a person's ability to recognize symptoms of medical problems early, when treatment is less expensive. Those with more education have healthier occupations; they eat better and are more efficient users of medical care.

financial risk The risk associated with contractual obligations that require fixed monetary outlays.

With its complex system of private and public insurance programs, the United States has developed a system of third-party insurance to spread the **financial risk** associated with sickness and injury. Third-party payers, including private insurance and the government, cover 80 percent of all medical care spending. Patients who are not directly responsible for their spending decisions tend to demand more medical care than they would otherwise purchase with their own money. Medical care that carries no out-of-pocket cost is treated as if it had no underlying resource cost. The result is moral hazard, demanding more than the social optimum. (See Chapter 7 for a more complete discussion of moral hazard.)

deductible The amount of money that an insured person must pay before a health plan begins paying for all or part of the covered expenses.

Recognizing that health insurance acts to increase the level of demand, health insurance providers offer policies with features that serve to reduce moral hazard. The features typically include **deductibles**, **coinsurance**, and **copayments**. The deductible is the initial amount the policyholder must pay before the insurance coverage begins paying. Coinsurance is the percentage of the total, beyond the deductible, that the policyholder pays. A copayment is a fixed dollar amount charged directly to the patient at the time of treatment.

coinsurance A standard feature of health insurance policies that requires the insured person to pay a certain percentage of a medical bill, usually 10 to 30 percent, per physician visit or hospital stay.

The impact of health insurance on medical care demand is depicted in Figure 5.3. D_{100} represents the demand for medical care for a person with no insurance (subscript indicates the percentage of medical care paid out of pocket). D_{50} is that same individual's demand curve with a policy that requires a 50 percent coinsurance rate. With 50 percent coinsurance, the insurance company pays half, the policyholder pays half, and the policyholder demands Q_1 at price P_0. Without insurance, the individual would pay the full price for the medical care, P_0, and demand only Q_0. Thus, the availability of insurance, or more generally reducing the coinsurance rate, increases the demand for medical care by rotating the demand curve upward.[10] In the case of full insurance, with a coinsurance rate equal to zero,

copayment A standard feature of many managed care plans that requires the insured person to pay a fixed sum for each office visit, hospital stay, or prescription drug.

---

[8]With no adjustment for health status, individuals with less than $14,000 in income had 7.3 physicians' visits on average in 1993. Individuals with over $50,000 had 5.8 (Health United States, 1994, Table 75, p. 169). The differential narrows when health status is considered. The poor and near poor still see the doctor more often than the nonpoor, with 5.7, 5.3, and 5.1 annual visits for each group (Health United States Chartbook, 1993, Figure 26, p. 36).

[9]See the human capital discussion in Chapter 8.

[10]More technically, the availability of insurance also makes the policyholder less sensitive to changes in the price of medical care. Demand is more inelastic when consumers spend a smaller percentage of their budgets on an item. Remember, as you move downward and to the right on a straight-line demand curve, demand becomes more inelastic (price elasticity falls).

FIGURE 5.3 The Effect of Insurance on Medical Care Demand

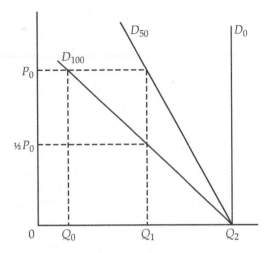

the demand curve would rotate to the vertical and become D_0, and quantity demanded would be equal to Q_2 at a zero price to the patient.

Even as insurance coverage has expanded, approximately 10 percent of the population is without medical insurance at any one point in time. This situation presents an interesting dilemma for policy makers. Those who are fully insured are probably using more medical care than they really need. At the same time, those who have no insurance are probably using less.

The presence of insurance has changed the nature of medicine over the past half century by changing the incentive structure encouraging the purchase of medical care. Insurance, to a degree, has distorted the medical market by creating a bias toward acute care instead of preventive care, specialty care instead of primary care, and hospital care instead of home care (Weisbrod, 1991). Insured patients demand new medical treatments if the expected benefits exceed the expected out-of-pocket costs they must pay. New medical treatments can be profitable even if the added benefits are less than their full social costs. This over investment in technology is further exacerbated by providers' desires to remain competitive by using the newest technologies. The direction of medical research and development is determined by what insurance will buy. As new technology and procedures become available, pressure mounts to include them under covered services. Efforts to restrain demand by deductibles and coinsurance, provider networks, and alternative delivery mechanisms result from a growing awareness of the distortions caused by the third-party payment mechanism.

Of all the factors that affect the demand for medical care, the economic factors are more important for policy considerations because they are more readily affected by public policy. Demographic factors change gradually. The population grows older, more couples divorce, and fewer children are born, but these factors are not easily manipulated by public policy.

In addition to the personal factors, changing attitudes and preferences of the population have a tremendous impact on demand. Over the last 50 years, the public attitude toward medicine has become increasingly positive. Once viewed with a certain amount of distrust, the medical profession today is highly respected. Part of that increased respect is due to the increased ability to cure patients of their ailments. With each new drug, with each new procedure, faith in medicine continues to grow.

As quickly as attitudes toward the medical profession have improved, there began a new movement toward patient autonomy. Terminally ill patients are increasingly demanding the "right to die." Patients suffering poor outcomes are questioning the quality of their care

POLICY ISSUE
The availability of health insurance has changed the incentive structure within the medical care market.

POLICY ISSUE
The movement for more patient autonomy has created added pressures to increase medical care spending.

and turning to the tort system to rule on claims of malpractice. All these economic factors have contributed to a growing demand for medical care and increased medical spending.

Physician Factors   Even though only 20 percent of all medical spending goes for physicians' services, physicians determine the vast majority of total spending. Physicians prescribe the drugs, admit patients into hospitals, and order the tests. Their influence on demand stems from the physician's dual role as adviser to the patient and provider of services.

A vast economic literature has been developed examining the **principal-agent relationship**. An agency relationship exists where an individual, the principal, gives someone else, the agent, authority to make decisions on his or her behalf. Problems arise when the interests of the principal and the agent diverge. In medicine, patients are relatively uninformed concerning alternative diagnoses and treatments. They trust physicians to make choices for them because of the difficulty in gathering and understanding medical information. But the physician's role as supplier can create a conflict of interest.

A physician's ability to induce demand is greatly enhanced when patients have a difficult time gathering and processing information. Given this unique position, physicians can serve as imperfect agents, serving their own interests over those of their patients. In other words, they have the ability to influence their patients' demand for the services they personally provide. In theory, efficacy and cost guide a physician faced with alternative treatment options for a particular disorder. If two treatments are equally effective, the physician can choose the cheaper alternative and save the patient money or the more expensive alternative and buy a new flat screen television for the den.

Standard economic analysis assumes that the demand and supply curves are independent of one another. A given increase in supply results in a new equilibrium reached by moving down a stationary demand curve. The equilibrium price falls, and more output is purchased and supplied. Demand inducement posits, however, that a given exogenous shift in supply causes a shift in demand as providers advise their patients to buy more medical care.

principal-agent relationship A relationship in which one person (the principal) gives another person (the agent) authority to make decisions on his or her behalf.

⭐ **KEY CONCEPT 6**
Supply and Demand

FIGURE 5.4
Demand Inducement Associated with an Increase in Supply

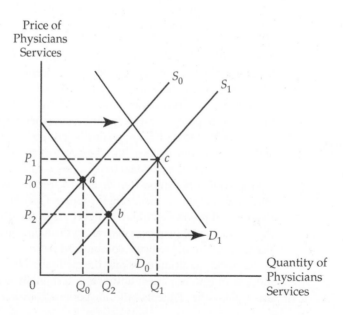

Beginning with demand curve D_0 in Figure 5.4, when the supply curve is S_0, equilibrium is at point a and price and quantity are P_0 and Q_0, respectively. An increase in supply to S_1 should result in a new equilibrium at point b with P_2 and Q_2. If the demand curve is inelastic, as expected, the new price/quantity equilibrium will be at a lower level of total spending.[11] In other words, P_2 times Q_2 will be less than P_0 times Q_0. More physicians and lower overall spending translate into lower average incomes, unless demand shifts at the same time.

The demand inducement hypothesis recognizes that physicians, rather than allow their incomes to fall, may recommend additional procedures, perform more surgeries, and schedule more follow-up visits—all increasing the demand for their services. This shift in the demand curve to D_1 results in a new equilibrium at point c with P_1 and Q_1 and an increase in total spending.

The potential for demand inducement is naturally limited. Patients will eventually detect a practice style that consistently over treats and will change providers if they do not agree with the practice. The potential for inducement is greatest in those areas where the procedure is a one-time event, such as a surgery.

The important issue is not whether physicians have the capability to induce demand, but whether they actually practice demand inducement. Studies examining the demand inducement hypothesis show mixed results. Early research focused on the association between the physician-population ratio and physician fees. Fuchs and Kramer (1986) concluded that the most important factor influencing the demand for physicians' services was the number of physicians. Reinhardt (1985) provided an alternative explanation for the observed positive association between the supply of physicians and the fees they charge. Physicians may simply be migrating into areas where the demand for their services is higher.

physician-induced demand A situation in which providers take advantage of uninformed consumers to purchase services that are largely unnecessary.

The confusing body of research on the subject of **physician-induced demand** represented by these two studies has several implications. First, the phenomenon is probably not as widespread as it was once thought to be. Physicians may have the ability to induce demand, but the extent to which they use this ability is difficult to estimate empirically. In any event, recent changes in the payment structure in medical care delivery, including capitation and bundled payments, have reduced the incentive to practice demand inducement. Second, because we are dealing with a complex phenomenon in an environment of imperfect information, we may never know empirically the full extent of physicians' ability to induce demand for their services (Pauly, 1988). As patients, payers, and lawmakers become more knowledgeable about medical practices and procedures, the phenomenon of demand inducement will likely become less of a concern.

Measuring Demand

Literally hundreds of studies have attempted to measure the impact of the various factors influencing the demand for medical care. Early research focused on the differences in utilization between individuals who had health insurance and those who did not.[12] Newhouse

---

[11]Proof of this assertion follows. Total revenue (TR) is calculated by multiplying the price of a good (P) times the quantity purchased (Q).

$$TR = P \times Q$$

Taking the total differential $\quad dTR = QdP + PdQ$

Factoring QdP $\qquad\qquad dTR = QdP\,[1 + (PdQ)/(QdP)]$

Or $\qquad\qquad\qquad\qquad dTR = QdP\,[1 + \varepsilon_p]$

Where ε_p is the price elasticity of demand.

When price falls (when dP is negative) and demand is inelastic ($\varepsilon_p < 1$), then total revenue falls (dTR is negative).

[12]See Donabedian (1976) for a comprehensive review of this literature.

(1978) has provided an excellent review of the early research quantifying the relationship between out-of-pocket payments and the amount of medical care demanded. Even individuals with comprehensive insurance coverage have different out-of-pocket payment requirements due to differences in deductibles and copayments. Deductibles and copayments may be treated analytically as subsidies to the unit price of medical care. As the subsidy varies, the effective unit price to the individual patient varies. The research focus is on the impact of these price variations on the quantity of medical care demanded, alternatively defined in the various studies as physicians' services, hospital services, dental services, and pharmaceutical services.

In addition to price variations and differences in income and insurance coverage, time costs measured by the hourly wage also affect the demand for medical care. You should recall from our discussion of price elasticity of demand in Chapter 2 that elasticity measures the responsiveness of quantity demanded to a change in the price. Empirical studies measuring medical care demand have focused on the calculation of the various elasticities. In addition to price elasticity, the medical care studies have also estimated income elasticity, insurance elasticity, time-cost elasticity, and **cross-price elasticity** among different types of medical care.

cross-price elasticity The sensitivity of consumer demand for good A as the price of good B changes.

Estimating Demand Functions Demand is typically estimated using regression analysis. The process is not nearly as straightforward as it may seem. The subject of the analysis can be the individual, the household, or an entire population. The unit of measurement may be the number of physicians' visits, the number of hospital admissions, the length of hospital stays, or total medical care spending, and variations in quality of services and intensity of services come into play. When studies include different countries, the way currency translations are made—either by using market exchange rates or purchasing power parity exchange rates—affects the results. Because of these variations, it should come as no surprise then that estimates of demand elasticities vary considerably across studies.

Calculating Elasticities The literature on this subject contains considerable disagreement regarding the magnitude of the various elasticity estimates. Table 5.3 provides a summary of the elasticity estimates from a number of representative studies. Mean estimates of price elasticity usually range from a low of −0.1 to a high of −1.5, depending on study design and dependent variables. Clearly, estimates indicate that demand for medical care in most cases is inelastic with respect to price. Additionally, the higher the patient's out-of-pocket spending, the greater the price elasticity of demand. The demand for outpatient visits is more elastic than the demand for hospital care (Davis and Russell, 1972). Increase the coinsurance rate, and demand becomes more price elastic (Rosett and Huang, 1973). Demand for preventive care is more price elastic than demand for hospital services (Manning et al., 1987), because individuals pay a larger share of the cost of preventive care than hospital care. (Of course, under the ACA preventive care is provided with zero copay, so these results may not hold today.)

income elasticity of demand The sensitivity of demand to changes in consumer income, determined by the percentage change in quantity demanded relative to the percentage change in consumer income.

Taking the empirical evidence as a whole, consumer demand seems to be relatively unresponsive to changes in the price of medical care. That does not mean that quantity demanded does not change when price changes, only that the percentage change in quantity demanded will be less than the percentage change in price. Based on the cited studies, a 10 percent increase in price will lead to a small decrease in quantity demanded, anywhere from 1 to 7 percent. When dealing with levels of expenditure that exceed $2.7 trillion, every 1 percent change in quantity demanded is as much as $27 billion.

TABLE 5.3 PRICE AND INCOME ELASTICITIES FROM SELECTED STUDIES

Study	Dependent variable	Elasticity
Price elasticities		
Davis and Russell (1972)	Outpatient visits	-1.00
	Hospital admissions	-0.32 to -0.46
Rosett and Huang (1973)	Hospital and physician spending	-0.35 to -1.50
Newhouse and Phelps (1976)	Hospital length of stay	-0.06 to -0.29
	Physicians' office visits	-0.08 to -0.10
Manning et al. (1987)	Overall spending	-0.22
	Hospital care	-0.14
	Preventive care	-0.43
Wedig (1988)	Level of care	-0.16 to -0.23
Eichner (1998)	Medical care	-0.62 to -0.75
Contoyannis et al. (2005)	Pharmaceuticals	-0.12 to -0.16
Income elasticities		
Newhouse (1977)	Per capita medical spending	1.15 to 1.31
Parkin, McGuire, and Yule (1987)	Per capita medical spending	0.80 to 1.57
Gerdtham and Jönsson (1991)	Per capita medical spending	1.24 to 1.43
Moore, Newman, and Fheili (1992)	Short-run per capita spending	0.31 to 0.86
	Long-run per capita spending	1.12 to 3.22
Murray, Govindaraj, and Musgrove (1994)	Total health expenditures	1.43
Manning and Marquis (1996)	Medical expenditures	0.22
Fogel (1999)	Health care expenditures	1.60
Okunade and Murthy (2002)	Per capita real health care spending	1.29 to 1.64
Herwartz and Theilen (2003)	Growth rate per capita health spending	0.74
Dormont et al. (2010)	Per capita health spending	0.75 to 1.59
Acemogln et al. (2013)	Per capita health spending	0.72 to 1.13

luxury or superior good Goods are considered superior if an increase in consumer income causes the percentage of the consumer's income spent on the good to increase and vice versa.

Estimates of the **income elasticity of demand** for medical care vary considerably, depending on whether the relationship being studied is the impact of individual income on personal medical expenditures or national income on aggregate medical expenditures. Research by Newhouse (1977) represents the conventional wisdom on income elasticities using national income and expenditure data. Using data from 13 developed countries, Newhouse found income elasticities to be greater than 1. If this is true, medical care is, at least on the margin, a **luxury or superior good.**[13] When income

---

[13]Income elasticity, defined as $e_m = \dfrac{Percentage\ change\ in\ quantity\ demanded}{Percentage\ change\ in\ income}$, is used to classify goods as inferior or normal, depending on whether it is negative or positive. Economists often classify goods as necessities if $e_M \leq 1$ and luxuries if $e_M > 1$.

POLICY ISSUE

Defining medical care as a necessity or a luxury may depend on whether the issue is being addressed to an individual or a nation.

necessity A good or service with income elasticity between zero and one.

increases, demand increases, and the percentage of income spent on luxury goods also increases.[14] The policy implications are far reaching. If medical care is a luxury good, countries with higher per capita incomes will spend a greater percentage of income on medical care. With little corroborating evidence that countries spending more on medical care have healthier populations, this additional spending on medical care may not improve physical health significantly.

Work by Parkin, McGuire, and Yule (1987) casts doubt on these earlier findings; concluding that the income elasticity of demand for medical care was actually less than 1, making it a **necessity** rather than a luxury good. However, their work does support the conclusion that income elasticities are greater when estimated across countries than when they are estimated across individuals within the same country. Gerdtham and Jönsson (1991) and Moore, Newman, and Fheili (1992) responded to the criticisms of Parkin, McGuire, and Yule. Using alternative models with different functional forms, and alternative ways of converting currencies to dollars, they concluded that the income elasticity of demand for medical care is greater than one, at least in the long run. More recently, Murray, Govindaraj, and Musgrove (1994) and Okunade and Murthy (2002) have calculated income elasticities that ranged from 1.29 to 1.64, indicating that when GDP (or per capita GDP) increases by 1 percent, health expenditures increase anywhere from 1.29 to 1.64 percent, implying that medical care is a luxury good.

Nyman (1999) provides an argument for income elasticity estimates significantly greater than those coming from the original RAND study and other studies that provide income elasticity estimates less than 1 (Manning and Marquis, 1996). According to his argument, the availability of health insurance provides an income transfer from those who are healthy to those who are ill. Reasonable estimates of this income effect could result in income elasticity estimates many times larger than the low estimates, even on the individual level. More remains to be done on this issue.

---

[14]Define the percentage of income (M) spent on good X as $P_X Q_X/M$. The issue being addressed is what happens to this percentage when there is a change in income (ΔM). If the percentage increases, the following ratio will be greater than 1.

$$\frac{\text{Percentage change } \Delta M}{\text{Percentage before } \Delta M} = \frac{P_X(Q_X + \Delta Q_X)}{M + \Delta M} + \frac{P_X Q_X}{M}$$

$$= \frac{P_X(Q_X + \Delta Q_X)}{P_X Q_X} \times \frac{M}{M + \Delta M} \qquad \text{multiply second term by } \frac{\frac{1}{M}}{\frac{1}{M}}$$

$$= [1 + (\Delta Q_X/Q_X)] \times \left[\frac{1}{1 + (\Delta M/M)}\right]$$

$$= \frac{1 + (\Delta Q_X/Q_X)}{1 + (\Delta M/M)} \qquad \text{multiply by } \frac{\frac{M}{\Delta M}}{\frac{M}{\Delta M}}$$

$$= \frac{\frac{M}{\Delta M} + \left[\frac{\Delta Q_X}{Q_X} \times \frac{M}{\Delta M}\right]}{\frac{M}{\Delta M} + 1} \qquad e_M = \frac{\Delta Q_X}{Q_X} \times \frac{M}{\Delta M}$$

$$= \frac{\frac{M}{\Delta M} + e_M}{\frac{M}{\Delta M} + 1}$$

The value of the ratio depends on the relationship between e_M and one. If $e_M > 1$, the percentage of income spent on good x increases when income increases. If $e_M < 1$, the percentage of income spent on good x decreases when income increases.

The RAND Health Insurance Study   The RAND Corporation conducted the most extensive randomized control trial (RTC) in health insurance from 1974 to 1982.[15] Over that period, approximately 7,000 individuals were randomly placed into one of the 14 separate insurance plans and one health maintenance organization. Some plans had deductibles and others did not. Copayments ranged from 0 to 95 percent. A maximum out-of-pocket outlay was set at 5 to 15 percent of income, up to a maximum of $1,000 per participant. Beyond the stop-loss participants received free care.

A number of studies have used data from the RAND Health Insurance Study, most notably Manning and colleagues (1987). Overall, the results indicate that individual demand responds to cost sharing. Manning's price elasticity estimate was approximately −0.17 when comparing individuals receiving free care with those paying a 25 percent coinsurance rate. Over the coinsurance range of 25 percent to 95 percent, the overall price elasticity of demand was estimated at −0.22, ranging from −0.14 for hospital care to −0.43 for preventive care. For those provided with free medical care, demand was about 45 percent higher than for those who had to pay 95 percent coinsurance. Plans providing free care had 23 percent higher spending relative to those with a 25 percent coinsurance. Finally, once admitted to the hospital, the type of plan had little effect on the level of spending.

From these results, it may be concluded that changes in out-of-pocket spending explain a small but significant portion of the overall change in medical care spending. Changes in deductibles and coinsurance can have an effect on the overall quantity of medical services demanded. Increasing the out-of-pocket spending required of individuals will have a dampening effect on medical care spending, with the notable exception of hospital spending once a person is admitted to the hospital. For most participants, assignment of plan had no measurable effect on health.

Summary and Conclusions

The demand for medical care is derived from the individual's desire for good health. Accessing medical care is only one of a number of ways that individuals can improve their health. In fact, when the other factors are taken into consideration, the marginal contribution of medical care is relatively small. The contribution of environmental, lifestyle, and genetic factors weighs heavily in determining overall health.

Individual patient factors play a key role in determining the demand for medical care. These patient factors include health and demographic characteristics. Seldom do individuals seek medical care unless there is at least a perceived illness. Age, race, and sex are also important contributors to medical care demand. Even though these patient factors are important, policy makers are more interested in economic factors that affect demand.

Individual incomes, the level of out-of-pocket spending, and the availability of medical insurance are more easily manipulated and thus studied more intensively.

The physician–patient relationship has been the subject of a number of studies. The dual role of the physician as adviser to the patient and provider of services places physicians in a unique position to influence demand for their services.

Empirical research on the demand for medical care has taught us a great deal:

- *Demand seems to be relatively insensitive to price changes, usually the result of changes in coinsurance rates. Even a modest coinsurance requirement from zero to 20 percent will reduce demand significantly.*

---

[15]Even though RAND did not totally eliminate self-selection in its experimental design, self-selection was reduced by making it costly for individuals to choose alternate plans.

[16]The case of preventive care is of course the major exception to this statement. Even with preventive care, however, the patient is attempting to avoid an illness.

■ *While individual income elasticities are low, probably less than 1, at the aggregate level they tend
to be higher, or somewhat greater than 1. In other
words, medical care may be treated as a necessity
good at the individual level and, at the same time,
as a luxury good at the national level.*

The most important lesson of this chapter may be
that economic incentives do matter in determining the
demand for medical care. Therefore, we must be careful
how we use incentives. In all fairness, we do not want
to exclude the sick and poor from medically necessary
care simply because they cannot afford to pay for it.

Questions and Problems

1. According to studies undertaken by the U.S.
Department of Agriculture, the price elasticity of
demand for cigarettes is between –0.3 and –0.4 and
the income elasticity is about +0.5.
   a. Suppose Congress, influenced by studies linking cigarette smoking to cancer, plans to raise
   the excise tax on cigarettes so the price rises
   by 10 percent. Estimate the effect the price
   increase will have on cigarette consumption and
   consumer spending on cigarettes (in percentage
   terms).
   b. Suppose a major brokerage firm advised its clients to buy cigarette stocks under the assumption that, if consumer incomes rise by 50
   percent as expected over the next decade, cigarette sales would double. What is your reaction
   to this investment advice?
2. In what ways is medical care different from other
commodities? In what ways is it the same?
3. If a wealthy person chooses to spend large sums of
money to increase the probability of surviving an
ordinarily fatal disease, should the rest of society
object? Explain.
4. It is difficult to argue against the scientific merit
of medical discoveries such as treatments for cancer or AIDS. Is scientific merit alone sufficient to
determine the rational allocation of medical funds
in such high-cost cases? What other kinds of information are relevant?
5. What does it mean to be on the "flat of the curve" in
health care provision? Why do some argue that the
United States is on the flat of the curve? Why is this
phenomenon not an issue in a developing country?
6. "Estimating a model of health care demand by the
individual patient is a futile exercise, because physicians determine what their patients use." Comment.
7. Does the model of a utility-maximizing consumer
have any application in medicine?
8. In what sense is health care an investment? In what
sense is it pure consumption?

9. Some argue that the price elasticity of demand
can be used to determine whether a good or service is a luxury or a necessity. In medical care, a
procedure with an elastic demand would be considered optional, or elective, and a procedure with
an inelastic demand would be a medical necessity.
Should planners use price elasticity of demand as a
guide to defining services that are medically necessary? What are the advantages of such a classification scheme? What are the drawbacks?
10. The stated premise behind the production function for health is that medical care, when combined
with other inputs and a person's own time, produces good health. What is the marginal contribution of medical care to the production of health in
the United States? Will spending more money on
medical care improve the health of Americans, or is
there another strategy that would work better? How
would your answer change if you were studying
health in a less-developed country?
11. Visit the website of the National Center for Health
Statistics. Spend some time studying the leading
causes of death for different age groups at *www.cdc.
gov/nchs/data/nvsr/nvsr56/nvsr56_05.pdf. What are
the three leading causes of death for each age cohort
listed? What are some of the policy implications?*
12. What has been the role of public health measures
in improving the health status of the population?
How can a less-developed country spend its limited health budget to maximize health outcomes?
Should policy makers concentrate on expanding
medical resources or focus on improving the water
supply and wastewater removal?
13. Demand studies in health care have provided estimates of both income and price elasticity. Estimates
of income elasticity are usually above +1.0 and
estimates of price elasticity typically range between
–0.1 and –0.75 (with hospital services at the lower
end and elective services at the upper end). What is
the significance of these estimates to policy makers?

PROFILE Paul J. Feldstein

"Health legislation arises from individuals, groups, and legislators acting in their own self-interest—usually economic self-interest." This statement by Paul J. Feldstein on the jacket of his book *The Politics of Health Legislation: An Economic Perspective* (Health Administration Press, 1996) stands in sharp contrast to the common notion that altruism and concern for the indigent are the driving forces behind the health care reform movement. It should come as no surprise that Feldstein would make this statement; it is a sentiment he shares with hundreds of other graduates of one of the most prestigious economics departments in the country, the University of Chicago.

After finishing his Ph.D. in 1961, Feldstein spent the first three years of his professional career as director of research for the American Hospital Association. He then joined the faculty at the University of Michigan. In 1987, he moved to the University of California at Irvine, where he is currently Professor and Robert Gumbiner Chair in Health Care management.

Feldstein has served as principal investigator on dozens of research grants, many funded by the Robert Wood Johnson Foundation. During several academic leaves of absence, he has served as a consultant with the Office of Management and Budget, the Social Security Administration, the World Health Organization, and the National Bureau of Economic Research. He regularly serves as an expert witness in legal cases involving health care antitrust issues.

Author of numerous books, journal articles, and book chapters on health care issues, Feldstein's current research focuses on the cost-containment strategies used by insurance companies. He has had a profound influence on thousands of students in health economics worldwide, primarily through his book *Health Care Economics*, (Delmar Publishers, 2011). First published in 1973, and now in its seventh edition (and translated into Chinese in 2004), this book has been required reading for over four decades for an entire generation of health economics students.

References

Acemogln, Daron, et al., "Income and Health Spending: Evidence from Oil Price Shocks," *Review of Economics and Statistics* 95(4), October 2013, 1079–1095.

Allison, David B., Kevin R. Fontaine, JoAnn E. Manson, June Stevens, and Theodore B. Van Itallie, "Annual Deaths Attributable to Obesity in the United States," *Journal of the American Medical Association* 282(16), October 27, 1999, 1530–1538.

Becker, Gary S., *Human Capital: A Theoretical and Empirical Analysis, with Special Reference to Education*, New York: Columbia University Press, 1964.

Brennan, Troyen A., "An Empirical Analysis of Accidents and Accident Law: The Case of Medical Malpractice Law," *St. Louis University Law Journal* 36, Summer 1992, 823–878.

Broome, John, "Good, Fairness, and QALYs," in J. M. Bell and Susan Mendus, eds., *Philosophy and Medical Welfare*, New York: Cambridge University Press, 1988, 57–73.

Contoyannis, Paul, et al., "Estimating the Price Elasticity of Demand for Prescription Drugs in the Presence of Non-Linear Price Schedules: An Illustration from Quebec, Canada," *Health Economics* 14(9), 2005, 909–923.

Culyer, Anthony J., "Commodities, Characteristics of Commodities, Characteristics of People, Utilities, and the Quality of Life," in S. Baldwin, C. Godfrey, and C. Propper, eds., *Quality of Life: Perspectives and Policy*, London and New York: Routledge, 1990, 9–27.

Cutler, David M., et al., "Why Have Americans Become More Obese?" NBER Working Paper No. 9446, Cambridge, MA: National Bureau of Economic Research, January 2003.

Davis, Karen and Louise B. Russell, "The Substitution of Hospital Outpatient Care for Inpatient Care," *Review of Economics and Statistics* 54(2), May 1972, 109–120.

Donabedian, A., *Benefits in Medical Care Programs*, Cambridge, MA: Harvard University Press, 1976.

Dormont, Brigitte, et al., "Health Expenditures, Longevity, and Growth," in *Ageing, Health, and Productivity*, P. Garibaldi et al., eds., Oxford, England: Oxford University Press, 2010.

Druss, Benjamin G., et al., "The Most Expensive Medical Conditions in America," *Health Affairs* 21(4), July/August 2002, 105–111.

Druss, Benjamin G., et al., "Comparing the National Economic Burden of Five Chronic Conditions," *Health Affairs* 20(6), November/December 2001, 233–241.

Eichner, Matthew J., "The Demand for Medical Care: What People Pay Does Matter," *American Economic Review Papers and Proceedings* 88(2), May 1998, 117–121.

Enthoven, Alain C., *Health Plan*, Reading, MA: Addison-Wesley, 1980.

Fogel, Robert W., "Catching Up with the Economy," *American Economic Review* 89(1), March 1999, 1–21.

Fuchs, Victor R., "Time Preference and Health: An Exploratory Study," in Fuchs, Victor R., ed., *Economics Aspects of Health*, Chicago: University of Chicago Press, 1982, 93–120.

Fuchs, Victor R. and Marcia J. Kramer, "Determinants of Expenditures for Physicians' Services," in Victor R. Fuchs, ed., *The Health Economy*, Cambridge, MA: Harvard University Press, 1986, 67–107.

Gerdtham, Ulf-G and Bengt Jönsson, "Conversion Factor Instability in International Comparisons of Health Care Expenditure," *Journal of Health Economics* 10(2), July 1991, 227–234.

Grossman, Michael, "On the Concept of Health Capital and the Demand for Health," *Journal of Political Economy* 80(2), March/April 1972, 223–255.

Guralnik, Jack M., Kenneth C. Land, Dan Blazer, Gerda G. Fillenbaum, and Laurence G. Branch, "Educational Status and Active Life Expectancy among Older Blacks and Whites," *The New England Journal of Medicine* 329(2), July 8, 1993, 110–116.

Herwartz, Helmut and Bernd Theilen, "The Determinants of Health Care Expenditures: Testing Pooling Restrictions in Small Samples," *Health Economics* 12(2), February 2003, 113–124.

Intriligator, Michael D., "Major Policy Issues in the Economics of Health Care in the United States," in J. van der Gaag and M. Perlman, eds., *Health, Economics, and Health Economics*, Amsterdam: North Holland Publishing, 1981.

Joyce, Geoffrey F., Emmett B. Keeler, Baoping Shang, and Dana P. Goldman, "The Lifetime Burden of Chronic Disease among the Elderly," *Health Affairs*–Web Exclusive, September 26, 2005, W5-R18-R29.

Kohn, Linda T., Janet M. Corrigan, and Molla S. Donaldson, *To Err Is Human: Building a Safer Health System*, Washington, DC: National Academy Press, 1999.

Lockwood, M., "Quality of Life and Resource Allocation," in J. M. Bell and S. Mendus, eds., *Philosophy and Medical Welfare*, New York: Cambridge University Press, 1988, 33–56.

Loomes, G. and L. McKenzie, "The Scope and Limitations of QALY Measures," in S. Baldwin, C. Godfrey, and C. Propper, eds., *Quality of Life: Perspectives and Policy*, London and New York: Routledge, 1990, 84–102.

Manning, Willard G. and Melinda S. Marquis, "Health Insurance: The Trade-Off between Risk Pooling and Moral Hazard," *Journal of Health Economics* 15, 1996, 609–640.

Manning, Willard G. et al., "Health Insurance and the Demand for Medical Care: Evidence from a Randomized Experiment," *American Economic Review* 77(3), June 1987, 251–277.

Marra, Biancarlo and C. Richard Boland, "Hereditary Nonpolyposis Colorectal Cancer: The Syndrome, the Genes, and Historical Perspectives," *Journal of the National Cancer Institute* 87(15), August 1995, 1114–1125.

McKeown, Thomas, *The Rise of Modern Population*, New York: Academic Press, 1976.

Mincer, Jacob, *Schooling, Experience, and Earnings*, New York: National Bureau of Economic Research, 1974.

Moore, William J., Robert J. Newman, and Mohammad Fheili, "Measuring the Relationship between Income and NHEs," *Health Care Financing Review* 14(1), Fall 1992, 133–139.

Murray, C. J. L., R. Govindaraj, and P. Musgrove, "National Health Expenditures: A Global Analysis," *Bulletin of the World Health Organization* 72(4), 1994, 533–692.

Mushkin, Selma J., "Health as an Investment," *Journal of Political Economy* 70(5, part 2), October 1962, 129–157.

Needleman, H. L. and D. Bellinger, "Low-Level Lead Exposure and the IQ of Children: A Meta-Analysis of Modern Studies," *Journal of the American Medical Association* 263(5), February 2, 1990, 673–678.

Newhouse, Joseph P., "Insurance Benefits, Out-of-Pocket Payments, and the Demand for Medical Care: A Review of the Recent Literature," *Health and Medical Care Services Review* 1(4), July/August 1978, 1–15.

Newhouse, Joseph P., "Medical Care Expenditure: A Cross-National Survey," *Journal of Human Resources* 12(1), Winter 1977, 115–125.

Newhouse, Joseph P. and Charles E. Phelps, "New Estimates of Price and Income Elasticities of Medical Care Services," in R. N. Rosett, ed., *The Role of Health Insurance in the Health Services Sector*, New York: National Bureau of Economic Research, 1976, 261–312.

Newhouse, Joseph P. and Lindy J. Friedlander, "The Relationship between Medical Resources and Measures of Health: Some Additional Evidence," *Journal of Human Resources* 15(2), Spring 1980, 200–218.

Newhouse, Joseph P. and the Insurance Experiment Group, *Free for All? Lessons from the RAND Health Insurance Experiment*, Cambridge MA: Harvard University Press, 1993.

Nyman, John A., "The Economics of Moral Hazard Revisited," *Journal of Health Economics* 18, 1999, 811–824.

Okunade, Albert A. and Vasudeva N. R. Murthy, "Technology as a 'Major Driver' of Health Care Costs: A Cointegration Analysis of the Newhouse Conjecture," *Journal of Health Economics* 21, 2002, 147–159.

Pappas, Gregory, Susan Queen, Wilbur Hadden, and Gail Fisher, "The Increasing Disparity in Mortality between Socioeconomic Groups in the United States, 1960 and 1986," *New England Journal of Medicine* 329(2), July 8, 1993, 103–109.

Parkin, David, Alistair McGuire, and Brian Yule, "Aggregate Health Care Expenditures and National Income," *Journal of Health Economics* 6(2), June 1987, 109–127.

Pauly, Mark V., "Is Medical Care Different? Old Questions, New Answers," *Journal of Health Politics, Policy and Law* 13(2), Summer 1988, 227–237.

Reinhardt, Uwe, "The Theory of Physician-Induced Demand: Reflections after a Decade," *Journal of Health Economics* 4(2), June 1985, 190–193.

Rogan, W. J., Beth C. Gladen, James D. McKinney, Nancy Carreras, Pam Hardy, James Thullen, Jon Tingelstad, and Mary Tully, "Polychlorinated Biphenyls (PCBs) and Dichlorodiphenyl Dichlor-Ethene (DDE) in Human Milk: Effects of Maternal Factors and Previous Lactation," *American Journal of Public Health* 76(2), February 1986, 172–177.

Rosett, Richard N. and Lien-fu Huang, "The Effect of Health Insurance on the Demand for Medical Care," *Journal of Political Economy* 81(2), March/April 1973, 281–305.

Shannon, M. W. and J. W. Graef, "Lead Intoxication in Infancy," *Pediatrics* 89(1), January 1992, 87–90.

Sindelar, Jody L., "Differential Use of Medical Care by Sex," *Journal of Political Economy* 90(5), October 1982, 1003–1009.

Somers, Anne R., "The Changing Demand for Health Services: A Historical Perspective and Some Thoughts for the Future," *Inquiry* 23(1), Winter 1986, 395–402.

Wedig, Gerald J., "Health Status and the Demand for Health: Results on Price Elasticities," *Journal of Health Economics* 7(2), June 1988, 151–163.

Weisbrod, Burton A., "The Health Care Quadrilemma: An Essay on Technological Change, Insurance, Quality of Care, and Cost Containment," *Journal of Economic Literature* 29(2), June 1991, 523–552.

Wessel, David, "We're Not Too Fat, It's Technology's Fault," *Wall Street Journal*, February 12, 2003, A2.

Woods, Robert and P. R. Andrew Hinde, "Mortality in Victorian England: Models and Patterns," *Journal of Interdisciplinary History* 18(1), Summer 1987, 27–54.

CHAPTER 6

Population Health

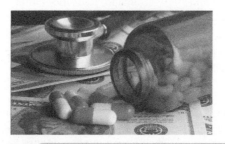

SUPERSIZE MINE

Obesity rates in the United States have been rising for the past five decades. Over one-third of the adult population is considered clinically obese (with a body mass index [BMI] greater than 30). Medical concerns stem from the increased risk of acquiring obesity-related illnesses such as type 2 diabetes, sleep apnea, hypertension, myocardial infarction, stroke, gallstones, gout, cancer, osteoarthritis, asthma, and acid reflux (Dixon, 2010).

Policy makers approach the problem by examining the association of obesity with medical care costs. Finkelstein et al. (2009) estimated that average medical spending among individuals with obesity-related diseases was $1,429 higher (41.5 percent more) than spending for the average healthy person. Generalizing to the entire population the aggregate medical spending associated with obesity-related diseases may be as much as $86 billion or 9.1 percent of total spending. Using more advanced modeling techniques Cawley and Meyerhoefer (2012) found that average obesity-related medical care spending was approximately twice the Finkelstein et al. (2009) estimate, or $3,115, which translates into an aggregate cost of $186 billion (16.5 percent of medical spending in 2008).

Alarmed at the growing obesity-related epidemic, public health officials suggest "common-sense" solutions to the problem, including taxes on fast foods and soda. Conventional wisdom accepts the argument that fast-food restaurants and sugared drinks are making Americans fat and the only way to fight the cause is to regulate and tax. Los Angeles City Council in 2008 approved a ban on new fast-food restaurants in 32 square miles of the city. New York and Seattle mandate that all chain restaurants with over 20 outlets must post nutrition information prominently in their establishments. State and federal policy makers are seriously discussing taxing nutritively sweetened beverages to combat the problem. Do these kinds of measures work? Will additional regulation lower the rate of obesity among Americans?

Anderson and Matsa (2010) challenge the conventional wisdom by examining whether fast-food restaurants are making Americans fat. Two possibilities guide their thinking. First, individuals consume more calories when they eat out and obese individuals may simply eat out more often. Thus, the correlation between eating out and obesity merely reflects consumer preferences. Second, individuals who consume more restaurant calories may offset the additional intake by eating less during the rest of the day. Studying two groups of people with different access to restaurants (one group living closer to fast-food restaurants than the other), they conclude that the group that eats more at restaurants compensates by limiting their caloric intake throughout the rest of the day.

Even though fast-food restaurants provide large portions with more calories at low prices, they are only one of the many sources of calories for obese individuals. A fast-food tax (or a soda tax) would merely result in these individuals finding substitutes, a different way to satisfy their preferences for their desired caloric intake.

Sources: John B. Dixon, "The Effects of Obesity on Health Outcomes," *Molecular and Cellular Endocrinology* 316, 2010, 104–108; Eric A. Finkelstein et al., "Annual Medical Spending Attributable to Obesity: Payer- and Service-Specific Estimates," *Health Affairs* Web Exclusive, July 27, 2009, W822–W831; John Cawley and Chad Meyerhoefer, "The Medical Care Costs of Obesity: An Instrumental Variables Approach," *Journal of Health Economics* 31(1), January 2012, 219–230; and Michael L. Anderson and David A. Matsa, "Restaurants, Regulation, and the Supersizing of America," *Regulation*, Fall 2010, 40–47.

Researchers, medical practitioners, and policy makers are all talking about population health. The concept is not new, but the crescendo has been fueled by the progressive movement that values group outcomes over individual achievements and results. Kindig and Stoddart (2003) are typically credited with the first formal attempt to define the term. They write that *population health* refers to "health outcomes of a group of individuals, including the distribution of such outcomes within the group." The concept has attracted more attention over the past two decades in Canada and Britain where policy makers began using it as a framework for studying outcome disparities among population groups (Young, 2005).

The World Health Organization (WHO) made use of this approach in their report ranking world health systems. The index developed in this report measured overall system performance based on four composite indicators measuring health, health disparities, system responsiveness, and fairness. Disability-adjusted life expectancy (DALE) was used to measure health, and disparities in DALEs were used to measure health inequality across groups (WHO, 2000). That next year, the Institute of Medicine released a report detailing the six dimensions of the patient experience: safety, effectiveness, timeliness, efficiency, equity, and patient centeredness, fully defining the patient experience that has become a critical component of how we evaluate the responsiveness of the health care delivery system as we know it today (IOM, 2001).

America's attention on population health was stimulated by the pioneering work of Porter and Teisberg (2006) who wrote about the concept of value in health care delivery. Simply speaking, they defined and measured value by health outcomes per dollar spent. The concept is not that much different from economic concepts already discussed: technical efficiency and cost-effectiveness. The focus on individual treatments or procedures was expanded to emphasize value in terms of the entire system; total population health relative to health care spending.

Not long after Porter and Teisberg published their contribution to the value discussion, Berwick, Nolan, and Whittington (2008) advanced the discussion by emphasizing the three elements that now define population health: the level of health of a well-defined population, the experience of care for members of that population, and the per capita cost of providing that care. These three dimensions of health care delivery are known as the "triple aim."

The passage of the Affordable Care Act (ACA) shifted the emphasis from treating the individual to managing the health of populations within delivery systems, such as health plans, medical homes, and accountable care organizations (ACO). With this added accountability, providers have expanded their perspective to include a broad array of confounding factors once considered outside the purview of health care delivery, namely, socioeconomic and environmental factors. Socioeconomic factors include income, wealth, education, employment, and social support. The environmental factors include urban design, food access, clean air and water, safety, and culture.

Individual determinants of health are still important and must not be ignored. They include genetic endowment, behavioral characteristics, physiological factors, spiritual health, and resilience. Clinicians have always been concerned with certain behavioral characteristics such as smoking, alcohol consumption, exercise, and diet and how they impact the health of their patients. Physiological factors such as hypertension, BMI, cholesterol levels, and blood glucose levels, markers for cardiovascular disease (CVD), cancer, and diabetes are included. With an overall policy goal of reducing disparities in outcomes and unequal access to care, delivery is taking on a clearly holistic focus.

As the emphasis shifts from the health of the individual to the health of the population, care should be taken that the needs of the individual are not sacrificed for the needs of the group. The mathematics of population health requires that we measure averages: average blood pressure, average cholesterol levels, and average blood glucose levels (Baicker et al., 2013). A focus on averages, however, can drive resource allocation decisions leading to our spending more money on preventive care to improve the health of the majority at the expense of specialty care at the expense of the acutely ill.

As we see, all these measures taken together underscore the importance of taking an analytical framework for examining population health. Measurement is a critical first step in understanding the relationship between inputs and outcomes. We must first have a firm understanding of the processes involved in improving population health. Only then can we go about the task of setting priorities and recommending policies to improve health and its distribution without harming certain vulnerable populations, namely, the seriously ill and elderly.

In this chapter, we will examine the analytics of population health by examining its basic dimensions. Using U.S. data, we will look at health outcomes and their disparities among certain ethnic groups. In turn, we will examine mortality measures, causes of death, and morbidity. The confounding risk factors associated with the socioeconomics and the physical environment will be discussed, followed by the individual risk factors. Finally, we will place U.S. health care experience in an international context, comparing these population health metrics with six developed countries across the world.

Health Outcomes

The most popular metrics used to evaluate population-based health outcomes are either mortality measures or morbidity measures. Despite their widespread acceptance, each has its drawbacks that policy makers should understand and consider.

Mortality Factors   There are many mortality measures that could be used; the most common indicator of health outcomes is life expectancy. Life expectancy provides a simple, but flawed, measure of well-being and often interpreted as a reflection of the quality and efficiency of a country's health care system.

Overall, life expectancy at birth has grown steadily over time. In 2001, life expectancy for the total population was 77.2 years, increasing 1.5 years to 78.7 in 2011. Over that decade, the gap between male and female life expectancy narrowed from 5.4 years to 4.8. While the story is the same for the white and black populations, blacks have experienced an increase in life expectancy that is more than two times that of whites. Still the racial gap is substantial with white life expectancy at 79.0 years and black life expectancy at 75.3 years. Of the three ethnic groups, Hispanics actually have the highest life expectancy at 81.4 years. The life expectancy gap between men and women remains significant at 4.8 years. Whites and Hispanics have similar gaps, 4.7 and 4.8 years. Black women live on

TABLE 6.1 MORTALITY OUTCOMES

2011	Total	White	Black	Hispanic
Life expectancy (years)				
At birth	78.7	79.0	75.3	81.4
Male	76.3	76.6	72.2	78.8
Female	81.1	81.3	78.2	83.7
At age 45	36.0	36.1	33.6	38.2
Male	34.0	34.2	31.1	36.0
Female	37.8	37.9	35.7	39.9
Causes of mortality (per 100,000)				
Coronary heart disease	116.1	117.7	141.3	86.5
Stroke	38.9	37.8	55.7	29.5
Drug induced	13.1	16.6	8.9	5.5
Homicides	5.5	2.6	19.9	6.6
Males (15–29 years old)	11.2	4.3	75.3	22.7
Motor vehicle accidents	11.7	12.1	12.0	10.4
Suicides	12.0	15.2	5.2	5.3
Infant mortality rate (per 1,000 live births)	6.6	5.5	12.7	5.6

Source: CDC (2013).

http://
The CDC provides health information and links to publications and statistics on disease prevention and control. Links are also available *to Mortality and Morbidity Weekly Report* and the journal *Emerging Infectious Diseases.* http://www.cdc.gov.

average 6.0 years longer than their male counterparts. By age 45 the gap between white and black life expectancy narrows, as do differences between men and women.

Causes of mortality tell an interesting story about the relative risks of death across ethnic groups. Whites are much more likely to die from drug-induced causes and suicide than either blacks or Hispanics. In contrast, blacks have a higher risk of coronary heart disease, stroke, and homicides. Of the seven categories listed in Table 6.1, Hispanics have the lowest risk of death in four.

A second measure of the overall effectiveness of a health care system is infant mortality. While the rate has steadily fallen over the past several decades, it is still stubbornly high by international standards, 6.6 per 1,000 live births in 2011. White and Hispanic rates are lower, 5.5 and 5.6, respectively, but black rates are over two times higher at 12.7. More will be discussed about this issue later in this chapter.

ISSUES IN MEDICAL CARE DELIVERY

THE INCOME/HEALTH GRADIENT

The evidence is strong and persistent, across time and across countries that a relationship exists between income and health outcomes. There is also a belief that health resources are more equitably distributed in those countries with a government-run system; and because personal financial resources do not determine access in those countries, health outcomes would be more equitably distributed. Many researchers have examined this issue, but most have not had the data required to estimate the health/income gradient at the individual level.

The usual results show a much steeper health-income gradient in the United States than in the comparison country. The greater variance in income in the United States biases the results when using above- and below-median income comparisons, forcing a steeper gradient on U.S. data.

O'Neill and O'Neill (2007) solve this problem by using Canadian and U.S. data on individuals that incorporate a continuous income variable into the analysis. They regress two health status variables, Health Utility Index and self-reported health status, on income for the two countries separately, and compare. In all of the models estimated, the income/health gradient is significantly steeper in Canada than in the United States. Regardless of the health care system, government-run or market-oriented, the health/income gradient is a reality. Free access to medical care does not translate into equal health outcomes.

Source: June E. O'Neill and Dave M. O'Neill, "Health Status, Health Care and Inequality: Canada vs. the U.S.," *Forum for Health Economics and Policy*, Berkeley Electronic Press 10(1), 2008.

The Relationship between Social Class and Health

Most of the research on health disparities across socioeconomic groups has centered on racial differences in health. There is no question that health disparities exist across race and ethnic groups, as seen in differences in the selected mortality rates in Table 6.2. While race is important in determining health status, there is growing evidence that social class may also play an important role.

Two studies of white-collar, government workers in the United Kingdom, known as the Whitehall studies, document the existence of a social gradient in mortality and morbidity (Marmot et al., 1997; Marmot, Shipley, and Rose, 1984). In both studies, the lower the grade level of the employee group, the higher the mortality rate from most major causes of death. The gradient is not represented by a threshold employment grade. As we move up the grade ladder, each subsequently higher grade has better health outcomes. Two important observations emerge. First, the social gradient is relatively stable over time. Income levels and life expectancy have risen over time in the developed world, but the health disparity remains. Second, the social gradient exists in Britain and most of the rest of the developed world, where there is some form of government-run health care, and in the United States, where there is not (Marmot, 2001).

TABLE 6.2 AGE-ADJUSTED MORTALITY RATES BY SEX AND RACE, SELECTED CAUSES, 2010 DEATHS PER 100,000

	White male	White female	Black male	Black female
Heart disease	222.9	140.4	280.6	185.3
Cerebrovascular	35.8	37.2	56.6	49.6
Cancer	208.2	146.9	264.8	167.1
Breast cancer	–	21.5	–	30.3
HIV	2.3	0.5	16.5	7.5
Homicide	4.7	1.8	31.5	5.0
Suicide	22.0	5.6	9.1	1.8
Diabetes prevalence (%)	9.5		19.6	
Obesity prevalence (%)	34.1	32.5	38.3	54.0

Source: National Center for Health Statistics, *Health, United States, 2012: With Special Feature on Emergency Care*, Hyattsville, MD: National Center for Health Statistics, 2013.

> ## APPLIED MICRO METHODS

DOES MORE INCOME LEAD TO LONGER LIFE EXPECTANCY?

Background

Substantial empirical evidence exists indicating that income and life expectancy are positively correlated with one another. In fact, at every stage of the life cycle health is associated with various measures of socioeconomic status (SES) such as income, wealth, education, and occupational status. While the association is clear, the causal link between SES and health (if one even exists) is not well understood.

Data and Methods

Chetty and colleagues (2016) use income data from federal tax records for the period 1999–2014 to examine the relationship between income and life expectancy. Mortality measures obtained from Social Security death records were used with a two-year lag to calculate mortality rates for 2001–2014. Differences in life expectancy were estimated across geographic areas defined by 741 commuting zones across the country. These geographic differences were evaluated correlating life expectancies (adjusted for race and ethnicity) for individuals in the top and bottom income quartiles.

Theories typically used to explain differences in life expectancies across socioeconomic groups were evaluated by correlating life expectancies of individuals in the top and bottom quintiles with local area characteristics. Measures of health behaviors included smoking, obesity, and self-reported exercise in the past 30 days. Access to medical care included the percent of the population uninsured, risk-adjusted per capita Medicare spending, quality of inpatient care (measured by 30-day hospital mortality rates), and the quality of primary and preventive care (measured by the percentage of the population with a routine primary care visit). Income inequality was measured using the Gini coefficient, residential income segregation was measured by using the Reardon rank order index, and social cohesion was estimated with a social capital index.

Several correlates were based on 2000 U.S. Census data: the percentage of the population that was black, local labor market conditions (using the unemployment rate), population change and labor force change between 1980 and 2000, population density, the percentage of the population that were college graduates, and median home values.

Results

The final sample consisted of 1.4 billion person-year observations of individuals between the ages of 40 and 76. Over the period 1999–2014 there were 4.1 million deaths among males and 2.7 million deaths among females. Individuals with higher incomes lived longer across the entire income distribution. For males, those in the top 1 percent of the income distribution had life expectancies of 87.3 years, those in the bottom 1 percent the expectation was 72.7 years (a differential of 14.6 years). For females in the top 1 percent of the distribution, the expected age at death was 88.9 years and those in the bottom 1 percent it was 78.8 years (a differential of 10.1 years). The gap between men and women was 1.6 years for those in the top income bracket and 6.1 years for those in at the bottom.

There was a substantial variation in life expectancies for low-income individuals (bottom 5 percent) across geographic areas and little difference for high-income individuals (top 5 percent). Using 4 major metropolitan areas, New York, San Francisco, Dallas, and Detroit, life expectancies ranged from 72.3 years to 78.6 years for those with low-incomes and 86.5 years to 87.5 years for high-income individuals. However, differences in life expectancy across geographic areas did not correlate with any of the socioeconomic variables that are typically used to explain them (access to medical care, residential segregation, income inequality, social cohesion, or labor market conditions). The differences did correlate with health behaviors (smoking, obesity, and exercise). Other factors were also positively correlated with life expectancy: percentage of the population that were immigrants, median home value, local government expenditures, population density, and the percentage of the population that were college graduates.

Discussion and Conclusions

Life expectancy is correlated with income, and differences in life expectancy across income categories are increasing over time. However, the correlation between life expectancy and income cannot be interpreted as a causal mechanism because income is also correlated with other factors that directly affect health. When these other confounding factors are taken into consideration, the causal impact of income on life expectancy is likely to be significantly smaller than the associated differences identified by this study.

Source: Raj Chetty et al., "The Association between Income and Life Expectancy in the United States, 2001–2014," *Journal of the American Medical Association* 315(16), 2016, 1750–1766.

Health might determine social position to some extent. While it is plausible that unhealthy people migrate to poor neighborhoods, it is unlikely that these migratory patterns are the sole reason for the observed differences. Lifestyle may be important, but that begs the question: Why are there socioeconomic differences in alcohol and tobacco use, physical activity, hypertension, diabetes, cholesterol levels, and obesity? This phenomenon is not simply a matter of one group, largely defined (i.e., the rich), living longer than everyone else (i.e., the poor). The social gradient indicates that everyone is affected. Whatever the causes, people in lower social classes die at younger ages and are more susceptible to whatever diseases are affecting the population.

Morbidity Factors　Morbidity is an intermediate outcome and is used as a measure of the disease burden for major chronic conditions. Expressed as disease prevalence or incidence rates, the term is a basic statistic measuring the percentage of a given population with a particular disease condition or the rate at which members of a group are newly diagnosed with the disease.

Table 6.3 provides disease prevalence information on several intermediate morbidity factors. Health-related quality of life (QOL) measures the self-perceived health status of

TABLE 6.3 MORBIDITY OUTCOMES

2011	Total	White	Black	Hispanic
Quality of life (% fair or poor)	16.1	13.3	23.3	28.1
Prevalence of asthma (%)	8.0	7.9	10.5	5.4/15.9
Prevalence of diagnosed diabetes (%)	7.9	6.8	11.3	11.5
Prevalence of periodontitis (%)	47.2	42.6	58.6	59.7
Tuberculosis rate (per 100,000)	3.6	0.9	7.0	6.5
HIV rate (per 100,000)				
Male	34.0	16.5	128.4	49.9
Female	8.6	2.2	45.3	10.2
HIV treatment ART (% with HIV)				
Male	89.9	92.5	87.1	90.7
Female	85.8	90.7	84.4	85.2

Source: CDC (2013).

http://

The Centers for Disease Control provides health information and links to publications and statistics on disease prevention and control. Links are also available to Mortality and Morbidity Weekly Report and the journal Emerging Infectious Diseases. http://www.cdc.gov

an individual or group. The Centers for Disease Control and Prevention (CDC) survey asked respondents to rate their general health status on a five-point scale of excellent, very good, good, fair, or poor. Approximately 16 percent of Americans rated their QOL as fair or poor, ranging from 13.3 percent of whites to 23.3 percent of blacks, and 28.1 percent of Hispanics. QOL is associated with younger ages and higher education. Those individuals who rated their QOL as fair or poor typically experienced more physically and mentally unhealthy days on average.

The prevalence of asthma, diagnosed diabetes, and periodontitis follows the same pattern with blacks and Hispanics having about the same prevalence for their respective groups but substantially higher rates than whites. Overall 8.0 percent of the population suffers from asthma, 7.6 percent of adults and 9.0 percent of children. Almost 8 percent of adults over the age of 18 have been diagnosed with diabetes. Almost one-half of all adults over the age of 30 have periodontitis, the largest factor leading to tooth loss.

The rate of tuberculosis (per 100,000) has declined substantially over the last decade and was 3.6 per 100,000 in 2010. The rate among whites is lower (0.9 per 100,000) compared to the rate among blacks (7.0) and Hispanics (6.5). The majority of new tuberculosis cases are in the foreign-born community causing some concern that our immigration policy may contribute to the spread of tuberculosis among the native population.

The prevalence of HIV infection is greatest among gay, bisexual, and other men who have sex with men (MSM). The overall rate is 8.6 per 100,000 for women and 34.0 for men. The rate for MSM is over 10 times higher at 382.6. Black men are eight times more likely to have HIV than white men (128.4 versus 16.5), and black women have 20 times higher prevalence than white women (45.3 versus 2.2). Treatment rates with antiretroviral therapy (ART) are about the same across ethnic groups, ranging from 85 to 90 percent of the affected population.

Confounding Risk Factors   Many argue that to manage population health fully, we need to begin the process further upstream by considering individual behavioral and physiological factors. Others will move further upstream examining the socioeconomic and physical environment.

Individual Behavioral and Physiological Factors   Because of its impact on health outcomes, health-related behavior is also measured by health systems. Table 6.4 provides data on factors relating to risky pregnancies, alcohol consumption, and smoking that are included in assessing risky behaviors.

Teen pregnancy is a concern among public health officials and policy makers because of the associated problems, including low birth weight, preterm deliveries, and the risk of infant mortality. Rates have been trending downward since the early 1990s; they are still high by standards present in the rest of the developed world. The overall pregnancy rate for teens between 15 and 19 years of age was 69.8 in 2011 but was 2–3 times higher among Hispanics and blacks than whites. These pregnancies resulted in 40.2 live births per 1,000 females, 17.8 induced abortions, and 11.8 fetal losses. Again, there were substantial demographic differences in the birth rates, 26.7 among whites, 60.4 among blacks, and 70.3 among Hispanics. Preterm births follow similar patterns with 10.8 percent of births to whites and Hispanics occurring preterm and 17.1 percent for blacks.

The health risks due to drinking and smoking are well documented. Excessive alcohol use is responsible for approximately 40,000 deaths per year. The percentage of the population that admits to binge drinking is 50 percent higher among whites than blacks. Overall,

TABLE 6.4 INDIVIDUAL RISK FACTORS

2011	Total	White	Black	Hispanic
Individual behavioral				
Pregnancy rate, 15- to 19-year-olds (per 1,000 females)	69.8	44.8	121.6	111.5
Birth rate, 15- to 19-year-olds (per 1,000 females)	40.2	26.7	60.4	70.3
Preterm births (% total live births)	12.0	10.8	17.1	10.8
Binge drinking ($\geq$4 in last 30 days, %)	18.4	21.1	14.2	17.7
Smoking prevalence				
12- to 17-year olds	8.6	10.2	5.0	7.7
$\geq$18 years old	24.9	25.8	25.4	22.9
Individual physiological				
Obesity rate, $\geq$18 years old (%)				
Male	33.0	33.0	37.0	35.0
Female	35.0	32.0	53.0	44.0
Hypertension rate (%)	29.6	28.6	41.3	27.7
Treatment for hypertension (% of diagnosed)	48.0	52.6	42.5	34.4

Source: CDC (2013).

almost one in five admit to consuming more than four drinks on an average of 4.1 occasions in the last 30 days. Smoking is the leading cause of preventable disease in the United States. About 25 percent of the adult population are regular smokers. Rates among young teens are twice as high among whites as blacks.

Individual physiological factors contribute substantially to poor health outcomes. Obesity prevalence in the United States is the highest in the developed world and has tripled since the 1960s. Not only is obesity present a serious health risk with links to CVD, cancer, and diabetes, individuals who are obese have higher health care spending than normal weight individuals (see following Applied Micro feature). Overall, the obesity rate is about 33 percent of the adult population with rates among black and Hispanic women reaching 53 and 44 percent, respectively.

http://
Calculate your body mass index. Go to the Centers for Disease Control web site to learn more: http://www.cdc.gov/nccdphp/dnpa/bmi/

APPLIED MICRO METHODS

THE COST OF OBESITY

Background

Over one-third of American adults are clinically obese (BMI > 30). Clinical research associates obesity with a higher risk of acute myocardial infarction (AMI), stroke, type 2 diabetes, cancer, hypertension, osteoarthritis, asthma, and depression. It also follows that many papers have tried to link obesity with increased medical spending. The problem with such research is that they are all observational studies, testing cross-sectional models with large data sets.

These studies share two major shortcomings. First, weight may be endogenous if obesity is due to a medical event (a disabling accident or the onset of depression).

Under these circumstances, the link between obesity and spending overstates the overall impact of obesity on health care spending. Likewise, if individuals with less access to medical care (due to socioeconomic considerations, for example) are also obese, they spend less on all medical care because of their circumstances and the impact of obesity on spending is understated. Obviously, correlation is not causation. In addition, weight is subject to serious reporting error. Most studies use self-reported weight rather than measured weight. Research evidence indicates that survey respondents typically understate their own weight. This reporting error further biases coefficient estimates.

Data and Methods

The obvious solution is to conduct a randomized trial, choosing one group to receive the treatment (gain weight to the point of obesity) and one (the controls) to stay at a normal weight. The ethics of this research approach is somewhat dubious so Cawley and Mayerhoefer (2012) use an alternative approach; estimate the treatment using an instrumental variable (IV) for the weight of the survey respondent. The IV model in this study takes advantage of the strong genetic component for weight and uses the weight of the oldest biological child (aged 11–20 years) as an instrument for the respondent's weight. It is a powerful instrument (with an F-value exceeding the conventional benchmark of 10), is uncorrelated with the respondent's excess medical cost (due to obesity), and is reported more accurately.

The research employs a two-part model, using log it to estimate the probability of any spending on health care and Gamma GLM (generalized OLS with Gamma distributed residuals) to estimate the amount of spending conditional on any spending. Controls used in the estimation are age, sex, race, education, geographic region, household size, employment status, and whether the respondent's weight is self-reported or proxy reported.

Results

The marginal effect on spending of obesity relative to normal weight (estimated from the entire sample of 9,852 males and 13,837 females) was $656 using the conventional approach and $2,741 using the IV approach. In summary, predicted spending using the IV model was $1,763 for nonobese individuals and $4,458 for obese. See the breakdown in the following table.

Sample population	Predicted spending for nonobese	Predicted spending for obese
Total sample	$1,763	$4,458
Men	$1,657	$2,907
Women	$1,928	$5,363
White	$2,026	$4,786
Non-white	$1,144	$3,900
Private insurance	$1,920	$4,393
Medicaid	$2,494	$6,455
Uninsured	$512	$3,271

The IV model passed several falsification tests, confirming the reasonableness of the estimates. The model showed a stronger impact on spending due to diabetes (an obesity-related disease) than conditions unrelated to obesity. Additionally, estimates indicate that the weight of biologically unrelated children was not a significant predictor of the respondent's weight, confirming that there is little connection between a shared household environment and BMI beyond genetics.

Discussion and Conclusions

The causal effect of obesity on health care spending using this IV approach is significantly higher than estimates based on the conventional approach from previous research. Estimated cost of treating obesity-related illness of the sampled population (adults with biological children between ages 11 and 20) was $209.7 billion (in 2008 dollars). The results suggest that health care spending due to obesity makes up 20.6 percent of national health care expenditures, more than twice the estimate of previous research (9.1 percent by Finkelstein et al., 2009).

Sources: John Cawley and Chad Meyerhoefer, "The Medical Care Cost of Obesity: An Instrumental Variables Approach," *Journal of Health Economics* 31, 2012, 219–230; and Eric A. Finkelstein et al., "Actual Medical Spending Attributable to Obesity: Payer- and Service-Specific Estimates," *Health Affairs* 28(5), September/October 2009, W822–W831.

Hypertension is a major risk factor for CVD and stroke. Almost 30 percent of Americans have chronic high blood pressure and less than half of that number are receiving regular treatment for the condition. Blacks have higher rates of hypertension and lower rates of control compared to whites. Hypertension rates are lower among Hispanics, but their rates of treatment are also lower.

Confounding Factors   Health systems must also deal with various environmental factors that make the provision of health even more challenging. The two areas most commonly addressed are socioeconomics and the physical environment.

The most common socioeconomic variable that contributes to health and its delivery is household income. As seen in Table 6.5, median household income was $50,054 in 2011, ranging from $55,412 for households headed by whites to $32,229 in black households. Related factors that contribute to income are similarly distributed. The high school dropout rate is 12.5 percent overall and 7.3 percent for whites. The black dropout rate is over two times higher and the Hispanic rate is five times higher. The unemployment rate is twice as high for blacks and Hispanics than whites, contributing to poverty rates that are one-third higher for blacks and Hispanics as well.

Living and working in a high-risk environment increases the probability of injury or death from exposure to those risks. In 2010, 16.0 percent of all private-sector workers were employed in a high-risk occupation. Men are disproportionately represented in these

TABLE 6.5 CONFOUNDING RISK FACTORS

2011	Total	White	Black	Hispanic
Socioeconomic				
Household income ($)	50,054	55,412	32,229	38,624
High school dropout rate (%)	12.5	7.3	16.1	37.7
Poverty rate (%)	13.3	12.4	16.4	16.0
Unemployment rate (%)	9.4	8.3	16.5	15.8
Physical environment				
Workers in high-risk jobs (%)	–	13.0	20.8	24.4
Fatal occupational injuries (per 100,000)	3.7	3.7	3.5	4.4
Living within 150 meters of major highway (%)	3.7	3.1	4.4	5.0

Source: CDC (2013).

occupations, 21.1 percent versus 8.9 percent for women. Over 25 percent of those individuals with only a high school education are in high-risk jobs. Those with more education have two-thirds that number in high-risk jobs. Only 13 percent of whites, but 20.8 percent of blacks and 24.4 percent of Hispanics, are employed in high-risk jobs. The likelihood of fatal workplace injury is 3.7 percent for the population as a whole, slightly lower for blacks (3.5) and higher for Hispanics (4.4).

Traffic-related air pollution is associated with chronic respiratory illnesses. Epidemiologists have difficulty modeling the interaction of environmental pollutants so they rely on measures such as proximity to major traffic arteries. Using proximity to major highways as a surrogate for exposure provides a measure of the likelihood of exacerbating the effects of asthma and other respiratory illnesses. Approximately, 4 percent of the population lives within 150 meters of a major highway—slightly fewer whites (3.1 percent) and more blacks (4.4) and Hispanics (5.0).

While these comparisons provide insight into the causes of differences in health across ethnic groups, most data sources provide countywide statistics (or information based on small samples). Whereas, providers and policy makers are more interested in data on smaller population groupings (by census tracts or zip codes) to more closely match their patient base. The challenge in managing population health goes beyond the delivery of health care to the relevant patient group. It includes the ability to collect and interpret the appropriate information for a well-defined patient population, information that is not always readily available through published sources.

International Comparisons

KEY CONCEPT 8
Efficiency

By any standard measure, overall spending, per capita spending, and spending as a percentage of gross domestic product (GDP) are far higher in the United States than any other country in the developed world. Using 2013 data provided in Table 6.6, we see that per capita spending in the United States was 38 percent higher than Switzerland's $6,325 and more than double per capita spending in France, Japan, and the United Kingdom. Relative to GDP, the story is much the same with U.S. spending of 16.4 percent almost double what is spent in the United Kingdom.

Is U.S. spending excessive? Many people closely equate price and quality when they purchase various items and do not mind paying more if they are getting higher quality items. Is this the case in health care? Are Americans getting their money's worth? In other words, is the experience of care received in the United States worth the extra spending?

TABLE 6.6 HEALTH CARE SPENDING

2013	Per capita spending[1]	Spending as a percentage of GDP
Canada	4,351	10.2
France	4,124	10.9
Germany	4,819	11.0
Japan	3,713	10.2
Switzerland	6,325	11.1
United Kingdom	3,235	8.5
United States	8,713	16.4

Source: OECD Health Data, 2016.

[1]USD purchasing power parity

Health Outcomes

Researchers and policy makers often refer to life expectancy and infant mortality rate when measuring the value of health care.

Life Expectancy   Using data provided in Table 6.7, the mortality gap between the United States and the rest of the developed world is apparent. Consider life expectancy at birth. Male life expectancy at birth trails Switzerland by 4.3 years and Germany by 2.2. Similarly, the gap in female life expectancy ranges from 1.7 years to 5.4 years. The rankings are largely unchanged at age 65, with the United States still trailing the comparison group.

What do these mortality differences mean? Measuring the gap is one thing. Explaining the gap requires that we look beyond the numbers. Ohsfeldt and Schneider (2006) argue that factors other than the health care system should be considered when making international comparisons of life expectancy. They use a standard regression model to estimate the impact of homicides, suicides, and accidental death (external causes of death) on life expectancy for 29 Organization for Economic Cooperation and Development (OECD) countries for the years 1980–1989. The results of their calculations for our comparison group are shown in Table 6.8.

The United States, with higher death rates from fatal injuries, rises from last to first in life expectancy when the differences in death rates from fatal injuries are omitted. Arguably,

TABLE 6.7 LIFE EXPECTANCY				
2013	Male life expectancy at birth	Female life expectancy at birth	male life expectancy at age 65	Female life expectancy at age 65
Canada[2011]	79.3	83.6	18.8	21.7
France	79.0	85.6	19.3	23.6
Germany	78.6	83.2	18.2	21.1
Japan	80.2	86.6	19.1	24.0
Switzerland	80.7	85.0	19.4	22.4
United Kingdom	79.2	82.9	18.6	20.9
United States	76.4	81.2	17.9	20.5

Source: OECD Health Data, 2016.

TABLE 6.8 LIFE EXPECTANCY AT BIRTH, ACTUAL AND ADJUSTED FOR DEATHS FROM EXTERNAL CAUSES, 1980–1989		
	Actual life expectancy at birth	Adjusted life expectancy at birth
Canada	77.3	76.2
France	76.6	76.0
Germany	75.4	76.1
Japan	78.7	76.0
Switzerland	77.6	76.6
United Kingdom	75.6	75.7
United States	75.3	76.9

Source: Ohsfeldt and Schneider (2006).

Ohsfeldt and Schneider use a relatively simplistic approach to the adjustment, but it does indicate, much like current population health proponents, that there are other factors that affect life expectancy; factors unrelated to the efficiency of the health care system.

This excess mortality from all external causes has a significant impact on the life expectancy of Americans. Lemaire (2005) estimates that in 2000, the U.S. life expectancy of 76.9 years would have been 1.2 years higher without these external causes. That same year, the population-weighted average life expectancy of the 33 richest counties in the world was 79.2 years. Thus, over half of the gap in life expectancy between the United States and the other developed countries of the world was due to external causes of death, primarily motor vehicle accidents and homicide.

Furthermore, focusing on life expectancy at birth fails to consider changes in the differential at later ages. Using life expectancy data from 2013, Table 6.9 compares the expected age at death at various points in the life cycle. Expected age at death provides a clear comparison using life expectancy at birth as the benchmark.

Careful examination of the table shows how changes in the causes of death at early ages affect the expected age at death for individual cohorts at ages 40, 60, and 80. A female living in Germany, for example, can expect to live to age 81.2 at birth and 84.6 if she survives to age 60. Males in the United States can expect to live to age 76.4 at birth and 81.7 at age 60. The gap between expected age at death for American men and women narrows from 4.8 years at birth to 2.9 years by age 60.

For international comparison purposes, we can examine the differences in expected age at death at the various age milestones. At birth the gap between German and American males is 2.2 years with Germans living longer. By age 60 the gap is 0.3 years and by age 80 the difference is 0.2 years. The story is the same for all comparison countries with the gap narrowing substantially as individuals survive beyond these age milestones. The biggest change takes place in the first 40 years of life, primarily because of cross-country differences in infant mortality rates and the incidence of fatal injuries at younger ages.

POLICY ISSUE
Better access to prenatal care will improve birth outcomes. Is free care the answer?

Infant Mortality Rate   Critics of U.S. medical care often cite high infant mortality rates as evidence of a breakdown in the current delivery system. One can make a very compelling argument linking poverty and poor access to care with high mortality rates. In 2012, the United States had the highest infant mortality rate among the seven advanced countries in Table 6.10. At 6.0 deaths per 1,000 live births (sum of the neonatal mortality rate and

TABLE 6.9 EXPECTED AGE AT DEATH, REFERENCE POINTS BIRTH AND AGES 40, 60, AND 80

	At birth		At age 40		At age 60		At age 80	
2013	Male	Female	Male	Female	Male	Female	Male	Female
Canada[2011]	79.3	83.6	80.9	84.6	82.8	86.0	88.9	90.6
France	79.0	85.6	80.4	86.4	83.1	88.0	89.2	91.6
Germany	78.6	83.2	79.7	83.9	82.0	85.3	88.5	89.5
Japan	80.2	86.6	81.3	87.3	83.1	88.5	88.6	91.5
Switzerland	80.7	85.0	81.8	85.7	83.5	86.8	88.6	90.4
United Kingdom	79.2	82.9	80.5	83.8	82.6	85.2	88.5	89.7
United States	76.4	81.2	78.7	82.6	81.7	84.6	88.3	89.7

Source: OECD Health Data, 2016.

TABLE 6.10 INFANT HEALTH

2012	Prenatal mortality rate[1]	Neonatal mortality rate[2]	Postneonatal mortality rate[3]
Canada[2011]	2.4	3.6	1.2
France	9.5	2.4	1.1
Germany[2010]	3.1	2.2	1.1
Japan	1.7	1.0	1.2
Switzerland	3.9	2.9	0.7
United Kingdom	4.1	2.9	1.2
United States	2.1	4.1	1.9

Source: OECD Health Data, 2016.
[1]Deaths (fetal age >28 weeks) per 1,000 live births (perinatal mortality rate minus neonatal mortality rate)
[2]Deaths (birth to 1 month) per 1,000 live births
[3]Deaths (aged 1–12 months) per 1,000 live births (infant mortality rate minus neonatal mortality rate)

the post-neonatal rate), the U.S. rate was twice that of Japan and 25 percent higher than Canada. However, the comparison is not that simple. The causes of infant mortality are complex, multidimensional, and misunderstood.

First, infant mortality reporting is plagued by inconsistencies in the definition of a live birth across countries (Atlas, 2011). The WHO has established a strict definition of a live birth as any infant, regardless of gestational age, that "breathes or shows any other evidence of life." While generally accepted, the WHO definition is not strictly followed in actual birth registration. Many European countries use a definition that takes into consideration gestational age (more than 28 weeks), birth weight (more than 1,000 grams), and length of survival (more than 24 hours).[1] In contrast, the United States strictly follows the WHO reporting guidelines, resulting in higher recorded infant mortality rates and complicating their direct comparison (Kramer et al., 2002). Approximately 40 percent of the differential may be attributed to reporting differences (Chen, Oster, and Williams, 2014). The fact that early deaths make up the majority of infant deaths, underreporting leads to large discrepancies in infant mortality rates across countries. In the United States, one-half of all infant deaths occur in the first 24 hours. A simple reclassification of these deaths from live births to still births would cut the U.S. infant mortality rate in half.

Second, infant mortality rates are much higher among racial and ethnic minorities, at least double that of the majority regardless of country or type of health care system. The racial-ethnic heterogeneity in the United States is far greater than in most western European countries, resulting in an overall higher rate.[2]

Finally, much of the evidence examining the cause of high infant mortality point to the high risk associated with low birth weight. The United States has the second highest rate of low-birth-weight infants with 8.2 percent of all infants born weighing less than 2,500 grams, considered a normal birth weight. Only Japan fares worse than the United States.[2]

---

[1]For example, in Switzerland live births require that the infant be greater than 12 inches in length, in France the babies must have a gestational age of at least 26 weeks, and in Germany babies must weigh at least 500 grams.

[2]Over the last decade, the incidence of low-birth-weight babies has been gradually trending upward in the United States. In 2000, 7.6 percent of all infants born weighed less than 2,500 grams: By race, the figure was 6.6 percent of white infants, 6.4 percent of Hispanic infants, and 13.0 percent of all black infants.

Low birth weight is associated with gestational age at birth. MacDorman and Mathews (2009) estimate that 12.4 percent of all births in the United States are classified as preterm (less than 37 weeks gestation). Preterm births account for 6.3 percent of the births in France, 7.5 percent in the United Kingdom, and 8.9 percent in Germany. Mortality rates for preterm infants are actually lower in the United States than in most countries. For infants born at 22–36 weeks gestation, only the Scandinavian countries of Finland and Sweden have lower mortality rates.

If the United States had the same birth-weight distribution as Sweden, its overall infant mortality rate would fall from 6.2 to 4.1 (MacDorman and Mathews, 2009). Using data from the late 1990s, O'Neill and O'Neill (2007) estimate that the U.S. infant mortality rate would have been 5.4 instead of 6.9 with the birth-weight distribution of Canada (which was actually lower than the Canadian rate of 5.5).

Kramer and colleagues (2005) estimate that the U.S. infant mortality rate for very low-birth-weight babies (those born weighing less than 1,500 grams) was 247.3 (in 1997), over 50 times the rate of 4.8 for infants born weighing more than 2,500 grams. At the same time, the Canadian infant mortality rate for these low-birth-weight babies was 262.2. Even though these very low-birth-weight babies make up only about 1.4 percent of all births, they account for over half of all infant deaths (MacDorman and Atkinson, 1999).

The United States has made great strides in improving the survival of very low-birth-weight infants and has made almost no progress in reducing the incidence of low birth weight. Some critics fault poor access to prenatal care in the United States. Admittedly, there are medical reasons that some women have low-birth-weight babies, but there are also personal reasons related to lifestyle where the medical care system has little impact. Tough, Siever, and Johnston (2007) report results of a randomized trial where pregnant women were offered supplementary prenatal care. Those women who participated in the program had better birth outcomes. Those who did not participate were disproportionately single, had higher incidence of drug use, reported more acute life events, and suffered more distress than those who participated in the program. These are factors related to education, income, and personal behavior.

Another measurement problem is the administrative handling of late fetal deaths (in the last trimester of pregnancy). *Perinatal mortality*, defined as late fetal deaths plus deaths in the first 30 days after birth, provides a slightly different picture of infant health. Because most infant deaths take place in the first 30 days after birth, the definition of what constitutes a live birth is less important when using this metric. The U.S. perinatal mortality rate is 6.2, below those found in France, Switzerland, and the United Kingdom.

An alternative explanation for the high incidence of low birth weight is the high rate of teen pregnancy in the United States (see Table 6.11), a sociological factor strongly correlated with low birth weight and infant mortality. In the United States 7.7 percent of total births are to teenage mothers, almost 10 times higher than the rate in Switzerland. Likewise, the birth rate for teenage mothers is 2–10 times higher than the six comparison countries.

Teen pregnancy and illegitimacy may actually serve as proxy variables for maternal behavior and attitude about the pregnancy.[3] Teen mothers are less likely to receive timely prenatal care and are more likely to smoke cigarettes, leading to inadequate maternal weight gain, lower birth weights, and a higher incidence of preterm births (Ventura, Curtin, and Mathews, 2000). The mortality rate of infants born to teenage mothers is 1.5–3.5 times the rate of infants born to 25- to 29-year-old mothers (Liu, 1992).

---

[3]Early research has shown that "mistimed or unwanted" babies were more likely to be born at low birth weights than those who were planned or "wanted" (Pamuk and Mosher, 1988).

TABLE 6.11 TEEN PREGNANCY		
	Births for women 15–19 years of age (% total births)	Birth rate for women 15–19 years of age (per 1,000 cohort population)
Canada (2009)	4.1	14.1
France (2012)	2.2	9.4
Germany (2013)	2.2	7.8
Japan (2013)	1.3	4.4
Switzerland (2013)	0.8	3.0
United Kingdom (2012)	4.2	17.3
United States (2012)	7.7	29.4

Source: *United Nations Demographic Yearbook,* available at http://unstats.un.org/unsd/demographic/products/dyb/dyb2.htm.

http://

The American Public Health Association provides a multidisciplinary environment of professional exchange, study, and action for those interested in personal and environmental health issues. http://www.apha.org

Other Factors

In this section, we will examine other individual behavioral and physiological factors that further complicate direct international comparisons of these commonly used metrics. The health problems associated with American lifestyles present a serious challenge for the U.S. medical sector. The cost to society can be measured in terms of the obvious health problems, such as heart disease, stroke, cancer, and other chronic conditions, but also in terms of the lost productivity due to disability and premature death. Discussions of relative performance of medical care delivery systems tend to focus on measures of health outcomes, when in truth, health outcomes may be more dependent on factors other than medical care that include lifestyle considerations and the burden of disease.

ISSUES IN MEDICAL CARE DELIVERY

IS ADDICTION RATIONAL?

When does a habit become an addiction? If you enjoy something and practice it regularly, are you addicted? People get addicted to all sorts of things: cigarettes, alcohol, drugs, work, food, sex, music videos, and computer games. Like many other interesting questions concerning human behavior, economists have discovered that the theory of rational choice can tell us a great deal about addictive behavior and the optimal public policy to deal with it.

A paper by Becker and Murphy (1988) influenced the early economic literature on addiction. They show that consumers of addictive goods are rational, meaning that they consistently maximize utility over time, and that the potential for addiction increases if past consumption increases current consumption. Their model is also able to explain the observed instability of consumption that manifests itself in "cold turkey" withdrawal and binge consumption. They also show that people who discount the future more heavily are more likely to become addicts.

This model relies on the premise that individuals recognize the total cost of their addictive behavior, both in terms of the current monetary price of the addictive good and the cost in terms of the future. Within this framework, forward-looking behavior has one problem: It requires individual behavior that is time consistent—in other words, the

KEY CONCEPT 3
Marginal Analysis

individual underestimates the difficulty of quitting or reducing consumption in the future. By failing to accurately estimate the future cost of addiction, the individual consumes too much of the addictive substance. The current self imposes added costs on the future self via mistaken expectations of the ease of quitting. Using the case of cigarette consumption, Gruber and Koszegi (2001) established that forward-looking behavior is not consistent over time. Incorporating time inconsistency into a model with forward-looking behavior, they show that the optimal government policy should take into consideration not only the externalities imposed on others but also the "internalities" imposed on the addict.

☆ **KEY CONCEPT 2**
Opportunity Cost

As interest in regulating addictive behavior grows, we have seen increased taxation, increased regulation of public consumption, and a rash of litigation against the tobacco industry. Using standard values for average age and life expectancy, Gruber and Koszegi estimate that an extra year at the end of a worker's life is worth almost $100,000. Since the typical smoker dies 6.1 years prematurely, the cost of smoking a pack of cigarettes in terms of life-years lost is $30.45. Thus, the internal costs are over 10 times the external costs. Policy conclusions based on the research are a significant departure from those based on the earlier model. Even if the government only considers a small portion of the internal costs in establishing tax policy, one can make a strong case for a substantial increase in the current federal excise tax of $1.01 per pack. Even if the external costs are also considered—secondhand smoke estimated at 19–70 cents per pack and the long-run costs of low birth weight due to maternal smoking estimated at 42–70 cents per pack—the internal costs still dwarf the calculation. This line of research has important implications for other forms of addictive behavior, in particular illegal drugs.

Sources: Gary S. Becker and Kevin M. Murphy, "A Theory of Rational Addiction," *Journal of Political Economy* 96(4), August 1988, 675–700; and Jonathan Gruber and Botond Koszegi, "Is Addiction 'Rational'? Theory and Evidence," *Quarterly Journal of Economics* 116(4), November 2001, 1261–1303.

Tobacco Use

The CDC estimates show that between 1997 and 2001, the health-related economic costs associated with tobacco use averaged $75 billion in direct medical costs per year and over $90 billion in lost productivity. Approximately 21 percent of the states' medical budgets and 14 percent of all Medicaid expenditures were related to tobacco use (CDC, 2005). Even though the economic cost has been staggering, any dollar amount reported pales in comparison to the toll in human suffering. It is estimated that over 440,000 deaths are attributable to tobacco use annually. When added to the 80,000 who die because of alcohol abuse, the total comes to over 520,000 premature deaths each year from these two substances alone. Based on past and current smoking patterns, 25 million Americans alive today will die prematurely from smoking. On average, smokers cut 10 years off their life expectancies due to the habit.

☆ **KEY CONCEPT 6**
Supply and Demand

Smoking patterns in the countries listed in Table 6.12 are similar with the United States being the outlier in terms of percentage smokers. The percentage of males who smoke exceeds 20 percent in most countries. Only Canada and the United States have fewer. In general, more males smoke than females, and in the case of Japan, the gap is 25 percentage points. Current smoking patterns are different today than in the 1980s when the United States had the highest percentage of adult, male smokers among these comparison countries; a factor reflected in the current high death rates among older Americans from smoking-related diseases.

TABLE 6.12 TOBACCO AND ALCOHOL USE

2013	Tobacco use (% age 15+ who smoke, males) 2009	Tobacco use (% age 15+ who smoke, females)	Alcohol consumption (liters per capita)
Canada	16.9	12.9	8.0
France	28.7[1]	20.2[1]	11.1
Germany	25.1	17.1	10.9
Japan	32.2	8.2	7.4
Switzerland	23.1[1]	17.8[1]	9.9
United Kingdom	22.0[1]	19.0[1]	9.7[1]
United States	15.6	11.9	8.8[1]

Source: OECD Health Data, 2016.
[1]2012

ISSUES IN MEDICAL CARE DELIVERY

ARE CIGARETTE AND ALCOHOL CONSUMPTION SENSITIVE TO PRICE INCREASES?

Conventional wisdom would have us believe that individuals who smoke and drink will do so at any price. Several economic researchers have offered evidence that may force us to rethink this common belief (Becker, Grossman, and Murphy, 1993; Chaloupka, 1991; Chaloupka et al., 1993). Taking into consideration the powerful reinforcing properties of addictive substances (increases in past consumption increase the marginal benefit of current consumption), this research finds evidence of rational addiction. In other words, consumers of addictive substances take into account the long-term harmful effects of their behavior when deciding how much of an addictive substance to consume.

As is the case with all goods, addictive and nonaddictive, long-run price elasticities are larger in absolute value than short-run elasticities. Consumers, when given enough time, have the ability to adjust to price changes by shifting to substitutes. The lesson from these studies is that in the long run, addictive behavior is price sensitive; that is, raising cigarette and alcohol prices will reduce consumption over time.

Sources: Gary S. Becker, Michael Grossman, and K. M. Murphy, "An Empirical Analysis of Cigarette Addiction," *NBER Working Paper No. 3322*, April 1990, revised March 1993; Frank J. Chaloupka, "Rational Addictive Behavior and Cigarette Smoking," *Journal of Political Economy* 99(4), August 1991, 722–742; and Frank J. Chaloupka, Michael Grossman, Gary S. Becker, and K. M. Murphy, "Alcohol Addiction: An Econometric Analysis," paper presented at the annual meeting of the American Economic Association, January 1993.

One of the reasons that women live longer in most societies is that they do not smoke with the same regularity as men. However, the gap between male and female smoking rates has narrowed substantially over the past four decades. Consequently, more than 500,000 women are dying worldwide every year of smoking-related illnesses. By the time today's young female population reaches middle age, more than one million females will be dying annually in the developed world alone.

BACK-OF-THE-ENVELOPE

Alcohol Consumption and Traffic Deaths: The Case for Higher Excise Taxes

Motor vehicle accidents are the leading cause of death for people under age 35. In over half of all fatal crashes, alcohol is a factor. A major dilemma for policy makers is how to reduce the number of alcohol-related traffic fatalities. In 1984, Congress passed the Federal Uniform Drinking Age Act raising the legal drinking age to 21. States were forced to conform or risk losing federal highway funding.

Another suggested strategy to reduce alcohol-related traffic fatalities is to raise the price of alcoholic beverages through an excise tax. Substantial evidence exists relating higher alcoholic beverage prices—and state excise tax rates on alcohol—to a lower incidence of youth alcohol consumption and, subsequently, to fewer deaths as a result of motor vehicle accidents (Chaloupka, Saffer, and Laizuthai, 1993). But raising excise taxes on alcohol to reduce consumption is a forgotten strategy. In 1991, the federal excise tax on beer and wine was raised for the first time since 1951, and the federal excise tax on distilled spirits was raised for only the second time over that same 40-year period. How would an increase in excise taxes affect alcohol consumption?

In the diagrams, the alcohol-dependent demand curve is drawn much steeper than that of the occasional drinker, indicating a more inelastic demand. An increase in the excise tax will shift the supply curve leftward (remember, the vertical distance between S_1 and S_2 represents the amount of the excise tax increase). In both cases, the resulting price increase causes the quantity demanded to decrease. However, in the case of the occasional drinker, quantity demanded falls considerably more than it does for the alcohol dependent.

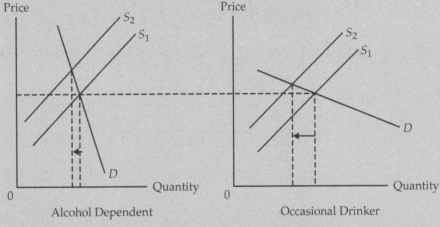

Alcohol Dependent   Occasional Drinker

Due partly to lagging federal excise taxes, the real prices of alcoholic beverages have actually fallen in recent years. Between 1975 and 1990, the real price of beer fell 20 percent, the real price of wine 28 percent, and the real price of distilled spirits 32 percent. If real alcohol prices had actually remained constant, youth alcohol consumption would have been lower, along with fewer traffic fatalities. Chaloupka, Grossman, and Saffer (1993) estimate that if the federal excise tax on beer had been indexed to the rate of inflation since 1951 that approximately 5,000 fewer traffic fatalities would have occurred annually. In addition, a uniform minimum drinking age of 21 would have saved more than 650 lives per year prior to the Federal Uniform Drinking Age Act of 1984. This and other research (Manning et al., 1989) suggest that excise taxes on alcoholic beverages are probably below optimal levels.

Sources: M. Grossman, F. J. Chaloupka, H. Saffer, and A. Laixuthai, "Effects of Alcohol Price Policy on Youth: A Summary of Economic Research," *Journal of Research on Adolescence*, 4(2), 1994, 347–364; F. J. Chaloupka, Michael Grossman, and H. Saffer, "Alcohol Control Policies and Motor Vehicle Fatalities," *Journal of Legal Studies* 22(1), January 1993, 161–186; and Willard G. Manning, Emmett B. Keeler, Joseph P. Newhouse, Elizabeth M. Sloss, and Jeffrey Wasserman, "The Taxes of Sin: Do Smokers and Drinkers Pay Their Way?" *Journal of the American Medical Association* 261, March 17, 1989, 1604–1609.

Alcohol Use

Compared to consumers in the rest of the developed world, Americans are relatively moderate drinkers, with per capita consumption of 8.8 liters in 2012. The prevalence of drinking, however, increases dramatically with age until early adulthood (aged 21–25) and then gradually declines. The cost of alcohol abuse in the United States was estimated at approximately $185 billion in 1998; the latest year sufficient data were available (Harwood, 2000). Over two-thirds of the costs are caused by the lost productivity due to alcohol-related illnesses and premature death. In over one million alcohol-related automobile accidents, over 10,000 die and 300,000 are injured. Additionally, alcohol plays a role in a significant proportion of all violent crime: assault, rape, murder, suicide, domestic violence, and child abuse.

Alcohol use is a double-edged sword. For some people, even moderate alcohol consumption carries with it severe health risks. However, there is substantial medical evidence that moderate consumption can actually be beneficial, the so-called French Paradox.[4] The medical evidence suggests that moderate daily consumption, one drink for women and two for men, offers some protection against heart disease and stroke (Abramson et al., 2001; Reynolds et al., 2003). Specifically, moderate alcohol consumption is associated with higher HDL (the good cholesterol), lower blood pressure, fewer blood clots, and protection against arterial damage caused by LDL (the bad cholesterol).

POLICY ISSUE

How will federal entitlement programs remain solvent as the percentage of the population over age 65 continues to expand?

KEY CONCEPT 5

Markets and Pricing

BACK-OF-THE-ENVELOPE

The Question of Drug Legalization

Many proponents of drug legalization use economics to make their case. They argue that banned drugs are just that: banned. With no distinction among illegal substances, young people may get the impression that one is no worse than the other is—phencyclidine (PCP), crack cocaine, heroin, or marijuana—they're all the same, aren't they? Consumers have no assurance regarding the quality of the drugs they buy, and the government can generate no tax revenue from the sale and purchase of the banned substances. Public costs are high with a large percentage of the costs of police, courts, and prisons directly or indirectly attributable to the war on drugs. Despite all the spending to stop drug trafficking, only 10 to 15 percent of all drugs entering the country are seized. Proponents of legalization suggest that we control the sale of drugs, tax the profits, supervise production, and at the same time discourage their use.

Citing the fact that increased spending for interdiction has little effect on the amount of drugs reaching the market, legalization proponents argue that the demand for drugs is likely to be inelastic. As depicted in the graph, when demand is relatively inelastic, increasing the cost to suppliers, and thus shifting the supply curve to the left, has little effect on the equilibrium quantity (reducing quantity from Q_0 to Q_1). The only thing the interdiction strategy accomplishes is to raise the price of drugs and increase the incentives for suppliers. In addition, those who use drugs are forced into lives of crime to support their expensive habit.

---

[4]The *French Paradox* refers to the observation that the French have less heart disease than Americans despite a high-fat diet. Red wine and olive oil are thought to be at least partially responsible.

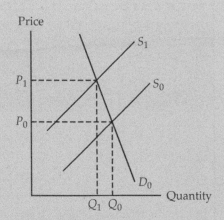

Opponents of legalization argue that prohibition may create crime by classifying certain activities as criminal, but it is not victimless crime. People under the influence of drugs are more likely to injure others, and the medical complications of drug use impose indirect costs on everybody. In any event, hard-core drug users were committing crimes long before they were using drugs. It is these hard-core users whose demand is price inelastic. For the millions who do not use drugs, demand is quite elastic. Any relaxation in standards will cause a substantial increase in use. The legal sanctions and the social stigma are enough to dissuade the curious. Therefore, the demand curve for these potential users is much flatter than the one shown above. Legalization will not only increase quantity demanded for this group but will also actually shift the demand curve to the right, further increasing consumption.

Organizations such as NORML (National Organization to Reform Marijuana Laws) argue that legalization of pot makes sense. They claim that it is nonaddictive, widely used, and no worse than alcohol. It is already the largest cash crop in the state of California. On the other hand, opponents ask the question: Do we need another social problem along the lines of tobacco and alcohol to add to the pathologies we already suffer? If we legalize, where do we draw the line? Do we stop at marijuana? Should PCP, crack, and lysergic acid diethylamide (LSD) be added to the list? How soon before proponents begin calling on governing bodies in sports to sanction the use of anabolic steroids? Should we try to legislate the moral behavior of society? Or should we follow the libertarian (some would say, libertine) principles and tolerate such behavior? Expect disagreement when you bring up this topic at your next social gathering.

Source: James W. Henderson, "Economic Impact of Cocaine and Crack Abuse: Private and Social Issues," in *Doing Drugs and Dropping Out: Assessing the Costs to Society of Substance Abuse and Dropping Out of School*, a Report Prepared for the Subcommittee on Economic Growth, Trade, and Taxes of the Joint Economic Committee, Congress of the United States, edited by Glen E. Lich, Washington, DC: U.S. Government Printing Office, August 1991.

KEY CONCEPT 6
Supply and Demand

Obesity and Its Consequences

Recent evidence from the WHO presented in Table 6.13 indicated that the United States is the world leader in obesity with close to 30 percent of Americans falling into that category.[5] In 2013, approximately 25 percent of Britons were considered obese, 15 percent of the French, and only about 4 percent of the Japanese.

---

[5]$\text{BMI} = \dfrac{\text{Weight (in kilogram)}}{\text{Height (in meters squared)}}$. Optimal BMI is between 20 and 25. A person with a BMI between 25 and 30 is considered overweight.

TABLE 6.13 OBESITY: ITS CAUSES AND CONSEQUENCES					
	Obesity (% male population BMI > 30)[1]	Obesity (% female population, BMI > 30)	Fat consumed per day (grams per capita)[1]	Calories consumed per day (per capita)[1]	Diabetes (% population with diagnosis)[2]
	2013	2013	2011	2011	2003
Canada	19.5	16.8	150.0	3,419	9.0
France	14.5[3]	14.6[3]	162.4	3,524	6.2
Germany	17.1	14.3	145.8	3,539	10.2
Japan	4.1	3.4	87.3	2,719	6.9
Switzerland	11.2[3]	9.4[3]	157.4	3,487	9.5
United Kingdom	24.4	26.0	138.1	3,414	3.9
United States	29.2	28.2	161.6	3,639	8.0

Source: [1]OECD Health Data, 2016.
[2]International Diabetes Foundation (2003), available at http://www.heartstats.org.
[3]2012
[4]2008

KEY CONCEPT 2
Opportunity Cost

Peeters and colleagues (2003) find a significant association between obesity and decreases in life expectancy. When compared with normal-weight nonsmokers, obese female smokers lost 7.2 years of life expectancy and obese male smokers lost 13.7 years. O'Neill and O'Neill (2007) estimate that over one-half of the male life expectancy gap and two-thirds of the female gap between the United States and Canada can be linked to increased mortality due to obesity-related diseases.

Why do Americans have a higher incidence of obesity than their counterparts in the rest of the developed world? Research by Cutler, Glaeser, and Shapiro (2003) explains the increase as a result of higher calorie consumption. Women today consume 9 percent more than they did 20 years ago, and men consume 13 percent more. The reason for these increases: Food is cheaper, not only in terms of the hours required to earn the money to buy it but also in terms of the time it takes to cook it. Remember, because demand curves slope downward, when something is cheaper, consumers demand more. Americans consume an average of 3,639 calories per day, more than any country in the comparison group.

Not only is calorie consumption increasing, much of what we buy to eat is processed before we get it, either in a restaurant or packaged and purchased in a grocery store. With more women working, they spend less time in food preparation. According to time-use surveys, married women (with no children in the household under age 18) who work outside the home spent an average of 32 minutes a day in food chores in 2009, compared to 85 minutes a day 40 years earlier. For those women without jobs outside the home, the average was 58 minutes in 2009 compared to 138 minutes in 1965. The same trends were also true for single individuals (BLS, 2011). Consumers usually view decreases in price as a good thing. In the case of food, however, lower prices coupled with a sedentary lifestyle can lead to consumption levels that have serious health consequences.

KEY CONCEPT 6
Supply and Demand

APPLIED MICRO METHODS

THE IMPACT OF A TRANS FAT BAN ON HEALTH

Background

The biological evidence relating the consumption of trans fat and the risk of CVD has been well established by the medical literature. In 2013, the American Medical Association indicated that the elimination of artificial trans fat would reduce the number of deaths from CVD between 30,000 and 100,000 per year. Despite the fact that the biological mechanisms are plausible, without randomized control trials, the link between CVD and trans fat may not be causal. Restrepo and Rieger (2016) provide evidence to support a causal link between the consumption of artificial trans fat and CVD by analyzing the impact of a ban on the use of trans fat on CVD mortality rates.

Data and Methods

Authors take advantage of the implementation of a ban on the use of artificial trans fat in restaurants in 11 of the 62 counties in New York State (NYS) between 2007 and 2011. Regression analysis relates the number of deaths due to CVD per 100,000 persons in a county with a number of county-specific covariates that may affect mortality rates (income, unemployment rate, obesity rate, smoking rate, alcohol consumption, and physical exercise) and a time-sensitive dummy variable identifying those counties that enacted trans fat bans. A further breakdown analyzes the number of deaths per 100,000 due to heart disease and stroke. The empirical strategy created synthetic control groups that closely mimic the pretreatment trends in CVD mortality rates realized in the treatment counties.

Results

Using time and county fixed effects, the model provided statistically significant estimates of the post treatment impact of trans fat bans on CVD mortality. The preferred model provided causal evidence that CVD-related mortality was reduced by 4.5 percent in the counties that enacted the trans fat bans.

A series of falsification tests (sometimes referred to as placebo studies) support the robustness of the results. Alternately estimating the impact on mortality rates from other diseases that would not be expected to change due to the bans and using the counties that did not enact trans fat bans as treatment counties did not result in statistically significant changes in CVD mortality rates, supporting the claim that the original results were not random.

Discussion and Conclusions

The size and significance of the estimated impact of trans fat bans on CVD mortality are consistent with the evidence presented in the medical literature. Based on the evidence provided in this study, the trans fat ban enacted in these 11 NYS counties likely prevented between 500 and 1,000 deaths per year due to CVD. In 2015, the FDA determined that partially hydrogenated oils, the principal source of artificial trans fat in U.S. diets, is unsafe. The action will likely eliminate partially hydrogenated oils from the U.S. food supply. Additionally, the WHO challenged lawmakers in Europe to remove artificial trans fat from European diets as well. The results of this study provide evidence that these policy recommendations will result in a reduction in CVD deaths in the United States and Europe.

Source: Brandon J. Restrepo and Matthias Rieger, "Trans Fat and Cardiovascular Disease Mortality: Evidence from Bans in Restaurants in New York," *Journal of Health Economics* 45, 2016, 176–196.

Summary and Conclusions

In this chapter, we discussed a number of factors used to measure the overall health of the population. Disparities between population groups and differences across countries were discussed to provide insight into understanding overall health outcomes. More importantly, these comparisons bring into focus how these commonly used health metrics can be used to improve our understanding of the role of the medical care delivery system in improving the overall quality of a health care system and the value of the medical care received.

PROFILE Jonathan Gruber

If the number of publications is a measure of the influence of a scholar, Jonathan Gruber may be the most influential health economist of the past decade. Since he received his Ph.D. in 1992, Gruber has published more than 150 articles in refereed journals and numerous research volumes and book chapters. Accomplishing this body of work in a lifetime is no minor feat; accomplishing it at such a young age is remarkable. In 2006, the American Society of Health Economists named him the leading health economists in the United States under age 40.

Born in New Jersey, Gruber received his undergraduate degree in economics from the Massachusetts Institute of Technology (MIT) in 1987 and then moved to Harvard University. Introduced to the power of policy-oriented economics at an early age, Gruber spent two summers at the Brookings Institution in Washington, DC. At Brookings, he began applying his knowledge of economics to inform policy makers on issues of importance to ordinary Americans.

After graduating from Harvard, he returned to his undergraduate alma mater, a move that some view as dangerous for a scholarly career, especially for a first academic appointment. Whatever the possible pitfalls, Gruber's progression through the ranks was just short of amazing—a promotion to associate professor after three years and then to full professor two years later. In addition to his position at MIT, he is a research associate at the National Bureau of Economic Research and director of their program on children. He is currently coeditor of the *Journal of Public Economics* and associate editor of the *Journal of Health Economics*.

Trained in public finance and labor economics, Gruber's early work reflected that perspective to examine the impact of health insurance mandates on labor markets. His research interests turned quickly to more standard health economics issues. With articles published in some of the most prestigious journals in economics, Gruber is not relying on accomplishments to guide public policy. His future research will focus on some of the most important issues in health policy, including the impact of public insurance programs (Medicaid and SCHIP [State Children's Health Insurance Program]) on health outcomes, the impact of reimbursement rates on the quality of nursing home care, and the impact of religion and religiosity on well-being.

Gruber has always had a penchant for looking at a well-discussed problem from a different perspective. Until his work on unemployment insurance, the focus in the literature was primarily on the labor market distortions of the program. Instead, Gruber studied the issue from the workers' perspective, looking at the impact on family consumption, savings, and labor supply decisions. His research on smoking and other addictive behavior has introduced a more realistic assumption of human behavior into the model (see "Is Addiction Rational?" in Issues in Medical Care Delivery earlier in this chapter). Because of this improvement, the normative implications for government policy options differ significantly from previous research.

He was a key adviser during the Massachusetts health reform effort and was appointed to the inaugural board of the state's Health Connector. *Modern Healthcare Magazine* named him the 19th most powerful person in health care in the United States in 2006. During the 2008 presidential campaign, he was a consultant for Hillary Clinton, John Edwards, and eventually Barack Obama. The *Washington Post* called him "possibly the [Democrat] party's most influential health-care expert."

Despite his scholarly success, Gruber's main avocation is his family. Whether it is spending time at the beach or just wrestling with his kids in the playroom, his goal is to strike a balance between a successful professional career and a fulfilling family life. Jonathan Gruber serves as an inspiration to any discouraged economists who think that what they do does not matter.

Source: Curriculum vitae and personal correspondence.

Questions and Problems

1. How important is the deterioration of the social system in contributing to the health care spending crisis, assuming one exists?

2. Is it important to characterize such social problems as alcoholism and drug abuse as diseases rather than behavior disorders? What are the implications of treating other social problems as diseases? What about anorexia? Obesity? Domestic violence? What are the implications for the medical care system of the proliferation of these new "diseases"?

3. What are the costs to society of cocaine use? Alcohol use? Tobacco use? Which of these presents the biggest problem? Explain.

4. "Drug use is a classic example of a victimless crime. Therefore it should not be prohibited." Comment.

5. How serious is the issue of medical malpractice in the United States today?

6. What are the intended purposes of medical malpractice? Does the threat of a lawsuit accomplish these purposes?

7. "It is impossible to place a dollar value on life. In other words, life is priceless." How does this view create a dilemma for social decision making and effective resource allocation?

8. Environmentalists and economists often find themselves at odds with each other. The conflict between the romantics and the rationalists surfaced again in the debate over air-quality standards set under the Clean Air Act of 1990. Under the law, the Environmental Protection Agency (EPA) must establish standards that promote public health. The EPA's cost-benefit analysis assigns a value for each life saved of $4.8 million. Is $4.8 million a reasonable value to place on a life? What questions would economists consider relevant in determining the value of a life? How would environmentalists react to the questions economists ask?

9. The term *iatroepidemic* describes a practice introduced into medicine without sound scientific evidence to establish its efficacy. Such practices result in systematic harm to large numbers of patients. Bloodletting during the fifteenth and sixteenth centuries, tonsillectomies in the 1950s, and the practice of psychosurgery have been identified as practices with little therapeutic value that actually harmed many patients. Can you think of other examples of iatroepidemics? When systematic medical error imposes costs on individuals, whom do we blame? Should individual physicians be liable for injuries under these situations?

References

Abramson, Jerome L., et al., "Moderate Alcohol Consumption and the Risk of Heart Failure among Older Persons," *Journal of the American Medical Association* 285(15), April 18, 2001, 1971–1977.

Atlas, Scott W., "Infant Mortality: A Deceptive Statistic," *National Review Online*, September 14, 2011, available at http://www.nationalreview.com/node/276952.

Baicker, Katherine, et al., "The Oregon Experiment—Effects of Medicaid on Clinical Outcomes," *New England Journal of Medicine* 368(18), May 2, 2013, 1713–1722.

Berwick, Donald M., Thomas W. Nolan, and John Whittington, "The Triple Aim: Care, Health, and Cost," *Health Affairs* 27(3), May/June 2008, 759–769.

BLS (Bureau of Labor Statistics), "American Time Use Survey—2010 Results," USDL-11-0919, June 22, 2011.

Cawley, John, and Chad Meyerhoefer, "The Medical Care Costs of Obesity: An Instrumental Variables Approach," *Journal of Health Economics* 31(1), January 2012, 219–230.

CDC (Centers for Disease Control and Prevention), "CDC Health Disparities and Inequalities Report—United States, 2013," *Morbidity and Mortality Weekly Report* 62(3) Supplement, November 22, 2013.

_____, "Preventing Tobacco Use," *Preventing Chronic Diseases: Investing Wisely in Health*, October 2008, available at http://www.tobaccofreemaine.org/ channels/parents/documents/Preventing TobaccoUse.pdf (Accessed March 15, 2017).

Chen, Alice, Emily Oster, and Heidi Williams, "Why Is Infant Mortality Higher in the US than Europe?" NBER Working Paper 20525, Cambridge, MA: National Bureau of Economic Research, September 2014.

Cutler, David M., Edward L. Glaeser, and Jesse M. Shapiro, "Why Have Americans Become More Obese?" NBER Working Paper No. 9446, Cambridge, MA: National Bureau of Economic Research, January 2003.

Harwood, Henrick, "Updating Estimates of the Economic Costs of Alcohol Abuse in the United States: Estimates, Update Methods, and Data," Report prepared by The Lewin Group for the National Institute on Alcohol Abuse and Alcoholism, 2000.

IOM (Institute of Medicine), Committee on the Quality of Health Care in America, *Crossing the Quality Chasm: A New Health System for the 21st Century*, Washington, DC: National Academy Press, 2001.

Kindig, David, and Greg Stoddart, "What Is Population Health?" *American Journal of Public Health* 93(3), March 2003, 380–383.

Kramer, Michael, et al., "Does Reducing Infant Mortality Depend on Preventing Low Birth Weight? An Analysis of Temporal Trends in the Americas," *Pediatric and Perinatal Epidemiology* 19(6), November 2005, 445–451.

Kramer, Michael, et al., "Registration Artifacts in International Comparisons of Infant Mortality," *Pediatric & Perinatal Epidemiology* 16(1), January 2002, 16–22.

Lemaire, Jean, "The Cost of Firearm Deaths in the United States: Reduced Life Expectancies and Increased Insurance Costs," *Journal of Risk and Insurance* 72(3), 2005, 359–374.

Liu, Korbin, et al., "International Infant Mortality Rankings: A Look Behind the Numbers," *Health Care Financing Review* 13(4), Summer 1992, 105–118.

MacDorman, Marian F., and Jonnae O. Atkinson, "Infant Mortality Statistics from the 1997 Period Linked Birth/Infant Death Data Set," *National Vital Statistics Reports* 47(23), Hyattsville, MD: National Center for Health Statistics, 1999.

MacDorman, Marian F., and T. J. Mathews, "Behind International Rankings of Infant Mortality: How the United States Compares to Europe," *NCHS Data Brief No. 23*, U.S. Department of Health and Human Services, Centers for Disease Control and Prevention, November 2009.

Marmot, Michael, "Inequalities in Health," *New England Journal of Medicine* 345(2), July 12, 2001, 134–136.

Marmot, Michael, M. J. Shipley, and G. Rose, "Inequalities in Death: Specific Explanations of a General Pattern?" *Lancet* 323, 1984, 1003–1006.

Marmot, Michael, et al., "Contributions of Job Control and Other Risk Factors to Social Variations in Coronary Heart Disease Incidence," *Lancet* 350, 1997, 235–239.

Ohsfeldt, Robert, and John E. Schneider, *The Business of Health*, Washington, DC: AEI Press, 2006.

O'Neill, June E., and Dave M. O'Neill, "Health Status, Health Care and Inequality: Canada vs. the U.S." *Forum for Health Economics & Policy* 10(1), Article 3, 2007, 1–45.

Pamuk, E. R., and W. D. Mosher, *Health Aspects of Pregnancy and Childbirth, United States 1982*, Hyattsville, MD: National Center for Health Statistics, Series 23, No. 16, 1988, 52–53.

Peeters, Anna, et al., "Obesity in Adulthood and Its Consequences for Life Expectancy: A Life-Table Analysis," *Annals of Internal Medicine* 138(1), January 7, 2003, 24–33.

Porter, Michael E., and Elizabeth Olmstead Teisberg, *Redefining Health Care: Creating Value-Based Competition on Results*, Harvard Business School Press, 2006.

Restrepo, Brandon J., and Matthias Rieger, "Trans Fat and Cardiovascular Disease Mortality: Evidence from Bans in Restaurants in New York," *Journal of Health Economics* 45, 2016, 176–196.

Reynolds, Kristi, et al., "Alcohol Consumption and Risk of Stroke: A Meta-Analysis," *Journal of the American Medical Association* 289(5), February 5, 2003, 579–588.

Tough, Suzanne C., Jodi E. Siever, and David W. Johnston, "Retaining Women in a Prenatal Care Randomized Controlled Trial in Canada: Implications for Program Planning," *BMC Public Health* 7, July 2007, available at http://www.biomedcentral.com/content/pdf/1471-2458-7-148.pdf.

Ventura, Stephanie J., Sally C. Curtin, and T. J. Mathews, "Variations in Teenage Birth Rates, 1991–98: National and State Trends," *National Vital Statistics Reports* 48(6), Hyattsville, MD: National Center for Health Statistics, 2000.

World Health Organization, "Health Systems: Improving Performance," The World Health Report 2000, Geneva: WHO, 2000.

Young, T. K., *Population Health: Concepts and Methods*, Oxford, England: Oxford University Press, 2005.

CHAPTER 7

The Market for Health Insurance

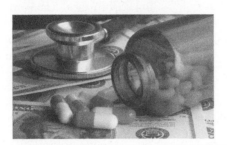

THE IMPACT OF THE AFFORDABLE CARE ACT ON HEALTH INSURANCE PREMIUMS

Prior to the passage of the Affordable Care Act (ACA), President Obama assured Americans that the price of insurance would fall after the law was implemented. Standard economic theory would suggest otherwise. Expanded benefits, free preventive care, and pooling individuals with known chronic conditions with everyone else make insurance pools riskier. What actually happened?

Dallas County, Texas	2013 Coverage Esurance.com (Pre-ACA Plan)	2014 Coverage Esurance.com (ACA Compliant)	2014 Coverage Texas Exchange (ACA Compliant)
27-year-old male, nonsmoker			
Plans offered	41	40	38
Annual premiums	$819–$2,823	$1,901–$4,480	$1,832–$4,644
Median premium	$1,648	$3,308	$3,189
50-year-old male, nonsmoker			
Plans offered	41	37	38
Annual premiums	$2,024–$6,771	$3,261–$8,800	$3,123–$7,686
Median premium	$3,696	$4,916	$5,436

Source: http://www.esurance.com/. Accessed December 18, 2013 and http://healthcare.gov.

Examining data from the individual insurance markets in Dallas County, Texas provides insight into the relevancy of standard theory. Available plans and their premiums for males (ages 27 and 50) are summarized in the earlier table. Before the end of the year 2013, individuals had the opportunity to purchase pre-ACA insurance plans that did not comply with the new legislation. As long as coverage went into effect prior to the end of 2013, plans were priced under standard underwriting rules (with premiums based on age, sex, and health status).

For comparison purposes two different sources for ACA-compliant plans are provided: Both series summarize data for plans that offer the expanded benefits and place limits on insurance underwriting (including a ban on preexisting conditions exclusions). Using either series the plans available through Esurance or the plans on the federal health insurance exchange available for residents of Dallas County, the results are similar. ACA-compliant premiums for the median priced plan are 94–100 percent higher for the 27-year-old male and 33–47 percent higher for the 50-year-old male.

Purchasers of ACA-compliant plans saw other differences in their plans, including higher deductibles, higher out-of-pocket maximums, and narrower provider networks. (Remember the president's promise "if you like your doctor, you can keep your doctor"? Well, maybe not.) Which approach is fairer? Should we promote solidarity and force everyone to purchase the same policy? Or is it better to pool risk by age, sex, and health status, and charge according to expected spending?

Source: Mary Lu Carnevale, "Obama: 'If You Like Your Doctor, You Can Keep Your Doctor,'" *Wall Street Journal*, June 15, 2009.

The Market for Health Insurance

The large number of people without insurance has weighed heavily on the national conscience for decades. It has now been over three years since full implementation of the ACA and the problem still persists. To address this problem rationally, we must understand the principles that govern the provision of insurance.

POLICY ISSUE
Over 50 million Americans are uninsured.

This chapter examines the development of employer-based insurance in the United States. A discussion of the theory of risk and insurance will serve as the basis for understanding the demand for private health insurance. We will then address the issue of market failure in the provision of medical care, focusing on the institutional features in the U.S. setting. Finally, we will examine the primary concern of reformers—the uninsured. Who are they? How does the lack of insurance coverage affect them? How do they pay for medical care?

Historical Setting

Insurance coverage for health services in the United States was first made available in 1798. Funded by mandatory payroll deductions, the U.S. Marine Hospital Services provided prepaid hospital care for eligible seamen. Although the first company to offer sickness insurance was organized in 1847, most of the early insurance policies covered loss of income due to accidents or disability rather than health services due to illness.

HTTP://
The Health Insurance Association of America (HIAA) is a trade association whose members are insurance companies and managed care companies. Visit this site at http://www.hiaa .org/.

Plans offering medical benefits became more prevalent in the 1870s and 1880s, offering coverage to workers in certain industries and to individuals who suffered from certain diseases. By the beginning of the twentieth century, a handful of insurance companies were actively writing policies covering accidental injury and disability.

Group health insurance was first offered in 1910 to the employees of Montgomery Ward and Company. The policy, written by the London Guarantee and Accident Company in New York, provided cash benefits in the event of disability or illness.

During the 1920s, hospitals began offering individual prepaid plans that covered hospital benefits. This practice was expanded in 1929 by Baylor University Hospital in

Dallas, Texas. In what is considered the forerunner of the Blue Cross plans, the hospital agreed to provide a group of Dallas teachers 21 days of hospital care and related services annually for a fixed monthly premium.

The Great Depression challenged the hospital sector to maintain its solvency. With people unable to afford hospital care, hospital occupancy rates fell to 50 percent. In 1932, a group of Sacramento, California, hospitals combined resources to offer the first area-wide plan supported by more than one hospital. Within three years, similar plans in 13 states provided a guaranteed cash flow to financially strapped hospitals. The California Physicians Service first introduced prepayment for physicians' services in 1939. Later known as Blue Shield, the plan provided medical and surgical benefits for a fixed monthly fee for members of employee groups earning less than $3,000 annually.

In the aftermath of the Second World War, group health insurance became a major feature of the collective bargaining process. A wage-price freeze during the war forced firms to offer nonwage benefits to attract and keep employees. A 1954 ruling by the Internal Revenue Service exempted employer contributions to health insurance benefits from employee taxable income. Today the tax exemption is a significant feature of the health insurance market in the United States, and it is responsible for the predominance of employer-sponsored group insurance (Thomasson, 2000). The next two decades witnessed improvements in insurance coverage. **Major medical** benefits were introduced in 1949, and dental care, prescription drugs, and vision care were added to many plans in the 1950s.

In 1965, after repeated failures to pass a nationwide universal insurance plan, Congress passed comprehensive coverage for the elderly and indigent—Medicare and Medicaid. A new era of government involvement in medical care financing saw its beginnings. Much of the upward pressure on health care spending can be traced to this legislation. As spending increased, so did pressure to control the cost spiral. The Health Maintenance Organization Act in 1973, the Employee Retirement Income Security Act (ERISA) in 1974, and the Medicare Catastrophic Care Act in 1988 were all attempts to curb runaway costs and improve access to those without insurance. Reform legislation that increased the role of the federal government in health care delivery and finance included the Health Insurance Portability and Accountability Act (HIPAA), State Children's Health Insurance Plan (SCHIP), and the Medicare Modernization Act (MMA). HIPAA established rules for insurance portability and patient privacy, SCHIP expanded coverage for low-income children who did not qualify for Medicaid, and MMA added outpatient prescription drug coverage to Medicare. MMA also expanded private insurance options by increasing access to health savings accounts.

Respecting the importance of employer-based insurance, legislators left the system largely intact when they passed the Patient Protection and ACA in 2010. The simultaneous expansion of Medicaid in some states to families with incomes below 138 percent of the federal poverty level established a uniform eligibility standard in the 30 states (and the District of Columbia) that voluntarily expanded coverage.

Types of Insurance

The current policy debate over health care reform is based on two opposing views to health care financing: the indemnity, or casualty, insurance approach and the **social insurance** approach. Private insurance has adopted the indemnity approach, providing reimbursement for certain medical expenditures or direct payments to those unable to work due to accident or injury. This category of insurance includes fire, theft, casualty, life, and in the United States, health insurance. It is based on the premise that the premium determined

major medical Health insurance to provide coverage for major illnesses requiring large financial outlays, characterized by payment for all expenses above a specified maximum out-of-pocket amount paid by the insured (often $2,000–$5,000).

social insurance An insurance plan supported by tax revenues and available to everyone regardless of age, health status, and ability to pay.

by the underwriting process should reflect expected medical spending. In principle, those individuals who have higher expected spending pay higher premiums. In practice, insurance premiums are determined by the expected spending of groups of individuals separated into insurance pools, the majority of which are established by employers.

Social insurance is the basis of all assistance programs associated with the welfare state: cash assistance, public education, and in most developed countries health care. The social insurance model ignores expected spending when calculating premiums. Instead of high-risk individuals paying higher premiums, individuals with higher incomes pay higher premiums. Subsidies are used extensively across risk categories to ensure that high-risk, low-income individuals have adequate insurance coverage.

The United States uses a combination of the two approaches. Prior to the implementation of the ACA, everyone covered by private insurance had premiums determined to a large extent by the expected medical care spending of their risk pool. Most policies are still written as group policies, and premiums are relatively uniform within groups, varying primarily by size of family. Premiums are **experience rated**, largely determined by past spending. So policies are **community rated** within groups and experience rated across groups, which means that everyone within the group pays the same premium, but premiums differ across groups. Groups with higher health care spending pay higher premiums. Proponents of this approach argue that not only is it is more efficient, it is more equitable. To the extent that medical costs are based on lifestyle choices, individuals should pay for the choices they make. Groups populated with individuals who practice a healthy lifestyle and are more cost conscious are rewarded with lower premiums. Those who choose to indulge in unhealthy behavior pay higher premiums.

The elderly, the disabled, the indigent, and those suffering from certain diseases, such as kidney failure, have their medical coverage provided by social insurance. Medicare and Medicaid are the two major social insurance programs in the United States. Proponents of this approach argue from the premise of individual rights and social responsibility. Some argue that justice dictates that all individuals be provided with medical care as an individual right. If indeed access to medical care is a right, its provision is the socially responsible thing to do. And because participation is mandatory, proponents claim the savings in administrative costs offset any loss in efficiency caused by a departure from the indemnity approach.

In general, health insurance may be classified into two broad categories: medical expense insurance that provides reimbursement for actual expenditures, and disability income insurance that provides periodic payments when the insured individual is unable to work. Although the combination of policies is virtually endless, all contain certain basic health insurance benefits that may be offered separately or in combination with other benefits, including hospitalization, physicians' services, outpatient services, dental, vision, disability income, and long-term care.

Health Insurance Providers

Providers are generally classified as commercial insurance carriers, Blue Cross and Blue Shield associations, and managed care organizations. Over 1,000 commercial insurance companies provide health insurance coverage to over 200 million people. Most operate nationally. Some offer only health insurance, but many also offer property and casualty insurance, liability coverage, and life insurance.

Managed care organizations—in particular, health maintenance organizations and **preferred provider organizations (PPOs)**—offer comprehensive health care coverage where the provider is responsible for the health care services of enrollees for a fixed fee. More will be covered about this arrangement in Chapter 8.

---

experience rated Basing health insurance premiums on the utilization experience of a specific insured group. Premiums may vary by age, sex, or other risk factors.

community rated Basing health insurance premiums on the health care utilization experience of the entire population of a specific geographic area. Premiums are the same for all individuals regardless of age, gender, risk, or prior use of health care services.

POLICY ISSUE
Is access to medical care an individual right? Should it be?

preferred provider organization (PPO) A group of medical providers that has contracted with an insurance company or employer to provide health care services to a well-defined group according to a well-defined fee schedule. By accepting discount fees, providers are included on the list of preferred providers.

In addition, an increasing number of health insurance plans are handled directly by the sponsoring employers through self-insurance. By 1985 over half of company-sponsored group insurance plans were operated under Administrative Service Only (ASO) arrangements. Under ASO arrangements, third-party administrators (TPAs) process claims and handle paperwork for a set fee.

Approximately 90 percent of the civilian population under age 65 has hospital insurance, surgical health insurance, or both. Of the population over 65 covered by Medicare, approximately 60 percent carry private supplemental coverage (Medigap insurance). Thus, an estimated 9.1 percent of the civilian population is uninsured.

Private Insurance Demand

risk A state in which multiple outcomes are possible, and the likelihood of each possible outcome is known or can be estimated.

Individuals enter insurance contracts to spread **risk**. The insurance contract is sold for a premium based on the expected cost incurred if a specific event takes place. In the seventeenth century, Lloyds of London started as a coffee house where ship owners contracted with wealthy merchants to underwrite the expenses incurred if a ship was lost at sea.

The most straightforward application of the traditional indemnity insurance contract is term life insurance. A policy is purchased for a given premium and pays a predetermined amount to named beneficiaries in the event the insured person dies. Another application is property casualty insurance. In this case, when an insured asset is damaged, the policy pays to restore its value to the undamaged state.

HTTP://
The Blue Cross and Blue Shield Association website with links to all the regional associations can be found at http:// www.bluecares.com/.

Health insurance is similar to term life insurance and property casualty insurance with a few notable exceptions. When first developed, the typical health insurance policy paid a specified amount for a given medical condition, such as a broken leg or a severed limb. The major problems with this arrangement were (1) the difficulty in verifying the seriousness of the medical condition and (2) the wide variation in the cost of treating similar medical conditions. These two problems placed too much risk on the insured and led to the development of the service-benefit policy, which covers billed expenses. This form of insurance became the predominant form of health insurance throughout the 1980s.

The Theory of Risk and Insurance

uncertainty A state in which multiple outcomes are possible but the likelihood of any one outcome is not known.

probability The likelihood or chance that an event will occur. Probability is measured as a ratio that ranges in value from zero to one.

The theory of risk and insurance is based on the pioneering work of Friedman and Savage (1948). Individuals enter into insurance contracts to share the **uncertainty** of financial risk with others. It is impossible to determine whether one particular individual will suffer from a medical condition, such as a heart attack or stroke. When individuals are combined into large enough groups, or risk pools, the **probability** that someone in the group will suffer from heart attack or stroke can be systematically estimated. The estimated probability of an event is based on its past frequency of occurrence. Larger groups improve the accuracy of the prediction.

Tracing health care spending back to 1928, Berk and Monheit (2001) show a remarkable stability in distribution of health care expenditures over time. Using national survey data, they estimated that in 1996, 5 percent of the population was responsible for 55 percent of the aggregate health care spending. Furthermore, the top 10 percent of the users accounted for 69 percent of the spending, the top 30 percent accounted for 90 percent, and the top half accounted for 97 percent of the total spending. These percentages have remained remarkably stable over time.

Some individuals are more willing to take chances than others. But even people who willingly take chances generally prefer less risky situations. The dominant attitude among

KEY CONCEPT 3
Marginal Analysis

expected value of an outcome The weighted average of all possible outcomes, with the probabilities of those outcomes used as weights.

the population is risk aversion. Attitudes toward risk may be depicted by the marginal utility of income. When evaluating two alternatives with the same **expected value**, a risk-averse individual will choose a certain prospect over the uncertain prospect. Risk aversion is shown by a diminishing marginal utility of income, measuring the rate of change of the total utility of income.

The more income a person has, the higher that person's level of utility. In addition, each additional increment to income increases utility by an amount smaller than the previous increment. Figure 7.1 depicts the total utility of income curve for a risk-averse person. Total utility is drawn concave from below, that is, increasing at a decreasing rate. As income increases from w_0 to w_1, total utility increases from u_0 to u_1. As the level of income increases, each increment to income increases utility by a smaller amount. In other words, as income increases from w_1 to w_2, the change in utility is less than it was when income increased an equivalent amount from w_0 to w_1.

When actual outcomes are uncertain, individuals do not know where they will end up on their utility-of-income curve. Even though no one can know with certainty the actual income they will receive in a given time period, their expected income can be estimated. *Expected utility* is the average of all possible utilities weighted by their respective probabilities. When making a choice under conditions of uncertainty, individuals attempt to maximize expected utility. Assume there are two possible health states: sick and healthy. A probability of being sick equal to 5 percent means a 95 percent probability of being healthy. (The sum of the probabilities of all possible health states must equal 100 percent.) If the cost of treating the illness is equal to $20,000, a person with an annual income of $50,000 has an expected net income (after medical expenses) of $49,000.[1]

Risk is costly, and a risk-averse person will pay to avoid the consequences of risk. To illustrate this principle, take the case of health insurance. An individual facing the uncertainty of an illness has two choices: (1) purchase insurance and voluntarily reduce income by the amount of the premium, or (2) self-insure, facing the small probability of a financial loss should an illness occur. It is impossible to know the actual probability that any one person will suffer from an illness. With a large number of people pooled together, the

FIGURE 7.1
The Total Utility-of-Income Curve

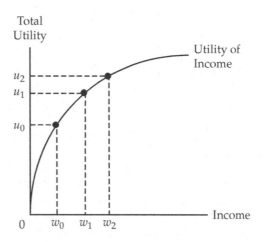

---

[1]Expected income is the weighted average of the two possible outcomes. The calculation is the sum of the income at each health state weighed by the probability that state will occur, or $E(Y)$ = ($50,000 × 0.95) + ($30,000 × 0.05) = $47,500 + $1,500 = $49,000.

proportion of the population that suffered from the illness in a previous time period can be used to estimate the probability.

Risk pooling will work as long as the group purchasing insurance, the risk pool, has the same probability of illness as the overall population used to estimate the probability. Insurance actuaries usually do a pretty good job in estimating these probabilities if group membership is predictable and stable over time. In that case, they are able to share the costs of treating the illness by collecting premiums from everyone and paying benefits to those who become ill. For this arrangement to work, the insurance company must collect enough in premiums to pay out all claims, cover all operating and administrative costs, and have a reasonable profit left over for the owners of the company.

To illustrate how this works, consider the following example: Suppose our prospective insurance customer faces a 4 percent probability of suffering from an illness that would result in a catastrophic financial loss equal to an entire year's income of $50,000. Under these circumstances, the range of uncertainty extends from a net income of zero (if ill) to $50,000 (if healthy). The expected utility of income is depicted by a straight line from the origin, where net income is zero because of illness, to the point on the actual utility-of-income curve corresponding to $50,000: the net income for a healthy person.[2] The concave utility of income depicts the level of utility associated with a guaranteed income (i.e., no uncertainty). The straight-line expected utility-of-income curve depicts utility adjusted for the different probabilities of illness. In other words, this straight line represents the expected utility of the $50,000 loss associated with the illness at all the probabilities between zero and one. The vertical distance between the two curves measures the reduction in utility associated with the risk of illness.

Choice under conditions of uncertainty means that a person tries to maximize expected utility. Because the probability of illness is 4 percent, the probability of not being ill is 96 percent. Referring to Figure 7.2, expected wealth in this case is $48,000, and expected utility is $96U$.[3]

Given the utility-of-income curve shown in the figure, our prospective insurance customer has the same level of utility (equal to $96U$) with a guaranteed income of $45,000 or an expected income of $48,000. In other words, this person's actual level of utility is the same when she has a 100 percent probability of an income level of $45,000 or a 96 percent chance of $50,000 coupled with a 4 percent chance of zero income (comparing point C with point A). The difference between $48,000 and $45,000 (or $3,000) is the price of uncertainty. In this case, if insurance can be purchased for less than $5,000, the individual will be better off; that is, the individual will be at a higher level of utility.

Obviously, many people have similar utility-of-income curves, all risk averse; otherwise insurance companies would not sell millions of insurance policies annually. Using these probabilities, if a group of 1,000 people seek insurance, an insurer can expect that 40 will become ill and make claims totaling $2 million. The insurer must charge at least $2,000 per person to cover the expected payout, but it can charge up to $5,000 per person: the expected payout plus the price of uncertainty. Remember, the difference between the maximum value of the insurance and the minimum cost of the insurance is the value of the risk reduction: the price of uncertainty. As long as the administrative costs and profit of the insurance company are less than the price of uncertainty, insurance can be successfully marketed to this group. With no insurance, each individual in the group has an expected utility of $96U$. When insurance costs less than $5,000, utility is higher. The person is better off insured (depicted by points B and C and all points in between), than uninsured (depicted by point A).

---

[2]Expected utility is calculated by summing the utility enjoyed at each health state adjusted (multiplied) by its respective probability. The expected utility curve is derived by varying the probability of each health state, from zero to one, and plotting the results.

[3]$E(Y) = (0.96 \times \$50,000) + (0.04 \times \$0) = \$48,000. \ E(U) = (0.96 \times 100U) + (0.04 \times 0U) = 96U.$

FIGURE 7.2
The Choice of Insurance

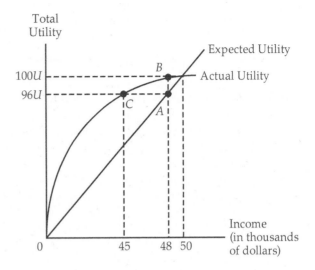

Several factors affect the decision to buy insurance. The shape of the utility-of-income curve is important. Obviously, individuals who are risk seekers or risk neutral will not buy insurance.[4] The magnitude of the loss also plays a key role in the decision. When the range of uncertainty is large (i.e., when the potential financial loss is large relative to the actual level of income), the distance between the actual utility curve and the expected utility curve is greater than when the range of uncertainty is small. The greater the expected loss, the greater the maximum value of the insurance, and the higher the likelihood that the individual will purchase insurance. As the probability of the loss changes, the likelihood of buying insurance changes. Even those who are risk averse do not buy insurance when the probability of a loss is at one of the extremes. The perceived cost of the risk is too low to stimulate demand at low probabilities, and minimum cost of the insurance is too high as the probability of illness approaches 100 percent. As with the demand for any product, it goes without saying that the price of the insurance and the level of income also play important roles in determining whether or not insurance will be purchased.

Health Insurance and Market Failure

An insurance pool is designed to spread the risk of high-cost, low-probability events across its participants. Hospitalization falls into this category, and insurance pays 97 percent of all hospital expenses. Coverage for low-cost, high-probability events—such as dental care, eyeglasses, and prescription drugs—is typically not as generous. Insurance covers about 50 percent of the overall spending for eyeglasses, about 60 percent for dental care, and 85 percent for prescription drugs (CMS, 2016). The premium paid by the policyholder is equal to the insured's expected spending plus a markup called loading to cover administrative overhead and profit—on average, approximately 15 percent of total premiums. For an individual to purchase insurance, the markup must be less than the price of uncertainty.[5] In situations where the likelihood of use is high and the costs are relatively low, the markup exceeds the value of the risk reduction, and the customer chooses not to buy insurance.

POLICY ISSUE

The health insurance tax subsidy distorts the salary package in favor of nontaxable benefits.

---

[4]For the risk seeker, risk contributes to utility. The actual utility function falls below the expected utility function, implying that risk adds to the level of utility. The risk-neutral person is indifferent to uncertainty. Risk has neither benefit nor cost associated with it.

[5]This statement assumes that the insurer and the policyholder place the same value on the expected payout.

KEY CONCEPT 9
Market Failure

POLICY ISSUE
*The health insurance
tax subsidy distorts the
salary package in favor of
nontaxable benefits.*

The dominant feature in the medical marketplace is the reliance on third-party payment. Just as insurance has shaped the market for medical care, the emergence of health insurance as an employment-based, tax-free benefit has shaped the market for health insurance. This feature has expanded coverage to medical services that normally would not be covered if insurance were purchased individually, creating a strong incentive for overconsumption (Pauly, 1986).

The aggregate value of this tax subsidy was an estimated $600 billion in 2017. In other words, if employer-based health insurance were treated as a taxable benefit, federal income tax receipts would rise by that amount. The tax savings ranges from $2,828 for those employed in firms that have a predominantly low-wage workforce to $4,131 for those employed in predominantly high-wage firms. Over 60 percent of the tax savings go to the highest-paid 20 percent of the population. The average private sector worker with employment-based health insurance saves about $3,340 per year in taxes (Miller and Selden, 2013). The progressivity of the tax benefit is the result of the progressivity of the income tax rate structure.

There is widespread agreement among economists that this favorable tax treatment distorts the composition of the typical employee compensation package. The theoretical argument is strong. For a person in the 28 percent tax bracket, it takes $1.39 in gross income to provide $1 in after-tax income. With the tax exemption, it only takes $1.17 in insurance coverage to provide $1 in health benefits.[6] This kind of subsidy provides a strong incentive to accept a compensation package disproportionately weighted in favor of nontaxable health benefits. Individuals in the lower income tax brackets have less incentive to substitute health insurance for income. Although it is clear that the tax subsidy matters, the empirical estimates of its impact are less precise.

As health benefits have expanded to cover routine care, the goal of insurance has expanded from spreading risk to insulating against all out-of-pocket spending. In 2013, out-of-pocket spending in the United States was 11.8 percent of total medical care spending.[7] Under these circumstances, providers have less incentive to provide care efficiently, which limits competition, raises costs, and lowers the quality of services.

APPLIED MICRO METHODS

EMPLOYER SPONSORED INSURANCE AND THE GENDER WAGE GAP

Background

Recent empirical evidence points to a persistent wage gap between men and women in the US. Although it has narrowed considerably over the last 30 years, the typical female makes only 79% as much as the typical male. Even after controlling for persistent differences between men and women (education, work experience, labor market attachment, occupation, and industry) the overall wage gap remains at about 10%.

Evidence points to the fact that women, during their primary working years, have annual medical care spending that are between $1,000 and $2,000 higher than men. This paper explores whether these differences in medical care spending play a factor in explaining the wage gap.

---

[6] Every $1 in premiums purchases $0.85 in expected health care benefits.

[7] A similar situation exists in the rest of the developed world. Out-of-pocket spending is higher in Canada, Germany, Japan, and Switzerland, ranging from 13.2 percent in Germany to 25.8 percent in Switzerland.

Data and Methods

Before the ACA was passed, risk rating by sex was permitted in the individual insurance market, resulting in women paying higher premiums than men. Since passage of the ACA, this type of risk rating has been banned and women can no longer be charged higher premiums. The employer-sponsored insurance (ESI) market where most Americans get their insurance was different. For tax and legal reasons employers did not charge women higher premiums or require higher cost sharing, even though women had higher medical costs. Employers simply absorbed the added cost (at least they appeared to do so).

This practice created an incentive for firms that offered ESI to prefer hiring men unless women's wages or other forms of compensation adjusted accordingly. Firms that did not offer ESI did not face this dilemma. Taking advantage of this distinction, the authors used a difference-in-difference (DiD) strategy to compare compensation of workers who receive ESI and those who did not.

The study used data from the 2002–2008 National Longitudinal Survey of Youth, 1979 cohort, resulting in 13,687 person-year observations. The baseline empirical model used workers' hourly wages as the dependent variable to estimate whether there was a differential wage offset (wage penalty due to higher health care spending) for women with ESI compared to women without ESI. Covariates included survey year, race, marital status, children in the household, age, education, Armed Forces Qualification Test score, job tenure, geographic location of residence, size of firm, industry, and occupation.

Results

Wages for women who did not receive ESI were $1.80 less than their male counterparts. Women who received ESI (in their own name) earned $3.33 less than men. Thus the DiD estimate of the wage penalty associated with ESI was $1.53. Research by Gruber (1994) supports the findings by pointing out that if employees fully value the benefit they are receiving, wages will fall to offset the full cost of the benefit to the employer and there will be no efficiency cost (no change in labor supply).

Discussion and Conclusions

Even though ESI premiums do not vary between men and women, wage differences fully account for the fact that women have higher medical risks and spend more on medical care than men. In situations where the employer pays a larger proportion of the medical expenses, the pay gap between men and women is larger. Female employees who receive ESI experience a larger wage gap relative to men than females who do not receive ESI. The annual pay differential between $1,000 and $3,000 for a full-time worker, accounting for roughly 10% of the overall wage gap. For the typical woman, the ESI penalty is responsible for the over one-half of the remaining wage differential.

Sources: Benjamin Cowan and Benjamin Schwab, "Employer-Sponsored Health Insurance and the Gender Wage Gap," *Journal of Health Economics* 45, 2016, 103–114; and Jonathan Gruber, "The Incidence of Mandated Maternity Benefits," *American Economic Review* 84(3), June 1994, 622–641.

Information Problems

Although the medical care sector in the United States has many problems, it is difficult to say how many of these problems can be traced directly to the traditional reliance on markets. The perceived failure of the medical marketplace to efficiently allocate resources and control spending has led most developed nations worldwide to adopt a system of extensive, collective involvement through social insurance. One of the most promising routes to understanding the functioning of the medical marketplace is to trace the implications of widespread information problems in that market. Information costs are a central factor in economic decision-making. The most challenging problems that arise because of costly information are due to unequal access to information. Often one party to an economic transaction has more and better information than all other parties. Several issues arise when access to information is not distributed equally: consumer information problems, moral hazard, and adverse selection.

Consumer Information Problems   For a market to work, consumers must behave rationally, have income to spend, and know their own preferences. When consumers have trouble gathering and understanding information, the ability to make informed decisions is compromised (Rice, 1998). The quality of information in health care markets tends to be poor: most information is passed from consumer to consumer by word-of-mouth with little formal advertising. Not only is medical information difficult to gather, it is also difficult to understand. A great deal of medical decision-making is based on highly technical information. Physicians spend a great deal of time in medical school to learn how to interpret the technical data on which they base diagnosis and treatment. Some patients strive to close this information gap through extensive use of medical information sites on the Internet. Many patients are not well equipped to make informed decisions and rely primarily on the medical provider who fills the dual role of supplier and adviser.

Cost-conscious decision-making also requires that consumers know the prices paid for the services they buy. This requirement is important and, at the same time, controversial. Prices of goods and services should reflect the value placed on them by individual consumers or society as a whole. However, many question the ethics of placing a monetary value on improved health status. The information issue is not what the price should be, but whether consumers should know the prices they are expected to pay. Better information on prices, often referred to as *price transparency*, would allow consumers to make price comparisons across providers and result in more efficient markets.

★ **KEY CONCEPT 9**
Market Failure

★ **KEY CONCEPT 4**
Self-Interest

The Economics of Moral Hazard   Information about the present and future is costly. Economic modeling once utilized the assumption of perfect and costless information exclusively, but has since attempted to recognize information costs as a central factor in decision-making. Nobel laureate George Stigler's (1961) thoughts are no longer accurate when he wrote, "Information occupies the slum dwelling in the town of economics." Now it seems that all of the interesting problems in economics are due to the fact that information is costly.

Information costs present problems during economic transactions. All contracts involve expectations of future behavior. Moral hazard occurs anytime there is an opportunity to gain from acting differently from the implied principles of a contract. There is always a chance that a contract will change the risk-taking behavior of one or both parties involved. The problem arises when parties to a contract cannot monitor each other's performance. Because private actions are hidden from view, both parties have an opportunity to gain from unpredictable behavior. If people were perfectly honest, writing contracts would be easy. But people are often opportunistic. People who are moral in most ways may still take advantage of situations when their behavior cannot be monitored. By exploiting the imbalance of information existing between the two parties to the contract, a person is engaging in economic opportunism—attempting to secure more utility than would be permitted or anticipated by a particular agreement.

BACK-OF-THE-ENVELOPE

The Economics of Opportunistic Behavior

In market transactions, there is a high probability that one or both parties to a transaction has knowledge of certain traits, characteristics, or behavior not readily available to the other party and will try to exploit this advantage. A person who purchases an insurance contract is likely to engage in opportunistic behavior, knowingly or unknowingly. Without the policyholder's knowledge, the insurance company may establish guidelines or create incentives to encourage providers to limit access to certain costly tests and procedures, a form of opportunistic behavior. One could argue that this sort of behavior is unethical or even immoral. Regardless of its origin, taking unfair advantage of private information when there is a potential for personal gain impedes the efficient workings of markets.

We can illustrate this inefficiency using a simple prisoner's dilemma game. Suppose the insurer and policy owners have two options: predictable or opportunistic. The payoffs shown represent different levels of utility or satisfaction with the outcome.

		Insurer	
		Predictable	Opportunistic
Policy	**Predictable**	80, 80	30, 100
Owner	**Opportunistic**	100, 30	50, 50

In the above case, both parties to the insurance contract have a dominant strategy; the best response is opportunistic behavior. If the insurer's behavior is predictable, the policy owner will be at a higher level of utility (100 instead of 80) by being opportunistic. The same is true for the insurer. When both play their dominant strategies (Opportunistic, Opportunistic), their combined utility is 100. The optimal payoff would be for them to cooperate, share private information, and practice predictable behavior where combined utility is 160.

It may be possible to set up a situation in which, through penalty or reward, the cooperative behavior (Predictable, Predictable) can be achieved, and welfare can be maximized. Suppose that predictable behavior is rewarded in such a way that utility increases by 25. In this case, the dominant strategy changes for each party and predictable behavior can be achieved all around.

		Insurer	
		Predictable	Opportunistic
Policy	**Predictable**	105, 105	55, 100
Owner	**Opportunistic**	100, 55	50, 50

The reward may be structured by providing a rebate to the policy owner, if medical care spending is below a certain threshold, or if no claims are made during the year. For the insurer, it may mean rewarding carriers that get high marks from enrollees or that satisfy certain benchmarks for preventive services.

The fact that a person has insurance coverage increases expected medical care spending. Two aspects to moral hazard affect both patient and provider. Having insurance (1) increases the likelihood of purchasing medical services and (2) induces higher spending in the event of an illness.[8]

These information problems affect the structure of insurance contracts. The person with insurance recognizes that the service is "sale priced." Patients experience net prices as low as 3 to 25 cents on the dollar for most medical services. It naturally follows that people pursue the rational tendency of purchasing more services than they would if they paid the full price. Lowering the cost of medical care to the individual through the availability of insurance increases the amount purchased.

It is easy to understand how this happens: A person visiting a physician for a battery of diagnostic tests will behave differently when fully insured. A patient with full insurance coverage will ask about the benefits of the tests, the nature of the complications, and the amount of time required for the entire procedure. A physician with a fully insured patient will provide the tests knowing that the insurance company will pay the bill. Seldom will cost enter the discussion. On the other hand, the uninsured patient will ask about the cost of the tests, the cost of alternative tests, whether the tests are absolutely necessary, and the likely consequences if they are postponed or skipped completely. And the physician of a patient without insurance will take the patient's financial situation into consideration when choosing which tests to run.

Studies by the RAND Corporation and others have shown that individuals who receive free care use more medical services than those who are required to pay a portion of the cost. It is widely understood that health insurance, by lowering the out-of-pocket cost of medical care to the individual, may increase the amount demanded. In other words, people demand more medical care when it is covered by insurance.

From a strictly economic perspective, we can argue that the response of seeking more medical care when one has insurance than when one does not is a result of rational economic behavior, not moral turpitude. The quantity of medical care demanded by an individual is a function of

- tastes and preferences for medical care,
- income,
- the extent of the illness, and
- the price charged for medical services.

Insurance reduces the price paid for medical care by the individual, from a positive market price to some lower price. Even if illness is a perfectly random event, the presence of medical insurance will alter the randomness of medical expenditures, unless the demand for medical care is perfectly inelastic.

Pauly (1968) presented these ideas more formally. Consider that there are three health events that can take place during a particular time period:

I_1 = a person will not be sick (with probability $p_1 = 0.5$)
I_2 = a person will be moderately ill (with probability $p_2 = 0.25$)
I_3 = a person will be seriously ill (with probability $p_3 = 0.25$)

Using Figure 7.3, the position of the individual's demand curve for medical care during any time period depends on which health event occurs. Assume perfectly inelastic demand

---

[8]In practice, economists view moral hazard as one aspect of the law of demand. Patients respond to lower net prices by purchasing more. Providers recognize that demand for their services is price inelastic and thus charge higher prices and prescribe more services.

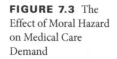

FIGURE 7.3 The Effect of Moral Hazard on Medical Care Demand

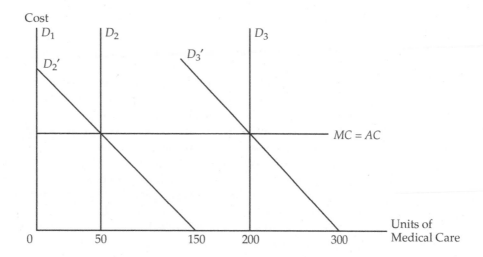

curves D_1 (along the vertical axis), D_2, and D_3 corresponding to the three events. With no medical insurance, the individual faces the probability p_1, that he will incur no medical expenses; p_2, that he will need 50 units of medical care at a cost of $50MC$; and p_3, that he will require 200 units of medical care at a cost of $200MC$, where MC is the cost of one unit of medical care.

The expected value of the individual's medical care expenses equals $62.5MC$. The calculation is $(0.5 \times 0) + (0.25 \times 50MC) + (0.25 \times 200MC)$. Arrow's (1963) welfare proposition indicates that the risk-averse individual will prefer paying a premium of $62.5MC$ for medical insurance to risking the probability distribution with the mean equal to $62.5MC$.

Suppose, however, that the individual's demand curves are not perfectly inelastic. If, instead, they are as D_2' and D_3'; the individual without insurance faces the probability distribution as above with mean $62.5MC$. However, to fully indemnify against all medical costs (with no out-of-pocket spending), the actuarially necessary insurance premium will be equal to $(112.5MC)$, which is equal to $(0.5 \times 0) + (0.25 \times 150MC) + (0.25 \times 300MC)$. In such a case, the individual may prefer taking the risk instead of purchasing the insurance.

The presence of demand curves that are not perfectly inelastic implies that the individual will alter his or her desired expenditures for medical care when insurance is present. The individual who has insurance that covers all cost demands medical care as though it had a zero price. If the demand for medical care has a price elasticity greater than zero, forcing individuals to purchase insurance will create inefficiencies. For an efficient solution, some form of price rationing at the point of service may be necessary; that is, deductibles and coinsurance.

Adverse Selection   Adverse selection arises because individuals have more information about expected medical expenditures than insurance companies. The ability of prospective insurance customers to conceal their true risks can result in some insurance risk pools having a disproportionate number of insureds who use medical care more frequently than might be expected. This leads to higher-than-average premiums for the group and creates an incentive for low-risk individuals to drop out of the group in search of lower-cost coverage elsewhere.

Adverse selection may be illustrated using the following example: Assume that there are 1,000 individuals, each with a 4 percent chance of a $50,000 loss. The insurer expects 40 claims or a total loss of $2,000,000, and requires a premium of $2,000 plus loading costs (overhead and profit). Suppose the original pool of individuals is merged with one that has 1,000 people, each with a 30 percent chance of making a $50,000 claim. There will be 300 additional claims and an additional $15,000,000 in medical spending. If the insurer cannot distinguish between the two groups (or is forced by law to charge the same premium to both), the premium must rise for everyone, because the minimum cost of insuring each of the 2,000 people is now $8,500. If members of the high-risk segment were pooled separately, their premium would be $15,000, so $8,500 is a bargain for them. For members of the low-risk segment of the pool, the premium increase is staggering.

The problem is shown using Figure 7.4. Assuming that risk preferences are the same for individuals in each group, we can use the same utility function to illustrate their situations. Low-risk individuals can self-insure, ending up at point A with the 4 percent risk of a $50,000 loss; or, when pooled separately, they may purchase insurance for $2,000 plus loading costs as long as they end up no lower than point B on their (income certain) utility curve. They enjoy a utility level of at least U_2 in either case. High-risk individuals (whose expectations have them situated closer to the origin on the expected utility curve) may choose to self-insure and end up at point E with a 30 percent risk of catastrophic loss; or when pooled separately, they may purchase insurance for $15,000 plus loading costs as long as they end up no lower than point F on their (income certain) utility curve. The utility level of the high-risk group can be no lower than U_0.

When the two groups are pooled together, a premium of $8,500 plus loading allows all members of the two groups to end up at point D and experience a utility level of U_1 with certainty. High-risk group members have two options: they may choose to go without insurance and end up at point E with utility of U_0, or they may buy pooled insurance and end up at point D with utility of U_1. Low-risk users also have two options: they may buy pooled insurance and end up at point D with utility of U_1, or choose not buy insurance at all and end up at point A with utility level U_2. In this example, low-risk users will forgo insurance and self-insure, leaving high-risk users in a separate pool with the higher premium of $15,000 plus loading costs. Without a significant tax subsidy, the only way to guarantee the solvency of the high-risk insurance pool is to force members of the low-risk group to remain in the pool. The fine for not participating in the insurance pool would have to approach the cost of insurance in the combined pool.

FIGURE 7.4 The Impact of Adverse Selection on Risk Pooling

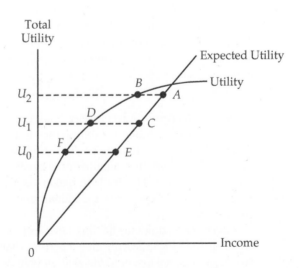

Insurers' Response to Information Problems   Moral hazard and adverse selection are information problems. Both arise due to the inability of insurers to monitor customer behavior and identify prospective risk. The typical insurer's response to the overspending associated with moral hazard is to charge deductibles and coinsurance. Deductibles are set amounts of spending before the insurance pays any part of the claim. Deductibles for individuals in the new insurance exchanges are anywhere from $1,000 to $7,150 (double that amount for families). Whether the deductible works to discourage spending depends on the probability that total spending will exceed the deductible. In practice, deductibles seem to have some depressing effect on spending when expected spending is below the deductible. Otherwise, they have little impact. Obviously, one way to increase the impact of the deductible is to increase its size. Deductibles of $7,150 will reduce spending more than deductibles of $1,000.

In most cases, the insured patient pays a fixed percentage of every claim. The typical coinsurance rate of 10 to 20 percent provides a measure of discipline to the cost-conscious patient. Higher coinsurance rates raise the marginal cost to the insured and serve to restrain spending to a greater degree. This cost sharing usually stops after total out-of-pocket spending reaches some predetermined limit. For coverage purchased in the newly created insurance exchanges, maximum out-of-pocket spending (in 2017) is $7,150 for individual coverage and $14,300 for family coverage.

Prior to the passage of the ACA, the insurer's response to adverse selection is twofold: insurance companies will only underwrite prospective risk and will refuse to provide insurance for known ailments. The insurer will try to determine the expected level of spending prior to entering into the contract and refuse to cover a **preexisting condition** (one associated with an extremely high probability of use, often approaching 100 percent). Without the ability to spread risk, the insurance premium would likely exceed the expected spending. High-risk consumers experience no gain from joining a risk pool with other high-risk consumers, so they have little demand for this high-cost insurance.

The failure of the free market to provide opportunities for the chronically and congenitally ill to purchase insurance at average premiums should come as no surprise. The purpose of insurance is to share risk, not redistribute income. Policymakers, even those not interested in income redistribution, have used market failure to justify the provision of social insurance as a safety net. However, the private insurance markets can provide adequate insurance for high-risk individuals through high-risk pools subsidized by taxpayers for those with preexisting conditions, or health status insurance for those with existing coverage who get sick.

Other policymakers justify the provision of social insurance because of the external costs associated with the uninsured (e.g., high-cost emergency room use, cost-shifting, and social unrest). Social insurance makes a pooling solution possible. Low risks are required to support the risk pool through compulsory participation, higher taxes, or higher insurance premiums. This approach to insurance is used in the United States in means-tested Medicaid, age-tested Medicare, and now the insurance exchanges created by the ACA.

The Optimal Insurance Plan

Insurance plan design must address the information problems. The optimal insurance plan design would only pay for medical care that would be chosen by self-insured individuals. Suppose a person is faced with a 10 percent probability of incurring a $20,000 medical expense. A risk-averse individual would be willing to pay a premium of at least $2,000 rather than self-insure. (The additional amount over $2,000 that the person would be

POLICY ISSUE
Should the government provide insurance for high-risk individuals with preexisting conditions?

preexisting condition
A medical condition caused by an injury or disease that existed prior to the application for health insurance.

willing to pay for the insurance depends on the degree of risk aversion.) After purchasing insurance, if the person becomes ill and spends $30,000, the additional $10,000 spending is due to moral hazard.

Using standard demand theory, the implications of moral hazard are simple. The reduced net price that an insured person pays for medical care has both a substitution effect and an income effect. Moral hazard is the substitution effect, the additional spending beyond the amount that a fully informed person would, prior to the illness, voluntarily contract to cover. The income effect is the systematic transfer of income from the pool of healthy persons to those who become ill. The transfer allows individuals who become ill to purchase medical care that would be unaffordable without insurance.

Insurers use deductibles and coinsurance in response to moral hazard. This form of risk sharing encourages patients to compare the marginal cost of medical care to its marginal benefit. Risk sharing provides incentives for providers and insurers to offer the medically appropriate amount of care. Individuals with generous insurance coverage seek more care than those who are uninsured and providers recommend higher levels of care.

The optimally designed insurance plan balances the benefits of greater risk sharing with the costs of moral hazard (Cutler and Zeckhauser, 2000). If the goal is to control over-spending, the solution is to make people responsible for more of their own care. Higher deductibles and larger copays will result in cost-conscious behavior on the part of both patients and providers.

Third-party insurance requires some method of assigning individuals to risk pools. Adverse selection arises because insurers find it difficult to identify prospective risk and charge premiums that accurately reflect the average risk of pool participants. The new health insurance exchanges created by the ACA use heterogeneous risk pooling where young and old, chronically ill and healthy are pooled together. Premiums are set using a modified community rating where they can vary no more than 300 percent between young and old and health status may not be taken into account. Efficient pooling requires that individuals be grouped into homogeneous risk pools (with others of similar risk) and charged premiums to reflect that risk.

In the United States, about 84 percent of Americans with private insurance are covered under group policies sold to employers or employee associations. Such pools are created without regard to individual risk categories. The sick are pooled with the healthy, the young with the old. The only thing they share in common is the fact that they work for the same employer. The policy implications of employer-sponsored insurance are important. Unless plan premiums are based on employee income, everyone pays the same premium. Younger employees pay the same premium as older employees, even though they use less medical care. Sorting people into pools based on expected spending means that those with low risk pay lower premiums than those with high risk.

Additionally, group insurance means that individuals do not own their own insurance policies. Without individual ownership, portability among employer groups has been a chronic problem. Because the ACA does not allow insurance underwriting to take into consideration any preexisting condition, the portability issue should be mitigated.

When plans set premiums according to community ratings, commercial insurers are forced to look for ways to offer low-risk groups better rates. To successfully attract groups with lower-than-average risks, plans must offer insurance at lower premiums. Because high-risk individuals are attracted to more generous plans, low-risk individuals will choose less generous plans to avoid subsidizing the sick, and plans will try to attract them by offering insurance with fewer benefits. This practice is often referred to as **cream skimming**. Two studies suggest that individuals are attracted to plans with lower premiums (Buchmueller, 1998; Cutler and Reber, 1998). When individuals are willing to switch plans

---

☆ **POLICY ISSUE**
Most Americans receive their health insurance through employer-sponsored plans.

☆ **POLICY ISSUE**
Should U.S. health care reform take a collectivist approach involving more government or focus on private sector solutions?

cream skimming A practice of pricing insurance policies so that healthy (low-risk) individuals will purchase coverage and those with a history of costly medical problems (high-risk) will not.

for small premium savings, plans become vulnerable to a death spiral resulting from adverse selection. Healthy individuals switch from comprehensive plans to less generous plans, leaving the generous plans with individuals who, on average, have higher levels of spending. Their departure results in even higher premiums for the generous plans, more dropout, and premiums rise further. Ultimately, the generous plan has problems attracting anyone because of high premiums and is cancelled.

Assume 1,000 individuals are pooled together to purchase a generous health insurance plan and each pays an annual premium of $3,450. Average expected spending is $3,000 with a 15 percent loading for overhead and profit. One-half of the group members are low risk and the rest are high risk. Members of the low-risk group spend on average $2,000 per year and those with high risk spend $4,000. The result of this pooling arrangement is that low risks pay $1,150 more than the actuarially fair premium for their group while the high-risk pay $1,150 less. Cream skimming involves members of the low-risk group opting for less generous and cheaper coverage or choosing to opt out and forego insurance completely. When all the low risks leave the pool, those left pay the actuarially fair premium of $4,600 for their risk class. If one-half left in the high-risk pool spend an average of $3,500 and the rest spend an average of $4,500, those with the relatively lower risk can leave the pool and choose less generous coverage or no coverage at all. The high spenders must then pay a premium of $5,175 to maintain their coverage. The process will continue as long as those with lower risk can secure coverage elsewhere at actuarially fair premiums or self-insure. Those with higher relative risk will see their premiums continuously spiral upwards until their insurance becomes unaffordable.

Risk adjustment is not the problem. Efficiency dictates that premiums reflect expected spending. In other words, those with higher risk should pay higher premiums. Pooling by age, sex, and geographic location is appropriate. If those with higher expected spending cannot afford their premiums, the problem is lack of income and the solution is an appropriate subsidy to pay for their excess medical spending. Those with lower expected spending are usually younger, making lower incomes. Forcing the young to subsidize the old is in practice transferring income from those with lower incomes to those with higher incomes.

BACK-OF-THE-ENVELOPE

Adverse Selection in Health Insurance Markets

The Marketplace Insurance & Casualty Organization (MICO) does business in the state's health insurance exchange, where individual health insurance, also called Obamacare is sold. However, the ACA requires that MICO must offer full coverage and charge the same premium to all of its policyholders. For simplicity, assume the premium must be set such that the dollar value of MICO's expected profit from selling insurance is equal to $0.

MICO estimates that the probabilities of a medical event for the five risk types are as follows (for simplicity, assume that there the same number of participants of each risk type):

Risk type	Probability of medical event
Low risk	10%
Moderate risk	25%
Average risk	30%
Above average risk	34%
High risk	50%

The dollar value of initial wealth and lost income due to illness for all risk types are $100,000 and $40,000 respectively. This implies that if an illness occurs, then the dollar value of uninsured wealth falls to $60,000. Furthermore, utility $U = W^{0.5}$ for all risk types. All participants pay the same insurance premium (P) which will fully cover catastrophic illness−related losses.

1. MICO must establish an initial premium (P) that will enable it to comply with ACA's insurance regulations.
   When all risk types purchase insurance, the initial premium will be:

   $P = 0.10(40,000) + 0.25(40,000) + 0.30(40,000) + 0.34(40,000) + 0.50(40,000)$
   $P = 4,000 + 10,000 + 12,000 + 13,600 + 20,000 = 59,600/5 = 11,920$

   When insurance is offered at $P = \$11,920$, the Low Risk participants realize that their utility is higher if they remain uninsured, even if they pay the tax penalty for not purchasing insurance (assumed equal to \$2,000).
   The expected utility for Low Risk participants if they are uninsured (UI) is

   $$EU_{Low\ Risk}^{\ UI} = 0.90(100,000 - 2,000)^{0.5} + 0.10(60,000 - 2,000)^{0.5}$$
   $$= 0.90(313.05) + 0.10(240.83)$$
   $$= 281.75 + 24.08 = 305.83$$

   The expected utility for all risk types (including Low Risk) if they pay a premium equal to \$11,920 and buy insurance is

   $$EU_{Buyers} = 1(100,000 - 11,920)^{0.5} = 1(88,080)^{0.5} = 296.78.$$

   Low Risk will not buy insurance because $305.83 > 296.78$.
   Note that even Moderate Risk participants will prefer insurance, since expected utility of being insured (296.98) exceeds expected utility of being uninsured (UI):

   $$EU_{Mod\ Risk}^{\ UI} = 0.75(100,000 - 2,000)^{0.5} + 0.25(60,000 - 2,000)^{0.5}$$
   $$= 0.75(313.05) + 0.25(240.83)$$
   $$= 234.79 + 60.21 = 295.00.$$

   Furthermore, the other three risk categories all have higher medical risk probabilities than the Moderate Risk group and their expected utilities from being uninsured are lower, so they too purchase insurance.

   $$EU_{Ave\ Risk}^{\ UI} = 0.70(100,000 - 2,000)^{0.5} + 0.30(60,000 - 2,000)^{0.5}$$
   $$= 0.70(313.05) + 0.30(240.83) = 291.38.$$

   $$EU_{Above\ Ave\ Risk}^{\ UI} = 0.66(100,000 - 2,000)^{0.5} + 0.34(60,000 - 2,000)^{0.5}$$
   $$= 0.66(313.05) + 0.34(240.83) = 288.50.$$

   $$EU_{High\ Risk}^{\ UI} = 0.50(100,000 - 2,000)^{0.5} + 0.50(60,000 - 2,000)^{0.5}$$
   $$= 0.50(313.05) + 0.50(240.83) = 276.94.$$

2. Because the Low Risk group will not purchase insurance when $P = \$11,920$, MICO must raise its premium to $P = \$13,900$ in order to comply with regulatory requirements. When the premium rises to \$13,900, the Moderate Risk group does *not* purchase insurance. The $EU_{Mod\ Risk}^{\ UI} = 295.00$. The expected utility of the Moderate Risk group (and all higher risk groups) if they purchase insurance at \$13,900 is

   $$EU_{Buyers} = 1(100,000 - 13,900)^{0.5} = 1(86,100)^{0.5} = 293.43.$$

   Because the Moderate Risk group has higher utility from not buying insurance (295.00), when $P = \$13,900$, they will voluntarily drop out of risk pool.
   Note that the Average Risk group will prefer insurance, because their expected utility of being insured (293.43) exceeds their expected utility of being uninsured (291.38). Both the Above Average and High Risk groups have even higher illness probabilities than the Average Risk group. Thus, their expected utility from being insured (293.43) is greater than their expected utility from being uninsured (288.50 and 276.94 respectively).

3. Because the Moderate Risk group does not purchase insurance when $P = \$13,900$, MICO must now raise its premium to $P = \$15,200$ in order to comply with regulatory

requirements. The Average Risk group *will not* purchase insurance when P = $15,200, but that the two highest risk groups *will* purchase insurance.
When the premium rises to $15,200, the expected utility of buyers is:

$$EU_{Buyers} = 1(100,000 - 15,200)^{0.5} = 1(84,800)^{0.5} = 291.20.$$

Because the Average Risk group has higher utility from not buying insurance at that premium (291.38), they will voluntarily drop out of the risk pool. Note that Above Average Risks will prefer insurance, since their expected utility of being insured (291.20) exceeds his expected utility of being uninsured. High Risks have an even higher accident probability than Above Average Risks, they will also have higher expected utility from being insured (291.20) than uninsured (276.24).

4. Average Risk will not purchase insurance when P = $15,200. MICO must raise its premium even further in order to comply with regulatory requirements; the new "breakeven" premium will P = $16,800. Above Average Risks will not purchase insurance at this price. When the premium rises to $16,800, the expected utility of buyers is:

$$EU_{Buyers} = 1(100,000 - 16,800)^{0.5} = 1(83,200)^{0.5} = 288.44.$$

Because Above Average Risk has higher utility from being uninsured (288.50), the group drop out of the risk pool and the High Risk group whose utility from not being insured is 276.94 will remain in the pool.

5. Above Average Risk will not purchase insurance when P = $16,800. MICO must raise its premium even further in order to comply with regulatory requirements; the new "breakeven" premium will P = $20,000. When the premium rises to $20,000, the expected utility of buyers is:

$$EU_{Buyers} = 1(100,000 - 20,000)^{0.5} = 1(80,000)^{0.5} = 282.84.$$

Only the High Risk group has higher utility from being insured (282.84) than being uninsured (276.94) and remain in the risk pool. The death spiral is over and the pool evolves into a high risk pool.

Many policymakers mistakenly believe that insurance companies make money by denying coverage to those identified as high risks. If insurance companies were free to set premiums according to strict actuarial principles, then high-risk individuals would pay higher premiums, and there would be no incentive to cream skim. Cream skimming is the result of regulation in the insurance industry, not competition (Pauly, 1984). Without an efficient mechanism of risk-adjusted premium differentials, the likelihood of cream skimming exists. If those with higher risk cannot afford higher premiums, the issue is an income problem and not an insurance problem. The solution is not community-rated premiums; it is appropriate subsidies to those who cannot afford the actuarially fair premium.

KEY CONCEPT 8
Efficiency

ISSUES IN MEDICAL CARE DELIVERY

HEALTH STATUS INSURANCE

Guaranteed renewability allows health insurance policy holders to renew their policies after they develop costly medical conditions. This benefit is not costless and can be priced into the premium. In fact, prior to the passage of HIPAA in 1997 approximately 80 percent of the non-group health insurance policies sold in the United States carried guaranteed renewability clauses (Pauly et al., 1999).

To support guaranteed renewability, health insurance policies would need a separately priced feature protecting the insured person from risk reclassification should
the individual develop a medical condition that results in the permanent reclassification into a high-risk category. This so-called health status insurance would provide
protection against the increase in premiums that accompanies such a reclassification (Cochrane, 1995; Herring and Pauly, 2006). Everyone in the risk pool would pay
a slightly higher premium (based on the per capita share of the expected increase in
group spending caused by those who are reclassified). In return, continuous coverage
would result in uniform premiums for everyone in the pool. The arrangement must
start with homogeneous risk pools (ideally created at birth) that are risk rated according to age and sex.

State-Level Insurance Regulation

As concerns over access and quality continue to mount, both the federal and state governments have intervened to correct the perceived deficiencies in the health insurance
market. Government policymakers have generally responded by introducing additional
regulation. State governments, historically responsible for insurance regulation, have
passed over 2,000 health insurance mandates with most states having between 40 and 60
mandates.

Passage of the ACA changed the dynamics of insurance regulation. The ACA required
that the Secretary of Health and Human Services define the benefit packages for all qualified health plans. As a result, all qualified plans provide a guaranteed set of benefits and a
legislated level of cost sharing. Individuals who purchase insurance from the exchanges will
be able to choose among four metallic tiers of plans. The four tiers are defined as Bronze
(covering 60 percent of the full actuarial value of the benefits), Silver (covering 70 percent),
Gold (80 percent), and Platinum (90 percent).

guaranteed issue
A requirement that
insurers must issue a
policy to anyone who
applies for one with no
consideration of health
status.

The legislation includes certain provisions that dictate how insurance companies manage their enrollment. These requirements include **guaranteed issue**, guaranteed renewability, restrictions on the exclusions of preexisting conditions, the requirement that adult
children under the age of 26 may receive coverage under their parents' plan, and the imposition of modified community-rated premiums.

The Economics of Mandates

These mandates are not free. They impose significant economic and social costs on their
intended beneficiaries. The regulations determining what benefits to offer, which providers to include, and how insurance companies manage their enrollment will have long-term
consequences on the ability of the health care system to provide access to quality care at
affordable prices.

From a public interest perspective, these regulations are designed to correct deficiencies in the health insurance market. Insurers and purchasers may unknowingly undervalue
the benefits of certain types of care, such as substance abuse treatment and mental health
treatment, resulting in a demand for treatment that is too low from a societal perspective. Without mandates, adverse selection is a significant problem with high-risk individuals choosing to enroll in plans offering more extensive coverage and low-risk individuals
choosing low-benefit plans.

APPLIED MICRO METHODS

WHO PAYS FOR THE ACA'S DEPENDENT MANDATE?

Background

Major portions of the coverage provisions of the ACA did not become operational until January 2014. However, one aspect went into effect almost immediately (September 23, 2010), the dependent coverage mandate stipulating that adult children up to age 26 be covered on their parents' insurance policies. Goda et al. (2016) examine the effect this type of mandate on employee incomes. The impact depends largely on how many dependents take advantage of this insurance option (crowd-out) and whether the cost is shared among employees regardless of parental status (pooling).

Data and Methods

The study takes advantage of the variation in dependent coverage across the states prior to the passage of the ACA. The state-level mandates already in place in 37 states had many restrictions. Some required that dependents live with their parents, that they be full-time students, unmarried, or that they be financially dependent on them. The federal mandate had no such restrictions; it applied to all young adults. Additionally, insurance plans could not charge higher premiums for the coverage and self-insured firms (exempt under state laws) had to provide the coverage.

Using the 2008 Survey of Income and Program Participation (SIPP) longitudinal data, states were divided into mandate states (MS) and non-mandate states (NMS) based on their pre-ACA status. Taking advantage of this discontinuity in the data, a DiD approach was taken with the MS as the control group, allowing the researchers to difference out unobserved factors unrelated to either the existing trends in income or the ACA mandate.

Results

With over 400,000 person-month observations, the study found that after the mandate went into effect monthly earnings for individuals in the NMS were $103 lower than their predicted earnings without the mandate. Results of several robustness tests suggest that there are no detectable trend differences in earnings across treatment and control states.

Discussion and Conclusions

The decrease in earnings due to the mandate to cover dependent children up to age 26 seems to be the result of at least moderate crowd-out (a large number of 19–25 year olds switching to their parents' plans from other coverage) or a disproportionate number of those who switch being sicker than average. Additionally, the results suggest at least some pooling between parents and non-parents indicating that the cost of the mandate is borne by all workers and not just those who are affected by the mandate.

A number of other studies have examined other implications of the ACA's dependent care mandate. Barbaresco et al. (2015) concluded that the provision increased the probability of having health insurance and a primary care physician while reducing body mass index at the same time. However, it also increased risky drinking and did not increase the use of preventive services. Depew and Bailey (2015) found that the mandate increased premiums in health plans covering children by 2.5–2.8 percent relative to single coverage plans. And Colman and Dave (2015) found that young people with coverage on their parents' plans reduced the amount of time they worked and reallocated time savings to socializing, sleeping, and other activities they view as more meaningful.

Sources: Gopi Shah Goda, Monica Farid, and Jay Bhattacharya, "The Incidence of Mandated Health Insurance: Evidence from the Affordable Care Act Dependent Care Mandate," NBER Working Paper 21846, January 2016; Silvia Barbaresco et al., "Impacts of the Affordable Care Act Dependent Coverage Provision on Health-Related Outcomes of Young Adults," *Journal of Health Economics* 40, 2015, 54–68; Briggs Depew and James Bailey, "Did the Affordable Care Act's Dependent Coverage Mandate Increase Premiums?" *Journal of Health Economics* 41, 2015, 1–14; and Gregory Colman and Dhaval Dave, "It's About Time: Effects of the Affordable Care Act Dependent Coverage Mandate on Time Use," NBER Working Paper 21725, November 2015.

Some policymakers view the addition of mandates as a way of improving insurance coverage without the costs that usually accompany the improvements. But these regulations impose economic and social costs on the same people they intend to benefit. These costs can include higher premiums, lower wages, higher unemployment, and an increase in the number of people who choose to go without insurance.

The evidence from studies on the cost of mandates creates an interesting problem for policymakers. Mandates are popular among certain well-defined constituencies: providers of clinical services, patient advocacy groups, and other political interest groups. Faced with pressure from the various special interest groups and the hidden cost of mandates, legislation passes easily. Mandated benefits attempt to make marginal improvements in the insurance benefits of those with insurance, but often at a price.

BACK-OF-THE-ENVELOPE

The Economics of Employer Mandates

employer mandate
A requirement that employers must offer a qualified health plan to every employee or pay a penalty (usually in the form of a payroll tax).

Proponents of a universal system assume that mandatory participation must be part of the system. Mandatory participation may take the form of government provision or some type of mandate, employer or individual. As a tool of social policy, mandates occupy the middle ground between the status quo and government provision. Conservatives prefer mandates to government provision, and liberals prefer mandates to the status quo. The **employer mandate** has occupied the compromise position in U.S. public policy debates as far back as the Nixon administration.

The case for mandating the employer provision of benefits is clear. The argument goes something like this: As with all merit goods, individuals underestimate the value of health insurance by underestimating the probability of a catastrophic loss due to illness. Because of the difficulty in making these kinds of intertemporal calculations, participation in a health insurance program should be mandatory. In the case of medical care, society may value equal consumption more highly than in the case of other goods and thus may mandate that a certain level of benefits be available to everyone. Finally, the externalities associated with medical care may be considerable. Even though the prevention of the spread of contagious disease is one aspect of this argument, the inability to pay for medical care creates pressures on society to pay the bills. This unwillingness to deny medical care to those in need is evidenced by the fact that uninsured Americans receive free care that amounts to approximately half of the per capita medical care received by the privately insured (Hadley and Holahan, 2003).

Those who argue against the employer mandate point out that it helps only the 60 percent who have some labor force attachment. The mandate places a wedge between the marginal cost of hiring an additional worker and the wage that can be offered. In other words, as the cost of mandates increases, benefits increase and actual wages decrease. Unable to adjust the wages of workers earning close to the minimum wage, employers are forced to eliminate some unskilled jobs, thereby creating unemployment in some sectors. Low-wage industries such as retail, construction, restaurants, agriculture, and personal and household services are affected more than the rest of the economy.

Economists tend to view mandated benefits as a disguised tax. Even though the viewpoint is true to a certain extent, it is not quite that simple. In the diagram, consider the original equilibrium of D_0 and S_0 with employment of E_0. A mandatory benefit that costs x dollars per hour shifts the employer's demand for workers down by that amount. If the worker values the mandated benefit at $\$x$ per hour, then the supply curve shifts out by the same amount, wages fall by $\$x$ per hour, and employment remains at E_0. However, workers are notorious for underestimating the value of health insurance, so the supply curve shifts by less than $\$x$. Wages fall by some fraction of $\$x$ per hour, but employment also falls from E_0 to E_1.

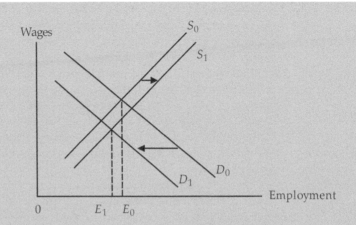

It is an issue without an easy policy stance. Because of the externalities associated with health insurance, and the tendency of workers to underestimate its value, some argue that it is appropriate for government to intervene and mandate coverage. Others focus on the potential job losses and the associated dislocations that they will cause. The lesson may be that there are no solutions, only competing alternatives with their own individual drawbacks.

Sources: Lawrence H. Summers, "Some Simple Economics of Mandated Benefits," *American Economic Review* 79, May 1989, 177–183; Carlos Bonilla, "The Price of a Health Care Mandate," *Wall Street Journal*, August 20, 1993; and Jack Hadley and John Holahan, "How Much Medical Care Do the Uninsured Use, and Who Pays for It?" *Health Affairs – Web Exclusive* (W3), February 12, 2003, 66–81.

The economics of mandates are clear. If firms already offer the mandated benefit, there is no tangible effect on the availability of insurance or premium costs. However, firms that do not voluntarily offer the mandated coverage are required to add it to their employees' benefit package, which increases the cost of health insurance for those firms. Advocates of additional mandates argue that the new coverage benefits recipients. But recipients end up paying for the new coverage. Evidence presented by Jensen and Morrisey (1999) indicates that workers pay for mandated benefits in three ways: lower wages, fewer non-health benefits, and higher premiums. Given ERISA exemptions, larger firms avoid mandates by self-insuring. Because owners of small businesses do not have the option of self-insuring, they are disproportionately affected by mandates (Jensen et al., 1995). Additionally, one in four uninsured Americans is without health insurance because of mandates.

One reason that a large percentage of the working poor remain uninsured is that mandates make private insurance unaffordable for many. This is especially true for small business owners, their employees, and their families, who represent the majority of the employed uninsured in this country.

The Practice of Self-Insurance

underwriting The insurance practice of determining whether or not an application for insurance will be accepted. In the process, premiums are also determined.

As insurance premiums rise, private sector employers have increasingly looked to self-insurance as a means of reducing the cost of providing health insurance to their workers. Currently, over half of all private insurance is provided in plans where the employer of the group assumes all or a significant part of the financial risk. The growth of self-insurance is easy to understand. Most private insurance **underwriting** is based on experience rating in the first place. After experiencing a large number of medical episodes, an employer may be able to accurately predict medical expenses from year to year. Thus, it is practical for large employers to self-insure. The predictability of expenses and the ability to spread risk over a large group makes self-insurance feasible.

Firms that self-insure do not actually contract with an insurance company to assume the financial risk. Instead, they accept this responsibility internally by simply placing funds previously paid in insurance premiums into a reserve account to pay medical claims directly. Many self-insured firms arrange for commercial insurance companies to administer their plans and handle claims processing, actuarial services, and utilization reviews. A large percentage of the plans limit risk through **reinsurance**, a cap on spending at some stop-loss threshold.

reinsurance Stop-loss insurance purchased by a health plan to protect itself against losses that exceed a specific dollar amount per claim, per individual, or per year.

Government regulation provides a strong incentive for firms to self-insure. Most states levy a tax on premiums that insurers must pass on to their customers. This extra premium expense does not apply to self-insured plans. Firms that self-insure are not subject to state-level mandates. Specifically, the provisions of the ERISA of 1974 supersede state laws and prohibit the application of state mandates to self-insured plans.

The increased popularity of self-insurance has changed the nature of risk rating. Firms that are large enough to self-insure do so. Community rating is no longer a viable way to determine premiums for groups with below-average levels of risk. Even Blue Cross-Blue Shield, traditionally a proponent of community rating, has been forced to abandon the practice in favor of experience rating for large firms that have the option of self-insuring.

POLICY ISSUE
State regulations create incentives for firms to set up self-insured plans.

Medical Care for the Uninsured

It is important to understand the nature and extent of the problems associated with being uninsured. The most recent estimates from the U.S. Census Bureau place the number of uninsured at 29 million (Barnett and Vornovitsky, 2016). Providing affordable coverage for the uninsured is a formidable task. Understanding who the uninsured are and the reasons they lack insurance coverage is critical in developing policy to deal with the problem.

POLICY ISSUE
Over 50 million Americans do not have a health insurance.

A large percentage of the uninsured can be categorized as working poor. Almost 25 percent make less than $25,000 per year. Many work for smaller firms where health insurance is not part of the employee benefit package. Others choose not to take up the insurance offered by their employer, because they do not consider the purchase of health insurance a very good buy for the money. Prior to the passage of ACA, many of these were the individuals who earned too much to qualify for Medicaid.

HTTP://
Health insurance statistics are available from the U.S. Census Bureau website at http://www .census.gov/hhes/www/ hlthins/hlthins.html.

Not everyone without health insurance is poor. Over 20 percent of the uninsured have incomes at least three times the official poverty level. While the number of uninsured poor has remained fairly stable in recent years, the higher-income uninsured have seen the most dramatic increase in numbers. In fact, households with over $50,000 in income have experienced the greatest growth in the number of uninsured of all income groups. Under ACA individuals who earn up to 250 percent of the federal poverty level are eligible for premium and copayment subsidies designed to keep their insurance premiums under a specified percent of income (2–6 percent of income). Individuals with incomes up to 400 percent of the FPL are eligible for premium subsidies only, keeping their net premiums under 9.5 percent of their income.[9]

---

[9]Over one-third of the 19 million uninsured 18–34 year olds are offered health coverage at their place of employment but decline the coverage because it is too expensive.

Counting the Uninsured

There is a great deal of confusion about the actual number of uninsured in the country. The most commonly cited estimates of the number of uninsured originate from the Census Bureau's Current Population Survey (CPS). Based on a nationally representative sample, the survey has been conducted annually since 1980. The CPS estimate is intended to measure the number of Americans uninsured for the entire year. Based on evidence available from other surveys, the CPS estimate likely overstates the number of uninsured Americans.

There are at least 6 national surveys that gather information on the characteristics of the uninsured. In addition to the CPS, other surveys, including the Survey of Income and Programs Participation (SIPP), the National Health Interview Survey (NHIS), and the Medical Expenditure Panel Survey (MEPS), address many of the same issues. Short (2001) tackles the methodological problems associated with estimating the number of uninsured to show how different survey techniques can result in different estimates. One of the major differences across the surveys is the frequency of data collection. CPS data comes from a survey conducted in March of each year, and it asks questions about insurance status for the previous year. CPS asks for insurance status over the previous year and calculates the uninsured as the residual. Many analysts argue that individuals underreport their insurance status, especially those covered by Medicaid (Pascale, Roemer, and Resnick, 2009; Plotzke, Klerman, and Davern, 2010).[10] SIPP interviews every four months, asking questions about insurance status for each month since the previous interview. The MEPS survey is conducted every three to five months, so the reference period varies across participants.

A study by the Congressional Budget Office analyzed data from the four surveys to estimate the number of uninsured in 1998. In that year, CPS estimated that 43.9 million Americans were uninsured for the entire year, or 18.4 percent of the population. Using MEPS, the estimate was 31.1 million, or 13.3 percent of the population. SIPP estimates placed the number at 21.1 million, or 9.1 percent of the population. When these latter two surveys were used to estimate the number of uninsured on a specific date, SIPP estimated the number at 40.5 million and MEPS put it at 42.6—both very close to the CPS estimates for the number uninsured the entire year.

The Duration of Uninsurance

The most persistent finding in studies of the composition of the uninsured population is that the pool of uninsured is constantly changing. The people who are uninsured today are not the same people who were uninsured last year. Being uninsured is a temporary phenomenon for most people. Using the 1993 SIPP panel, Bennefield (1998) estimated that half of all spells without health insurance lasted less than 5.3 months. Similarly, Copeland (1998) estimated that approximately two-thirds of America's uninsured are without coverage for less than one year.

While it may look as though being uninsured is a temporary phenomenon, it should be remembered that one-third of the uninsured are without coverage for over one year. Even this number may be overstated, because many survey respondents who identify themselves as uninsured are eligible for Medicaid coverage and either do not realize it or simply have failed to apply.

---

[10]Studies indicate that individuals do not recall whether they or others living in the same household are enrolled in Medicaid. Comparing CPS results with administrative records from CMS suggests that the undercount may approach 36 percent of enrollees or as many as 13 million.

Another way to look at this problem is to count the number of people who cycle into and out of the pool of uninsured each year. Instead of 20 million, or even 45 million, Short and Graefe (2003) estimated that there were almost 85 million Americans who were without insurance coverage for at least one month from 1996 to 1999. One out of every three nonelderly Americans found themselves without coverage at some point during that four-year period. But only 4 percent, or 10 million, were without coverage the entire four years and could be considered chronically uninsured.

Demographics of the Uninsured

Many people have the mistaken impression that most people without insurance are unemployed. On the contrary, 54.9 percent of all uninsured people were employed in full-time or part-time jobs in 2015. Approximately one in four was a nonworking adult, with the rest being dependent children. If dependent children were distributed proportionately according to employment status, it is a fair approximation to say that over 75 percent of the uninsured had some labor force connection—through their own employment or that of a family member.

Table 7.1 provides information on individuals without insurance. An estimated 29 million were uninsured in 2015, 9.1 percent of the total U.S. population. For those under 19 years of age, 5.3 percent were uninsured. For 19- to 25-year-olds, the percentage jumped to 14.5 and for those between 26–34 years old it reached 16.3 percent. The percentage without insurance steadily fell in cohorts of older people. Older individuals have a higher demand for medical care and more money to spend on luxuries such as health insurance.

Insurance is closely associated with level of income. Almost 15 percent of the population with incomes below $25,000 did not have coverage. Less than 5 percent of those with incomes over $100,000 were uninsured. Individuals with annual incomes less than two times the official poverty level are more likely to be uninsured than those making more than that amount. More than 45 percent of all uninsured have household incomes that exceed $50,000.

Race is also a factor in the likelihood that a person will have insurance. Even though only 6.7 percent of whites are uninsured, they make up 45 percent of those who do not have coverage. One in nine blacks and one in six Hispanics are uninsured. A related issue is nativity, or country of origin. Approximately 7.7 percent of Americans born in the United States are uninsured, and 8.7 percent of naturalized citizens. However, 26.4 percent of all noncitizens go without coverage.

What does all this mean? The starting point (and unfortunately for most policymakers, the ending point) is 29 million people uninsured. Out of that number, 6.1 million are non-citizens, indicating that 22.9 million of the uninsured are Americans. From previously cited research, around 8–10 million of this number are actually covered by Medicaid (the Medicaid undercount), making the actual number of uninsured more like 15 million, closer to the estimate using SIPP data.

Small Group Factors

The fact that over 75 percent of the uninsured have some sort of labor force attachment is both troubling and reassuring. It is troubling in the sense that most people who are uninsured have a job, and at the same time reassuring because they are already connected to the primary mechanism used in this country to provide health insurance.

TABLE 7.1 INDIVIDUALS WITHOUT HEALTH INSURANCE BY SELECTED CHARACTERISTICS, 2013–2015

Group	2015 Uninsured (000)	2015 Percentage of group	2015 Percentage of total	2014 Uninsured (000)	2014 Percentage of group	2014 Percentage of total	2013 Uninsured (000)	2013 Percentage of group	2013 Percentage of total
All persons	28,966	9.1	100.0	32,968	10.4	100.0	41,795	13.2	100.0
American citizen	22,900	7.7	79.1	25,964	8.8	78.8	33,439	11.5	80.0
Nativity:									
Native	21,150	7.7	73.0	23,955	8.7	72.7	30,500	11.2	73.0
Naturalized citizen	1,750	8.7	6.0	2,008	10.2	6.1	2,939	15.4	7.0
Noncitizen	6,066	26.4	20.9	7,004	31.2	21.2	8,356	38.7	20.0
Age:									
Under 19 years	4,158	5.3	14.4	4,858	6.2	14.7	5,843	7.5	14.0
19–25 years	4,414	14.5	15.2	5,212	17.1	15.8	6,728	22.1	16.1
26–34 years	6,337	16.3	21.9	6,990	18.2	21.2	9,020	23.7	21.6
35–44 years	5,489	13.7	18.9	6,163	15.4	18.7	7,519	18.9	18.0
45–64 years	8,062	9.6	27.8	9,115	11.0	27.6	12,030	14.6	28.8
65 years and over	506	1.1	1.7	629	1.4	1.9	655	1.5	1.6
Income:									
Less than $25,000	7,713	14.8	26.7	9,145	16.6	27.7	11,611	20.9	27.8
$25,000–$49,999	8,143	12.5	28.1	9,477	14.1	28.8	12,759	19.0	30.5
$50,000–$74,999	5,318	9.6	18.4	5,957	10.7	18.1	7,352	13.3	17.6
To $75,000–$99,999	3,150	7.3	10.9	3,296	8.0	10.0	4,023	9.7	9.6
Over $100,000	4,642	4.5	16.0	5,094	5.3	15.4	5,717	6.1	13.7
Income to FPL:									
Below 100% FPL	7,489	17.4	25.9	9,018	19.3	27.4	10,877	23.5	26.0
Below 138% FPL	10,586	16.4	36.5	12,503	18.1	37.9	15,444	22.6	37.0
100–199% FPL	7,838	13.6	27.1	8,851	15.1	26.8	11,980	20.4	28.7
200–299% FPL	4,880	9.8	16.8	5,996	11.7	18.2	7,848	15.8	18.8
300–399% FPL	3,062	7.3	10.6	3,427	8.4	10.4	4,219	10.3	10.0
Over 400% FPL	5,662	4.5	19.5	5,646	4.8	17.1	6,537	5.6	15.6
Race:									
White, non-Hispanic	13,100	6.7	45.2	14,824	7.6	45.0	19,032	9.7	45.5
Black	4,627	11.1	16.0	4,847	11.8	14.7	6,450	15.9	15.4
Asian	1,360	7.5	4.7	1,659	9.3	5.0	2,342	13.8	5.6
Hispanic origin	9,235	16.2	31.9	11,059	19.9	33.5	13,257	24.4	31.7

Source: Barnett and Vornovitsky, 2016.

Why is it that so many workers lack coverage? Broadly speaking, there are three primary reasons that a worker does not have health insurance (Holahan and Kim, 2000):

- The employer does not offer a health plan.
- The employer offers a health plan, but the employee is not eligible for the plan because of part-time status or some other rule.
- The employer offers a plan, and the employee is eligible for that plan, but the employee chooses not to participate because the plan is either too expensive, the employee can get a better plan elsewhere (usually through a spouse's employment), or the employee does not perceive a need for a health plan.

Bundorf and Pauly (2006) present evidence that as many as 75 percent of the uninsured can actually afford insurance coverage (by two different standard definitions of affordability), but they choose to spend their money on other things.

Many of the uninsured are employed by small firms that do not provide health benefits. Small firms are at a distinct disadvantage when buying health insurance; it simply costs too much. In setting premiums for group plans, insurers usually charge small firms more per employee than they charge large firms. The estimated administrative costs for small-group plans (those with less than five employees) are about 40 percent of claims. For large-group plans (those with more than 10,000 employees), the comparable number is about 5.5 percent of claims. General and administrative expenses are higher for small-group plans, along with selling expenses and commission costs (Helms, Gauthier, and Campion, 1992).

Insurers perceive a higher level of risk in the small-group setting. The private insurance market is fragmented in nature. Instead of the concept of community rating, in which everyone in a particular geographic area pays the same premium, different groups pay different premiums based on perceived risk. Perceived risk is higher for the smaller group. One large claim can have a catastrophic impact on the calculated premium for them, effectively pricing the group out of the market or making insurance unavailable at any price.

For the same reason, small firms are not able to take advantage of self-insuring. According to a 1992 survey by Foster Higgins, over 80 percent of all private sector companies with more than 1,000 workers self-insure. Even smaller firms see the benefits offered by this practice. Half of all self-insured companies have fewer than 100 employees (Thompson, 1993). With so many firms self-insuring, up to half of all private sector employees are now in self-insured pools. Self-insurance carries with it a substantial risk of adverse selection for small firms. Sound underwriting principles would suggest a minimum of 100 to 300 employees before self-insurance is recommended.

Taking all the relevant small-group factors into consideration, it is not surprising that many small firms do not offer health benefits to their employees. In addition, small firms usually pay comparatively low wages.

The problem associated with providing affordable coverage to small groups was the primary reason that ACA established the health insurance exchanges for those who do not purchase insurance through an employer. Firms that have fewer than 50 employees may participate in the Small Business Health Options Program (SHOP) and receive tax credits if they contribute at least 50 percent of the premium.

The Relationship between Insurance and Health

⭐ **POLICY ISSUE**
Poor access to medical care often results in poor health, especially for the chronically ill poor.

The connection between lack of insurance and poor health may be decomposed into two parts. First, how does the lack of health insurance affect access to medical care? Second, does poor access result in poor health outcomes? Significant differences of opinion weigh in on whether the lack of insurance contributes to poor health. Evidence from the RAND

Health Insurance Experiment suggests that more generous health insurance benefits have little effect on health outcomes (Newhouse, 1993). Brook (1991) provides additional evidence that the absence of insurance does not reduce the health status of the average American. While the uninsured have only about two-thirds the number of physicians' visits per year as those with insurance, and about half the number of hospital days per year, these differences in utilization do not translate into significant differences in health status. Considering the fact that the uninsured are on average younger and healthier, this result may be at least in part due to self-selection. With the exception of those who were poor and sick, there seems to be no relationship between health status and insurance status.

These differences could be due to the fact that up to one-third of the care provided to the insured is considered inappropriate or equivocal. In other words, the medical benefit does not exceed the medical risk. Because of the questionable nature of such a large percentage of the medical care provided to the insured, differences in the amount of care may not be responsible for differences in health status.

Other research suggests that those without insurance have trouble accessing the medical care system, resulting in poorer health outcomes. The access problem manifests itself in a lower likelihood of having a regular source of care (Berk, Schur, and Cantor, 1995; Bindman et al., 1995; Zuvekas and Weinick, 1999), delays in seeking care (Burstin et al., 1998; Weissman et al., 1991), and receiving fewer services than those with health insurance (Berk and Schur, 1998; Brown, Bindman, and Lurie, 1998). Even those individuals with health problems find that a lack of insurance significantly affects their access to the system (Berk, Schur, and Cantor, 1995).

Lack of insurance may lead to lower levels of utilization, but establishing a connection between reduced access and poor health outcomes is a more difficult task. The literature supporting the connection generally fails to overcome several important empirical problems.[11] Results from the RAND Health Insurance Experiment cited above (Manning et al., 1987) show that those individuals who receive free care have better control of their blood pressure and have better vision. Other studies indicate that those without insurance delay seeking needed medical care, resulting in avoidable hospitalizations (Billings, Anderson, and Newman, 1996; Bindman et al., 1995), higher than expected mortality rates (Franks, Clancy, and Gold, 1993; Hadley, Steinberg, and Feder, 1991), and poor birth outcomes (Currie and Gruber, 1996). The argument that individuals without insurance experience poorer health outcomes is powerful, but not supported by the empirical evidence.

ISSUES IN MEDICAL CARE DELIVERY

DOES INSURANCE IMPROVE HEALTH?

Paul Krugman (2012) argued that the repeal of the ACA would result in "thousands, and probably tens of thousands, of excess deaths of Americans each year." Given Krugman's stature as a former Nobel Laureate in economics, his words tend to carry a lot of weight. Is he right? Would repeal of the ACA result in needless suffering and death? How could anyone favor its repeal?

---

[11]The most notable problem is endogeneity bias, a situation in which the empirical data are unable to determine whether lack of insurance leads to poor health or whether poor health decreases the probability of being insured. Additionally, the research suffers from selection bias where omitted variables that jointly determine the availability of insurance and health status are not included in the analysis.

The basis for Krugman's statement is a 2002 report from the Institute of Medicine (IOM) on the consequences of being uninsured. In it the authors estimated that the uninsured have a 25 percent higher mortality rate than the insured, resulting in 18,000 excess deaths annually. The Urban Institute actually updated that report in 2006 and raised that estimate to 22,000.

At the time of the original IOM study, there were only two empirical studies on the mortality consequences of being uninsured (Franks et al., 1993; Sorlie et al., 1994). The two observational studies used similar methodology and not surprisingly came up with similar results: being uninsured was "associated with" a 25 percent higher mortality rate. Both studies share the same methodological weakness, making it impossible to determine causality. In other words, any inferences about the causal relationship between lack of insurance and mortality using the observational approach are dubious. Even more questionable is the large statistical error associated with the estimates. Both studies found the 95 percent confidence interval to range from no increase in mortality to a 50 percent increase, or between zero excess deaths to 36,000 excess deaths. Instead of saying there are 18,000 excess deaths from uninsurance, IOM could have easily said going without insurance may have no impact on mortality or it could result in as many as 36,000 excess deaths.

Richard Kronick (2009) looked at the mortality differences between the insured and uninsured using a much larger data base than either of the previous studies. After a series of adjustments controlling for difference between the two groups, including age, sex, race, education, and income, the difference in mortality rates narrowed. When smoking status, obesity, self-reported health status, and physical activity were added, the difference vanished completely. Kronick concluded that "the IOM's estimate that lack of insurance leads to 18,000 excess deaths each year is almost certainly incorrect."

The only credible way to identify health differences between the insured and the uninsured would require a randomized experiment. The 2008 Medicaid expansion in Oregon (Baicker et al., 2013) provided a good opportunity for such a study. In 2008, Oregon used a lottery to expand Medicaid coverage to over 6,000 adults who were previously uninsured. These individuals served as the treatment group in the experiment. A similarly sized group who registered but were not chosen in the lottery served as the control group. The results surprised many and resulted in a firestorm of controversy. Medicaid recipients used more health care but had no significant differences in physical health outcomes (hypertension, cholesterol, and hemoglobin levels) linked to three of the most common causes of death in the United States (heart disease, stroke, and diabetes). Compared to those without insurance, those with Medicaid had higher drug use, more outpatient visits, more emergency room visits, and higher overall health care spending (Taubman et al., 2014). Proponents of the expansion were undeterred. Expanding access was sufficient justification for the added spending, even if there were no perceptible differences in health outcomes.

Trying to prove causality using observational studies is dubious at best. Taking advantage of quasi-randomized experiments, however, provides a way to address causality with more accuracy, but it does have its drawbacks. We don't always get the answers we want.

Sources: Paul Krugman, "Death by Ideology," *New York Times*, October 14, 2012; P. Franks et al., "Health Insurance and Mortality: Evidence from a National Cohort," *Journal of the American Medical Association* 270(6), 1993, 737–741; P. D. Sorlie et al. "Mortality in the Uninsured Compared with That in Persons with Public and Private Health Insurance," *Archives of Internal Medicine* 154, 1994, 2409–2416; Richard Kronick, "Health Insurance Coverage and Mortality Revisited," *Health Services Research* 44(4), August 2009, 1211–1231; and Katherine Baicker et al., "The Oregon Experiment—Effects of Medicaid on Clinical Outcomes," *New England Journal of Medicine* 368(18), May 2, 2013, 1713–1722; and Sarah L. Taubman et al., "Medicaid Increases Emergency-Department Use: Evidence from Oregon's Health Insurance Experiment," *Science Online*, January 2, 2014.

The Safety Net for the Uninsured

Since 1985, it has been illegal for a hospital emergency department—public or private—to deny care to anyone requesting care. The Emergency Medical Treatment and Active Labor Act (EMTALA) requires a hospital to provide medically appropriate screening to determine the nature of the medical condition and either treat the condition or stabilize and transfer the patient to a facility that can. Private hospitals have been systematically reducing

POLICY ISSUE

Competitive pressures are jeopardizing the ability of hospitals and physicians to provide free care to the uninsured. Budget pressures are forcing state and local governments to rethink how they will pay for indigent care.

their free care in non-acute cases, forcing the public hospitals to absorb the burden of the responsibility of providing care to the uninsured. Estimates indicate that fewer than 10 percent of the nation's public hospitals provide almost half of all hospital care for the uninsured. Much of this uncompensated care is provided in the hospital emergency department or as a result of a hospital admission from the emergency department.

Coughlin et al. (2014) estimated that uninsured Americans received $84.9 billion in uncompensated care in 2013. Most of this "free" care is financed from municipal budgets, Medicaid subsidies for the treatment of the indigent poor, or Medicare disproportionate share payments. As the number of uninsured increases, and medical costs continue to climb, government budgets at all levels are coming under closer scrutiny. Competitive pressures make it almost impossible for hospitals to pass the cost of care for the uninsured on to private patients. Private insurers, employers, and payers of all kinds are increasingly unwilling to pay for the treatment of the uninsured. Payers are refusing to accept cost shifting and are negotiating discounts in return for guaranteed patient volume.

Universal insurance coverage requires accepting the principles of subsidization of those who cannot afford coverage and offering participation incentives to those who can. The chronically ill cannot afford risk-rated insurance premiums. If the insurance market is to provide a solution, the high risk must receive subsidies of some kind. The solution is not as simple as mandating that all insurance premiums be based on community rating, thus forcing low-risk insureds to subsidize those who are high risk. Under community rating, the healthy may face premiums that exceed the maximum value of the insurance. If the purchase of insurance is based on voluntary choice, many of the healthy will choose not to buy unless provided with strong incentives, such as tax credits when insurance is purchased, or penalties when it is not.

KEY CONCEPT 7
Competition

KEY CONCEPT 9
Market Failure

BACK-OF-THE-ENVELOPE

The Welfare Loss from a Subsidy

Insured customers compare benefits of services with the out-of-pocket costs incurred directly (where true costs are the sum of out-of-pocket costs and charges covered by insurance). By ignoring total cost, the decision calculus results in overuse of resources; that is, using more than the socially desirable amount. This may be the single most important factor in the escalation of total medical care expenditures.

The economics of an insurance subsidy can be shown graphically. Initial demand for medical care is shown by the demand curve D_0E. Access to insurance, and the subsidy it provides, causes the demand curve to become more inelastic (D_1E). Insurance consumer surplus is P_0AD_0. Because insurance only changes the price of medical care to the individual, but not its value, consumer surplus with insurance is evaluated using the actual demand curve D_0E and will be P_2D_0C. Likewise, producer surplus increases with insurance, from P_0AS to P_1BS.

Economic concept	Before insurance	After insurance
Consumer surplus	P_0AD_0	P_2CD_0
Producer surplus	P_0AS	P_1BS
Cost of insurance	—	P_1BCP_2
Net gain to society	D_0AS	$D_0AS - ABC$
Deadweight loss	—	ABC

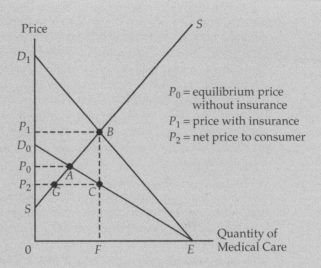

Note the overlap of surpluses with insurance, the area D_0AGP_2. The cost of the insurance, P_1BCP_2, erases the overlap and part of both consumer surplus *(ACG)* and producer surplus *(P_1BAD_0)*. Is society better off with the subsidy? Actually, the insurance subsidy reduces surplus by *ABC*. Instead of D_0AS, surplus is now D_0AS–*ABC*.

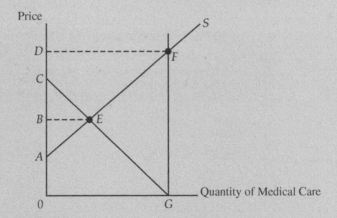

If the government provides insurance that covers 100 percent of the cost of medical care with no coinsurance requirement, the demand curve for medical care becomes perfectly inelastic. This is shown in the lower diagram, where the new demand curve is *FG* instead of *CG*. The price of medical care becomes $0D$, and the quantity demanded becomes $0G$. Total cost to the taxpayers is $0DFG$, consumer surplus is $0CG$, and producer surplus is *ADF*. Expenditures exceed the combined surplus by *FEG–ACE*, representing a net welfare loss to society when *FEG* is greater than *ACE* and a net gain if the opposite is true.

In both the case of insurance with copayments and taxpayer-financed insurance with no copayments, the loss to society is caused by the consumption of medical care where the cost of care to society exceeds the net benefit to the patient.

Summary and Conclusions

Medical care in the United States, predominantly a private out-of-pocket expense as recently as 1965, is now overwhelmingly financed by third parties: government and private insurers. Government at all levels directly finances almost 50 percent of all medical care. Coupled with the tax subsidy provided to purchasers of private insurance, taxpayers finance over half of all medical care spending in this country.

The private sector insures over 214 million people, not including the 20 million Medicare recipients who obtain their insurance through Medicare Advantage or buy private supplementary insurance. Commercial insurance companies, the Blue Cross-Blue Shield plans, self-funded employer plans, and prepaid health plans provide the vast majority of this coverage. The two primary government health programs, Medicare and Medicaid, provide health care coverage to over 100 million

Americans. Medicare enrollment topped 55 million elderly and disabled in 2015, and Medicaid served more than 68 million.

This patchwork coverage provides health insurance to approximately 90 percent of the American population but still leaves approximately 29 million without insurance.

Advocates of more government involvement may have preferred a single-payer option instead of the ACA reform package. Advocates of a private sector solution prefer a focus on reducing the cost of private insurance to make it more affordable, especially to the 18–34-year-old age cohort representing over 40 percent of the uninsured. Across the political divide there is little agreement on whether ACA has done much to improve the situation. One thing is certain. This is a great time to be studying health economics.

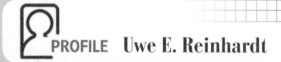

PROFILE   Uwe E. Reinhardt

Once introduced at a conference by U.S. Representative Pete Stark (D – Calif.) as an "expert on contrariness," Uwe (pronounced *oo-vuh*) Reinhardt is regarded by many as the "bad boy" of the health care reform debate. Born in 1937, Reinhardt's formative years were spent in war-torn Germany, where his family literally lived in a tool shed. During those years of abject poverty, Reinhardt grew to appreciate universal health care financed primarily through taxation. "I grew up in countries where health care was treated as a social good, where the rich paid significantly more than their health care costs to subsidize the poor," he says. "I found that a civilized environment."

Reinhardt migrated to Canada in 1956, where he attended the University of Saskatchewan. After graduation in 1964, he came to the United States to study at Yale University, where he received his Ph.D. in economics in 1970. He also holds an honorary doctorate from the Medical College of Pennsylvania. As an academic, Reinhardt is a bit unusual, in that he has taught at Princeton his entire career.

A recognized authority on health economics and health policy, most of his scholarly work has been in health care economics. He is on the editorial board of several journals, including *Health Affairs, New England Journal of Medicine, Journal of the American Medical Association, Milbank Memorial Quarterly*, and *Health Management Quarterly*. He has also served as associate editor of the *Journal of Health Economics*. This is quite a contrast for someone who was considering a Ph.D. dissertation topic on optimal tolls on the Connecticut Turnpike. Fortunately, one of Reinhardt's Yale professors suggested the economics of health care, and the rest is history.

His fascination for the topic has continued to grow over the last three decades. He has served on a number of government commissions and advisory boards including the Physician Payment Review Commission and the National Advisory Board of the Agency for Health Care Quality and Research. In 2010, he was awarded the William B. Graham Prize for Health Services Research given by the Association of University Programs in Health Administration. Reinhardt has become a devout advocate for the uninsured. Prone to black humor about many health-related issues, Reinhardt never jokes about the plight of the uninsured. Although he does not see, nor does he want to see, health care defined as a constitutional right, he firmly believes that health care plays a social role. It is a right "implied in the social contract … It's not a consumer good. It's a quasi-religious commodity … It's the cement that makes a nation out of people."

Ever controversial, Reinhardt has earned the respect of individuals on both sides of the health care debate. Equally comfortable in front of a class or a congressional committee, he leaves little doubt about where he stands on the important issues surrounding health care reform.

Source: Personal curriculum vitae; and Julie Rovner, "MM Interview: Uwe Reinhardt," *Modern Maturity* 37(6), November/December 1994, 64–72.

Questions and Problems

1. In what way is insuring for a medical loss different from insuring for any other loss?
2. Define the following concepts. How important are they in determining the efficient functioning of medical markets?
   a. moral hazard
   b. adverse selection
   c. asymmetric information
   d. third-party payer
   e. cream skimming
3. What are the major reasons that health insurance policies have deductibles and coinsurance features? Are they really necessary?
4. What are the four types of medical insurance? Briefly describe the coverage available with each one.
5. Should insurers be allowed to refuse health insurance policies to individuals who are genetically predisposed to certain diseases? To those whose lifestyles place them in high-risk categories for certain diseases? Support your answers.
6. One of the major issues driving the health care reform debate is the number of uninsured Americans and their limited access to medical care. Describe the typical person in the United States without insurance. Does lack of insurance mean the uninsured have no access to medical care?
7. What is asymmetric information? How does it present a problem to medical providers and health insurers?
8. Why do firms self-insure?
9. Does the availability of free health care improve health status? Explain.
10. What is the purpose of deductibles and coinsurance? To what problem are insurers responding?
11. You heard someone state "If the purpose of insurance is to protect people against large financial losses, then requiring patients to make co-payments and pay co-insurance defeats the purpose of insurance." Clearly explain why health plans require patients to pay a portion of their medical expenses out-of-pocket.

References

Arrow, Kenneth J., "Uncertainty and the Welfare Economics of Medical Care," *American Economic Review* 53(5), December 1963, 941–973.

Barnett, Jessica C. and Marina S. Vornovitsky, "Health Insurance Coverage in the United States: 2015, Current Population Reports, P60-257, September 2016, available at https://www.census.gov/library/publications/2016/demo/p60-257.html. Accessed April 10, 2017.

Bennefield, Robert L., "Dynamics of Economic Well-Being: Health Insurance 1993 to 1995, Who Loses Coverage and for How Long?" U.S. Census Bureau, *Current Population Reports*, P70–64, August 1998, 1–6.

Berk, Mark L. and Alan C. Monheit, "The Concentration of Health Care Expenditures, Revisited," *Health Affairs* 20(2), March/April 2001, 9–18.

Berk, Mark L. and Claudia L. Schur, "Access to Care: How Much Difference Does Medicaid Make?" *Health Affairs* 17(1), January/February 1998, 169–180.

Berk, Mark L., Claudia L. Schur, and Joel C. Cantor, "Ability to Obtain Health Care: Recent Estimates from the Robert Wood Johnson Foundation National Access to Care Survey," *Health Affairs* 14(3), Fall 1995, 139–146.

Billings, John, Geoffrey M. Anderson, and Laurie S. Newman, "Recent Findings on Preventable Hospitalizations," *Health Affairs* 15(3), Fall 1996, 239–249.

Bindman, A. B., et al., "Preventable Hospitalizations and Access to Care," *Journal of the American Medical Association* 274, 1995, 305–311.

Brook, Robert H., "Health, Health Insurance, and the Uninsured," *Journal of the American Medical Association* 265(22), June 12, 1991, 2998–3002.

Brown, M. E., A. B. Bindman, and N. Lurie, "Monitoring the Consequences of Uninsurance: A Review of Methodologies," *Medical Care Research and Review* 55, 1998, 177–210.

Buchmueller, Thomas, "Does a Fixed-Dollar Contribution Policy Lower Spending?" *Health Affairs* 17, 1998, 228–235.

Bundorf, M. Kate and Mark V. Pauly, "Is Health Insurance Affordable for the Uninsured?" *Journal of Health Economics* 25, 2006, 650–673.

Burstin, H. R., K. Swartz, A. C. O'Neil, E. J. Orav, and T. A. Brennan, "The Effect of Change of Health Insurance on Access to Care," *Inquiry* 35(4), 1998, 389–397.

Centers for Medicare and Medicaid Services, National Health Expenditures by Type of Service and Source of Funds: Calendar Years 1960 to 2015, 2016, available at https://www.cms.gov/Research-Statistics-Data-and-Systems/Statistics-Trends-and-Reports/NationalHealthExpendData/NationalHealthAccountsHistorical.html. Accessed April 10, 2017.

Cochrane, John H., "Time-Consistent Health Insurance," *Journal of Political Economy*, 103(3), June 1995, 45–473.

Copeland, Craig, "Characteristics of the Nonelderly with Selected Sources of Health Insurance and Lengths of Uninsured Spells," *EBRI Issue Brief* No. 198, June 1998.

Coughlin, Teresa A., et al., "Uncompensated Care for the Uninsured in 2013: A Detailed Examination," Kaiser Family Foundation, The Kaiser Commission on Medicaid and the Uninsured, May 2014.

Currie, Janet and Jonathan Gruber, "Saving Babies: The Efficacy and Cost of Recent Expansions of Medicaid Eligibility for Pregnant Women," *Journal of Political Economy* 104(6), December 1996, 1263–1296.

Cutler, David and Sarah Reber, "Paying for Health Insurance: The Tradeoff between Competition and Adverse Selection," *Quarterly Journal of Economics* 113, 1998, 433–466.

Cutler, David M. and Richard J. Zeckhauser, "The Anatomy of Health Insurance," in *Handbook of Health Economics*, Volume 1, edited by A. J. Culyer and J. P. Newhouse, North Holland: Elsevier Science, 2000, 563–643.

Franks, P., C. M. Clancy, and M. R. Gold, "Health Insurance and Mortality: Evidence from a National Cohort," *Journal of the American Medical Association* 270, 1993, 737–741.

Friedman, Milton and Leonard J. Savage, "The Utility Analysis of Choices Involving Risk," *Journal of Political Economy* 56(4), August 1948, 279–304.

Hadley, Jack and John Holahan, "How Much Medical Care Do the Uninsured Use, and Who Pays for It?" *Health Affairs — Web Exclusive*, 12 February 2003, W3–W66 to W3–W81.

Hadley, Jack, Earl P. Steinberg, and Judith Feder, "Comparison of Uninsured and Privately Insured Hospital Patients: Conditions on Admission, Resource Use, and Outcome," *Journal of the American Medical Association* 265(3), January 16, 1991, 374–379.

Helms, W. David, Anne K. Gauthier, and Daniel M. Campion, "Mending the Flaws in the Small-Group Market," *Health Affairs* 11(2), Summer 1992, 7–27.

Herring, Bradley and Mark V. Pauly, "Incentive-Compatible Guaranteed Renewable Health Insurance Premiums," *Journal of Health Economics*, 25, 2006, 395–417.

Holahan, John and J. Kim, "Why Does the Number of Uninsured Americans Continue to Grow?" *Health Affairs* 19(4), 2000, 188–196.

Jensen, Gail A., Kevin D. Cotter, and Michael A. Morrisey, "State Insurance Regulation and Employers' Decisions to Self-Insure," *Journal of Risk and Insurance* 62(2), 1995, 185–213.

Jensen, Gail A. and Michael A. Morrisey, "Employer-Sponsored Health Insurance and Mandated Benefit Laws," *Milbank Quarterly* 77(4), 1999, 425–459.

Manning, Willard G., et al., "Health Insurance and the Demand for Medical Care: Evidence from a Randomized Experiment," *American Economic Review* 77(3), June 1987, 251–277.

Miller, G. Edward and Thomas M. Selden, "Tax Subsidies for Employer-Sponsored Health Insurance: Updated Microsimulation Estimates and Sensitivity to Alternative Incidence Assumptions," *Health Services Research* 48(2, Pt 2), April 2013, 866–883.

Newhouse, Joseph, *Free for All? Lessons from the RAND Health Insurance Experiment*, Santa Monica, CA: RAND Corporation, 1993.

Pascale, Joanne, Mark I. Roemer, and Dean M. Resnick, "Medicaid Underreporting in the CPS: Results from a Record Check Study," *Public Opinion Quarterly* 73, 2009, 497–520.

Pauly, Mark V., "Is Cream Skimming a Problem for the Competitive Medical Market?" *Journal of Health Economics* 3(1), April 1984, 87–95.

———, "Taxation, Health Insurance, and Market Failure in the Medical Economy," *Journal of Economic Literature* 24(2), June 1986, 629–675.

———, "The Economics of Moral Hazard: Comment," *American Economic Review* 58(2), June 1968, 531–538.

Pauly, Mark V., Allison Percy, and Bradley Herring, "Individual versus Job-Based Health Insurance: Weighing the Pros and Cons," *Health Affairs* 18(6), 1999, 28–44.

Plotzke, Michael R., Jacob A. Klerman, and Michael Davern, "How Does Medicaid-Managed Care Impact Reporting of Medicaid Status?" *Health Services Research* 45(5, Pt 1), October 2010, 1310–1323.

Rice, Thomas, *The Economics of Health Reconsidered*, Chicago, IL: Health Administration Press, 1998.

Short, Pamela Farley, "Counting and Characterizing the Uninsured," ERIU Working Paper 2, University of Michigan, Economic Research Institute on the Uninsured, December 2001.

Short, Pamela Farley and Deborah R. Graefe, "Battery-Powered Health Insurance? Stability in Coverage of the Uninsured," *Health Affairs* 22(6), November/December 2003, 244–255.

Stigler, George, "The Economics of Information," *Journal of Political Economy* 69(3), June 1961, 213–225.

Thomasson, Melissa A., "The Importance of Group Coverage: How Tax Policy Shaped U.S. Health Insurance," NBER Working Paper 7543, Cambridge, MA: National Bureau of Economic Research, February 2000.

Thompson, Roger, "Going, Going, ... Gone?" *Nation's Business* 81(7), July 1993, 24.

Weissman, J. S., R. Stern, S. L. Fielding, and A. M. Epstein, "Delayed Access to Health Care: Risk Factors, Reasons, and Consequences," *Annals of Internal Medicine* 114, 1991, 325–331.

Zuvekas, S. H. and R. M. Weinick, "Changes in Access to Care, 1977–1996: The Role of Health Insurance," *Health Services Research* 34(1 Pt 2), 1999, 271–279.

CHAPTER 8

Managed Care

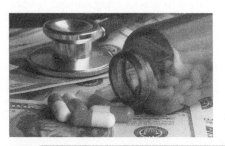

PUBLIC EMPLOYEES SHIFTING INTO CONSUMER-DIRECTED PLANS

The term "consumer-directed health plan" (CDHP) typically refers to an insurance plan that combines a "high-deductible health plan" (HDHP) with a "health savings account" (HSA). The Medicare Prescription Drug Improvement and Modernization Act of 2003 authorized the provision of HSAs as part of the same bill that created the Medicare out-patient prescription drug benefit. They have grown in popularity since first available in January 2005. By 2016, most large employers were offering an HSA/CDHP option and almost 30 percent of workers with employer-sponsored insurance had enrolled in one. Largely their popularity is due to two factors: coverage and cost. If set up properly, they meet the minimum requirements of a qualified plan under the Affordable Care Act (ACA; equivalent to a Bronze Plan) and their premium levels (around $16,000 for a family plan) are 10–15 percent lower than the alternative options.

Their popularity is not limited to the private sector. With states struggling to save tax-payer money, 28 states now offer CDHP options to public-sector employees. Indiana pro-vides one of the more generous state offerings of the HSA/HDHP, contributing as much as $1,375 annually into an individual's HSA and $2,750 into a family plan.

The first year the plan option was available to Indiana state employees (2006), only 4 percent signed up. By 2010, over 70 percent had signed up. That year the state saved $20 million in health care costs, representing an 11 percent savings.

HSA holders experience two-thirds fewer visits to the emergency department, have one-half the hospital admissions, use more generic drugs, and spend one-third less over-all than those employees in traditional plans. These savings are common among HSA/HDHP participants. The traditional system, built on cost-plus reimbursement and first dol-lar coverage, is by design built to encourage consumption and spending. The top-down approach to spending control is a formula for failure. Cost-conscious behavior begins with consumers spending their own money. Only then will providers see it in their own self-interest to recommend cost-effective procedures and services. This may be the only way to "bend the cost curve."

Source: Mitch Daniels, "Hoosiers and Health Savings Accounts," *Wall Street Journal*, March 1, 2010.

As recently as 1975, almost the entire insured population in the United States received medical care services financed under traditional indemnity insurance arrangements. With favorable legislation in place, the 1980s witnessed major growth in managed care along with other related changes in medical care financing and delivery. These changes were, in part, a response to the high and rising cost of medical care and the increase in the number of Americans receiving their health insurance coverage from self-insured group plans.

Managed care is a term used to describe any number of contractual arrangements that integrate the financing and delivery of medical care. Purchasers (usually employers) contract with a select group of providers to deliver a specific package of medical benefits at a predetermined price. The wide variety of financing and delivery arrangements in the market today makes it difficult to classify managed care organizations precisely, thus complicating attempts to evaluate the efficiency and effectiveness of managed care.

Numerous differences mark the way managed care plans are organized: How physicians are paid, how financial risk is shared, whether physicians see only managed care patients, or whether they also see fee-for-service patients. This chapter will focus on the historical development of managed care and its emergence as an important element of the health care delivery system in the United States and worldwide.

We begin our discussion with a brief history of the emergence of managed care as an alternative to traditional fee-for-service delivery, and then we turn to the basic categories of managed care. We will also look at the cost-saving features of managed care and the practical evidence that this form of delivery actually saves money. Finally, the future of managed care will be discussed.

HTTP://

Kaiser-Permanente is the largest not-for-profit HMO in the country, with 8.7 million members. http://www .kaiserpermanente.org.

health maintenance organization (HMO) A type of managed care organization that functions like an insurer and also arranges for the provision of care.

HTTP://

Group Health Cooperative of Puget Sound, the nation's sixth largest not-for-profit HMO, serves over 700,000 members in the northwestern United States. http:// www.ghc.org.

History of Managed Care

Although the concept of the prepaid medical plan can be traced back to the nineteenth century, the first health plans with the organizational structure of today's **health maintenance organization (HMO)** were formed in the 1920s (Friedman, 1996). Industrialist Henry J. Kaiser organized one of the first managed care plans. Kaiser-Permanente, the largest managed care organization in the country today, was established to provide medical care in geographically isolated areas of northern California. Physicians working on a fixed salary provided medical care for employees of Kaiser's steel mill and shipyards, a group of relatively high-risk workers, in Kaiser-owned clinics and hospitals. The idea of using HMOs for cost-containment purposes was not an issue at the time and would not become one until the 1970s.

When Kaiser opened the plan to other patient groups in 1947, the HMO concept was still untested in the greater community. By 2016, Kaiser-Permanente was the nation's largest not-for-profit HMO, serving more than 10.2 million members in nine states and the District of Columbia and generating more than $60.7 billion in operating revenue. Kaiser medical facilities included 38 hospitals, 622 medical offices, 186,000 employees, and over 18,000 physicians. The pioneering efforts of Kaiser and others on the West Coast served as a model for prepaid medical care.

Many physicians were opposed to the concept of prepaid medical care, calling it "contract medicine," and they organized to ban the practice entirely. Their efforts were successful in slowing the growth of managed care, limiting the number of HMOs nationally to less than 40 throughout the 1960s (Gruber, Shadle, and Polich, 1988). As recently as 1980, enrollment in managed care plans was less than 10 million, 4 percent of the population.

Passage of Medicare and Medicaid in 1965 led to more direct federal involvement in the provision of medical care and a growing political concern for escalating costs. Research by

InterStudy proposed a health maintenance strategy based on the HMO as an alternative to traditional fee-for-service medicine.[1] Despite strong opposition from provider groups and the American Medical Association, the Nixon administration embraced the concept of the **prepaid group practice** to control medical care costs.

Working with congressional leaders, primarily from the Democrat Party, President Richard Nixon was successful in passing legislation that defined the HMO, including a list of covered benefits, pricing and enrollment practices, physician organization, and requirements regarding financial risk. The Health Maintenance Organization Act of 1973 provided over $364 million in subsidies to nonprofit groups to establish HMOs. Even with this funding, the government fell far short of its goal of establishing 1,700 HMOs and enrolling 40 million participants by 1976. The episode sent a clear message to the medical industry: The federal government was concerned with the high cost of medical care and was willing to intervene through the legislative process. Nevertheless, the real lesson was that government action alone (short of overt coercion through mandatory participation) may not be sufficient to push people into prepaid health plans. That task was not accomplished until corporate America began its move to managed care as a cost-control measure in the late 1980s. It took another decade of rising costs to emphasize the role of cost-effective behavior and spur the development and expansion of managed care arrangements through the private sector.

The initial popularity of managed care was due to the perception that it could provide significant cost savings over the more traditional fee-for-service delivery mechanism. Between 1984 and 1991, the average health insurance premium per employee increased 119 percent. At the same time, the overall increase in the inflation level, as measured by the change in the consumer price index, was 31 percent. With insurance premiums outpacing inflation by almost four to one, the pressure to control costs mounted accordingly.

prepaid group practice An arrangement through which a group contracts with a number of providers who agree to provide medical services to members of the group for a fixed, capitated payment.

HTTP://
The America's Health Insurance Plans (AHIP) represents more than 1,300 HMOs and other network-based plans, serving over 200 million Americans nationwide. http://www.ahp.org.

KEY CONCEPT 7
Competition

KEY CONCEPT 4
Self-Interest

Types of Managed Care Plans

Managed care has many aspects of the familiar all-you-can-eat buffet—a single price, paid in advance, good for everything on the board. Just as the buffet must price its product based on the expected behavior of likely diners, managed care must be sure that its pricing is sufficient to cover all the medical needs of its enrollees. One way the buffet can guarantee the "right" price is by offering plenty of the low-cost basics and limiting the availability of expensive entrees. Similarly, a successful pricing strategy in managed care must provide easy access to low-cost primary and preventive care as a way to discourage the use of expensive services, including specialty care and hospitalization.

Enlisting the services of a "gatekeeper" to steer diners to the cheaper alternatives and limit access to expensive entrees may not be harmful to most consumers. In the case of the buffet, a diet of soup and salad may be healthier than red meat and potatoes in the long run. Those diners accustomed to meat and potatoes will find the transition painful. Those with special dietary needs may actually end up worse off if their choices are limited.

Most diners understand the rules of the all-you-can-eat buffet. They do not pay $8.95 expecting steak and lobster. However, expectations are much different in the U.S. medical care sector. Therein lies the challenge to managed care. Americans have developed a taste for unlimited access to expensive treatments. Traditional fee-for-service medicine financed through indemnity insurance is like dining with a group of coworkers on a business trip.

---

[1]InterStudy is a research and policy institute headed by Paul M. Ellwood. For years, Ellwood invited a group of individuals interested in health policy to his Jackson Hole, Wyoming, retreat to discuss medical care reform. Out of this gathering, details of Alain Enthoven's proposal for managed competition emerged. Collectively, the group was referred to as the Jackson Hole group.

point-of-service (POS) plan A hybrid managed care plan that combines the features of a prepaid plan and a fee-for-service plan. Enrollees use network physicians with minimal out-of-pocket expenses and may choose to go out of the network by paying a higher coinsurance rate.

consumer-directed health plans A health plan that combines an HSA with a high-deductible insurance policy.

group-model HMO A group of physicians that agrees to provide medical care to a defined patient group in return for a fixed per capita payment or for discounted fees.

staff-model HMO A managed care organization that serves as both payer and provider, owns its own facilities, and employs its own physicians.

network-model HMO A managed care organization that contracts with several different providers, including physicians' practices and hospitals, to make a full range of medical services available to its enrollees.

independent practice association (IPA) An organized group of health care providers that offers medical services to a specified group of enrollees of a health plan.

practice guideline A specific statement about the appropriate course of treatment that should be taken for patients with given medical conditions.

Instead of ordering from the menu and paying separately, one member of the group agrees to pay the bill using one's expense account. In other words, the boss is now paying for the meal and individual accountability is virtually nonexistent. In this situation, the incentive structure encourages overeating. We tend to be more extravagant when someone else pays the bill. In other words, we seldom practice economizing behavior when someone else will benefit from our prudent actions.

Types of Managed Care Organizations

Approximately 99 percent of all enrollees in group health insurance plans are in managed care organizations of one type or another, including HMOs, preferred provider organizations (PPOs), **point-of-service (POS) plans**, and **consumer-directed health plans** (CDHPs). Some plans pay only for care received through an established network of providers. Others, including most PPOs and POS plans, offer options for enrollees to obtain medical care outside the established network but at higher out-of-pocket costs.

HMOs are classified as: (1) group model, (2) staff model, (3) network model, or (4) the independent practice association (IPA).[2] The **group-model HMO** contracts with a multispecialty group practice to provide all medically necessary care for its enrollees. The **staff-model HMO** is usually a closed panel where access to clinical services is restricted to facilities owned by the HMO and physicians employed by the HMO. Physicians are usually paid a fixed salary that often includes bonuses based on some measure of performance (usually work effort or patient satisfaction scores). The **network-model HMO** utilizes contracts with many different providers, including physicians' practices and hospitals, to make a full range of medical services available to its enrollees. The **independent practice association (IPA)** contracts with individual physicians or small group practices to provide care to enrolled members. Physicians practicing in IPAs often contract with one or more managed care plans and, at the same time, maintain their own private practice where they treat non-HMO patients on a fee-for-service basis.

The PPO has emerged as one of the more popular types of managed care plans. The PPO is a health care organization that serves as intermediary or broker between the purchaser of medical care and the provider. The PPO establishes a network of providers (physicians, hospitals, dentists, pharmacies, rehabilitative services, home health care, etc.) who agree to provide medical services to a specific group of enrollees at discounted rates. In most cases, providers agree to a set of utilization controls—that is, **practice guidelines**—in order to be included on the preferred list. Despite the lower fees and utilization controls, participating providers view the arrangement as a means of securing a steady volume of patients. Even though enrollees are free to use any provider, incentives and disincentives are used to encourage them to choose from the preferred list. Enrollees find their out-of-pocket costs to be higher, in the form of higher deductibles and copayments, when they receive care from providers who are not on the preferred list.

The typical arrangement provides discounts of billed charges for most services. The patient is usually required to make a modest copayment when using preferred providers. When using nonpreferred providers, however, patients are subject to higher out-of-pocket costs. Often a small copayment is required when using a preferred hospital and a much larger one when not.

The PPO typically lacks the strict cost-control features of the closed-panel HMO. With no risk sharing, providers have no direct incentive to control utilization in the short run.

---

[2]Those interested in a more comprehensive discussion on the types of HMOs are directed to Kongstvedt (1997) and Glied (2000).

The key to controlling costs is not the discounts offered by providers, but the selection of cost-conscious providers and the threat of dropping any physician who refuses to follow the practice guidelines established by the plan.

The POS plan is a mixed-model health plan. It incorporates many of the cost-control features of HMOs along with the provider-choice features of PPOs. Enrollees' choice of plan does not have to be made at the time of enrollment. It is made at the point of service; each time the enrollee seeks medical treatment. POS enrollees choose a primary care "gatekeeper" to coordinate all network-based care. Offering incentives in the form of better benefits and lower copayments encourages use of the network providers.

Network-based managed care dominates health care delivery in the United States. Managed care networks are similar to group-model HMOs but with one major difference: Instead of contracting with one multispecialty group practice, the network plan contracts with several. Therein lies the primary challenge to network-based care—the very success of the network depends on the ability to control costs. Without rigorous policies to control utilization, including provider risk sharing, **utilization review**, and limiting access to nonpreferred providers, such organizations will have a difficult time surviving.

Provisions included in the Medicare Modernization Act passed in 2005 have paved the way for the development of HDHPs with a savings option. The HDHP is characterized by a higher deductible than would normally be found in a typical policy. For 2016, the Internal Revenue Service requires a minimum deductible of $1,300 for an individual policy and $2,600 for a family policy (maximums are $6,550 and $13,100). The policy is often based on either an HSA or a health reimbursement account (HRA), in which individuals set aside pretax dollars designated to cover routine care. The maximum allowed contribution in 2016 was $3,350 for an individual and $6,750 for a family. Out-of-pocket spending (including the deductible) is limited to $6,550 for an individual and $13,100 for a family. (See IRS Revenue Procedure 2013–25, http://www.irs.gov/publications/p969/ar02 .html#en_US_publink1000204045.)

Most private sector employees who have group health insurance coverage are enrolled in some type of managed care plan. Table 8.1 provides dramatic evidence of the popularity of managed care for private sector employees. In 1979, over 98 percent of all group insurance policies were traditional indemnity insurance arrangements with few restrictions on choice of provider or service options. As medical care costs escalated in the 1980s, employers sought to reduce costs by moving away from traditional fee-for-service care to managed care. By 2000, less than 10 percent of the private sector had traditional indemnity

---

☆ **KEY CONCEPT 7**
Competition

☆ **KEY CONCEPT 8**
Market Failure

utilization review An evaluation of the appropriateness and efficiency of prescribed medical services.

TABLE 8.1 HEALTH PLAN COVERAGE FOR PRIVATE EMPLOYERS WITH GROUP INSURANCE (PERCENTAGE BY TYPE OF PLAN)

Type of plan	1979	1988	1993	1996	2000	2005	2006	2010	2014	2015	2016
Traditional Indemnity	98	73	46	27	8	3	3	1	<1	<1	<1
HMO	2	16	21	31	29	21	20	19	13	14	15
PPO	*	11	26	28	42	61	60	58	58	52	48
POS	*	*	7	14	21	15	13	8	8	10	9
HDHP	*	*	*	*	*	*	4	13	20	24	29

*No data available
Source: Kaiser Family Foundation, *Employer Health Benefits 2016 Annual Survey.*

plans. Employees seem to be moving into the less-restrictive managed care option, the PPO. Between 1993 and 2005, the percentage of employees enrolled in PPOs rose from 26 percent to 61 percent, slipping to 48 percent by 2016. After steady growth throughout the 1990s, HMO enrollment dropped from a high of 29 percent of all covered employees in 2000 to 15 percent in 2016. POS membership has likewise fallen from a 21 percent to 9 percent. Since 2005, the HDHP movement has gained momentum, reaching 4 percent of the covered population by 2006 and 29 percent in 2016. Just as employees moved out of traditional indemnity plans in the 1990s, many consider this move into HDHP as the first wave of consumerism in the twenty-first century.

The Theory of Managed Care Savings

The theoretical underpinnings of managed care suggest that medical care costs and spending may be affected by changing patient utilization, physicians' practice styles, and the introduction of new technology. Managed care arrangements are similar to traditional indemnity health insurance in many ways. A premium is charged to cover a prescribed set of medical benefits. Both use demand-side cost-sharing provisions, such as deductibles and coinsurance, to reduce moral hazard. In addition, managed care utilizes a combination of provider-side provisions to control moral hazard and the spending associated with it. These provider-side provisions include (1) selective contracting, (2) risk-sharing arrangements, and (3) utilization review.

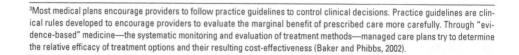

KEY CONCEPT 9
Market Failure

Selective Contracting

To varying degrees, managed care limits the patient's choice of provider for a given medical service. The limits include the use of gatekeepers, **closed panels**, and preferred providers. A gatekeeper is a physician responsible for providing all primary medical care and coordinating access to high-cost hospital and specialty care. Patients who wish to see a specialist must first get a referral from their primary care gatekeeper. A closed panel further limits a patient's choice of physician to a list of participating providers. To be part of a panel, physicians must agree to a set of standards established by the sponsoring organization. Networks that contract with **any willing provider** ensure enrollees a wide choice of physicians, but exclusive networks result in better cost controls. The criteria for inclusion vary depending on the selectivity of the plan. At minimum, providers are usually board certified, professionally accredited, and meet medical liability standards. Networks that are more selective consider practice styles and use only those providers who agree to follow "best practices" guidelines.[3] The PPO allows the patient to choose a provider who is not part of the panel. Patients who use physicians who are not part of the panel usually pay higher coinsurance rates, further discouraging off-panel utilization.

closed panel A designated network of providers that serves the recipients of a health care plan. Patients are not allowed to choose a provider outside the network.

any willing provider A situation in which a managed care organization allows any medical provider to become part of the network of providers for the covered group.

Risk-Sharing Arrangements

The method of reimbursement is an important mechanism in controlling costs. Managed care utilizes various reimbursement schemes with the common goal of shifting some of the financial risk to providers. Shifting risk discourages overutilization of services, primarily

---

[3]Most medical plans encourage providers to follow practice guidelines to control clinical decisions. Practice guidelines are clinical rules developed to encourage providers to evaluate the marginal benefit of prescribed care more carefully. Through "evidence-based" medicine—the systematic monitoring and evaluation of treatment methods—managed care plans try to determine the relative efficacy of treatment options and their resulting cost-effectiveness (Baker and Phibbs, 2002).

the use of expensive technology, brand-name prescription drugs, referrals to specialists, and inpatient hospital procedures.

Many managed care plans contract with primary care physicians using prospective payment or capitation—lump-sum payments per enrollee determined in advance. Prepayment shifts the financial risk to the providers. Instead of payment on a per-service basis, primary care physicians receive a fixed payment determined in advance to provide all the medically necessary primary and preventive care for a specific group of patients. Some managed care plans withhold a percentage of the authorized payment to ensure that providers control utilization and cost.[4] Primary care physicians serve as gatekeepers and may be subject to strict budgets for hospital services, specialty referrals, and prescription drugs for their covered patients. Physicians who provide care within the predetermined budgets receive bonuses. Those who do not are penalized by forfeiting part or all of their withholdings to the plan. This risk-sharing arrangement provides strong incentives to physicians to control utilization.

Figure 8.1 provides a schematic depiction of the allocation of premiums for a hypothetical capitated arrangement. In this example, primary care physicians serve as gatekeepers to more advanced services. Enrollees, most likely employees working at the same firm, are charged a premium of $500 per member per month (PMPM) for a defined package of medical benefits. The managed care organization uses $75 of the PMPM payment to cover operating expenses, administrative overhead, and profit. The remainder goes into four separate categories: primary care, pharmaceuticals, specialty care, and hospital care.

KEY CONCEPT 4
Self-Interest

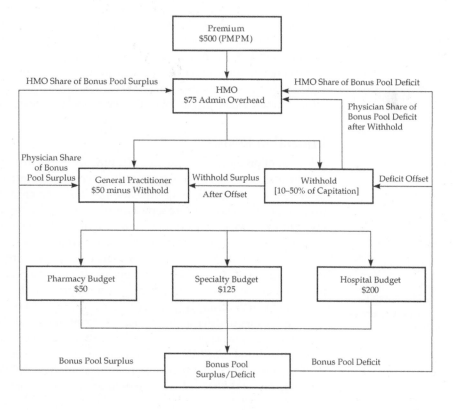

FIGURE 8.1 Typical Allocation of a $500 Premium under a Capitated Contract

---

[4]In the past these withholdings have been as high as 50 percent of the capitated payment. Recently, regulations that are more aggressive have brought the amount of capitated payment at risk to levels that are more manageable.

The general practitioner serving as gatekeeper receives a capitated payment of $50 PMPM for each enrollee who designates him or her as their primary care physician. Some plans withhold a percentage of this capitated payment as insurance against expense overruns in the other three budgetary categories. The pharmacy budget receives $50 PMPM, the specialty budget receives $125 PMPM, and the hospital budget receives $200 PMPM.[5] A bonus pool is created with the surpluses or deficits in each expense category. The providers and the plan share surpluses and deficits according to a specified formula, often on a 50/50 basis. Bonus-pool deficits are covered by the physician's withholding account. Any surplus in the withholding account is paid to the physician directly. If the physician's share of the bonus pool deficit is greater than the funds in the physician's withholding account, he or she is often responsible for reimbursing the plan for the difference. Recent changes in the bonus arrangement have added positive inducements for physicians to modify their practice patterns. These inducements include a target percentage of the enrolled children receiving their inoculations in a timely manner, a target percentage of enrolled women receiving appropriately timed cancer screenings, and specific scores on patient satisfaction surveys. Mixed bonus arrangements are much more popular than those based solely on cost considerations.

Providers paid according to the traditional fee-for-service arrangement are more likely to recommend and perform only reimbursed services. When given an option, providers are more likely to perform services reimbursed more generously relative to their resource cost. Because an insured patient's share of the total cost of care is relatively small, some services are provided that have little marginal value.

In contrast, the managed care organization structures the financial arrangements to shift some of the financial risk onto physicians. Providers are incentivized to practice in a more cost-effective manner. When a cheaper care option exists, providers are rewarded for choosing it. Such an arrangement changes the incentive structure completely. Instead of encouraging the provision of too many services, as is the case with traditional fee-for-service payment, this type of risk-sharing arrangement can, if not properly monitored, create pressures to do just the opposite and provide too few services.

Utilization Review

Selection of providers who follow "best practice" guidelines and the sharing of financial risk are often insufficient to control medical care expenditures. More than 90 percent of all health plans use some form of utilization review. The most popular technique for controlling utilization is to require some type of authorization for the use of hospital services: a preadmission review, concurrent review, or retrospective review. In addition, second surgical opinions and **case management** are used to control costs associated with surgeries.

Utilization management focuses primarily on services provided in the hospital sector. Preadmission review establishes the appropriateness of a procedure. Either the admitting physician or the patient must receive approval prior to the hospital admission. Often a maximum length of stay is specified at the same time. Concurrent review utilizes established guidelines to determine whether a hospital stay should be continued. Retrospective review examines the appropriateness of care after it has been completed. Inappropriate care is recognized, and providers who deviate from the established standards are identified.

Many managed care plans require second surgical opinions before recommended surgeries can be performed. This method of utilization control forces the physician who

---

[5]The numbers used in this example are representative of the typical allocation of a $500 premium. If the premium is higher, $625 for example, the appropriate adjustment would be to multiply each number by 1.25.

HTTP://

The National Committee for Quality Assurance (NCQA) is an independent, not-for-profit organization that serves as the accrediting agency for the nation's managed care plans. NCQA maintains Healthcare Effectiveness Data and Information Set (HEDIS), the standard report card used to rate and compare managed care plans. Links to HEDIS may be found at the NCQA website http://www.ncqa.org.

recommends the surgery to seek the opinion of a second physician before authorization is granted. Another commonly used utilization review technique is case management. In situations where costs and risks are high, case management is used to monitor resource use and thus lower the overall cost of treatment. A case manager, usually a member of the hospital nursing staff, often coordinates hospital care for costly conditions, such as coronary artery bypass surgery, organ transplantation, and the treatment of chronic conditions.

Overall, managed care plans use these three mechanisms—authorization review, second opinion, and case management—to varying degrees and with different rates of success. The ability to control moral hazard depends on the combination of features utilized and how strictly they are applied. These mechanisms can also affect the choice of technology by encouraging less technology-intensive practice styles. When patients and providers are required to share in the costs of care, the use of expensive technologies is discouraged (Cutler and Sheiner, 1998).

Managed Care Strategies

Medical care, whether in the United States or some other country, has traditionally been provided on a fee-for-service basis. Because of spiraling expenditures, fee-for-service medical plans began taking on cost-containment features during the 1980s. Frequently, these features include various aspects of the traditional managed care system: the use of a gatekeeper required second surgical opinions, prior certification before hospital admissions, utilization reviews, and preadmission hospital testing. These cost-control measures approach the issue from different perspectives. Nevertheless, their common goal is to ensure the provision of medically necessary services in the appropriate setting at the appropriate levels and prices.

The results of these strategies are to restrict access to certain kinds of medical care (such as hospital and specialty care), to redirect medical care delivery to less-expensive locations (such as outpatient and ambulatory settings), and to monitor the use of medical products, supplies, and services (such as prescription drugs and prosthetic devices). Not only has fee-for-service adopted many of the cost-savings features of managed care, but managed care has also increased its flexibility to better compete with fee-for-service. Instead of forcing recipients to use a closed panel of providers, more managed care systems offer open plans in which recipients are allowed to use providers outside the panel, subject to higher deductibles and coinsurance rates. Thus, managed care and fee-for-service systems are looking for the right mix of cost control and flexibility to compete in a changing medical care environment.

Market Alternatives

Claiming that government intervention was unnecessary and counterproductive, opponents of a government-run system argue that market alternatives are available. Market advocates claim that no one spends money more wisely than an individual spending his or her own money. Demand-side strategies include options that give the consumer patient more responsibility in the decision-making process. Patients would personally pay for the more routine care—relatively low-cost procedures that occur with regularity. These might include annual physical examinations, routine screening, and immunizations, often referred to as preventive care. The financial model would include a high-deductible insurance policy supported by an HSA.

Consumer-Directed Health Plans

For many who believe that free enterprise works and that the market is the best way to organize the delivery of goods and services, medical care delivery presents a conundrum. Many are content to argue market failure and recommend reliance on a government-run plan, but government action has proven susceptible to many of the same failings of the market, plus others that are more difficult to correct.

Defenders of the market believe that if the market is to work in medical care, individuals must have "skin in the game"—they must spend their own money when they receive care. Even though holders of a private insurance policy spend their own money on premiums—or their employer spends it for them—once paid, they represent a sunk cost and are irrelevant in the decision-making process. Faced with a low or zero marginal cost of care, individuals tend to overconsume; that is, they demand care that does little to improve medical outcomes. For the consumption decision to be optimal in the economic sense, individuals must take into consideration the alternative uses of the resources. If individuals are to economize on the use of resources, they must realize a direct benefit from their own economizing behavior.

For the market to work in medical care, consumers must spend their own money for routine (high frequency, low cost) medical services. In turn, to protect against catastrophic (low frequency, high cost) expenses, individuals would purchase a high-deductible insurance policy. Insurers use deductibles and coinsurance to get policyholders to spend their money more wisely, but often even small deductibles and low coinsurance rates create problems. For a single mother with three children, even a trip to the doctor to treat an earache can mean a financial hardship. Without money to pay the deductible, the earache often goes untreated, resulting in higher spending for an emergency room visit at a later date, and possibly long-term hearing loss for the child.

Quite possibly the most important advance in health insurance since the managed care movement in the 1990s was the introduction of CDHPs. A few small insurers began linking high-deductible coverage with HRAs in the late 1990s. This arrangement allowed individuals and their employers to make tax-free contributions into accounts designated for out-of-pocket medical spending. The movement was slow to develop until Congress passed the Medicare Modernization Act in 2003, which allowed insurers to offer HSAs to those with high-deductible policies. The major difference between the two accounts is portability. Typically, in the HRA arrangement, ownership of the account rests with the employer. If the holder of an HRA leaves employment for any reason, the balance in the HRA stays with the employer. In contrast, the HSA is treated more like a 401(k) investment plan, in which ownership rests with the employee.

The basic idea behind the HSA is simple. Instead of buying a traditional insurance policy, individuals purchase a high-deductible policy, say $2,500 that would cover only medical spending above that amount. Each year, approximately 90 percent of all claims and 70 percent of all medical spending are for amounts totaling less than $2,500. Annual deductibles in this range would result in significant savings on insurance premiums.[6]

The individual would have the HSA to pay for the first $2,500 for an individual or $5,000 for a family. The catastrophic insurance policy would cover all expenses in excess of some stated out-of-pocket maximum. Accumulations in these accounts would be available to pay future medical expenses. The important aspect of the plan is that the savings account belongs to the individual and does not have to be depleted at the end of each year. It would grow through annual deposits and earn interest.

---

[6]Total assets in HSAs increased from $11.3 billion in 2012 to $16.6 billion in 2013. The average balance in an HSA was $2,311 (Fronstin, 2014).

The major advantage of the HSA is that it puts the individual in control of his or her own medical spending. Proponents of HSAs assert that the main reason medical markets fail is that there is no incentive to practice economizing behavior—for either the provider or the patient. With HSAs, patients are spending their own money, at least up to the out-of-pocket maximum, so they have an incentive to economize. Rather than being indifferent to the prices they pay, consumers will benefit from shopping around. Such an environment is representative of consumer sovereignty in the real sense of the classical economic concept.

At a point, individual self-interest would take over. With patients benefiting from their own economizing behavior, savings balances would grow as spending moderated. Estimates of reduced spending are based primarily on the experience of individual employers. The movement to consumer-directed plans progressed slowly at first. The first HSAs became available in 2004, and by 2016, about one out of every three workers covered by private insurance had a CDHP.

APPLIED MICRO METHODS

LONG-TERM EFFECT OF CDHP ENROLLMENT ON HEALTH SPENDING

Background

CDHPs, where high-deductible plans are matched with either an HSA or other tax-advantaged personal medical account, are promoted as part of a strategy to reduce medical spending. Increasingly popular, enrollment in the employer-sponsored market has risen from 4 percent to 24 percent over the past decade alone. Empirical evidence supports the claim that CDHPs are responsible for at least part of the recent slowdown in U.S. medical care spending (Bundorf, 2016). The estimated impact on spending of a new CDHP offering is a reduction of between 5 percent and 24 percent in the first year. Whether the CDHP effect is more than a short-run phenomenon remains an unanswered question and is the focus of this research.

Data and Methods

This study utilizes enrollment and claims data from 54 large U.S. employers from 2003 to 2007, covering 13 million person years of data, 4 million from firms offering CDHPs and 9 million from those who did not. Total (all-payer) medical spending was categorized as either inpatient, outpatient, pharmaceutical, or emergency department. A difference-in-differences (DiD) strategy was used to estimate differences in spending growth over time between firms offering CDHPs (treatment group) and those not offering CDHPs (control group). To control for individual-level selection bias (where only healthy individuals choose CDHPs), an intent-to-treat design was employed. Instead of comparing spending differences between those who chose to enroll in a CDHP and those who did not, the intent-to-treat design compares spending differences of those who were offered a CDHP (whether they enrolled on one or not) and those who were not offered one.

Because of year-to-year fluctuations in the composition of a firm's employment base, the estimated CDHP effect may be biased simply due to the retention of young, healthy employees by the treatment group. To control for this possibility, the study uses a machine-learning approach that creates a weighted set of individuals within each firm whose demographic characteristics are invariant over time. The approach provides assurance that the estimated spending differences are due to the CDHP offer and not changes in the composition of the workforce between treatment and control firms.

Results

In the time period studied, spending growth in control firms is similar to spending growth experienced in private insurance nationally. The parallel trends assumption of the DiD strategy is also supported with the treatment group experiencing similar spending growth. Relative to control firms, those offering a CDHP significantly lower spending in the three years after an offer (ranging from 6.6 percent to 3.4 percent). This decrease translated into a $208 per capita savings in the first year gradually falling to $107 by the third year. The savings are concentrated in 2 spending categories: Pharmaceuticals spending growth was 5–9.5 percent lower in the first 3 years and outpatient spending was 3–6.8 percent lower. Inpatient spending growth was marginally lower in the first two years for firms offering CDHPs but no different in the third year. Spending growth in emergency department care was no different. If the CDHP effect results solely from reduced spending among employees who actually chose CDHPs (with no spillovers to those who remained in PPOs), the reduction in overall spending ranges from 7 percent to 22 percent.

Discussion and Conclusions

This paper is the first large multiemployer study examining the longer-term spending implications of firms offering CDHPs to their employees. The results suggest that the savings due to employees choosing CDHPs persist over time. There is weak evidence that the impact moderates over time but stronger evidence that it does not increase over time.

Sources: Amelia M. Haviland et al., "Do 'Consumer-Directed' Health Plans Bend the Cost Curve over Time?" *Journal of Health Economics* 46, 2016, 33–51; and M. Kate Bundorf, "Consumer-Directed Health Plans: A Review of the Evidence," *Journal of Risk and Insurance* 83(1), January 2016, 9–41.

Many do not believe that the HSA concept can work on a nationwide scale, dismissing the idea because it allows too much individual discretion in choosing medical care. Critics think that most people are incapable of making informed decisions about the quality and quantity of the health care they need. They argue that nothing short of universally mandated free care provides the proper incentives for individuals to seek the correct mix of primary and preventive care. They fear that individuals with medical savings accounts would be tempted to save their money rather than spend it when they or their children are sick (United States House of Representatives, 1993).

Many are hesitant to back the concept of the HSA for fear that what may work for a small segment of the community may not work for the whole population. HSAs may work well for those who are healthy, but what about the small percentage of the population that gets sick? How would those unfortunate enough to have large medical bills be protected at a reasonable cost? Others worry that individual HSA holders would be no match for the more powerful provider networks.

Proponents argue that holders of CDHP plans will be smarter consumers of health care and will demand better price and quality information from providers. Additionally, early evidence does not support the claim that holders of high-deductible plans will underuse preventive services and drive up spending in the long run (Rowe et al., 2008). Under any circumstance, greater cost sharing by policyholders is inevitable and, short of overt price controls, the CDHP model is better equipped to moderate spending than the alternatives.

Innovative Delivery Concepts

Changes on the supply side focus on increasing competition in health care delivery. As part of the managed care movement in the mid-1990s, managed care plans increased the use of capitation, shifting some of the financial risk to providers and encouraging the incorporation of cost-reducing strategies into the delivery system. Individual providers were not prepared to absorb the additional risk and found that they were unable to make the necessary adjustments without jeopardizing the quality of care.

Competition can also serve as the catalyst for innovative behavior on the part of providers to lower cost and improve quality. The best example of innovative behavior on the delivery side is the advancement of the accountable care organization (ACO). An ACO is an integrated delivery system that coordinates the delivery of care for a well-defined group of beneficiaries. Providers may be affiliated with each other in group practices, provider networks, partnerships, or joint venture arrangements. In any case they are accountable for providing all the medically necessary care for their patients for a set payment determined in advance. Medical organizations like the Mayo Clinic and the Geisinger Clinic (discussed in the Issues in Medical Care Delivery on pages 260–261) are examples of an ACO.

The Accountable Care Act provides incentives for provider groups to establish ACOs to better coordinate the delivery of care, improve quality, and lower cost. Under the demonstration project that began in 2012, ACOs that accomplish these goals may keep part of the savings they generate.

Evidence of Managed Care Savings

Evidence provided in Table 8.2 suggests that managed care offers employers savings over the traditional indemnity option. A survey by the Kaiser Family Foundation (2016) estimated the average annual premium across all plans for a single person to be $6,435 in 2016, and for a family, the average premium was $18,142, both 15 percent higher than the 2012 premium. The PPO premiums were highest, averaging $6,800/$19,003. For HMO plans premiums were $6,576/$17,978, and HDHP premiums averaged $5,762/$16,737.

Empirical evidence supporting managed care's savings potential is complicated by the difficulty in classifying plans according to their cost-saving features. The extensive combination of features utilized by the various plans makes it difficult to control for the differences, making comparisons tricky. By designing benefit packages that appeal to low-risk users, plans can successfully segment their market and avoid high-risk users. Thus, cost differences across plans may be a phenomenon due in part to enrollee selection.

Empirical research on the effectiveness of managed care has examined several important issues: selection bias, utilization of services, quality of care, and ability to control costs (Glied, 2000). Hellinger (1995) examined the differences between the characteristics of managed care and traditional indemnity insurance enrollees. Overall, the research suggests that managed care plans attract a healthier group of enrollees than indemnity

TABLE 8.2 AVERAGE PREMIUMS FOR SINGLE AND FAMILY PLANS, 2012, 2016

	Single plans		Family plans	
	2012	2016	2012	2016
All plans	$5,615	$6,435	$15,745	$18,142
HMOs	5,668	6,576	15,729	17,978
PPOs	5,850	6,800	16,356	19,003
HDHPs	4,928	5,762	14,129	16,737

Source: Kaiser Family Foundation, 2012, 2016.

plans. However, the evidence is mixed. It is difficult to determine how health differences affect utilization and cost because of differences in characteristics between groups (Newhouse, 1996).

A number of studies have attempted to estimate the difference in medical care utilization between managed care and traditional indemnity insurance. Luft (1981) conducted one of the earliest studies on HMO utilization. Using data from 1959 through 1975, he concluded that managed care plans had 10–40 percent lower costs per enrollee than conventional health plans such as Blue Cross. Although HMO enrollees experienced as many ambulatory visits, they had 25–45 percent fewer hospital days per capita. The reason was fewer admissions, not shorter hospital stays.

The most extensive study of the cost-saving potential of HMOs was the RAND Health Insurance Experiment (see Manning et al., 1984). This study avoided selection bias by randomly assigning individuals to a staff-model HMO or to one of several indemnity plans. The results of this study confirmed the cost-savings potential of managed care. The HMO had per capita costs that were 28 percent lower than the indemnity plan without cost sharing. This difference was due largely to enrollees in HDHPs initiating fewer episodes of care.

Miller and Luft (1994, 1997) analyzed more recent literature comparing HMO and fee-for-service costs. Their findings suggest that HMOs provide care comparable to traditional fee-for-service care at savings of 10–15 percent. Savings are due to shorter hospital stays, fewer tests, and the use of less costly medical procedures. HMOs are able to accomplish these savings in spite of higher rates of physician office visits and more comprehensive benefits packages than fee-for-service plans.

A few studies have attempted to explain the savings features of the newer forms of managed care with mixed results. Using data from the Medical Outcomes Study of 20,000 adult patients, Greenfield and colleagues (1992) found no statistically significant difference in four treatment categories between three types of managed care organizations and two fee-for-service arrangements.[7] Murray et al. (1992) examined two small, private group practices that treated both HMO and fee-for-service patients diagnosed with hypertension and found that HMO patients had fewer laboratory tests and consequently lower spending. Smith (1997) found that preferred provider plans reduced costs and Hosek, Marquis, and Wells (1990) found that they increased costs.

RAND research has examined the preliminary savings resulting from the adoption of consumer-directed plans (Buntin et al., 2011; Haviland et al., 2011, 2012). Their research analyzed data from 800,000 households over the period 2003–2007. Key findings indicate that families switching from traditional low-deductible plans saved an average of 21 percent when they enrolled in high-deductible plans for the first time. (Cost savings were significant only in cases where the deductibles were at least $1,000.) Unlike results from RAND's health insurance experiment in the 1970s, approximately one-third of savings estimates were due to lower spending per episode of care. Additionally, a significant share of the savings was due to enrollees increased use of generic drugs, fewer visits to specialists, and fewer hospital admissions.

This research concluded that 25 percent of Americans enrolled in consumer-directed plans would result in an annual reduction in health care spending of $57 billion. One-third of the population enrolled in such plans would result in a savings of $85 billion annually (Haviland et al., 2012).

Overall, the evidence suggests that managed care can reduce health care spending, even after controlling for enrollee characteristics and type of plan. In most cases, these

---

[7]The four treatment categories were the percent of enrollees hospitalized, the use of office visits, the number of prescription drugs utilized, and the number of tests per patient per year.

savings have been accomplished primarily through the initial reduction in hospital use and a decrease in spending per episode of care. As summarized in Glied (2000), the evidence is far from conclusive, but the savings potential of managed care (especially consumer-directed plans) is potentially significant.

Evidence of Quality Differences between Managed Care and Fee-for-Service Care

Another issue explored by the empirical literature is whether there are quality differences between managed care and traditional fee-for-service care. Building on their earlier research, Miller and Luft (1997) summarized the research on the relationship between the type of plan and quality of care. In their review of 15 studies comparing quality of care, they found equal numbers of statistically significant positive and negative effects of managed care on quality. Four studies found significantly better quality in managed care, and four found worse. The others found insignificant differences or were inconclusive.

Robinson (2000) reviewed 24 studies, mostly from 1988 to 1995. The overall patterns identified by these studies suggested lower levels of utilization for managed care plans. In most cases, managed care had fewer hospitalizations, shorter hospital stays, and lower levels of discretionary services. Another important difference was the relative emphasis on preventive care as evidenced by more diagnostic screening and testing among managed care plans. Once again, Robinson found little conclusive evidence that managed care quality was lower than that found in fee-for-service plans.

Even though managed care has not decreased the overall effectiveness of care, certain vulnerable subpopulations—including older patients, sicker patients, and patients with low incomes—may have less favorable outcomes under managed care (Ware et al., 1996). Robinson (2000) identified five studies that compared quality of care for Medicare enrollees under fee-for-service and managed care plans. He found some evidence that managed care fared worse than fee-for-service, but most of the studies were inconclusive. Hellinger (1998) reported that managed care enrollees are less satisfied with their health plans than fee-for-service enrollees. Their lower levels of satisfaction resulted from difficulties in accessing specialized care, leaving enrollees with the perception that the overall quality of care was somewhat lower.

The strongest disincentive for providing quality care is for the sickest and costliest patients. Plans that provide quality care for their sickest patients will attract sicker patients. At average premiums, this strategy leads to losses. If premiums rise to cover higher costs, the plans lose enrollment.

To summarize, the empirical research does not provide definitive evidence about the overall effect of managed care on quality of care.

Managed Care and Its Public Image

HTTP://
The accounting firm Pricewaterhouse Coopers maintains an active consulting practice in the managed care industry. Access survey and research information through their website at http://www.pwc.com.

Accustomed to the lack of restrictions in fee-for-service medicine, the American consumer has found it difficult to adjust to the limitations of managed care delivery. Everybody has a favorite HMO story they like to tell. The anecdotes abound. In the movie *As Good as It Gets*, Helen Hunt treats the viewing audience to a diatribe against a fictitious HMO that has denied care to her asthmatic son. The fee-for-service physician who finally diagnoses and treats him is viewed sympathetically. In light of the lack of evidence suggesting poor quality of care, why does managed care have such a poor public image?

Miller and Luft (1997) offer one possible answer to this question. They note the inevitable time lag for published research to get into print. The most recent research findings do not make it to publication in a timely manner due to the delay. As a result, available research results do not relate well to current market conditions.

A second possible explanation relates to the diversity of managed care arrangements. Few studies to date have taken into consideration the newer types of managed care plans and the preponderance of cost-cutting rules and financial incentives that have affected providers since the early 1990s. Anecdotal evidence abounds, but generalizations are difficult because of the lack of reliable empirical research. Additionally, many of the newer managed care organizations are for-profit in nature and thus place a greater emphasis on cost-saving strategies, which eventually may affect managed care quality. To the extent that they exist, these differences will not show up in the research for years.

Finally, the role of medical providers in influencing public perception about managed care should not be ignored. Managed care is unpopular among health care professionals. Their clinical autonomy is challenged and their incomes are lower because of certain managed care strategies. When physicians complain loudly about the restrictions of managed care, their patients are likely to notice the discontent and mimic the criticism. This combination has resulted in a powerful force that has found a sympathetic hearing among policy makers at all levels of government.

ISSUES IN MEDICAL CARE DELIVERY

THE MANAGED CARE "BLUES"

For over 75 years, Blue Cross and Blue Shield were virtually synonymous with health insurance. A network of 38 independent, community-based plans nationwide (and two international plans in Panama and Uruguay), they have dominated the industry, covering over 100 million people, or about one-third of the total U.S. population. In addition, the federal employee program plan covers over 5 million federal workers.

Their nationwide dominance does not accurately reflect their importance. Through administrative services contracts with the federal government, the plans process over 80 percent of Medicare Part A claims and 70 percent of Part B claims. And in many states, a single Blue Cross entity covers over half the population. Nationwide, over 95 percent of all community hospitals and 90 percent of all private-practice physicians have contracts with at least one of the Blues.

These nonprofit companies, once considered the insurer of last resort for many, are rapidly changing their operating practices and drawing sharp criticism from some circles. Over the first half of the 1990s, the market had witnessed the private, for-profit health insurers transforming themselves into managed care companies. While the "Blues" have not reacted as quickly as many of the commercial insurers—such as Prudential, CIGNA, and Aetna—many have adopted an aggressive strategy for setting up managed care networks.

Simply by virtue of their size, the Blues are the largest providers of managed care in the country, covering over two-thirds of all managed care enrollees nationwide. The system is also the largest provider of managed care to Medicare and Medicaid.

The most controversial step by plan administrators was the approval in July 1994 of a change in organizational status. Traditionally nonprofit in nature, the plans can now become for-profit entities or establish for-profit subsidiaries. This change will affect more than their tax-exempt status; it will allow the Blues greater access to the private capital market and increase their ability to expand, which is essential if they are to be competitive with the commercial carriers.

No one is quite sure what the new health care environment will look like. But one thing is certain: The Blues, once dominant players in the health insurance market, are not sitting around, waiting to be swallowed up by the system. They are merging, partnering, and integrating; in general, they are preparing for the new health care environment of the twenty-first century.

Source: Steven Findlay, "The Remaking of the Blues; Blue Cross and Blue Shield Association; Company Profile," *Business and Health* 12(8), August 1994, 37ff.

The Future of Managed Care

The future of managed care is dependent in many ways on the changes ushered in by the ACA. Payment and delivery reform imbedded in the ACA may in fact take managed care in an entirely new direction. Important among these changes is the emphasis on encouraging the development of the ACO. The Centers for Medicare and Medicaid Services (CMS) defines the ACO as "an organization of health care providers that agrees to be accountable for the quality, cost, and overall care of [a group of assigned] Medicare beneficiaries who are enrolled in the traditional fee-for-service program" (CMS, 2016). The development of the ACO concept is not new, but its resurgence is a response to changes in the Medicare payment design. Different from traditional Medicare fee-for-service and the fully capitated payment to Medicare Advantage providers, ACO payments will include a "shared savings" component where the ACO will be rewarded for reduced spending by receiving a share of the savings or bonus payments.

POLICY ISSUE

A health care system that focuses on cost containment will tend to short-change other important goals, including quality and access.

In order to accomplish the program's objectives, providers will try to become fully integrated delivery systems by consolidating primary, specialty, and hospital care in one delivery system. Several collaborative options come to mind immediately: Geisinger Health System in Pennsylvania, the Mayo Clinic in Minnesota, and the Baylor-Scott and White Health System in central Texas. The change brings with it concern about the competitive impact of consolidation in the industry. Integration, both horizontal (hospitals acquiring hospitals) and vertical (hospitals acquiring physicians' practices and post-acute care facilities), will reduce competition and potentially raise prices (Burns and Pauly, 2012).

To function effectively as an ACO will require a significant change in physician and patient behavior. Physicians will have to change their approach to treating patients by switching to evidence-based protocols. Few U.S. physicians are willing to give up their clinical autonomy and follow clinical pathways designed to provide optimal care for the typical patient.

Patients will need to be more engaged in their treatment and accountable for the cost of care they receive. Incentives must direct patients to the most cost-effective procedure and provider. Limited patient choice was not popular when it was introduced by managed care in the 1990s. It's not likely to be popular today.

The big question is whether the ACO will save money. Even the most optimistic interpretation of pilot program results does not show significant savings. With an additional 30 million Americans covered initially, any savings are likely to be swamped by increased demand from the previously uninsured.

Even with all these changes, the cost-conscious consumer is still the best defense against excess spending. While an exclusively consumer-driven health care system seems unlikely, as premiums continue to soar, the consumer-driven health plan with an HSA supported by a high-deductible insurance plan will continue to see increased popularity.

Summary and Conclusions

In this chapter, we have examined how managed care emerged as the alternative payment and delivery mechanism to traditional fee-for-service indemnity insurance. What began as an experiment is now the choice of more than 90 percent of all insured Americans under the age of 65.

Stakeholders learned valuable lessons from the experience of the past decade.

■ *Patients learned that a one-size-fits-all solution to medical care is too restrictive. As medical technology provides more treatment options, the definition of what constitutes medical care also expands. Rising expectations against a backdrop of access restrictions create tension.*

■ *Providers learned that risk sharing presents a challenge to their clinical autonomy and financial security. Forced into a double-agent role (as agent for both patient and plan), providers dislike the restrictions as much as patients do.*

■ *Payers learned that cost control is unpopular. The backlash against managed care presented not only an image problem but was dangerous for corporate survival.*

■ *Employers learned that there is no magic pill to solve the health care cost problem. Overly aggressive measures to control costs are not only unpopular among employees, but they can lead to litigation problems as plaintiffs search for deep pockets.*

■ *Politicians learned that restrictions on access and limits to spending are unpopular and cost votes. They also learned that expansions of treatment options and increases in spending are popular and win votes.*

PROFILE William B. Schwartz

Trained as an internist, William B. Schwartz had invested a lifetime in academic medicine and became a respected biomedical researcher and national authority on kidney disease. So when this distinguished scholar announced his plans for a mid-career change from clinical medicine to health policy, it raised more than a few eyebrows. Many of his colleagues probably thought he was taking the midlife crisis thing a bit too far. They could understand gold chains and a red sports car, but giving up a medical career to study economics seemed a bit extreme.

Schwartz's medical career reads like a Who's Who in academic medicine. He graduated from Duke medical school in 1945. Five years later, he settled at Tufts University, where he became head of the Nephrology Division at the New England Medical Center. In 1971, he was appointed chair of the Department of Medicine and Physician-in-Chief at the medical center. That same year, he spent the first of several summers working with health economists Charles Phelps and Joseph Newhouse at the RAND Corporation. Under their tutelage, Schwartz was introduced to the economic concepts of scarcity and opportunity cost, and his professional career as a health policy analyst began to bud.

Because his administrative and clinical duties at Tufts required most of his energies, he had little time left to devote to his research interests. Lack of research opportunities and a newly acquired interest in health care policy analysis provided enough incentive to convince Schwartz to resign as department chair and pursue an alternative career path.

After shifting to health policy, his research interests focused on applying economics to problems in medical care delivery. His first article on health policy was published in *Science* in 1972. Since that time, Schwartz has devoted his efforts to explaining the role of market forces and competition in promoting efficiency in medical care delivery.

One of his most widely read works, *The Painful Prescription: Rationing Health Care*, was coauthored in 1984 with Brookings economist Henry J. Aaron. The publication examines nonprice rationing of hospital services in the United Kingdom. His book is not a criticism of the National Health Service, but an honest attempt to understand resource allocation within that system and learn from the British experience. The consummate iconoclast, Schwartz has also challenged the conventional wisdom on physician supply in the United States. Instead of forecasting a surplus of 150,000 physicians by the year 2000, he made a solid case for a balance between supply and demand.

Most scholars work a lifetime to make a contribution in a single preferred field of study, but Schwartz distinguished himself as a clinician and health policy analyst. Emeritus professor of medicine at Tufts Medical Center in Boston, Schwartz died of Alzheimer's disease in 2009. He had the good fortune of contributing in two areas, and his accomplishments stand as an inspiration to clinicians and economists everywhere.

Sources: John K. Iglehart, "From Research to Rationing: A Conversation with William B. Schwartz," *Health Affairs* 8(3), Fall 1989, 60–75; and William B. Schwartz, Frank A. Sloan, and David N. Mendelson, "Why There Will Be Little or No Physician Surplus between Now and the Year 2000," *New England Journal of Medicine* 318(14), April 1988, 892–897.

Questions and Problems

1. Define each of the following terms used regularly by the major third-party payers, and explain how they are supposed to affect providers' incentives, fees, and overall utilization:
   a. fee-for-service
   b. assignment
   c. capitation
   d. risk sharing

2. "As the health care delivery system becomes increasingly cost conscious, physicians are no longer able to serve as advocates for their patients' medical needs." In light of this concern, discuss the changing role of the physician in the managed care environment.

3. What are the distinguishing characteristics of an HMO? How do HMOs differ from other insurers operating in the health insurance industry?

4. What are the primary cost-saving features of managed care?

5. How will the expansion of managed care produce competitive effects throughout the health care system?

6. In theory, how is managed care expected to affect patient and provider incentives, and hence, the cost and use of medical care? What is the evidence?

7. In a series of articles in the February 10, 1993, issue of the *Journal of the American Medical Association*, researchers were said to have estimated that 2.4 percent of all bypass surgeries are inappropriate, and 7 percent are clearly unnecessary—roughly, one-fourth as much as previously estimated. Results were similar for coronary angioplasty and coronary angiography. Some analysts are using these results to claim the problem is now underuse instead of overuse. How do you define terms such as "inappropriate" and "unnecessary"? What are the lessons to be learned about the use of outcomes research?

8. Explain how the theory of managed care with prospective payment was expected to affect patient and provider incentives, and the consequent effect on the cost and use of medical care.

References

Baker, Laurence C. and Ciaran S. Phibbs, "Managed Care, Technology Adoption, and Health Care: The Adoption of Neonatal Intensive Care," *RAND Journal of Economics* 33(3), Autumn 2002, 524–548.

Buntin, M. B., et al., "Healthcare Spending and Preventive Care in High-Deductible and Consumer-Directed Health Plans," *American Journal of Managed Care* 17(3), March 2011, 222–230.

Burns, Lawton R. and Mark V. Pauly, "Accountable Care Organizations May Have Difficulty Avoiding the Failures of Integrated Delivery Networks of the 1990s," *Health Affairs* 31(11), 2012, 2407–2416.

Centers for Medicare and Medicaid Services (CMS), "Summary of the June 2015 Final Rule Provisions for Accountable Care Organizations (ACOs) under the Medicare Shared Savings Program," March 2016.

Cutler, David M. and Louise Sheiner, "Managed Care and the Growth in Medical Expenditures," in A. M. Garber, ed., *Frontiers of Health Policy Research*, Vol. 1, Cambridge, MA: MIT Press, 1998.

Friedman, E. S., "Capitation, Integration, and Managed Care: Lessons from Early Experiments," *Journal of the American Medical Association* 275(12), 1996, 957–962.

Fronstin, Paul, "Health Savings Accounts and Health Reimbursement Arrangements: Assets, Account Balances, and Rollovers, 2006–2013," EBRI Issue Brief, No. 395, January 2014.

Glied, Sherry, "Managed Care," in *Handbook of Health Economics, Vol. 1*, edited by Anthony J. Culyer and Joseph Newhouse, North Holland: Elsevier, 2000, 707–753.

Greenfield, Sheldon, et al., "Variations in Resource Utilization among Medical Specialties and Systems of Care," *Journal of the American Medical Association* 267(12), March 25, 1992, 1624–1630.

Gruber, Lynn R., Maureen Shadle, and Cynthia L. Polich, "From Movement to Industry: The Growth of HMOs," *Health Affairs* 7(3), Summer 1988, 197–208.

Haviland, A. M., et al., "Growth of Consumer-Directed Health Plans to One-Half of All Employer-Sponsored Insurance Could Save $57 Billion Annually," *Health Affairs* 31(5), May 2012, 1009–1015.

___, "The Effects of Consumer-Directed Health Plans on Episodes of Health Care," *Forum for Health Economics and Policy* 14(2), Article 9, September 2011, 1–27.

Hellinger, Fred J., "The Effect of Managed Care on Quality: A Review of Recent Evidence," *Archives of Internal Medicine* 158, April 27, 1998, 833–841.

___, "Selection Bias in HMOs and PPOs: A Review of the Evidence," *Inquiry* 32, Summer 1995, 135–143.

Hosek, S. D., M. S. Marquis, and K. B. Wells, *Health Care Utilization in Employer Plans with Preferred Provider Organizations*, RAND Corporation, February 1990.

Kaiser Family Foundation, "Employer Health Benefits: 2016 Annual Survey," 2016, available at http://files.kff.org/attachment/Report-Employer-Health-Benefits-2016-Annual-Survey. Accessed March 17, 2017.

_____, "Survey of Employer Health Benefits: 2012," 2012, available at http://kff.org/health-costs/report/employer-health-benefits-2012-annual-survey. Accessed August 6, 2013.

Luft, Harold S., *Health Maintenance Organizations: Dimensions of Performance*, New York: Wiley, 1981.

Manning, Willard, et al., "A Controlled Trial of the Effect of a Prepaid Group Practice on Use of Services," *New England Journal of Medicine* 310(23), June 7, 1984, 1505–1510.

Miller, Robert H. and Harold S. Luft, "Does Managed Care Lead to Better or Worse Quality of Care?" *Health Affairs* 16(5), September/October 1997, 7–25.

___, "Managed Care Plan Performance since 1980: A Literature Analysis," *Journal of the American Medical Association* 271(19), May 18, 1994, 1512–1519.

Murray, J., et al., "Ambulatory Testing for Capitation and Fee-for-Service Patients in the Same Practice Setting: Relationship to Outcome," *Medical Care* 30(2), March 1992, 252–261.

Newhouse, Joseph, "Reimbursing Health Plans and Health Providers: Selection versus Efficiency in Production," *Journal of Economic Literature* 34(3), September 1996, 1236–1263.

Robinson, Ray, "Managed Care in the United States: A Dilemma for Evidence-Based Policy?" *Health Economics* 9(1), January 2000, 1–7.

Rowe, John W., et al., "The Effect of Consumer-Directed Health Plans on the Use of Preventive and Chronic Illness Services," *Health Affairs* 27(1), January/February 2008, 113–120.

Smith, D. G., "The Effects of Preferred Provider Organizations on Health Care Use and Cost," *Inquiry* 34, Winter 1997, 278–287.

United States House of Representatives, *The President's Health Care Reform Proposal*, Hearings before the Committee on Ways and Means, House of Representatives, 103rd Congress, 1st Session, Washington, DC: U.S. Government Printing Office, 1993.

Ware, J. E., et al., "Differences in Four-Year Health Outcomes for Elderly and Poor, Chronically Ill Patients Treated in HMO and Fee-for-Service Systems: Results from the Medical Outcomes Study," *Journal of the American Medical Association* 13, 1996, 1039–1047.

The Physicians' Services Market

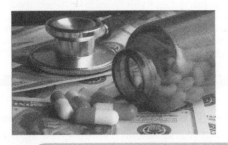

THE FUTURE PHYSICIAN SHORTAGE

The Affordable Care Act (ACA) is expected to increase the number of Americans with insurance by 30 million over the next decade. Medical infrastructure, including imaging facilities and hospital capacity, is expected to keep pace with the increased demand. However, physician workforce shortages continue to plague the system, particularly in primary care and general surgery.

The shortages are already manifesting themselves in the form of increased waiting times for routine medical exams. Surveying 15 major metropolitan areas, Merritt Hawkins & Associates (2014) found an average waiting time of 18.5 days in the five specialty areas studied (cardiology, orthopedics, family medicine, dermatology, and obstetrics/gynecology), ranging from 9.9 days in orthopedics to 28.8 days in dermatology. Regional differences were also significant with average waits ranging from 10.2 days in Dallas to 45.4 days in Boston. The forerunner of the ACA has been in place in Massachusetts since 2006, pointing to increased challenges in acquiring an appointment for routine services as the new law becomes operational nationwide.

In addition, the expansion of Medicaid added almost 14 million new enrollees from 2013–2016. In the 15 cities surveyed, less than one-half of the physicians (45.7 percent) currently accept patients insured through that government entitlement program.

The passage of the ACA is not the only demand shock expected in the next decade. Aging baby boomers will increase the number of Americans eligible for Medicare by 36 percent while at the same time one-third of the physician workforce will reach retirement age, making the looming physician shortage even more daunting.

The Association of American Medical Colleges (AAMC) estimated that the physician shortage was 62,900 in 2015, with most of the shortfall in primary care and general surgery. The situation is not expected to improve over time. Shortages are estimated to increase to 91,500 by 2020 and 130,000 by 2025 (Reuters, 2010).

Many hospitals are resorting to hiring surgical temps (locum tenens) to address their short-term needs and finding a surprisingly large number of general surgeons willing to work in that capacity. Full-time surgical temps can earn $250,000 annually with none of the expenses of the traditional practice, including malpractice insurance that is covered in the temp contract (Fuhrmans, 2009).

The shortage could be addressed by immediately creating 15–20 percent more residency positions nationwide. This would enable the system to graduate an additional

4,000 physicians per year, cutting the projected shortages by one-half in a decade. The AAMC strategy is to increase the size of medical school classes and build new medical schools. But the real bottleneck is the funding source for residencies, 75 percent coming from Medicare that experienced $740 billion in budget cuts as a result of the ACA. To address the shortage immediately will require better integration of medical practices, doctors seeing more patients, and more efficient use of physician assistants and nurse practitioners.

Sources: Vanessa Fuhrmans, "Surgeon Shortage Pushes Hospital to Hire Temps," *Wall Street Journal*, January 13, 2009; Merritt Hawkins & Associates, "2014 Survey of Physician Appointment Wait Times," 2014, available at https://www .merritthawkins.com/uploadedFiles/MerrittHawkings/Surveys/mha2014waitsurvPDF.pdf (Accessed March 20, 2017); Reuters Business & Financial News, "Health Reform to Worsen Doctor Shortage," 2010, available at http://dailycaller .com/2010/10/01/health-reform-to-worsen-doctor-shortage-group/ (Accessed January 31, 2011).

Physicians occupy the central role in the provision of medical services. Even though physicians receive less than one-fourth of total medical spending, they determine how much money is spent on medical care. Physicians are responsible for admitting patients to the hospital, recommending treatment, writing prescriptions, and scheduling and performing surgeries. In addition to the details of patient care, physicians also control other important aspects of the decision-making process in medical care delivery, including the acquisition of medical equipment in hospitals, the direction of biomedical research, and medical school curricula.

The past decade was an unsettling period for both active physicians and those hoping to someday practice the healing arts. Major changes in the market include a movement away from traditional fee-for-service practice toward other payment options and shifts from retrospective to prospective payment. During this period, physicians experienced increased intrusion into medical practice from both public and private payers. We begin with a brief discussion of the theory of labor markets, and then we focus our analysis on the physicians' services market. The final two sections will explore briefly the markets for nursing services and dental services.

The Theory of Labor Markets

KEY CONCEPT 6
Supply and Demand

The standard economic theory of labor markets views individual marginal productivity as one of the main determinants of labor income. Because productivity determines wages, higher productivity is translated into greater demand for labor services, and in turn, higher wages.

Input Pricing

Broadly speaking, the theory of input pricing is no different from the theory of pricing goods and services presented in Chapter 2. Both are based on the interaction of demand and supply. However, several important differences arise. First, an input's marginal contribution in the production process determines its demand. The second important difference between input demand and product demand is related to the first: Inputs are not consumed directly; therefore, the quantity of the input demanded will depend on the amount of the final product desired for consumption. Thus, input demand is derived from the demand for the final product and affected by the prevailing conditions in the market for the final product.[1]

---

[1]When examining the demand for physicians' services, keep in mind that the final product is a desired level of health.

The economic model of input pricing is based on a firm's decisions concerning the input combination used to produce a given level of output, or in the case of physicians' services, an individual's decisions concerning the combination of medical services used to produce a given level of health. Once the firm (individual) decides on a level of production (health), the level of input demand is simultaneously determined. The process involves determining the optimal or least-cost combination of inputs required to produce the profit-maximizing (utility-maximizing) level of output (health). Generalizing from the discussion in Appendix 3B, the least-cost combination of inputs in the production process $Q = Q (X, Y, \ldots, Z)$ may be written as the following equilibrium condition:

$$\frac{MP_X}{P_X} = \frac{MP_Y}{P_Y} = \cdots = \frac{MP_Z}{P_Z}$$

KEY CONCEPT 8
Efficiency

where MP_i is the marginal product of the ith input ($i = X, Y, \ldots, Z$) and P_i is its price.

It can also be shown that the reciprocal of each of the ratios is equal to the marginal cost of production (MC), or

$$\frac{P_X}{MP_X} = \frac{P_Y}{MP_Y} = \cdots = \frac{P_Z}{MP_Z} = MC$$

To prove this equality, consider that the use of one more unit of input X, holding the other inputs constant will increase output by MP_X units. Thus, using an additional $1/MP_X$ units of input X will increase output by one unit. If one unit of input X costs P_X, then $1/MP_X$ units of X costs P_X/MP_X, which is the cost of producing an additional unit of output, or marginal cost.

If firms are maximizing profit, they are producing an output level at which marginal revenue (MR) equals marginal cost. Thus, it follows that

$$\frac{P_X}{MP_X} = \frac{P_Y}{MP_Y} = \cdots = \frac{P_Z}{MP_Z} = MR$$

By rearranging terms and writing a separate equation for each input, it follows that

$$P_X = MP_X \cdot MR$$
$$P_Y = MP_Y \cdot MR$$
$$\vdots$$
$$P_Z = MP_Z \cdot MR$$

marginal revenue product The change in total revenue resulting from the sale of the output produced by an additional unit of a resource.

Interpreting these results, we see that in a world where buyers are profit (utility) maximizers, inputs used in a production process are paid an amount—in this case P_X, P_Y, and P_Z—equal to each input's **marginal revenue product** (MRP). Thus, the value of an input in the production process is calculated by multiplying marginal product of the input by the marginal revenue generated by the production and sale of an additional unit of the final product. This result serves as the underlying principle for deriving the demand curve for an input.

Demand for Inputs

In order to derive the demand curve for an input, first determine the maximum price buyers are willing to pay to obtain the desired amount of the input. The incremental value placed on an additional unit of the input in the production process determines the maximum price that buyers are willing to pay.

FIGURE 9.1
Marginal Wage Revenue
Product

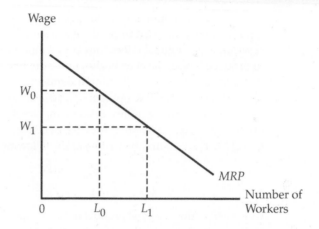

Figure 9.1 represents the MRP for any given input. It is downward sloping for the same reason that the marginal product curve is downward sloping: the law of diminishing returns. If the input is labor, the market wage rate determines the number of workers hired. At wage rate W_0, L_0 workers are hired. If the wage rate falls to W_1, more workers are hired (L_1). Thus, the MRP curve is the input demand curve, reflecting the two important concepts that determine input demand: the marginal productivity of the input and the level of product demand.

More productive inputs command higher prices in the market, as do inputs that are used in the production of highly valued commodities. It is no wonder that most medical inputs carry such high price tags. They are very effective in improving health status, something consumers value highly.

Human Capital Investment

One of the most popular ways for an individual to improve his or her marginal productivity is to attend school. Presumably, school attendance enables a person to learn a set of skills that enhances productivity. Schooling affects income in two important ways. First, while a person is attending school, income is lower due to forgone earnings. The time spent in school could have been used in gainful employment. In other words, the opportunity cost of attending school is the income that could have been earned if the individual had chosen to work. Second, after completing school, the individual's income will be higher. Individuals who attend school make more money than those who do not. The time spent in school valued by the opportunity cost measured in terms of the income forgone is called *human capital investment*.

KEY CONCEPT 5
Markets and Pricing

Investment in Medical Education   Medical education is a time-consuming process—four years of undergraduate study followed by four years of medical school. That is only the beginning. After eight years of formal education, the medical school graduate must complete a clinical residency program that lasts a minimum of three years before beginning a medical practice. Forgone income is obviously a major expense of attending medical school (estimated as high as $675,000). Even though tuition and fees make up less than 20 percent of the median cost of attending medical school, 86 percent of the graduates of the class of 2012 had educational debt. Median debt was $170,000, and 17 percent had debt totaling over $250,000 (*AAMC Data Book*, 2010).

No one undertakes such a course of action without considering the payoff. The potential earnings must be enough to overcome the huge cost of the investment. As is the case with many investments, the costs are borne early in a person's life, and the returns are realized later on. Is attending medical school a good economic investment? To answer this question, we must compare the value of forgone earnings early in a person's life with the value of the extra earnings later in life. One major complication comes into play: Most individuals exhibit a positive rate of time preference, meaning that one dollar invested today has a higher value than one dollar earned tomorrow.

The Rate of Return to Investment   To determine whether medical school attendance is a good economic investment, we can calculate the **rate of return** on that investment. Recall from our discussion on present-value discounting from Chapter 4, the net present value of a human capital investment can be calculated by comparing the present value of the costs with the present value of the benefits over the lifetime of the investment.

rate of return The amount earned on an investment translated into an annual interest rate.

The present value of a net-benefits stream over time (NB) is defined by the difference between the annual benefits (B_t) and the annual costs (C_t) of the investment.

$$NB = \sum_{t=1}^{n} \frac{B_t - C_t}{(1 + r)^t}$$

The costs of pursuing a medical degree tend to be front-loaded and take the form of forgone income, tuition, and fees. The benefits are realized later in the form of increased earnings. The value of the investment depends on the discount rate: The higher the discount rate, the smaller the present value of the net-benefit stream. The rate of return on an investment is the discount rate that results in a net-benefit stream summing to zero.

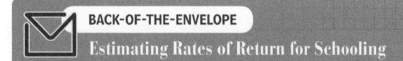

BACK-OF-THE-ENVELOPE
Estimating Rates of Return for Schooling

For the past four decades, economists have used an approach popularized by Jacob Mincer (1974) to estimate rates of return for education. The returns for schooling are calculated by comparing the age-earnings profiles of individuals with different levels of schooling. In the following diagram, Y_0 represents the earnings profile of an individual with no schooling, and Y_1 represents the profile of someone with one year of schooling.

Ignoring the direct costs of training, which are usually small relative to forgone income, an additional year of schooling will cost the individual Y_0 income for one year. In return, the individual will receive an increment $Y_1 - Y_0$ for the remainder of his or her work life.

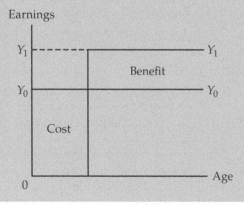

The rate of return for the additional year of schooling can be estimated as follows:

$$r_1 = \frac{Y_1 - Y_0}{Y_0}$$

Solving for Y_1, we get

$$Y_1 = Y_0(1 + r_1)$$

Similarly, the return to the second year of schooling, r_2, would be

$$r_2 = \frac{Y_2 - Y_1}{Y_1}$$

Likewise,

$$Y_2 = Y_1(1 + r_2)$$

Substituting from above,

$$Y_2 = Y_0(1 + r_1)(1 + r_2)$$

After s years of schooling,

$$Y_s = Y_0(1 + r_1)(1 + r_2) \ldots (1 + r_s)$$

If the returns to schooling are small (i.e., less than 100 percent) and similar in size from year to year, then:

$$Y_s = Y_0 e^{rs}$$

The estimated rate of return is calculated by taking the natural logarithm (*ln*) of both sides of the equation, resulting in:

$$\ln Y_s = \ln Y_0 + rs$$

Empirical tests are conducted by gathering data on earnings and schooling for a cross section of individuals. Regressing the logarithm of income on the number of years of schooling results in a coefficient estimate for the schooling variable, r, interpreted as the estimated rate of return for additional schooling.

Source: Jacob Mincer, *Schooling, Experience, and Earnings,* New York: National Bureau of Economic Research, 1974.

KEY CONCEPT 2
Opportunity Cost

How does the income physicians receive compare to that of other professionals? Higher rates of return for a medical education will encourage more students to pursue medicine as a career. Is the investment a good one from the individual's perspective? Even with the high salaries of physicians, the forgone income during the long investment period may discourage many from pursuing medicine and instead attend business or law school. Should society encourage more students to pursue medicine as a career? Greater subsidies in the form of grants to medical schools and loan forgiveness programs lower the cost of attending medical school and increase the rate of return on the investment.

What is the rate of return for a medical education? Weeks and colleagues (1994) compared the rate of return on the investment made by the typical physician, both primary care and specialist, with those of college graduates entering business, law, and dentistry. Estimated returns were adjusted for the amount of time required to train for the chosen profession and the average number of hours worked.

Empirical results indicated that the annual rate of return on the educational investment made by primary care physicians was 15.9 percent. Dentists and medical specialists fared substantially better, enjoying a 20.7 and 20.9 percent return, respectively. However, attorneys and those entering business fared much better with 25.4 and 29.0 percent rates of return. Even though these are crude estimates for the respective rates of return, it is clear that despite their high incomes, individuals who choose medical careers receive lower economic returns on their educational investments than other professionals. The lower returns are due to much higher training costs, 7–12 years of postgraduate forgone income, and the resulting shorter payoff periods.

The perception that high physicians' salaries are a contributing factor in the high cost of medical care is widely shared by the public and policy makers. A better understanding of the market for physicians' services is essential for a sound policy-making approach to the health care spending problem.

The Market for Physicians' Services

POLICY ISSUE
IMGs make up 25 percent of the physician workforce in the United States.

The changing demographics of the population have played an important role in determining demand and supply in the physicians' services market. The population in the United States was 203 million in 1970 and increased to 318 million by 2013, or approximately 50 percent. At the same time, the number of active physicians increased 175 percent, from 310,929 to 854,698. The result, clearly shown in Table 9.1, was a 75 percent increase in the ratio of physicians per 100,000 population from 154 to 268, indicating a greater relative supply of physicians today than 40 years ago.

In 2013, the United States had 141 medical schools with a first-year enrollment of 20,803 students and 40 schools of osteopathic medicine with a first-year enrollment of 6,636. That same year, these medical schools graduated 23,075. The AAMC wants to expand the number of medical school admissions by 30 percent by increasing existing class sizes and through the creation of new medical schools. Approximately 21 percent of U.S. physicians graduated from foreign medical schools. Reliance on graduates of foreign medical schools has increased modestly over the past 30 years and remains a vital part of the physician workforce. By 2010, international medical graduates (IMGs) filled about 23 percent of all residency positions. Much of the attraction of the U.S. medical market may be attributable to higher relative salaries and fewer practice restrictions than in other countries.

KEY CONCEPT 6
Supply and Demand

Another important aspect of physician supply has been the number of U.S. citizens attending foreign medical schools. As the ratio of applicants per opening in U.S. medical schools rose to 2.8 in the mid-1970s, many Americans were attracted to the option of studying in foreign countries. Some schools in Mexico and the Caribbean began accepting large numbers of American citizens, causing concern about the future quality of medical school graduates to fill residency positions in academic health centers.

POLICY ISSUE
Many rural and inner-city hospitals rely on foreign-trained physicians to staff their facilities.

Anyone trained in a foreign medical school and seeking admission to a residency-training program in the United States must pass an examination and be certified by the Educational Commission for Foreign Medical Graduates. The number of U.S. citizens receiving certification increased steadily until 1984, when a more rigorous exam was administered. The number certified for residency programs has fallen dramatically, from over 1,500 per year in the mid-1980s to less than 500 in recent years.

TABLE 9.1 ACTIVE PHYSICIANS IN THE UNITED STATES

Year	Active physicians	Rate per 100,000 residents	General and primary care physicians	Primary care as a percent of active physicians
1960	247,257	138	125,359	50.7
1970	310,929	154	137,515	43.2
1980	414,916	183	187,347	41.1
1990	547,310	220	244,425	39.0
2000	692,368	246	326,947	39.7
2005	762,438	257	365,420	39.4
2010	794,862	257	304,687	38.3
2013	854,698	268	319,881	37.4

Source: Centers for Disease Control and Prevention, *Health, United States,* various years.

KEY CONCEPT 6
Supply and Demand

POLICY ISSUE
About 40 percent of the active physicians in the United States are involved in primary care compared with 50–70 percent in most developed countries.

HTTP://
The AAMC provides access to medical schools and colleges. The website is located at http://www.aamc.org.

HTTP://
The Accreditation Council for Graduate Medical Education is responsible for the accreditation of post-MD medical training programs within the United States. Visit their website at http://www.acgme.org.

POLICY ISSUE
Should the United States rely on market forces to adjust the specialty mix, or should government adjust residency financing to bring about the desired mix?

Given the long training period for physicians, one would expect the supply of physicians to be inelastic in the short run. The slow supply response means that changes in physicians' incomes do not translate into immediate adjustments in the number of physicians practicing medicine. U.S. immigration laws, however, currently place relatively few restrictions on the entry of foreign-trained physicians, especially during times of perceived shortages. This allows physician supply to remain responsive to market conditions. The importance of foreign-trained physicians in staffing many rural and inner-city facilities highlights the potential impact of changes in U.S. immigration policy on physician supply.

Increases in relative supply do not tell the entire story. Policy makers have voiced concern over certain aspects of the supply side of the market, including the distribution of physicians across specialty areas and regions of the country, the relative salaries of physicians, the pricing of their services, and the organizational structure of physicians' practices.

Specialty Distribution

Many policy analysts and health maintenance organizations (HMOs) have established a goal to increase the number of physicians in the primary care specialties to 50 percent of the physician workforce. In the rest of the developed world, this percentage is common. In fact, primary care physicians make up 50–70 percent of the total number of active physicians in most developed countries (OECD, 2013). In the United States, however, less than 40 percent of all active physicians are in primary care.[2]

The percentage of physicians in general primary care has been on a gradual downward trend since 1960. Referring again to Table 9.1, between 1960 and 1990, the number of primary care physicians increased from 125,359 to 244,425, or 95 percent. Over the same period, the number of specialists increased from 121,898 to 302,855, or 148 percent. Since 1990, the percentage of physicians in primary care has fallen slightly to 37.4 percent. The number of active physicians has steadily increased to 268 per 100,000. There are now approximately 100 primary care physicians per 100,000 and 168 specialists.

---

[2]For purposes of this discussion, *primary care* is defined as family practice, general internists, and pediatricians.

The appropriate percentage of primary care physicians is not easy to determine. Policy concerns are based on the projected number of patients compared to the number of physicians required to provide for their primary care needs. Several studies have examined the physicians' services market and identified a mismatch between supply and demand.

- The AAMC Center for Workforce Studies (2010) forecasts a shortage of 130,000 physicians across the country by 2025. The additional coverage due to the Medicaid expansion will add an additional 31,000 to that number.
- The American Academy of Family Physicians projects a shortage of 149,000 by 2020 (Worth, 2010).
- Health Services and Resources Administration (HSRA) projects a shortage of 65,560 primary care physicians by 2020 (Worth, 2010).
- HSRA has designated over 6,000 areas in the United States as Health Professional Shortage Areas (HPSA) for primary care. They project it would take 17,000 additional primary care physicians to achieve a physician-to-patient ratio of 1 to 2,000 and eliminate the shortages (O'Reilly, 2010).
- Patterson et al. (2012) estimate that an additional 52,000 primary care physicians are required by 2025 due to population growth, population aging, and the new health care law.

While estimates vary, most studies reach similar conclusions, pointing to some challenging policy issues.

Geographic Distribution

Even as the concern for the falling percentage of generalists grows, so does the concern for the declining number of physicians willing to practice in rural and inner-city areas. The problem of providing medical care in many rural areas has reached near critical stages. Overall, over 62 million people, almost 20 percent of the U.S. population, live in rural areas, where the physician–population ratios are substantially lower.

The nation's inner cities face the same challenge in attracting and keeping qualified physicians. With large minority and indigent populations, inner cities depend heavily on hospital emergency rooms and public clinics, staffed by IMGs, for a substantial portion of their medical care.

Pennsylvania provides a good example of the problem of attracting physicians to rural areas. According to the most recent census, Pennsylvania has the largest rural population in the country; *rural* is defined as an area with fewer than 2,500 population. The three counties surrounding the state's two major urban centers, Pittsburgh and Philadelphia, comprise approximately 25 percent of the state's population and over one-half of its physicians (Rabinowitz, 1993). The remaining 64 counties, with over 75 percent of the state's population, are severely underserved.

Nationwide, individuals living in the smaller market areas have fewer physicians per 100,000 than those living in more populated markets. The physician–population ratio in the 700 counties with fewer than 10,000 inhabitants was one-third that of the rest of the country. Nurse practitioners and physicians' assistants are filling some of these gaps. A number of physicians operate satellite offices in rural areas, some at permanent sites and others using mobile units. Providing medical care to these low-density, remote areas will be a continuing challenge for the medical care delivery system.

ISSUES IN MEDICAL CARE DELIVERY

AN ENDANGERED SPECIES: THE MALE GYNECOLOGIST

Obstetrics was once a field dominated by women. At one time, the local midwife delivered most babies. Modern medicine has changed that relationship in most urban areas. Over the course of the twentieth century, childbirth became an integral part of a medical practice, and midwifery lost much of its clientele.

Obstetricians deliver most of the babies born in the United States today. Obstetrics and gynecology (OB–GYN) has become a popular specialty, primarily because it is one of only a few that combines primary care with surgery. Women today are deserting their male gynecologists in increasing numbers and turning to female OB–GYNs. Just as men prefer a same-sex physician almost two to one, an increasing number of women are beginning to voice a similar preference. As recently as 1980, women filled less than 30 percent of the residency positions in OB–GYN. Today, almost 75 percent of OB–GYN residents are women and by 2020 over one-half of all practicing OB–GYN will be female.

The increase in supply of female OB–GYNs may be in part a response to the rapidly expanding demand for their services. This shift in preferences has several major implications, all indicative of a shortage of female OB–GYNs in the market.

- Initial salaries for women within the specialty are $20,000 a year more than for men.
- While the median salary for female physicians is about 70 percent of the male median, female OB–GYNs enjoy pay parity with their male counterparts.
- Patients have shown a willingness to wait for appointments with their female OB–GYNs who are booked months in advance.

For women this preference shift may not be solely an issue of seeing a same-sex physician. There seems to be a significant difference in practice styles between the sexes. Male gynecologists are more likely to perform hysterectomies, and patients of female gynecologists are more likely to be current on their Pap tests and mammograms. Whether female gynecologists are more sensitive to their patients' needs, or whether the practice styles of more recent graduates—male and female—are simply different, is an unanswered question.

For whatever reason, many newly trained female gynecologists are opening all-female practices and marketing them as such. This trend has opened up a completely different set of questions dealing with reverse discrimination. Can an obstetrical practice seeking to fill a vacancy on its staff advertise for females only? When patients are voicing a preference for female physicians, is it legal for employers to discriminate against male applicants? Is sex a legitimate qualification? When it comes to performing a gynecological exam, is patient preference an appropriate concern? It is only a matter of time, given our litigious society, before our judicial system addresses this issue. How will the courts respond? Is the desire for a same-sex provider for a gynecological exam different from wanting a same-sex stockbroker or sales clerk in a shoe store?

Source: Andrea Gerlin, "The Male Gynecologist: Soon to Be Extinct?" *Wall Street Journal*, February 7, 1996, B1, B5.

Physician Compensation

To a large degree, the strength of the U.S. health care system is due to the dominance of specialty care. The increasing number of specialists has been accompanied by a more frequent use of the latest diagnostic, therapeutic, and surgical procedures. This approach has contributed to improving the quality of care, but it has also consumed large quantities of resources and has served as a primary cost driver (Schroeder and Sandy, 1993).

KEY CONCEPT 5
Markets and Pricing

TABLE 9.2 MEDIAN COMPENSATION IN SELECTED SPECIALTIES, VARIOUS YEARS

	1995	2000	2005	2010	2014
All primary care:	$133,329	$147,232	$168,111	$202,392	–
Family practice (without OB)	129,148	145,121	160,729	189,402	$221,419
Internal medicine	139,320	149,104	176,124	205,379	238,227
Pediatrics	–	–	167,178	192,148	226,408
All specialists:	215,978	256,494	316,620	356,885	–
Anesthesiology	240,666	280,353	359,699	407,292	443,859
Invasive cardiology	337,000	365,894	463,801	500,993	505,794
Dermatology	176,948	213,876	334,277	430,874	462,500
Emergency medicine	176,439	198,423	243,449	277,397	317,972
Gastroenterology	209,913	281,308	384,015	463,995	504,492
OB–GYN	215,000	223,007	256,485	281,190	217,496
Orthopedic surgery	301,918	335,646	428,119	514,659	568,319
Psychiatry	132,477	156,486	189,409	200,694	245,673
Diagnostic radiology	247,505	298,824	426,346	471,253	491,679
General surgery	216,562	245,541	300,800	343,958	395,456

Source: *Physician Compensation and Production Survey*, various years, Englewood, CO: Medical Group Management Association.

Many critics of the U.S. system have focused on physicians' incomes as the primary cause of high and rising health care spending, even though physicians' compensation consumes only 20–25 percent of total spending. Based on Medical Group Management Association (MGMA) surveys, median compensation for most physicians has been steadily increasing over the past 20 years (see Table 9.2). There is a substantial variation in the median incomes across specialties. At the lower end of the spectrum, family practice physicians without an OB practice earned $221,419 in 2014, compared to those in internal medicine, who earned $238,227. Specialists' salaries range from $217,496 in OB–GYN to over $500,000 in invasive cardiology, gastroenterology, and orthopedic surgery.

Alternative Payment Practices

Traditionally, the fee-for-service model has dominated physician payment where compensation is based on the volume and intensity of services provided. See more patients, perform more procedures, provide more complicated services, and you make more money.

Increasingly, however, physicians' compensation is tied to productivity metrics. Many are volume based, such as the number of patients treated, billed charges, or revenue collected. An alternative approach finding favor in many health care settings is an attempt to measure and reward the amount of work performed rather than the number of patients seen and procedures provided. The measure of work is the relative value unit (RVU). Simply stated, an RVU is the relative amount of time, skill, training, and intensity required to provide a specific service or procedure.

resource-based relative value scale (RBRVS) A classification system for physicians' services, using a weighting scheme that reflects the relative value of the various services performed. The RBRVS considers time, skill, and overhead cost required for each service. When used in conjunction with a monetary conversion factor, medical fees are determined.

Every procedure has an RVU assigned to it by the Center for Medicare and Medicaid Services (CMS). The CMS has been using a **resource-based relative value scale (RBRVS)** since 1993 to calculate physicians' compensation when treating Medicare patients. The practice of using the RVU to calculate productivity payments has gained favor among physicians' groups over the past several years. In 2007, about one-third of all physicians had their compensation tied to RVUs in some way. By 2010, almost two-thirds received some sort of bonus based on RVUs. (More information of the RBRVS is provided later in this chapter.)

The successful application of an RVU-based compensation model is straightforward in theory; simply pay each physician an amount based on the total number of "work RVUs" generated.[3] Benchmarks for work RVUs expected by specialty are readily available from medical practice organizations and can be modified to fit individual circumstances.

Nevertheless, volume-based bonus metrics, including RVUs, are still fee-for-service, with all the associated incentives that drive up health care spending. The future transition toward evidence-based practice encouraged by the ACA will require bonus payments based on patient satisfaction, the use of cost-effectiveness principles, and other quality-based measures.

BACK-OF-THE-ENVELOPE

Is There an Optimal Physician–Population Ratio?

How many physicians do we need? In theory, an optimal physician–population ratio can be determined. In practice, however, determining that ratio is not so easy. Even though other inputs in the medical care process must be considered, most medical services require at least one physician input. Some inputs complement physicians; others are substitutes. The list of other labor inputs includes nurses, physicians' assistants, receptionists, bookkeepers, lawyers, medical technicians, and therapists. Nonlabor inputs include the office and its equipment, computers, supplies, electricity, and, of course, medical malpractice insurance. Medical care can be provided using different combinations of physicians' services and these other inputs. The optimal combination depends on the relative price of the inputs and the preferences of the decision makers responsible for combining the inputs and making the medical care available.

Using the production isoquants developed in Appendix 3B, we can show how prices and preferences affect the optimal number of physicians used in the production of medical care. The isoquant mapping in the following diagram depicts the preferences of a managed care organization with a greater willingness to substitute other inputs for physicians' services. Increases in the price of physicians' services relative to the prices of the other inputs create an incentive to use fewer physicians' services and more of the other inputs. The isocost curve rotates inward due to the increase in price, and the equilibrium number of physicians used falls from S_1 to S_0.

---

[3]The work RVU is one element of the total RVU concept created by CMS, where total RVUs are equal to the sum of work RVUs, practice expense RVUs, and malpractice insurance RVUs, adjusted by an index based on practice costs in the geographic region where the service is provided.

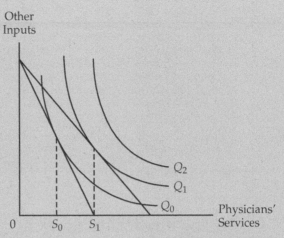

Decision makers with a strong preference for using physicians in the production process will have steeper isoquants. Other things equal, any given increase in the price of physicians will have much less of an impact on the use of physicians' services than indicated in the diagram. The second diagram depicts the preference mapping of a physicians' group practice. Using the same starting point, S_1, defined as the equilibrium quantity of physicians' services, the same increase in the price of physicians' services (as shown in the previous diagram) has less of an impact on the use of physicians' services, lowering utilization to S_0'. The obvious implication deals with the use of physicians in a tightly controlled managed care environment. A good example is the staff-model HMO, in which substitution for high-cost physicians' services is more widely practiced, resulting in a flatter isoquant mapping (as shown in the first diagram) and a demand for physicians' services that is relatively price elastic. A difference in staffing patterns between the staff-model HMO and traditional fee-for-service physicians' practice (as shown in the next diagram) supports this view. Based on a nationwide survey of HMOs, Dial and colleagues (1995) estimated that the staff-model HMO uses about 140 physicians per 100,000 enrollees, with 40 percent of those being involved in primary care. HMOs are also more likely to utilize nonphysician providers, advanced practice nurses (APNs), and physician assistants (PAs) to supplement their clinical staffing needs. The median number of APNs per 100,000 of the responding HMOs was 19.7. Overall, the median number of PAs was 8.1.

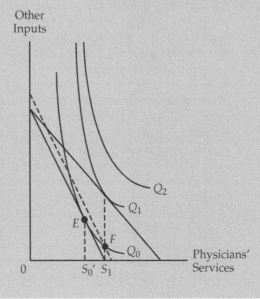

In contrast, the overall physician–population ratio stood at 220 per 100,000 in 1992, with only about 40 percent practicing primary care. Additionally, Kronick and colleagues (1993) reported that the ratio of physicians to population is 10–200 percent higher in the fee-for-service sector compared to the classic HMO, depending on specialty examined.

Restrictions on the minimum number of physicians used to produce a given level of care generally lead to higher costs. Suppose S_1 physicians' services are required by law to provide Q_0 medical care. Precluded from using the least-cost combination of inputs at point E, providers must use a minimum of S_1 at point F, resulting in equilibrium on a higher isocost curve.

Sources: Thomas H. Dial et al., "Clinical Staffing in Staff- and Group-Model HMOs," *Health Affairs* 14(2), Summer 1995, 169–180 and Richard Kronick et al., "The Marketplace in Health Care Reform—the Demographic Limitations of Managed Competition," *New England Journal of Medicine* 328(2), January 14, 1993, 148–152.

Pricing Physicians' Services

Prior to widespread health insurance coverage, most patients made direct payment for physicians' services out of pocket. Physicians, on the other hand, practiced a form of Ramsey (1927) pricing, charging patients different prices based on their relative demand elasticities. As insurance became more popular, payers' concern over rapidly increasing medical spending resulted in a pricing model that limited physicians' fees to usual, customary, and reasonable (UCR) levels. Under the UCR standards, physicians could charge the minimum of the usual charge, defined as the median charged during the past year, and the customary charge, defined by some percentile of the fees charged by other physicians in the area; and physicians were allowed reasonable increases from year to year. It is easy to understand the inflationary nature of UCR (Frech and Ginsburg, 1975). There is no reason for a physician's usual price to be below the customary price charged by other physicians in the area. If it were, the price received would be below prevailing prices in the area. Thus, physicians had an incentive to make sure that their usual fee was not the minimum in the formula.

KEY CONCEPT 5
Markets and Pricing

Under the old fee-for-service system, physician payment had a built-in inflationary bias. Physicians had no incentive to compete on price. If a physician's actual charges were less than the prevailing charge in the area, the physician received the actual charge. The incentive was to raise fees to the prevailing charge. As fees escalated, physician and patient behavior was distorted. Some physicians criticized the system as complex and unpredictable. Others argued that it was irrational, inequitable, and open to abuse.

As prices for physicians' services continued to escalate, payers looked for other ways to control spending. Since 1992, Medicare has paid physicians according to a fee schedule based on a relative value scale (RVS) that translates costs into payments. Under RVS, physicians' fees were divided into three cost components: work effort, practice expense, and malpractice expense. RVS actually translates into a dollar fee schedule by multiplying the relative values of over 7,000 procedure codes by a monetary conversion factor. The government influence is so prominent that many private insurers base their payment schedules on Medicare's relative values, typically using a percentage of the Medicare fee. Thus any change in the Medicare payment cascades throughout the entire system.

Since 2000, the consumer price index (CPI), not including medical care, rose 2.18 percent per year, and the medical services component of the CPI rose 3.99 percent per year. Using the latter measure, many observers argue that medical inflation is the primary reason that medical spending is a growing problem, increasing twice as fast as everything else. As discussed in the appendix to Chapter 1, several problems are inherent in using the CPI as a measure of inflation. These same problems may be applied to the use of the medical services CPI as a measure of inflation in the medical services market.

Establishing a Relative Value Scale

In 1986 Congress commissioned a study to determine the feasibility of developing a RBRVS for physician payment. Hsiao and colleagues (1988) conducted a two-year study of physician compensation and developed resource-based relative values for physicians' services in 18 specialty areas.

RVSs were first developed in the United States by individual state medical societies in response to the increased complexity of medical practice and the need to develop a means of determining the amount to charge for various services provided. In other countries, Japan, for example, RVS is used in various forms to establish a technical basis for the established fee schedules. The RVS provides guidelines in establishing weights that reflect the time it takes to perform a procedure and its complexity. In theory, weighting should reflect changing technologies. As methods of treating various conditions change, so should the weighting.

Today, Medicare physician payment is based on the principle that differences in payments should reflect differences in work effort. Physicians incur three types of costs to produce medical services for their patients: 1) work effort measured by their own time, energy, and skill level; 2) the overhead cost of their practice; and 3) professional liability insurance premiums. The Medicare fee schedule calculates a total RVU for each service based on these costs.

Determining a Payment Schedule from Relative Values

An RVS translates directly into a fee schedule by simply applying a monetary conversion factor to the scale. Theoretically, once the conversion factor is set, the payment schedule is determined by applying it to each procedure weighted by the appropriate RVU. Under the old Medicare method of payment, physicians were paid more for performing invasive medical procedures than for general medical services.

The fee system based on the RVS was designed to reduce the disparities between procedures and services. Such a system focuses on the time and effort involved in providing the medical procedure or service. Allowable fees for invasive procedures fell under this system, while those for the general services rose. It is not surprising that specialists whose practices were primarily in the former group were vehemently opposed to the new system. General practice physicians, whose practices fell predominantly in the latter group, strongly supported the changes.

monetary conversion factor A monetary value used to translate relative value units into dollar amounts to determine a fee schedule.

When the Medicare fee schedule was first implemented in 1992, the **monetary conversion factor** was $31 per RVU. A medical service with a relative weighting of 5 units would be paid $155 ($31 × 5). Congress has raised and lowered the conversion factor annually. In 2017, it was $35.89, down slightly from $36.08 in 2010.

The desire to control medical spending has resulted in a moderation in the escalation of Medicare fees for many procedures. Table 9.3 provides Medicare pricing information on several common procedures using Current Procedure Terminology (CPT) codes as identifiers. This listing, while not randomly chosen, is representative of recent experience with Medicare pricing. The prices of procedures such as total hip replacement, single artery bypass, treatment of a retinal lesion, and a complete electrocardiogram have fallen or risen only slightly. Prices of other procedures have risen at higher rates but have not kept pace with the CPI. These include upper endoscopy biopsy, new patient office visits, and initial hospital care. Explaining the reason for the overall increase in medical care spending in the United States is not as simple as saying, "It's the prices." More likely, the increase in the overall utilization of services also plays a big role—more people are using more services.

TABLE 9.3 CHANGES IN MEDICARE FEES FOR SELECTED PHYSICIANS' SERVICES, SELECT YEARS

CPT code	Description	2000	2005	2010	2015	Annual percentage change from 2005
27130	Total hip replacement	$1,423	$1,292	$1,378	$1,401	+0.81
33533	Single coronary artery bypass graft	1,853	1,794	1,952	1,943	+0.80
43239	Upper GI endoscopy biopsy	223	300	325	410	+3.17
67210	Treatment of retinal lesion	599	560	628	524	−0.66
93000	Electrocardiogram	26	24	20	17	−4.16
99203	Office visit, new patient	83	90	98	109	+1.93
99213	Office visit, established patient	44	49	65	73	+4.07
99223	Initial hospital care	147	151	198	205	+3.10
99292	Additional 30 minutes of critical care	90	108	116	124	+1.39

Source: Centers for Medicare and Medicaid Services, Physician Fee Schedule Search, http://www.cms.hhs.gov/pfslookup/ (Accessed December 19, 2016).

KEY CONCEPT 5
Markets and Pricing

POLICY ISSUE
How do physicians respond when the government sets the prices they can charge for their services?

The Economic Impact of a Fee Schedule for Physicians' Services   In theory, a RBRVS approximates the relative fee schedule that would emerge in perfectly competitive equilibrium. Hence, the RBRVS could provide a fair and equitable approach to compensating physicians for the services they provide. By removing the distortions in current fee structure, the RBRVS would provide a neutral incentive structure for physicians in making medical decisions. By altering physician practice patterns, the rates of surgery, invasive diagnostic tests, and hospital use could be reduced significantly. Such an outcome would enhance the cost-effectiveness of medical care, leading to a reduction in the overall cost of health care.

In the long run, fee schedules based on the RBRVS would even change the supply of physicians according to specialty. Changes in the relative rewards across specialties would alter the specialty choices of medical school graduates. It might even alter the geographic distribution of physicians, thus affecting the accessibility, cost, and quality of care in currently underserved areas.

Physician response is easy to predict. Those who have a solid patient base in the private sector will begin to refuse new Medicare patients. The elderly will find it increasingly difficult to secure the services of a primary care physician. In 2014, almost 25 percent of U.S. physicians were not accepting new Medicare patients (Merritt Hawkins & Associates, 2014). Hospital emergency rooms will become the best alternative source of care for a great number of the elderly population. Shortages of health services for the elderly will begin to develop as resources are shifted into the unregulated, private sector. Physicians will encounter the same forces with private patients insured by HMOs and preferred provider organizations (PPOs). In either case, the lesson is clear: If you do not ration via price, you will ration by queuing.

> ### APPLIED MICRO METHODS

DOES DEFENSIVE MEDICINE REDUCE MALPRACTICE CLAIMS?

Background

In a national survey of U.S. physicians (Carrier et al., 2010), over 60 percent reported that they practiced defensive medicine (defined as providing medical care solely to reduce the risk of malpractice liability). Studies confirm the practice of defensive medicine among U.S. physicians, although size estimates vary considerably. Jena et al. (2015) explore whether greater resource use in a given year is associated with a reduction in claims of malpractice in subsequent years.

Methods

Data for the study came from two sources: The Florida Agency for Health Care Administration and the Florida Office of Insurance Regulation. Individual patient information from nearly 19 million hospital discharges in all Florida acute care hospitals was collected for the period 2000–2009. Data on medical malpractice claims totaling 4,342 that closed between 2000 and 2013 were collected covering 24,637 physicians from six specialties (internal medicine, family practice, pediatricians, general surgery, specialty surgery, and OB–GYN). In addition to a general measure of resource use (average hospital spending per patient for each physician), a more clinically specific measure (risk-adjusted rate of cesarean births) was utilized for obstetricians. Obstetrics provides an interesting application of the methodology because OB–GYN consistently ranks in the top five in both the number of medical malpractice claims and the average size of damages awarded.

The study utilized two statistical approaches: First, within each specialty physicians were classified into quintiles according to average hospital spending per patient. Average medical malpractice incidence rates were then calculated for each quintile. Likewise, obstetricians were classified into quintiles based on risk-adjusted cesarean rates and average malpractice incidence rates were calculated for each quintile. Additionally, regression models were estimated with physician fixed effects to control for differences in resource use and medical malpractice risk due to differences in unobserved physician characteristics.

Results

Across all specialties in the study, physicians in the top spending quintile had significantly lower medical malpractice rates than those in the lowest spending quintile. For example, in general surgery the medical malpractice rate for physicians in the top spending quintile was 0.4 percent while the rate for those in the lowest spending quintile was 2.3 percent. For OB–GYN the medical malpractice rates were similar, 0.4 percent for the highest spenders and 1.9 percent for the lowest.

The data included 1.5 million deliveries (14.8 percent cesarean rate) performed by 1,625 obstetricians. Almost 500 malpractice claims were filed (4.8 percent of the total deliveries). Similar to results using overall hospital spending, obstetricians in the quintile with the highest frequency of cesarean deliveries (31.6 percent of all births) had a medical malpractice rate of 2.7 percent. Those in the lowest frequency quartile (5.1 percent of all births) had a medical malpractice rate of 5.7 percent.

Discussion

Higher resource use (whether measured in terms of hospital spending or cesarean delivery rates) was associated with a statistically significant lower incidence rate of medical malpractice claims. If higher resource use is associated with fewer medical errors (and thus fewer malpractice claims), then it may be money well spent. If the additional resource use is not associated with fewer medical errors and adds no real clinical bene-fit, then it is wasteful. Without evidence on the rate of medical errors, it is impossible to determine if defensive medicine actually improves medical outcomes and patients have less reason to bring lawsuits or whether the outcomes are the same and the additional spending simply reduces the incidence of lawsuits.

The study results fall short of claiming a causal relationship between higher resource use and lower malpractice rates. Unobserved differences in physician practice style or patient characteristics may confound the relationship and result in biased estimates. To address these limitations, further work should focus on the mechanisms at work that result in the negative association between resource use and malpractice claims.

Sources: Anupam B. Jena et al., "Physician Spending and Subsequent Risk of Malpractice Claims: Observational Study," *BMJ* 351(h5516), 2015, 1–9 and Emily R. Carrier et al., "Physicians' Fears of Malpractice Lawsuits Are Not Assuaged by Tort Reforms," *Health Affairs* 29(9), September 2010, 1585–1592.

Organization of Physicians' Practices

Research indicates that there are modest economies of scale in the provision of physicians' services (Escarce and Pauly, 1998; Reinhardt, 1972). The number of physicians in solo practice has steadily declined over the last decade. Survey evidence (Hing and Burt, 2007) indicates that about one-third of practicing physicians are now in solo practices, while over 50 percent are in groups of three or more.

Organizing into group practices not only lowers the overhead cost for each physician, but it also increases the range of services offered within the practice. The extra services may include a pharmacy, a clinical laboratory, radiology and ultrasound equipment, and even CT scanning and MRI facilities. The shift to group practice has enhanced the full-service capabilities of physicians' practices and has contributed to the shift in services from the hospital to the ambulatory setting.

The potential benefits of taking advantage of economies of scale in a medical practice are clearly shown in Figure 9.2. *LAC* depicts the long-run average cost of a typical medical practice. The small-group practice is able to carry a patient load equal to Q_S. At this service level, SAC_S represents the short-run average cost of the practice and AC_S the actual average cost per patient. Larger practices can combine activities and spread administrative over-head over a larger number of patients. The larger practice is able to move down the LAC, utilizing a larger physical plant (larger offices, more equipment, an on-site laboratory, etc.). The short-run average cost of the larger operation is SAC_L and represents, in this case, the optimal plant size. Average cost per patient is lower at AC_L.

FIGURE 9.2

Economies of Scale in a Medical Practice

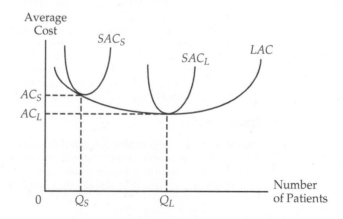

Patients will benefit from the lower operating costs when there is competition in the market. Competition forces providers to charge prices reflecting these lower costs. If, however, these consolidations lead to the concentration of market power, providers will be able to act more like monopolists, restrict the availability of services, and charge higher prices.

Quite possibly the most notable trend in physician practices is the growth of hospital ownership. As recently as 2002, approximately 20 percent of physician practices were owned by hospitals. Since that time, the market has witnessed a steady upward trend in hospital ownership and by 2008 over one-half of medical practices were owned by hospitals. Today we see over two-thirds of established physicians employed in hospital practices and almost half of all physicians find themselves employed by hospital practices when they leave their residencies. There are several reasons for continuation of this trend. Foremost is the looming uncertainty surrounding changes in payment practices that will accompany health care reform.

KEY CONCEPT 7
Competition

Geographic Variations in Practice Patterns

Geographic Variations in Practice Patterns   Regional variations in the incidence of surgery and other inpatient procedures are well documented (Dartmouth Atlas of Health Care, 2010). Small-area variations (SAVs) refer to the wide dispersion in per capita utilization rates for many common medical procedures found among otherwise similar health care markets across the country. These cross-regional differences do not seem to be the product of demographic differences in education, income, and insurance coverage or the underlying pattern of diseases. Physicians faced with symptoms and syndromes are expected to make decisions on the appropriateness of care with the scientific accuracy of *Star Trek*'s Doctor Leonard McCoy. Patients do not always come to their physicians with readily identifiable diseases. Even if they did, the outcome of a particular treatment is not always predictable.

POLICY ISSUE
Variations in practice patterns across geographic regions result in patients with similar health conditions being treated differently.

McPherson and colleagues (1982) compared the utilization rates for several common surgical procedures within New England and observed wide variations, even after adjusting for differences in the age and sex composition of the population. Procedures showing the most variation included hysterectomy, prostatectomy, and tonsillectomy. Additionally, they found significant differences in utilization rates when comparing New England with Norway and England.

Wennberg (1984) speculated that the observed variations in practice patterns across regions could be explained by the degree of scientific uncertainty associated with diagnosis and treatment. A lack of consensus on the efficacy of a medical procedure will lead individual physicians and groups of physicians to follow clinical rules of thumb to determine who needs surgery. Consistent application of these rules leads to the "surgical signature" phenomenon—rates of surgery in a region that are consistent over time and differ dramatically from those observed in otherwise similar regions.

A second reason for differences in the rates of surgery may be patient preferences for specific treatments. However, when patients are uninformed, they tend to delegate the decision-making responsibility to the physician, which leads to decisions that closely mirror the preferences of the provider.

The important public policy issue deals with the costs and consequences of these variations. Do regional variations mean that some physicians overtreat and others undertreat? Do different treatment patterns indicate inappropriate and unnecessary care? From the individual's perspective, appropriate care is a level of care that the fully informed patient would demand by comparing the marginal benefit of the care with the out-of-pocket marginal cost of the care. Therein lies the problem. From society's perspective, the level of care demanded by the individual patient may be an inefficient use of scarce resources, since the fully insured patient bears only a small fraction of the total cost.

KEY CONCEPT 3
Marginal Analysis

Eddy (1990) explored the role of patient preferences in explaining the variations in treatment across regions. Figure 9.3 provides a framework for examining the role of patient preferences in determining the level of care provided in treating certain medical conditions. In the diagram, D_1 and S_1 represent the demand and supply conditions in Region 1, and P_1 and Q_1 represent the equilibrium price and quantity. Suppose there is a second region with the same physician supply, but where consumers have a different demand, D_2, for the same medical procedure. The different level of demand may be due to differences in income, insurance coverage, or other demographics, or it may be due to different health preferences or attitudes toward risk, pain, and discomfort. Information about these different demand preferences is communicated to providers specializing in this procedure. They, in turn, increase the quantity supplied to Q_2, receiving higher prices for their services, P_2. Assuming easy mobility between the two regions, there is an incentive for physicians to relocate to Region 2. Under these circumstances, utilization rates are even higher than Q_2.

Weinstein and colleagues (2004) examined utilization patterns for major orthopedic procedures including total hip replacement, total knee replacement, and back surgery. Rates of surgery differed more than five times between the high-rate regions and

⭐ **KEY CONCEPT 6**
Supply and Demand

FIGURE 9.3
Small-Area Variations

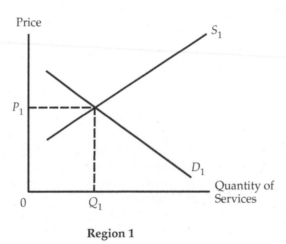

Region 1

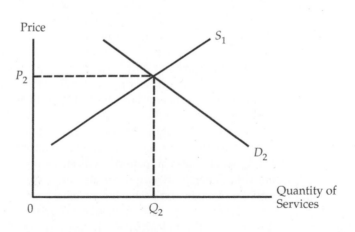

Region 2

the low-rate regions, and the interquartile ratio—surgery rates for regions ranked in the 75th quartile relative to those ranked in the 25th quartile—was 1.31 for knee replacement and 1.45 for hip replacement. They also observed differences in overall medical spending across local communities. Per capita Medicare spending (adjusted for differences in age, sex, and race) was 1.65 times greater in Miami than in Fort Myers, Florida.

Improving the scientific basis for clinical decisions through outcomes research should serve to reduce the variations over time. Old habits are difficult to change, and there is no reason to indicate that changing medical practice patterns will be easy. With few exceptions, medical services are highly localized in their delivery. As a result, the usual market forces that serve to eliminate inefficiencies in manufacturing, for example, are not as active in medical care markets.

Whether any gains are to be made by a more standardized approach to treatment remains to be seen. In a sense, patient welfare may actually be enhanced by the variations because of the treatment alternatives available across regions. The goal is to determine whether the gains in the efficacy and efficiency of medical care delivery outweigh the losses to patients caused by limiting the choice of treatment that will follow from the standardization of services.

Models of Physician Behavior

KEY CONCEPT 9
Market Failure

To adequately model physician behavior, we must take into consideration the characteristics of the market for physicians' services. Many urban markets have a substantial number of physicians practicing in the same specialty area; however, a large percentage of Americans live in geographic areas that are considered underserved. As we have seen in earlier discussions, certain imperfections in medical markets (lack of transparency, barriers to entry, and third-party insurance) result in markets where providers have a certain degree of market power.

The Physician as Monopolistic Competitor

The physicians' services market shares many of the characteristics of the standard model of monopolistic competition with many sellers, each providing a slightly different product or service. Physicians strive to differentiate their practices by various means—location, hospital affiliations, and quality of care are but a few differences. At the same time, patients have little information to judge physicians and rely mainly on the recommendations of friends and family. As a result, physicians are imperfect substitutes for one another.

The major implication of market power is downward-sloping demand curves. Physicians are not price takers; instead, they experience differences in patient demand depending on the prices they charge. In other words, demand is less than perfectly elastic.

The large percentage of patients with health insurance complicates the development of a model to explain physician pricing. Ignoring for the moment the impact of health insurance on the demand for physicians' services, Figure 9.4 depicts the pricing strategy of a physician with a degree of market power.[4] A physician with the goal of maximizing profit will provide services as long as marginal revenue is greater than marginal cost. Profit is maximized where $MR = MC$ with the physician providing Q^* services and charging the maximum price that patients will pay to get those services, or P^* in this instance.

---

[4]Refer to Figure 5.3 and the related discussion on the impact of insurance on the demand for medical care.

FIGURE 9.4
Pricing and Output
Decision of Physician
in Monopolistic
Competition

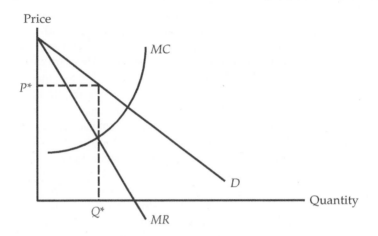

The availability of health insurance affects patients' responsiveness to changes in price. Less concerned about the prices they are charged, patients with insurance have demand curves that are more price inelastic. Inelastic demand, however, does not change the basic implications of the standard model. It merely provides the physician with the opportunity to charge patients different prices for the same services based on the extent of their insurance coverage. Patients with more elastic demand are charged lower prices, and patients with more inelastic demand are charged higher prices.

BACK-OF-THE-ENVELOPE

Price Discrimination in Medical Care

When suppliers have market power, they are faced with downward-sloping demand curves. The price searcher will frequently discover that in searching for the profit-maximizing price, the opportunity arises to charge customers different prices for the same product. A successful price discriminator must be able to:

- Classify customers according to willingness to pay and providers must have some way to distinguish which customers are willing to pay higher prices. Conceptually, the provider attempts to determine each group's price elasticity of demand for the product.
- Make **arbitrage** difficult. Those customers who are able to buy at the low price must have no easy way to resell the product to those charged the higher price.

arbitrage The practice
of simultaneously buy-
ing a commodity at one
price and selling it at a
higher price.

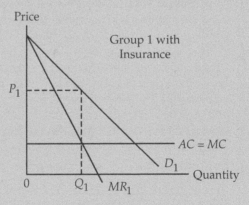

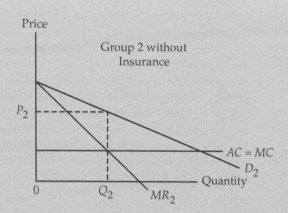

Medical care delivery provides a classic case in which conditions exist that allow providers to practice **price discrimination**. Patients approach providers with certain identifiable characteristics that help determine their willingness to pay, most notably, the type of insurance they have. As with any service, it is difficult for a patient paying the lower price to resell a medical procedure to a patient paying the higher price.

The preceding diagram provides a graphical depiction of how a supplier with market power becomes a price discriminator. Suppose that the medical provider identifies two distinct groups of patients—one with insurance and one without. Those patients with insurance (Group 1) are less price-sensitive than those paying out of pocket (Group 2) and thus have a steeper demand curve. To simplify the analysis, assume that marginal cost (MC) is constant and equal to average cost (AC). The profit-maximizing level of output for each group is determined by equating marginal revenue (MR) with marginal cost. For Group 1, $MR_1 = MC$ at Q_1. For Group 2, $MR_2 = MC$ at Q_2. At these respective output levels, the provider charges the highest price that the groups are willing to pay, P_1 for Group 1 and P_2 for Group 2.

Clearly, Group 2 pays a lower price for the same medical care: $P_2 < P_1$. Why? Without insurance, their demand is more elastic. Recognizing this, providers charge them less for the same services. Does this happen in medical care delivery? Over six decades ago, Kessel (1958) showed how the model of price discrimination applied to medical care. One of the more interesting conclusions of Kessel's research was the implication that the growing popularity of prepaid medical plans will reduce the ability of providers to practice price discrimination. More competition will mean less price discrimination.

Source: Reuben A. Kessel, "Price Discrimination in Medicine," *The Journal of Law and Economics* 1, 1958, 20–53.

The Physician as Imperfect Agent

Another key assumption when using standard economic theory to model physicians' behavior is that supply and demand are independently determined. As we discussed in Chapter 5, the relationship between the patient and the physician can be described using a principal-agent model. The patient (principal) seeks out the physician (agent) for advice on a medical problem. The physician behaving as a perfect agent will recommend only the treatment that a fully informed patient would demand. The problem arises because the physician not only serves as an adviser to the patient but is also the provider of the recommended services. This dual role as adviser and provider creates a potential conflict of interest between what is best for the patient in terms of clinical efficacy and what is best for the physician in terms of financial reward. By law, the physician must act in the best interests of the patient. Due to the uncertainty of diagnosis and the question of best treatment alternative, the best interests of the patient are not always clear.

Physicians acting as imperfect agents may recommend unnecessary procedures, especially if they pose little clinical risk to the patient and the patient is fully insured. This practice of demand inducement may occur for different reasons: to augment falling incomes or simply to reduce the risk of a potential lawsuit. In the latter case, it may be referred to as defensive medicine. Reinhardt (1999) presents a model of physician behavior that incorporates the potential for demand inducement as one of the factors that affects a physician's well-being or utility. In this model, a physician's utility depends on three factors: income, hours worked, and the extent of demand inducement. Income and leisure time increase a physician's utility. The practice of demand inducement reduces utility; presumably because of guilt feelings due to a professional code of ethics or the stigma associated with the behavior should it become public knowledge. Physicians are faced with a trade-off among income, leisure, and conscience.

Influencing Physician Behavior

Patients delegate medical decisions to their physicians because physicians have better information about the causes and consequences of medical conditions. However, physicians' motives are unobserved and may not correspond perfectly with those of the patient and the payer. The physician is faced with competing incentives. One is the financial arrangement between the payer and the provider, designed to control for moral hazard. The other is the moral obligation between patient and provider, designed to guarantee the provision of all medically necessary care. Both payer and patient compete for the provider's loyalty to advance their competing goals.

In search of ways to influence provider behavior, health plans have designed incentive mechanisms to influence the way physicians practice medicine. These mechanisms include capitation, withholdings and bonuses, diagnosis-related groups, clinical rules, and utilization reviews. To encourage cost-conscious practice patterns, some health plans pay primary care physicians on a capitation basis and make them responsible for the cost of referring patients to approved specialists. Under capitation, physicians are responsible for the management of care within a fixed budget. In other words, they accept some of the financial risk in making clinical decisions. When the managed care plan establishes a risk-sharing plan, using withholdings and bonuses, the result limits the independence of participating physicians. Management tends to focus on costs, and with few exceptions, the trade-off is between controlling costs and improving the quality of care.

Do Physicians Respond to Incentives?

Efforts to control spending have led many health plans to adjust the way physicians are paid. One popular approach establishes reduced fee-for-service rates for all covered procedures. When physicians are paid in this manner, many increase the dollar volume of services by changing the way they bill (e.g., **unbundling** of services and/or upcoding) and by providing more services (Holahan, Dor, and Zuckerman, 1990; Lee, Grumbach, and Jameson, 1990; Wedig, Mitchell, and Cromwell, 1989). Canada has learned that controlling physician fees does not lower expenditures on physicians' services. Fee schedules lead to changed patterns of medical care delivery, including an increased number of follow-up visits (Hughes, 1991; Lomas et al., 1989).

unbundling
Separating a number of related procedures and treating them as individual services for payment purposes.

When financial incentives exert pressures, no matter how subtle, clinical decisions may be influenced (Hillman, 1990). Managed care places the physician's clinical judgment on a collision course with his or her pecuniary interests. Theoretically, physicians well schooled in economic principles will consider the costs to society when making clinical decisions.

But in practice, the payment scheme used by many managed care plans induces physicians to take into consideration the impact of their clinical decisions on their own income. Because many physicians share financial risk with managed care plans, they share the same incentives with insurance companies to avoid sick patients (Stone, 1997).

Strong financial incentives result in a physician taking on some of the responsibilities of an insurer, usually without an adequate patient base to spread actuarial risk. In a fixed-budget environment, physicians who withhold care can earn higher incomes. Placing physicians at financial risk mixes two types of risk: probability risk and efficiency risk. Probability risk measures the likelihood that patients will utilize medical care based on the characteristics of the patient pool, including age, sex, and health status. Efficiency risk measures how effectively the physician treats the patient. Although physicians control their own efficiency risk, they have no control over probability risk. It is appropriate to hold physicians responsible for efficiency risk; it is inappropriate to hold them responsible for probability risk.

By adjusting compensation for population characteristics, at least part of the probability risk is transferred back to the insurer. But most plans adjust for only two variables, age and sex, even though these account for less than 20 percent of the annual costs of medical care among patients (Goldfield et al., 1996).

Managed care attempts to shape physician behavior through either clinical rules or financial incentives. **Clinical rules** establish guidelines that encourage physicians to adopt a particular practice style. The effectiveness of clinical rules depends on the ability of managed care plans to educate physicians about the appropriate practice style, to use peer pressure to ensure compliance, and to select the physicians who may participate in the provision of care. In contrast, financial incentives leave the treatment choice to the physician. However, financial incentives create a conflict of interest by compromising the physician's fiduciary responsibility or exercise of independent clinical judgment. Both approaches share the goal of encouraging less-expensive care.

Less-expensive care, however, does not necessarily mean poor-quality care. Hellinger (1998) cites evidence that the cost-cutting measures practiced by managed care may adversely affect the health of certain vulnerable subpopulations, including older and sicker patients, and that managed care enrollees may suffer because of problems accessing certain specialized services. In fact, the strongest disincentive for quality care is for the sickest and most expensive patients. Physicians who provide quality care for their sickest patients will find their practices attracting the sickest patients. Because most capitation rates are adjusted only for age and sex, not health status, this strategy results in lost income for the provider. The alternative strategy is to offer a level of care that encourages sick patients to change providers. This strategy, called "patient dumping," does not have to be overt. It may be accomplished in more subtle ways, including delays in scheduling appointments for certain types of procedures, refusal to refer sick patients to specialists, and failure to meet patient expectations on treatments prescribed and provided.

In other research, Hellinger (1996) examined the impact of financial incentives on physician behavior, specifically capitation and the use of withholdings and bonuses, and concluded that financial incentives are a key element in explaining lower levels of spending and utilization in managed care plans. It is important to recognize that all of the studies comparing utilization rates in managed care with those in fee-for-service care are unable to differentiate between the impacts of financial incentives and those of clinical rules. To the extent that plans with strong financial incentives also include stringent clinical rules, it is difficult to separate the impact of the two. However, it is possible to conclude that plans with strong financial incentives and strong clinical rules have lower utilization rates compared to plans that do not.

POLICY ISSUE

Risk-sharing contracts, which subject physicians to financial incentives to limit health care spending, may adversely affect quality of care.

clinical rule Is a specific practice required of all participating physicians, such as a policy to refer patients only to a specific panel of specialists.

gatekeeper A primary care physician who directs health care delivery and determines whether patients are allowed access to specialty care.

Empirical Evidence on the Impact of Financial Incentives   The empirical literature examining the impact of financial incentives on physician behavior may be divided into three categories: randomized trials, same-disease studies, and same-physician studies. The largest and most widely cited randomized trial is the RAND Health Insurance Experiment (Manning et al., 1984). Results of this study concluded that participants in a group-model HMO had fewer inpatient hospital days and lower overall medical expenditures than did participants in a traditional fee-for-service plan. Martin and colleagues (1989) examined the impact of a **gatekeeper** operating under a risk-sharing contract and concluded that physicians at risk for budget deficits had lower spending per enrollee, attributable to lower specialist referral costs.

A limited number of same-disease studies have examined the treatment decisions of physicians facing different financial incentives. These studies looked at the treatment and diagnostic services provided to patients with a variety of health conditions, including heart disease, colorectal cancer, childbirth, and acute myocardial infarction. These studies concluded that patients treated by HMO physicians received fewer procedures, diagnostic tests, and treatments than patients who used physicians paid under traditional indemnity insurance arrangements. Epstein, Begg, and McNeil (1986) studied the practices of 27 physicians certified in internal medicine, 10 with fee-for-service practices, and 17 in prepaid group practices. They concluded that patients treated in fee-for-service practices received 50 percent more electrocardiograms than patients treated in prepaid practices.

Finally, the same-physician studies avoid some of the potential biases inherent in other approaches. Because practice styles may differ substantially among physicians, by contrasting an individual physician's practices with fee-for-service patients and managed care patients, same-physician studies control for many of the sources of variation that incorrectly affect results. Using this approach, Welch, Pauly, and Hillman (1990) and Murray and colleagues (1992) conclude that physicians used more services in treating patients enrolled in fee-for-service plans than patients enrolled in prepaid plans. Melichar (2009) found that physicians spend less time with their patients covered under capitated plans than their noncapitated patients.

ISSUES IN MEDICAL CARE DELIVERY

DIFFERENCES IN TREATMENT PATTERNS: MEDICARE VERSUS PRIVATE INSURANCE

Supporters of the ACA relied on the critical estimate that the legislation would reduce Medicare spending by $741 billion. These savings would come largely from reductions in unnecessary care and thus painlessly provide a large portion of the funds required to finance the coverage of millions of previously uninsured individuals. The savings potential is based on research published in the *Dartmouth Atlas of Health Care* identifying large variations in Medicare spending in different regions of the country.

The popular press picked up on the spending differences when a *New Yorker* article (Gawande, 2009) compared Medicare spending in two Texas border towns—McAllen and El Paso—both located on the Rio Grande River separating Texas from Mexico. Gawande found that price-adjusted per capita Medicare spending was 86 percent higher in McAllen than in El Paso and 75 percent higher than the national average. His explanation for the differences was a greater "entrepreneurial spirit" among McAllen's physicians and a "culture of money" manifesting itself there.

Franzini et al. (2010) explored the same medical spending patterns among privately insured patients in the two cities. With the same physicians treating Medicare and privately insured patients, this study explored whether the spirit and culture identified by Gawande carried over from Medicare to the privately insured.

Using 2008 Blue Cross/Blue Shield claims data, Franzini and colleagues found that among the privately insured, total annual spending per enrollee was 7 percent lower in McAllen than in El Paso. The results do not disprove the existence of an entrepreneurial spirit or culture of money, only that private insurance plans with their more stringent spending restraints may control that spirit and culture more effectively.

Sources: Dartmouth Institute for Health Policy and Clinical Studies, Dartmouth Atlas of Health Care, 2011, available at www.dartmouthatlas.org (Accessed February 1, 2011); Atul Gawande, "The Cost Conundrum," *New Yorker*, June 1, 2009, available at www.newyorker.com/reporting/2009/06/01/090601fa_fact_gawande (Accessed February 1, 2011); and Luisa Franzini et al., "McAllen and El Paso Revisited: Medicare Variations Not Always Reflected in the Under-Sixty-Five Population," *Health Affairs* 29(12), 2010, 2302–2309.

Not all studies conclude that financial incentives systematically affect physician behavior. Cangialose and colleagues (1997) and Conrad and colleagues (1998) are two of the most often cited studies that reach the opposite conclusion. However, these studies have methodological problems that bring their results into question. Cangialose and colleagues (1997) published in a managed care industry journal, bringing into question the objectivity of the peer-review process. Conrad and colleagues (1998) chose health plans in which 96 percent of the enrollees were being treated by primary care physicians who shared in the financial risk of treatment. In their own words, this choice "eliminated the influence of health plan payment in this sample" (p. 857).

All of the studies on incentives are subject to certain biases. Patients may select physicians who practice the style of medicine they prefer. Healthy patients may cluster in prepaid practices. Moreover, virtually every study that adjusted for the available information on differences in type of enrollee, physician, and plan concluded that physicians facing financial incentives provided fewer services, diagnostic tests, and procedures than did physicians who were not faced with them. The robustness of these findings suggests that when faced with financial incentives, specifically capitation and the use of withholds and bonuses, physicians alter their practice style to provide fewer services, diagnostic tests, and procedures. This practice may not affect the health status of healthy patients; however, certain vulnerable patients—those who are poor or suffer from chronic conditions—may receive lower quality care.

Most physicians practice in a setting where a variety of insurance arrangements exist simultaneously, variations of both managed care and fee for service. Theory suggests that managed care patients will receive less intensive care than fee-for-service patients. However, a physician may find it difficult to modify his or her practice style based on the type of plan that covers the patient. Empirical findings by Glied and Zivin (2002) indicate that financial incentives in fact do affect treatment intensity among patients according to method of payment. Additionally, and more importantly, variations in treatment intensity depend on the relative mix of managed care and fee-for-service patients in the physician's practice. Physicians with a large percentage of their patients covered by managed care plans change their practice styles across the board, treating all patients with the lower, managed care intensity.

The Market for Nursing Services

A number of different occupational groups may provide nursing services. The two that have specific educational and licensing requirements are registered nurses (RNs) and licensed practical nurses (LPNs). RNs make up the largest component of the nursing workforce. To qualify for the basic RN license, one of three educational programs must be completed—a two-year associate degree, a three-year hospital diploma, or a four-year baccalaureate degree. None of the attempts to raise the minimum educational requirement for the RN license to a baccalaureate degree have gone very far. LPNs generally have only 12–14 months of training usually offered at technical schools and community colleges and earn about two-thirds of the average annual income of an RN.

ISSUES IN MEDICAL CARE DELIVERY

DO WE REALLY WANT LOW-COST PRIMARY CARE?

The shortage of primary care physicians and the increased popularity of managed care, with its emphasis on cutting costs, have provided momentum to those who advocate greater autonomy for nurses in treating patients. By allowing advanced-practice nurses to take over some of the more routine duties now reserved for physicians, the United States could save billions of dollars in medical care costs annually. Advanced-practice nurses comprise nurse practitioners, nurse anesthetists, and nurse midwives; they usually have two years of clinical training beyond the four-year baccalaureate degree. As such, even without experience, they have more training than first-year residents who provide a great deal of the primary care in the nation's teaching hospitals.

Legislation dating back to the 1930s restricts nurses in two important ways. First, nurse practitioners do not have prescriptive authority in many states, which means they are unable to write prescriptions unless they are in a collaborative practice with a licensed physician. Second, not all payment sources recognize nurse practitioners as qualified providers and thus do not directly reimburse them for their services.

Still, more than 100,000 advanced-practice nurses nationwide offer physical exams, immunizations, preventive screening, and treatment for minor illnesses such as ear infection, sore throat, and the flu. Many see nurse practitioners, who offer their services at a 30–70 percent cost-saving compared to general practitioners, as a way to lower costs and improve access to primary care in many underserved areas. Critics, however, feel that lowering the barriers to nurse practitioners will only drive more physicians from general practice into the higher-paying specialties and, in the long run, will do little to lower costs and improve access.

How many of the restrictions on nursing are based on concerns over quality of care, and how many are merely a cultural artifact of an era when female nurses assisted male physicians? One thing is certain: As concern over cost cutting grows, the barriers to an expanded role for nurses will gradually disappear. It is simply a matter of time until economics once again promotes a more effective use of scarce resources.

Source: Adrienne Perry, "Nurse Practitioners Fight Job Restrictions," *Wall Street Journal*, September 3, 1993, B1, B8.

KEY CONCEPT 7
Competition

KEY CONCEPT 7
Competition

RNs held almost 2.7 million jobs in 2014, an increase of almost 23 percent over the decade (see Table 9.4). Approximately 70 percent of those jobs were in hospitals, and one-fourth were part time. In 2013, over 850 nursing programs nationwide that maintained membership in AACN, the American Association of Colleges of Nursing. First-year nursing enrollment numbered over 240,000 with over 72,000 graduating that same year.[5]

---

[5]First year enrollment includes baccalaureate, master's, and doctoral students.

TABLE 9.4 RNs IN THE UNITED STATES

	Active RNs (000)[2]	RNs per 100,000	First-year enrollment[1]	Nursing graduates[1]
1970	750	368	NA	43,103
1980	1,273	560	105,952	75,523
1990	1,790	714	108,580	66,088
1995	2,116	798	127,184	97,052
2000*	2,218	788	138,885	68,709
2005	2,368	799	213,868	64,990
2006	2,417	807	240,082	72,159
2010	2,655	858	NA	NA
2014	2,687	842	NA	NA

[1]Beginning in 2000, RNs seeking baccalaureate, master's, and doctoral degrees.
[2]Numbers in column are in thousands of active RNs.
Source: *Statistical Abstracts of the United States 1999*, Table No. 196; U.S. Department of Health and Human Services, *Health, United States*, various years.

Efforts to curb the growth of health care costs are likely to have significant effects on the market for nursing services. By redesigning the medical workplace, hospitals will be able to use more nursing aides to provide much of the low-skill, routine care. Using lower-paid aides can save as much as $25,000 for each job converted from an RN to an LPN (average RN salary of $78,000 versus average LPN salary of $43,000). In addition, demand will increase for advanced-practice nurses to help providers cut costs for routine primary and preventive care.

BACK-OF-THE-ENVELOPE
Monopsony Power in the Market for Registered Nurses

Chronic shortages have often plagued the labor market for nurses. Public policy has traditionally focused on the supply side of the market, offering recommendations to increase the number of nursing graduates. Economists examine the problem from a different perspective. Chronic and persistent shortages may be an indicator of monopsony power. In competitive markets, a shortage results when wages are set below their equilibrium level. Employers compete to attract and retain workers by bidding up the wage until demand and supply are back in balance.

The market for RNs may not work this way. Several aspects of the market contribute to the development of monopsony power among employers. The hospital industry is the largest employer of nursing services. Over 70 percent of all nurses in the United States are employed in this setting. This institutional feature establishes a single-buyer model in many local labor markets with the hospital as the dominant purchaser of nursing services. Mobile workers can overcome local market monopsony. If enough nurses were willing to move to other communities where wages are higher, or if they transferred their skills and experience to other types of work within the local labor market, competition would raise local wages.

Historically, these normal checks and balances on monopsony power are relatively inoperative in the nursing market. Nursing skills are very job-specific and do not readily transfer to other occupations. The wholesale exodus of nurses leaving the profession for jobs in some other industry poses little threat to the local hospital employer. Additionally, geographic mobility among nurses is also low. Most nurses are married females and often earn less than their spouses. As the secondary income earner within the family, the typical nurse is restricted to the geographic location chosen by the higher-paid spouse.

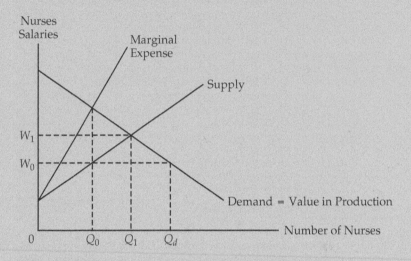

What do these factors mean for nurses in general? Using the diagram, we can see that the monopsonistic employer equates the workers' value in production with their marginal expense, and therefore only Q_0 are hired. To hire that number, the monopsonist pays a wage equal to W_0, substantially less than the competitive wage of W_1 determined by the intersection of supply and demand. With wages below the competitive equilibrium, a shortage $(Q_d - Q_0)$ exists. Normally, competitive pressures bid wages back up to W_1, but in this case—without competitive pressures—wages remain at W_0, and the shortage persists. Nursing unions and the increased mobility of professional women can improve salaries and reduce shortages. In fact, by demanding the competitive wage W_1, the union actually increases the quantity of nurses demanded to Q_1.

Sources: Lavonne A. Booten and Julia I. Lane, "Hospital Market Structure and the Return to Nursing Education," *Journal of Human Resources* 20(2), 1985, 184–196; and Julia Lane and Stephan Gohmann, "Shortage or Surplus: Economic and Noneconomic Approaches to the Analysis of Nursing Labor Markets," *Southern Economic Journal* 61(3), January 1995, 644–653.

KEY CONCEPT 6
Supply and Demand

KEY CONCEPT 7
Competition

HTTP://
Nursing World is the official website of the American Nurses Association. In addition to legislative updates on issues affecting the profession, regular news releases, and job search information, the site provides access to the Online Journal of Issues in Nursing published at Kent State University. The address is http://www.nursingworld.org.

The Market for Dental Services

Most of the 186,100 dentists actively practicing in the United States are general practitioners. The remainder practice as specialists. Orthodontists, who make up the largest group of specialists, straighten teeth. The next largest group is oral and maxillofacial surgeons, who specialize in surgery of the mouth and jaw. Other specialties include pediatric dentistry, periodontics, prosthodontics, endodontics, dental public health, and oral pathology.[6]

More than 80 percent of dentists practice privately as "solo practitioners." They own their own businesses and employ a small staff of assistants to complement their work effort. Some dentists practice in partnership with others, and a small percentage are employed as associates in a larger group practice.

---

[6]Dentists in these areas specialize in the practice of children's dentistry, the treatment of diseases of the gums and supporting bone structure, making dentures and artificial teeth, root canal therapy, epidemiology, and the study of diseases of the mouth.

TABLE 9.5 DENTISTS IN THE UNITED STATES

	Active dentists	Dentists per 100,000 population	Dental schools	First-year enrollment	Dental graduates
1970	96,000	47	53	–	3,749
1980	121,900	54	60	6,132	5,256
1985	133,500	57	60	5,047	5,353
1990	147,500	59	58	3,979	4,233
1995	153,300	61	54	4,121	3,908
2000	166,400	61	55	4,327	4,367
2005	–	–	56	4,688	4,515
2006	172,603	58	–	–	–
2010	–	–	58	5,170	4,996
2011	186,025	60	–	–	–
2013	191,347	60	65	5,904	5,491

Source: *Statistical Abstracts of the United States 1999*, U.S. Department of Health and Human Services, *Health, United States,* various years.

HTTP://

ADAONLINE is the offi-cial website of the Amer-ican Dental Association (ADA), providing access to educational opportu-nities, current research, and other clinical issues of interest to dentists. The ADA Newsstand fea-tures news releases and links to other websites. The address is http://www.ada.org.

As summarized in Table 9.5, there are 65 dental schools enrolling over 5,900 new students each year in four-year programs. Most dental schools require a minimum of two years of predental education at an accredited undergraduate institution. Most dental students, however, have at least a four-year baccalaureate degree in one of the physical sciences. The course work in dental school is similar to the medical school curriculum. The first two years are spent learning the basic sciences through classroom instruction and lab-oratory training. The final two years are spent in clinical work, treating patients under the supervision of licensed dental professors.

Occupational Employment Statistics provided by the Bureau of Labor Statistics esti-mates that the average annual income for dentists was $177,130 in 2015. The amount var-ies considerably by state with dentists in Wisconsin, North Carolina, North Dakota, New Hampshire, Alaska, and Delaware making over $200,000 annually. The job outlook for the dental profession looks relatively good. Demand for dental services will grow as the baby boom generation ages. On average, this group has retained more of its teeth than previous generations and has more disposable income. Thus, the demand for preventive care will remain solid.

ISSUES IN MEDICAL CARE DELIVERY

THE DEMAND FOR DENTAL CARE

Dental care, hospital care, physicians' services, and pharmaceuticals—all are medical care, so they must be the same. Right? If all these medical services are the same, why do most health insurance plans treat them differently? Out-of-pocket payments for medical care averaged roughly 12 percent of total spending in 2011. That percentage differs signifi-cantly when viewed by category of spending. It stands at 3 percent of hospital spending, 18 percent of physicians' services, 30 percent of pharmaceuticals, and 48 percent of den-tal services. Why do these percentages vary so dramatically?

The demand for dental care is associated with the same variables that affect the demand for other types of medical care—prices, income, tastes and preferences, and health status. But there are elements of dental care that are different from other types of medical care. A large portion of dental services is preventive in nature; some consider them elective. Because teeth are a durable good, much of the normal demand for dental care is for maintenance or repair. Roughly, 85 percent of the services performed are comprised of fillings, extractions, cleanings, and examinations. Much of the rest is performed for cosmetic reasons. We want good teeth so we can chew our food without pain and look good at the same time.

Insurance coverage for dental services has been slow in developing because of the individual's ability to postpone care, plus the fact that it is sometimes difficult to delineate the difference between maintenance and repair on the one hand and pure cosmetics on the other. Because of these characteristics, even partial insurance coverage results in a substantial increase in demand for services. The insured population spends roughly 1.8 times more on dental services than the population at large.

In terms of economics, the demand for dental care is more price elastic than the demand for other forms of medical care. Elasticity estimates vary by type of service and demographics. White females have the price elasticities of demand that range from −0.5 to −0.7. In general, demand of white males and children is more elastic than that of females. This means that adults with free dental care will spend twice as much as adults with no insurance, and fully insured children will spend three times as much as children with no insurance.

Any improvement in dental insurance coverage must be carefully coordinated with policies to increase the supply of dentists. Improved insurance coverage will mean increased demand for dental care. Increased demand coupled with an inelastic supply of dentists will mean increased prices, increased queues, and higher quasi-rents for dentists. Markets will ration scarce resources, and that rationing will take the form of higher prices or longer waiting times for office visits.

Source: Willard G. Manning and Charles E. Phelps, "The Demand for Dental Care," *The Bell Journal of Economics* 10, Autumn 1979, 503–525.

Summary and Conclusions

Policy makers speak with near unanimity in their claim that residency programs in the United States are turning out too few generalists and too many specialists. The imbalance, if one actually exists, may be corrected by imposing more regulations on the medical education establishment or by relying on market forces. Those who would rely on regulation do not believe that the current system will respond to market incentives and change the proportion of residents entering general practice. Advocates of the market approach argue that regulators do not have enough information to predict the needs of the medical care delivery system and probably would not get it right if they tried. They argue that the proper specialty mix and geographic distribution are better determined through market incentives.

In any event, managed care is already bidding up the salaries of primary care physicians; a phenomenon that many believe is the beginning of the adjustment process.

Another important topic in this chapter is the changing incentive structure of the physicians' services market. In a fee-for-service environment, the most valuable patient in the physician's practice is the sickest patient. More office visits, more services, and more procedures all translate directly into more income for the physician. In a capitated environment, the most valuable patient is the healthiest patient. Sick patients consume costly medical resources without contributing any additional income. Healthy patients generate the same income and do not consume valuable resources.

PROFILE   Gary S. Becker

Considered an imaginative, original thinker by his supporters—and accused of intellectual imperialism by his detractors—Gary S. Becker, more than any other scholar, has inspired a revolution in economic thought that is extending the boundaries of economic inquiry and ultimately redefining what economists do. Beginning with his dissertation research published in 1957 under the title *The Economics of Discrimination*, Becker's theoretical work has opened to economists the fertile research fields of the other social sciences. An entire generation of economists challenged by his insights has used his theories as a springboard for their own policy-oriented research.

In addition to his early work on discrimination, Becker is responsible for pathbreaking research on important social issues such as fertility and demographics, education, crime and punishment, and marriage and divorce—all aspects of human behavior once considered outside the scope of economics. He is best known for his contribution to a symposium "Investment in Human Beings," published in a special issue of the *Journal of Political Economy* in 1962. This work, expanded into a book in 1964 entitled *Human Capital*, is recognized as a classic piece of research by economists and serves as the theoretical foundation for a field of study under that same title. Within this framework, individuals spend and invest in themselves and their children with the future in mind. Education and training, job search, migration, and medical care are all viewed as investments in human capital. The decision to spend is based on a comparison of the present value of the expected benefits with the present value of the costs.

Becker's innovative thought did not end there. His later research into crime and punishment and the economics of the family has been equally revolutionary, affecting not only economics but also criminology and sociology. In 1992, he became the third straight University of Chicago economist awarded the Nobel Prize in Economic Science. Becker was honored for extending "the domain of microeconomic analysis to a wide range of human behavior and interaction including nonmarket behavior."

Born in Pottstown, Pennsylvania, Becker graduated from Princeton in 1951. He completed his doctoral training at the University of Chicago in 1955 and was asked to remain there as a member of the faculty. Except for 12 years at Columbia University and the National Bureau of Economic Research, Becker has maintained his Chicago affiliation throughout his professional career. Probably more than any other proponent of the Chicago School of Economics, he has developed and applied the ideas of classic free-market economics in ways his predecessors never considered.*

Becker appeared on the academic scene in the 1960s, when neoclassical economics was under attack from all fronts. The resurgence of the Marxist critique of capitalism challenged the orthodoxy from the outside, and a subtle movement toward a less rigorous analysis (as exemplified by the work of John K. Galbraith) challenged it from within. Becker's unrivaled imagination saved the discipline from irrelevancy. For that, we are all deeply thankful.

Sources: J. R. Shackleton, "Gary S. Becker: The Economist as Empire Builder," in J. R. Shackleton and G. Locksley, eds., *Twelve Contemporary Economists*, London: Macmillan, 1981, 12–33; Jonathan Peterson, "Chicago's Lock on the Nobel: Economics Professor Is University's Third Winner in Three Years," *Los Angeles Times*, Home Edition, October 14, 1992, D1; and Peter Passell, "New Nobel Laureate Takes Economics Far Afield," *The New York Times*, Late Edition, October 14, 1992, D1.

*The Chicago School is more than a geographic location. It is a school of thought based on a methodology rooted in the microeconomic foundations of all of economics. Its theoretical basis is one of self-interested decision makers, market equilibrium, the universal application of the concept of capital, and a healthy skepticism for government-based solutions to economic problems.

Questions and Problems

1. If surgeons really have the ability to increase the demand for surgeries, which kinds of surgeries will be most affected? Can you think of a way to determine which surgeries are unnecessary? Provide several examples from your own readings or experience.

2. If the theory of supplier-induced demand is valid, what are the implications for public policy?

3. How does the dual nature of the physician's role as both adviser and provider support the demand-inducement hypothesis? What institutional mechanisms support the possibility of demand inducement? How does health insurance reinforce this effect? What are the natural limits to the alleged problem?

4. Why is the supply of physicians a major cause of concern? How would you expect the supply of physicians to affect physicians' incomes and the price and quantity of medical services provided? What is the actual evidence?

5. The AMA has been actively involved in shaping the regulation of nursing and other health care practitioners. What are the arguments for and against the AMA determining the scope of legitimate activities for other health care practitioners?

6. "High salaries are essential if we are to have the most capable students pursuing medical careers." Comment.

References

AAMC Center for Workforce Studies, *The Impact of Health Care Reform on the Future Supply and Demand for Physicians Updated through 2025*, Washington, DC: Association of American Medical Colleges, June 2010.

AAMC Data Book: Statistical Information Related to Medical Education, Washington, DC: Association of American Medical Colleges, 2010.

Cangialose, Charles B., S. J. Cary, L. H. Hoffman, and D. J. Ballard, "Impact of Managed Care Arrangements on Quality of Care: Theory and Evidence," *American Journal of Managed Care* 3(8), August 1997, 1153–1170.

Conrad, Douglas A., et al., "Primary Care Physician Compensation Method in Medical Groups: Does It Influence the Use and Cost of Health Services for Enrollees in Managed Care Organizations?" *Journal of the American Medical Association* 278, March 18, 1998, 853–858.

Dartmouth Atlas of Health Care, 2010, available at http://www.dartmouthatlas.org/ (Accessed June 28, 2013).

Eddy, David M., "Clinical Decision Making: From Theory to Practice," *Journal of the American Medical Association* 263(3), January 19, 1990, 441–443.

Epstein, A. M., C. B. Begg, and B. J. McNeil, "The Use of Ambulatory Testing in Prepaid and Fee-for-Service Group Practices: Relation to Perceived Profitability," *The New England Journal of Medicine* 314, April 24, 1986, 1089–1094.

Escarce, Jose J. and Mark V. Pauly, "Physician Opportunity Costs in Physician Practice Cost Functions," *Journal of Health Economics* 17(2), April 1998, 129–151.

Frech, H. E. and Paul Ginsburg, "Imposed Health Insurance in Monopolistic Markets: A Theoretical Analysis," *Economic Inquiry* 13(1), 1975, 55–70.

Glied, Sherry and Joshua Graff Zivin, "How Do Doctors Behave When Some (but Not All) of Their Patients Are in Managed Care?" *Journal of Health Economics* 21(2), March 2002, 337–353.

Goldfield, N., et al., "Methods of Compensating Managed Care Physicians and Hospitals," in *Physician Profiling and Risk Adjustment*, edited by N. Goldfield and P. Boland, Gaithersburg, MD: Aspen Publishers, 1996.

Hellinger, Fred J., "The Effect of Managed Care on Quality: A Review of Recent Evidence," *Archives of Internal Medicine* 158, April 27, 1998, 833–841.

Hellinger, Fred J., "The Impact of Financial Incentives on Physician Behavior in Managed Care Plans: A Review of the Evidence," *Medical Care Research and Review* 53, September 1996, 294–314.

Hillman, A. L., "Health Maintenance Organizations, Financial Incentives, and Physicians' Judgments," *Annals of Internal Medicine* 112(12), June 15, 1990, 891–893.

Hing, Esther and Catharine W. Burt, "Office Based Medical Practices: Methods and Estimates from the National Ambulatory Medical Care Survey," Centers for Disease Control, Advance Data from Vital and Health Statistics, No. 383, March 2007.

Holahan, J., A. Dor, and S. Zuckerman, "Understanding the Recent Growth in Medicare Physician Expenditures," *Journal of the American Medical Association* 263(12), March 23–30, 1990, 1658–1661.

Hughes, J. S., "How Well Has Canada Contained the Costs of Doctoring?" *Journal of the American Medical Association* 265(18), May 8, 1991, 2347–2351.

Lee, P., K. Grumbach, and W. Jameson, "Physician Payment in the 1990s: Factors That Will Shape the Future," *Annual Review of Public Health* 11, 1990, 297–318.

Lomas, J., C. Fooks, T. Rice, and R. Labelle, "Paying Physicians in Canada: Minding Our P's and Q's," *Health Affairs* 8(1), Spring 1989, 80–102.

Manning, W. F., A. Leibowitz, G. A. Goldberg, W. H. Rogers, and J. P. Rogers, "A Controlled Trial of the Effects of a Prepaid Group Practice on Use of Services," *New England Journal of Medicine* 310(23), June 7, 1984, 1505–1510.

Martin, D. P., P. Diehr, K. F. Price, and W. C. Richardson, "Effect of a Gatekeeper Plan on Health Services Use and Charges: A Randomized Trial," *American Journal of Public Health* 79(12), December 1989, 1628–1632.

McPherson, Klim, John E. Wennberg, Ole B. Hovind, and Peter Gifford, "Small-Area Variations in the Use of Common Surgical Procedures: An International Comparison of New England, England, and Norway," *New England Journal of Medicine* 307(21), November 18, 1982, 1310–1313.

Melichar, Lori, "The Effect of Reimbursement on Medical Decision Making: Do Physicians Alter Treatment in Response to a Managed Care Incentive?" *Journal of Health Economics* 28(4), July 2009, 902–907.

Merritt Hawkins & Associates, "2014 Survey of Physician Appointment Wait Times," 2014, available at https://www.merritthawkins.com/uploadedFiles/MerrittHawkings/Surveys/mha2014waitsurvPDF.pdf (Accessed March 20, 2017).

Murray, J. P., S. Greenfield, S. H. Kaplan, and E. M. Yano, "Ambulatory Testing for Capitation and Fee-for-Service Patients in the Same-Practice Setting: Relationships to Outcomes," *Medical Care* 30(3), March 1992, 252–261.

O'Reilly, Kevin B., "New Medical Schools Open but Physician Shortage Concerns Persist," *American Medical News*, March 29, 2010.

Organization of Economic Cooperation and Development, OECD Health Data, 2013, available at http://www.oecd-ilibrary.org/social-issues-migration-health/data/oecd-health-statistics_health-data-en (Accessed March 20, 2017).

Patterson, Stephen M., et al., "Projecting U.S. Primary Care Workforce Needs: 2010–2025," *Annals of Family Medicine* 10(6), November/December 2012, 503–509.

Rabinowitz, Howard K., "Recruitment, Retention, and Follow-Up of Graduates of a Program to Increase the Number of Family Physicians in Rural and Underserved Areas," *New England Journal of Medicine* 328(13), April 1, 1993, 934–939.

Ramsey, Frank P., "A Contribution to the Theory of Taxation," *Economic Journal* 37(145), 1927, 47–61.

Reinhardt, Uwe E., "A Production Function for Physician Services," *Review of Economics and Statistics* 54(1), February 1972, 55–66.

Reinhardt, Uwe E., "The Economist's Model of Physician Behavior," *Journal of the American Medical Association* 281(5), February 3, 1999, 462–465.

Schroeder, Steven A. and Lewis G. Sandy, "Specialty Distribution of U.S. Physicians—the Invisible Driver of Health Care Costs," *New England Journal of Medicine* 328(13), April 1, 1993, 961–963.

Stone, D. A., "The Doctor as Businessman: The Changing Politics of a Cultural Icon," *Journal of Health Politics, Policy and Law* 22(2), April 1997, 533–556.

Wedig, G., J. B. Mitchell, and J. Cromwell, "Can Price Controls Induce Optimal Physician Behavior?" *Journal of Health Politics, Policy and Law* 14(3), Fall 1989, 601–620.

Weeks, William B., Amy E. Wallace, Myron M. Wallace, and H. Gilbert Welch, "A Comparison of the Educational Costs and Incomes of Physicians and Other Professionals," *New England Journal of Medicine* 330(18), May 5, 1994, 1280–1286.

Weinstein, James N., Kristen K. Bronner, Tamara Shawver Morgan, and John E. Wennberg, "Trends and Geographic Variations in Major Surgery for Degenerative Diseases of the Hip, Knee, and Spine," *Health Affairs—Web Exclusive*, October 7, 2004, VAR-81–VAR-89.

Welch, W. P., Mark V. Pauly, and Alan L. Hillman, "Toward New Topologies for HMOs," *Milbank Quarterly* 68(2), 1990, 221–230.

Wennberg, John E., "Dealing with Medical Practice Variations: A Proposal for Action," *Health Affairs* 3(2), Summer 1984, 6–32.

Worth, Tammy, "Agencies Warn of Coming Doctor Shortage," *Los Angeles Times*, June 7, 2010.

Medical Malpractice

Modern medicine is inherently a dangerous undertaking. A medical care system that takes the responsibility for more ambitious interventions in the case of increasingly sicker patients will see the incidence of *iatrogenic disease* or injury increase, in turn increasing the number of tort cases. Medicine is continuously developing new techniques and more sophisticated medical technology, and placing them in the hands of imperfect human agents. It is no wonder errors result, leading to harm to patients. In this appendix, we will explore the impact of medical malpractice medical care delivery.

The Purpose and Function of Tort Law

Medical malpractice law is designed to encourage physicians to act as responsible agents for their patients and only expose them to a level of risk that a fully informed patient would accept willingly. In this context, medical malpractice law serves three functions: compensation, deterrence, and retribution.

Tort law has evolved as a method of compensating individuals who are injured due to the negligent behavior of others. Compensatory damages are awarded to compensate the successful plaintiff for actual losses, both economic and noneconomic. Economic losses include lost income and any tangible expenses, including all medical and rehabilitation expenses. Noneconomic losses or general damages include pain and suffering, disfigurement, shock, and loss of association.

Medical providers use private third-party liability insurance to spread the risk of loss among policyholders through the payment of malpractice insurance premiums. The losses are actually spread among patients who pay higher prices for medical care services. Thus, the cost of risk avoidance falls primarily on patients as providers pass through the cost of medical malpractice insurance to their customers in the form of higher fees.

Another important function of tort law is to deter specific behavior that causes injuries. In fact, if the tort system is evaluated according to a standard of economic efficiency, then its justification is based solely on its ability to deter injurious behavior. Compensation and the spreading of risk can actually be accomplished at a lower cost and more equitably through a mechanism of first-party liability in which the patient buys health and disability insurance.

Injuries are costly. Likewise, steps taken to avoid injuries are also costly. The goal is not the avoidance of all accidents, but that only the optimal number of accidents will take place. Suppose that a $20,000 injury can be avoided by the medical provider, taking steps costing $1,000, or by the patient spending $10,000. In this case, it is in society's best interest for the provider to take the responsibility for accident prevention. Likewise, if prevention costs either provider or patient more than $20,000, then failure to take steps to prevent the injury should not be considered negligent behavior.[7]

The rules of tort will deter negligent behavior if the responsibility for compensating the victims of injurious behavior rests squarely on those who can prevent the losses at the lowest cost. Holding the low-cost avoider

---

[7]The legal standard of negligence has been laid down by Judge Learned Hand, 159 Federal Reporter 2d 169 (1947), where he defines *negligence* as the failure to take precautions (measures to avoid injury) if the cost of taking precautions is less than the expected cost of damages averted. In other words, as an economist would say, if the marginal costs are less than the marginal benefits. According to this principle, *negligence* is defined as failure to take adequate precautions in a situation where $C < pD$; where C is the cost of taking precautions, p is the probability that damages will occur without intervention, and D is the amount of the damages.

responsible for the costs of the injury should guarantee that efficient precautions will be taken to prevent such accidents in the future.

A third function of the tort system is to exact retribution on those guilty of negligent behavior. Many legal scholars will argue that the law should punish anyone responsible for an injury to another person for his or her actions. To the extent that the actions are intentional, only by assigning responsibility can we be sure that justice will be served.

The argument for punitive damages is based on the retribution function. Punitive damages serve the same purpose as criminal and civil penalties, such as jail sentences and fines, in the event that someone is guilty of particularly egregious or malicious behavior. In the case of large damage awards, punitive damages often make up a large percentage of the total compensation to the victim.[8] The U.S. legal system does fulfill the three functions of tort law—compensation, deterrence, and retribution—but at a very high administrative cost, upwards of 50–60 percent of the total amount awarded.

International Differences

The legal system for dealing with medical malpractice claims is markedly different in the United States than in other developed countries. These differences are, at least in part, responsible for the differences in the liability costs imposed on medical practitioners. As a percentage of gross domestic product, the United States spends two to three times more than the other advanced countries in the world to settle tort disputes.[9] Even though the legal climate abroad is generally less favorable to potential plaintiffs, the upward trend in the frequency and severity of claims seems to be a worldwide phenomenon.

Data on malpractice claims in other countries are less comprehensive than data available in the United States. The information in Table A9.1 indicates that the number and severity of malpractice claims is much higher in the United States than in either Canada or the United Kingdom. The number of claims per physician is roughly eight times higher in the United States than in Canada. Claims frequency in the United Kingdom, measured in terms of the population, varied across regions from 21 to 70 percent of the U.S. frequency.

Several important differences contribute to the differences in the size and frequency of claims. These include differences in legal rules, social values, and the costs of filing litigation. The differences are difficult to measure empirically, but their influence on the incentive structure affects the costs and benefits of filing lawsuits.

In theory, there is little difference in the negligence rule of liability across countries. Regardless of country, plaintiffs must show that negligent care from a medical provider caused an injury. More specifically, it must be shown that a duty of care existed, that the defendant failed to conform to the required standard of care either by act or by failure to act, that the plaintiff sustained damages, and that the breach of duty was the proximate cause of the injury.

Some evidence indicates that differences in the rate of surgical procedures have some bearing on the frequency of malpractice lawsuits. But differences in the rate of lawsuits cannot be fully explained by differences

TABLE A9.1 INTERNATIONAL COMPARISONS OF MALPRACTICE AWARDS ANNUAL CLAIMS FREQUENCY AND SEVERITY, 2001

	United States	Australia	Canada	United Kingdom
Claims per 100 physicians	7.67	4.72	1.90	6.00
Claims per 100,000 population	18	12	4	12
Average claim awarded (PPP U.S. dollars)	$265,103	$97,014	$249,750[1]	$411,171

Source: Anderson et al. (2005).
[1]Excluding a single large class action suit. If included, the value would be $309,417.

---

[8]Of course, if the defendant has insurance coverage that includes the payment of punitive damages, this function is not served efficiently.
[9]Tillinghast-Towers Perrin's (2006) analysis tracks tort costs worldwide and has found that in 2003, the U.S. system cost 250 percent of the average in the industrialized world. Tort costs amounted to 0.69 percent of GDP in the United Kingdom, 0.74 percent in France, 0.75 percent in Switzerland, 0.80 percent in Japan, 1.14 percent in Germany, and 2.22 percent in the United States.

in the rate of adverse surgical outcomes. Major differences in rules governing compensation determine the expected payoff from a lawsuit. Differences in punitive damages, caps on payments for pain and suffering, contingency fees for attorneys, and the U.S. rule on costs provide a greater incentive to sue.

Punitive damages, often a substantial portion of large awards in the United States, are rare in other countries. Awards for pain and suffering are typically subject to judicial caps. The cap in Canada, set at $100,000 (Canadian) in 1978 and indexed to the rate of inflation, has reached around $200,000. The contingency-fee system, used extensively in the United States, is used infrequently in Canada and is illegal in the United Kingdom. The English rule of costs, by which the loser pays court costs and all attorneys' fees, is the standard rule everywhere except the United States. The combined effect of these features lowers the expected return for a successful lawsuit and increases the expected cost of litigation for plaintiffs, which tends to discourage the initiation of lawsuits with little chance of success.

Most countries have uniform rules that govern tort claims nationwide. In contrast, the U.S. system has fostered the development of a diverse standard of law in each of the 50 states. A judge alone, without the aid of a jury, decides almost all medical malpractice cases in Canada. Canadian judges tend to hand out more modest awards than American juries in similar situations.

The major impact of the tort system on health care spending is not the direct cost of litigation. Roberts and Hoch (2007) estimate the direct cost of malpractice settlements may be as high as 0.3 percent of total health care spending. The link between malpractice litigation and health care spending is through the practice of "defensive medicine," defined as marginally beneficial care designed primarily to lower the risk of being sued. In practice, defensive medicine manifests itself in excess testing, diagnostic screening, and medical procedures.

Evidence from multiple studies provides a range of estimates measuring the impact of the threat of litigation on health care spending. Roberts and Hoch (2009) estimate that litigation adds at minimum 2.6 percent and as much as 10 percent to overall health care spending. Mello et al. (2010) estimate overall liability costs at 2.4 percent of total spending. Not only does the threat of litigation affect spending, Currie and MacLeod (2008) show that it affects clinical decision making and outcomes. Others indicate that this effect manifests itself primarily on diagnostic rather than therapeutic decision making (Kessler and McClellan, 2002; Sloan and Shadle, 2009). The threat of tort has grown with the growth in imaging technology (Baicker et al., 2007).

No one has a bigger stake in the outcome of this debate than the patients who ultimately pay the bills. If meaningful change is to happen, it will require our sincere efforts to ensure that the public interest is served instead of merely the special interest.

ISSUES IN MEDICAL CARE DELIVERY

SILICONE BREAST IMPLANT LITIGATION: A CASE OF RENT-SEEKING BEHAVIOR

Economic rent is the payment to a resource that exceeds its true opportunity cost. Ann O. Krueger (1974) introduced the concept as a way of explaining the use of scarce resources to secure monopoly profits as shown in the following diagram.

In a competitive environment, price, depicted by *PP*, reflects the underlying average cost of production. With demand *DD,* output would equal *Q.* Any distortion introduced into the market to raise price to *P'P'* will lower output to *Q'.* The dotted triangle depicts the social cost of the distortion measured by the lost consumer surplus. The shaded rectangle represents a transfer from consumers to producers or economic rent.

The case of the silicone-gel breast implant provides a classic case of rent-seeking behavior. From 1962 to 1992, somewhere between 1.0 and 2.2 million women received breast implants in the United States and Canada. A large percentage of these implants were provided for reconstructive surgery following mastectomy, but most were strictly for cosmetic augmentation.

In the early 1990s, a number of reports surfaced linking implants with a variety of illnesses, including lupus, scleroderma, joint swelling, and chronic fatigue. A December 10, 1990, broadcast of the CBS television show *Face-to-Face* entitled "Hazards of Silicone Breast Implants" heightened public awareness. The show presented a number of case reports claiming that implants were the cause of silicone poisoning in implant recipients. Those women whose implants were not yet leaking or ruptured were said to be carrying around "ticking time bombs."

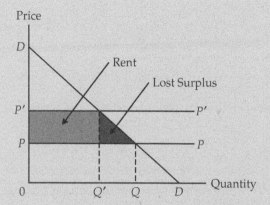

Where are the rents? As you might guess, the publicity sparked a firestorm of litigation. In addition to over 45 class action lawsuits, individual plaintiffs filed more than 19,000 individual product liability lawsuits nationwide, most claiming unspecified economic damages. In suits that specified damages, they ranged from $100,000 to $140 million. Although a number of these lawsuits were settled separately, a settlement in a national class action lawsuit provided a $4.5 billion settlement to members of the class of plaintiffs. Individual awards ranged from $105,000 to $1.4 million, based on the severity of the injury and age of the recipient.

Rents represent surplus transferred from customers of implant manufacturers to successful plaintiffs, their attorneys, and all the expert witnesses providing litigation support services in these cases. These "expert" witnesses included toxicologists, pathologists, and economists who made up to $500 per hour; many received over $250,000 for their testimony. Attorneys paid by the contingency-fee system received up to 40 percent of the damage awards. According to *Forbes* magazine, one Houston firm had over 2,000 implant clients, and a partner in that firm reportedly made over $40 million in 1994 on implant litigation (Alster, 1999).

An interesting feature of this episode in tort history is how silicone implants were ever approved for human use in the first place. The product, never tested on human subjects, had been in use for more than a decade when the FDA inherited jurisdiction with the passage of the Medical Devices Act in 1975. The product remained in use until 1992, pending the filing of safety data that were in fact never filed. The FDA, under intense pressure from the mounting case evidence concerning the product's safety, banned further use of the device in April 1992.

From a scientific viewpoint, case evidence is useful in formulating a theory but inadequate for testing a hypothesis. In other words, the 300 plus medical case studies in the English literature, while compelling emotionally, are merely descriptive and prove nothing. The scientific issue is causation. The only way to prove causation is to compile scientific evidence showing that implants contribute to the diseases in question—an issue that has so far been avoided by the courts.

Several basic research studies have shown how silicone gel may influence the immune system. Three notable attempts studied the impact of silicone implants on the immune system. The Nurses' Health Study (Sanchez-Guerrero et al., 1995) and the Women's Health Study (Hennekens et al., 1996) used self-reporting data to examine the relationship. To date the only major epidemiological study on the issue was performed at the Mayo Clinic (Gabriel et al., 1994). Based on these studies, it is clear that there is little or no evidence of an "association between breast implants and connective-tissue disease" and no evidence of "large risks of connective-tissue diseases following breast implants."

These studies have their critics, and, admittedly, such studies cannot be considered definitive. The original claim that silicone implants cause autoimmune diseases became implants cause "atypical" disease. This claim presents a problem for science, because atypical disease remains undefined. If it cannot be defined, it cannot be studied systematically. It therefore presents an even bigger problem for defendants in the courts, because the association between silicone implants and atypical disease cannot be disproved. To clear up the confusion, a federal judge appointed an independent panel of experts to examine the evidence and provide an opinion as to whether there is a connection between silicone implants and autoimmune diseases. Based on the panel's recommendation, the National Academy of Sciences' Institutes of Medicine declared in 1999 that implants—saline or silicone—do not cause disease. Still, concerns about the safety of implants and their related side effects abound. Recent studies indicate that most women will have at least one rupture within 11–15 years. Despite the warnings, at least 130,000 women have received implants annually between 1999 and 2003.

Moreover, the saga is not over. In 2003, an FDA committee recommended that silicone implants be made available to women who want them. The FDA lifted the ban on their use completely in 2006, and breast augmentation soon became the most frequently performed cosmetic procedure in the United States. In 2012 "gummy bear" implants were approved providing the market with "form stable" implants that will not leak even if ruptured. In that year over 70 percent of the 330,000 augmentation procedures used some type of silicone implant.

Sources: Ann O. Krueger, "The Political Economy of the Rent-Seeking Society," *American Economic Review* 64(3), June 1974, 291–303; Jorge Sanchez-Guerrero, et al., "Silicone Breast Implants and the Risk of Connective-Tissue Diseases and Symptoms," *The New England Journal of Medicine* 332(25), June 22, 1995, 1666–1670; Charles H. Hennekens, et al., "Self-Reported Breast Implants and Connective-Tissue Diseases in Female Health Professionals: A Retrospective Cohort Study," *Journal of the American Medical Association* 275(8), February 28, 1996, 616–621; and Sherine E. Gabriel, et al., "Risk of Connective-Tissue Diseases and Other Disorders after Breast Implantation," *The New England Journal of Medicine* 330(24), June 16, 1994, 1697–1702. Those interested in reading further on this topic may look at Marcia Angell, *Science on Trial: The Clash of Medical Evidence and the Law in the Breast Implant Case,* New York: Norton, 1996; and Norm Alster, "Getting the Middleman's Share," *Forbes* 154, July 4, 1999, 108–109.

References

Anderson, Gerald F., et al., "Health Spending in the United States and the Rest of the Industrialized World," *Health Affairs* 24(4), July 2005, 908–914.

Baicker, Katherine, et al., "Malpractice Liability Costs and the Practice of Medicine in the Medicare Program," *Health Affairs* 26(3), June 2007, 841–852.

Currie, Janet and W. Bentley MacLeod, "First Do No Harm? Tort Reform and Birth Outcomes," *Quarterly Journal of Economics* 123(2), May 2008, 795–830.

Hsiao, William C., et al., *A National Study of Resource-Based Relative Value Scales for Physician Services: Final Report* to the Health Care Financing Administration, publication 17-C-98795/1-03, Boston: Harvard University School of Public Health, 1988.

Kessler, Daniel P. and Mark B. McClellan, "How Liability Law Affects Medical Productivity," *Journal of Health Economics* 21(6), November 2002, 931–955.

Mello, Michelle M., et al., "National Costs of the Medical Liability System," *Health Affairs* 29(9), September 2010, 1569–1577.

Roberts, Brandon and Irving Hoch, "Malpractice Litigation and Medical Costs in the United States," *Health Economics* 18, 2009, 1394–1419.

Roberts, Brandon and Irving Hoch, "Medical Malpractice Litigation and Medical Costs in Mississippi," *Health Economics* 16, 2007, 841–859.

Sloan, Frank A. and John H. Shadle, "Is There Empirical Evidence for 'Defensive Medicine'? A Reassessment," *Journal of Health Economics* 28, 2009, 481–491.

Tillinghast-Towers Perrin, "U.S. Tort Costs and Cross-Border Perspectives: 2005 Update," 2006, available at http://www.legalreforminthenews.com/Reports/Tort_Costs_2005_Update.pdf (Accessed March 20, 2017).

CHAPTER **10**

The Hospital Services Market

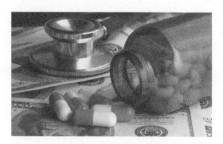

ISSUES IN MEDICAL CARE DELIVERY

THE HOSPITAL AS A FACTORY: LESSONS FROM INDIA

The U.S. Medicare price of coronary artery bypass surgery ranges between $20,000 and $40,000 depending on the complexity. Imagine a situation where you could purchase the same operation for one-tenth the cost. Impossible, you say. Look no further than the Narayana Health (NH) in Bangalore, India. What began as a 280-bed hospital has grown into a network of 26 hospitals with almost 7,000 beds in 16 cities across the country. One of over 20 fully accredited hospitals in India, the 1,000-bed Bangalore facility is part of a growing segment of international hospitals accredited by Joint Commission International employing the same standards used to judge the quality of U.S. hospitals.

Dr. Devi Shetty, director of NH, stepped onto the world stage in the early 1990s as Mother Teresa's personal cardiac surgeon. Trained in London at Guy's Hospital, one of the top medical facilities in Europe, Shetty returned to India in 1989 to open a heart hospital. NH now employs over 1,500 physicians, who have performed 100,000 cardiac surgeries and 250,000 cath lab procedures since 2001. A world leader in pediatric medicine, surgeons at the hospital perform more pediatric heart surgeries (almost 50 per day) than physicians at Children's Hospital, Boston.

The hospital's approach takes advantage of the **economies of scale** that come with the high volumes. The hospital uses the same diagnostic imaging equipment familiar to most U.S. facilities, but uses them more intensively, up to five times the rate at a typical U.S. hospital. And surgeons perform more procedures (four per day, six days a week), up to two times the average for U.S. surgeons. More volume does not place quality at risk. In fact, evidence seems to indicate that as doctors perform more surgeries, outcomes improve. Narayana reports lower 30-day mortality after bypass surgery (1.27 percent) than the U.S. average.

India's growing private hospital system targets the country's growing middle class. Pricing strategies allow the hospital to compete on both price and quality. Differential pricing is the norm, charging different segments of the population different prices based on ability to pay. This tiered pricing model allows the hospital to engage in value-based competition. High volumes, low overhead, and subsidies across segments of the patient population result in profit margins that exceed those of most U.S. hospitals.

In many ways, the expansion of the private hospital system in India mirrors the explosive growth of physician-owned hospitals in the United States in the early 2000s. Passage of the Affordable Care Act (ACA) in 2010 further regulated the U.S. hospital sector

economies of scale A situation in a production process where long run average costs decline as output expands.

 **KEY CONCEPT 8**
Efficiency

305

and actually stopped the licensing of additional beds in this segment of the market. U.S. regulation impedes the kind of organizational innovation that is so effective in the Indian market. However, these impediments do not extend beyond U.S. borders. Market forces in other parts of the world will eventually find a way to impact the U.S. market. Narayana has built a 200-bed hospital in the Cayman Islands, a one-hour flight from Miami, with plans to expand it to a 2,000-bed general hospital. With prices at one-half U.S. levels, it is only a matter of time before Americans demand that their health plans begin covering these foreign alternatives.

Sources: Greta Anand, "The Henry Ford of Heart Surgery," *Wall Street Journal*, November 25, 2009; Barak D. Richmond et al., "Lessons from India in Organizational Innovation: A Tale of Two Heart Hospitals," *Health Affairs* 27(5), September/October 2008, 1260–1270; and M. Madhaven, "Compassionate Heart, Business Mind," *Business Today*, May 25, 2014.

Flexner Report A 1910 report published as part of a critical review of medical education in the United States. The response of the medical establishment led to significant changes in the accreditation procedures of medical schools and an improvement in the quality of medical care.

The publication of the **Flexner Report** in 1910 served as a catalyst for general reform in medical care delivery. Nowhere are the effects more noticeable than in the hospital services industry. Hospitals, once notorious places more likely to spread diseases than cure them, are now the focal point of the medical care delivery system.

This chapter examines the market for hospital services. The first two sections provide a brief history of hospitals and an examination of the institutional setting in the United States. Following this is a discussion of the role of the private, not-for-profit hospital as the dominant organization in the industry. The chapter also examines several popular theories of hospital behavior, and finally, recent developments in the industry, in particular the trend toward multihospital systems.

A Brief History of American Hospitals[1]

Three important factors served to transform hospitals into the modern medical institutions they have become: the germ theory of disease, advances in medical technology, and increased urbanization. These changes have been accompanied by a dramatic change in patient expectations. No longer do patients seek a caring environment exclusively; they have come to expect a cure.

HTTP://

The AHA news is a weekly online publication of the AHA. Access this site at http://www.ahanews.com/ahanewsapp/index.jsp.

The development of the germ theory of disease, first articulated by Louis Pasteur in 1870, revolutionized the treatment of patients. His research recognized that diseases had specific causes rather than merely being effects of disequilibria or the result of moral turpitude. The search for causal factors required more elaborate testing and diagnostic services. Centralized medical care, bringing the patient to the practitioner, became a necessity.

New hospital technology, especially advances in surgical and diagnostic imaging, provided physicians with the tools that would revolutionize medical intervention. Anesthesia was first used in surgery in 1846. However, it was not until the adoption of antiseptic procedures, beginning in 1867, that the high rates of death from infection following surgery began to fall. The introduction of X-ray technology in the late 1800s, and more recently the development of more advanced imaging tools—such as computed tomography (CT) scans and magnetic resonance imaging (MRI)—have vastly improved the ability to diagnose injury and illness.

A third factor, urbanization, also played an important role in the centralization of medical facilities. Migration to the urban centers meant more one-person households and fewer extended-family living arrangements. People could no longer count on treatment at home.

---

[1]A more complete development of the history of the modern hospital can be found in Stevens (1989).

Home was an apartment building or boarding house and likely inappropriate for convalescence. Without family nearby, patients had no one to serve as caregiver anyway.

The modern hospital began to emerge in the twentieth century. Early in the century, the distinguished Flexner Report (1910) served as a pointed condemnation of medical education. In its wake, bogus medical schools were closed, standards became more stringent, and the goal of "scientific medicine" was formulated, leading to medical schools affiliating with hospitals and ultimately creating the teaching hospital.

The reforms continued throughout the 1920s, aimed at driving incompetent physicians out of the profession. Physician licensing became more structured, and hospital admission privileges were restricted to members of certain medical societies. The decade also saw the role of a nurse change dramatically. Prior to the 1928 reforms in nursing education, poorly trained volunteers or nurses in training did most of the in-hospital nursing. Trained nurses established community practices that directly competed with hospitals. After the reforms, nurses were no longer competitors with the hospitals, they were employees.

The reliance on patient fees caused severe financial problems for hospitals during the Great Depression. The introduction of private health insurance during the decade of the 1930s would later transform medical care financing. Developed by Baylor University Hospital in Dallas, Texas, and modeled after a prepaid hospital plan for Dallas schoolteachers, the American Hospital Association (AHA) established the first Blue Cross plan—and soon had a virtual monopoly in hospital insurance. The decade also saw a revolution in the pharmaceutical industry. The most important advance was the development of sulfa drugs and penicillin. For the first time, physicians had the power to cure diseases that resulted from infection.

Wartime demands resulted in a sharp increase in the number of physicians and nurses in the 1940s. World War II provided a unique opportunity to improve skills and to develop new techniques. The federal government became actively involved in providing hospital care. The passage of the Hill-Burton Act of 1946 dedicated the government to replacing an aging hospital infrastructure that had deteriorated during the Depression and war. With priority given to hospital construction in rural and poor parts of the country, Hill-Burton served to create a climate in the hospital sector that made uncompensated care an expected element of the overall health care financing mechanism.

collective bargaining
The negotiation process whereby representatives of employers and employees agree upon the terms of a labor contract, including wages and benefits.

Precluded from offering higher wages because of rigid price controls, companies were forced to compete for workers by offering better benefit packages that included group health insurance. A ruling by the National Labor Relations Board in 1948 made health insurance a permanent feature in labor negotiations by ruling that it was subject to **collective bargaining**. Tax deductible for the employer and tax exempt for the employee, group health plans now cover over one-half of all workers with private health insurance.

Vaccines against polio and rubella discovered in the 1950s marked the true beginning of high-technology medicine. These developments, combined with the widespread use of antibiotics, helped change the image of medicine. Physicians were no longer practitioners with limited knowledge, who were able only to ease suffering. We now expect to leave the doctor's office with a cure. The anticipated number of doctor and hospital visits during a person's lifetime increased significantly, along with the concern over how to pay for them. The result was an increased demand for private health insurance.

In 1964, Congress passed legislation creating Medicare and Medicaid, making the federal government a major purchaser of health care services. No longer did providers have to worry about whether the elderly and the indigent would have money to pay their bills; provider earnings rose rapidly. Today, over half of provider income originates from government sources.

The decade also witnessed the beginnings of the investor-owned, for-profit hospital system. Prior to the 1960s, for-profit hospitals were small, rare, and established to benefit clearly defined patient groups. Until the creation of Medicare and Medicaid, the general population with large numbers of elderly and uninsured was not a dependable source of revenue. Thus, Medicare and Medicaid, serving as a stable funding source, actually facilitated the development of the for-profit hospital sector.

The 1970s witnessed the expansion of hospitals and clinics, medical school admissions, foreign-educated doctors, open-heart surgery, organ transplantation, and the use of technology. The total number of surgical procedures increased from 14.8 million in 1972 to 51.4 million in 2010. Much of the increase may have been essential. Nevertheless, it was an ominous sign when the procedures most lucrative to physicians under the payment system in place escalated at the fastest rate.

The intensity of medical interventions also increased dramatically. Intensive care units (ICUs) became widely used. Trauma centers were established in most areas. Although the trauma center is one of those expenses that may be worth the cost, the ICU in contrast has created a painful dilemma. Originally designed for temporary use following shock or surgery, its function has been extended to the terminally ill and the declining elderly—patients with little likelihood of recovery.

All the developments of the decade shared one thing: They were expensive. Health care expenditures increased at an average annual rate of 13 percent during the 1970s. By the end of the decade, Medicare expenditures were growing at an annual rate of over 20 percent.

certificate-of-need
Regulations that attempt to avoid the costly duplication of hospital services. Providers are required to secure a CON before undertaking major expansion of facilities or services.

Concerned by the spending growth, state rate-setting legislation and certificate-of-need (CON) laws were used more frequently. CON laws required governmental approval for capital expansion projects in hospitals, including increases in bed capacity and acquisition of new medical equipment. The avoidance of costly duplication of services and the reduction of excess capacity were used to justify such restrictions. In practice, CON laws served to reduce competition and actually limited the entry of HMOs and nursing homes into some markets (Mayo and McFarland, 1989).

By 1982, health care expenditures exceeded 10 percent of gross domestic product (GDP) for the first time. To slow the rate of growth in federal expenditures, Medicare initiated a new hospital reimbursement scheme based on the principal diagnosis rather than services performed. Implemented in 1983, diagnosis-related groups (DRGs) have had profound effects on the hospital industry, moving a large percentage of the financing from retrospective to **prospective payment**.

prospective payment
Payment determined prior to the provision of services. A feature of many health plans that provide capitated payment to providers.

Managed care was the dominant factor affecting medical care delivery during the decade of the 1990s. Hospitals are no longer the revenue generators they once were; instead, they have become cost centers. **Horizontal integration**, characterized by hospital mergers and consolidations, transformed an industry that was once highly fragmented with many stand-alone facilities into one in which multihospital systems are common. An industry characterized by underutilization and overstaffing now experiences a move toward integrated systems. With administrators downsizing in the name of efficiency, many are concerned about the quality of care and the provision of indigent care.

horizontal integration
The merger of two or more firms that produce the same good or service.

The new millennium has witnessed expansions in government involvement in health care with Congress enacting an outpatient prescription drug benefit for Medicare recipients and attempting to provide coverage to virtually all uninsured children through the State Children's Health Insurance Plan. Physicians, searching for ways to boost their income, became active investors in physician-owned facilities, including specialty hospitals and ambulatory surgery centers (ASCs). The presidential elections of 2008 proved to be a watershed event that resulted in major reform for the U.S. health care system with the eventual passage of the ACA in 2010.

The U.S. Institutional Setting

Hospitals are by far the most important institutional setting for the provision of medical services. In 2015, U.S. hospital expenditures totaled more than $1.04 trillion, approximately one-third of national health care spending and almost 6 percent of GDP.

Hospital Classification

Hospitals are classified according to the length of stay, the major type of service delivered, and the type of ownership. Hospitals with an average length of stay of less than 30 days are short-term hospitals. Long-term hospitals are those with an average length of stay of over 30 days.

Community Hospitals   Community hospitals are the most common hospital classified by types of services offered. Under the current classification scheme adopted in 1972, a *community hospital* is defined as a short-stay hospital, providing not only general services, but also specialty care, including cardiology, obstetrics and gynecology; eye, ear, nose, and throat care; and rehabilitation and orthopedic services. Other hospitals are classified according to specialized services offered. These include hospitals that provide psychiatric services and hospitals that treat individuals with tuberculosis and other respiratory diseases.

Community hospitals are also classified according to control or ownership. The most prominent form of ownership is the private not-for-profit hospital, which represented 58.4 percent of all hospitals in 2013. This figure understates somewhat the importance of this organizational form, which tends to be larger on average than the other hospital types, controlling 68 percent of all beds. For-profit hospitals represent 21.3 percent of all community hospitals and 16.9 percent of all beds. The remaining 20.3 percent of community hospitals and 14.7 percent of beds are government owned, usually by the states. Community hospital figures do not include 213 federal hospitals with 38,747 beds.

Over 90 percent of all nonfederal hospitals are community hospitals. Table 10.1 provides selected measures for the community hospital. The number of community hospitals in existence peaked in the early 1980s. Since that time, the decline has been about 1 percent per year, until 2014 when the number stood at 4,926. Most of the decline has come from the small and rural hospitals, many of which had been government owned. The number of beds experienced a similar downward trend. In fact, since the mid-1980s, the number of beds has declined faster than the number of hospitals. The number of beds per 1,000 population stood at 4.4 in 1980. The steady decline since then left the United States with 2.5 beds per 1,000 in 2014.

Despite the number of hospitals declining, the number of beds falling, and physicians admitting fewer patients, the average occupancy rates have also fallen dramatically. In 1980, on average over three-fourths of all beds were occupied. That fraction had fallen to barely two-thirds by 1990 and further decreased to 62.9 percent in 2013.

The goal of cost control is responsible for the other major trends evident from the table. Between 2000 and 2013, the cost per hospital day increased from $1,149 to $2,184. This increase translates into an annual compound rate of 4.6 percent, almost twice the annual increase in consumer prices. Cost per stay increased from $6,649 to $12,015 or an annual compound rate of 4.1 percent. To counter the rising costs, the focus has been on controlling inpatient hospital stays, the most expensive episode of care usually encountered. With admissions down, outpatient visits have increased substantially, from 202.3 million in 1980 to 693.1 million in 2014. Almost 90 percent of all hospitals have outpatient departments that perform 65.9 percent of all surgical operations. As a result, the average length of stay for inpatient services has fallen from 7.6 days to 5.5 days over the same period.

TABLE 10.1 SELECTED CHARACTERISTICS OF COMMUNITY HOSPITAL CHARACTERISTICS, VARIOUS YEARS

Measure	1970	1980	1990	2000	2005	2010	2014
Number of hospitals	5,859	5,904	5,420	4,915	4,936	4,985	4,926
Beds (000)	848.2	992.0	929.4	823.6	802.3	804.9	786.9
Beds per 1,000 population	4.2	4.4	3.7	2.9	2.7	2.6	2.5
Admissions (000)	29,252	36,143	31,181	33,089	35,239	35,149	33,067
Admissions per 1,000 population	144.0	159.6	125.4	117.6	118.9	113.8	103.7
Resident U.S. population (millions)	203.2	226.5	248.7	281.4	296.4	308.7	318.9
Average length of stay (days)	7.7	7.6	7.2	5.8	5.6	5.4	5.5
Percent occupancy	78.0	75.4	66.8	63.9	67.3	64.5	62.9
Outpatient visits (millions)	133.5	202.3	301.3	521.4	584.4	651.4	693.1
Outpatient visits per admission	4.57	5.60	9.66	15.76	16.6	18.5	21.0
Outpatient surgeries as a percent of total	–	16.3	50.5	62.7	63.3	63.6	65.9
Cost per day ($)	74	245	687	1,149	1,522	1,910	2,184
Cost per admission ($)	605	1,851	4,947	6,649	8,535	10,314	12,015

Sources: *Statistical Abstracts of the United States*, various years and National Center for Health Statistics, *Health, United States*, various years.

POLICY ISSUE
Compared with not-for-profit hospitals, for-profit clinics operate under a different set of requirements with respect to the provision of free care.

Physician-Owned Facilities   Even as the number of hospitals has decreased, the number of physician-owned ASCs, diagnostic testing facilities, and specialty hospitals have increased dramatically. In 2000, physicians had ownership interest in over 3,028 ASCs, 1,784 diagnostic testing facilities, and 56 specialty hospitals (Iglehart, 2005). By 2003, the number of ASCs had increased 23 percent to 3,735 and the number of diagnostic testing facilities had increased 35 percent to 2,403. Today, there are over 5,000 ASCs performing over 23 million surgeries annually.

The Government Accountability Office (GAO) defines a *specialty hospital* as one in which more than two-thirds of its Medicare patients were treated in no more than two DRG categories or were classified in one of the surgical DRGs. Five types of specialty hospitals were identified: cardiac, orthopedic, surgical, women's, and other. Not surprisingly, these areas are among the most profitable for hospitals in general.

Physician ownership has increased competition in the hospital industry, encouraging improvements in efficiency and productivity and potentially lowering costs to everyone involved. The bigger issue, however, may be the impact of these facilities on the ability of hospitals to provide free care for the indigent and uninsured, an expense estimated at over $35 billion in 2015, or about 4.2 percent of total hospital revenue (AHA, 2016b). Many are for-profit and do not have a legal requirement to provide charity care. By taking only fully insured patients—a practice called *cream skimming*—they reduce the operating base of not-for-profit hospitals.

There are currently 238 physician-owned specialty hospitals in the United States, down from 265 before passage of the ACA (which prohibits the establishment of new physician-owned facilities). About two-thirds are located in seven states, including Arizona, California, Kansas, Louisiana, Oklahoma, South Dakota, and Texas—states that do not require CON permission to open new facilities. Most are located in urban areas, are organized as for-profit entities, lack emergency departments, and generally do not accept

Medicaid patients or the uninsured. Specialty hospitals tend to have higher financial margins than general hospitals due primarily to greater efficiencies and higher productivity.

In general, for patients covered by Medicare and Medicaid, federal law does not permit referrals to freestanding facilities by the physician owners of those facilities. One exception to this prohibition is called the *whole-hospital exception*, in which physicians are allowed to hold ownership interest in an entire hospital. Competing directly with hospitals, freestanding facilities may have a competitive advantage, but both rely on referrals from physicians. Concerned with the rapid growth of physician-owned specialty hospitals, in 2003 Congress enacted an 18-month moratorium on new facilities to allow the Centers for Medicare and Medicaid Services (CMS) to study the effects of these entities on general hospitals. The ACA included an outright ban on further expansion of the physician ownership in specialty hospitals that treat Medicare and Medicaid patients. Facilities that treat only private-pay patients are free to build and expand.[2]

Teaching Hospitals   About 20 percent of all hospitals in the United States have an affiliation with one or more of the nation's 141 medical schools and sponsor at least one residency training program. More than 400 hospitals are members of the Council of Teaching Hospitals of the Association of American Medical Colleges. To qualify for membership in this association, a hospital must participate in at least four approved residency programs. Nationwide, 80 of these teaching hospitals are university owned, and 70 are operated by the Department of Veterans Affairs (AAMC, 1999).

Most of the teaching hospitals are located in major metropolitan areas with populations in excess of 1 million. On average, they have more beds, longer patient stays, and higher occupancy rates than their nonteaching counterparts, with predictable results—higher costs. Not only are teaching and research expensive, these facilities have a significant presence in the inner city and often find their emergency rooms and outpatient clinics filled with uninsured patients seeking free care.

Recognizing the legitimacy of these higher costs of education and research, the federal government provides subsidies, both direct and indirect, to supplement hospital revenues. Direct subsidies include stipends for residents, salaries for teaching physicians, grants for research, and overhead payments for administrative expenses. Indirect subsidies are provided in the form of higher reimbursement rates for Medicare patients. Nevertheless, with cutbacks in Medicare reimbursements, teaching hospitals are finding that they, too, must respond to the prospects of a more competitive marketplace.

POLICY ISSUE

The nation's teaching hospitals shoulder a disproportionate share of the burden of providing free care to the indigent and uninsured.

KEY CONCEPT 7

Competition

Hospital Spending

The growth in the hospital sector can be seen more clearly upon examining the change in expenses for community hospitals (excluding new construction) and the total hospital sector. Hospital spending has increased from $9.2 billion in 1960 to over $1.04 trillion in 2015. The average growth rates in spending were well over 10 percent per year through much of the 1980s. Since then spending has abated somewhat, increasing about 6 percent annually since 2000.

The moderation in spending growth may be in part attributable to the introduction of prospective payment in 1983. Hospital spending had increased to almost 40 percent of

---

[2]Physician Hospitals of America and Texas Spine and Joint Hospital filed a lawsuit in February 2011 that the courts declare unconstitutional the section of the ACA prohibiting any new construction or expansion of existing physician-owned facilities. Construction at 45 different facilities around the country stopped at the end of 2010 due to licensing restrictions, including facilities owned by the plaintiffs.

total health care expenditures by 1985. Since that time, hospital spending has fallen to 32.3 percent of total health care expenditures.

Third-party payers cover most hospital services. Government sources pay 47.8 percent of all hospital spending, and Medicare and Medicaid provide over 80 percent of that amount. Private insurance pays about 39 percent, and patients pay 3 percent out of pocket. The remainder is paid from other private funds, primarily from charitable donations and miscellaneous hospital revenues (gift shops, parking, and cafeterias). The patient share of hospital spending, 3 cents out of every dollar, has fallen over the past half-century from almost 21 cents in 1960.

With Medicare and Medicaid paying such a large percentage of the total hospital bill, government reimbursement rules play a big role in determining the financial stability of the hospital sector. Pressure from Congress to slow the rate of spending has contributed to a complicated system of subsidies and cross-subsidies among payers. The AHA (2016a) reported that in the aggregate Medicare paid 88.5 percent of the actual costs incurred by hospitals in 2014, and Medicaid paid 90 percent. In addition to these underpayments, hospitals provided billions of dollars in uncompensated care to the uninsured. Patients covered by private insurance paid 144 percent of actual costs incurred in treating them, a practice that some call *cost shifting*.

★ **KEY CONCEPT 5**
Markets and Pricing

Cost Shifting: Theory and Practice

How do hospitals provide free care to the uninsured? How can a hospital afford to provide care to some patients at prices substantially below the price paid by those who have private insurance? One popular claim is that hospitals merely shift the cost of care for the uninsured and underinsured to private pay patients. Is this practice merely a form of price discrimination, or are privately insured patients paying higher prices to subsidize care for everyone else?

Cost shifting assumes that capacity-constrained medical providers are able to offer free care to some patients knowing that they can pass the excess costs on to privately insured patients. The cost-shift theory is used in policy arguments because of its intuitive appeal, but like much of the conventional wisdom in health care, it is essentially unsubstantiated (Reinhardt, 2011).

The Theory of Cost Shifting

★ **KEY CONCEPT 6**
Supply and Demand

We can gain insights into the issues surrounding the cost-shift theory using a simple model of hospital behavior. In the diagram, a hospital treating only private patients will have a demand curve of D_P and a marginal revenue curve of MR_P. Assuming profit (or surplus) maximization, the hospital will set MR_P equal to MC and provide Q_1 services at P_1.

Legally, a hospital is obligated to accept patients that do not cover the fully allocated cost of their care. Consider the case of Medicare patients (the largest group of below-cost patients in most hospitals). The actual Medicare payment is a fixed price P_M, represented by the demand curve D_M and marginal revenue curve MR_M. The hospital is faced with a new demand curve equal to D_P down to point a, dropping down to D_M thereafter. More importantly, the new marginal revenue curve is MR_P to point b and then becomes MR_M. Profit is maximized where $MR_M = MC$, providing Q_T services. The hospital sees Q_2 private patients and charges them a higher price P_2 $(>P_1)$. The $(Q_T - Q_2)$ Medicare patients will be provided medical care at a price equal to P_M. (Note, beyond point b the marginal revenue from Medicare patients, MR_M, is greater than that from private patients, MR_P.)

★ **KEY CONCEPT 3**
Marginal Analysis

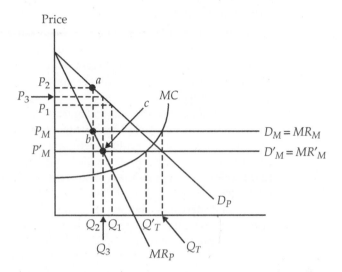

What happens when Medicare lowers the payment rates to hospitals? In the diagram earlier, the Medicare price falls to P'_M and the Medicare demand and marginal revenue curves fall accordingly. The hospital's marginal revenue curve changes to MR_p down to point c and MR'_M thereafter. Now, more private patients are seen (Q_3) and the price they pay (P_3) is lower but still greater than P_1. Likewise, fewer Medicare patients are served ($Q'_T - Q_3$).

This analysis seems to indicate that in theory the government payment mechanism has an impact on the amount private patients pay for hospital services. When Medicare lowers the rates paid to hospitals for treating the elderly, there is downward pressure on prices paid by everyone else.

A separate line of reasoning views the price differentials between private insurance and Medicare as classic price discrimination. Suppose that the hospital had constant marginal cost and significant excess capacity. In that case, the hospital would treat each payer group as separate markets. Under those conditions, changes in the payment structure for Medicare would have no impact on prices paid by the private sector. A second issue that could be examined deals with how low the Medicare price can fall before the elderly find themselves priced out of the market. If payment rates are set below the intersection of MR_p and MC, the hospital will find it unprofitable to treat Medicare patients, period, and will likely do everything legally possible to discourage their admission.

The alternative explanation is the standard model of price discrimination. The first requirement for a firm to practice some form of price discrimination is a degree of market power, the ability to charge higher prices without losing all your customers. The ability to charge different prices to different customers requires that the firm must be able to segment its market by some measure of willingness to pay. Classic Ramsey pricing (1927) accomplishes this by identifying market segments with different price elasticities and charging progressively higher prices to those customers with more inelastic demand. Additionally, those customers who pay lower prices must not have the ability to resell their purchases to those customers who are required to pay higher prices. Finally, the firm must have the capacity to absorb the segment that pays the lower price without crowding out the segment that pays the higher price. Cost shifting is a form of price discrimination, but price discrimination is not necessarily cost shifting.

The Practice of Cost Shifting

It is easy to understand why a person might think that private insurance is covering the shortfall caused by low payment rates from Medicare and Medicaid. The fact that the two public programs pay only 90 percent of hospital costs while private insurance pays 140 percent, however, does not prove cost shifting. It simply shows price discrimination across categories of payers.

Taken at face value, the data in Figure 10.1 suggest a negative correlation between the payment-to-cost ratios paid by privately insured patients and Medicare and Medicaid patients. The simple correlation coefficient between private payers' payment to cost ratio and that of Medicare is −0.91; for Medicaid it is −0.68, both statistically significant. Frakt (2011) cautions accepting the cost-shift theory based on this univariate approach because other factors may play a more causal role. Institutional reputation or differences in market size and share may play an important role in a hospital's ability to negotiate favorable payment rates with private payers. These price differentials may look like cost shifting, but they are primarily the result of differences in bargaining power between providers of medical care and those who pay for medical care.

For this reason, many economists are skeptical about the cost-shift theory because it implies that providers do not fully use their market power when bargaining with private payers over prices and somehow tap into this pool of unexploited revenues only when government lowers Medicare payment rates.

The empirical evidence examining the extent of the cost shift is inconclusive. Dranove (1988) found that 50 percent of Medicare payment cuts in Illinois were shifted, but later Dranove et al. (1998) found no evidence of cost shifting in California. Using data from the late 1980s to early 1990s, Cutler (1998) estimates 100 percent cost shifting. Others using data from the same period find only modest cost shifting (Clement, 1998; Zwanziger et al., 2000). And using more recent data, the cost-shift estimates range from 0 to 50 percent (Cutler, 1998; Zwanziger and Bamezai, 2006).

The wide variation in empirical estimates has not deterred proponents of the cost-shift theory from spreading their message. A Milliman report (Fox and Pickering, 2008) commissioned jointly by health insurance and hospital industries is widely presented as evidence of

FIGURE 10.1
Hospital Payment-to-
Cost Ratios

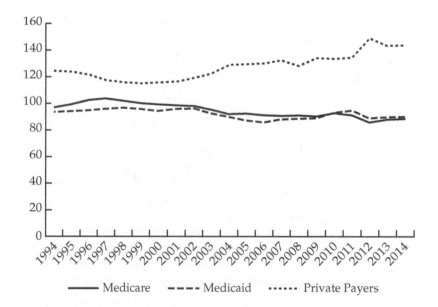

the extent of cost shifting. Results are based on the assumption that in the absence of cost shifting operating margins would be the same for all payers. As a result, the estimated cost shift to private payers in 2007 was $51 billion in the hospital sector and $38 billion by physicians. Of course, low Medicare and Medicaid payments are blamed for the shift.

APPLIED MICRO METHODS

ARE HOSPITALS ABLE TO COST SHIFT?

Background

Even with the large number of theoretical and empirical studies attempting to explain and measure the extent of hospital cost shifting, experts still disagree on its economic rationale and whether hospitals engage successfully in the practice. In light of the mixed evidence, Wu (2010) took advantage of a natural experiment created by the Medicare spending cuts implemented by the Balanced Budget Act (BBA) of 1997. Did hospitals respond to the Medicare payment cuts by shifting costs to private payers or did they address the challenge in some other way?

Two possible explanations for cost shifting serve as the basis of most empirical studies: the market power model and the strategic behavior model. Advocates of the market power approach argue that two conditions must exist for cost shifting to be possible: Hospitals must have some degree of market power and prices to private payers must be below profit-maximizing price levels. The strategy approach models a sequential pricing game played by public and private payers. In it the public payer strategically sets prices low knowing that private payers will compensate the hospitals for the shortfall.

Methods

Combining data from eight sources, Wu was able to construct a database of 1,400 urban hospitals for her analysis. The paper makes two important contributions to the cost-shift literature. First, it measures variations in the BBA revenue shocks according to a hospital's share of privately insured patients. Second, it simulates a Medicare financial loss index to capture the exogenous revenue losses due to changes in the Medicare DRG payment rates and uses it as an instrumental variable (IV) for the actual change in Medicare price and revenue from 1996 to 2000.

The IV regression controls for the possible endogeneity between changes in Medicare revenues and changes on private revenues. The outcome variable is the change in private payment per discharge between 1996 and 2000. The treatment effect is the instrumented BBA revenue shock. Covariates include the importance of private payers, hospital ownership (for profit or not for profit) at the individual and market level, HMO penetration, hospital bed size, and market concentration (measured by the Hirschman-Herfindahl index).

Results

Wu's empirical approach is a direct test of the market power hypothesis and the strategic behavior hypothesis. If the market power hypothesis is true, hospitals with a larger percentage of privately insured patients are better able to cost shift because of greater bargaining power. If the strategic behavior hypothesis is true, hospitals with a greater percentage of private patients are less able to shift costs, because they have already made the price/quality decision. The results are summarized as follows:

- *The ability to cost shift depends on the hospital's bargaining power with private payers. Hospitals with a favorable payer mix (large volume of privately insured patients relative to Medicare patients) are better able to cost shift.*
- *Hospitals in market areas with a higher percentage of for-profit hospitals are less likely to practice cost shifting, regardless of individual ownership type.*

■ *Hospitals with average reliance on privately insured patients were able to shift 21 per-cent of the BBA revenue shock to private payers. Hospitals at the 90th percentile of the private/Medicare payer mix were able to shift 37 percent of the BBA shortfall. Those at the 10th percentile shifted only 5 percent.*

Discussion

Cost shifting does exist to some extent, but the majority of hospitals have a limited ability to shift costs to private payers. Cost shifting is greater in hospitals with a large volume of privately insured patients and is less in hospitals in areas dominated by for-profit hospitals. Hospitals absorbed most of the BBA revenue shock of 1997 through changes in hospital operations and services: reducing operating costs to improve efficiency, eliminating less profitable service lines, reducing the provision of free care, and selectively lowering the quality of care in some cases. A hospital's market power dominates all other factors in its ability to negotiate prices with private payers.

Source: Vivian Y. Wu, "Hospital Cost Shifting Revisited: New Evidence from the Balanced Budget Act of 1997," *International Journal of Health Care Finance and Economics* 10, 2010, 61–83.

Structure of the Hospital Market

KEY CONCEPT 7
Competition

Economics predicts that competition in most markets improves economic welfare. This improvement in economic welfare comes about as a result of lower prices, improved efficiency, and higher quality. But does this prediction hold true in the hospital sector? Before answering that question, maybe we should explore how competitive the hospital sector is in the first place.

Competition may be viewed from the perspective of how well a market fits the characteristics of the perfectly competitive model. Applying the discussion from Chapter 2, competition depends on the number of firms operating in the market, the nature of the product or services offered, the relative ease of entering the market with a competing firm, and the amount of information available to consumers.

HTTP://
HCA owns and operates over 164 hospitals and 106 outpatient surgery centers in 20 states and Great Britain. A for-profit corporation, HCA's strategy is to build comprehensive networks of medical services in local markets and to integrate various services to deliver patient care with maximum efficiency. Check it out at http://hcahealth-care.com/.

Hospital markets may not fit the competitive model very well, because so many of the structural characteristics of perfect competition are violated. Local markets, where most hospital services are purchased, typically have a limited number of hospitals.[3] Services are not standardized across hospitals. In fact, hospitals expend a considerable amount of resources to differentiate themselves from their rivals. Relatively uninformed consumers, who for the most part leave the decision making to their physicians, characterize the decision-making process. Third-party insurance pays for most of the care, leaving patients insensitive to price differences.

No theoretical basis is available for determining the minimum number of hospitals needed to sustain a competitive environment. How many providers are needed to promote competition? In many metropolitan areas, numerous hospitals provide a complete range of medical services, conveniently located within a short distance of perhaps several hundred thousand residents. For example, the Dallas-Fort Worth metroplex, with a population of 6.5 million in 2011, had 134 hospitals, most located within a reasonable commute of one another. In fact, over 45 percent of the population of the United States lives in metropolitan areas with over a million inhabitants. Based on the number of hospitals per 1,000 inhabitants nationwide, a metropolitan area of this size would have approximately 65 hospitals.

KEY CONCEPT 9
Market Failure

---

[3]The markets for both primary and secondary care tend to be local in nature. The market for tertiary care, in contrast, is regional or even national in scope.

TABLE 10.2 POPULATION DISTRIBUTION, UNITED STATES, 2000

Number of inhabitants	Percent of population
Rural	20.8
Urban less than 50,000	10.5
Urban 50,000 to 200,000	10.4
Greater than 200,000	58.3

Source: U.S. Census Bureau, 2000.

Approximately 60 percent of the U.S. population live in areas with more than 200,000 inhabitants (see Table 10.2), a minimum size necessary to provide a full range of acute care hospital services to the surrounding community. This size area could likely support three to four community hospitals.

ISSUES IN MEDICAL CARE DELIVERY

POPULATION REQUIRED TO SUPPORT A HOSPITAL

The gap in the availability of health care services between urban and rural areas has increased substantially with the recent changes in health care delivery, including improved transportation services, expanded use of outpatient services, and the increased use of medical technology. Access to health care services in a community is largely determined by the presence of a hospital. The empirical evidence seems to indicate that rural communities are underserved relative to their urban counterparts. Does it make more sense to bring medical services to rural communities, or is it more efficient to bring rural residents to urban centers, where medical services can be delivered more effectively?

Using 1996 cross-sectional data on hospital locations in Texas, Henderson and Taylor (2003) estimated the impact of patient demand and rural isolation on the availability of hospital services. Drawing from a large body of literature called *central place theory*, they estimated the minimum market size, or population threshold, needed to support any given number of hospitals. Their results suggest that the number of hospitals in a given geographic area depends on area demand patterns, usually measured by population size, population density, per capita income, and factors affecting transportation costs, measured by rural isolation.

The empirical results suggest that the typical community in Texas, one that is 47 miles from the nearest metropolitan area with a per capita income of $18,000, must have a population of 35,675 to support a single community hospital and a population of over 80,000 to support two. Results also identify a noticeable trade-off between per capita income and population. Communities with higher per capita income require fewer residents to support a hospital. As per capita income approaches $30,000, the number of residents required to support a hospital falls below 20,000.

Many of the services available in the hospital setting are considered *higher-ordered services*, those services that are expensive to offer and require specialized resources to provide. Theory predicts that higher-ordered services will cluster in geographic areas that can support them, driving down the average cost of providing the service. As a result, the number of people required to support a hospital actually declines as a community becomes more urbanized due to these so-called agglomeration economies.

Source: James W. Henderson and Beck A. Taylor, "Rural Isolation and the Availability of Hospital Services," *Journal of Rural Studies* 19, 2003, 363–372.

The fact that physicians make most of the important decisions regarding hospital care may be a problem if demand inducement is extensive. As you may recall, most of the research has shown that physicians tend to be responsible agents for their patients. Even though patients pay only a small percentage of their hospital bills and may be unconcerned about prices, the third-party payers are concerned and expend a great deal of time and resources to control spending.

Is the hospital market competitive? Several attempts have been made to examine the issue empirically. Held and Pauly (1983) found little evidence of price competition among hospitals. They do seem to compete, but competition is based on quality of care and other amenities, not price. Robinson and colleagues (1988) could find competition only on certain nonprice aspects of the hospital stay, in particular, longer stays in regions where there are more hospitals. Following this line of reasoning, research indicates that as competition increases in the hospital sector, spending tends to increase (Luft et al., 1986; Robinson and Luft, 1987).

Feldman and Dowd (1986) approached the question from a different perspective. They suggested that the answer to the question could be determined by estimating the price elasticity of demand for individual hospitals. Price elasticities close to infinity, or at least those significantly greater than 1, would provide evidence for competitive markets. Using data from the early 1980s, they concluded that certain patient groups, especially Medicare patients, had no price sensitivity at all. Thus, hospital markets did not seem to be competitive.

Although early empirical evidence does not seem to support the hypothesis that hospital markets are competitive, the research was conducted prior to the recent expansion of managed care as a way of organizing and financing medical care delivery. As you may recall from Chapter 8, these changes have had a significant impact on the nature of competition in medical care delivery. The use of DRGs began to put pressure on hospitals in the mid-1980s to limit the use of nonprice competitive strategies that had become so prevalent. The expanded use of prospective payment in managed care has resulted in more price competition. The relationship between payer and provider is changing dramatically, characterized by aggressive negotiation over prices. Some hospital markets may be more competitive than others, but all are experiencing increased competition.

Back to the original question: Will increased competition in the hospital sector improve economic welfare? The answer to this question is rife with policy implications, particularly with respect to mergers, acquisitions, and collaborative decisions regarding services offered. There are two views on this issue. The first argues that increased competition leads to a "medical arms race" and the provision of services of questionable medical necessity. Two factors play an important role in this race: First, patients pay only a small percentage of their hospital costs; second, the prices paid for services are highly regulated with over half of hospital services paid by Medicare and Medicaid. Because patient demand is price inelastic, hospitals do not practice price competition. Rather they compete for patients by providing more services and higher-quality services than patients would demand under more normal conditions. Excessive quality is inefficient and does not always improve economic welfare. The alternative view argues that increased competition in the hospital sector yields the same benefits to economic welfare that it does in any other market; namely, lower prices, increased efficiency, and improved quality.

Early empirical research by Feldstein (1971) and Robinson and Luft (1985) provided support for the existence of a medical arms race in the hospital sector. Later research by Pauly (1987) and Dranove, Shanley, and Simon (1992) supported the alternative view that competition in the hospital sector actually improved economic welfare by lowering prices and costs. Recent empirical evidence has cleared up this ambiguity to some extent. Dranove and White (1994) identified a trend beginning in the mid-1980s in which increasing competition in the U.S. hospital sector lowered both price and cost. More recently, Gaynor and Haas-Wilson (1999) and Keeler, Melnick, and Zwanziger (1999) confirmed these results. Together, their research documented the price-reducing effects of competition in both the for-profit and not-for-profit sectors. Kessler and McClellan (2000), correcting for certain empirical shortcomings of the previous research, found that increased competition in the hospital sector did increase prices and costs in the 1980s, lending support to the medical arms race explanation. At the same time, this quality-based competition resulted in improvements in medical outcomes for some patients, leaving unanswered the question of whether competition improved economic welfare. However, they proceeded to find that competition in the 1990s not only increased quality in the hospital sector but also lowered costs, unequivocally improving economic welfare. Testing the hypothesis that more efficient firms grow faster, Frech and Mobley (2000) confirmed that concentration in the hospital industry, via merger and consolidation, has improved efficiency in that industry.

The best evidence available at this time leads us to conclude that competition in the hospital sector during the 1980s did result in a medical arms race that improved the quality of care for some patients but also drove up costs substantially. Furthermore, as competition continued to escalate in the 1990s, quality continued to improve and costs began to fall in spite of increased concentration, supporting the predictions of traditional economic analysis.

Cost-Containment Strategies in the United States

As medical prices continue to escalate, the pressure on policy makers to find new approaches to contain health care spending continues to grow. Instead of developing policies that encourage market solutions, policy makers are more likely to propose government solutions that include price controls.

The U.S. government pays for almost half of all the medical care in this country; therefore, government solutions have focused on controlling federal outlays, especially for Medicare and Medicaid. The temptation facing policy makers is the simplistic appeal of price controls to limit expenditures, which is much like trying to limit the spread of the flu by passing a law against running a temperature greater than 98.6 degrees. You cannot legislate an illness out of existence. Likewise, you cannot legislate price increases out of existence. Price controls bring about unintended consequences that are potentially more difficult to deal with than the price increases they were designed to limit. Changes in Medicare reimbursement for hospitals and physicians over the past decade provide a good case study in the limitations of price controls in restraining the growth in medical spending.

KEY CONCEPT 6
Efficiency

Diagnosis-Related Groups

Until 1983, Medicare reimbursed hospitals on a cost-plus basis for all inpatient services. The hospital provided services to an eligible recipient and billed Medicare for the cost of that care. Thus, payment was determined retrospectively, based on per-unit or per-service charges determined by what the hospital billed for the services provided. This payment mechanism, coupled with private, third-party financing, was largely responsible for the increased volume and intensity of services observed in the hospital sector, and to varying degrees, for the growing inefficiencies within the industry evidenced by overinvestment in capital equipment.

To counter the increased spending and growing inefficiencies, federal strategy focused its cost-containment efforts on the supply side, devising a prospective payment mechanism for the hospital sector. Introduced in 1983, prospective payment took the form of flat-rate reimbursement for hospitals based on principal diagnosis of the patient. In principle, prospective payment will provide economic incentives to conserve scarce medical resources, which will in turn hold down the growth in expenditures.

Currently known as Medicare Severity–Diagnosis-Related Groups, MS-DRGs have actually redefined the unit of measure used in determining Medicare payments. No longer are charges determined on a per-item or a per-service basis. Now charges are determined in advance on a per-case basis. Payment is based on a point system and is determined by a reimbursement rate that is set for each case-weighted point. These relative weights are set nationally and adjusted for wage differences by location and a number of other factors including the costs associated with graduate medical education, the share of low-income patients treated, and the cost of living. The standard payment is calculated as follows:

$$\text{Payment} = (\text{MS-DRG case weight}) \times (\text{Adjusted payment rate})$$

In the case of MS-DRG 286, circulatory disorder except acute myocardial infarction (AMI; i.e., heart attack) with cardiac catheterization and major complications, the case weight was 2.0360. If the hospital's adjusted payment rate is $5,850, the payment will be $11,910.60.

The Nature of DRGs   It is instructive to examine the organization of the DRG classification scheme. Medicare initially set up 467 DRG categories based on principal diagnosis, age of the patient, presence of comorbidity conditions, use of surgical procedures, and discharge status of the patient. There are currently over 750 MS-DRGs and each is assigned a relative weight to approximate the resource usage of the average case within that diagnosis category.

Figure 10.2 provides details on the classification system and MS-DRG usage weight for a pregnant female who presents herself to the labor and delivery area of a hospital. Under these circumstances, the two possibilities are either the female is experiencing labor or she is not. A female in labor may or may not be experiencing complications and may end up delivering the baby in the normal manner (i.e., vaginal delivery) or may have a cesarean section. The normal delivery without complications or other procedures is MS-DRG 775 with a DRG weight of 0.5283. The cesarean delivery with complications is MS-DRG 765 and has a DRG weight of 1.2255, implying a little over two-and-one-half times the resource use of a normal delivery. These eight-related MS-DRGs have DRG weights ranging from 0.1947 for false labor to 1.8180 for a normal delivery with complications and a procedure requiring the operating room.

Economic Impact of DRGs on Hospital Behavior   The stated goals of introducing prospective payment for hospitals were to control the growth in hospital spending under Medicare and promote cost efficiencies in the provision of hospital services. Early evidence indicated that prospective payment succeeded in reducing Medicare hospital expenditures (Russell and Manning, 1989). Using 1990 prices, the savings from prospective payment amounted to approximately $18 billion from what had earlier been projected for that year. Much of the savings can be attributed to decreases in the number of hospital admissions and the average length of a hospital stay. Between 1982 and 1985, the average length of stay for a Medicare patient fell 15 percent. In fact, the number of admissions and the average length of stay fell in response to these changes in reimbursement, an indication of system-wide inefficiencies.

In general, hospital reimbursement under Medicare is determined at the point of diagnosis. If the cost of treatment is less than the DRG reimbursement rate, the hospital keeps

POLICY ISSUE
How does the change to prospective payment affect medical care delivery?

FIGURE 10.2
DRGs for Labor and
Delivery

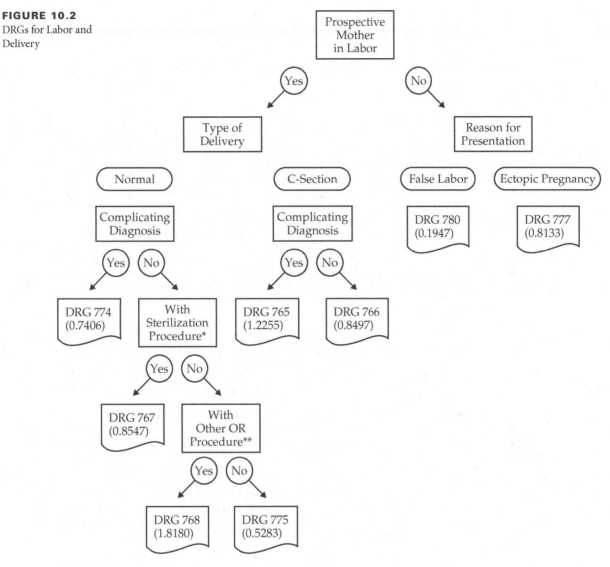

*and/or dilation and currettage

**Operating Room

the surplus.[4] If costs exceed reimbursement, the hospital absorbs the loss. In theory, hospitals that treat a large number of Medicare recipients in each diagnostic category should be able to cover costs with overall reimbursements. During the first few years after implementation of the program, hospitals experienced healthy operating margins on Medicare patients, ranging from 8 to 15 percent (Sheingold, 1989). These margins were due primarily to aggressive cost reductions and clever gaming of the DRG system.[5]

KEY CONCEPT 5
Markets and Pricing

---

[4]The correct term is *surplus* in a not-for-profit hospital. In a for-profit hospital the same concept is called *profit*.

[5]In the late 1990s, the federal government investigated Columbia/HCA for fraudulent practices in classifying patients and billing Medicare. In December 2000, they paid the U.S. government $850 million in criminal and civil penalties related to guilty pleas as the first stage in the settlement for the fraud actions against it.

APPLIED MICRO METHODS

CAN PRICE TRANSPARENCY REDUCE HEALTH CARE COSTS?

Background

Prices for U.S. hospital services vary widely across the country. Mammography screening, a test performed over 38 million times annually, costs commercial insurers in the Los Angeles and the San Francisco Bay regions anywhere from $128 to $694 (Aliferis, 2015). The cost of the same MRI can vary between $300 and $3,000 within some geographic areas (Hussey et al., 2013). Factors contributing to the observed price variation include the type of facility performing the scan (hospital-based or freestanding) and the market power of the provider (relative bargaining power when negotiating prices with insurers).

Because of the complexity of plan benefit designs, patients find it difficult to obtain accurate prices before receiving health services. Price transparency initiatives have uniformly failed to reduce price variations because patient engagement is difficult and deductibles and copays obscure price data. When patients do not have access to accurate information, there is little reason for them to search for the lowest prices.

Methods

The failure of most transparency projects stems from the fact that they rely on the patient to initiate any change. The Wu et al. study (2014) is based on a project undertaken by AIM Specialty Health, a specialty benefit management company, and aimed at elective imaging procedures. Taking advantage of preauthorization requirements for elective imaging, the staff identified situations where the price difference between the referred provider and other suitable alternatives was at least $400. When a suitable alternative was available, the staff phoned the patient with information on the alternative.

Patients with at least one MRI scan during the pre-implementation year (2010) or the post-implementation year (2012) were included in the study. Approximately, 61,000 patients were in the treatment group (whose insurer offered the price transparency program) and 44,000 were in the control group (no program available). The study was designed to evaluate patients' responses to the transparency information. The main outcome measure was the change in the average cost of an MRI scan from 2010 to 2012.

The primary results were based on difference-in-differences regression analysis to measure the impact of the transparency program on MRI unit prices between the two groups. Covariates included type of scan and the Medicare adjustment factor (measuring the differences in operating expenses across geographic regions).

Results

The adjusted cost of an MRI scan decreased $95 for the treatment group ($1,053–$958) and increased $124 for the control group ($868–$992).

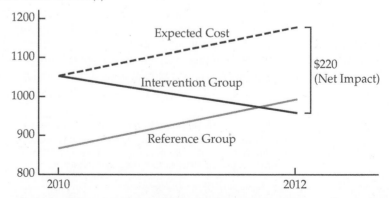

A major factor contributing to the cost reduction was a shift from hospital-based facilities to freestanding, outpatient facilities. The proportion of scans conducted at hospital-based facilities declined from 53 percent in 2010 to 45 percent in 2012 in the treatment group. In contrast, the proportion for the control group remained essentially the same.

Discussion

When provided with similar-quality and lower-priced scanning options, patients were willing to switch to the lower-priced option. Average cost per scan decreased, patients switched from hospital-based facilities to freestanding, outpatient facilities, and price variation between hospital-based facilities and freestanding outpatient facilities decreased. Price transparency programs targeting nonurgent procedures involving direct patient outreach have the potential to lower health care costs.

Sources: Lisa Aliferis, "Variation in Prices for Common Medical Tests and Procedures," *JAMA Internal Medicine* 175(1), January 2015, 11–13; P. S. Hussey et al., "The Association between Health Care Quality and Cost: A Systematic Review," *Annals of Internal Medicine* 158(1), 2013, 27–34; Sze-jung Wu et al., "Price Transparency for MRIs Increased Use of Less Costly Providers and Triggered Provider Competition," *Health Affairs* 33(8), 2014, 1391–1398.

Pricing Hospital Services

By the time Blue Cross and Blue Shield became household names in the health insurance industry in the 1950s, hospitals were paid on a per diem basis, an amount determined by the average cost of a hospital day plus a small increment. Medicare and Medicaid adopted cost-plus pricing from their inception in 1965, solidifying this approach as the standard method of payment for hospital services for the next two decades. By 1983, the government abandoned the cost-plus pricing model in favor of a fixed payment per case determined by the principal diagnosis at the time of admission. The price of a DRG is the product of the relative weight and a monetary conversion factor. The monetary conversion factor is set nationally, updated annually, and adjusted for geographic location and other factors that affect the cost of providing care. Private insurance went an entirely different direction, paying negotiated prices based on discounts from billed charges. These two approaches exist simultaneously, with little regard to the billed charges established by the individual hospital.

After an initial period of overly generous payment rates, hospitals saw average Medicare margins drop from a high of 11.9 percent in 1997 into negative territory by 2003, falling as low as −7.3 percent by 2008. Margins improved slightly to −5.8 percent by 2014 and were positive in only 30 percent of all hospitals. In contrast, all-payer margins were +7.3 percent in 2014 (MedPac, 2016).

With the growth of managed care and the bargaining power it represented, hospital pricing moved from charged-based rates to negotiated rates determined by contract. The result was a shrinking percentage of patients paying billed charges and a growing gap between billed charges and the prices paid by most payers. The shrinking pool of self-paying patients is still an important revenue source, so hospitals continue to raise charge-based rates. The AHA (2016a) estimated that U.S. community hospitals charge 2.6–4.7 times the amount actually received from payers.

Hospitals keep track of the prices they charge for procedures through a file system referred to as the *chargemaster*. While the form and content of the chargemaster may vary from hospital to hospital, the goal of a successful pricing policy is to cover resource costs and generate a positive margin to guarantee flexibility for future operations. Moreover, when billed charges have little in common with the actual prices paid for services, these charges cease to serve as market signals to guide optimal resource allocation. Differential pricing, instead of being based on Ramsey principles, charges those payers with the most purchasing power the lowest prices and forces the self-payers, including the uninsured, to pay the inflated prices stipulated by the chargemaster.

KEY CONCEPT 5
Markets and Pricing

Table 10.3 provides a detailed example of how this complicated pricing system is practiced in hospitals across the country. In 2007, the official charge for a simple procedure, a diagnostic bilateral mammogram, varied from $240 in a Portland hospital to $460 in Los Angeles, a 92 percent differential. Medicare paid anywhere from $50 to $156 for the procedure while Medicaid paid between $59 and $173. The Medicare and Medicaid prices take into consideration such things as the number of uninsured patients treated at the hospital and the number of residents training at the hospital. Private health plans pay varying amounts for the same service and in most cases more than the public plans pay. In all cases, private payers' charges are discounted from the official charge by as much as 90 percent.

Almost all hospitals have a policy for pricing of services to the uninsured. The policy is either a discount based on ability to pay or a sliding fee schedule based on income. Because of bad publicity in the past, seldom do hospitals try to collect the chargemaster price from the uninsured.

In 2000, Congress mandated an ambulatory payment classification (APC) scheme in which outpatient services are categorized into 600 distinct groupings that represent clinically similar procedures. Thus, prices for outpatient services are determined by multiplying the relative weight of the APC (determined by resource use) by a monetary conversion factor.

As originally envisioned, the hospital pricing mechanism was an elaborate system designed to subsidize the cost of medical care provided to the indigent poor by charging

TABLE 10.3 CHARGES AND DISCOUNTS FOR DIAGNOSTIC BILATERAL MAMMOGRAM

Hospital (Location)	Official charge	Medicare	Medicaid	HMOs, Health plans	Policy on uninsured
UCLA Medical Center (Los Angeles)	$460	$127	$90	Up to $242	Gives discounts based on individual's ability to pay
Oregon Health & Science University (Portland)	$240	$65	$59	Average $128	Works with uninsured patients to help them find financial aid; offers sliding scales, payment plans
Jamaica Hospital (Queens, N.Y.)	$351	$50	$96	$40 to $78	Has sliding fee scales for uninsured
Johns Hopkins Hospital & Health System (Baltimore)	$261	$156	$173	$186	State regulation of charges reduces disparity between bills to insured and uninsured
Grinnell Regional Medical Center (Grinnell, Iowa)	$285	$73	$79	$119 to $190	Works with uninsured to set a payment schedule

Source: Lucette Lagnado, "A Young Woman, an Appendectomy, and a $19,000 Debt," *Wall Street Journal*, March 17, 2003, A1.

privately insured patients more than the cost of their care. This cost shifting, as originally envisioned, is nothing short of a *de facto* tax on those with private insurance. The economic environment has changed over time with private payers aggressively challenging the status quo. Those payers with substantial market shares wield enough market power to turn hospitals into classic price takers for covered patients (Tompkins, Altman, and Eilat, 2006). Those patients without a powerful payer backing them in the market must rely on the hospital's collection policy to determine what they pay for services. If hospitals are to continue to provide free or discounted care to a significant portion of its customers, hospitals must have the ability to practice price discrimination; otherwise, the system as we have come to know it will have to change.

HTTP://

The Shriners Hospitals for Crippled Children provides pediatric care to needy children at no charge. The organization operates 19 orthopedic units and three burn institutes. In addition, three of the hospitals specialize in treating spinal cord injuries. A guide to the Shriners Hospitals can be found at http://www.shrinershq.org/.

The Role of the Not-for-Profit Organization in the Hospital Industry

Using the neoclassical model with profit-maximizing decision makers may seem inappropriate in an industry dominated by not-for-profit institutions. Physicians receive their training in not-for-profit medical schools. Almost 80 percent of all hospitals are not-for-profit in nature, and for many years, the regional not-for-profit carriers, Blue Cross and Blue Shield, dominated the health insurance industry.

At the beginning of the twentieth century, most hospitals were not-for-profit institutions. Their main responsibility was the provision of free care for the poor and indigent. Hospitals were notorious institutions—avoided at all costs by any self-respecting person. Medical reform during the interwar period enhanced the quality and respectability of the industry. Paying customers provided the incentive for the development of the proprietary, for-profit institution. The financial challenges of the Great Depression, and government policy favoring the not-for-profit structure, led to the dominance of the private, not-for-profit hospital after the Second World War. With their tax-exempt status, not-for-profit hospitals were able to accept tax-deductible, charitable contributions. Many also received construction subsidies from the federal government under the Hill-Burton Act.

Some state legislatures even made the for-profit form illegal altogether. As a result, by 2000, over three-fourths of all community hospitals were either government owned or not-for-profit. Data presented in Table 10.4 show that the percentage of for-profit hospitals has been increasing steadily since 1980, when it stood at 12.5 percent of the total, until 2013, when it was 21.3 percent. For-profit hospitals have increased their share of the total beds to 16.9 percent, at the expense of a shrinking share for government-owned hospitals.

The Not-for-Profit Organizational Form

The institutional constraints facing for-profit and not-for-profit hospitals are substantially different. For all practical purposes, the differences are simply differences in the right to transfer assets. A not-for-profit hospital does not have shareholders in the typical sense of the term. Thus, equity capital does not come from the sale of stock but from donations. Without shares of stock, there are no dividends to be paid. Surplus funds are restricted and may not be used to provide *ex post* incentives to managers. In other words, hospital administrators may not receive dividends or other distributions of residual earnings. Finally, in the event of liquidation or sale of assets, no individual owner receives the proceeds.

POLICY ISSUE

Is the provision of services through not-for-profit hospitals desired over provision through for-profits?

KEY CONCEPT 4
Self-Interest

TABLE 10.4 NUMBER OF COMMUNITY HOSPITALS AND BEDS BY OWNERSHIP TYPE, SELECTED YEARS

Year	Number of hospitals	For profit		Nongovernment, nonprofit		Government	
		No.	%	No.	%	No.	%
1975	5,875	775	13.2	3,339	56.8	1,761	30.0
1980	5,830	730	12.5	3,322	57.0	1,778	30.5
1985	5,732	805	14.0	3,349	58.5	1,578	27.5
1990	5,384	749	13.9	3,191	59.3	1,444	26.8
1995	5,194	752	14.5	3,092	59.5	1,350	26.0
2000	4,915	749	15.2	3,003	61.1	1,163	23.7
2005	4,936	868	17.6	2,958	59.9	1,110	22.5
2010	4,985	1,013	20.3	2,904	58.3	1,068	21.4
2013	4,974	1,060	21.3	2,904	58.4	1,010	20.3

Year	Number of beds (000)	For profit		Nongovernment, nonprofit		Government	
		No.	%	No.	%	No.	%
1975	941.8	73.5	7.8	658.2	69.9	210.2	22.3
1980	988.4	87.0	8.8	692.5	70.0	208.9	21.2
1985	1,000.7	103.9	10.4	707.5	70.7	189.3	18.9
1990	927.4	101.4	11.0	656.8	70.8	169.2	18.2
1995	872.7	105.7	12.1	609.7	69.9	157.3	18.0
2000	823.6	109.9	13.3	583.0	70.8	130.7	15.9
2005	802.3	113.5	14.1	561.1	69.9	127.7	15.9
2010	804.9	124.7	15.5	555.8	69.0	124.5	15.5
2013	795.6	134.6	16.9	543.9	68.4	117.0	14.7

Source: *Health, United States*, various years.

ISSUES IN MEDICAL CARE DELIVERY

FOR-PROFIT OR NOT-FOR-PROFIT: THAT'S A GOOD QUESTION

The practice of converting not-for-profit hospitals to investor-owned, for-profit hospitals has received a great deal of attention recently. State attorneys general have the oversight responsibilities in these cases, because such cases involve the disbursement of charitable assets. Over half the states and Congress are considering legislation to regulate the conversion process. A Kaiser Family Foundation survey conducted in March 1997 provides evidence of public distrust for these for-profit conversions. By a margin of 42 percent to 20 percent, Americans responded that such conversions are bad for health care.

Between 1994 and 1996, over 100 not-for-profit community hospitals were taken over by for-profit hospital chains with Columbia/HCA (Hospital Corporation of America) leading the way with over 50 acquisitions. Along with these conversions came the largest transfer of charitable assets in U.S. history—over $9 billion. The sale of Presbyterian/

St. Luke's (P/SL) in Denver provides a good example of the magnitude of these conversions. In 1995, Colorado Trust was created with assets of $310 million from the proceeds of the sale of P/SL, making it the largest single trust in Colorado. The purchase of Rose Medical Center by Columbia endowed the Rose Community Foundation with more than $175 million. The planned conversion of Blue Cross and Blue Shield into a for-profit entity may spin off over $300 million into a charitable foundation. Staggering as they may be, these numbers pale in comparison to the conversion of California Blue Cross, which created two new trusts with $3.2 billion in assets.

Critics have a number of legitimate concerns in the wake of these conversions, including proper valuation of charitable assets, impact on the community's access to health care services, continued provision of uncompensated care, and governance issues of the newly created charitable trust.

Proponents argue that these conversions are introducing an element of competition into markets characterized by complacency and inefficiency. Regardless of how you feel personally about these conversions, expect more as hospitals, both for-profit and not-for-profit, find that they must become part of larger, integrated systems to ensure their own survival as competition heats up.

Sources: John Leifer, "Inside the Predator: Former Columbia Executive Tells How to Avoid Becoming the Giant's Next Victim," *Modern Healthcare*, April 14, 1997, 46; Tamar Lewin and Martin Gottlieb, "Health Care Dividend—a Special Report; In Hospital Sales, an Overlooked Side Effect," *The New York Times*, April 27, 1997, Section 1, page 1; and Stuart Steers, "Roll On, Columbia; The Nation's Largest for-Profit Hospital Chain is out to Flatten its Denver Competition," *Denver Westword*, April 24, 1997.

Nature of Competition in the Not-for-Profit Sector

The popularity of the not-for-profit organizational form in the hospital industry may seem a bit odd given the dominance of the for-profit organizational form in the rest of the U.S. economy. Sloan (1988) addressed the conventional wisdom regarding the prevalence of not-for-profit hospitals. The first argument was based on asymmetric information in the hospital market. Because patients have a difficult time evaluating the quality of medical care, they prefer to purchase their medical care from providers who do not suffer from the profit motive. If this is true, however, there is no good explanation why virtually every other provider—physicians, optometrists, pharmacists, and dentists—works in the for-profit sector.

KEY CONCEPT 7
Competition

A second argument is based on the notion that profit-maximizing hospitals will not undertake any activity in which the marginal revenue is less than the marginal cost. Activities such as biomedical research, medical education, and public health measures would not be provided at optimal levels. In addition, patients without insurance or other means of paying would be less likely to receive care. This line of reasoning, while relevant for teaching hospitals and large public hospitals, cannot explain why the rest of the not-for-profit sector engages in little research, undertakes few public health activities, and provides no more uncompensated care than hospitals in the for-profit sector (Sloan, Valvona, and Mullner, 1986).

KEY CONCEPT 4
Self-Interest

Based on arguments by Pauly and Redisch (1973) and Shalit (1977), hospitals are not-for-profit because this form of organization provides the most benefits for physicians. Patients do not purchase hospital services directly. Their physician agents do it for them. Rather than competing for patients, hospitals actually compete for physicians who admit the patients.[6] Physicians interested in maximizing their own productivity will have more control over decisions relating to input mix in the absence of the profit motive.

---

[6]Competition for physician referrals is more important than ever for hospital survival, particularly as system consolidations and for-profit conversions create integrated networks of medical care services.

Many argue that even with the preponderance of not-for-profits in the industry, the profit-maximizing objective is a reasonable operating assumption. Operating margins (operating revenues minus operating expenses) are positive for 75 percent of all hospitals. In fact, 25 percent have all-payer margins that exceed 9 percent. This operating surplus has many uses. It can be used to increase the incomes of staff physicians or other personnel, or it can be used to promote desired activities, such as teaching and research. To the extent that hospitals are run to further the interests of physicians, financial and otherwise, the use of the profit-maximizing model may be reasonable.

Thus, decision making in a not-for-profit hospital could resemble decision making in a for-profit hospital (Danzon, 1982). Newhouse (1970) has noted that in an environment of free entry and free exit, all hospitals—for-profit or not-for-profit—are required to produce efficiently in order to survive. The empirical evidence is far from unanimous on the issue. Zelder (1999) reviewed 24 studies comparing for-profit and not-for-profit performance in the hospital sector. Half of the studies found no significant differences in operating behavior between the two organizational forms. The other 12 studies were split on the issue, with 7 favoring the for-profit form and 5 favoring the not-for-profit form. Pauly (1987) best summarized these results when he observed that holding size, quality, and teaching status constant, there is little difference in the provision of hospital care attributable to ownership status. The one exception is the operating performance of public, not-for-profit hospitals. Zelder (1999) reviewed 15 studies comparing public and private hospital performance and found compelling evidence that private hospitals are more efficient than public hospitals.

KEY CONCEPT 8
Efficiency

Alternative Models of Hospital Behavior

Accepted alternatives to the profit-maximizing model share a common approach: utility maximization. In practice, profit maximization is simply a special case of utility maximization. The only practical difference between the two models is the way residual earnings are distributed. Because utility is unobservable, the challenge is to specify a model with an objective function that is observable.

KEY CONCEPT 4
Self-Interest

Utility-Maximizing Models

According to these models, decision makers in a not-for-profit environment maximize utility subject to a break-even constraint. The objective of the decision makers may be their own utility. In this case, they will operate the hospital to maximize their own pecuniary and nonpecuniary benefits. Pecuniary benefits include salary and fringe benefits. Nonpecuniary benefits include the prestige and authority that go along with the position. Empirical research has explored many possible elements in the utility function for hospital administrators. The most popular elements include output and quality or some combination of the two.

The utility-maximizing approach assumes that the hospital decision maker's objective is to be in charge of the largest or the highest-quality hospital possible given the resources available. Studies by Newhouse (1970), Sloan (1980), and Danzon (1982) use this approach to modeling the behavior of not-for-profit hospital managers. Quality is typically measured by the level of technology, the type of facility and services, the quality of the staff, and the number of specialists. Running a hospital that ranks high in these quality measures provides a great deal of prestige to the manager. Recruiting quality staff is easier, as is generating charitable donations for further enhancements to quality.

In practice, the assumption of quality maximization is merely a variant of profit-maximizing (and cost-minimizing) behavior to support other objectives. Short-run

FIGURE 10.3
The Impact of Quality Improvements on Average Cost and Demand

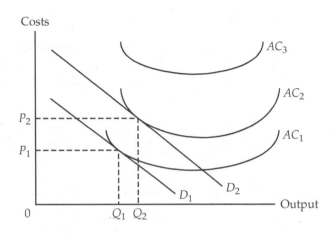

FIGURE 10.3
The Impact of Quality Improvements on Average Cost and Demand

profit-maximizing behavior may be pursued in order to invest profit in quality. Adding quality in most cases serves to increase costs and shift demand. Quality enhancements are not free, and consumers have a demand for quality. Figure 10.3 provides an illustration of the hypothesized relationship between quality enhancements and the average cost and demand curves.

Suppose a not-for-profit hospital has average costs and demand depicted by AC_1 and D_1. The not-for-profit assumption implies that the hospital will operate where price and average cost are equal, indicating an output of Q_1 and price of P_1. An increase in quality moves the average costs up to AC_2. If the enhancement also increases demand, the demand curve shifts to D_2, and output and price increase to Q_2 and P_2. At some point, however, further increases in quality will only increase costs (to AC_3) without changing demand. At this point, patients are unwilling to pay for quality improvements, and hospital charges fall short of average costs. In other words, over investing in certain quality improvements begins to produce a product of higher quality than consumers are willing to buy. These models explain certain behavior, such as the investment in technology to increase prestige, but they shed little light on the important role that physicians play in the hospital setting.

KEY CONCEPT 2
Opportunity Cost

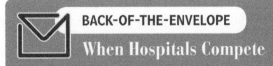

BACK-OF-THE-ENVELOPE

When Hospitals Compete

Hospitals rarely engage in price competition. Medical care consumers gained insight into the pricing practices of the nation's hospitals when the federal government released price information on the 100 most common inpatient procedures in May 2013 (Kliff and Keating, 2013). You might expect price differentials across regions, but prices for services such as lower joint replacements vary considerably within the same city. For example, Las Colinas Medical Center near Dallas billed Medicare, on average, over $160,000 for the replacement of a lower joint (hip or knee). Nearby Baylor Medical Center billed, on average, just over $42,000 for the same procedure.

If hospitals do not compete on price, how do they compete? Calem and Rizzo (1995) believe that hospitals engage in competition for physicians and patients and choose a service mix and quality that advances the hospital's mission; a practice that was referred to as a "medical arms race" over a decade ago. Because prices are largely determined by third-party payers, hospitals use the factors that they control to attract customers.

Calem and Rizzo use a game theoretic framework to examine the two-part decision: First choose a service mix and then engage in quality competition. The decision fits the framework of the standard prisoner's dilemma as shown in the next payoff matrix (values depict hospital profit/surplus). After deciding what services to provide (cardiology, obstetrics, joint replacement, etc.), the hospital chooses a level of quality (high, low) measured by technology mix, optimal mortality rate, or 30-day readmission rate.

		Hospital B	
		High	**Low**
Hospital A	High	150, 150	250, 0
	Low	0, 250	200, 200

When both hospitals pursue their dominant strategies (High, High), they both invest in costly technology to increase perceived quality, resulting in a suboptimal outcome (150, 150). For the hospitals, a cooperative strategy (Low, Low) would generate an outcome that would result in a socially optimal service mix and quality level and result in greater profit/surplus (200, 200).

Sources: Paul S. Calem and John A. Rizzo, "Competition and Specialization in the Hospital Industry: An Application of Hotelling's Location Model," *Southern Economic Journal* 61(4), April 1995, 1182–1198 and Sarah Kliff and Dan Keating, "One Hospital Charges $8,000—Another $38,000," *The Washington Post*, May 8, 2013.

Physician-Control Models

If physicians are the relevant decision makers, they have a stake in what combination of inputs is used. Staff physicians may have a financial stake in maintaining an efficient operation. In contrast, private practice physicians with hospital-admitting privileges may be more concerned about their own productivity than hospital efficiency. Excess hospital capacity enables physicians to maximize their own incomes. Because the prices of other inputs are effectively zero to nonstaff physicians, they have little concern for the productivity or the actual prices of these inputs. Thus, any increase in demand is met by increases in hospital capacity rather than increases in physician staff. The excess capacity enables physicians to maximize the use of their own time.[7]

Physician control leads to technical inefficiency in production. When the physician faces a zero price for other inputs, too many other inputs are used relative to physician inputs. This suggests that physicians are interested in the hospital investing in additional services to increase hospital capacity, such as interns and residents who provide services for which the physician can charge, additional operating rooms and obstetric facilities, and any other investment that will serve to economize on their own time.

⭐ **KEY CONCEPT 8**
Efficiency

The physician wants the hospital to price complementary services with the goal of increasing the demand for physicians' services. They also want the hospital to provide outpatient services and preventive care. The former reduces the risk of treating nonpaying patients. The latter is time intensive for the physician and is avoided.

Certain services provided by physicians and hospitals are somewhat substitutable for one another. As the number of physicians increases, more services will be provided in

---

[7]This phenomenon is unique to the American hospital system. In most countries, a distinct line is drawn between hospital physicians and private-practice physicians. Mobility between the two categories is controlled, and there are few opportunities to practice in both simultaneously.

physicians' offices than in hospitals. When medical services are bundled, the lower the hospital charges, the greater the residual for the physician.

Payment for hospital services is separated from payment for physician services, making the physician neither financially responsible to the hospital nor accountable to the patient for the cost of the hospital portion of the care. Any attempt to control costs without the cooperation of physicians has little chance of success.

BACK-OF-THE-ENVELOPE

Measuring Efficiency

In this chapter we've talked a lot about efficiency, but said little about how to measure it. The concepts of technical and allocative efficiency were introduced in Chapter 3 with very little analysis. In order to understand how to measure efficiency, we need to provide a little more detail to the discussion. There are two ways to define technical efficiency: One is maximizing output with a given level of resource use and the other is producing a given level of output with a minimum of resources.

The next graph helps us visualize the first approach. Consider a production function for Q (number of surgeries performed) that requires a single resource X (time in the operating room) or $Q = Q(X)$. Points like A and B lie on the production frontier and represent the technically efficient use of resource X to produce output levels Q_A and Q_B, respectively. Points like C that lie below the production frontier are technically inefficient with the degree of inefficiency measured by the distance to the frontier.

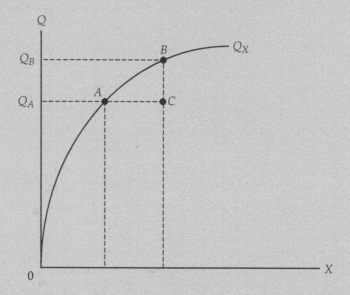

The alternative way to look at technical efficiency is to consider a production process with two inputs, X and Y, using isoquants (refer to Appendix 3B). The isoquant shown in the next diagram represents the level of $Q = Q^*$. Input combinations represented by points A, B, and D are technically efficient and points like C are inefficient. We can measure inefficiency along the ray from the origin to point C or OC. The distance CD represents the degree of technical inefficiency.

Allocative efficiency requires the optimal response to relative input prices, producing the output Q at minimum cost. Refer once again to the earlier diagram where EF

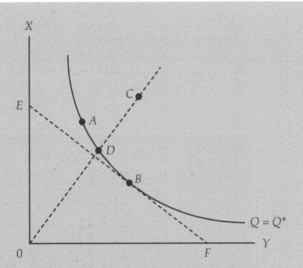

represents the lowest cost of producing Q*. While A and D are both technically efficient, only B is both technically and allocatively efficient. At the relative prices of inputs X and Y, the cost of producing Q* is lower at point B than at point A or D.

The empirical approach to study technical efficiency uses a technique called "Data Envelopment Analysis" or DEA. After collecting production information on a number of firms, the approach estimates the efficient frontier using linear programming. Valdmanis (1990) was the first to use this approach to measure the degree of inefficiency in the hospital industry. Magnusson (1996) and Sloan and colleagues (2001) used it to estimate efficiency differences between for-profit and not-for-profit hospitals. These studies reached the same conclusions, that hospitals are surprisingly efficient in a technical sense and that there is little difference in the level of efficiency between for-profit and not-for-profit hospitals. Examining allocative efficiency represents a different challenge. Because most hospital prices are not competitively driven, they have little meaning in terms of optimal resource allocation decisions.

Sources: Vivian G. Valdmanis, "Ownership and Technical Efficiency of Hospitals," *Medical Care* 28, 1990, 552–561; Jon Magnusson, "Efficiency Measurement and the Operationalization of Hospital Production," *Health Services Research* 31, 1996, 21–37; and Frank A. Sloan et al., "Hospital Ownership and Cost and Quality of Care: Is There a Dime's Worth of Difference?" *Journal of Health Economics* 20, 2001, 1–22.

The Trend Toward Multihospital Systems

One of the most important trends in the hospital market during the past two decades has been the increase in multihospital systems (see Ermann and Gabel, 1984; Morrisey and Alexander, 1987). In 1975, one out of every four hospitals in the United States was part of a multihospital system.[8] Merger activity increased dramatically in the late 1980s; over 1,300 separate hospital acquisitions took place between 1989 and 1993 (Danzon, 1994). By 1993, one out of every two hospitals was part of a multihospital system. Between 2007 and 2012 there were 316 mergers affecting over 550 hospitals. Between 2013 and 2015 there were 389 mergers affecting 733 hospitals. Today, over 60 percent of all community hospitals are in multihospital systems. The largest for-profit hospital system in the country is the HCA, comprising 169 hospitals and 116 free-standing surgery centers in 20 states and the United Kingdom. Community Health Systems is the second largest with 118 hospitals and Tenet Healthcare System has 20 short-stay surgical hospitals and 79 acute-care hospitals in 14

---

[8]A multihospital system is defined as two or more hospitals that are owned, managed, or leased by a single entity.

states (plus 9 facilities in the United Kingdom). The two largest not-for-profit health systems are Ascension Health (131 hospitals) and Catholic Health Initiatives (103 hospitals).

The Theory of Consolidation

Mergers, acquisitions, and other forms of consolidation occur in the hospital industry for the same reasons they occur in any other industry. Horizontal integration allows businesses to take advantage of economies of scale, reduce administrative costs, and improve customer access to information.[9]

Firms experience economies of scale when long-run average costs fall as the size of the operation expands. The notion of scale economies can be seen more clearly in Figure 10.4. The figure depicts short-run average costs of producing a product with five different-size plants, shown as AC_1 through AC_5. The average cost of production (LAC) falls as the scale or size of the operation increases up to a point. In this case, AC_3 represents the most efficient plant size, the one where economies of scale are exhausted and average cost minimized. Beyond that point, average costs increase as plant size increases, and the firm experiences diseconomies of scale.

If economies of scale are to improve efficiency, increased size must lead to a number of technical advantages. These advantages may include the ability to secure discounts through bulk purchasing and the ability to take advantage of specialization and division of labor, especially in the use of highly skilled personnel. Because case mix differs so dramatically from hospital to hospital, the relationship between cost and output is difficult to measure. Larger hospitals tend to treat more seriously ill patients and thus have higher average costs (Cowing, Holtman, and Powers, 1983; Vitaliano, 1987).

The relationship between cost and size may resemble more closely the average cost curves in Figure 10.5. Hospital A is on a higher long-run average cost curve (LAC_2) than Hospitals B and C because it provides services that are more complicated and treats sicker patients. Merely looking at the level of average cost would indicate that Hospital C is more efficient than Hospital A, which would be incorrect. With Hospital B yet to fully capture all its economies and Hospital C experiencing diseconomies of scale, Hospital A is more efficient relative to its service mix than either of the other two hospitals.

KEY CONCEPT 8
Efficiency

FIGURE 10.4 The
Long-Run Average Cost
Curve

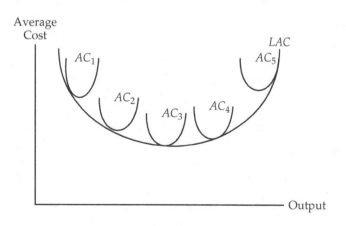

---

[9]Horizontal integration occurs when two or more firms that make the same product or provide the same service combine.

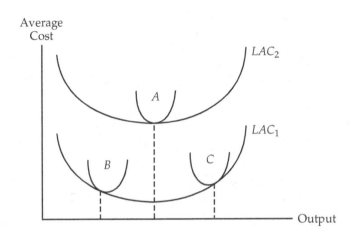

The Empirical Evidence on Consolidation

Most of the empirical research on the growth of hospital systems and efficiency is based on data from a time when cost-plus reimbursement was the standard practice. Under such conditions, hospitals had little incentive to lower costs (Renn et al., 1985; Santerre and Bennett, 1992).

As hospital reimbursement shifted from retrospective to prospective payment beginning in the mid-1980s, the efficiencies of the multihospital system have become more evident. Research by Dranove, Shanley, and Simon (1992) suggests that there may be substantial unexploited opportunities for economies of scale in the hospital industry, especially in smaller markets. Although antitrust policy has shown a tendency to reject the efficiency argument, these potential economies may serve as a justification for future hospital mergers.

Dranove and Shanley (1995) focused on the marketing strategy used by hospital chains to promote brand-name identity. This strategy, similar to the one used by international franchises in the fast-food industry, has as its goal creating a perception of standardized quality in the minds of potential customers. Danzon (1994) argued that chains have a comparative advantage in providing information on product quality that customers value in their decision-making process. Given the uncertainties of the hospital market, customers seek out inexpensive information on quality and service. Identification with an established chain of respected hospitals improves customer access to information, in turn increasing demand and allowing higher margins over cost.

Mobley (1997) examined the differences in merger activities between for-profit and not-for-profit hospitals. Her findings indicated that for-profits and not-for-profits seem to have different motives for consolidating. For-profits apparently seek lucrative niche markets sheltered from competition. In contrast, the not-for-profit acquisitions seem to be more focused on markets in which managed care penetration is higher. By consolidating in markets with substantial managed care penetration, hospitals position themselves to bargain with managed care plans. In addition, hospitals can take advantage of the economies of scale without having to expand any one facility beyond its maximum level of efficiency. By satisfying the demand of the managed care plans for a full range of services, they are better able to compete in these market areas.

Consolidation activity presents an interesting challenge to antitrust policy. If consolidation leads to efficiency gains, then patients could benefit from higher-quality care at lower prices. With the volume of consolidation activity that has taken place in the past decade, it is surprising how little consensus exists on the extent of scale economies in this industry.

KEY CONCEPT 10
Comparative Advantage

POLICY ISSUE
Will consolidation in the hospital industry benefit patients or providers?

> ### ISSUES IN MEDICAL CARE DELIVERY
>
> ## THE GEISINGER APPROACH
>
> National health reform has created opportunities for innovative changes in the way health care is delivered. Geisinger Health Systems, a fully integrated health services organization in northeastern Pennsylvania, is uniquely positioned to take advantage of the changes in health care delivery and finance brought about by the ACA. Founded in 1915, Geisinger, with almost 1,600 employed physicians and 30,000 employees, operates 12 hospitals and 2 research centers serving a population of over 3 million people in 45 counties.
>
> Innovation at Geisinger begins with the 510,000 members of the Geisinger Health Plan (GHP). Over the years major innovative initiatives have included Geisinger's Proven-Health Navigator, its "advanced medical home" designed to improve patient health by coordinating primary and specialty care. Focusing on the highest utilizers, nurse care coordinators are each assigned 24-hour triage responsibility for 150 of the sickest chronic disease patients.
>
> Other initiatives include the use of a single-bundled payment for acute care procedures such as coronary artery bypass, hip replacement, cataract surgery, and bariatric surgery. The so-called ProvenCare program provides care using a single episode package price that includes preoperative evaluation, all hospital and physicians' charges, routine post-discharge care, and management of any postoperative complications for 90 days.
>
> Care for patients with high-prevalence chronic conditions is tracked using an "all-or-none approach" where only full compliance with best clinical practices is scored as a success. Geisinger uses integrated electronic health records (EHR) to monitor workflows and eliminate duplication.
>
> It is not yet clear whether Geisinger and other organizations such as the Mayo Clinic and Kaiser Permanente are examples of the integrated delivery systems of the future. It is clear that without the innovative spirit that is pervasive at Geisinger, the future of health care delivery in the United States will mimic systems around the world where spending trends are unsustainable. If we are unable to control spending, the U.S. system will find itself squarely on the road to price controls, global budgets, and resource rationing.
>
> Sources: Susan Dentzer, "Geisinger Chief Glenn Steele: Seizing Health Reform's Potential to Build a Superior System," *Health Affairs* 29(6), June 2010, 1200–1207 and Ronald A. Paulus, Karen Davis, and Glenn D. Steele, "Continuous Innovation in Health Care: Implications of the Geisinger Experience," *Health Affairs* 27(5), September/October 2008, 1235–1245.

Summary and Conclusions

Hospital care tends to be the most expensive aspect of medical care delivery. Dominated by the private not-for-profit hospital, the hospital industry is responsible for approximately one-third of all medical care spending. Of interest for policy purposes has been the recent increase in consolidations and mergers, particularly the high profile, not-for-profit to for-profit conversions. Lessons to be learned from this chapter include the following:

- *A cost-plus environment does not reward efficiency. Thus, finding little difference in efficiency between for-profit hospitals and not-for-profit hospitals is not surprising, or at least it should not be.*

With the increasing popularity of managed care and prospective payment, only recently have hospitals been given an incentive to be efficient.

- *The economic models predict that competition on the payment side will eventually eliminate the inefficiencies in the market. Inefficient hospitals become prime targets for acquisition by multihospital chains.*
- *As the inefficiencies are eliminated, so too is the ability to subsidize medical education and charity care for the uninsured. With increased pressure on hospitals to provide care to nonpaying patients, hospitals in turn will increase pressure on public*

policy makers to improve the social safety net for the more vulnerable population groups, including the elderly, pregnant women, children, and the poor in general.

■ *Increased hospital competition in the 1980s promoted quality enhancement, not cost efficiency, which led to a medical arms race. Further competition in the 1990s continued to see quality improvements and, at the same time, increased cost efficiencies.*

The changes that began in the 1980s pushed hospitals to become competitive and profit oriented. This corporate mentality has led to extensive local marketing, leveraging with debt, multihospital chains, and administrators earning salaries rivaling those of corporate executives. Will the industry become money oriented and self-serving, or will the changes lead to an industry that is technologically innovative and caring?

PROFILE   Frank A. Sloan

After receiving an undergraduate degree from Oberlin College and a Ph.D. from Harvard, Frank Sloan spent the first three years of his professional career as a research economist with the RAND Corporation. While at RAND, he explored the implications and extensions of his dissertation research on the supply of physicians. An academic appointment at the University of Florida brought him back to the East Coast. After five years at Florida, he moved to Vanderbilt University in Nashville, Tennessee, where he spent the next 17 years as chair of the department and Centennial Professor of Economics. Three decades after first leaving his home state, Sloan returned to North Carolina in 1993 to become a member of the faculty at Duke University near his hometown of Greensboro. In addition to his appointment as the Alexander McMahon Professor of Health Policy and Management, he is also Professor of Economics and Senior Research Fellow at the Center for Demographic Studies.

With over 200 publications in some of the profession's most prestigious journals, including the *American Economic Review, Journal of Health Economics, Journal of the American Medical Association,* and *New England Journal of Medicine,* Sloan shows few signs of slowing down. If anything, the pace of his scholarly activities has actually increased in the past few years.

Sloan's early work focused on physicians and their workshops—the nation's hospitals. His article in the 1983 *Journal of the American Medical Association,* "More Doctors: What Will They Cost?" challenged the conventional wisdom that increasing the supply of physicians would lower the cost of medical care. The paradox was striking. Although economic theory suggests that more supply lowers costs, the physicians' service market did not seem to follow the same discipline as other markets.

In the mid-1980s, Sloan's research interests began to shift. With separate articles on medical malpractice and medical care for the elderly, both published in 1985, a gradual change in research emphasis began. Today his scholarship interests lean heavily toward issues of tort liability and elder care.

Sloan's research exhibits a practical side as well. Over the years, he has shown that economics is relevant to real-world problems by lending his expertise as a private consultant to dozens of public and private organizations, including individual hospitals and hospital associations, pharmaceutical associations, physicians' associations, and federal agencies. He also provides litigation support for a number of law firms across the country, using his expertise as a forensic economist to testify in lawsuits requiring estimates of economic damages.

Over the years, Sloan has been the principal investigator on dozens of research grants, generating millions of dollars for his affiliated institutions. He is a member of the Institute of Medicine, National Academy of Science. Equally productive in his many roles—teacher, writer, reviewer, and consultant—his influence within health care circles knows no boundaries.

Source: Frank A. Sloan curriculum vitae and Duke University website.

Questions and Problems

1. What are the major criticisms of the for-profit hospital?
2. In theory, describe the different operating characteristics of the for-profit and the not-for-profit hospital.
3. The critical issue in the debate over the merits of the for-profit hospital structure is whether the profit motive has a negative impact on quality of care and access for the poor and uninsured. Is there a significant difference in quality and access between for-profit and not-for-profit hospitals?

What is the empirical evidence? (Clearly distinguish between private not-for-profit hospitals and public hospitals.)
4. Does the not-for-profit structure in a hospital eliminate for-profit behavior? Explain.
5. What is cost-plus pricing? How does cost-plus pricing affect supplier behavior?
6. What is a horizontal merger? A vertical merger? Provide examples of each in the current hospital marketplace.

References

AAMC Council of Teaching Hospitals: Geographic Listing, Washington, DC: Association of American Medical Colleges, 1999.

AHA (American Hospital Association), *Trendwatch Chartbook 2016: Trends Affecting Hospitals and Health Systems*, Chicago: AHA, October 2016a.

———, "Uncompensated Hospital Care Cost Fact Sheet," December 2016b, available at http://www.aha.org/content/16/uncompensatedcarefactsheet.pdf.

Clement, J. P., "Dynamic Cost Shifting in Hospitals: Evidence from the 1980s and 1990s," *Inquiry* 34, 1998, 340–350.

Cowing, Thomas G., Alphonse G. Holtmann, and Susan Powers, "Hospital Cost Analysis: A Survey and Evaluation of Recent Studies," in *Advances in Health Economics and Health Services Research*, Volume 4, edited by Richard M. Scheffler and Louis R. Rossiter, Greenwich, CT: JAI Press, 1983, 257–303.

Cutler, David M., "Cost Shifting or Cost Cutting? The Incidence of Reductions in Medicare Payments," in *Tax Policy and the Economy* 12, edited by J. M. Poterba, Chicago: University of Chicago Press, 1998, 1–27.

Danzon, Patricia, "Hospital 'Profits': The Effects of Reimbursement Policies," *Journal of Health Economics* 1(1), May 1982, 29–52.

———, "Merger Mania," *Health Systems Review* 27(6), 1994, 18–28.

Dranove, David, "Pricing by Nonprofit Institutions: The Case of Hospital Cost-Shifting," *Journal of Health Economics* 7, 1988, 45–57.

Dranove, David and Mark Shanley, "Cost Reductions or Reputation Enhancement as Motives for Mergers: The Logic of Multihospital Systems," *Strategic Management Journal* 16(1), January 1995, 55–74.

Dranove, David and William D. White, "Recent Theory and Evidence on Competition in Hospital Markets," *Journal of Economics and Management Strategy* 3(1), Spring 1994, 169–209.

Dranove, David, Mark Shanley, and Carol Simon, "Is Hospital Competition Wasteful?" *RAND Journal of Economics* 23(2), Summer 1992, 247–262.

Dranove, David, et al., "Determinants of Managed Care Penetration," *Journal of Health Economics* 17, 1998, 729–745.

Ermann, Dan and Jon Gabel, "Multihospital Systems: Issues and Empirical Findings," *Health Affairs* 3(1), Spring 1984, 50–64.

Feldman, Roger and Bryan Dowd, "Is There a Competitive Market for Hospital Services?" *Journal of Health Economics* 5(3), September 1986, 277–292.

Feldstein, Martin S., "Hospital Price Inflation: A Study of Nonprofit Price Dynamics," *American Economic Review* 61(5), December 1971, 853–872.

Flexner, Abraham, *Medical Education in the United States and Canada*, Bulletin No. 4, The Carnegie Foundation for the Advancement of Teaching, Boston: D. B. Updike, 1910.

Fox, W. and J. Pickering, "Hospital and Physician Cost Shift: Payment Level Comparison of Medicare, Medicaid, and Commercial Payers," Milliman, December 2008, available at http://www.aha.org/content/00-10/081209costshift.pdf.

Frakt, Austin B., "How Much Do Hospitals Cost Shift? A Review of the Evidence," *Milbank Quarterly* 89(1), 2011, 90–130.

Frech, H. W. III and Lee R. Mobley, "Efficiency, Growth, and Concentration: An Empirical Analysis of Hospital Markets," *Economic Inquiry* 38(3), July 2000, 369–384.

Gaynor, Martin and Deborah Haas-Wilson, "Change, Consolidation, and Competition in Health Care Markets," *Journal of Economic Perspectives* 13(1), Winter 1999, 141–164.

Held, Philip and Mark Pauly, "Competition and Efficiency in the End Stage Renal Disease Program," *Journal of Health Economics* 2(2), August 1983, 95–118.

Iglehart, John K., "The Emergence of Physician-Owned Specialty Hospitals," *New England Journal of Medicine* 352(1), January 6, 2005, 78–84.

Keeler, Emmett B., Glenn Melnick, and Jack Zwanziger, "The Changing Effects of Competition on Nonprofit and for-Profit Hospital Pricing Behavior," *Journal of Health Economics* 18(1), January 1999, 69–86.

Kessler, Daniel P. and Mark B. McClellan, "Is Hospital Competition Socially Wasteful?" *Quarterly Journal of Economics* 115(2), May 2000, 577–615.

Luft, Harold S., et al., "The Role of Specialized Clinical Services in Competition among Hospitals," *Inquiry* 23(1), Spring 1986, 83–94.

Mayo, John W. and Deborah A. McFarland, "Regulation, Market Structure, and Hospital Costs," *Southern Economic Journal* 55(3), January 1989, 559–569.

MedPac, "Data Book: Beneficiaries Dually Eligible for Medicare and Medicaid," January 2016, available at http://medpac.gov/docs/default-source/publications/january-2016-medpac-and-macpac-data-book-beneficiaries-dually-eligible-for-medicare-and-medicaid.pdf?sfvrsn=0.

Mobley, Lee R., "Multihospital Chain Acquisitions and Competition in Local Healthcare Markets," *Review of Industrial Organization* 12(2), April 1997, 185–202.

Morrisey, Michael A. and Jeffrey A. Alexander, "Hospital Participation in Multihospital Systems," in *Advances in Health Economics and Health Services Research*, Volume 7, edited by Richard M. Scheffler and Louis R. Rossiter, Greenwich, CT: JAI Press, 1987, 59–82.

Newhouse, Joseph, "Toward a Theory of Nonprofit Institutions: An Economic Model of a Hospital," *American Economic Review* 60(1), March 1970, 66–74.

Pauly, Mark V, "Nonprofit Firms in Medical Markets," *American Economic Review Proceedings* 77(2), May 1987, 257–262.

Pauly, Mark V. and Michael Redisch, "The Not-for-Profit Hospital as a Physicians' Cooperative," *American Economic Review* 63(1), March 1973, 87–99.

Ramsey, Frank, "A Contribution to the Theory of Taxation," *Economic Journal* 37, 1927, 47–61.

Reinhardt, Uwe E., "The Many Different Prices Paid to Providers and the Flawed Theory of Cost Shifting: Is It Time for a More Rational All-Payer System?" *Health Affairs* 30(11), 2011, 2125–2133.

Renn, Steven C., et al., "The Effects of Ownership and System Affiliation on the Economic Performance of Hospitals," *Inquiry* 22(3), Fall 1985, 219–236.

Robinson, James C. and Harold S. Luft, "Competition and the Cost of Hospital Care, 1972 to 1982," *Journal of the American Medical Association* 257(23), June 19, 1987, 3241–3245.

———, "The Impact of Hospital Market Structure on Patient Volume, Average Length of Stay, and the Cost of Care," *Journal of Health Economics* 4(4), December 1985, 333–356.

Robinson, James C., et al., "Hospital Competition and Surgical Length of Stay," *Journal of the American Medical Association* 259(5), February 5, 1988, 696–700.

Russell, Louise B. and Carrie Lynn Manning, "The Effect of Prospective Payment on Medicare Expenditures," *New England Journal of Medicine* 320(7), February 16, 1989, 439–444.

Santerre, Rexford E. and Dana C. Bennett, "Hospital Market Structure and Cost Performance: A Case Study," *Eastern Economic Journal* 18(2), Spring 1992, 209–219.

Shalit, Sol S., "A Doctor-Hospital Cartel Theory," *Journal of Business* 50(1), January 1977, 1–20.

Sheingold, Steven H. "The First Three Years of PPS: Impact on Medicare Costs," *Health Affairs* 8(3), Fall 1989, 191–204.

Sloan, Frank A., "Property Rights in the Hospital Industry," in *Health Care in America: The Political Economy of Hospitals and Health Insurance*, edited by H. E. Frech III, San Francisco: Pacific Research Institute for Public Policy, 1988, 103–141.

———, "The Internal Organization of Hospitals: A Descriptive Study," *Health Services Research* 15(3), Fall 1980, 203–230.

Sloan, Frank A., Joseph Valvona, and Ross Mullner, "Identifying the Issues: Statistical Profile," in *Uncompensated Hospital Care: Rights and Responsibilities*, edited by Frank A. Sloan, James F. Blumstein, and James M. Perrin, Baltimore, MD: Johns Hopkins University Press, 1986, 16–53.

Stevens, Rosemary, *In Sickness and in Wealth: American Hospitals in the Twentieth Century*, New York: Basic Books, 1989.

Tompkins, Christopher P., Stuart H. Altman, and Efrat Eilat, "The Precarious Pricing System for Hospital Services," *Health Affairs* 25(1), January/February 2006, 45–56.

Vitaliano, Donald F., "On the Estimation of Hospital Cost Functions," *Journal of Health Economics* 6(4), December 1987, 305–318.

Zelder, Marvin, "How Private Hospital Competition Can Improve Canadian Health Care," Online Public Policy Source Paper No. 35, Vancouver, BC: The Fraser Institute, 1999.

Zwanziger, Jack and Anil Bamezai, "Evidence of Cost Shifting in California Hospitals," *Health Affairs* 25(1), 2006, 197–203.

Zwanziger, Jack, et al., "Can Cost Shifting Continue in a Price Competitive Environment?" *Health Economics* 9, 2000, 211–225.

CHAPTER 11

The Market for Pharmaceuticals

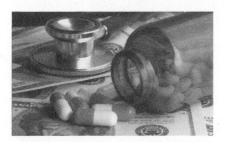

ISSUES IN MEDICAL CARE DELIVERY

PHARMA'S SEARCH FOR A NEW RESEARCH STRATEGY

Some pharmaceutical industry analysts mark 2010 as the year of the "patent cliff," the beginning of a three-year period when drugs with over $50 billion in annual sales saw their patents expire. The trend has continued over the past several years, leaving the pharmaceutical industry struggling to discover a new research strategy that will prove financially sound and scientifically successful. Lipitor (Pfizer), the most successful drug in terms of sales, experienced a 50 percent drop in sales when it went off patent in 2011. The same can be said for the Sanofi-Aventis anticoagulant Plavix when its patent expired the same year. In fact, 5 of the top 15 drugs in terms of annual sales lost their patents between 2013 and 2015. After 2015 the high-revenue drug patent expirations continued.

The pharmaceutical research firms are beginning to realize that the old blockbuster model may no longer work. Instead of targeting diseases that affect millions of people, the drug makers are considering treatments that help thousands. Changing the focus from marketing to science, the companies may no longer invest in copycat drugs that target the same conditions as drugs already under patent. Instead, they will likely try to diversify their drug portfolios into those areas where the science is well understood, regardless of the size of the affected population.

The recent experience with drugs like Vioxx (Merck) and Baycol (Bayer) has resulted in a public that is less tolerant of drug risk. (The FDA recalled both drugs due to unacceptable mortality risk.) The result is a Food and Drug Administration (FDA) that now approves about 35 new drugs annually (average number accepted in 2010–2015).

Drugs that treat the diseases that we understand well have already been discovered. We have options for treating high cholesterol, hypertension, asthma, bacterial infections, diabetes, depression, and migraine. However, the conditions where we have a large affected population like Alzheimer's and cancer are poorly understood, and may be several diseases and not one. Joint ventures, outsourcing, and acquisitions/mergers may be seen with increasing frequency. Competitive pressures are high and success depends on the ability to adapt and adjust to a changing environment.

PATENT EXPIRATIONS, BLOCKBUSTER DRUGS, 2015–2017		
BRAND	MANUFACTURER	INDICATION
2015		
38 drugs including:		
Lovaza	Reliant	Cholesterol
Ambilify	Bristol-Myers Squibb	Depression
Gleevec	Novartis	Cancer
Celebrex	Pfizer	Pain/inflammation
2016		
30 drugs including:		
Crestor	Astra Zeneca	Cholesterol
Nuvigil	Cephalon	Narcolepsy
Rituxan	Biogen Idec/Genentech	Cancer
Zetia	Schering-Plough	Cholesterol
Celebrex	Pfizer	Pain/inflammation
2017		
25 drugs including:		
Tamiflu	Roche	Viral infections
Velcade	Takeda	Cancer
Vytorin	Merck	Cholesterol

Source: "Pharma Is at Pains to Replace Blockbusters: Has It Found the Cure?" *Knowledge@Wharton*, February 3, 2010, available at knowledge.wharton.upenn.edu/article.cfm?articleid=2424 (Accessed October 4, 2010).

Economists began studying the pharmaceutical industry in response to questions that arose from the 1959 Congressional investigations of the Kefauver committee. The main issues that concerned the committee dealt with pricing, profitability, competition, product safety, and outlays for research and development (R&D). Over five decades have passed since the Kefauver investigation, but the issues remain the same. Fueled by concern over the high out-of-pocket spending by the elderly and rising government outlays through Medicare and Medicaid, many reformers today are targeting the pharmaceutical industry for more stringent drug-price regulation in an effort to curb overall health care spending.

For all the attention that the industry receives in the medical care reform debate, it is actually relatively small, about 10 percent of total health expenditures in 2015. Americans spend twice as much on computers and three times as much on automobiles as they do on prescription drugs. That figure is less than every European country except Sweden and Norway and far less than the Japanese, who spend 40 percent more per capita on drugs than Americans. The low percentage spent on pharmaceuticals in the United States is somewhat deceiving, because working-aged adults with low hospitalization rates spend 20–25 percent of their individual health care dollars on pharmaceuticals. The Centers for Medicare and Medicaid Services (CMS) project national pharmaceutical spending to remain around 10 percent of total health care spending. The effects of the expansion of the Medicare outpatient prescription drug program will be offset by increased generic competition as important blockbuster drugs lose their patent protection over the next decade and cost sharing increases as private insurance copays rise.

In this chapter, we will examine the market for pharmaceuticals. We will look at the structure of the industry, discussing the R&D process, the role of patents, and issues relating to pricing in the global market.

The Structure of the Industry

Traditionally, the United States has relied on private sector initiative and market mechanisms to influence the direction of R&D in the overall economy. The pharmaceutical industry provides an interesting case study in which government, private philanthropy, and academia have become intimately involved in the process of new product development. In most cases, the U.S. government sponsors very little **applied research**, the purpose of which is usually commercialization of a product. Through a network of nationally owned laboratories, such as the National Institutes of Health (NIH), and through grants to universities, government and private philanthropy have taken a direct role in funding **basic research**, the purpose of which is to advance fundamental knowledge.

Basic research is essential. Denison (1985) argued that it is the primary source of the innovative technologies responsible for a substantial portion of economic growth. The U.S. leadership position in pharmaceuticals is due, at least in part, to a commitment to basic research, but ultimately the success of the pharmaceutical industry depends on its ability to discover, develop, and market new drugs.

applied research
Research whose purpose is typically the commercialization of a product.

basic research
Research whose purpose is to advance fundamental knowledge.

The Role of Research in the Age of Technology

The pharmaceutical industry relies heavily on R&D to discover new chemical compounds that save lives and improve the quality of life. Innovative research and the discovery of new compounds are becoming increasingly important in a world where government price controls are responsible for falling prices in many markets. The 40 member companies of Pharmaceutical Research and Manufacturers of America (PhRMA; the world's largest pharmaceutical manufacturers) have spent over $500 billion on R&D since 2000, and $51.2 billion in 2014 alone, or 17.9 percent of their combined sales of $286 billion. Approximately 75 percent of the world's total R&D spending in pharmaceuticals is concentrated in the United States, where firms must innovate in order to survive (PhRMA, 2015).

U.S. supremacy in the development of new drugs is clear. Data from PhRMA reported by Weidenbaum (1993b) show that over 60 percent of the 1,265 new drugs introduced into the U.S. market between 1940 and 1990 were developed by U.S. firms. Switzerland was second with 89 new drug introductions, followed by the United Kingdom, Germany, and France. Furthermore, 45 percent of the 152 drugs introduced worldwide between 1975 and 1994 were developed in the United States. The United Kingdom was the country of origin in 14 percent of the cases, Switzerland in 9 percent, and Japan and Germany in 7 percent each (PhRMA, 2010). This trend has continued well into the twenty-first century. In 2010, there were almost 3,000 compounds in development in the United States—three times the number in the entire European Union and six times the number in Japan. Europe's once thriving pharmaceutical industry has largely migrated to the United States. Since 1995, Pharmacia (Sweden), Novartis (Switzerland), Avantis (France/Germany), and GlaxoSmithKline (United Kingdom) have moved some aspect of their operations to the United States.

HTTP://
NIH, one of the world's foremost biomedical research centers and the federal focal point for biomedical research in the United States. http://www.nih.gov.

HTTP://
PhRMA provides facts and figures on pharmaceutical research and drugs in development. http://www.phrma.org.

return on sales A financial measure of a firm's ability to generate after-tax profit out of its total sales. Calculated by dividing after-tax profit by total sales.

The introduction of new drugs is a major determinant in profitability (Baily, 1972). The longer a drug is on the market, the lower its **return on sales**. 5 Firms earn normal profits on older drugs and higher profits on newer drugs. The importance of discovering new chemical compounds leads pharmaceutical firms to spend a high percentage of their sales revenue on R&D. Biopharmaceutical companies consistently spend 15–20 percent of sales revenue on R&D. In comparison, the U.S. industry average, excluding drugs and medicine, is less than 5 percent. In 2015, 8 of the top 20 corporations ranked according to R&D spending were pharmaceutical companies.

Between 2001 and 2015, the U.S. FDA approved 411 new medicines or about 27 per year. In 2015 alone 45 new molecular entities (NMEs) were approved (the most in a single year since 53 approvals in 1996) targeting various diseases affecting millions of people worldwide. More than one-third of the medications approved in 2015 were considered first in class treatments, taking an entirely new approach to treating a disease. The list includes drugs to treat chronic conditions such as asthma, diabetes, and high cholesterol, and a new wave of targeted treatments for cancer. Eleven of the drugs launched in 2015 are expected to reach annual sales of at least $1 billion by 2020. (New drug applications [NDAs] accepted slowed considerably in 2016, falling to 22.)

Prior to the mid-1970s, pharmaceutical research was based primarily on trial and error. Natural compounds were extracted from dirt samples or plants and then injected into animals to see what would happen. Scientists might try as many as 60,000 compounds in order to develop a drug with annual sales of $100 million. Not until the late 1970s did scientists begin to understand the role of receptors in the body that block or trigger biochemical responses. It then became possible to fashion molecules to fit those receptors. Tagamet, developed by SmithKline, was one of the first chemical compounds developed this way. This ulcer medication works by blocking a histamine receptor in the intestines that triggers the secretion of acid. It has proven far more effective than ordinary antacids, virtually eliminating the need for ulcer surgery.

APPLIED MICRO METHODS

CAN THE USE OF STATINS REDUCE THE RISK OF HEART ATTACK?

Background

Several large randomized control trials (RCTs) in the United States and abroad show that the use of statins reduces the level of low-density lipoprotein (LDL) and the risk of acute myocardial infarction (AMI). However, RCTs have yet to establish the efficacy of fluvastatin (brand name Lescol) in reducing AMI risk.

Data and Methods

Enrollees in the Fallon Community Health Plan (FCHP) with recorded LDL levels exceeding 130 mg/dl at any time from 1994 to 1998 were eligible for this study. Researchers combined enrollment files and pharmacy claims data to identify 52 coronary heart disease (CHD) risk factors. Using logistic regression, they estimated propensity scores measuring the probability of initiating statin use. Using these propensity scores, they matched statin initiators (SI) with statin non-initiators (SNI) and followed them for 54 months for the occurrence of AMI.

Results

Descriptive statistics indicated that the unmatched cohorts of SI and SNI had no statistically significant differences in over 80 percent of the CHD risk factors. Among the unmatched cohorts (see left-hand side of the next figure), the SI cohort had a higher incidence of AMI than the SNI cohort. Each cohort numbered 4,144 enrollees with the SI group experiencing 325 cases of AMI compared to 124 in the SNI cohort (hazard ratio of 2.11).

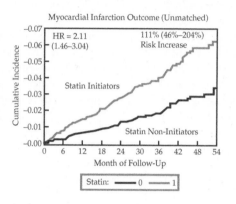
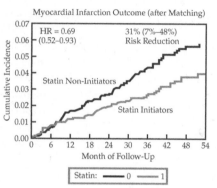

Each SI was paired with an SNI with a similar propensity score (difference of less than 0.01). Over 70 percent of SI were matched with an SNI indicating that there were no statistically significant differences in CHD risk factors across the cohorts (2,901 in each). The SI cohort had a decreased LDL of approximately 20 percent more than their matched SNI cohort and 13 percent fewer AMIs (77 versus 114, hazard ration of 0.69).

Discussion and Conclusions

Clearly, statin use significantly reduces not only LDL levels but also the risk of AMI. Using only the results of the observational analysis would result in the wrong conclusions, highlighting the limitations of observational analysis. Propensity score matching provides a more accurate understanding of the benefits of statin use (primarily fluvastatin), closely replicating the results achieved in RCTs.

Source: John D. Seeger et al., "A Propensity Score-Matched Cohort Study of the Effect of Statins, Mainly Fluvastatin, on the Occurrence of Acute Myocardial Infarction," *American Journal of Cardiology* 92, December 15, 2003, 1447–1451.

In 1986, less than 10 years after its introduction, Tagamet became the first billion-dollar-a-year drug in worldwide sales. By 1992, four drugs had reached this blockbuster status. In 1998, there were 29 and in 2000 there were 55. Since 2012, the top-selling drug worldwide has been the biologic Humira produced by AbbVie. Used for the treatment of rheumatoid arthritis and other autoimmune disorders, its annual sales were $15.7 billion in 2016. The hepatitis C treatment Harvoni was second on the list. Produced by Gilead, it had sales of $11.6 billion. Rituxan, produced by Roche and used to treat non-Hodgkin's lymphoma, had sales of $7.3 billion. Roche also produced Avastin, used to treat cancer, with sales of $7.0 billion. In fact, each of the top 10 drugs generated over $5 billion in worldwide revenues in 2016, and five are expected to remain on the list of top drugs through at least 2020.

ORPHAN DRUGS

patent An exclusive right to supply a good for a specific time period, usually 20 years. It serves as a barrier to entry, virtually eliminating all competition for the life of the patent.

Given the expense of developing new drugs, pharmaceutical firms seek to protect their intellectual property rights through the use of **patent** law. Patents provide exclusive rights to the production for a specified time period, usually 20 years. The long developmental period for the typical drug—12–15 years—means that the market benefit of the patent is usually only around 5–8 years.

The one important exception to this rule emerges when firms pursue "orphan drug" status for drugs used to treat rare diseases (defined by the FDA as those affecting less than 200,000 U.S. patients). Congress passed the Orphan Drug Act in 1983 to encourage the development of drugs that have limited commercial value. The status carries with it the exclusive marketing rights to the drug. As amended in 1984, the act makes it easier for firms to get orphan status for drugs that have market potential. For example, the drug Taxol (made from the bark of the Pacific yew tree) was approved for the treatment of ovarian cancer in 1992. With only 30,000 women affected by the cancer, orphan drug status seemed to make sense. Even before Taxol was designated an orphan drug, however, it was clear that its full market potential extended well beyond the treatment of ovarian cancer. The American Cancer Society speculated that Taxol's commercial potential extends to other cancers—including malignant melanoma, breast cancer, and lung cancer—with over 300,000 potential beneficiaries. Between 1993 and 2002, Taxol's sales revenue exceeded $9 billion.

Firms that receive orphan drug status for compounds that would have been developed without it stand to receive substantial economic rents, payments in excess of the minimum necessary to guarantee production. Granted, some drugs would never be developed without the provision of this status. However, one of the top-selling biotech drug—Epogen manufactured by Amgen and used to treat anemia—is an orphan drug. Epogen's sales of approximately $1.4 billion in 2015 make it one of the most successful biotech drug on the market.

Sources: Suzanne Tregarthen, "Pharmaceutical Firms Seek Monopoly Protection from the U.S. Government," *The Margin*, Fall 1992, 50–51 and Cynthia Smith, "Retail Prescription Drug Spending in the National Health Accounts," *Health Affairs*, 23(1), 2004, 160–167.

BIOTECHNOLOGY: WHAT IS A FAIR PRICE?

KEY CONCEPT 5
Markets and Pricing

The images that we have of gene splicing are, for the most part, the products of Hollywood movie magic. Cloning dinosaurs from DNA fragments found in prehistoric mosquitoes trapped in fossilized tree resin makes good science fiction, but a more realistic assessment of the current state of biotech research reveals the potential for far more important commercial applications.

Biotechnology is an attempt to understand the basic function of the human body and disease. As an industry, biotechnology is relatively new. In the early 1970s, scientists developed the capability of identifying specific genes and harnessing them to make the specific proteins the body uses to protect itself against disease. A 1980 Supreme Court ruling paved the way for the creation of biotechnology as an industry. The court ruled that scientists could patent the new life forms they developed by splicing genes and transforming them into other organisms or cells.

Over 1,400 biotech firms operate in the United States, generating $150 billion in revenues and spending over one-half that on R&D. Investors are pouring billions in equity capital every year into the search for the cures for such diseases as cancer, AIDS, and heart disease. The price of success is high. And no single product epitomizes the drug-pricing dilemma better than Ceredase, produced by Genzyme Corporation as a treatment for Gaucher's disease.

Gaucher's disease is a rare genetic disorder in which the body fails to produce an essential enzyme to break down fat deposits in cells. If left untreated, body functions degenerate, vital organs enlarge, and joints deteriorate. Ceredase provides the enzyme, reversing the damage caused by the disease. Originally extracted from human placentas, it took 20,000 placentas, or about 27 tons of afterbirth, to produce a year's supply for one person.

Given the obvious production challenges, Genzyme developed a genetically engineered version of the drug, Cerezyme, targeting the disease process itself. More recently in 2016, the FDA approved an oral alternative, Cerdelga, which is now available at an annual price of over $300,000. Unlike Sovaldi, used for the treatment of hepatitis C—a disease that affects over 3.2 million Americans (available at a cost of $89,000), Gaucher's only affects about 2,000 Americans (10,000 worldwide). Despite the individual cost, overall burden is actually lower; insurance companies actually consider the cost of Cerdelga sustainable.

Biotechnology as an industry is barely 30 years old. As new genetic discoveries are made, their economic implications are not always obvious. Discovery through basic research is one thing. Commercial application is a separate and oftentimes more complex issue. What is a fair price? Ask the sufferers of Gaucher's disease who are spared the costly surgeries to repair damage to vital organs and joints.

Sources: Elyse Tanouye, "What's Fair?" *Wall Street Journal*, May 20, 1994, R11; Michael Waldholz, "An Industry in Adolescence," *Wall Street Journal*, May 20, 1994, R4; and Robert Wiseman, "New Genzyme Pill Will Cost Patients $310,250 a Year," *Boston Globe*, September 2, 2014.

⭐ **KEY CONCEPT 5**
Markets and Pricing

HTTP://
Activities of the U.S. FDA may be found at their website http://www.fda.gov.

The R&D Process   The profit potential for successful new drugs is exceptionally good. This is due, at least in part, to the patent protection that grants monopoly rights to the firm that discovers a new chemical entity (NCE). This high-profit potential is offset to a large degree by the low probability that a chemical compound will find its way onto the shelves of the local pharmacy. The odds of getting a new drug approved by the FDA are extremely low. During the discovery phase, researchers will evaluate at least 5,000 compounds, out of which 250 will proceed to the preclinical testing phase. Only five of those will enter human trials, and only one will receive FDA approval. The odds of making a profit on an approved drug are even lower—only 2 in 10 generate enough sales to cover average R&D expenditures (Vernon, Golec, and DiMasi, 2010).

The R&D process for a typical drug approval takes about 12–15 years, approximately two times the 6.5 years it took in 1964. Testing progresses sequentially, and the drug's status is reviewed periodically to determine whether the process will continue. Table 11.1 summarizes the steps in the pharmaceutical R&D process for the typical drug.

The preclinical phase of the R&D process includes a significant amount of discovery research undertaken to develop new concepts in treating diseases. This phase includes the synthesis and extraction of a new chemical compound to determine whether it brings about the desired change in a biological system. After the new compound is synthesized, it is screened for pharmacological activity and toxicity in the laboratory. When firms identify a promising compound, they file an Investigational New Drug (IND) application with the FDA. After 30 days, the firm begins three phases of clinical testing on humans.

TABLE 11.1 STEPS IN THE PHARMACEUTICAL R&D PROCESS

Testing phase	Mean phase length (Years)	Out-of-pocket spending (Millions)	Capitalized spending (Millions)
Discovery—preclinical	5.0	$ 430	$1,098
Clinical trials		$ 965	$1,460
Phase 1	1.5		
Phase 2	2.0		
Phase 3	3.5		
FDA review and approval	1.5		
Post-approval testing	–	$ 466	$ 312
Total R&D	13.5	$1,861	$2,870

Source: DiMasi et al. (2016).

The FDA approves approximately 2 percent of these applications for human trials for the three phases of human testing. Phase 1 testing is performed on a small number of healthy volunteers, usually 20–100, to determine the drug's safety profile: toxicity to humans, absorption and distribution rates, safe dosage levels, metabolic effects, and other information needed to establish human tolerance to the compound. Phase 2 evaluation is the first of the two controlled clinical trials conducted on a small number (between 100 and 500) of volunteer patients who the drug is intended to benefit. Efficacy and safety are the primary issues examined during this phase. The final development phase involves large-scale testing in hospital and outpatient settings and usually involves 1,000–5,000 patients. By using a large number of patients, Phase 3 testing gathers essential effectiveness and safety information by approximating the actual manner of usage in the event that the FDA eventually grants marketing approval.

Throughout the clinical testing period, additional long-term toxicology experiments on animals are performed. The purpose of these experiments is to determine the teratologic and carcinogenic effects of the compounds. At the same time, formulation work and process development are conducted to determine if the compound can be manufactured in quantities that are sufficient to satisfy potential demand for the drug. If the firm is satisfied with the evidence compiled from the clinical studies, it will submit an NDA to the FDA. The NDA typically runs over 100,000 pages and contains all the scientific information gathered during the clinical trials. By law, the FDA has six months to review each NDA. In practice, the process takes 18 months. The FDA ultimately approves for human use only one out of five compounds that reach the clinical trial stage.

Once approved, the new medication becomes available for use. Even as marketing efforts begin, the pharmaceutical companies continue the testing process. Reports to the FDA track adverse health events, including deaths. In some cases, the FDA will require additional study to evaluate the long-term effects of the drug, often referred to as Phase 4 of the trial process.

The entire process is long and expensive. DiMasi, Grabowski, and Hansen (2016) studied 1,442 investigational drugs first tested on humans between 1995 and 2007, out of which only 7.1 percent had been approved for marketing. Their estimate for the fully capitalized cost for a newly approved drug was $2.6 billion (in 2016). Firms spend approximately one-half of the overall cost of developing a drug during the 7-year long clinical trials phase.

Required post-approval R&D discounted to approval date added $312 million (25 percent) to the total cost, bringing it to approximately $2.9 billion per approved drug.

This study is actually the fourth in a series of studies using similar methodology. Hansen (1979) looked at drugs first tested in humans in the 1970s and early 1980s and estimated the full cost to be 179 million. DiMasi et al. (1991) estimated total capitalized cost for drugs first tested in humans in the 1980s to early 1990s to be 413 million. The third study (DiMasi, Hansen, and Grabowski, 2003) found total cost to be $1.04 billion. Using constant dollars, the total capitalized cost of developing a newly approved drug has increased over 14 times across the 40-year time span of the four studies.

BACK-OF-THE-ENVELOPE
A Simple Estimate of the Cost of R&D

The pharmaceutical industry regularly cites the studies by DiMasi and colleagues (2003, 2016) as the source of the multibillion dollar estimate of drug development cost. Critics question the methodology and the math, but the real figure may actually be much higher. Herper (2012) takes a more direct approach to determine the estimate and simply calculates R&D spending over a given time period relative to the number of approved drugs during that period. There are issues with the approach; timing of spending and approvals is just one. Nevertheless, it does have its advantages, namely simplicity.

Company	Number of approved drugs (1997–2012)	Total R&D spending (billions)	R&D spending per approved Drug (billions)
Pfizer	16	$108.19	$6.67
Johnson & Johnson	16	88.29	5.89
Roche Holdings	11	85.85	7.81
Novartis	21	83.66	3.98
GlaxoSmithKline	11	81.71	7.43
Merck	17	68.36	3.96
Sanofi	10	63.28	6.33
Astra Zeneca	5	58.96	11.79
Eli Lilly	11	50.35	4.58
Abbott Labs	8	35.97	4.50
Total R&D	125	$724.62	$5.80

The earlier table shows the average R&D spending per approved drugs for the top 10 pharmaceutical manufacturers in terms of total R&D spending for the years 1997–2012. R&D spending averages between $4 billion and $12 billion per approved drug. The overall average of the 125 approved drugs was $5.8 billion. Why is the process so expensive? The drug industry would have us believe that it is expensive because it's difficult. It could be that the drug companies are going about the business of research the wrong way. They are simply displaying the inefficiencies inherent in all markets dominated by monopoly. Maybe it is time for a new paradigm.

Sources: Matthew Herper, "The Truly Staggering Cost of Inventing New Drugs," *Forbes*, February 22, 2012 and U.S. Food and Drug Administration, FY 2012 Innovative Drug Approvals, available at http://www.fda.gov/downloads/AboutFDA/ReportsManualsForms/Reports/UCM330859.pdf.

KEY CONCEPT 5
Markets and Pricing

Policy Toward Innovation   Encouraging innovation has long been an interest of government. Statutes traced back to seventeenth-century England rewarded innovation by granting special monopoly rights to the inventor. The U.S. patent system emerged as colonists in the New World recognized that rewarding individual innovators would benefit society as a whole. Patent policy was eventually codified in the U.S. Constitution. Article I, Section 8, grants Congress the authority "to promote the progress of science and useful arts, by securing for limited times to authors and inventors the exclusive right to their respective writings and discoveries." Policy change often outpaces implementation: It was not until 1836 that Congress authorized the U.S. Patent Office to determine if proposed inventions qualified for patent protection.

Regulation of pharmaceutical drugs became the responsibility of the FDA in the early twentieth century. Initially, concern focused primarily on drug safety. Then, with the passage of the Kefauver-Harris Drug Amendments in 1962, the scope of regulation expanded to include not only safety but also effectiveness. Adopted in the wake of the thalidomide tranquilizer disaster in Europe, where over 12,000 babies were born with severe birth defects, the Kefauver amendments required drug makers to prove the effectiveness of a drug in treating a specific disease or medical condition. In addition, the FDA was given strict control over investigational drug studies, Phase 2 and Phase 3 of human trials.

The most significant change in patent law, and its profound impact on the pharmaceutical industry, came in 1984 with the passage of the Drug Price Competition and Patent Term Restoration Act. The Hatch-Waxman Act extended the effective life of a drug patent up to five years and, at the same time, made it easier for generic drugs to enter the market. The patent-life extension was intended to restore part of the patent life lost to the expanded regulatory process; it is equal to the sum of the FDA review time for the NDA and half the time consumed by the clinical trials. Prior to the Hatch-Waxman Act, generic drug companies were required to submit their own safety and efficacy evidence to support their NDA. Because of the new law, if the generic company could demonstrate bioequivalence to the existing branded drug, it might rely on the original safety and efficacy evidence provided by the branded drug. This Abbreviated New Drug Application (ANDA) is a low-cost option compared to the earlier requirement, cutting at least two years off the application process and saving millions of dollars (Grabowski and Vernon, 1986). Since passage of the Act, the generic share of the unit volume increased from 19 percent to over 80 percent. Now, within months of patent expiration, a branded drug's market share falls substantially.

International property rights were further strengthened as part of the Uruguay Round in the General Agreement on Tariffs and Trade (GATT) negotiations in 1993. Patent infringement by developing countries had become a serious issue in trade negotiations. The Uruguay Round produced an agreement on Trade-Related Aspects of Intellectual Property (TRIPs) that brought about major changes in the patent policies of other countries. For U.S. domestic policy, the most important change was increasing the patent term, from 17 years from the date of grant to 20 years from the date of application. Other important changes included providing patent holders the right to prohibit the importation of products that infringe on a valid patent and a limit on the use of compulsory licensing policies that force patent holders to relinquish property rights on certain essential drugs (Barton, 2004; Jaffe, 2000).

Patents   The goal of the patent system is to insure adequate rewards for R&D consistent with the dissemination of the patented product and information related to it. The economic rationale for patents is based on the understanding that the primary product of R&D, scientific knowledge, has many of the attributes of a public good (Levin, 1986). Though patents create monopoly price distortions, this defect was overshadowed in the early years of the American republic by the advantage that the nation did not need to rely on its tax system for revenues: Inventors and authors generated their own rewards through selling their works.

Spence (1984) identified three issues that lead to market failure associated with large investments in R&D. First, the value of R&D is determined by what buyers are willing to pay for the product of R&D, and total revenues understate social benefits, both in the aggregate and at the margin. Thus, there is no a priori reason to think that unaided market outcomes will be optimal in any sense. Second, because R&D is often associated with significant fixed costs (certainly true in the case of pharmaceuticals), imperfect competition and its consequences are likely to characterize the industry. Third, substantial investment in R&D frequently is associated with an appropriability problem, thereby reducing the firm's incentive to conduct R&D.[1] As many have noted, solving the R&D incentive problem by creating a monopoly problem merely trades off one inefficiency for another.

With modern economics, we can better describe the flaws of the patent system:

- Patents do not transfer to the holder the social surplus that the invention generates. The failure to account for full consumer surplus may mean that the incentive to invent is inefficiently low.
- The well-known experiences of Louis Daguerre (Daguerreotype) and Eli Whitney (cotton gin), whose inventions were quickly stolen, or effectively expropriated, by the public show that the patent is often little defense against inventions being purloined by others (Kremer, 1998). Once a product has been manufactured, pharmaceutical knowledge is often easily reverse engineered.
- The patent system fails to account for beneficial externalities that result from the patent. Daguerre's photographic process had a tremendous impact on spurring the widespread development of photography, a positive externality never captured by the inventor. In the case of new drugs, knowledge spillovers resulting in imperfect appropriability diminish incentives for R&D. The marginal cost of the understanding required to produce a pharmaceutical drug is often close to zero, comprising only the cost of transmitting the scientific knowledge.
- Finally, by their nature, patents create monopoly rents. These distort research incentives and encourage inefficient efforts by other firms to create copycat inventions that undercut the patent holder in pursuit of the monopoly rents.

The point that patents respond in part to the appropriability problem but provide imperfect protection bears repeating. In its capacity as a barrier to entry, a patent increases the cost of supplying a perfect substitute, but it does not preclude the development of similar drugs designed to treat the same medical condition (Waterson, 1990). In 2000, there were six different proton pump inhibitors and six histamine H2 receptor antagonists under patent for the treatment of ulcers. Seven patented drugs were available for the treatment of high cholesterol, five patented antidepressants were available, and there were 27 different patented drugs for the treatment of hypertension (Spence, 2000). Taking into consideration the eventuality of in-class competition, the first mover can expect only a temporary advantage until follower drugs in the class are approved. For most classes of drugs, competitors are able to develop imitations or close substitutes in a short period. The process of filing for and receiving a patent sometimes discloses enough scientific knowledge to encourage further innovation, when combined with the prospect of economic rents. Even presuming

---

[1]Because many inventions are easily reverse engineered, they are relatively simple to duplicate, allowing rivals to appropriate, or rather expropriate, financial returns normally considered the property of the original inventor.

that markets are monopolistically competitive, patents create allocation problems, provide the innovator with market power, and cause pricing distortions.

A natural response to this dilemma is to ask whether we can improve social outcomes by adjusting the patent rules to create a system that provides the optimal balance between the short-run efficiency of marginal cost pricing and the long-run incentives to innovate. Unfortunately, it is unlikely that the patent system, as it is traditionally envisioned, can be fine-tuned to improve social welfare (Scotchmer, 1991). The number of instruments available to policy makers limits the scope of patent law to achieve the desired objectives. In addition to the length of the patent life (20 years for pharmaceuticals), policy is constrained by the breadth of protection, which connects to the likelihood that second-generation technology will infringe on the patent. Whether the patent is awarded to the first to invent, as is the case with the U.S./Canada priority rule, or to the first to apply, which is the case in the rest of the world, it remains a restricted instrument.

The Impact of Patents on Drug Prices

The special treatment of intellectual property through the patent system distorts drug prices, limits treatment options for individuals who do not have the means to pay, and causes American consumers to pay too much for their prescription medications. Lower prices on certain branded drugs purchased in Canada have many arguing for a public policy response targeting high U.S. prices.

KEY CONCEPT 7
Competition

The awarding of a patent provides the innovator with monopoly power—the ability to limit availability of the product and set prices above the marginal cost of production. A pharmaceutical patent holder (see Figure 11.1) facing a downward-sloping demand curve for its prescription drug, D_1, will set output at Q_1 and charge a price P_1. A competitive market that prices the drug at marginal cost, C_1 (equal to average variable cost, AVC, when MC is constant), improves welfare; output is higher, at Q_2, and the producer earns only normal profits.

The Impact of Insurance on Drug Prices Creating a prescription drug insurance plan with a copayment provision invites the monopolist's response, which is to raise the drug price in proportion to the inverse of the copay. A 50-percent copay, as shown in

FIGURE 11.1
Pricing a Patented Drug

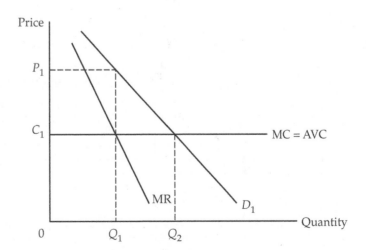

Figure 11.2, would imply that the monopolist would double prices from their initial level; the monopolist could adjust the resulting price-quantity point on the effective demand curve by moving from the initial quantity only if profits are thereby raised (Grinols and Henderson, 2007). In the figure, consumer demand without insurance is D_1 with its associated equilibrium price and quantity of P_1 and Q_1. With a 50-percent copay—insurance pays half of the cost—demand rises to D_2, and prices virtually double, to P_2.[2]

The monopoly response is important, because the percentage of prescription drug expenditures paid out of pocket by U.S. consumers has fallen from 60 percent in 1990 to about 20 percent today. In the absence of other market changes, this fact would predict an approximate increase in drug prices of 200 percent. From 1990 to 2016, the pharmaceutical component of the medical consumer price index (CPI) actually increased approximately 165 percent. Consumer advocates express concern that the prices of drugs, especially those consumed by the elderly, have surged since the Medicare drug program was first introduced in mid-2001 (Martinez, 2004). However, the industry's actions should elicit little surprise. They are the natural result of an inefficient and outmoded means of encouraging innovation.

Large sunk costs, high fixed costs, low variable costs, segmentable markets, and strong patent protection for drug discoveries characterize the pharmaceutical industry. Market power restricts competition and guarantees to patent holders a monopoly position for the effective life of the patent, currently about eight years after introducing the drug on the market. Pharmaceutical companies maintain that high prices are essential to support continued innovation and an uninterrupted flow of new products. Because of the high cost of developing a drug, patent protection does not guarantee that a drug will be economically successful. It is reported that the likelihood of recovering research expenditures on a marketable drug is less than one in three (Grabowski, Vernon, and DiMasi, 2002).

FIGURE 11.2

The Impact of Insurance on Monopoly Pricing

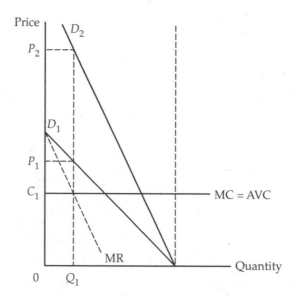

---

[2]For this statement to be true, the marginal cost of producing the drug would have to be zero. In reality, a slight quantity adjustment will take place to maximize profits, and the final equilibrium price will be somewhat lower than P_2.

Those who believe that our current patent system solves the problems associated with rewarding innovation are mistaken. Patents create monopolies, and monopolists effectively exercise market power, restricting output below its social optimum and charging high prices. Patents may not be the best way to reward successful innovation while spreading their benefits as quickly and widely as possible. The profit earned by the monopolist may not accurately reflect the optimal reward to ensure the optimal future R&D effort.

Take, for example, the question of calculating a reward. In principle, much of the benefits of a new invention should accrue to the inventor to ensure optimal effort toward possible future inventions.[3] In a static setting, this involves, among other things, knowing the consumer surplus associated with an invention. If patent rights are granted, consumer surplus information is not provided by the monopoly profits of the seller, and such information is not provided by other immediate price and quantity observations if the patent is not granted.

Pharmaceutical Pricing Issues

The cost of producing a modern pharmaceutical drug is high, primarily because of the high expenditures on R&D. The relevant question may be, are new drugs worth the high cost? If drug therapy reduces the need for more expensive treatments such as surgery, hospitalization, and long-term care, then it may be worth the price. Research evidence indicates that the appropriate use of pharmaceuticals can prevent or at minimum slow the progression of certain diseases.

KEY CONCEPT 2
Opportunity Cost

Lichtenberg (2002) examined data from 20 OECD countries over the period 1995–2003 and found that the use of cardiovascular drugs reduced hospital admissions and average length of hospital stay. Savings on hospitalization was 3.7 times the amount spent on drugs on a per capita basis. Sokol and colleagues (2005) examine the use of diabetes, cholesterol, and blood pressure medications and find that their use can lower overall health care spending by $4–$7 for every dollar spent on medications. Cutler and colleagues (2007) using data from the Framingham Heart Study estimated that the use of hypertensive drug therapy in the United States had an annual benefit cost ratio of 6:1 (in 1999–2000), eliminating 833,000 hospitalizations and 86,000 premature deaths.

Taking a somewhat different approach, Roebuck and colleagues (2011) studied health care utilization among patients suffering from congestive heart failure, high blood pressure, and diabetes. They found that the appropriate use of prescribed medications saved as much as $7,500 per patient by lowering emergency department visits and the length of inpatient hospital stays. Every dollar spent on prescription drugs saved between $3 and $10 on medical care overall. McWilliams and colleagues (2011) estimate that after implementation of Medicare Part D, the average senior who had no significant prior drug coverage realized an annual savings of $1,200 in nondrug spending.

The discovery of medicines to cure or significantly alter the progression of chronic and degenerative diseases represents the single best prescription for increasing profitability in the industry. Increased competition and government oversight have resulted in an environment where innovation is the key to survival. Finding a drug that deals effectively with diseases such as cancer, Alzheimer's disease, arthritis, and AIDS will not only save money, it will ensure healthy profit margins for successful innovators.

---

[3]It is sometimes asserted that, for this to happen, all of the future social value of an invention should go to the inventor, but this is not true if full inventive effort is reached short of this amount. Could it be that Paul McCartney might still have devoted all of his efforts to creating new songs for less than he actually earned for his work?

APPLIED MICRO METHODS

CAN A NEARBY WALMART STORE MAKE YOU HEALTHIER?

Background

Individuals with chronic health conditions are responsible for over 75 percent of all health care spending. Pharmacological therapy can delay or even prevent medical complications that result from conditions such as hypertension, diabetes, congestive heart failure, and asthma (together responsible for over 40 percent of all hospital admissions). Despite our ability to treat these chronic conditions, up to one-half of all individuals diagnosed with one of these chronic diseases fails to take medications prescribed by their physicians.

Evidence indicates that when prescription drug prices decline, utilization increases. Whether the increase in use leads to a reduction in the utilization of downstream services (such as hospitalizations) is less certain. Borrescio-Higa (2015) studied the impact of Walmart's $4 Prescription Drug Program. Launched in 2006, the program allows customers to purchase a 30-day supply of over 130 of the most frequently used generic drugs for only $4. The study examined the impact of cheaper drug prices on drug utilization and avoidable hospitalizations.

Methods

The study used drug utilization and hospital discharge data from the state of Florida for the period 2002–2009. In 2006, Walmart had 3,791 stores nationwide, 222 in Florida. Over 60 percent of the U.S. population lived within 5 miles of a Walmart store, 96 percent within 20 miles. Using a difference-in-differences approach, the study tested the nature of retail pharmacy markets by estimating differences in drug utilization rates (for hypertensive medications) based on an individual's proximity to a nearby Walmart. Specifically, are customers who live closer to a Walmart pharmacy more likely to purchase medications to control high blood pressure? Will increased utilization of antihypertension drugs reduce the likelihood of avoidable hospitalizations?

Results

The $4 generic price translated into an 80 percent decrease at Walmart pharmacies, while all other pharmacies actually raised their prices by 4.2 percent. The author is able to show that customers living closer to a Walmart pharmacy (the treatment group) increased their use of antihypertensive drugs by 7 percent compared to those living farther away (the control group). This increased utilization provides a mechanism to link the drug price reduction to the decrease in avoidable hospitalizations. Results suggest that the decrease in the price of drugs reduced the probability of an avoidable hospitalization by 6.2 percent. The results were larger for non-whites and older individuals (45–64 years old). Uninsured experienced a bigger response to the drug price reduction and had a larger decrease in the probability of an avoidable hospitalization.

Discussion

The results suggest that the introduction of cheaper generic drugs has the potential to reduce unnecessary hospitalizations. In the three years after the program introduction, between 412 and 520 hospitalizations were avoided. Based on the average billed charge for an avoidable hospitalization ($28,221), individuals living within one mile of a Walmart pharmacy saved between $13.5 and $17.3 million. Generalizing the results to the overall U.S. population suggests that the savings may be as high as $202 million nationwide.

Source: Florencia Borrescio-Higa, "Can Walmart Make Us Healthier? Prescription Drug Prices and Health Care Utilization," *Journal of Health Economics* 44, 2015, 37–53.

POLICY ISSUE

Do pharmaceutical companies make too much money? Should government control drug prices?

HTTP://

Center for Genome Research at the White-head Institute for Biomedical Research in Cambridge, Massachusetts, contains information on the Genome project. http://www.broad.mit.edu.

Protection of intellectual property through the patent system establishes a mechanism to keep prices significantly above the marginal cost of manufacturing. Predictably, covering the fixed costs of R&D requires high prices during the patent period. Once a patent expires, generic competitors emerge to offer chemically equivalent drugs at much lower prices. The prices that really matter for most consumers are the prices they actually pay at the pharmacy. Health plans including Medicare and Medicaid use benchmark prices based on average wholesale prices (AWP) to determine how much pharmacies are paying for drugs. Many plans use pharmacy benefit managers (PBMs) to administer their plans, and PBMs often use the AWP of a drug—adjusted by an estimated markup of up to 20 percent—to determine how much they will pay pharmacies.

As wholesalers became more efficient, they began selling drugs to pharmacies at much lower markups, as low as 2–3 percent; but a 20 percent markup was still commonly used as the wholesaler's drug acquisition cost. A shift to a 25 percent markup in 2002 brought the entire pricing system under attack (Martinez, 2004). Litigation settled in 2006 revealed that the survey used to determine the AWP of all drugs sold in the United States was based on information provided by a single national wholesaler and did not gather actual pricing data. In addition to a price rollback, as part of the settlement in the lawsuit, publication of the AWP stopped in 2008. PBMs and other payers had to come up with another way to determine how much they paid pharmacies for prescription drugs.

ISSUES IN MEDICAL CARE DELIVERY

GENE-BASED RESEARCH

Almost all of the new chemical entities discovered to date act on proteins, the chemicals that do the work in all living cells. But advances in basic research have pharmaceutical companies changing their focus to the development of drugs that act directly on human genes, not just the chemicals they produce.

A $3 billion international research effort called the Human Genome Project was undertaken to decode the estimated 100,000 genes that make up the human structure. As scientists discovered new genes, they were able to identify the molecular causes of certain inherited disorders and discern how genes trigger common illnesses. In 1980, only 40 genes were known. In 2000, the mapping of the entire human genome was completed. Recent discoveries include genes linked to lung cancer, osteoporosis, and Alzheimer's disease.

The basic notion behind gene research is that a defective gene—one that fails to produce a protein when it should, or one that produces a protein when it should not—is the cause of all illness. With the proper understanding of the genetic code, scientists hope to switch on genes to produce therapeutic proteins (gene therapy) and switch off genes so that they stop making harmful proteins (gene blocking).

Despite the fact that over 1,500 disease-related genes have been isolated, there is no conclusive scientific evidence that gene therapy works. Still the pharmaceutical industry is risking large sums of money, betting that it will pay off in the future. While the cost-savings potential is enormous, we may be years away from a developed technology. The near-term market potential is highly speculative at this time; industry analysts estimate that sales could be upward of tens of billions of dollars within the next two decades. Each gene produces its own protein, and each new protein is a potential new drug.

Sources: Clive Cookson, "Poised for the Big Switch-Off," *Financial Times*, April 22, 1993 and Laura Johannes, "Detailed Map of Genome Is Now Ready," *Wall Street Journal*, December 22, 1995, B1, B11.

Advertising and Promotion

Pharmaceutical companies have quickly learned the power of marketing. The industry spent $27 billion on marketing and promotion in 2010 (70 percent of which was free samples and promotion to physicians). That same year over $56 billion was spent on R&D. For all the money spent on R&D, many pharmaceutical firms, especially those that specialize in copycat drugs, spend twice as much on administration and marketing than they do on R&D. It is quite common for new drugs to sell at wholesale prices that are three to six times higher than their costs of production. These unusually high gross profit margins allow the drug companies to funnel large sums of money into advertising and promotion. Pharmaceutical companies direct most of the sales efforts at providers—sending representatives to see physicians, providing free samples, sponsoring seminars, and funding research—to educate them about the benefits of drugs.

Although most pharmaceutical advertising is directed at physicians, the fastest growing segment is advertising directed at the end consumers. This so-called direct-to-consumer advertising (DTCA) had reached $791 million in 1996 and rose to $6.1 billion in 2015, approximately 40 percent of the industry's promotion and advertising expense. The remaining promotional expense was for hospital and office promotion and journal advertising. DTCA, essentially illegal prior to 1996, has been sparked by a new FDA policy that allows television advertising to provide information on the benefits of specific drugs by name without also listing all of the side effects and warnings that normally accompany print ads. Wording is still under consideration for the so-called "major statement" of risks similar to the disclosures used in ads for over-the-counter drugs. Television commercials are required to list a toll-free telephone number or Web-page address for viewers to contact to get the full disclosure information. Print advertising is unaffected by the new policy.

The policy is extremely controversial. Pharmaceutical companies have always advertised in medical journals, read primarily by an audience that can understand the details of the disclosure statements. Some critics fear that the new advertising directed at consumers will simply motivate and not educate. The ads can urge consumers to read the fine print of the disclosure statements, call the toll-free number, access the website, or consult with a physician. Almost half of all physicians report an increase in specific drug requests, but less than 10 percent of patients ask for a specific drug. DTC provides vital information. Most physicians believe that DTCA informs and educates patients, and the vast majority of patients say ads increase awareness of new drugs and improve communication with physicians about health issues (Moser, 2003).

There is little evidence of a correlation between DTCA and the prices of drugs. Based on research by Rubin (2003) examining 33 drugs advertised directly to consumers and 43 that were not, there was no relationship between drug prices and advertising.

The DCTA strategy has proved to be very effective. According to IMS Health (Jenkins, 2000), the $1.8 billion spent on DTCA in 1999 generated an extra $9 billion in sales. That may seem like a lot of advertising relative to sales, but remember these are marginal dollars. The advertising is aimed at unsatisfied demand from patients who otherwise would go undiagnosed and untreated. These revenues would not exist without the advertising. Since marginal production costs are a fraction of the selling price, the difference is all profit. Attracting the marginal patient makes economic sense. More sales will spread the overhead costs of R&D over more users, allowing the pharmaceutical companies to sell at lower prices.

Jayawardhana (2013) examined the effect of DTCA on consumer welfare. In her model, DTCA plays an informative role and leads underdiagnosed patients to seek medical care. Using evidence from the market for statins (cholesterol-lowering drugs), overall consumer welfare is improved.

The next time you are watching television and one of these commercials comes on, instead of reaching for the remote, watch and learn. Notice the products that are being promoted. The pharmaceutical companies are not solely promoting the so-called lifestyle drugs in this manner (Viagra and Rogaine). They are promoting drugs for allergies, arthritis, depression, high cholesterol, asthma, insomnia, heartburn, depression, and many more conditions that go largely untreated. Research by Nielsen Company indicates that the five most heavily advertised drugs in 2015 were Lyrica and Prevnar (both Pfizer), Invokana (Merck), Humira (AbbVie), the top selling drug that year, and Eliquis (Bristol-Myers Squib/Pfizer).[4] Humira is the only one that was on the list five years earlier.

KEY CONCEPT 6
Supply and Demand

POLICY ISSUE
Is the FDA drug-approval process too long and costly?

Type I error Rejecting a hypothesis that is actually true.

Type II error Accepting a hypothesis that is actually false.

The Role of Government

The FDA has been criticized for being too cautious in the regulatory process and thus causing substantial delays in the approval of new drugs. Grabowski and Vernon (1983) examined the trade-off from a statistical perspective. They explained FDA behavior as an attempt to minimize **Type I error**, mistakenly allowing a harmful drug onto the market before it has been fully tested and determined to be safe. The success in keeping the drug thalidomide out of the U.S. market in the 1960s is an excellent example of the benefits of minimizing Type I error.[5] The market functions to minimize **Type II error**, delaying a beneficial drug from reaching the market until its safety and efficacy is fully understood. Excessive government regulation delays approval of the new drug, reduces competition to develop new drugs, and raises the overall development costs (Miller, 2010). Type I errors are highly visible. Type II errors receive little attention. The cost of delaying a potentially beneficial drug from reaching the market is real. A one-year reduction in Phase 1 testing would save millions in R&D expenditures. That cost does not even begin to take into consideration the vast numbers of people who die prematurely because of FDA delays. Kazman (1990) estimated that 10,000 Americans died prematurely between 1967 and 1976 because of the FDA delay in approving beta blockers for reducing the risk of heart attacks.

ISSUES IN MEDICAL CARE DELIVERY

WHY ARE PHARMACEUTICAL DRUG PRICES SO HIGH?

The obvious answer to the question of why drug costs are high is the substantial investment in time and money required to navigate through the FDA approval process. Nevertheless, like most controversies in economics, the obvious answer is not complete answer. The market exclusivity provided by the patent is short lived; on average only eight years of patent life remain after final approval. During this time, the pharmaceutical company sets its price at monopoly levels and consumers have little choice but to pay the high prices.

Competition provides the best restraint on price. Brand name drugs potentially face competition from two sources: The implications of loss of patent protection are well documented in the literature. When the first generic enters the market after a brand drug loses its patent, on average its price is 94 percent of the brand drug's price. When the second generic enters the market, the generic price is about one-half of the brand price. By the time there are five competitors, the generics sell for one-third of the branded price and prices continue to fall as more generics are approved. While the brand drug is still

---

[4]These drugs treat nerve pain; a pneumonia vaccine; diabetes; arthritis, plaque psoriasis, Crohn's disease, and ulcerative colitis; and an anticoagulant, respectively.

[5]This tranquilizer, used widely in Europe to combat the symptoms of nausea in pregnant women, was responsible for thousands of serious birth defects (children born without arms and legs).

under patent, the entrance of follow-on drugs into the market has the same effect on prices. When Sovoldi, the hepatitis C drug, was first approved in 2013, its list price was $1,000 per dose. As follow-on drugs entered the market, large purchasers received discounts of more than one-third off list.

Historically, competition from developers of similar drugs (of the follow-on or "me too" variety) usually emerges within 2–3 years. However, critics point out that the follow-on drugs offer little added benefit and that the money spent on their development is essentially wasted. Congress responded to the criticisms with the passage of the 21st Century Cures Act, signed into law in 2016. The act essentially streamlines the approval process for drugs labeled "first in class" by relaxing rules requiring double-blind clinical trials. The process of putting new drugs on a fast track to approval gets drugs to the market sooner. At the same time, fast tracking slows the development process for prospective competitors and increases the time that the first-in-class drug can charge monopoly prices.

The lack of competition contributes to high prices at every level of the supply chain. From raw materials to wholesalers to retail pharmacies, markets tend to be dominated by a handful of suppliers. The market solution for high prices is competition. Government policy should encourage competition from all sources. Placing developers of follow-on drugs at a disadvantage results in even higher prices.

Source: Devon Herrick, "How to Make New Drugs More Affordable," National Center for Policy Analysis, Issue Brief No. 203, January 5, 2017.

Future Directions for the Industry

The pharmaceutical industry has been widely criticized for high markups, high profit margins, and high and rising prices on its most popular products. Consumer advocates and certain members of Congress have long called for aggressive public policy to control the industry's ability to raise prices, thus limiting profitability.[6] According to a U.S. Government Accountability Office (GAO) report (1992), price controls on prescription drugs have resulted in substantially lower prices in Canada than in the United States. On average, the differential was reported to be 25 percent at the wholesale level. Price controls have had a choking effect on pharmaceutical research in Canada. Since price controls on prescription drugs were adopted in 1969, virtually no new pharmaceutical products have been developed in that country. In general, countries with the most stringent controls on pharmaceutical prices, for example, France and Austria, also do the least amount of research. A study by the GAO (1994) compared prices of 77 leading branded pharmaceuticals in the United States and abroad and concluded that U.S. prices were substantially higher than those found in the United Kingdom and other European countries.

Price controls take on different forms across the world. The United Kingdom places profit limits on pharmaceutical companies, Germany uses reference pricing (where prices are set for entire therapeutic categories of drugs equal to the cheapest one in the category), and Canada negotiates price ceilings. Whether prices fall below market levels is difficult to determine. Danzon and Furukawa (2003) estimate that disparities between U.S. prices and those of western Europe are roughly in line with differences in per capita GDP and, in turn, with the predictions of a Ramsey (1927) pricing scheme.

---

[6]Investment in the pharmaceutical industry is a high risk proposition. Rewards for success must be in line with risk, or shareholders will take their liquid capital elsewhere. As of January 2017, the average profit margin in the pharmaceutical industry was headed down due to generic competition. For the major drug manufacturers, it averaged around 21.4 percent (generic companies averaged –4.8 percent). At the same time, the average margin for health insurance companies was 7.6 percent, biotechnology companies 19.7 percent, wireless communications companies 29.8 percent, and real estate developers 38.7 percent.

Danzon (1994) probes the validity of the apparent price differentials by examining the methodology on which it is based. She concludes that GAO results are biased toward finding higher prices in the U.S. market. First, GAO research was based on an unrepresentative sample of drugs marketed in the United States. Only one of many possible dosage forms, strengths, and package sizes was included in the pricing survey. Second, it ignored the importance of generics, which accounted for almost 50 percent of the dispensed prescriptions in the U.S. market in 2001, up from almost 20 percent at the end of 1984 (CMS, 2003). Generic competition in the United States has increased significantly in the last decade. Today, a generic competitor will receive approximately half of the new prescription volume in less than two months after its introduction. Generics were quick to enter the market when the two leading ulcer medications lost their patent protection. Tagamet's patent expired in 1994 and Zantac, the best-selling drug worldwide in 1993 with sales of $3.5 billion, began feeling generic competition in 1996 because of patent expiration.[7] Branded drugs with worldwide sales of more than $50 billion lost their patent protection between 2010 and 2012. Such industry giants as Pfizer's Lipitor and Sanofi-Aventis's Plavix were included on the list (recall the Issues in Medical Care Delivery at the beginning of the chapter). Finally, the GAO study also ignored the practices of discounting and rebating, which are especially common in managed care, Medicaid, and other government programs.

Taking these issues into consideration, Danzon's 1996 study of drug prices in nine countries reached far different conclusions. When comparing unit prices (price per dose), Canada, Germany, Switzerland, and Sweden all had higher prices than the United States. Prices in the United Kingdom were 24 percent lower than in the United States—not 60 percent the GAO study had reported—and prices in France were even lower.

The OECD completed a comprehensive study of pharmaceutical pricing in 2008 examining drug-pricing strategies in the global market. Benchmarking a basket of drugs (75 percent branded) using data collected by OECD and Eurostat, they generated a retail price index of 181 of the top-selling drugs in Europe. The second column of Table 11.2 shows the index for the seven countries in our comparison group. While the United

HTTP://

Eli Lilly is developing a major advertising campaign to promote its antidepressant Prozac. The campaign, appearing in over 20 U.S. magazines, will remind consumers of the benefits of the drug. The Lilly website provides more information.
http://www.lilly.com.

TABLE 11.2 RELATIVE RETAIL PHARMACEUTICAL PRICE LEVELS, 2005

	Pharma price level	GDP per capita (2005)	GDP per capita level
Canada	134	$36,213	105
France	91	30,461	88
Germany	127	32,184	93
Japan	118	30,442	88
Switzerland	185	39,153	113
United Kingdom	92	34,623	100
United States	130	44,308	128
OECD average	100	34,520	100

Source: OECD Health Policy Studies (2008).

---

[7]Smith-Kline Beecham launched an aggressive counterattack on generics by releasing an over-the-counter version of its ulcer-treatment drug Tagamet before the expiration date of its patent.

States has prices that are 30 percent higher than the OECD average, prices in Switzerland and Canada are actually higher. Prices are over 40 percent higher in Canada and the United States than they are in France and the United Kingdom, but they are 100 percent higher in Switzerland.

The pharma price index and the per capita GDP index (shown in column 4) are highly correlated (correlation coefficient of $+0.51$), lending credence to the claim (Danzon and Furukawa, 2003) that pharmaceutical price differences are roughly in line with differences in per capita GDP.

spending cap A limit on total spending for a given time period.

Opponents of price controls, sometimes referred to as **spending caps** in policy discussions, claim that they have been uniformly disastrous, resulting in market distortions, shortages, poor quality, and black markets. In the case of the pharmaceutical industry, it is argued that price controls will limit innovation, lower quality and availability, and result in reduced well-being for Americans. Price controls still receive widespread popular support. Proponents focus on the monopoly rents and the high markups, and they have a legitimate case. Who is right? Who is to blame? It is important to study the evidence, understand its implications, and make informed judgments.

KEY CONCEPT 6
Supply and Demand

KEY CONCEPT 5
Markets and Pricing

BACK-OF-THE-ENVELOPE

The Economics of Regulating Drug Prices

Advances in pharmaceuticals normally receive patent protection for a period of 20 years. The patent serves as an effective barrier to entry that insulates the firm from competitive pressures and grants monopoly power in the area of pricing practices. It does not mean that the pharmaceutical company can set any price it desires; price changes are still limited by demand. A profit-maximizing pricing strategy may include establishing different prices in different markets (classic price discrimination), selling at prices many multiples of the actual cost of production (price is greater than marginal cost), and enjoying monopoly profits for the life of the patent.

Two additional features may help define the economics of drug pricing: the extremely high fixed costs of R&D and the extraordinarily long product development phase that extends through much of the patent protection period. The results are shown in the accompanying diagram. The demand curve for a patented drug is relatively inelastic (D). Marginal revenue (MR), marginal cost (MC), average variable cost (AVC), and average total cost (ATC) are defined in the usual manner.

The monopolist first determines the level of output that will maximize profitability (at point E, where $MR = MC$). In this case, the profit-maximizing quantity is Q_M. At this level of output, the pharmaceutical company will charge the maximum price that prospective customers are willing to pay (P_M in this example). The firm will earn monopoly profits, revenues in excess of fully allocated costs, including the opportunity costs of invested capital; the rectangular area $P_M ABC_0$.

From society's perspective, this pricing strategy results in a deadweight economic loss represented by the triangle ACE. This loss is caused by the voluntary quantity restrictions practiced by the monopolist to ensure the profit-maximizing price P_M.

The government response to this situation is often price regulation. A price fixed at the competitive price (P_C) would satisfy the efficiency criterion ($P = MC$) but would result in a loss to the firm, because the price would be less than the average total cost of production. This dilemma could be solved in one of the two ways: set the price at P_C and subsidize the firm by the amount of the loss, or set the price at P^* (where $P = ATC$ and the firm earns a normal profit) and sacrifice some efficiency.

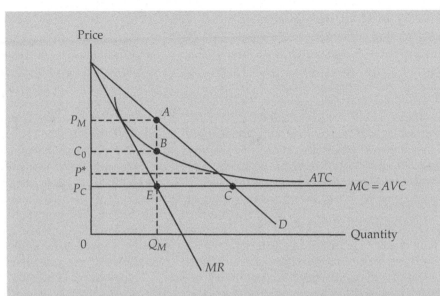

Although this regulating strategy may seem simple in theory, it is actually quite complex in practice. Because the demand and cost curves are not known with certainty, regulators must rely on accounting data to make their "fair" pricing determination. Two issues dominate regulatory deliberations: defining the fair rate of return and determining what to include in average cost of production. The issues are complex, and the stakes are high. Before venturing too far down the slippery slope of price regulation, it is important that we fully understand the implications of such policy changes.

International Issues

Supporting pharmaceutical R&D requires incentives that reach beyond the borders of a single country. A global challenge requires a global strategy. The fact that pharmaceutical R&D spending is a global joint cost that benefits consumers around the world creates a cost-allocation problem. The cost of R&D is a quasi-fixed cost. In other words, no matter how many consumers or how many countries receive access to the drug, R&D costs do not change. In most countries, government-run programs purchase drugs at regulated prices. Regulators tend to focus on country-specific costs in setting prices. However, cost structure provides little insight in determining how much of the R&D spending is attributable to any one specific country. The challenge is determining how much each country should contribute to the innovator for use of the patented drug.

The most direct way to cover global joint costs is to allow the patent holder to charge different prices in different countries. Equitable cost sharing across countries should be aimed at estimating the value of the drug to residents of each country. The appropriate price paid by each country then would replicate a Ramsey pricing strategy with each country paying a different price based on its price elasticity of demand (Ramsey, 1927). Paying a price equal to the marginal cost of producing the drug but not including a fair share of R&D expense is a classic example of free riding.

At stake is the ability to support pharmaceutical R&D equitably. Countries that try to acquire drugs through reimportation are merely trying to circumvent their obligation to share in the cost of developing innovative drugs that provide value to their residents.

KEY CONCEPT 3
Marginal Analysis

Summary and Conclusions

Analysts agree that one of the primary reasons for high health care spending is the third-party payment system. Individuals, both patients and providers, fail to practice economizing behavior because there is very little direct benefit to the individual who economizes. The availability of insurance, public or private, and the social mandate of providing free care to those who cannot afford to purchase it themselves result in patients demanding, and physicians supplying, a level of care that, at the margin, provides little benefit for the resources expended.

Over the past 50 years, insurance coverage has expanded to a larger segment of the population, providing a growing array of medical benefits. Better access to health insurance has also created a powerful incentive for industry to develop new, and often more expensive, technologies to deal with the maladies of modern society.

Medical research has accomplished countless miracles over the years, especially in the lifetimes of most of those who are reading this book. The most important pharmaceutical innovations include developments in the areas of the treatment of heart disease (including angiotensin-converting-enzyme [ACE] inhibitors to control high blood pressure, blood-thinning agents to control clotting, and statins to treat high cholesterol) and inhaled steroids to treat asthma (Fuchs and Sox, 2001).

Is technological change worth the cost? Cutler and McClellan (2001) try to answer this question by examining five conditions: heart attacks, low-birth-weight infants, depression, cataracts, and breast cancer. For each condition except breast cancer, the net benefits of the new treatment have been significantly positive due to substantial improvements in outcomes at reasonable costs.

It is important that we understand the close causality between the availability of medical technology and the ability to pay for it. In our desire to control expenditures, it is essential that we preserve the financial incentives that foster and promote scientific inquiry at its basic level. We must also reward the applied research that creates marketable products that enhance the quality of medical care for millions.

Using history as a guide, we might conclude that rapid technological change in medical care will lead to increased spending. If biotechnology provides for the effective treatment of genetic diseases, however, we could see a shift from cost-increasing technology to cost-saving technology. It is not just wishful thinking to expect advances in cell biology in the next few decades to lead to cures for specific types of cancers and heart disease. It is equally important that the price mechanism not put these products out of the reach of those who stand to benefit from the discoveries.

PROFILE   Patricia M. Danzon

If the makeup of a Ph.D. dissertation committee is an indicator of future success, then Patricia Danzon's climb to the pinnacle of her profession comes as no surprise. In addition to her supervising professor, Nobel Prize winner George Stigler, the other members of her committee included future Nobel laureates in economics Ronald Coase and Gary Becker.

Soon after she was born, Danzon's father moved the family from England to Pretoria, South Africa, where they lived until she was a teenager. Returning to England, Danzon graduated from Oxford University in 1968 with a Bachelor of Arts in politics, philosophy, and economics. She decided to attend graduate school in the United States and applied to the six best graduate programs in economics. Only one, the University of Chicago, accepted her, and they even provided a full fellowship to cover the cost of her studies.

Danzon received her Ph.D. in 1973 and began working for the RAND Corporation. She was able to turn her dissertation on exploring eminent domain into her first publication in the prestigious *Journal of Political Economy*. Her work with RAND initially dealt primarily with military work force issues. Even though the issue was of growing importance with the end of the Vietnam War and emergence of the all-volunteer army in the United States, Danzon was soon ready to tackle another challenge. At about this time, the first malpractice insurance crisis was gripping the medical community. Joseph Newhouse, then head of the health group at RAND, came to her suggesting that someone really ought to look into the problem from an economic perspective. Danzon saw this as an opportunity to combine several fields of study: health economics, insurance, law, and economics. She had to overcome one minor problem—her background was in law and economics, and she knew little about the other two. Undaunted by the limitation, she became self-taught in both health economics and insurance.

Danzon was assigned as the staff person on professional liability at the California Commission on Tort Reform. There she teamed up with Dennis Smallwood to publish empirical research on the property/casualty industry in the 1980 *Bell Journal of Economics*, the first of over 40 books, journal articles, and book chapters that she authored or coauthored on insurance and medical liability. Her work has been published in the most highly regarded journals in economics and health care, including the *American Economic Review*, the *Journal of Health Economics*, and *Health Affairs*. She is best known for her book *Medical Malpractice: Theory, Evidence, and Public Policy* (Harvard University Press, 1985).

Danzon left RAND in 1980. After relatively short stays at Stanford's Hoover Institute and Duke University, she moved to the University of Pennsylvania in 1985, where she is the Celia Moh Professor and Professor of Health Care Systems and Insurance and Risk Management at The Wharton School.

Danzon emerged as an international expert on medical malpractice, but the exclusive focus on one issue left her desiring a little variety in her scholarly pursuits. So in 1991, funded by a grant from the University Research Council, Danzon ventured into a new field of study: the pharmaceutical industry. She has turned her interest in health care and pharmaceutical pricing into consultancies with the World Bank, the Asian Development Bank, and the United States Agency for International Development, examining drug pricing in Europe and New Zealand. Danzon has maintained a practical focus in her scholarly pursuits. The testing of economic theory with empirical evidence is a way of thinking she acquired during her graduate studies under Stigler and developed in the years since. Everyone interested in the study of health care, insurance, and legal liability is richer for her efforts.

Source: Curriculum vitae and personal correspondence.

Questions and Problems

1. Pharmaceutical spending is about 10 percent of total health care spending in the United States. Why do you suppose the industry is the target of such severe criticism?

2. What are some of the important economic issues that help us understand availability and pricing in the pharmaceutical industry?

3. A person learns from a genetic test that she has a predisposition for a certain disease, say, Alzheimer's disease. Who should have access to that genetic information? Medical practitioners? Insurance companies? The individual? Would you want to know? Why?

References

Baily, Martin N., "Research and Development Costs and Returns: The U.S. Pharmaceutical Industry," *Journal of Political Economy* 80(1), January/February 1972, 70–85.

Barton, John H., "TRIPS and the Global Pharmaceutical Market," *Health Affairs* 23(3), 2004, 146–154.

(CMS) Centers for Medicare and Medicaid Services, "Health Care Industry Market Update: Pharmaceuticals," January 10, 2003, available at https://www.cms.gov/Research-Statistics-Data-and-Systems/Statistics-Trends-and-Reports/CapMarketUpdates/Downloads/hcimu11003.pdf.

Cutler, David M. and Mark McClellan, "Is Technological Change in Medicine Worth It?" *Health Affairs* 20(5), September/October 2001, 11–29.

Cutler, David M., et al., "The Value of Antihypertensive Drugs: A Perspective on Medical Innovation," *Health Affairs* 26(1), January 2007, 97–110.

Danzon, Patricia M., "Drug Price Controls, Wrong Prescription," *Wall Street Journal*, February 4, 1994, A10.

___, "International Drug Price Comparisons: Uses and Abuses," in *Competition Strategies in the Pharmaceutical Industry*, edited by Richard B. Helms, Washington, DC: The AEI Press, 1996.

Danzon, Patricia M. and Michael F. Furukawa, "Prices and the Availability of Pharmaceuticals: Evidence from Nine Countries," *Health Affairs Web Exclusive*, October 29, 2003, W3-521–W3-536.

Denison, Edward, *Trends in American Economic Growth*, Washington, DC: Brookings Institution, 1985.

DiMasi, Joseph A., Henry G. Grabowski, and Ronald W. Hansen, "Innovation in the Pharmaceutical Industry: New Estimates of R&D Costs," *Journal of Health Economics* 47, 2016, 20–33.

DiMasi, Joseph A., Ronald W. Hansen, and Henry G. Grabowski, "The Price of Innovation: New Estimates of Drug Development Costs," *Journal of Health Economics* 22, 2003, 151–185.

DiMasi, Joseph A., et al., "Cost of Innovation in the Pharmaceutical Industry," *Journal of Health Economics* 10(2), July 1991, 107–142.

Fuchs, Victor R. and Harold C. Sox, Jr., "Physicians' Views of the Relative Importance of Thirty Medical Innovations," *Health Affairs* 20(5), September/October 2001, 30–42.

GAO (U.S. Government Accountability Office), *Prescription Drugs: Companies Typically Charge More in the United States than in Canada*, Washington, DC: USGAO, 1992.

___, *Prescription Drugs: Spending Controls in Four European Countries*, Washington, DC: USGAO, 1994.

Grabowski, Henry G. and John Vernon, "Longer Patents for Lower Imitation Barriers: The 1984 Drug Act," *The American Economic Review Papers and Proceedings* 76(2), 1986, 195–198.

___, *The Regulation of Pharmaceuticals: Balancing the Benefits and Risks*, Washington, DC: American Enterprise Institute, 1983.

Grabowski, Henry G., John Vernon, and Joseph A. DiMasi, "Returns on Research and Development for 1990s New Drug Introductions," *Pharmaceutical Economics* 20(Suppl 3), 2002, 11–29.

Grinols, Earl L. and James W. Henderson, "Replace Pharmaceutical Patents Now," *Pharmacoeconomics* 25(5), 2007, 355–363.

Hansen, Ronald W., "The Pharmaceutical Development Process: Estimates of Current Development Costs and Times and the Effects of Regulatory Changes," in *Issues in Pharmaceutical Economics*, edited by R.I. Chen, Lexington Books: Lexington, MA, 1979, 151–187.

Jaffe, Adam B., "The U.S. Patent System in Transition: Policy Innovation and the Innovation Process," *Research Policy* 29, 2000, 531–557.

Jayawardhana, Jayani, "Direct to Consumer Advertising and Consumer Welfare," *International Journal of Industrial Organization* 31(2), March 2013, 164–180.

Jenkins, Holman W., Jr., "Lazy Insurers Hitch a Ride on the Drug Wars," *Wall Street Journal*, August 9, 2000, A23.

Kazman, Sam, "Deadly Overcaution: FDA's Drug Approval Process," *Journal of Regulation and Social Costs* 1, September 1990, 35–54.

Kremer, Michael, "Patent Buyouts: A Mechanism for Encouraging Innovation," *Quarterly Journal of Economics* 113(4), November 1998, 1137–1167.

Levin, Richard C., "A New Look at the Patent System," *American Economic Review Papers and Proceedings* 76(2), 1986, 199–202.

Lichtenberg, Frank R., "Benefits and Costs of Newer Drugs: An Update," *NBER Working Paper No. 8996*, Cambridge, MA: National Bureau of Economic Research, 2002.

Martinez, Barbara, "Drug-Price Surge May Erode Savings from Medicard Card," *Wall Street Journal*, March 24, 2004, B1.

McWilliams, J. M., et al., "Implementation of Medicare Part D and Nondrug Medical Spending for Elderly Adults with Limited Prior Drug Coverage," *Journal of the American Medical Association* 306(4), 2011, 402–409.

Miller, Henry I., "Type I Errors," *Regulation* 33(3), Fall 2010, 30–33.

Moser, Joe, "Direct-to-Consumer Advertising Informative, Spurs Conversation between Doctor and Patient," Galen Institute, May 28, 2003, available at http://galen.org/2003/direct-to-consumer-advertising-informative-spurs-conversation-between-doctor-and-patient/.

OECD Health Policy Studies, "Pharmaceutical Pricing Policies in a Global Market," September 2008, available at http://www.oecd.org/els/

pharmaceutical-pricing-policies-in-a-global-market.
htm (Accessed January 5, 2017).

PhRMA (Pharmaceutical Research and Manufacturers
of America), *Pharmaceutical Industry Profile 2010*,
Washington, DC: PhRMA, March 2010.

PhRMA (Pharmaceutical Research and Manufacturers
of America), *Pharmaceutical Industry Profile 2015*,
Washington, DC: PhRMA, March 2015.

Ramsey, Frank, "A Contribution to the Theory of Taxation," *Economic Journal* 37, 1927, 47–61.

Roebuck, M. C., et al., "Medication Adherence Leads
to Lower Health Care Use and Costs Despite
Increased Drug Spending," *Health Affairs* 30(1),
2011, 91–99.

Rubin, Paul H., "The Economics and Impact of
Pharmaceutical Promotion," *Economic Realities in
Health Care Policy* 3(1), December 2003, 6–17.

Scotchmer, Suzanne, "Standing on the Shoulders of
Giants: Cumulative Research and the Patent Law,"
Journal of Economic Perspectives 5(1), 1991, 29–41.

Sokol, M.C., et al., "Impact of Medication Adherence
on Hospitalization Risk and Healthcare Cost,"
Medical Care 43(6), 2005, 521–530.

Spence, Michael, "Cost Reduction, Competition, and
Industry Performance," *Econometrica* 52(1), 1984,
101–121.

_____ "The Top 500 Drugs by Class of Drugs," *Med Ad
News* 19(5), 2000, 77–82.

Vernon, John A., Joseph A. Golec, and Joseph A. DiMasi,
"Drug Development Costs When Financial Risk
Is Measured Using the Fama-French Three-factor
Model," *Health Economics* 19, 2010,1002–1005.

Waterson, Michael, "The Economics of Product
Patents," *American Economic Review* 80(4), 1990,
860–869.

Weidenbaum, Murray, *Restraining Medicine
Prices: Controls vs. Competition*, St. Louis, MO:
Washington University Center for the Study of
American Business, Policy Study No. 116, April
1993b.

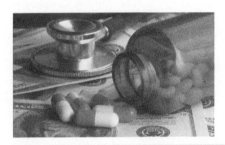

CHAPTER **12**

Medicare

ISSUES IN MEDICAL CARE DELIVERY

THE POLITICS OF MEDICARE

The 1965 legislation that created Medicare included aspects of the three major proposals that were popular at the time. Democrats favored a hospital trust fund that included mandatory participation and financing from a broad-based tax, which became Medicare Part A. Republicans wanted traditional indemnity insurance with voluntary participation, funded by a premium paid by all participants and subsidized out of general tax revenues, which became Medicare Part B. Finally, the medical community, led by the American Medical Association, wanted medical insurance for the indigent paid out of general tax revenues, which became Medicaid.

Since the creation of the program, numerous changes have expanded the system's coverage and method of paying providers. The end-stage renal program was added in 1972 and medical benefits for the disabled in 1975. Prospective payment to hospitals was established in 1983, and a relative-value scale to pay physicians was started in 1994. Outpatient prescription drug benefits were added in 2006.

In addition to expanding benefits, Congress addressed the major weakness of the program in 1988, namely, its inability to provide catastrophic financial protection, by passing the Medicare Catastrophic Coverage Act. Instead of a crowning achievement, this act represents one of the most embarrassing moments in congressional history.

The intent of the legislation was to guard against the high cost of a prolonged or debilitating illness. The unique feature of the plan was that the entire cost of a social welfare program was borne by the intended beneficiaries. After considering its effect, the majority of the elderly population, or at least an extremely vocal minority, determined that the extra benefits provided by the program were not worth the added costs. Most Medicare beneficiaries already had supplemental coverage that they considered superior to the benefits provided by the new legislation. The failure of the act to provide additional benefits—especially long-term care benefits—led to its ultimate demise. Protests by the elderly and reversals in positions by advocates of the elderly, including the American Association of Retired People, led to repeal in November 1989.

Subsequent legislation has attempted to address the expected shortfall in the hospital trust fund. According to the 1996 trustees' report, the trust fund was expected to become insolvent by 2001 if no changes to the system were adopted. Acting on this report, Congress included Medicare reform in the 1998 federal budget. Originally, the proposed reform package was designed to reduce Medicare spending growth by over $270 billion by reducing the fees paid to providers, increasing premiums and copayments to recipients, and extending the eligibility age to 67. Opposition quickly mobilized and defeated the proposal, reinforcing the perception that Medicare was politically untouchable.

Congress was able to address the short-term insolvency by cutting provider payments by $115 billion over the five-year time period beginning in 1998. The legislation encouraged enrollment in managed care plans and allowed the option of setting up medical savings accounts. Relief was only temporary. The changes were not enough to address the long-term structural deficiencies in the system, and Congress formed a bipartisan commission in 1998 to study the problem and recommend alternative solutions for Congress to consider. The commission agreed on a reform package designed along the same lines as the Federal Employee Health Benefit Plan that featured a choice of plans for all enrollees, along with a prescription drug benefit. A threatened veto by President Bill Clinton killed the bill in committee.

In 2006, President George W. Bush delivered the promised outpatient prescription drug benefit. It seems possible to expand coverage as long as the basics of the program remain intact. While everyone speaks about reform, it has been largely elusive.

The Patient Protection and Affordable Care Act (ACA) passed in 2010 cut $741 billion out of the 10-year Medicare budget and added $842 billion in new taxes (much of that in the form of increases in the Medicare tax on certain "high income" taxpayers) to pay for a new entitlement program to expand coverage for the nation's uninsured. Policy discussions have focused on the impact of these measures on the long-term sustainability of Medicare. ACA proponents argue that this move has strengthened Medicare by postponing the depletion of the trust fund well into the next decade. Skeptics contend that the money cannot be spent twice—using the same funds to expand coverage for the uninsured and to extend the program's solvency at the same time is an illusion. "Accounting gimmick" or not, politics never seems to take a back seat in the Medicare discussion.

Source: Thomas Rice, Katherine Desmond, and Jon Gabel, "The Medicare Catastrophic Coverage Act: A Postmortem," *Health Affairs*, 9(3), Fall 1990, 75–87.

The federal government's role in funding medical care in the United States continues to be defined and revised. Total government spending on health care—including federal, state, and local spending—was approximately $1.56 trillion in 2014. Together spending on Medicare and Medicaid alone total over $1.11 trillion, making them the largest health insurance plans in the United States. Now over 50 years old, the two combined will require more public spending than any other government program. Support for the two is unwavering among its constituents, while many question how long it will survive in its current form. When expenditures on public health, research, construction, and administration are included, government's share of total health care spending is well over 50 percent.

Passage of the ACA has not dampened the debate over the direction and shape of health care reform. The defining issue remains the extent to which we are willing to embrace the principle of universal entitlement to medical care. The principle is already in place in the form of a legal framework that guarantees medical care to certain vulnerable segments of the population; namely, the elderly, those living in low-income families, children under age 18, and military veterans with service-related disabilities.[1]

The development of government's role in the provision of medical care to these vulnerable populations is instructive when we examine health care policy. The government is instrumental in providing medical care to over 100 million people under two major

---

[1]A major provision of the ACA of 2010 expanded Medicaid eligibility to those living in households with incomes less than 138 percent of the federal poverty level.

programs: Medicare and Medicaid. The ACA will expand this number to well over 140 million by 2020, approximately 40 percent of the total population.

Medical Care for the Elderly

The elderly, defined as the adult population over the age of 65, are the fastest growing segment of the U.S. population. Approximately 13 percent of the total population accounting for over one-third of total health care spending, this politically active group is comprised of over 55 million voters who are not afraid to let policy makers know how they feel about issues that affect their well-being.

Medicare was not the first federal law that enhanced access to medical providers. Under the Hill-Burton Act, passed by Congress in 1966, hospitals were required to provide free care to those who did not have the means to pay. In return, federal, state, and local governments contributed more than $13 billion to increase hospital bed capacity by 500,000. Kerr-Mills, a means-tested program to provide access to low-income seniors was passed in 1960. By 1962, the majority of American workers had health insurance provided through their employers. The uninsured were primarily poor, elderly, or unemployed. Even so, more than 60 percent of the elderly purchased health insurance in a thriving individual market and those who did not had access to free care under Kerr-Mills. Almost all seniors had coverage of one kind or another.

Whether it was the government bureaucracy or an ideological distain for free markets, the voluntary nature of senior coverage options ran counter to the prevailing sentiments supporting mandatory, universal coverage. The death of President Kennedy in 1963 and the subsequent Democrat landslide victory in 1964 paved the way for the passage of the Medicare bill in 1965.

Medicare guaranteed elderly Americans access to health care regardless of their financial circumstances. When combined with Social Security, it represented an important source of economic security for our nation's elderly and disabled. Serving 19.1 million in 1966, Medicare enrollment reached over 55 million Americans in 2015 (over 16 percent of the total population), and is expected to grow to over 73 million by 2025 as the baby boom generation reaches eligibility age (see Table 12.1). This current figure included over 46.3 million senior citizens and approximately 9.0 million permanently disabled, including over 250,000 suffering from end-stage kidney failure. Although 75 percent of the beneficiaries of Medicare are between the ages of 65 and 84, the disabled and those over 85 are the fastest growing segments. In 1966, the first complete year of the program, total Medicare spending was $1.6 billion. Medicare spending reached $647.6 billion in 2015 and is expected to grow to $1.3 trillion by 2025 (Medicare and SMI Trustees Report, 2016). With overall Medicare spending growing twice as fast as U.S. gross domestic product (GDP), the long-term sustainability of the program in its current form is uncertain.

Institutional Features

Administered by the Centers for Medicare and Medicaid Services (CMS), Medicare provides benefits through four major programs depicted in Figure 12.1: Parts A, B, C, and D. Part A is medical hospital insurance, Part B is supplemental medical insurance (primarily covering physicians' services), Part C is Medicare Advantage (MA), and Part D is outpatient prescription drug insurance. Individuals who have paid into the Social

HTTP://

The Centers for Medicare and Medicaid Services (CMS), an agency of the Department of Health and Human Services, was created in 1977 to administer Medicare and Medicaid. This site links to both the Medicare and Medicaid home pages.
https://www.cms.gov/.

TABLE 12.1 ACTUAL MEDICARE SPENDING AND ENROLLMENT CALENDAR YEARS 1966–2015 WITH PROJECTIONS TO 2025

Year	Total enrollment (Millions)	Total spending (Billions of current dollars)	Annual rate of change in spending[1] (%)
1966	19.1	$ 1.6	–
1970	20.5	7.5	45.6
1975	25.0	16.3	16.9
1980	28.5	36.8	17.7
1985	31.1	72.3	14.5
1990	34.2	111.0	9.0
1995	37.6	184.2	10.7
2000	39.7	221.8	3.8
2005	42.6	336.4	8.7
2010	47.7	522.9	9.2
2011	48.9	549.1	5.0
2012	50.9	574.2	4.6
2013	52.5	582.9	1.5
2014	54.1	613.3	5.2
2015	55.3	647.6	5.6
Projections			
2020	64.1	899.4	6.8
2025	73.3	1,285.8	7.4

Source: 2016 Annual Reports of the Board of Trustees of the HI and SMI Trust Funds, Tables V.B1 and V.B4.
[1] Average annual change from the previous entry.

Security system for 10 years, and/or their spouses, are automatically enrolled in traditional fee-for-service Part A hospital insurance upon reaching their 65th birthday. Enrollment in Parts B, C, and D is voluntary. Over 95 percent of all those who are eligible enroll in Part B. Approximately 90 percent of all seniors have prescription drug benefits, either through a Part D plan (55 percent) or an employer-sponsored plan. Over one-third of those eligible for Medicare benefits are enrolled in MA (Part C), a comprehensive, private sector alternative that provides hospital, physicians, and drug coverage under a single plan.

The basic idea underlying Part A payments is simple. The patient pays a deductible approximately equal to the cost of the first day in the hospital. Medicare pays for days 2 through 60 with no coinsurance requirement; days 61 through 90 are covered, but the patient must pay coinsurance equal to 25 percent of the deductible. Days 91 through 150 are covered if the lifetime reserve days are available, but the patient pays coinsurance equal to 50 percent of the deductible amount.[2] After 150 days in the hospital (or 90 if lifetime days are already exhausted), Medicare pays nothing. This limitation is easily the most serious flaw in the current system, because it provides enrollees with no protection against catastrophic losses.

☆ **POLICY ISSUE**

The gaps in Medicare coverage include limited protection against catastrophic losses and poor coverage of long-term custodial care.

---

[2] Each enrollee is provided 60 lifetime reserve days with a daily copayment of $550. These are used to pay hospital expenses beyond the 90 days of coverage during each benefit period. Once a patient uses these reserve days, Part A benefits stop after 90 days in the hospital during a benefit period.

FIGURE 12.1
Structure of Medicare

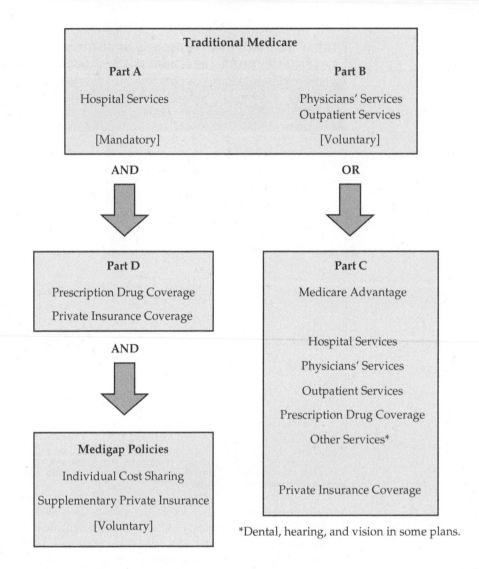

*Dental, hearing, and vision in some plans.

The 2016 figures translate as follows. The first 60 days of inpatient hospital care during each benefit period is provided to patients with the only out-of-pocket expense being a deductible payment equal to $1,288.[3] The patient is responsible for a copayment of $322 per day for the next 30 days. The daily copayment is $644 thereafter until reserve days are exhausted. When they are exhausted, the patient is responsible for all costs.

Additional benefits include 100 days in a skilled-nursing facility (SNF) during each benefit period. This benefit is provided as a supplement to hospital care and is only available after a minimum three-day hospitalization. The first 20 days are provided at no charge to the patient; days 21 through 100 require a daily copayment of $161 (one-eighth of the hospital deductible). Beyond 100 days, the patient is responsible for the entire bill. Inpatient psychiatric care is available for up to a 190-day lifetime maximum. Home health

---

[3]A benefit period is defined as the period that begins on the first day the patient is admitted into the hospital and extends to 30 days after that patient is discharged.

assignment A Medicare policy providing physicians with a guaranteed payment of 80 percent of the allowable fee. By accepting assignment, physicians agree to accept the allowable fee as full payment and forgo the practice of balance billing.

participating physician A physician who agrees to accept Medicare assignment.

benefits include up to four days of care per week with no limit and up to three full weeks of care per illness. Individuals with life expectancies of less than six months are eligible for 210 days of hospice care.

Participation in Part B is voluntary and pays for physicians' services and outpatient hospital services, including emergency room services, diagnostic testing, laboratory services, outpatient physical therapy, speech-pathology services, and durable medical equipment. Of interest to most participants is what Medicare does not cover: custodial nursing home care.

After the patient pays a $159.30 annual deductible, Part B pays 80 percent of the allowable fee set by Medicare. Individuals who earn incomes over $85,000 (and couples who earn over $170,000) pay increasingly higher premiums as their incomes rise (as much as $389.90). The majority of physicians who accept Medicare **assignment** accept Medicare's reimbursement as payment in full for the covered services. Approximately half of all practicing physicians accept Medicare assignment, and these **participating physicians** bill over 90 percent of Part B's covered charges (Gillis, Lee, and Willke, 1992).

BACK-OF-THE-ENVELOPE

The Impact of Medicare Assignment on Medical Practice

balance billing Billing a patient for the difference between the physician's usual charge for a service and the maximum charge allowed by the patient's health plan.

Physicians who provide care to Medicare patients must decide whether to accept the Medicare allowable fee as payment in full for the services provided. In other words, physicians must decide whether to take "assignment" on their Medicare patients. Physicians who take assignment bill Medicare and receive 80 percent of the allowable fee directly from the federal government. Those who do not take assignment bill their patients directly, but no more than 15 percent over the allowable fee (now 95 percent of the fee paid to physicians who accept assignment). Medicare will pay 80 percent of the allowable fee to the patient, who in turn is responsible for paying the physician. The excess charges over the allowable fee are referred to as **balance billing**. Physicians who take assignment are reasonably certain they will collect 80 percent of the allowable fee. Those who do not take assignment have no such assurances.

From the physician's perspective, the problem centers on the relationship between the fee usually charged for the service provided and the Medicare allowable fee, which is often much lower. The following diagram addresses the impact of assignment on the physicians' services market.

For those physicians who accept assignment, the market for a physician's services can be divided into two segments: private patients and Medicare. Private-patient demand is given by the downward-sloping demand curve labeled D_P. To maximize profits, the physician will set $MRP = MC$ and provide Q_0 services at a price of P_0. Profits are depicted graphically as the shaded area bounded by the points P_0ABC_0.

Physicians who accept Medicare assignment agree to a fixed price (P_M) for their Medicare patients. As a price taker, the demand curve for this segment of the market becomes $D_M = MR_M = AR_M$. Now the physician is faced with a more complicated decision. The new marginal revenue curve has a floor established at P_M. The combined marginal revenue curve is now MR_P to point E, where MR_P and MR_M intersect, and MR_M thereafter. The physician will see a total of Q_M patients (Q_1 private patients and $Q_M - Q_1$ Medicare patients). Private patients now pay a higher price for services, or P_1, which is sometimes called *cost shifting*. It is important to note that the only reason that the physician charges private patients higher prices is that the analysis implicitly assumes that the physician's

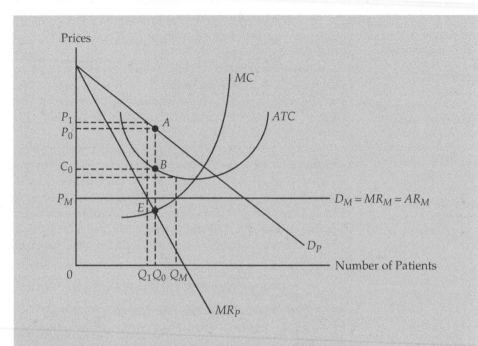

Source: Centers for Medicare and Medicaid Services, Medicare Program Payments 2008, Table 3.6.

KEY CONCEPT 3
Marginal Analysis

KEY CONCEPT 5
Markets and Pricing

KEY CONCEPT 6
Supply and Demand

practice has capacity limitations. In order to accept more Medicare patients, the physician has to limit the number of private pay patients served. If there is excess capacity, there is no opportunity to cost shift.

Physicians complain that the Medicare allowable fee is below their average cost of providing medical services. In the diagram, the shaded area between ATC and P_M shows this loss. Although providing care to the Medicare segment of the market may not cover fully allocated costs, each one of those transactions is reimbursed at a rate that covers the physician's opportunity cost: all relevant costs as measured by MC. Whether the physician is better off or worse off (determined by the change in profit) depends on whether the extra profits from private patients offset the losses incurred in providing care to Medicare patients.

Participants receive medical coverage through the traditional fee-for-service option or by joining privately administered MA plans. MA provides private insurance coverage to seniors, who pay a fixed premium. In addition to the standard benefits, many MA plans cover additional services including vision, dental, and outpatient prescription drugs, decreasing the need to purchase supplementary insurance. In addition, many offer protection against catastrophic medical costs. In 2016, over 17 million seniors participated in MA plans, or 31 percent of the eligible population, up from 5.3 million and 13 percent in 2003.[4]

Outpatient prescription drug coverage was added as Part D in 2006. By 2012, an estimated 31.5 million seniors were enrolled in Part D plans, with 78 percent covered by the 10 largest plans. Many seniors who are not enrolled in Part D plans have creditable drug coverage from some other source, such as an employer plan or the Veterans' Administration. Enrollees pay monthly premiums that vary depending on the plan chosen.

[4]Provisions of the ACA of 2010 will reduce the size of the capitated payment to private insurance companies as part of the overall cuts to Medicare. The Congressional Budget Office estimates that many seniors in MA plans will likely see benefit cuts that will make the plans less attractive.

Who Pays?

Medicare financing is set up on a pay-as-you-go basis. Program revenue comes from four major sources: payroll taxes, income taxes, trust fund interest, and enrollee premiums. Almost 90 percent of the funding comes directly and indirectly from individuals who are less than 65 years old. The remainder comes in the form of enrollee premiums from those who are over 65. A payroll tax of 2.9 percent is levied on the gross income of all employees and is collected along with the Social Security tax. (The tax increased to 3.8 percent for high-income earners because of changes initiated by the ACA.) This tax is divided equally between employer and employee. Until 1994, tax law included a cap on the income that was subject to the Medicare tax—initially $6,600, rising to $135,000 by 1993. Legislation passed in 1993 removed the income ceiling, subjecting all payroll income to the Medicare levy.

This 2.9 percent payroll tax on all workers in the U.S. labor force—over $227 billion in 2014—is dedicated entirely to the trust fund to pay Part A benefits. The ACA introduced an additional 0.9 percent tax surcharge effective in 2014 on individuals making more than $200,000 and couples who file joint returns making more than $250,000. Total program spending has exceeded payroll tax receipts since 2008, resulting in annual deficits that reduce the size of the Medicare trust fund.[5]

Who Benefits?

Medicare's Part A allocation pattern loosely fits the usual experience of underwriting medical care spending for large groups. Underwriters often refer to this pattern as the 80–20 rule: 80 percent of the spending benefits, 20 percent of the covered population. As illustrated in Table 12.2, about 33 million enrollees received hospital and supplemental benefits in 2012. Approximately 82 percent of the program's outlays of $345.4 billion purchased care for 23.3 percent of the population whose per capita medical care spending exceeded $10,000. Per capita spending for this high-cost group was over $36,500. An additional 60.3 percent of the enrollees spent $60.9 billion, 17.5 percent of the total outlays, or $3,034 per capita. The other 16.5 percent received Parts A and B benefits averaging $73 (approximately zero). Overall, average spending per recipient was $10,369.

Medicare has proven to be a good financial investment for the individual enrollee. A couple retiring in 1994, which had been paying the average Medicare tax since 1966, would have paid $20,000 in payroll taxes into the program (including the employer's share). Lifetime benefits, discounted to 1994, exceed the amount paid in premiums and taxes by an average of $117,200, or six times the amount paid into the system. Because Part B premiums account for only 25 percent of the outlays for medical benefits, an **actuarially fair premium** would have to be four times greater than the current $121.80, or $487.20 per month, to cover 100 percent of Part B spending.[6] Private insurance coverage for comparable benefits under Parts A and B would cost a 64-year-old male between $6,400 and $8,500 per year, or $600 to 800 per month.

actuarially fair premium Insurance premium based on the actuarial probability that an event will occur.

---

[5]Many argue that because the "trust fund" is invested in interest-bearing U.S. Treasury securities, it is not really a trust fund at all. To use the fund, the federal government must liquidate the securities by reissuing debt, raising additional tax revenues, or printing money.

[6]This premium schedule applies to individuals with taxable income less than $85,000. Income-related adjustments will raise premiums to $353.60 per month for those with taxable incomes over $214,000.

TABLE 12.2 MEDICARE (PARTS A AND B) PAYMENT ALLOCATION, 2012[1]

Payment range	Number of enrollees (Millions)	Percent of total	Spending (Billions)	Percent of total	Average per enrollee
Over $25,000	3.90	11.7	$221.2	64.0	$56,694
$20,000–$24,999	0.85	2.6	19.1	5.5	22,376
$10,000–$19,999	3.01	9.0	43.0	12.4	14,286
$5,000–$9,999	3.93	11.8	27.8	8.0	7,062
$2,000–$4,999	6.99	21.0	22.6	6.5	3,237
$1,000–$1,999	5.19	15.6	7.6	2.2	1,457
$500–$999	3.96	11.9	2.9	0.8	736
Less than $500	5.49	16.5	1.3	0.4	73
Total	33.31	100.0	$345.4	100.0	$10,369

Source: Centers for Medicare and Medicaid Services, *Medicare & Medicaid Research Review/2013 Statistical Supplement*, Table 3.6.
[1]Includes inpatient hospitalization, skilled-nursing facilities, home health care, hospice, physicians, and outpatient care.

APPLIED MICRO METHODS

WHAT DID MEDICARE DO?

Background

Research analyzing the benefits of health insurance has focused almost exclusively on the impact on health outcomes. Levy and Meltzer (2004) examined the empirical evidence and concluded that, for the adult population, health insurance coverage conveys only modest health benefits. In contrast, the risk-reduction potential of health insurance has received scant attention in the empirical literature. This study provides an empirical examination of the 1965 introduction of Medicare, providing near universal insurance coverage for the elderly.

Data and Methods

The study used individual mortality data from the National Center for Health Statistics Multiple Causes of Death micro-data to examine whether the introduction of Medicare had any measurable impact on mortality in its first decade. Using an age-based identification strategy, the authors examine trends in mortality rates for the near elderly (ages 55–64) who are not eligible for Medicare and compare them with trends for the young elderly (ages 65–74) who are.

Results

Data in the next figure show a decline in mortality rates for the young elderly that began at least a decade before 1965. The downward trend in mortality rates for the near elderly began at least a decade later, but both fell similarly after 1965.

Regression analysis does not show any evidence of an impact on the mortality of the young elderly relative to the near elderly. Additionally, there is no evidence of an impact on specific causes of death (e.g., cardiovascular disease), or for more vulnerable demographic groups (e.g., non-whites), or for individuals living in urban areas (where medical care is more accessible). Even though Medicare-induced hospital use increased significantly, the empirical results do not provide any evidence that Medicare played an essential role in the decline in mortality rates.

The authors exploit timing of Medicare's introduction into the segregated South (specifically the Mississippi delta region) to study the impact on non-whites. Deaths from all causes, pneumonia, and cardiovascular disease for both whites and non-whites were examined. In general, the introduction of Medicare had no impact on overall elderly mortality. However, it was associated with a significant decline in non-white mortality due to pneumonia (with no comparable decline among whites). Although statistically significant, the impact on pneumonia was relatively small, so the overall impact was less than a 1 percent reduction. The explanation is likely because only 25 percent of the counties in the Mississippi delta had a Medicare-certified hospital by the end of 1966. To receive Medicare funds, a hospital had to be desegregated. Medicare opened access for non-whites, whereas whites went to hospitals even if they had no prior insurance coverage.

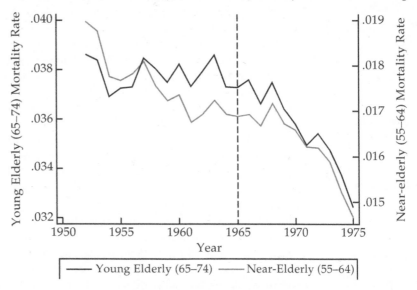

Mortality Rate Trends by Age Group

To estimate the impact of Medicare on out-of-pocket spending risk, the authors used data from the 1963 and 1970 Surveys of Health Service Utilization and Expenditures, focusing on individuals aged 55–74. Using a standard difference-in-difference framework, they compared changes in spending for the young elderly and the near elderly and found an insignificant impact of Medicare on the spending of the young elderly. However, further analysis indicated that the real impact of Medicare is in the right tail of the out-of-pocket spending distribution. They found that on average Medicare is associated with a statistically significant 40 percent decline in out-of-pocket spending for the top quintile spenders.

Discussion and Conclusions

Results demonstrate that even without any improvement in health outcomes, the introduction of Medicare was associated with a substantial decline in financial risk for its participants. Furthermore, these risk-reduction benefits are associated with an increase in social welfare approaching 40 percent of total Medicare spending especially among low-income households. The long-run benefits on mortality may be substantial due to the role that Medicare may have played in encouraging the introduction of many new life-saving technologies.

Sources: Amy Finkelstein and Robin McKnight, "What Did Medicare Do? The Impact of Medicare on Mortality and Out of Pocket Spending," *Journal of Public Economics* 92, 2008, 1644–1668; Helen Levy and David Meltzer, "What Do We Really Know about Whether Health Insurance Affects Health? In Catherine McLaughlin, ed., *Health Policy on the Uninsured: Setting the Agenda*, Washington, DC: Urban Institute Press, 2004.

Economic Consequences

Medicare's spending pattern highlights the fundamental flaw in Medicare coverage, the fact that it provides virtually no protection against low probability, catastrophic losses. For short hospital stays, Medicare pays virtually all the bill beyond the deductible. Longer hospital stays, in excess of 150 days, subject the individual to larger percentages of the total bill. This failure to cover very long but infrequent hospital stays is the result of the original "spell of illness" concept originally considered beneficial to participants. Under this concept, if a patient is discharged from the hospital and readmitted within 60 days, the readmission is considered part of the same illness. As part of the same illness, the patient does not have to pay the deductible again. The intent is to save the patient from the financial burden of paying the deductible over and over and to guarantee that elders will seek care when it is needed. The unintended consequence of this provision is to increase the chance that a long hospital stay will expose the individual to the risk of a catastrophic financial loss, in which the patient is responsible for the entire bill after the 60 lifetime reserve days are exhausted.

Overall, Medicare pays 87 percent of inpatient hospital charges and 67 percent of physician's services but only 0.5 percent of long-term care. Because of gaps in coverage, an active supplementary insurance market has developed. In 2007, approximately 92 percent of Medicare enrollees had supplemental insurance benefits from an employer-sponsored plan (33 percent), MA (22 percent), a supplemental "Medigap" policy (18 percent), or Medicaid (14 percent). Many of the so-called Medigap policies have the same problem as Medicare itself: an upside-down structure. In other words, they cover the up-front costs—deductibles and copayments—and provide for some non-covered expenses, but they do not provide protection against catastrophic financial risk.

Federal laws passed in the 1980s to regulate this growing insurance market failed to address this flaw completely. Congress created minimum standards for all **Medigap insurance** policies, but rather than provide true catastrophic coverage for the extremely rare, long hospital stay, the government has forced the private insurance market to provide Medigap policies that offer first-dollar coverage. This practice is inefficient and encourages participants to overutilize medical resources and drives up the premium costs without providing genuine catastrophic insurance coverage. As a result, the typical senior spends approximately one-fourth of his or her income either out-of-pocket or through private insurance premiums (Cubanski et al., 2014). In addition, Medicare does not cover most long-term care or mental illness treatment and does not provide protection against catastrophic losses due to extended illnesses.

The Future of Medicare

Every year the trustees of Medicare submit a detailed analysis on the financial condition and the long-term sustainability of the program. Based on the 2016 report, Medicare spending grew from less than 1 percent of GDP in 1975 to 3.5 percent in 2015 and is expected to grow to over 5 percent of GDP in the next decade. Medicare Trustees estimate that Medicare spending will grow to over 6 percent of GDP by 2040, rising to over 9 percent by 2090 (Boards of Trustees, 2016). These estimates may actually understate future spending growth because of the difficulty of sustaining the ACA's productivity adjustments for hospitals and the resulting low payment updates that are built into the estimates.

Given its pay-as-you-go funding structure, there is no permanent funding where each recipient group saves and invests for its own medical spending. Each generation of seniors relies on the next generation of workers to pay for their medical care. The

---

POLICY ISSUE

Medicare coverage provides little protection against catastrophic illnesses.

KEY CONCEPT 9

Market Failure

KEY CONCEPT 8

Efficiency

Medigap insurance

A supplemental insurance policy sold to Medicare-eligible individuals to pay the deductibles and coinsurance that are not covered by Medicare.

KEY CONCEPT 5

Markets and Pricing

arrangement worked pretty well at its inception because there were few seniors receiving benefits relative to the number of workers paying taxes. A contemporary philosopher once said, "The times they are a-changing."[7] People have fewer children, retire earlier, live longer, and demand more medical care than ever. With the number of workers per retiree shrinking dramatically, the long-term outlook for a pay-as-you-go system is not favorable.

Since 2008, the annual Trustees Report has painted a grim picture of the long-term viability of the Medicare program as we know it. Table 12.3 summarizes the 75-year horizon for the net present value of the future obligations to pay the medical expenses for today's living cohorts. The infinite horizon looks at the obligations to pay the medical expenses for everyone who will ever receive benefits. With no change in the law, future Congresses must appropriate taxes to pay these amounts. To illustrate this point, the hospital insurance trust fund is projected to become insolvent in 2028. Without additional revenue sources (or a reduction in spending on hospital services), the program will only be able to pay 87 percent of the promised benefits. By law, Medicare is unable to borrow money to cover the annual deficits, and the only option to pay all promised benefits is to raise the payroll tax.

To provide the long-term perspective on the challenges ahead, the report estimates the unfunded obligations and the general revenue obligations necessary to pay for future spending. The net present value of GDP of the U.S. economy over the 75-year horizon (beginning in 2016) was estimated at $1,189 trillion. These 75-year unfunded obligations of $33.7 trillion represent 2.8 percent of total GDP over that period. Unfunded obligations under the infinite horizon of $58.6 trillion are 2.6 percent of total GDP of $2,294 trillion over that same period.

The Trustees recognize that the estimate of the accumulated budget shortfall is likely a serious understatement of the true shortfall. Supporters of the new health care reform plan point to these estimates as proof that the ACA has gone a long way in taking care of the Medicare shortfall (as promised). The Trustees are not so sure.

TABLE 12.3 NET PRESENT VALUE OF MEDICARE'S UNFUNDED OBLIGATIONS (IN TRILLIONS OF U.S. DOLLARS)

Category	2009	2010	2013	2016
75-year horizon				
Part A. Hospital insurance[1]	$13.8	$ 2.7	$ 4.6	$ 3.8
Part B. Physicians' insurance[2]	17.2	12.9	15.7	20.0
Part D. Prescription drug insurance[3]	7.2	7.2	7.8	9.9
75-year unfunded obligations	$38.2	$22.8	$28.1	$ 33.7
Infinite horizon				
Part A. Hospital insurance[1]	$36.8	$ (0.3)	$ 3.5	$ (2.8)
Part B. Physicians' insurance[2]	37.0	21.1	25.0	36.9
Part D. Prescription drug insurance[3]	15.5	15.8	16.2	24.5
Infinite unfunded obligations	$89.3	$36.6	$44.7	$58.6

Source: Medicare Trustees Reports (2010–2016).
[1]Unfunded obligations, Table III.B10 (2010); Table V.G1 (2013); Table V.F2 (2016).
[2]Required general revenue contributions, Table III.C15 (2010); Table V.G4 (2013 and 2016).
[3]Required state tax and general revenue contributions, Table III.C23 (2010); Table V.G5 (2013 and 2016).

[7]Bob Dylan, *The Times They Are a-Changin'*, Columbia Records, 1964.

It is important to note that the actual future costs for Medicare may exceed the projections shown in this report, possibly by substantial amounts. Use of an alternative projection can illustrate the potential magnitude of this difference (2016 Medicare Trustees Report, p. 195).

Even Medicare's chief actuaries have provided an illustrative alternative scenario with what in their opinion are more realistic assumptions of expected productivity growth and the subsequent payment rates for Medicare services (Shatto and Clemens, 2016).

The current-law projections should not be interpreted as the most likely expectation of actual Medicare financial operations in the future but rather as illustrations of the very favorable impact of permanently slower growth in health care costs, if such slower growth can be achieved. The illustrative alternative projections shown here help to quantify and underscore the potential understatement of the current-law projections in the 2016 Trustees Report (p. 17).

The alternative report views the physician payment reductions as implausible and the hospital productivity adjustments required by current law unsustainable. To reach the target spending levels, physician payment rates must fall from 75 percent of private health insurance rates to 50 percent by 2040 (and 25 percent by 2090). Hospital rates must fall from the 2016 level of 60 percent of private health insurance to about 50 percent also by 2040. The thinking is that the projections in the Trustees Report are overly optimistic because Congress will modify them at some point in the future.

The conventional wisdom from health policy experts is that further reductions in Medicare payments to physicians would jeopardize access to mainstream physicians' services (Newhouse, 2010). Thus, if the difference between private insurance rates and Medicare continues to grow, "providers may very well abandon Medicare" (Jost, 2010).

In addition, the assumed productivity adjustments for hospital services projected to lead to lower hospital payments are overly ambitious and based on historical evidence not likely to occur. If the legislated changes in hospital payments actually happen, an additional 15 percent of hospitals will experience negative margins by the end of the decade and one-half will see negative margins by 2040 (Foster, 2010). Moreover, if the two changes are overridden, Medicare spending will increase significantly, wiping out most of the projected reduction in unfunded obligations shown in the 2010 report (when they dropped to 40 percent of the previous estimate).

Medicare was unsustainable before passage of the ACA, and it is still unsustainable. To fix the health care system, we must secure Medicare's financial future.

Reform Options

When the Beatles released the classic album *Sgt. Pepper's Lonely Hearts Club Band*, the first wave of baby boomers were in their early 20s and Medicare was barely a year old. "When I'm Sixty-Four," written by Paul McCartney when he was 16 years old, expressed concerns about how future relationships change as we get older. Now, 50 years later many of these same individuals are 64 (and older) and signing up for Medicare in record numbers. Like the boomers themselves, Medicare is beginning to show its age.

Medicare was largely ignored by the ACA. There were changes in the Medicare tax and adjustments in benefits relating to preventive care and prescription drugs, but the biggest change was a cut of more than $740 billion from Medicare spending over the next decade and redirecting it to pay for the Medicaid expansion and the exchange subsidies. Possibly, the most controversial change to Medicare is the creation of the controversial Independent Payment Advisory Board (IPAB) designed to reduce the growth in Medicare spending.

In order to achieve legislated spending targets, IPAB can cut Medicare payments to providers and the private insurers that participate in the MA and prescription drug programs. The board can also change Medicare's payment structure from fee-for-service to capitation or some hybrid form to achieve its targets. It may not propose any structural changes to the program, nor ration care, restrict benefits, modify eligibility rules, or make changes in cost sharing that affect enrollees.

With hospitals and hospice payments exempted from IPAB oversight until 2020, changes will disproportionately affect payment for physicians' services. For example, over the period 2013 through 2018 per capita Medicare spending is targeted to grow at a maximum rate equal to the average of the consumer price index (CPI) and the medical CPI. The board will develop an annual plan to keep Medicare spending below the target. From 2011 through 2015, the CPI grew at an annual rate of 1.76 percent and the medical CPI grew 3.60 percent (an average of 2.68 percent). At the same time, per capita Medicare spending grew 0.84 percent annually. As long as the growth in per capita Medicare spending lags the CPI averages, payment cuts will not be necessary. However, these results may be short lived. Per capita Medicare spending is projected to grow at a much higher rate in the next five years, outpacing the CPI average by as much as 1 percent. If these results continue into the future, the IPAB would have to cut Medicare spending by that amount without touching hospital spending. Thus, spending on physicians' services and other nonexempt categories would have to decrease by as much as 1–2 percent.

Despite the language of the act, rationing will be inevitable. The board can set prices for specific services so low that no provider will offer them, or at least fewer will offer them. Many physicians already refuse to see new Medicare patients, and as payment rates fall below those of Medicaid more will follow. While hospitals escape the impact of IPAB until 2020, they too will find it more difficult to remain solvent because of low payment rates.

Most researchers agree that Medicare is unsustainable in its current form. But that is where the agreement ends. Demographic trends are not encouraging. The number of workers per beneficiary has fallen to historically low levels and is expected to continue to fall as the baby boom generation becomes eligible for benefits. Even though their actual contributions amount to only one-third of their expected lifetime spending, Boomers have supported the program their entire working lives and expect to receive benefits (Steuerle and Quakenbush, 2013).

The only fair solution to the problem is one that considers the needs and expectations of both seniors who will receive the benefits and workers who are expected to pay for them. Several simple steps can solve some of the structural issues. First, place limits on the ability of recipients to purchase first dollar coverage through private supplemental insurance policies. Currently, these policies are front-loaded and allow policyholders (92 percent who have them) to avoid deductible and copays completely. With virtually no cost-sharing, moral hazard results in excess spending on low-value care.

Next, the benefit structure is overly complicated. Combine the three separate insurance plans (A, B, and D) covering hospitals, physicians, and prescription drugs into one plan. Add an out-of-pocket maximum that solves the problems that the absence of catastrophic insurance creates, leaving too many frail elderly vulnerable for medical expenses that they are unable to pay.

Another straightforward change would be to raise the eligibility age gradually much like the changes that were made to Social Security eligibility. When the program was enacted in 1965, the average life expectancy for males was 67 and that for females was 74. Now 50 years later, males can expect to live to 76 and females to 81. Extending the eligibility age could be coupled with means testing similar to the current income-based premium schedule that exists in Part B.

The open-ended nature of the original entitlement is the primary focus of the debate surrounding its sustainability. Another option preferred by those who favor a more market-oriented approach would completely restructure Medicare from defined benefit to defined contribution. Instead of an open-ended entitlement that results from a promised benefit (regardless of its cost), Medicare would provide a direct subsidy to individuals allowing them to purchase the coverage of their choice. Often referred to as premium support, this change would eventually shift most seniors into private insurance plans (Schwartz and Merlis, 2012).

The original idea of defined contribution in health care was managed competition introduced by Enthoven (1978) and modified to incorporate a competitive bidding process to establish a benchmark premium that sets the subsidy level. Competitive bidding is simply a reverse auction where the second lowest premium becomes the benchmark. Some suggest that the plan incorporate an important safety mechanism: A plan with the benefits and out-of-pocket costs of traditional Medicare would be available at a premium that does not exceed the required premium for Part B. Additionally, overall program spending may be limited by some set amount (some suggest the growth in GDP plus 0.5 percent). For all practical purposes, the premium-support plan would establish a Medicare exchange similar to the insurance exchanges created by the ACA.

Because the benchmark premium is determined by competitive bidding, the Congressional Budget Office is unable to score the proposed plan and critics are left to criticize versions that recommended a fixed-dollar benchmark premium. Does competitive bidding work to lower the cost of medical care? MA and Medicare Part D already use aspects of the competitive bidding process. Experience with competitive bidding in the MA program provides evidence that it can lower costs. Song, Cutler, and Chernew (2012) estimated that in 2009 the second lowest MA bid in Massachusetts was 9 percent below traditional Medicare. Feldman, Coulam, and Dowd (2012) also examined MA pricing and estimated a 9.5 percent savings with competitive bidding.

Because the premium support sets a fixed contribution paid directly to beneficiaries, concerns arise that the benefit will slowly erode over time leaving many low-income elderly, in particular those with significant health problems, unable to afford their premiums. For this vulnerable population the subsidy can easily be adjusted to take into consideration their increased risk. Proponents of premium support maintain that these concerns are overly pessimistic because the bidding process will introduce price competition that will restrain medical costs. Experience with the prescription drug benefit program reflects the more likely outcome of more competition in Medicare. Part D premiums have not changed appreciably for the past several years, and MA premiums in 2013 actually fell from 2012 levels. In any event, the sustainability of the entire program depends on our willingness to make structural changes in the way it is administered.

Summary and Conclusions

The history of American health care cannot be understood without careful consideration of the government's expanding role in providing medical care. Medicare and Medicaid (discussed in the next chapter), created in 1965 to provide access to medical care for the elderly and indigent, have proven to be a mixed blessing. Both have been successful in fulfilling their stated missions, providing care to over 100 million of the nation's poor, elderly, and disabled, but the success has come at a tremendous cost with the government spending well over $1.3 trillion on health care in these two programs alone.

Even with the passage of the ACA, Medicare and Medicaid reform will receive a great deal of attention in future congressional sessions. Still, the electorate applies substantial pressure to maintain a balanced federal budget, and the perception is that medical care spending must be controlled for that to happen.

The introduction of prospective payment to hospitals with DRGs and physician payment reform via the relative-value scale represented major changes on the spending side. Short of asking the elderly to accept a more moderate benefits package or pay more out of pocket—something most policy makers are unwilling to do—workers could simply pay more taxes. Only recently have policy makers given consideration to more seniors enrolling in private insurance plans using premium support to help them pay their premiums.

The 2016 Medicare Trustees Report, using assumptions based on "current law," estimates that the Medicare Trust Fund depletion will occur in 2028. According to the illustrative alternative projection submitted by the Office of the Actuary of the CMS, this optimistic outlook may not be the most likely (Shatto and Clemens, 2016). If more realistic assumptions on future payments for both hospital and physicians' services are used, the depletion date will occur sooner and the long-term gap between spending and revenues will continue to grow into the near future. The Trustees do project small surpluses in 2016–2020 but will run an annual deficit thereafter. Further evidence of the program's underfunding is the reality that the trust fund does not meet the legal requirements of financial adequacy. Program assets fell to 71 percent of annual spending in 2015, well below the recommended level of 100 percent. The trust fund has not met this minimum level of adequacy since 2003.

Policy makers have still not addressed the long-term demographic problem facing the system—the aging baby boom generation—and the fact that Medicare is still insulated from the market forces that serve as a moderating influence on the rest of the health care sector. Medicare suffers from the same structural deficiencies brought on by a third-party payment system that insulates its recipients from any incentives to economize. Reforms targeting incentives address cost sharing from a defined contribution approach. Whatever is included in the reform plan, if the system is to be put on a sound financial basis, its structural deficiencies must be addressed (Gokhale, 1997). Medicare as we know it is unsustainable. Either we change it or we lose it.

PROFILE   John K. Iglehart

When listing individuals who have had a profound influence on intellectual thought in the area of health policy, the name of John K. Iglehart makes everyone's top 10. Born in Milwaukee, Iglehart received his Bachelor of Science in journalism at the University of Wisconsin-Milwaukee in 1961. After four years with the *Milwaukee Sentinel,* he spent six years with the Associated Press in Chicago and eventually was promoted to night city editor. In 1969, he took a position with the *National Journal* in Washington, DC, where he is still one of their contributing editors.

In addition to the numerous articles, he has written in health and medical journals, Iglehart is the journalist in residence at the Harvard School of Public Health and national correspondent for the *New England Journal of Medicine.* In 1981, William B. Walsh, the founder of Project HOPE (Health Opportunities for People Everywhere), recruited him to guide the creation of a new health policy journal, *Health Affairs.* Under his direction, the journal's circulation rose to over 10,000—the largest for a journal of its type. Dedicated to the goal of Project HOPE, *Health Affairs* has become a highly respected journal among academicians, policy makers, and journalists. Faculty members all over the country are using the journal as a textbook in their health economics and policy classes. Policy makers have come to rely on it as a source of background information on the complexities of health care delivery and finance. Journalists quote its pages regularly, using it as a source of breaking news in health policy research. Because of his important contribution to the dissemination of health services research to a diverse audience, he was awarded the 2016 William B. Graham Prize sponsored by the Association of University Programs in Health Administration.

Iglehart is widely known for his research on the medical care delivery systems of Canada, Germany, and Japan. His series in the *New England Journal of Medicine* on "The American Health Care System," with subtitles ranging from "Private Insurance" to "Medicare" to "Managed Care," provides an excellent introduction into the diverse viewpoints, proposals, and perspectives on the problems faced by the U.S. medical care delivery system today.

Source: Project HOPE website, available at http://www.projecthope.org/, and Who's Who in America.

Questions and Problems

1. Comment on the following statement: "The proposal to increase Medicare cost sharing (increasing premiums, deductibles, and coinsurance) will deprive the elderly poor of needed medical services."

2. You have recently been hired as a research assistant to the Secretary of Health and Human Services. To keep the administration informed on health care issues, your supervisor has asked you to research options for changing the Medicare system. Current concerns stem from the fear that if Medicare remains an open-ended entitlement program, its share of the federal budget will continue to increase over time. Prepare a brief memo to the secretary examining one or more of the following proposed changes. Use your best economic reasoning.
   a. A freeze in physicians' fees and a requirement of mandatory assignment.
   b. A plan to enroll everyone eligible for Medicare in managed care networks and pay a fixed, capitated amount per enrollee equal to the current per capita Medicare spending level.
   c. Allowing all Medicare recipients to buy high-deductible insurance policies and use the premium savings to set up medical savings accounts.

3. One of the major problems in dealing with any welfare program is the tension between individual and social responsibility—Medicare is no different. Should adult children be responsible for the medical expenses of their parents? Where does individual and familial responsibility end and social responsibility begin?

4. What is Medigap insurance? How does the existence of Medigap policies affect the cost of providing medical services to the elderly? Was Mark Pauly correct when he observed that the provision of some insurance might be suboptimal? (See "The Economics of Moral Hazard: Comment," *American Economic Review* 58(2), June 1968, 531–538.)

5. Define the following terms and describe the effect of each on the provision of medical care for the elderly:
   a. mandatory assignment
   b. balance billing
   c. capitation
   d. free choice of provider

References

Boards of Trustees, Federal Hospital Insurance and Federal Supplementary Insurance Trust Funds, "2016 Annual Report of the Federal Hospital Insurance and Federal Supplementary Insurance Trust Funds," June 22, 2016, available at https://www.cms.gov/Research-Statistics-Data-and-Systems/Statistics-Trends-and-Reports/ReportsTrustFunds/Downloads/TR2016.pdf.

Cubanski, Juliette, et al., "How Much Is Enough? Out-of-Pocket Spending among Medicare Beneficiaries: A Chartbook, Kaiser Family Foundation, June 2014, available at http://files.kff.org/attachment/how-much-is-enough-out-of-pocket-spending-among-medicare-beneficiaries-a-chartbook-report (Accessed September 9, 2016).

Enthoven, Alain C, "Consumer Choice Health Plan," *New England Journal of Medicine* 298(12 and 13), March 23 and March 30, 1978, 650–658 and 709–720.

Feldman, Roger, Robert Coulam, and Bryan Dowd, "Competitive Bidding Can Help Solve Medicare's Fiscal Crisis," American Enterprise Institute for Public Policy Research, No. 2, February 2012, available at www.aei.org.

Foster, Richard S., "Estimating Financial Effects of the 'Patient Protection and Affordable Care Act,' as Amended," April 22, 2010, available at https://www.cms.gov/Research-Statistics-Data-and-Systems/Research/ActuarialStudies/downloads/PPACA_2010-04-22.pdf.

Gillis, Kurt D., David W. Lee, and Richard J. Willke, "Physician-Based Measures of Medical Access," *Inquiry* 29(3), Fall 1992, 321–331.

Gokhale, Jagadeesh, "Medicare: Usual and Customary Remedies Will No Longer Work," *Economic Commentary*, Cleveland, OH: Federal Reserve Bank of Cleveland, April 1, 1997, available at https://www.clevelandfed.org/en/newsroom-and-events/publications/economic-commentary/economic-commentary-archives/1997-economic-commentaries/ec-19970401-medicare-usual-and-customary-remedies-will-no-longer-work.aspx.

Jost, Timothy, "The Independent Payment Advisory Board," *New England Journal of Medicine* 363(2), 2010, 103–105.

Newhouse, Joseph P., "Assessing Health Reform's Impact on Four Key Groups of Americans," *Health Affairs* 29(9), September, 2010, 1714–1724.

Schwartz, Anne and Mark Merlis, "Health Policy Brief: Premium Support in Medicare," *Health Affairs*, March 22, 2012.

Shatto, John D. and M. Kent Clemens, "Projected Medicare Expenditures under an Illustrative Scenario with Alternative Payment Updates to Medicare Providers," Office of the Actuary, Centers for Medicare and Medicaid Services, June 22, 2016, available at http://www.cms.gov/Research-Statistics-Data-and-Systems/Statistics-Trends-and-Reports/ReportsTrustFunds/Downloads/2016TRAlternativeScenario.pdf.

Song, Zirui, David M. Cutler, and Michael E. Chernew, "Potential Consequences of Reforming Medicare into a Competitive Bidding System," *Journal of the American Medical Association* 308(5), August 1, 2012, 459–460.

Steuerle, C. Eugene and Caleb Quakenbush, "Social Security and Medicare Taxes and Benefits over a Lifetime, Urban Institute," November 2013, available at http://www.urban.org/sites/default/files/alfresco/publication-pdfs/412945-Social-Security-and-Medicare-Taxes-and-Benefits-over-a-Lifetime.PDF.

Changing Demographics: The Aging of America

Economic theory often cites changing demographics as a major factor in determining the demand for goods and services. The popular notion that demand changes as an individual, family, or nation grows in size and matures is familiar to most students of economic theory. In fact, partly because of his pioneering research in life-cycle changes in savings, investment, and consumption, Franco Modigliani was awarded the Nobel Prize for Economic Science in 1985. When exploring the causes of high and rising medical care spending, the aging population makes everyone's top 10 list.

In this appendix, we will examine the changing demographics of the population and its impact on overall medical care spending. As Americans live longer, the changing age and sex structure will have a significant effect on medical care demand in the coming century.

The Aging Population

Since 1950, the percentage of the U.S. population over the age of 65 has increased from 8.1 percent to 13.1 percent. Due primarily to low fertility rates, the percentage of the population less than five years of age has fallen from 10.8 percent to just under 8.0 percent. The baby boom generation (those born between 1946 and 1964) may get a lot of attention regarding their demand for goods and services, but to date, they have had only a modest effect on demand for medical care services, largely fertility related. As this cohort becomes Medicare eligible (which began in 2010), the percentage of the population over the age of 65 will become a concern of health policy analysts. The percentage of the population over the age of 65 will rise to over 20 percent, or almost 70 million, by 2030. The major concern for policy makers is that a growing working-age population will not match this rapidly growing, aged population. The imbalance will jeopardize the solvency of the entire federal old-age entitlement apparatus, particularly Social Security and Medicare.

Up until now, the age and sex composition of the population has contributed little to the growth in health expenditures in the United States. Studies examining the causes of the rise in medical care spending attribute less than 10 percent to the change to the age and sex composition of the population (Aaron, 1991; Gordon, 1992).

To date, population aging has been much more of an issue in Europe than in North America (see Table 12A.1). In most European countries, higher life expectancies and lower fertility rates have resulted in 16–20 percent of their populations falling in the over-age-65 category. The United States and Canada are about 20 years behind Europe and Japan in feeling the impact of an aging population.

TABLE 12A.1 POPULATION AGING

	Percent of population over age 65 (2010)
Canada	14.2
France	16.8
Germany	20.6
Japan	23.2
Switzerland	17.4
United Kingdom	15.8
United States	13.1

A number of individuals in their sixties and seventies are frail and impaired, but most are healthy, active, and relatively well off. The rapid growth in the population over age 85 presents a challenge to policy makers concerned with the rise in medical care spending. Individuals in the ninth and tenth decades of life begin to show their age. They are more prone to chronic conditions that lead to disability and the need for long-term care: Alzheimer's disease and other forms of dementia, Parkinson's disease, hypertension, diabetes, osteoarthritis, hip fractures, and peripheral vascular diseases. Today, an estimated 100,000 Americans are over 100 years old—the fastest growing age cohort in the country. By 2020, centenarians will likely number 240,000 and by 2050, one million.

The increasing number of the oldest old raises certain bioethical issues. There is already talk of rationing medical care to the oldest old (Callahan, 1987). Assisted suicide, euthanasia, and denial of treatment are all cutting-edge ethical issues. These issues are not unique to the United States. Throughout history, every culture and every society has had to deal with how to allocate scarce resources. Whenever resources were in short supply, the elderly were the first to see their shares limited. The old Eskimo accepted his fate and willingly stepped onto the ice floe, never to be seen again.

Medical Care Costs for the Elderly

Seniors make up only 13.1 percent of the population and consume over one-third of all medical resources. Figure 12.A1 provides details of medical care utilization by age group for 2006. Health spending exhibits a significant upward trend over the life cycle. Younger cohorts spend less than their elders. Individuals in their fifties spend $4,000–$5,000 on average while those in their early twenties spend on average $1,000–$2,000. The highest spenders are over the age of 65, each spending over $7,500 (see Jung and Tran, 2010).

What is true for spending across age groups is also evident when comparing spending between males and females. Starting at age 19 and continuing through age 60, on average women spend about $1,000 per year more per men. Undoubtedly, this difference is primarily fertility related, reproductive services and obstetrics. From age 60 to 70, average spending by males exceeds that of females.

The reason that the elderly spend more on health care than the young is due partially to the increased frequency of medical encounters: emergency department visits, outpatient procedures, days of hospital care, and physician office visits. Table 12A.2 details the life-cycle pattern. In all cases individuals over the age of 65 see the physician more often, are admitted to the hospital more often, and when admitted stay in the hospital longer. The typical person over age 65 visits the physician more than seven times annually, three times the rate of the typical 18- to 44-year-old. The older cohort has five times the number of hospital days and half again as many outpatient visits. Increased frequency of physician visits and increased intensity of care contribute to the higher spending.

FIGURE 12A.1 Personal Medical Care Expenditures by Age and Sex, 2006

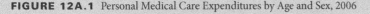

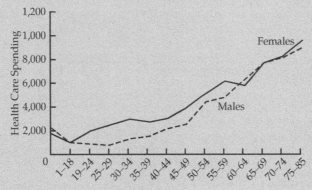

Source: Medical Expenditure Panel Survey, 2006.

TABLE 12A.2   UTILIZATION OF MEDICAL CARE RESOURCES ANNUALLY BY AGE GROUP, 2007

Age group	Emergency department visits per 100 population	Outpatient visits per 100 population	Days of hospital care per 100 population (2006)	Physician office visits per 100 population
Less than 18	36	26	19	264
18 to 44	43	27	34	233
45 to 54	34	32	47	325
55 to 64	29	36	73	438
Over 65	48	38	192	712
65 to 74	36	41	132	669
Over 75	62	36	254	761
All persons	39	30	56	336

Source: National Center for Health Statistics, *Health, United States, 2009.*

ISSUES IN MEDICAL CARE DELIVERY

HAVE WE DISCOVERED THE MYTHICAL FOUNTAIN OF YOUTH?

The quest for immortality is fueled by our inherent fear of the unknown. Early explorers of the New World led by Ponce de Leon searched for the Fountain of Youth. Even the fictional archeological explorer Indiana Jones survived his third crusade to see the restoration of life to those who drank from the Holy Grail used by Jesus to celebrate the Last Supper. Current exploration, somewhat more scientifically based, has taken the form of medical research into the gene that controls the aging process and the fierce debate that it fosters.

The current medical approach to the study of mortality is based on a model of disease. From this viewpoint, death results from disease. Except for trauma and violence, without disease there is no death. Actuarial data from the Social Security Administration predict that life expectancies will continue to climb throughout the next century. According to these estimates, white females born in 2080 can expect to live over 90 years.

Fries (1980) advocates a different viewpoint. From his perspective, the human life span is genetically determined. Organs that have substantial reserves to restore health after an illness at age 30 have very limited capacity at older ages. Thus, the elderly die, not from disease as much as from the body's inability to restore health after an illness. Fries' perspective suggests a maximum life expectancy of 85 years.

Proponents of the theory of ever-increasing life expectancies must face the prospect that living longer does not necessarily mean living better. Aging still has its consequences. Currently, those consequences involve living a longer proportion of our lives affected by chronic disease. Unless we find a way to treat or minimize the effects of these chronic diseases, we will be faced with an increasing number of frail elderly in need of partial or total assistance for longer periods.

Proponents of a limited life expectancy see things differently. As life expectancies reach their upper limits, the period of diminished activity due to chronic illnesses diminishes, along with the need for costly medical care. Depending on which viewpoint is correct, the implications for future resource needs will be quite different.

Sources: James F. Fries, "Aging, Natural Death, and the Compression of Morbidity," *New England Journal of Medicine* 303(3), July 17, 1980, 130–135; Edward L. Schneider and Jacob A. Brody, "Aging, Natural Death, and the Compression of Morbidity: Another View," *New England Journal of Medicine* 309 (14), October 6, 1983, 854–856.

The Challenge of Treating Chronic Diseases

The conventional wisdom attributes much of the medical cost explosion to the high cost of treating the elderly, particularly during the last year of life. Dying is expensive, and the United States devotes about $100 billion per year to medical care treatment during the last six months of life. The real issue is not the cost of dying but the multiplicity of illnesses that affect us as we age and the increased use of services to treat those illnesses. Chronic problems strike with increased frequency and severity as we age.

Medical progress has resulted in improved longevity and a change in the focus of medical research. The acute medical problems experienced at earlier ages no longer occupy our attention. Influenza, small pox, diphtheria, and polio, once feared, are no longer major concerns. Developments in medicine have exchanged these acute problems for chronic ones. Individuals once struck down by an acute illness early in life are surviving to experience chronic problems later in life. The trade-off is a low-cost, early death for a more expensive, later death.

As Americans live longer, the focus of attention shifts from responding to acute illnesses to treating chronic conditions such as hypertension, diabetes, heart disease, depression, and arthritis. In fact, these five chronic conditions were among the 15 most expensive conditions treated in 1997 (Cohen and Krauss, 2003). The combined cost of treating these five conditions was $141.4 billion, or 12.9 percent of total health care spending.

Hwang and colleagues (2001) estimated that over 125 million Americans suffer from one or more chronic conditions, a disability, or a functional limitation. About 10.7 million of these have functional limitations, in combination with one or more chronic conditions or a disability, and need assistance to perform certain activities of daily living (ADL).[8] The cost of treating these individuals consumes approximately 75 percent of total health care spending. Health insurance generally provides better coverage for the treatment of acute care episodes than for ongoing care for a chronic illness. As a result, services designed to slow the progression of chronic illnesses may not be covered or may have only limited coverage. Moreover, those needing assistance with ADL will find that most insurance plans do not pay for these services at all.

The Cost of Long-Term Care

The issue of long-term care is a growing concern in modern industrial societies. As societies develop and mature, they have more elderly and fewer children to provide elder care. The only option available for many families is institutional care, sending the aging parent to a nursing home.

Those reaching the age of 85 today can expect to live longer, but chronic health problems will be increasingly dominant their remaining years. As we age, episodes of illness increase in frequency and severity, along with the need for medical care for longer periods. The two major problems facing this age group are hip fractures and the various forms of dementia, including Alzheimer's disease. The incidence of dementia doubles every five years after age 65. The median prevalence is 2.8 percent for those of ages 65–74, increasing to 9 percent for those of ages 74–84, and 28 percent for those over age 85 (Schneider and Guralnik, 1990).

Many view long-term care as the ticking medical care time bomb, especially as the baby boom generation begins to enter the oldest-old age category beginning in 2020. In 2010, over $150 billion was spent on nursing home care for the elderly—almost 6 percent of total health care spending. By 2040, we can expect to spend three to five times that amount in real terms. Federal and state governments are the largest payers for long-term care, financing over 50 percent of the total spending primarily through Medicaid.

In 2008, more than 1.41 million elderly residents lived in nursing homes across America; 50 percent were over age 85. The probability of residing in a nursing home increases with age. For Americans between the ages of 65 and 74, 1 percent lives in a nursing home. That figure increases to 3.6 percent of those between 75 and 84 and almost 13.9 percent of those over the age of 85 (*Health, United States*, 2010). By 2040, the nursing home population may reach as high as 5.9 million, with at least 2 million of those over the age of 85. Over the next five decades, the 85-plus nursing home population

---

[8]*Activities of daily living* are defined as the activities of basic self-care, including feeding, washing, and toileting.

will become twice as large as the total number of current nursing home residents.

Comments on Aging

In part, our attitude toward death drives us to treat terminally ill patients aggressively, fueling the debate. Survey results by the Robert Wood Johnson Foundation show that Americans are not nearly so willing to accept this aspect of life as are citizens of other countries. When asked what they would do if told by their personal physician that they had an incurable and fatal disease, 90 percent of Americans over age 65 said they would seek a second opinion. One-third of Britons and one-half of Australians responded similarly ("The Immortal American," 1995).

As a result, Americans receive four times the number of bypass operations of the Japanese, Germans, and Britons. We have higher rates of use of all the major high-tech treatment and diagnostic services, including chemotherapy, kidney dialysis, and advanced imaging. The higher usage rates are due in part to the fact that the United States has very few supply restrictions, unlike the crude triage system used in Britain or the regionalized services in Canada.

For most middle-aged baby boomers, the prospect of living longer and healthier is appealing. (Bypass surgery may not lengthen my life, but if it enables me to enjoy tennis in my retirement years, who is to say it is not worth it?) The policy issue is clear and continues to grow in critical importance who should bear the costs of our desire for longer, happier lives?

Researchers at the Cleveland Federal Reserve Bank provide a unique look at how the burden of paying for government spending on goods and services is distributed among current and future generations (Auerbach, Gokhale, and Kotlikoff, 1995). Using the 1993 benefit and tax structure, the typical 65-year-old American male could expect to receive transfers from Social Security, Medicare, and Medicaid, net of any taxes paid, in excess of $100,000 over his remaining lifetime. That same year, the typical 65-year-old female could expect net transfers of almost $140,000 before her death. In fact, males over the age of 55 and females over the age of 50 could expect a positive net transfer over the remaining years of their lives. In contrast, younger Americans could expect a net tax payment. For example, a 25-year-old male had a prospective net tax burden (taxes over transfers) of $200,000 over his expected lifetime. Nowhere is fairness such an issue as when dealing with this generational imbalance.

The apparent relationship between health care spending and the proximity to death is due primarily to the relationship between age and mortality. The end-of-life medical episode tends to be expensive. As we live longer, it is increasingly likely that this event will take place after age 65. Is it cost effective to provide certain services to individuals once they reach a particular age—for example, should kidney dialysis, organ transplantation, or joint replacement be available after age 65? The United States is still a long way from establishing a formal rationing scheme for medical care based on age. If cost-effective care were the sole criterion for access to the medical care system, we would end up with a society where euthanasia at retirement was the norm. What are the chances that we will one day initiate the end-of-life episode shown in the 1960s movie *Logan's Run*? In the futuristic society depicted, when people reached 30, they submitted to the Carousel for the final death spiral. Are the actions of Dr. Jack Kevorkian merely a glimpse of that future?

ISSUES IN MEDICAL CARE DELIVERY

LIFE IS SHORT: MAKE IT COUNT

As for the days of our life, they contain seventy years,
Or if due to strength, eighty years,
Yet their pride is but labor and sorrow;
For soon it is gone and we fly away.
Psalms 90:10

References

Aaron, Henry J., *Serious and Unstable Condition: Financing America's Health Care*, Washington, DC: The Brookings Institute, 1991.

Auerbach, Alan J., Jagadeesh Gokhale, and Laurence J. Kotlikoff, "Restoring Generational Balance in U.S. Fiscal Policy: What Will It Take?" *Economic Review* 31(1), Quarter 1, 1995, 2–12.

Callahan, Daniel, *Setting Limits: Medical Goals in an Aging Society*, New York: Simon and Schuster, 1987.

Cohen, Joel W. and Nancy A. Krauss, "Spending and Service Use among People with the Fifteen Most Costly Medical Conditions, 1997," *Health Affairs* 22(2), March/April 2003, 129–138.

Gordon, John Steele, "How America's Health Care Fell Ill," *American Heritage*, May/June 1992, 49–65.

Hwang, Wenke, et al., "Out-of-Pocket Medical Spending for Care of Chronic Conditions," *Health Affairs* 20(6), November/December 2001, 267–278.

Jung, Juergen and Chung Tran, "Medical Consumption over the Life Cycle: Facts from a U.S. Medical Expenditure Panel Survey," UNSW Australian School of Business Research Paper No. 2010 ECON 08, June 24, 2010. At ssrn.com/abstract=1566095 (Accessed January 15, 2011).

Schneider, Edward L. and Jack M. Guralnik, "The Aging of America: Impact on Health Care Costs," *Journal of the American Medical Association* 263(17), May 2, 1990, 2335–2340.

"The Immortal American," *Wall Street Journal*, May 31, 1995, A14.

Questions and Problems

1. As individuals grow older, how does their demand for medical care change? How does aging affect the provision of medical services?

2. How will an aging population influence health policy makers in the twenty-first century?

3. In 1993, the Census Bureau estimated that elderly men were nearly twice as likely to be married and living with their spouses as elderly women (75 percent versus 41 percent). What are the economic and medical care implications of this phenomenon?

4. Since the passage of Medicare in 1965, what has happened to overall medical spending for the elderly? Per capita spending? Out-of-pocket spending? How does this compare with health care spending by the nonelderly?

5. Some policy makers have identified the high cost of dying as a primary reason for increased medical spending by the elderly. What is the evidence?

CHAPTER 13

Medicaid

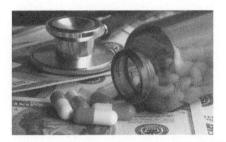

MEDICAID EXPANSION WILL STIMULATE THE ECONOMY AND CREATE JOBS, OR NOT

Now providing coverage for over 70 million low-income Americans, Medicaid is one of the largest health care systems in the developed world. In 2014, the Affordable Care Act (ACA) expanded coverage by providing 100 percent funding for states that increased the income threshold to 138 percent of the federal poverty level (FPL). Thirty states plus the District of Columbia accepted the funds and three years after implementation, approximately 5 million participants were covered under the new eligibility standards.

Repeatedly, proponents of the ACA expansion and their forecasting models claimed that it would create jobs and stimulate economic activity at little or no cost to the states. The Council of Economic Advisers (2014) projected that expansion would increase employment in the expansion states by 356,000 job years through 2017 resulting in a $62 billion increase in economic activity. States that did not expand coverage would forego 379,000 job years and $66 billion in economic activity. The Kaiser Family Foundation (2013) summarized the results of 32 studies on the impact of Medicaid expansion on the economies of 26 different states. Study results predicted an increase in economic activity in each state, along with significant growth in employment. For example, in the case of Texas the state could expect an increase in gross state product of $270 billion over the first decade of implementation along with an increase in employment of almost one million.

Estimates of this type showing the economic benefits of the Medicaid policy change are based on a category of simulation models called regional input-output models. The accuracy of these models depends critically on the basic assumptions buried in their estimating equations, and when used improperly can be manipulated to provide just about any answer you want. Input-output models with their demand-side orientation ignore capacity constraints in the health care system and the opportunity cost of resources. Ignoring these factors will result in an overestimation of the economic impact of the policy change.

The impact estimates derived from these models are difficult to accept when compared to the actual experience of many of the states that expanded Medicaid. Overall, enrollment surged and program costs increased much faster than projections, even with 19 states refusing to participate in the expansion. New enrollees are costlier than expected. Initial expectations were that the expansion enrollees would be healthier and have per capita costs that were 30 percent below those previously enrolled. Instead, new

enrollees spent 23 percent more than previous enrollees, or 49 percent more than predicted. A program, already the second largest spending category in most states' budgets,
is taking up even larger share (Cassidy, 2015).

A study published by the American Action Forum (Book, 2014) provides a different
(and more complete) perspective of the state-by-state macroeconomic effects of the Medicaid policy change. Correcting the methodological drawbacks of the input-output models discussed earlier, Book estimates a 10-year loss in economic activity of $174 billion
and a loss of 206,000 jobs between 2014 and 2017 if all states were to expand Medicaid
coverage. In Book's estimates, some 20 states gain economic activity and jobs and the
remainder lose. It is also interesting to note that these estimates of job loss are similar
to those provided by the Congressional Budget Office (CBO) in 2014 that projected an
ACA-induced reduction in the U.S. labor force of 2.5 million by 2024.

Sources: Council of Economic Advisers, *Missed Opportunities: The Consequences of State Decisions Not to Expand
Medicaid*, July 2014, available at https://obamawhitehouse.archives.gov/sites/default/files/docs/missed_opportunities_
medicaid_0.pdf; Henry J. Kaiser Family Foundation, *The Role of Medicaid in State Economies and the ACA*, Issue Brief
#8522, November 2013; Christina A. Cassidy, *Medicaid Enrollment Surges, Stirs Worry About State Budgets*, Associated
Press, Big Story, July 19, 2015; and Robert Book, *Expanding Medicaid Will Not Stimulate the Economy or Create Jobs*,
American Action Forum, December 11, 2024.

As the cost of medical care rises, policy makers throughout the world have had to face
difficult decisions concerning the Triple Aim of quality, access, and cost. The problems of
medical care delivery affect the quality of life of millions of people, particularly the poor
and elderly. Concern for this segment of the population has resulted in the provision of
universal coverage in most developed countries around the world. With access guaranteed,
spending becomes the primary concern.

This chapter examines the primary safety net coverage for the low-income population
in the United States, Medicaid. The basic institutional features of the program, including
the Children's Health Insurance Program (CHIP), are the topic of the first section. The
following section presents a discussion of the economic consequences of Medicaid. The
changes in eligibility resulting from the passage of the ACA are discussed in the next section. Explanation of the impact of Medicaid on its participants is followed by a section on
the future of the program. Summary and conclusions end the chapter.

Medicaid: Medical Care for the Poor

Medicaid was passed in 1965 as part of the same legislative package with the federal
Medicare program. The program served approximately 4 million low-income Americans
in 1966, increasing to over 70 million by 2016. Medicaid spending amounted to $0.9 billion
in 1966 and grew to almost $600 billion by 2016 (see Table 13.1). Enrollment is expected to
reach over 77 million and spending to exceed $900 billion as the ACA expansion reaches
its 10th year in 2024.

Institutional Features

Medicaid is an open-ended, means-tested entitlement program, administered by the states
and financed jointly with state and federal funds. Each state's per capita income relative
to national per capita income determines the federal portion of Medicaid payments. The
national average for the federal matching rate was 58 percent in 2012, rising to 61 percent
with the eligibility expansion in 2014 and will remain at about that level for the next decade.

TABLE 13.1 MEDICAID SPENDING SELECT YEARS, 1966–2024

Year	Total enrollment (millions)	Total spending (billions of current dollars)[1]	Annual rate of change in spending[2] (in percentages)	Average federal share (in percentages)
1966	4.0	$ 0.9	—	50
1970	14.0	5.1	54.3	54
1975	20.2	13.1	20.8	55
1980	19.6	25.2	14.0	55
1985	19.8	41.3	10.4	57
1990	22.9	72.2	11.8	57
1995	33.4	159.5	17.1	57
2000	34.5	206.2	5.3	57
2005	46.3	315.9	8.9	57
2010	54.5	401.5	4.9	67
2011	55.8	427.4	6.5	63
2012	57.3	431.2	0.9	58
2013	58.6	455.6	5.7	58
2014	64.0	494.5	8.7	61
Projections				
2015	68.9	554.3	12.1	63
2016	70.5	582.8	5.1	63
2017	71.6	607.2	4.2	62
2020	74.7	728.2	6.2	61
2024	77.5	920.5	6.0	61

Source: Office of the Actuary, CMS, 2015 Actuarial Report on the Financial Outlook for Medicaid.
[1]Includes administration expense.
[2]Average annual change from the previous entry.

State shares range from 50 percent in 13 states to 25.2 percent in Mississippi.[1] The law sets no upper limit on total Medicaid spending and thus, states do not take full responsibility for effectively managing the program. There is limited spending discipline because the federal government pays the majority of new spending and shares in any program savings at the same rate. A state receiving 60 percent federal matching money will return 60 percent of any savings to the federal treasury.

Traditionally, the states had some flexibility in designing their own programs as long as certain federal guidelines were met, specifically that a basic medical benefits package be provided to specific population groups, primarily low-income groups traditionally eligible for welfare. Eligibility standards varied considerably from state to state, resulting in unequal coverage. Individuals eligible for benefits in one state would not be eligible, under similar circumstances, for benefits in another. Even with passage of the ACA these differences continue. States that expanded Medicaid coverage were required to enroll all individuals making less than 138 percent of the FPL income. In return, the federal government covered 100 percent of the increased spending through 2016, at which time the federal

[1]The federal share, or federal medical assistance percentage (FMAP), is determined by the formula $FMAP = 1 - \{[(\text{State per capita income})^2/(\text{U.S. per capita income})^2] \times 0.45\}$.

share adjusts to 90 percent. States that did not expand Medicaid continue to set their own eligibility standards. States still have flexibility in determining the level of payment to providers.

The original legislation provided coverage for recipients of public assistance, primarily single-parent families and the aged, blind, and disabled. Since its original enactment, over 20 major legislative actions have expanded benefits to additional groups and have covered additional services (Gruber, 2000b). These steps have resulted in the dramatic escalation in spending over the original projections. After moderating somewhat in the 1980s, spending increased over 10 percent per year in the early 1990s and has only recently settled down to single-digit annual increases.

Since 1987, most of the changes in the program have increased the income threshold for eligibility. The first major change allowed states to cover children who met the financial standards but lived in two-parent households. By 1992, states were required to provide pregnancy-related benefits for pregnant women and children under age 6 who had family incomes that were less than 133 percent of the FPL.[2] The program also covers children aged 6–18 if their family income was less than 100 percent of the poverty level.

In the summer of 1996, Congress enacted a sweeping welfare reform bill that included legislation dealing with the treatment of legal immigrants. Legal immigrants arriving in the country after August 22, 1996, are eligible for Medicaid benefits after they have resided in the United States for five years.

Passage of the ACA in 2010 (and amended by the Supreme Court in 2012) created a uniform eligibility standard applied to all states that voluntarily participated. The eligibility threshold for all legal residents was raised to 138 percent of the FPL in the 30 participating states.

State Children's Health Insurance Program

Passage of the Balanced Budget Act of 1997 created the State Children's Health Insurance Program (SCHIP) and subsidized states to fund health insurance for low-income children who did not qualify for Medicaid. In 2016, Medicaid and SCHIP covered approximately 35 million low-income children. State programs must provide enrollees with the same benefits under each. Patient out-of-pocket costs are allowed in SCHIP but are limited to 5 percent of family income. SCHIP is not set up as an entitlement program. Participants must pay monthly premiums for their coverage.

Premium assistance programs and coverage waivers have also been passed in a number of states. States have used these waivers to cover other uninsured individuals in addition to eligible children, including parents of eligible children, childless adults, and pregnant women. Under these programs, states are allowed to subsidize employers who offer insurance to otherwise eligible participants and in some cases to purchase family coverage if it is proven cost effective.

Economic Consequences

Results of a study by the Kaiser Commission on the Future of Medicaid (1995) concluded that most of the increase in Medicaid spending since 1988 was due to three factors: 1) program expansions mandated by the federal government that have led to dramatic increases

---

[2]States are allowed to establish eligibility standards that extend benefits to families with incomes up to 185 percent of the poverty level.

in enrollment; 2) the overall increase in medical care costs; and 3) increases in reimbursement rates to hospitals and other providers. The three factors remain the primary reasons for spending growth to this day.

Congress moved to expand Medicaid eligibility as part of the Deficit Reduction Act of 1984. In an attempt to reduce infant mortality and improve access to child health services, the act was the first in a series of seven legislative steps that extended eligibility to all pregnant women and children under the age of 19.

At the same time, Congress also required the states to add new services to the mandatory benefits package. States must cover the services of nurse practitioners, care provided in community and migrant health centers, and any service needed to treat a condition discovered during a diagnostic screening, even if the treatment is considered an optional benefit.

In addition, Congress acted to improve reimbursement levels for providers. The 1980 Boren amendment allowed states to deviate from Medicare's cost-reimbursement system for hospitals and nursing homes but also required that reimbursement levels be sufficient to allow for their efficient and economical operation.

disproportionate share A payment adjustment under Medicare and Medicaid that pays hospitals that serve a large number of indigent patients.

In order to increase physician participation and advance the goal of increasing health services for children and pregnant women, legislation was passed to improve payments to pediatricians and obstetricians. Hospitals that serve a **disproportionate share** of Medicaid patients receive supplemental payments as part of the Disproportionate Share Hospital Program, in part to make up for low initial reimbursement rates.

Currently, about 60 percent of all Americans younger than age 65 living below the poverty level receive assistance through Medicaid. Because of the non-expansion states setting their own income eligibility standards, the percentages vary considerably from state to state and are as low as 17 percent of the FPL. Federal law established the eligibility threshold for pregnant women with children at a minimum of 133 percent of the poverty level for all states.

Since the early origins of federal involvement in medical care for the needy, spending per enrollee has varied considerably across regions (see Table 13.2). In fiscal year (FY) 2011, over 55 million were enrolled and spending was $427 billion, with almost half concentrated in the seven most populous states. Nationwide, the average spending per eligible person was $5,496, compared to $8,558 for the 10 states with the highest spending per eligible person and $3,962 for the 4 states with the lowest. Payment per eligible person in highest spending states is over two times that of the lowest spending states.

Congress originally established the Medicaid program to provide basic medical benefits, including hospital and physicians' services, for those who were receiving cash assistance through state welfare programs. Although medical payments for welfare recipients remain a key element of the program, nursing home care and home health care, primarily for the Medicare-eligible population, constitute approximately 20 percent of the total outlays. Table 13.3 summarizes program spending by eligibility category. Approximately 56 percent of the program spending in FY 2016 was for care to the elderly and disabled. Per capita spending for these two groups was over $19,000. Children received 27.4 percent of the total program outlays. Per capita payments were $3,471. The 15 million adults eligible under pre-ACA standards spent an average of $5,431. Newly eligible adults (due to the Medicaid expansion) numbered over 10 million and spent on average 10 percent more or $5,910.

Many of those who are eligible for Medicaid have a difficult time finding a physician who will treat them. The expansion of the eligible population resulting from the newly passed ACA exacerbated this problem. Even with the federal government picking up 100

TABLE 13.2 MEDICAID PAYMENTS BY STATE, 2011[1]

State	Total expenditures (in billions)	Number eligible (in millions)	Payment per eligible
Ten highest per capita			
Rhode Island	$ 2.13	0.23	$ 9,145
New York	52.74	5.82	9,062
Alaska	1.31	0.15	8,819
District of Columbia	2.10	0.24	8,780
Pennsylvania	20.49	2.23	8,096
North Dakota	0.73	0.09	8,019
Connecticut	6.00	0.79	7,641
New Hampshire	1.37	0.18	7,613
Minnesota	8.02	1.11	7,237
New Jersey	10.37	1.46	7,105
Ten lowest per capita			
Oklahoma	4.27	0.91	4,699
Florida	18.35	3.99	4,605
Louisiana	6.37	1.41	4,528
Utah	1.79	0.40	4,520
Alabama	4.70	1.06	4,424
Nevada	1.57	0.39	4,032
Georgia	8.44	2.15	3,921
Illinois	12.15	3.13	3,879
Idaho	1.67	0.46	3,640
California	42.64	11.83	3,606
Total U.S.	$ 397.33	72.06	$ 5,496

Source: Medicaid Statistical Supplement, *2013*, Table 13.3.

TABLE 13.3 MEDICAID SPENDING BY ELIGIBILITY CATEGORY, FY 2016[1]

Category	Payment per capita	Number eligible (millions)	Percent of total eligible population	Total spending (billions)	Percent of total spending
Aged	$ 16,299	5.7	8.1	$ 92.9	17.0
Disabled	20,633	10.4	14.8	214.6	39.3
Children	3,471	27.4	38.9	95.1	17.4
Adults	5,431	15.1	21.4	82.0	15.0
Expansion adults	5,910	10.5	14.9	62.1	11.3
Total	$ 7,903	69.1	100.0	$546.7	100.0

Source: *Medicare and Medicaid Research Review: 2013 Statistical Supplement*, Tables 13.5–13.11.
[1]Projections.

percent of the increase in spending over the first three years of the expansion, many states have shown an unwillingness to participate in the expansion due to added cost. For example, expansion in Texas was projected to add an additional $4 billion in state spending and $55 billion in federal spending over the first six years (United Health, 2010).

States have a limited range of responses to rising costs. Program cutbacks jeopardize federal funding, and tax increases jeopardize political careers. To date, only Oregon has moved to ration care by prioritizing services and restricting access to services that are not cost effective (see more about that later in, "Is Medicaid Worse than No Insurance at All?"). Most states are turning to managed care to reduce Medicaid spending. In fact, over 75 percent of the Medicaid population was enrolled in managed care plans in 2014, making the Centers for Medicare and Medicaid Services (CMS), the agency that administers Medicare and Medicaid, the nation's largest purchaser of managed care in the country.

Medicaid Expansion under the ACA

Medicaid expansion, a critical element of ACA, has increased the number of low-income Americans enrolled in the program by approximately 14 million as of 2016. That number is down significantly from earlier CBO estimates because of the June 2012 Supreme Court ruling that made the expansion optional for the states.

Proponents argue that in the long run state treasuries are only responsible for $1 of every $10 in new spending. Furthermore, providing coverage to low-income patients will eliminate the need for hospitals to shift costs from those who do not pay for their care to those with insurance. Moreover, the stimulus provided by the federal spending will increase economic activity in the state enough to increase state tax revenue by more than the state's required contribution for the expansion itself.

Proponents of the Medicaid expansion ignore at least two important considerations. The first is the formula for calculating the federal medical assistance percentage (FMAP) for a state. Under the current formula, the federal share of Medicaid spending ranges from 50 percent to 75 percent, with states picking up the remainder. The income threshold for eligibility is a state decision and varies from 17 percent to 275 percent of the FPL. The Medicaid expansion is designed to cover all families with incomes less than 138 percent of the FPL, and for the years 2014–2016, the federal government covered the total cost of the expansion. Beyond 2016, the federal share will settle at 90 percent of the expansion cost, with the state paying the other 10 percent. Non-expansion states were promised, if they do expand eligibility, three years of 100 percent federal coverage before the 10 percent state match goes into effect.

Will the federal money be available at this rate forever? The concern is whether the federal government will continue to spend money that it does not have. The time will come and is coming soon when Congress must address the problem of excess spending. With entitlements responsible for a large share of the deficit, reform of the FMAP formula cannot be ruled out. Maintaining programs will likely require the states to absorb a larger share of the financing.

The second consideration is the expansion's effect on the existing Medicaid program. The adult take-up rate in the current program is 65–70 percent, indicating that a large fraction of the eligible population does not participate at all. Policy makers expect that the take-up rate will rise to 85 percent with the expansion. In Texas, for example, only 800,000 of the 1.23 million adults eligible under the pre-expansion criterion are enrolled. If the state were to expand Medicaid eligibility, not only will an additional 1.5 million newly eligible individuals enroll, but an estimated 365,000 of those currently eligible will emerge out of the "woodwork" and enroll. The state will be responsible for 40 percent of the cost of their health care, effectively doubling the state's share of the overall expansion costs.

Taking a more practical approach to the argument, proponents claim that if the state refuses the federal funding to expand Medicaid then tax dollars will simply flow to some other state. That logic is flawed. The number of eligible enrollees in a state determines Medicaid spending. The only way that California (an expansion state) gets the Medicaid expansion money targeted for Texas (a non-expansion state) is for otherwise eligible residents in Texas to move to California to receive benefits. Research by Schwartz and Sommers (2014) suggests that interstate migration will not be a common way for individuals to qualify for Medicaid coverage.

How does expanding Medicaid further the efforts to reaching the goals established by the Triple Aim: access, value, and affordability? The focus of the ACA is universal coverage, but insurance coverage does not guarantee access to care. Medicaid payment rates are significantly below those paid by private insurers with predictable results. Access is reasonable in parts of the country but relatively poor overall. Merritt Hawkins (2014) surveyed physicians in 15 U.S. metropolitan areas and reported Medicaid acceptance rates for five specialties (cardiology, dermatology, obstetrics/gynecology, orthopedic surgery, and family practice).

Table 13.4 summarizes the results. Less than one-half of surveyed physicians accept new patients with Medicaid coverage. The rate varies from a high of 73 percent in Boston to a low 23 percent in Dallas/Fort Worth. Overall, the story is marginally better for family practice access with 52 percent accepting new Medicaid patients, varying from 86 percent in San Diego to 20 percent in Denver. Those cities with higher physician-to-population ratios tend to have higher acceptance rates (correlation coefficient of 0.56) but also significantly higher average wait times (correlation coefficient of 0.85).

TABLE 13.4 PHYSICIAN-TO-POPULATION RATIOS, MEDICAID ACCEPTANCE RATES, AND AVERAGE WAIT TIMES FOR 15 U.S. METROPOLITAN AREAS, 2013

Metropolitan area	Physicians per 100,000 population	Medicaid acceptance rate (%)	Average wait times (days)
Atlanta	212.5	37.0	14.0
Boston	450.1	73.0	45.4
Dallas/Fort Worth	197.2	23.0	10.2
Denver	271.9	34.4	23.6
Detroit	268.1	63.4	17.8
Houston	235.2	55.8	14.0
Los Angeles	253.9	36.4	12.2
Miami	253.7	53.8	13.6
Minneapolis	264.1	23.6	19.2
New York	344.6	39.8	16.8
Philadelphia	322.4	47.3	20.6
Portland	297.6	63.5	19.4
San Diego	270.2	39.4	16.2
Seattle	297.8	48.0	16.0
Washington, DC	320.1	43.1	17.8
United States	226.0	45.7	18.5

Source: Merritt Hawkins, Physician Appointment Wait Times and Medicaid and Medicare Acceptance Rates, 2014 Survey.

As far as value is concerned, new Medicaid spending provides relatively low value to recipients. In their welfare analysis of the Oregon Medicaid expansion, Finkelstein, Hendren, and Luttmer (2015) found that Medicaid's value to its recipients is less than the overall cost of the program. They estimate that the welfare benefit to its recipients is only 20–40 percent of Medicaid spending and that approximately 60 percent of the overall spending is merely a transfer from government to providers. These results are in sharp contrast to those of the CBO that values Medicaid benefits at total spending.

Finally, the expansion has proven costlier than the CBO originally projected. As stated earlier, per enrollee spending in 2015 was 49 percent higher than projected a year earlier. Enrollment in the expansion states is 50 percent higher than anticipated. Combining higher than expected enrollment with higher than expected per capita spending, overall spending was 62 percent higher in 2015 than expected.

Poor access, low value, and higher than expected costs add to the mounting evidence that those states that chose not to simply expand Medicaid eligibility may have made the correct decision. Adding the fact that Medicaid fails to produce physical health outcomes compared to no insurance at all, many states are exploring different alternatives for covering the low-income population.

APPLIED MICRO METHODS

IS MEDICAID WORSE THAN NO INSURANCE AT ALL?

Background

In 2008, Oregon initiated a limited expansion of Medicaid—from a waiting list of 90,000, about 30,000 names were drawn by lottery. The "Oregon Experiment" presented a unique opportunity to study the effects of Medicaid coverage on medical care use and outcomes. Random assignment was able to isolate the causal effects of program coverage without the confounding factors that might otherwise differ between the insured and the uninsured.

Data and Methods

The Oregon Health Plan (OHP) Standard is a Medicaid program for legal Oregon residents, uninsured for at least six months and ineligible for other public insurance, whose incomes are below the FPL. OHP Standard provides a comprehensive package of benefits with zero cost sharing at a low monthly premium. Closed to new enrollees in 2002, the OHP Standard was opened to new enrollees via a waiting list in 2008. The state conducted a series of lottery drawings from the waiting list. Individuals selected were able to apply for insurance for themselves and their family members, and satisfying the eligibility criteria enroll in the program.

The study collected data with in-person interviews on a wide variety of outcome measures from over 20,000 individuals (approximately 10,000 each from a treatment group of lottery winners and a control group of lottery losers). Approximately two years later a second interview took place to assess changes in medical care use and health outcomes.

Results

In the final sample, the characteristics of the two groups (age, race, and sex) were similar. Recorded outcomes measured in the study include blood pressure, cholesterol levels (LDL, HDL, and total), glycated hemoglobin levels, and depression. Medicaid coverage had no significant statistical effect on blood pressure, hypertension (either diagnosis or use of medication), cholesterol levels, or hemoglobin levels. There was a significant increase in the probability of receiving a diagnosis of diabetes and the use of diabetes medications. Medicaid coverage led to an increase in the diagnosis of depression, but there was no change in the use of medications for treatment.

Predicted 10-year risk of cardiovascular episodes was measured with the use of the Framingham risk score (measuring the risk among persons older than 30 years). After two years, there was no significant change in the 10-year predicted risk among those with Medicaid coverage.

Discussion and Conclusions

After two years, the Oregon Experiment confirms that Medicaid coverage resulted in higher prescription drug use, more preventive screening, better access to primary care, and higher health care spending. The study did not detect a significant improvement in the quality of life related to measured physical health (measured blood pressure, cholesterol levels, or glycated hemoglobin levels) or in self-reported levels of happiness. Medicaid enrollees reported improved financial security and the near elimination of catastrophic medical expenditures.

Source: Katherine Baicker et al., "The Oregon Experiment—Effects of Medicaid on Clinical Outcomes," *New England Journal of Medicine* 368(18), May 2, 2013, 1713–1722.

Medicaid's Impact on Enrollees

POLICY ISSUE

To what extent does better access to medical care improve health outcomes?

As with any other entitlement program, researchers are interested in its impact on the behavior and well-being of its participants. Research has examined the economic impact of the Medicaid program to determine its effect on health outcomes, enrollment in private insurance, labor supply, family structure, and savings.

Health Outcomes

One of the stated goals of the Medicaid program is to improve the health of the eligible population. Although policy makers cannot legislate better health, they can improve access to providers in hopes that better access will result in better health outcomes. Expansions in eligibility since the mid-1980s have focused primarily on enrolling pregnant women and children. A number of studies have examined the connection between Medicaid eligibility and health outcomes for these two groups. Currie and Gruber (1996a) found evidence that Medicaid eligibility expansions among pregnant women improved prenatal care utilization and resulted in a reduction in the proportion of low-birth-weight deliveries and an improvement in birth outcomes. They estimate that a 10 percent increase in Medicaid eligibility leads to a 2.8 percent decrease in infant mortality rates for the affected population. Currie and Gruber (1996b) also found that expansions in eligibility for children increased hospitalizations but reduced avoidable hospitalizations. An increase in eligibility of only 10 percent resulted in a 3.4 percent decrease in child mortality rates, due to better access to primary and preventive care.

POLICY ISSUE

Does Medicare pay high enough fees to attract a sufficient number of physicians who are willing to treat eligible participants?

Dubay and colleagues (2001) found that Medicaid expansions increased medical care utilization by pregnant women. However, their research showed no significant impact on the incidence of low birth weight. They concluded that their results were because expansions in the early 1990s included mainly pregnant women with higher family incomes. Better birth outcomes are normally associated with higher family incomes in the first place. The lesson may be that further expansions to women with higher incomes will have even smaller marginal effects on birth outcomes.

Many policy makers are convinced that the shortage of physicians willing to serve the Medicaid population is due to low reimbursement rates. Research has shown that higher fees increase physician participation in the program (Hadley, 1979; Mitchell, 1991; Sloan, Mitchell, and Cromwell, 1978), especially among physicians specializing in obstetrics and gynecology (Adams, 1994; Mitchell and Schurman, 1984). This research, however, does not make the connection between higher physician participation rates and better health outcomes.

Other research has shown that patients with Medicaid coverage have worse outcomes than virtually all other patients (those with private insurance, Medicare, and even the uninsured). For example, studies indicate that Medicaid enrollees had more complications and a lower chance of survival after colon cancer surgery (Kelz et al., 2004); were more likely to die in the hospital after surgery (LaPar et al., 2010); were more likely to suffer complications while in the hospital and spend more per hospital stay (LaPar et al., 2010); had worse outcomes after stroke (Shen and Washington, 2007); and received lower-quality treatment for asthma (Ortega et al., 2001).

A word of warning. While the preponderance of research questions the quality of care received by Medicaid patients, it is possible, even likely, that the research results may be biased. The reason is that observational studies seldom control every relevant variable that might be correlated with the specified health outcome. These uncontrolled factors will likely vary across groups and influence health outcomes in predictable ways (Kronick, 2009).

At minimum, the evidence seems to indicate that Medicaid coverage is associated with worse health outcomes when compared to individuals with other forms of insurance (and even no insurance at all). The differences are difficult to ignore.

Enrollment in Private Insurance

As the value of free, public insurance coverage increases, holders of costly, private insurance are likely to drop private coverage and enroll in Medicaid. Cutler and Gruber (1996) examine the economics of crowding out and conclude that hundreds of thousands of women have dropped private insurance as Medicaid expands eligibility. The decision to drop private insurance coverage is often encouraged by employers who decrease their own share of the private insurance premium, creating an incentive for employees to drop private coverage "voluntarily."

Labor Supply

For individuals on public welfare assistance, Medicaid eligibility is a valuable benefit. Many hesitate to accept jobs, fearing the loss of free, public health insurance. This so-called welfare lock has been documented by Yelowitz (1995) and Winkler (1991) and is especially profound in the case of women with small children. This literature is summarized by Gruber (2000a).

Family Structure

Another important aspect of Medicaid eligibility is its impact on family structure—the marriage decision and the decision to have children. Yelowitz (1998) showed that the Medicaid program as traditionally structured created a bias favoring single-parent families. Women with children remained single to qualify for the program, because potential marriage partners may not have been able to provide health insurance for the family. Between 1987 and 1992, the fraction of women of childbearing age eligible for Medicaid doubled, and the fraction of children eligible increased by 50 percent (Cutler and Gruber, 1996). Medicaid's pregnancy coverage lowers the cost of childbearing, and its generous child coverage lowers the discounted present value of raising a child. These two factors resulted in a significant increase in fertility among eligible women (Joyce, Kaestner, and Kwan, 1998). In fact, Medicaid expansions were estimated to be responsible for up to a 10 percent increase in the birth rate for this group (Bitler and Zavodny, 2000).

Savings

POLICY ISSUE

Easing Medicaid eligibility standards results in several important unintended consequences and their associated negative implications.

Finally, Gruber and Yelowitz (1999) discuss the channels whereby Medicaid expansions have an impact on individual savings decisions. By reducing the financial risk associated with an illness, the need for precautionary savings is diminished. Research by Kotlikoff (1988) provides the empirical evidence supporting this claim. Most public assistance programs include an asset test, whereby family wealth is a determining factor of eligibility. Hubbard, Skinner, and Zeldes (1995) show that the Medicaid asset test is empirically important. The wealth holdings of Medicaid families are 16.3 percent lower because of the asset test. Another potentially important concern for policy makers is the possibility that the elderly will transfer assets to their children to qualify for Medicaid financing for nursing home care. While the evidence is mixed, at least a portion of the elderly engages in this activity (Cutler and Sheiner, 1994; Norton, 2000).[3]

Critics of Medicaid contend that eligibility standards create incentives and disincentives that lead to serious socioeconomic disruptions. Basing eligibility standards on marital status promotes family breakups. Eligibility standards based on income provides a disincentive for work. Using disability for categorical eligibility encourages dependence. Illegitimate births are encouraged by tying eligibility to pregnancy and the presence of children in single-parent families. Possibly the single greatest disruption is the minimum asset requirement for eligibility. This forces many elderly females into poverty in order to qualify for long-term care.

KEY CONCEPT 4

Self-Interest

Those who defend the system contend that Medicaid provides coverage for millions of Americans who would otherwise have no health insurance. Those who are eligible for Medicaid are among the most vulnerable population subgroups in the country.

APPLIED MICRO METHODS

DID MEDICAID EXPANSION LEAD TO INCREASED EMERGENCY DEPARTMENT USE?

Background

Less than one year after the publication of their paper on the Oregon Experiment in the *New England Journal of Medicine*, many of the same authors published the results of a related study on the effects of Medicaid coverage on emergency department (ED) use. The results of their original study that showed Medicaid coverage led to improved outcomes (improved general health, reduced depression, and reduced ED use) were based on self-reported measures. The current study, based on administrative data from all 12 Portland-area hospitals, examines disparities in self-reported ED use and actual ED use.

---

[3]In Germany, the incomes of the children of elderly parents are counted when calculating the resource base for government-provided nursing home care.

Data and Methods

The current study matched actual ED data with the Oregon Health Insurance Study data, counting actual ED visits and characterizing the nature of each visit. The results compared the outcomes between the treatment and control groups. The causal effect of Medicaid coverage was estimated using a standard instrumental variables (IV) approach. Lottery selection was used as an instrument for Medicaid coverage (not everyone selected by the lottery enrolled in Medicaid), removing the possible selection bias resulting from individuals choosing not to enroll due to confounding factors.

Results

Medicaid coverage increased ED use. Approximately 35 percent of the control group (those with no insurance) visited the ED during the study period at least one time. Whereas those with Medicaid coverage were more likely to visit the ED with a 7 percentage point increase. Medicaid coverage also increased the number of ED visits by 0.41 visits per patient (1.02 versus 1.63), about a 40 percent increase. Both results were statistically significant

Medicaid coverage increased visits of all types. Visits were characterized into four groups: non-preventable emergent, preventable emergent, primary care treatable, and non-emergent. There was no significant change in the number of non-preventable emergent visits. However, visits in the other three categories were higher among Medicaid enrollees whose ED use was 50 percent higher in all cases. The calculations were replicated with self-reported data and results did not produce statistically significant changes in ED use with Medicaid coverage.

Discussion and Conclusions

Whether Medicaid coverage should increase or decrease ED use is open to discussion. By reducing out-of-pocket spending, Medicaid coverage should increase use of all types of medical care, including the ED. Improvements in access (real or perceived) should also increase ED use. However, improvements in primary care access and preventive care should lead to improvements in health and decreases in ED use.

Results of this study indicate that Medicaid coverage increased ED use among low-income, uninsured adults. Using $435 as the average cost of an ED visit (based on 2002–2007 Medical Expenditure Panel Survey data), Medicaid increased annual spending in the ED by approximately $120 per covered individual. Based on the findings of the prior research, one possible interpretation of the results of this study is that Medicaid coverage did not improve the actual physical health of the covered population or improve their access to primary and preventive care.

The same authors (Finkelstein et al., 2016) extended the study by a year and determined that the increased ED use persists over time. In fact, Medicaid coverage increased the joint probability of having both an ED visit and a regular office visit to a physician by 13.2 percentage points. In other words, newly covered individuals will increase the use of medical care in all settings.

Sources: Sarah L. Taubman et al., "Medicaid Increases Emergency-Department Use: Evidence from Oregon's Health Insurance Experiment," *Science* 343, January 2, 2014, 263–268; and Amy N. Finkelstein et al., "Effect of Medicaid Coverage on ED Use—Further Evidence from Oregon's Experiment," *New England Journal of Medicine* 375(16), October 20, 2016, 1505–1507.

The Future of Medicaid

The biggest design flaw in Medicaid is that it is set up to provide open-ended federal reimbursement for state spending with no limits placed on that spending. On average states receive a 61 percent subsidy from the federal government on the total amount spent on care for participants. In 2010, the ACA expanded Medicaid eligibility to everyone with a family income less than 138 percent of the FPL. Two years later the Supreme Court reinterpreted the statute and made participation optional for the states. A total of 30 states plus the District of Columbia have chosen to adopt the federal standard and expand eligibility, adding to the unsustainable spending trajectory already in place.

Expansion of eligibility is not reform, and Medicaid needs to be reformed. The free market prerequisite to reform is the assumption that the individual state, free from unnecessary federal regulations, is better able to design, manage, and deliver medical benefits to its residents. Changes aimed at improving the administrative efficiency of Medicaid include dispensing federal support in the form of block grants to the states in the form of either lump sum or per-capita grants. An alternative would be to base the grant on the number of state residents under the FPL. This along with waivers allowing the states to experiment with design options would provide incentives to improve administrative efficiency. Overall spending would be controlled by establishing caps in the growth in funding to limit taxpayer liability (similar to what the ACA did with Medicare spending).

The Medicaid-eligible population can be divided into four categories: 1) the Medicare-eligible elderly (many receiving long-term care benefits), 2) the disabled, 3) children, and 4) adults. In the non-expansion states, adults without dependent children find it difficult to qualify. Income thresholds are as low as 17 percent of the FPL. But even in these states single mothers with dependent children (or pregnant women without dependents) qualify for enrollment if their incomes are below 100–180 percent of the FPL. The ineligible population is comprised mostly of able-bodied, working-age, childless adults (primarily men), leading many to suggest a work requirement for this group.

It seems logical that this latter group would benefit from some degree of privatization by opening up the exchanges to their participation. By adding a cost-sharing requirement based on income and ability to pay, states could contribute to health savings accounts for participants (without it being treated as a direct cash grant). Such change would go a long way to solve the eligibility problem as individuals' incomes rise and fall around the income threshold. Program eligibility could be permanent or transitory depending on income.

Simple program expansion made possible by the passage of the ACA has not solved the long-term problems of Medicaid. It will take some creative thinking and bold leadership by policy makers to place the program on a trajectory to become the broad safety net coverage that Congress originally intended.

KEY CONCEPT 6
Efficiency

Summary and Conclusions

Entitlement reform presents overwhelming political challenges, as President Bill Clinton discovered in 1996. The reform challenge we face with Medicaid begins with agreeing upon a clear understanding of the program's primary mission. Is Medicaid a medical program designed to provide good health care to the poor, or is it a social program designed to eliminate the financial risk associated with the provision of health care services? Do we measure the success of the program by the relative improvement in the health of its participants or by the redistributive impact the program has on some measure of income?

How much money we spend should not be the measure of our compassion. Using resources inefficiently is not only wasteful but focuses on supporting health care interests and not individuals. Within the next decade, the United States will be spending over one trillion dollars on Medicaid annually. We must not find ourselves chasing social goals while delivering mediocre health care to the poor.

PROFILE   Mark B. McClellan

It took Republican President George W. Bush almost two years to find a commissioner for the Food and Drug Administration (FDA) that the Democrats in Congress would accept. The long wait ended in November 2002, when the U.S. Senate confirmed Mark B. McClellan unanimously. After a brief stint as FDA Commissioner, McClellan is now Senior Fellow and Director of the Engelberg Center for Health Care Reform and holds the Leonard D. Schaeffer Chair in Health Policy Studies at the Brookings Institution.

McClellan has a unique pedigree, Ph.D. economist and board-certified physician. He received his undergraduate education at the University of Texas at Austin and graduate degrees in public administration, medicine, and economics at Harvard and the Massachusetts Institute of Technology. Board certified in internal medicine, he received his clinical training at Brigham and Women's Hospital in Boston.

Upon finishing his residency, McClellan took a position as attending physician with Stanford Health Services and soon became the director of the Program on Health Outcomes Research at the Stanford Center for Health Policy. After a brief stint as Deputy Assistant Secretary for Economic Policy with the U.S. Department of Treasury, he was promoted to associate professor in the departments of economics and medicine at Stanford. He is associate editor of the *Journal of Health Economics* and visiting scholar with the American Enterprise Institute.

His publications include articles, books, and book chapters in some of the most prestigious journals in economics and health policy, including *American Economic Review*, *Journal of Health Economics*, *Health Affairs*, *RAND Journal of Economics*, and *Journal of Economic Perspectives*. In 1995, he received the Review of Economic Studies Award for his outstanding dissertation in economics, and in 1997, the International Health Economics Association awarded him with the Kenneth Arrow Award for Best Paper in health economics. He also received Griliches Award for Best Empirical Paper in both the *Quarterly Journal of Economics* and *Journal of Political Economy* in 1999. His current research includes working papers on quality of care, health outcomes, medical productivity, managed care report cards, and end-of-life care.

Before his appointment as FDA chief, he served on the President's Council of Economic Advisors, and at the same time was senior policy director for health care and related economic issues for the White House. McClellan is no stranger to politics. His mother, Carole Keeton Strayhorn, was the Comptroller of Public Accounts for the state of Texas. McClellan's brother, Scott, is the former White House press secretary for President George W. Bush.

McClellan's grandfather, former dean of the University of Texas Law School, once told him: "If you haven't made anybody mad, you haven't done anything." If his grandfather's words ring true, there must be some pretty mad folks around the country right now.

Sources: Personal vitae and Department of Health and Human Services biography, available at https://www.fda.gov/AboutFDA/WhatWeDo/History/Leaders/Commissioners/ucm093717.htm.

Questions and Problems

1. Compared to fee-for-service payment, what are the advantages and disadvantages of payment based on diagnosis-related groups?

2. What was the motivation for changing the way the Medicare system compensates physicians? What are the implications for physicians' behavior as the resource-based relative value scale is fully implemented?

3. In his testimony before the House Ways and Means health subcommittee, Robert Reischauer stated that CBO research concluded that price controls could severely limit the quality and quantity of medical care in the United States. He also argued that the only way to control medical care spending is by imposing global health care budgets at the national level. Explain how price controls can be bad and global budgets good.

4. Advocates of a market orientation argue that exclusive reliance on the visible hand of government will never bring spending under control. The missing component has been the invisible hand of the market-pricing mechanism. Patients spending their own money have an incentive to control spending. Comment.

5. In 1994, 565 economists sent President Bill Clinton a letter warning against the economic consequences of price controls that played such a prominent role in his health care reform plan. The price controls included mandated fee schedules for fee-for-service medical plans, prospective budgets for regional health alliances, increases in health insurance premiums tied to the cost of living, and price ceilings on prescription drugs. Discuss the economics of price controls. Under what circumstances do they accomplish their intended purpose? When do they fail?

References

Adams, E. Kathleen, "The Effect of Increased Medicaid Fees on Physician Participation and Enrollee Service Utilization in Tennessee," *Inquiry* 31(2), Summer 1994, 173–189.

Bitler, Marianne and Madeline Zavodny, "The Effect of Medicaid Eligibility Expansions on Births," Federal Reserve Bank of Atlanta Working Paper 2000-4, Atlanta, GA, March 2000.

Currie, Janet and Jonathan Gruber, "Saving Babies: The Efficacy and Cost of Recent Changes in the Medicaid Eligibility of Pregnant Women," *Journal of Political Economy* 104(6), December 1996a, 1263–1296.

___, "Health Insurance Eligibility, Utilization of Medical Care, and Child Health," *Quarterly Journal of Economics* 111(2), May 1996b, 431–466.

Cutler, David M. and Jonathan Gruber, "Does Public Insurance Crowd Out Private Insurance?" *Quarterly Journal of Economics* 111(2), May 1996, 391–430.

Cutler, David M. and Louise Sheiner, "Policy Options for Long Term Care," in David Wise, ed., *Studies in the Economics of Aging*, Chicago, IL: University of Chicago Press, 1994, 395–434.

Dubay, Lisa, Theodore Joyce, Robert Kaestner, and Genevieve Kenney, "Changes in Prenatal Care Timing and Low Birth Weight by Race and Socioeconomic Status: Implications for the Medicaid Expansions for Pregnant Women," *Health Services Research* 36(2), 2001, 373–398.

Finkelstein, Amy, Nathaniel Hendren, and Erzo F. P. Luttmer, "The Value of Medicaid: Interpreting Results from the Oregon Health Insurance Experiment," NBER Working Paper No. 21308, Cambridge, MA: National Bureau of Economic Research, June 2015.

Gruber, Jonathan, "Health Insurance and the Labor Market," in Joseph P. Newhouse and Anthony J. Culyer, eds., *Handbook of Health Economics*, Amsterdam: North Holland, 2000a.

___, "Medicaid," National Bureau of Economic Research Working Paper 7829, Cambridge, MA: National Bureau of Economic Research, August 2000b.

Gruber, Jonathan and Aaron Yelowitz, "Public Health Insurance and Private Savings," *Journal of Political Economy* 107(6 Part 1), December 1999, 1249–1274.

Hadley, Jack, "Physician Participation in Medicaid: Evidence from California," *Health Services Research* 14, 1979, 266–280.

Hubbard, R. Glenn, Jonathan Skinner, and Stephen P. Zeldes, "Precautionary Saving and Social Insurance," *Journal of Political Economy* 103(2), April 1995, 360–399.

Joyce, Theodore, Robert Kaestner, and Florence Kwan, "Is Medicaid Pronatalist: The Effect of Eligibility Expansion on Abortions and Births," *Family Planning Perspectives* 30(3), 1998, 108–113.

Kaiser Commission on the Future of Medicaid, "Medicaid and Federal, State, and Local Budgets," Washington, DC: Kaiser Commission on the Future of Medicaid, May 1995.

Kelz, Rachel Rapaport, et al., "Morbidity and Mortality of Colorectal Carcinoma Surgery Differs by Insurance Status," *Cancer* 101(10), November 2004, 2187–2194.

Kotlikoff, Laurence J., "Health Expenditures and Precautionary Saving," in Laurence J. Kotlikoff, ed., *What Determines Saving?* Cambridge, MA: MIT Press, 1988, 141–162.

Kronick, Richard, "Health Insurance Coverage and Mortality Revisited," *Health Services Research* 44(4), 2009, 1211–1231.

LaPar, Damien J., et al., "Primary Payer Status Affects Mortality for Major Surgical Operations," *Annals of Surgery* 252(3), September 2010, 544–551.

Mitchell, Janet B., "Physician Participation in Medicaid Revisited," *Medical Care* 29, 1991, 645–653.

Mitchell, Janet B. and Rachel Schurman, "Access to Private Obstetrics/Gynecological Services under Medicaid," *Medical Care* 22, 1984, 1026–1037.

Norton, Edward C., "Long Term Care," in Anthony Culyer and Joseph Newhouse, eds., *Handbook of Health Economics*, Amsterdam: North Holland, 2000.

Ortega, Alexander N., et al., "Use of Health Services by Insurance Status among Children with Asthma," *Medical Care* 39(10), 2001, 1065–1074.

Schwartz, Aaron L. and Benjamin D. Sommers, "Moving for Medicaid? Recent Eligibility Expansions Did Not Induce Migration from Other States," *Health Affairs* 33(1), January 2014, 88–94.

Shen, Jay J. and Elmer L. Washington, "Disparities in Outcomes among Patients with Stroke Associated with Insurance Status," *Stroke* 38(3), March 2007, 1010–1016.

Sloan, Frank, Janet Mitchell, and Jerry Cromwell, "Physician Participation in State Medicaid Programs," *Journal of Human Resources* 13(Supplement), 1978, 211–245.

United Health, "Coverage for Consumers, Savings for States: Options for Modernizing Medicaid," Center for Health Reform & Modernization Working Paper 3, April 2010.

Winkler, Anne E., "The Incentive Effects of Medicaid on Women's Labor Supply," *Journal of Human Resources* 26(2), Spring 1991, 308–337.

Yelowitz, Aaron, "The Medicaid Notch, Labor Supply, and Welfare Participation: Evidence from Eligibility Expansions," *Quarterly Journal of Economics* 110(4), November 1995, 909–939.

Yelowitz, Aaron, "Will Extending Medicaid to Two-Parent Families Encourage Marriage?" *Journal of Human Resources* 33(4), Fall 1998, 833–865.

A Note on "Projections"

One of the intriguing questions that puzzle those with inquiring minds is, "Just where do they come up with these numbers anyway?" Anyone who forecasts for a living knows that change is the order of the day. Seldom do things stay the same. Underlying economic conditions change, and institutional characteristics change. About the only thing that stays the same is human nature, and that is sometimes the most unpredictable piece in the entire puzzle.

Forecasting, by its very nature, has an element of extrapolation associated with it. Examining trends and extending those trends into the future is a common technique used to project all sorts of economic variables. Currently, an estimated 4 million Americans are afflicted with Alzheimer's disease. With 1 percent of all 65-year-olds and 25 percent of all 85-year-olds diagnosed with the disease, as the number of elderly increase—especially those who reach their 85th birthday—the number of people with Alzheimer's disease will skyrocket. Over 15 million people are expected to have the disorder by 2050 if an effective form of prevention and treatment is not found. Extrapolation plays a key role in this kind of prediction. There is nothing inherently wrong with making these predictions as long as we understand the qualifying statement: "if an effective form of prevention and treatment is not found."

Predictions of health care spending absorbing 25–40 percent of GDP by the year 2030 are political fodder in policy making circles (Waldo et al., 1991). The spending scenarios necessary to bring about these results make little intuitive sense when examined closely. CMS projections shown in Table 13A.1 are based on actuarial models using trend analysis. According to CMS projections, personal health care spending will increase to over $5 trillion by 2022, representing 19.9 percent of GDP and $14,664 per capita. Actuarial projections assume a continuation of current laws, policies, and trends. In other words, current programs, regulations, and practices remain unchanged. In addition, economy-wide shocks, all technological innovation, and any reform of health care delivery and finance are ruled out.

In 1992, the CBO, known for its "fair" numbers, projected medical care spending at 18 percent of GDP by the year 2000 (Lemieux and Williams, 1992) when it actually reached 13.2 percent of GDP. Policy based on these projections would call for immediate action, but for medical care spending to reach, say, 25 percent of GDP, substantially more than 25 percent of the annual changes in GDP must be spent in the health care sector. Except for recessionary periods, the change in health care spending relative to the change in GDP rarely

TABLE 13A.1 NATIONAL HEALTH CARE EXPENDITURES 2010, WITH PROJECTIONS TO 2022

Category	2010	2012	2013	2014	2015	2022
National Health Expenditures (NHE)	$2,600.0	$2,806.6	$2,914.7	$3,093.2	$3,273.4	$5,008.8
NHE per capita	$8,417	$8,948	$9,216	$9,397	$10,172	$14,664
NHE as percent of GDP	17.9	17.9	18.0	18.3	18.4	19.9

Source: Gigi A. Cuckler et al., "National Health Expenditure Projections, 2012–22: Slow Growth until Coverage Expands and Economy Improves," *Health Affairs* 32(10), October 2013, 1820–1831.

reaches 0.15, placing an upper bound on the ratio of health care spending to GDP at 15 percent. In fact, from 1984 to 1990, the change in health care spending represented 15.5 percent of the total change in GDP and was never greater than 17 percent.

The key phrase in the above scenario is "except for recessionary periods." Over the past 35 years, only twice has the change in medical care spending exceeded 17 percent of the GDP change. The recessions of 1981–1982 and 1990–1991 saw this figure rise to over 30 percent.

It is easy to criticize those who make predictions for a living. Meteorologists have difficulty forecasting what the weather will be like tomorrow morning. The economist always seems to have an explanation for why those interest rate predictions were incorrect. Moreover, when is the last time Jean Dixon or even the Amazing Kreskin got it just right? Most projections are based on some variant of extrapolation, analyzing trends based on certain assumptions about the state of the world at some future date. The further that date is into the future, the more careful we need to be about relying too heavily on those predictions. Remember what they say: "The only two things certain in this world are death and taxes."

References

Lemieux, Jeffrey A. and Christopher Williams, *Projections of National Health Expenditures*, Congress of the United States, Congressional Budget Office, October 1992.

Waldo, Daniel R., Sally T. Sonnefeld, Jeffrey A. Lemieux, and David R. McKusick, "Health Spending Through 2000: Three Scenarios," *Health Affairs* 10(4), Winter 1991, 231–242.

CHAPTER 14

Medical Care Systems Worldwide

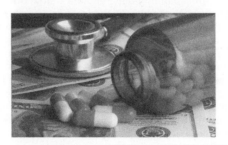

ISSUES IN MEDICAL CARE DELIVERY

WHO HAS THE BEST HEALTH CARE SYSTEM?

In 2000 the World Health Organization (WHO) released a report (based on a 1997 survey) ranking the health care systems of the world's 191 countries. The first attempt of its kind, the report attracted a great deal of media attention and surprised many health experts in its findings and is still widely quoted today. The WHO based its rankings on four composite indicators each weighted equally: 1) level of health, 2) health inequality, 3) health system responsiveness and its distribution across groups, and 4) financial fairness. This composite index was compiled from surveys administered to 1,791 public health experts in 35 selected countries.

The health of the population was measured in terms of disability-adjusted life expectancy (DALE) and disparities in DALEs across groups. Health system responsiveness measured how well patients are served and the degree of service disparity across different groups. Financial fairness measured the percentage of household income beyond subsistence spent on health care. Countries with highly progressive tax systems that finance health care via taxation rated high on fairness. Reliance on private insurance lowered the rankings of high-income countries.

WORLD HEALTH ORGANIZATION HEALTH CARE SYSTEM RANKINGS

	Overall performance	Overall attainment	Responsiveness
Canada	30	7	7
France	1	6	16
Germany	25	14	5
Japan	10	1	6
Switzerland	20	2	2
United Kingdom	18	9	26
United States	37	15	1

Source: WHO (World Health Organization), "Health Systems: Improving Performance," The World Health Report 2000, Geneva: WHO, 2000.

The ranking based on the overall performance is the most frequently reported index. Using this measure, the French health care system was rated number one. The only other country examined in this chapter that made the top 10 was Japan, finishing at number 10. The next large, developed country on the list was the United Kingdom at number 18; Germany finished 25th, Canada 30th, and the United States 37th.

Because of the subjective nature of the performance indicators, rankings vary by the indicator used. Using overall achievement instead of overall performance changes the rankings considerably with Japan number 1 and the United States number 15.[†] Basing the rankings on responsiveness to patient needs and desires also changes the outcome considerably. Responsiveness is another way of saying whether the system is patient centered. The defining criteria were choice of provider, timeliness of care, patient autonomy, quality of care, and confidentiality of patient information. Using this index, the United States ranked first and France was 16.

Additionally, WHO reports 80 percent confidence intervals and finds that the rankings are highly sensitive to measurement error. For example, there is no statistically significant difference in the overall attainment index for countries ranked 2 through 21. This indicates that Japan was number one in overall attainment and the other six tied for second place. For obvious reasons statistical clarity and objectivity were not constraining features of the WHO rankings.

Sources: Glen Whitman, "WHO's Fooling Who? The World Health Organization's Problematic Ranking of Health Care Systems," Briefing Paper No. 101, Washington, DC: CATO Institute, February 28, 2008 and WHO (World Health Organization), "Health Systems: Improving Performance," The World Health Report 2000, Geneva: WHO, 2000.

[†]The primary difference between the two indices is an emphasis on financial fairness in the overall performance index (defined as the percentage of health care spending through government sources). The overall attainment index is a more objective measure looking at how well a system is achieving its goals; the overall performance index is a subjective measure examining how well it is doing relative to available resources. This difference injects a strong ideological component into the ranking.

Anyone involved in the debate on health care reform in the United States will eventually get around to comparing the U.S. private insurance model to the social insurance model used in most of the developed world. Care must be taken when making comparisons across systems. As we learned in Chapter 6, differences in socioeconomics, population demographics, and individual behavioral and physiological risk factors often make direct comparisons difficult to interpret.

In the following sections, we will discuss the health care delivery systems of seven major developed countries across the globe. Each of these countries, no matter how its medical care delivery is organized and financed, struggles with a common problem—controlling the growth in medical care spending. These problems will be carefully documented, not for rating the delivery mechanisms of those countries, but to show that health care delivery takes on a structure that uniquely fits the culture of each individual country. What are the insights that we can gain for our own reform alternatives?

POLICY ISSUE

What lessons can we learn from studying health care delivery in other countries?

International Comparisons

Table 14.1 provides a listing of several key statistics on population demographics, health spending, and the use of medical resources for the United States and the six countries discussed in this chapter: Canada, France, Germany, Japan, Switzerland, and the United Kingdom. In 2013, national populations ranged from 8.1 million in Switzerland to 316.1 million in the United States. The U.S. population is approximately 40 times the population

TABLE 14.1 KEY STATISTICS

2013	Canada	France	Germany	Japan	Switzerland	United Kingdom	United States
Demographics							
Population (millions)	35.3	65.7	80.6	127.3	8.1	64.1	316.1
GDP per capita[1]	42,839	37,670	43,887	36,235	56,940	38,255	53,042
Health Expenditures							
Health care spending per capita[1]	4,351	4,124	4,819	3,713	6,325	3,235	8,713
Health care spending (percent of GDP)	10.2	10.9	11.0	10.2	11.1	8.5	16.4
Medical Resources							
Number of physicians (per 1,000)	2.5[2]	3.1	4.1	2.3[2]	4.0	2.8	2.6
GPs (per 1,000)	1.2	1.6	1.7	—[3]	1.1	0.8	0.3
Acute care beds (per 1,000)	1.7[2]	3.4	5.3	7.9	2.9	2.3	2.5[2]
Acute care average length of stay (days)	7.6[2]	5.7[2]	7.7	17.2	5.9	5.9	5.4[4]
Occupancy rate (%)	89.0[2]	75.0[2]	79.3	75.9[2]	83.6	84.3[5]	64.4[4]
Excess beds (per 1,000)[6]	0.2[2]	0.9	1.1	1.9	0.5[3]	0.4[5]	0.9
CT scanners (per million)	14.7	14.5	18.7	101.3[4]	36.6	7.9	43.5
MRI (per million)	8.8	9.4	11.6	46.9[4]	19.9	6.1	35.5

Source: *OECD Health Data*, OECD, Paris, 2016.

[1] In U.S. purchasing power parity dollars—the exchange rate at which different currencies purchase the same bundle of goods.

[2] 2012

[3] Virtually all physicians in Japan, regardless of specialty, practice as GPs.

[4] 2011

[5] 2010

[6] Equal to [1 − (inpatient utilization rate)] × [number of acute care beds per 1,000 population].

of Switzerland, 5 times that of both France and the United Kingdom, 4 times that of Germany, and 2.5 times that of Japan. The United States has the largest economy as measured by gross domestic product (GDP), more than twice the size of the second largest, Japan. The widely used measure for relative standards of living, per capita GDP adjusted for purchasing power parity, is 7.3 percent higher in Switzerland than in the United States and 20–45 percent higher in the United States than the other five countries.

Health care spending, whether measured in U.S. per capita dollars or as a percentage of GDP, is significantly higher in the United States than in any other country. Switzerland, Germany, and Canada are ranked second, third, and fourth according to the two measures. Per capita spending in the United Kingdom is barely 37 percent that of the United States. Physicians per 1,000 population range from a low in Japan of 2.3 to a high in Germany of 4.1. The United States is slightly below the median in terms of acute care hospital beds per 1,000, at 2.5 beds. In terms of average length of hospital stay, no country has fewer than the 5.4 days in the United States. Japan tops the list in both of these categories, with 7.9 beds per 1,000 and an average hospital stay of 17.2 days.[1]

Consensus research concludes that medical technology is responsible for much of the increase in medical care spending over the past several decades (Baker et al., 2003; Fuchs, 1996; Newhouse, 1992; Weisbrod, 1991). If medical spending is indeed determined to a great extent by the availability and use of medical technology, then differences in its availability and use may signal quality differences as well as spending differences across countries. Limiting access to expensive technology and procedures may be one strategy to control medical care spending.

The United States ranks at or near the top in access to medical technology in terms of computed tomography (CT) scanners and magnetic resonance imagings (MRIs) per million population. The United States has more CT scanners than any country except Japan, almost 3 times the number found in Canada and France and 5.5 times the number in the United Kingdom. Analyzing the availability of MRI equipment tells a similar story.

Expenditures across OECD Countries

As we have already seen, medical care spending in the United States is the highest in the world, both in per capita terms and as a percentage of GDP. Although health care spending as a percentage of GDP—the spending-to-GDP ratio—is the most widely used performance measure for the health care sector, it is important to remember that there are actually two components to this ratio. Comparisons at a given point in time tend to focus on the ratio alone. When comparing countries over time, however, it is important to examine both the change in health spending and the change in GDP. In other words, changes in both the numerator and the denominator of the ratio are important.

Table 14.2 presents a comparison of the growth rates for health care sector components for the past 35 years, 1980 through 2015. Annual growth rates in health care spending were considerably higher in the 1980s than in the 1990s in all countries. The average growth rate in nominal health care spending was 7.73 percent in the 1980s, ranging from 4.19 percent in Germany to 9.78 percent in the United States. Nominal spending growth slowed to an average of 5.16 percent in the 1990s, ranging from 3.82 percent in France to 6.80 percent

KEY CONCEPT 2
Opportunity Cost

HTTP://
OECD provides information on economic issues, activities, and events for all member countries. http://www.oecd.org.

HTTP://
The World Bank reports regularly on health and health care issues worldwide. Their publications, including an annual world development report, provide data on economic, demographics, and infrastructure. The data are particularly useful in studying less-developed countries. http://worldbank.org.

---

[1]Several cultural reasons explain why the Japanese average length of stay is so long—the sick are more pampered, more conditions are considered illnesses, and the Japanese place an emphasis on bed rest as a cure for most illnesses. For example, in contrast to the situation in the United States, where Congress must legislate a mandatory two-day hospital stay after childbirth, the length of stay following childbirth in Japan approaches two weeks. In addition, rehabilitation services after an inpatient hospital stay is provided primarily in the hospital setting, substantially increasing length-of-stay calculations.

TABLE 14.2 ANNUAL COMPOUND GROWTH IN HEALTH SECTOR COMPONENTS, 1980 THROUGH 2015, PERCENTAGES

	Canada	France	Germany	Japan	Switzerland	United Kingdom	United States
1980–1989							
Nominal health care spending	9.64	9.64	4.19	4.73	7.17	8.91	9.78
Nominal per capita health care spending	8.47	9.06	4.11	4.19	6.59	8.78	8.90
Real health care spending[1]	4.68	3.59	1.63	2.94	2.99	3.13	5.69
Real per capita health care spending[1]	3.57	2.72	1.54	2.42	2.47	2.97	4.84
1990–1999							
Nominal health care spending	3.89	3.82	6.87	3.83	5.13	6.80	5.76
Nominal per capita health care spending	2.89	3.48	4.12	3.57	4.38	6.58	4.59
Real health care spending[1]	2.55	2.31	4.95	3.52	3.07	3.82	3.76
Real per capita health care spending[1]	1.57	1.97	2.24	3.26	2.43	3.61	2.61
2000–2009							
Nominal health care spending	7.03	4.64	3.06	2.12	4.02	8.08	6.97
Nominal per capita health care spending	5.92	3.95	3.08	2.05	3.19	7.67	5.96
Real health care spending[1]	4.52	2.66	2.19	3.38	2.76	5.81	4.51
Real per capita health care spending[1]	3.43	1.97	2.21	3.31	1.94	5.41	3.52
2010–2015							
Nominal health care spending	3.26	2.27	3.44	3.95	3.23	5.92	4.30
Nominal per capita health care spending	2.17	1.78	3.59	4.07	2.17	5.21	3.51
Real health care spending[1]	1.56	1.31	1.87	4.28	3.53	4.04	2.70
Real per capita health care spending[1]	0.48	2.82	2.02	4.40	2.47	3.33	1.91

Source: OECD Health Data 2013, Paris: OECD.
[1]Spending adjusted by the GDP price deflator.
Note: Measurements based on changes denominated in national currencies.

POLICY ISSUE
Of all the major developed countries in the world, which one does the best job in controlling health care spending?

KEY CONCEPT 2
Opportunity Cost

POLICY ISSUE
How can a health care system that relies on third-party insurance control spending?

global budget A limit on the amount of money available to a health care system during a specified time. All medically necessary care must be provided to all eligible patients within the limits of a fixed budget.

POLICY ISSUE
Are price ceilings and spending caps the best way to control the problem of rising health care spending? What are the unintended consequences?

in the United Kingdom. Growth rates in the decade beginning in 2000 turned upwards in four of the seven countries—Canada, France, the United Kingdom, and the United States— averaging 6.68 percent. A portion of the increased spending is due to increased population, as evidenced by slightly lower per capita growth rates over the entire 35-year period. Regardless of measure, spending continued to slow in four of the seven countries in the latest five-year period.

Deflating health care expenditures by the GDP deflator adjusts nominal spending into real terms, providing a measure of the opportunity cost of resources absorbed by the health care sector. Canada and the United States have experienced the most substantial slowdown in real growth over the entire period, implying that Canadians and Americans have experienced the largest reduction in opportunity cost to accommodate spending in their health sectors.[2]

Cost Containment Strategies

Systems that guarantee free access to medical care must eventually confront the issue of increasing costs and growing expenditures. The way most health care delivery systems are organized, relying on the third-party payment system, no natural mechanisms to control cost and spending exist. Policy makers usually rely on one of two basic strategies: either provide incentives for people to use less medical care, usually through cost sharing, or increase regulation to control access and spending. Most governments have chosen the regulatory option, relying on a combination of approaches to rein in spending growth, including mandatory fee schedules, **global budgets**, and resource rationing. All three classified under the general heading of price controls share a common element—they interfere with the normal workings of the market.

With only limited success of these supply-side measures, policy makers around the world are beginning to consider the role of the consumer in holding down the growth in spending. The two independent variables in the spending identity are price and quantity.[3] To control spending, you must control both. Direct limits on the quantity of services available are too easily identified as *rationing*. Thus, the three cost-control measures go hand in hand. Once fee schedules are mandated (set P), global budgeting soon follows (restrict TE). Inevitably, the unintended consequence of fee schedules and global budgeting is resource-rationing (limit Q).

Many countries, including Switzerland and the United States, are trying a more consumer-directed approach. As consumers take more responsibility for their own care, the challenge becomes how to maintain access when financial considerations enter the decision. Early evidence seems to indicate a slowdown in spending, at least in the United States, but it is still too early to assess whether the expansion of the integrated delivery approach in the form of the accountable care organization, encouraged by certain provisions of the Accountable Care Act, has played a significant role. While promising in theory, it remains to be proven if the successes of Mayo Clinic, the Geisinger Clinic, and Kaiser-Permanente can be replicated on a larger scale. There is yet no single solution to the cost-control challenge.

Mandated Fee Schedules

Almost every government-run system has resorted to some form of price setting in an attempt to control spending. Whether referred to as a *price freeze* or a *price ceiling*, the

---

[2]Note that during the 2000 through 2015 period, Japan's real spending was actually higher than nominal spending. This phenomenon is due to a period of deflation in the Japanese economy, where overall prices have actually declined.
[3]In other words, TE = $P \times Q$, where TE is total expenditures, P is price, and Q is quantity.

price schedules are commonly negotiated between the government and representatives of the medical community. They may be interim, voluntary, or mandatory. Sometimes the prices are loosely determined through a relative-value schema that attempts to place a value on services according to some comparative scale (theoretically based on some measure of resource use). More often than not, this scale measures the political influence of the various specialties and not relative resource use.

Providers can still maintain their profit margins by lowering their own expenses. If there is waste in the system, price controls serve as a stimulus toward more efficient resource use. Thus, price controls can provide some short-term relief from the upward spiral of medical spending, but over time, the short-term beneficial effects are exhausted. Providers often find that they can get around the controls, and the associated erosion in their incomes, by seeing more patients and treating them more intensively. Thus, physician-induced demand may actually increase the demand for medical services, resulting in a higher level of spending and an increase in the physician's income. This shift means less time spent with each patient, so more patients can be seen, and more follow-up visits scheduled.

Another common practice used to avoid the heavy hand of price controls is the unbundling of services. *Unbundling* refers to the practice of breaking down a service into its various component parts. Instead of billing for the service, the provider bills for each part of the treatment. The practice defies logic, because the sum of the parts is greater than the whole. Standard care for treating a broken bone, when decomposed into its component parts with a separate bill for each, will cost more than the complete item. Providers can bill for an office visit, two X-rays, and a follow-up visit, often greater than the bill for the total package including the cast and its removal. A patient billed separately for the component parts of a wheelchair—wheels, armrests, cushions, and so on—will pay more than the cost of the complete item. A glucose monitoring kit may cost $12 at the local pharmacy but several times that amount when unbundled.

Controlled prices seldom result in the desired level of spending. In almost every situation in which price controls have been tried, the government authority ultimately revises the fee schedule downward, either through some automatic mechanism or unilaterally. A system of negotiated fee schedules eventually becomes one of regulated fee schedules with an elaborate government mechanism, often punitive in nature, to ensure compliance.

Global Budgeting

Unable to control spending with fee schedules, and desiring to avoid the direct plunge into rationing, the next step historically has been to establish a global budget. Global budgets are nothing more than spending caps. These caps may be established either as targeted or mandatory budgets. In politics, targeted caps serve merely as "backstop" measures. In other words, they are not binding in the sense that they would force rationing. In reality, however, the targets soon become mandatory budgets, and what was never intended becomes part of the apparatus of control.

Global budgets may be used in various ways. Canada and Germany set global budgets for hospitals, providing each institution with a set amount of money to be used to provide services to all comers. If actual spending exceeds budgeted spending, hospital providers are then faced with a dilemma. Providers handle this situation in a straightforward manner. Anything that can be delayed is delayed. Hospital wards are closed, operating rooms are unused, and nonessential personnel take unpaid furlough. All elective surgery is wait-listed until the next budget period. Available resources are used to treat only life-threatening conditions.

BACK-OF-THE-ENVELOPE

The Elements of Cost Control in Medical Care

Controlling medical care spending begins by controlling medical care costs. Cost control depends on the ability to control the major elements of costs: resource prices, resource productivity, and utilization of services. The derivation of the cost-control identity follows. In a standard two-input production process, output (Q) is a function of inputs A and B.

$$Q = Q(A, B) \tag{1}$$

Production of Q using the most efficient combination of A and B results in total cost (C) calculated as

$$C = P_A A + P_B B \tag{2}$$

where P_A is the price of input A, and P_B is the price of input B. *Average cost* (AC) is defined as total cost divided by output or

$$AC = C/Q \tag{3}$$

Substituting (2) into (3), we get

$$AC = \frac{P_A A}{Q} + \frac{P_B B}{Q} \tag{4}$$

$$AC = P_A\left(\frac{A}{Q}\right) + P_B\left(\frac{B}{Q}\right)$$

Note that (3) implies $C = AC \times Q$. Thus, when (4) is restated, generalizing to n inputs, we find that

$$C = \left[P_A\left(\frac{A}{Q}\right) + P_B\left(\frac{B}{Q}\right) + \ldots + P_N\left(\frac{N}{Q}\right)\right]Q \tag{5}$$

From (5), the first element in the cost-control identity is the level of input prices, P_A through P_N. If you want to reduce costs, you must control input prices. The second element is input productivity, shown by the inverses of the technical efficiencies of the inputs, A/Q through N/Q. As input productivity increases, efficiency improves and costs fall. The final element is output, Q. Control the size of Q, limit utilization, and costs can be reduced.

The static world of cost identities may not provide much encouragement to would-be cost containers. Fuchs (1988), for one, argues against placing too much hope in our ability to moderate input prices, improve efficiency, or reduce utilization. Our ability to control cost may go back to equation (1), the production function for medical care itself. Cost-saving technological improvements and changes in the production mix from higher-priced to lower-priced inputs may provide some hope for continued moderation of medical costs.

Source: Victor R. Fuchs, "The Competition Revolution in Health Care," *Health Affairs* 7(3), Summer 1988, 5–24.

KEY CONCEPT 8
Efficiency

Resource Rationing

Frustrated with their inability to control medical spending with price controls even in a fixed-budget system, policy makers are left with their last alternative—resource rationing.[4] Policy makers rarely use the term *rationing*. However, for all its various names, its results are the same: Rationing limits access to the desired commodity or service.

The first step toward resource rationing begins with improving access to primary and preventive care by encouraging, or possibly even mandating, more physicians to practice primary and family medicine.[5] As the system evolves, primary care physicians become the gatekeepers. Patients must first go through them before they are admitted to a hospital or are allowed to see a specialist.

To ensure cost containment, access to high-cost medical technology must be restricted. Designating certain facilities as technology centers usually accomplishes this task. Rationing takes the form of waiting lists and increased cost of travel to distant facilities, especially for patients living in rural areas.

In summary, price controls in medical care seem to benefit patients at the expense of providers, at least in the short term. Initially, this may seem desirable to many policy makers. The beneficial effects are immediate, but the harmful effects take longer to materialize and are difficult to understand. The lessons, however, are clear. After the initial cost efficiencies are realized, the lower prices associated with the fee schedules lead to fixed budgets and eventually limits on services. Targets become mandates and, eventually, nonprice rationing becomes prevalent, resulting in an inefficient allocation of services among patients. Quality of care does not improve with controls; in fact, it deteriorates. In the end, controls actually increase costs, because the distortions created by controls stifle the innovative activities that would lower costs. So the root cause of increased spending, limited cost-conscious behavior on the part of buyers or sellers, is never addressed.

★ POLICY ISSUE
Is resource rationing a feasible alternative to control medical spending when fee schedules and global budgets fail?

★ POLICY ISSUE
Are price ceilings and spending caps the way to control the problem of rising health care spending?

★ KEY CONCEPT 8
Efficiency

ISSUES IN MEDICAL CARE DELIVERY

MEDICAL CARE SPENDING AND INTERNATIONAL COMPETITIVENESS

General Motors (GM) spends $5.6 billion for worker health insurance on 1.1 million beneficiaries, making GM the largest private purchaser of health care in the United States. The level of spending amounts to over $1,600 for every car produced in North America, more than the amount spent on steel in each vehicle. Is medical care spending making American business less competitive in the global marketplace? This popular notion has a great deal of intuitive appeal, especially when members of the business community make the arguments.

The microeconomic argument examines the issue from the perspective of an individual firm. This argument assumes that the relevant price of labor is the cash wage paid to workers, and it treats fringe benefits as an add-on cost. Under this scenario, the firm has only two options when faced with increasing fringe costs: shift the costs forward to the firm's customers by raising product prices, or shift the costs backward to the firm's owners by reducing the firm's profits. The first option makes the firm's products less competitive in the marketplace; the second makes the firm's stock less attractive in the equity capital market.

---

[4]A system in which payment is based on prospective payment, including a significant portion of the managed care systems in the United States (public and private), is a fixed budget system.
[5]Establishing quotas for residency programs or paying all providers according to the same fee schedule creates strong incentives to specialize in primary care.

⭐ **POLICY ISSUE**
Does the high cost of health insurance handicap U.S. business in the global market?

⭐ **KEY CONCEPT 5**
Markets and Pricing

⭐ **KEY CONCEPT 2**
Opportunity Cost

⭐ **POLICY ISSUE**
Is the United States getting its money's worth in terms of health outcomes for the money spent on health care?

The macroeconomic argument examines the issue from the perspective of the entire economy. Much of our medical care spending represents pure consumption. By devoting a large fraction of GDP to medical care, less is available for savings and capital formation. In addition, spending less on medical care would allow the shifting of resources to more productive activities that would enhance economic efficiency and international competitiveness.

Overall, the argument that high medical care costs reduce competitiveness does not stand up under careful scrutiny. In particular, the microeconomic argument ignores a third option available to firms faced with rising fringe costs, namely, to shift the costs of increased fringe benefits to the workers who receive them. This option may be accomplished by merely paying the workers lower cash wages. To understand this perspective, realize that the relevant market-clearing wage is not solely the cash wage but the value of the total compensation package, including cash wages, health benefits, retirement benefits, the firm's share of social security taxes, and other payroll taxes. It makes little sense to single out any one component of the total compensation package and blame it for the lack of competitiveness in the global marketplace. Instead, it is important to realize that workers who receive fewer fringe benefits will merely demand higher cash wages.

On the other hand, the macroeconomic argument is based on the assumption that consumer spending in every other economic sector is "more productive" than spending on medical care. Because of the dominance of third-party payment in the medical care sector, a large percentage of medical care spending may be wasteful. Patients who do not pay the true incremental costs of the procedures they receive demand services that provide little benefit. Suggesting that spending in one sector is more productive than spending in any other, however, begs an important consideration: Who decides what type of spending is more productive? Would we be better off if half of the lawyers left their chosen profession and got jobs that are "more productive" in other sectors? Why not shift half of all college professors engaged in scholarly research into activities that are "more productive," for example, undergraduate teaching?

The business sector's motivation to control medical care spending goes beyond the global competitiveness argument. Every dollar spent on medical care affects at least one of the firm's stakeholders: customers pay higher prices, workers accept lower cash wages, and/or owners receive reduced profits. It is important to use resources wisely, not just in the medical care sector but also throughout the economy.

Sources: Uwe E. Reinhardt, "Health Care Spending and American Competitiveness," *Health Affairs* 8(4), Winter 1989, 5–21 and Lee Hawkins, Jr., "As GM Battles Surging Costs, Workers' Health Becomes Issue," *Wall Street Journal*, April 7, 2005.

Health System Classification

The developed countries of the world have each taken a somewhat different approach in establishing their own health care delivery system. Table 14.3 provides a summary of nine key characteristics relating to health care delivery. The four basic models adopted by these can be described as national health insurance (NHI; Canada), Bismarck (France, Germany, Japan, and Switzerland), Beveridge (United Kingdom), and mixed (United States).

The Beveridge model is characterized by government ownership of the medical infrastructure; most clinical personnel are public employees. Funds are generated through general taxation, and medical care is free at the point of service. Private insurance is available and duplicates services provided in the public system. The Bismarck approach, first developed in Germany, provides universal insurance coverage through not-for-profit insurance companies selling mandated benefit packages. France and Germany finance insurance coverage through payroll taxes, while the Swiss require individuals to purchase their own plans paying fixed premiums. Japan uses a combination of financing through

TABLE 14.3 CLASSIFICATION OF HEALTH SYSTEMS

2013	Canada	France	Germany	Japan	Switzerland	United Kingdom	United States
Model	NHI	Bismarck	Bismarck	Bismarck	Bismarck	Beveridge	Mixed
Source of funds	General taxes	Payroll taxes	Payroll taxes	Combination	Fixed premium	General taxes	Combination
Role of private insurance	Suppl	Compl	Primary (high income)	Compl	Primary; Suppl	Duplicate	Primary; Compl
Population with private coverage (%)	68	96	43	>70	100	11	64
Cost sharing	Drugs	Hospital physician drugs	Hospital physician drugs	Hospital physician drugs	Hospital physician drugs	Drugs	Hospital physician drugs
Plan deductible	N	N	N	N	Y	N	Y
Out-of-pocket maximum	N	N	Y	Y	Y	N	Y
Uniform fee schedule	Y	N	N	Y	Y	N	N
Prescription drug benefit	N	Y	Y	Y	Y	Y	Y

Suppl = Supplementary private insurance
Compl = Complementary private insurance
Source: OECD, *Health at a Glance*, 2012.

payroll taxes and fixed premiums, depending on the type of plan. Canada's system, classified as NHI, uses elements of both Beveridge and Bismarck. Sometimes referred to as "single payer," this model is characterized by government-run NHI sold at the provincial level.

Each country allows some form of private insurance coverage. In Switzerland and the United States private insurance is the primary type of insurance. Private insurance in Germany is the primary coverage for those with high incomes. Canada and Switzerland allow supplementary private policies that cover services beyond the mandated benefits package, including private hospital rooms, dental care, and travel insurance. In Canada prescription drugs are covered by supplemental policies. France and Japan allow participants to purchase complementary insurance that covers out-of-pocket payments for deductibles, copays, and balance billing. In the United States Medigap policies are sold to cover most out-of-pocket payments for seniors on Medicare. All such policies in the United States require some form of cost sharing, usually in the form of deductibles and copays.

The public sector is responsible for a substantial portion of overall spending, above two-thirds in all countries except the United States (see Table 14.4). The Swiss system is unique. Even though the Swiss purchase private insurance, because it is mandatory and universal, Organization for Economic Cooperation and Development (OECD) includes the premiums in the public spending category. Excluding private insurance premiums, public spending is only about 16.5 percent of total expenditures instead of almost two-thirds. Private spending is surprisingly high, exceeding 20 percent of total spending in each country except the United Kingdom.

Variation in the 15 quality indicators shown in Table 14.5 does not seem to be highly correlated with the model followed in the respective countries. Two things determine five-year survival rates: early diagnosis and a minimally invasive screening option. Colorectal cancer has the highest mortality rate, likely due to the invasive nature of the preferred method of screening. The United States fares well in terms of cancer survival, consistently ranking near the top of the comparison group. In fact, the U.S. results are consistently better when compared to the all-European average for breast (79.0 percent), colorectal (56.2 percent), and prostate cancer (77.5 percent).

The United States fares quite well in terms of in-patient, 30-day mortality rates for heart attack and stroke. Immunization rates and cancer screening rates show little variance across countries. Japan may be the only exception, likely due to the invasive nature of the tests. The rates of coronary artery bypass surgery and total knee replacements are higher in the U.S. than in the comparison countries. Canada tends to lag the other countries in these three areas, including hip replacements, considerably.

TABLE 14.4 HEALTH CARE EXPENDITURES BY SOURCE, PERCENTAGES

2013	Canada	France	Germany	Japan	Switzerland	United Kingdom	United States
Public	67.3	74.5	74.7	80.0	66.1[1]	83.3	46.2
Private	32.7	25.5	25.3	20.0	33.9	16.7	53.8
Private insurance	14.3	13.8	11.1	3.2	0.9	0.1	37.9
Out-of-pocket	13.6	6.4	13.2	13.5	25.8	9.5	11.8
Other private[2]	4.8	5.3	1.0	3.3	7.2	7.1	4.1

[1]Mandatory insurance is purchased from private firms but counted as public spending. Only 25 percent of premiums are paid out of public funds. The public–private breakdown is actually 16.5 percent public and 83.5 percent private with private insurance covering 50.5 percent of spending.
[2]Includes capital formation by providers and uncategorized spending.
Source: OECD Health Data 2015.

TABLE 14.5 HEALTH SYSTEMS QUALITY AND ACCESS INDICATORS

2013 or nearest year available	Canada	France	Germany	Japan	Switzerland	United Kingdom	United States
5-Year cancer survival rates							
Cervical	74.0[1]	62.7[1]	62.0[1]	70.5[1]	66.0[1]	70.0[1]	67.8[1]
Breast	81.0[1]	70.6[1]	78.2[2]	83.1[1]	84.5[2]	77.8[2]	90.1[2]
Colorectal	60.0[1]	59.9[2]	61.2[2]	67.5[1]	63.8[2]	51.8[2]	65.5[2]
Prostate	–	–	85.3[2]	–	87.3[2]	–	99.3[2]
In-hospital 30-day mortality rate (%)[3]							
AMI	6.7	7.2	8.7	12.2	7.7	7.6	5.5
Stroke:							
Hemorrhagic	27.3	26.9	16.7	11.8	20.0	26.5	22.0
Ischemic	10.0	7.9	6.4	3.0	6.9	9.2	3.6
Diagnostic imaging rate (per 1,000)[3]							
MRI	52.8	90.9	95.2	–	–	–	106.9
CT	131.5	192.8	117.1	–	–	–	240.4
Immunization rate (%)[3]							
Measles (children)	95	89	97	95	93	95	91
Influenza (seniors)	64	52	59	50	46	76	66
Screening rate (%)[3]							
Breast cancer (Age 50–69)	72.2	75.4	71.3	41.0	47.4	75.9	80.8
Cervical cancer (Age 20–69)	73.4	73.6	52.8	42.1	74.5	78.1	84.5
Other utilization (per 1,000)[3]							
CABG	56.1	30.0	67.6	–	45.6	28.7	79.0
Hip replacement	135.6	235.5	282.9	–	301.4	182.6	203.5
Knee replacement	165.8	145.4	190.0	–	210.1	141.4	225.8
Physicians' visits per capita[4]	7.7	6.4	9.9	–	3.9	5.0	4.0
Primary care access (%)[4]							
Same or next day	45	62	66	–	93	70	57
6 days or more	33	17	16	–	2	8	19
Specialist access (%)[4]							
Less than 4 weeks	41	53	83	–		72	80
More than 2 months	41	28	7	–	82	19	9
Elective surgery[4]							
Less than 4 weeks	35	46	78	–	55	59	68
More than 4 months	25	7	0	–	7	21	7

Sources:

[1]Armesto et al. (2007).

[2]Verdecchia et al. (2007).

[2]OECD Health Data (2016).

[4]Schoen, Pierson, and Applebaum (2010).

Japan and Germany top the list in terms of physicians' visits per capita, 12.9 and 9.9, respectively. Primary care access is quite good in Switzerland with 93 percent of patients receiving same or next day appointments. Over 80 percent of patients receive specialist access in less than four weeks in Germany, Switzerland, and the United States. Over two-thirds of patients in Germany and the United States receive elective surgery in less than four weeks. In terms of these three access measures, Canada's performance lags the others significantly.

Canadian National Health Insurance: Medicare

Canada is divided into ten provinces and two territories. Its total population is 35.3 million with most living within 100 miles of its southern border with the United States. These demographics create quite a challenge for health care delivery in the rest of the country, where low population densities, long-distance travel requirements, and provider shortages are the norm. Only two provinces have populations exceeding one million, and only four metropolitan areas have sufficient population to support integrated delivery systems. Canadian policy makers have responded to these challenges by creating a **national health insurance** system that has demonstrated an ability to deliver high-quality medical care to the entire population at about one-half of the per capita spending of U.S. health care.

The 1984 Canada Health Act defines the health care delivery system as it currently operates. Provisions of the act require that each provincial health plan be publicly administered; portable across provinces, accessible, and that each provide comprehensive first-dollar coverage of all medically necessary services. With some exceptions (most notably, pharmaceuticals), health coverage is available to all residents with no out-of-pocket charges. Most physicians are paid on a fee-for-service basis and enjoy a great deal of practice autonomy.[6]

The Canadian health care system began to take on its current form when the province of Saskatchewan set up a hospitalization plan immediately after the Second World War. In 1944, provincial voters elected a socialist-leaning government, the Cooperative Commonwealth Federation, or CCF (now called the New Democratic Party). The province was plagued by the kind of medical problems that one might expect in a predominantly rural, low-income population—shortages of both hospital beds and medical practitioners. By 1947, two years after coming into power, the CCF delivered on its campaign promise and enacted the Saskatchewan Hospital Services Plan. The main feature of this plan was the creation of a regional system of hospitals: local hospitals for primary care, district hospitals for more complex cases, and base hospitals for the most difficult cases.

British Columbia, Saskatchewan's western neighbor, enacted its own hospital insurance plan in 1949, providing momentum for the creation of a national hospital insurance system. In 1956, the federal parliament enacted the Hospital and Diagnostic Services Act, laying the groundwork for a nationwide system of hospital insurance. By 1961, all ten provinces and the two territories had hospital insurance plans of their own with the federal government paying half of the costs.

Within a year, Saskatchewan moved to provide for the funding of physicians' services. The Saskatchewan Medical Care Insurance Act of 1962 was passed; its main provision was a binding fee schedule for physicians' services. As a result, physicians in the province orchestrated the first-ever physicians' strike in North America to protest the fixed-fee schedule. To settle the dispute, the provincial government allowed the practice of "extra billing," which allowed physicians to charge fees in excess of those scheduled. Within two years, the average physician income moved from last among the provinces to first, fueling the engine of reform.

national health insurance A government-run health insurance system covering the entire population for a well-defined medical benefits package. Usually administered by a government or quasi-government agency and financed through some form of taxation.

HTTP://
The Canadian Health Network provides links to over 30 health sites with information on Canadian medical care. http://www.hc-sc.gc.ca.

KEY CONCEPT 4
Self-Interest

---

[6]About 90 percent of all primary care is provided by fee-for-service GPs. The rest is provided by salaried GPs working in local community health centers.

The other provinces began to fall in line, but this time national legislation was enacted in half the time—four years instead of nine. By 1971, Canada had its NHI plan, providing coverage for both hospitalization and physicians' services. To receive matching funds from the federal government, each provincial plan had to meet certain national standards. This included universal eligibility, coverage of all medically necessary services (inpatient, outpatient, and physician), public administration, portability between provinces, and no financial barriers to service—that meant no hospital user charges and no extra billing by physicians.

National coverage focuses primarily on hospital and physicians' services. Most Canadians have some form of supplementary private insurance that covers dental, vision, and prescription drugs. Dominated by Blue Cross organizations across the country, private insurance coverage pays for almost one-half of medical spending on these uncovered services.

KEY CONCEPT 3
Marginal Analysis

BACK-OF-THE-ENVELOPE

Negotiating Fee Schedules: Bilateral Monopoly in Canada

In practice, each province in Canada offers a separate health care system. While the federal government helps finance these systems through an income tax, most of the money is raised at the provincial level through general tax revenues, payroll taxes, or premiums. Each provincial health ministry tightly controls hospital spending through global budgets. Hospitals receive a fixed operating budget at the beginning of each fiscal year. Spending on physicians' services is controlled in a number of different ways across the country. The basic tool for controlling spending on physicians' services is a mandatory fee schedule negotiated between the provincial health ministry, representing patients, and the provincial medical society, representing physicians. This is a classic case of bilateral monopoly. Here is how it works.

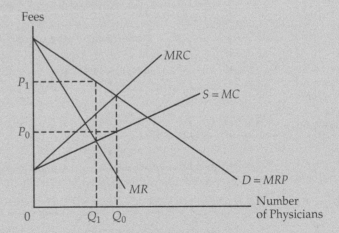

In the diagram, the demand curve for physicians' services is the marginal revenue product curve (MRP). This is the demand curve facing the medical association representing all the physicians in the province. The medical association functions in much the same way as a union and behaves like a labor monopolist. The marginal revenue (MR) curve is derived from the demand curve. The supply curve S represents the opportunity cost, or marginal cost (MC), of making an additional physician available to the market. If the medical association behaves like a profit (or economic rent) maximizer, it sets $MR = MC$ and offers Q_1 physicians at a fee schedule equivalent to P_1.

The health ministry, acting as a monopsonist, maximizes profit where $MRP = MRC$. From its perspective, the optimal equilibrium will have Q_0 physicians available at a fee schedule equal to P_0. The final equilibrium will find fees somewhere between P_0 and P_1 and the number of physicians between Q_0 and Q_1.

In this situation, negotiations will likely begin with the medical association offering to make Q_1 physicians available and the health ministry refusing to pay fees higher than P_0. If the health ministry wants more physicians, then higher fees must be paid. The trade-off will be made, and a bargain will eventually be reached. In the Canadian case, it is likely that the medical association is in a weaker position. If the demand curve in the earlier figure is more inelastic and the supply curve more elastic, then Q_0 is less than Q_1. The health ministry wants fewer physicians in practice than the medical association is willing to provide. No longer is a bargaining trade-off possible. In this case, the provincial health ministries set utilization targets to control overall spending. If these targets are exceeded in one year, the next year's fees are lowered accordingly, or physicians are forced to work for reduced fees until budgets are met, or income ceilings are established for individual physicians.

The federal government abandoned the 50-50 cost-sharing arrangement in the original legislation in 1977 and replaced with a per capita grant to the provinces. The result has been steady erosion in the percentage of the costs covered by the federal government. The federal share has fallen to about 20 percent currently. The shifting financial burden has created a strong incentive to reduce spending and shift some of the expense onto the private sector. The public sector financed 67.3 percent of total health care spending in 2013 with private insurance covering 14.3 percent and patient out-of-pocket spending 13.6 percent.

Public sector medical spending comes primarily from personal income and consumption taxes. Two provinces, British Columbia and Ontario, actually charge income-based premiums and four others collect payroll taxes. Government spending on medical care has grown faster than GDP since 1975, putting additional pressure on provincial budgets. The two largest provinces, Ontario and Quebec, already spend over 50 percent of all revenues on medical care, and four more are projected to do so by 2017.

"single-payer" system Usually associated with Canada, a system of financing medical care in which payment comes from a single source, typically the government.

Many feel that it is inaccurate to characterize the Canadian system as a **"single-payer" system**, because there is considerable variation among the provincial health plans. In spite of the differences, it is fair to say that each provincial plan is a public sector monopsony, serving as a single buyer of medical services within the province and holding medical care prices below market rates.

Theoretically, physician fee schedules are determined through bilateral negotiations at the provincial level between the Ministry of Health and the medical association. Practically, several provinces have reduced unilaterally the binding fee schedules. Five provinces, with 80 percent of the population, have mechanisms to control service volume by placing a limit on the quarterly gross billings allowed for the individual practitioner. Billings above the limit are reimbursed at one-fourth the prescribed fee schedule (Evans et al., 1989; Wolfe and Moran, 1993).[7] Several provinces have initiated an across-the-board, 25 percent reduction in fees for new physicians practicing in urban areas, for reducing crowding in

---

[7]Quebec has the strictest limitations, with the billing threshold at $180,000 (USD).

HTTP://

Many of the provincial health ministries in Canada have their own websites. The British Columbia Ministry of Health site address is http://www.gov.bc.ca/health/.

urban areas and scarcity in rural areas. To confront the fee problem head-on, the Ministry of Health for British Columbia has begun setting fee schedules unilaterally.

By U.S. standards, physicians' incomes are on average low. In 2010, the income of general practitioners (GPs) averaged $136,236 and specialists averaged $215,714 (OECD, 2016). The average GP's income is about 2.9 times the average wage, while specialists incomes are about 4.6 times average wage. Both are less than two-thirds that of comparable U.S. physicians.

If cost control is defined in terms of health care spending as a share of economic output, Canada has done far better in controlling health care costs than the United States. In 1970, Canada's health care spending as a share of GDP was 7.2 percent, compared to the U.S. figure of 7.4 percent. Over the next three decades, the increase in the spending-to-GDP ratio was significantly lower in Canada than in the United States. In 2013, the health care sector represented 10.2 percent of GDP in Canada and 16.4 percent in the United States.

HTTP://

The Ontario Ministry of Health also has its own website. http://www.health.gov.on.ca/.

The key element in the Canadian strategy to control overall spending is the regionalization of high-tech services. Government regulators make resource-allocation decisions. This control extends to capital investment in hospitals, the specialty mix of medical practitioners, the location of recent medical graduates, and the diffusion of high-tech diagnostic and surgical equipment. In 2013, there were 312 magnetic resonance imagers in all of Canada, one for every 114,000 citizens. Contrast that to over 11,200 in the United States, one for every 28,000 Americans. That same year, there were 518 CT scanners in Canada, one for every 68,600 citizens. The United States had over 13,700 CT scanners, one for every 23,000 Americans.

It can be argued that U.S. hospitals have excess capacity in these technology areas while, at the same time, Canada experiences a shortage. Waiting lists for certain surgical and diagnostic procedures are common in Canada. In 2016 there were approximately 973,500 Canadians waiting for surgical procedures (assuming one patient per procedure), 2.7 percent of the population. Nationwide, the median wait from referral by a GP to treatment was 20 weeks, up from 9.3 weeks in 1993. Median waits ranged from 15.6 weeks in Ontario to 38.8 weeks in New Brunswick and 34.8 weeks in Nova Scotia. Median waiting times are longest for orthopedic surgery (38.0 weeks), neurosurgery (46.9 weeks), and opthalmology (28.5 weeks). Urology, general surgery, and oncological services have the shortest waits, ranging from 3.7 to 12.1 weeks (Ren and Barua, 2017). Comparisons between reasonable and actual waiting times were made for all 10 provinces and 13 specialties. The median waiting time was longer in 66 percent of the cases than Canadian physicians consider clinically reasonable (Barua, 2015).[8]

⭐ **KEY CONCEPT 6**
Supply and Demand

The problem does not end there. When care requires diagnostic imaging, waiting times are even longer. In 2016 patients had to wait an average of 3.7 weeks for a CT scan, 11.1 weeks for an MRI, and 4.0 weeks for an ultrasound. Treatment delays are causing problems for certain vulnerable segments of the Canadian population, particularly the elderly who cannot get reasonable access to the medical care they demand, including hip and knee replacement (median wait of 26.3 weeks, ranging from 18 to 44 weeks across the provinces) and cataract surgery (18.5 week median, ranging from 9 to 31.5 weeks). Patients requiring non-emergent cardiac bypass surgery wait an average of 7.6 weeks (ranging from 1 to 29 weeks). Thus, Canadians are sacrificing access to modern medical technology for first-dollar coverage for primary care.

Ren and Barua (2017) estimated the cost of waiting in terms of foregone income. In 2016, the cost was estimated at $1.7 billion. If only working hours are included in the

---

[8]A clinically reasonable wait as defined by Canadian physicians is one-third to one-half longer than is considered reasonable by American physicians.

calculation, the per capita cost of waiting for medical procedures is $1,759. If, however, total time is used in the calculation (hours awake), the per capita opportunity cost of waiting is $5,360.

The cost of government-provided health is more than waiting for access. While Canadians are not billed directly for their health care, they pay for services via taxation. The average two-parent household pays close to $12,000 per year in taxes of one kind or another to pay for their health care. This amount varies by income with households in the lowest decile paying an average of $477; those in the decile representing mean income ($59,666) pay $5,684. Top earners, those in the top decile, pay $37,180 (Barua and Ren, 2016).

Another cost-control measure is global budgeting. Hospitals receive annual budgets to cover their operating expenses. They are expected to serve every patient within the level of funding provided by this budget. The resource allocation decision falls squarely on hospital administrators across the country, who must decide service availability given funding levels.

★ **KEY CONCEPT 2**
Opportunity Cost

Several lessons can be learned from the Canadian experience. When government provides a product "free" to consumers, inevitably, demand escalates and spending increases. Products provided at zero price are treated as if they have zero resource cost. Resource allocation decisions become more inefficient over time, and government is forced either to raise more revenue or curb services.

A second lesson is that everything has a cost. When care requires major diagnostic or surgical procedures, the "free" system must find a mechanism to allocate scarce resources. The Canadian system delegates this authority to the government. Resource allocation is practiced not through the price mechanism but by setting limits on the investment in medical technology. Proponents will argue that using waiting lists as a rationing measure is reasonable and fair. Opponents find the lists unacceptable and an unwelcome encroachment on individual decision making in the medical sector.

★ **KEY CONCEPT 1**
Scarcity and Choice

Proponents of the single-payer alternative must deal with the fact that Canadians face waiting lists for some medical services, especially for high-tech specialty care. To avoid delays in treatment, many Canadians are able to travel abroad for more advanced treatment, legitimately viewed as a safety valve for wait-listed Canadians.

★ **POLICY ISSUE**
What are the economic and political consequences of changing the U.S. health care delivery system to a Canadian-style single-payer system?

These cross-border transactions reached record levels in the early 1990s. Until 1991, Canadians were reimbursed for 100 percent of all emergency care received abroad and 75 percent of the cost of all elective surgery. These generous benefits were lowered to a flat per diem for emergency services and elective surgery. Since the change, the number of Canadians seeking care in the United States has sharply declined. Still, a large number of Canadians (over 30 million individual and group policies) have extended health care insurance that cover them while traveling abroad. Esmail (2011) estimated that approximately 45,000 Canadians traveled abroad for elective procedures in 2010.

The system faces a significant challenge: How to respond to the Canadian Supreme Court ruling that the prohibition of private insurance for publicly insured services is unconstitutional. In other words, "access to a waiting list is not access to health care" (*Chaoulli v. Quebec*, 2005). The ruling became effective in June 2006 and states that unless the provincial plan meets patient needs without undue waits, the government can no longer ban private insurance (Steinbrook, 2006). While this ruling technically affects only the province of Quebec, it opens up the opportunity to challenge the law in other provinces. It seems that it is only a matter of time before this patient backlash affects all provinces and leads to a growing private insurance sector and possibly a two-tiered system with shorter waiting times in the private insurance sector, increased demand for services, and more spending for those with private insurance.

The purpose of a safety valve is to relieve pressure. How is the notion of a safety valve relevant in analyzing medical care markets? Consider two medical care markets separated in some manner: the primary market and the safety valve. Supply is restricted through limits on the number of operating rooms, imaging devices, and other procedures requiring sophisticated medical technology. To keep prices and spending down, the governing authorities place a price ceiling in the primary market as shown in the left-hand side of the diagram.

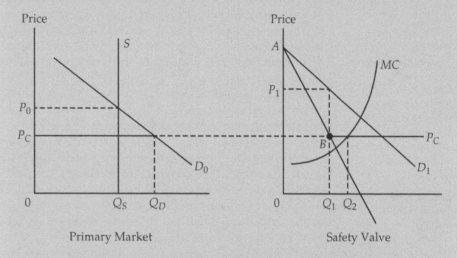

Primary Market   Safety Valve

The vertical supply curve S fixes the quantity supplied at Q_s. Instead of allowing the market price P_0 to prevail, government sets a price ceiling at P_c and creates a shortage of $Q_D - Q_S$. The excess demand causes problems with waiting lists and frustrated patients. Given a certain degree of geographic mobility, patients in the primary market can travel to the unrestricted market, the safety valve, and receive treatment.

Suppose the payer in the primary market agrees to finance the care received in the safety valve at the controlled price P_c. Providers in the unrestricted market face a marginal revenue curve with a downward-sloping segment, AB, and a horizontal segment, BP_c. Marginal cost crosses this combined marginal revenue curve at Q_2. If capacity in the unrestricted market is less than Q_1, all of the available capacity will be devoted to consumers in that market, because they willingly pay P_1. If providers in the unrestricted market have capacity beyond Q_1, those consumers shut out of the primary market can get care through the safety valve at price P_c. Providers in the unrestricted market practice price discrimination, charging P_1 to the original customers and P_c to the overflow from the primary market.

HTTP://

Information about the Pasteur Institute's contributions, conferences, and publications—much of it in English—may be found at their website. http://www.pasteur.fr/ english.html; https:// www.pasteur.fr/fr.

France: Equality, Liberty, Fraternity[9]

Even though France is often depicted as the birthplace of European democracy, the nation actually adopted a highly centralized system of government during the reign of Napoleon Bonaparte. Since that time, the French have tried to maintain a delicate balance between individual freedom and collective action. Economic and social policy is based, in varying

---

[9]This section is loosely based on Henderson (1993).

degrees, on three principles that the French hold dear: a national spirit of egalitarianism, a respect for individual freedom, and a commitment to minimal state intervention. In other words, the French attempt to strike a balance between solidarity, choice, and competition.

The potential for conflict among these principles is easy to recognize, and nowhere is it more evident than in the nation's complex system of medical care delivery. The national spirit of egalitarianism is manifested in the preamble to the French Constitution: "The nation guarantees to all protection of health." The social security system serves not only to provide health insurance for everyone, but also serves as a mechanism to redistribute income and provide social solidarity. Respect for individual freedom is evident in the provision for patient choice and physician autonomy. Patients are free to choose their own physicians and may see a specialist without referral.[10]

As economic theory would suggest, unconstrained pursuit of these two principles has led to escalating spending. Again, patients who are provided with care at zero price use it as if it had zero resource cost. Providers who are free to treat with little consideration for cost effectiveness tend to overprescribe. In 1960, the government intervened with regulatory reform, maintaining the principles of liberty and solidarity but compromising the principle of **laissez faire**. In its place, state control over prices and budgets was substituted in an effort to moderate spending.

As in many other European countries, NHI in France grew out of a nineteenth-century system that provided certain industrial workers and miners with insurance through mutual aid societies (MAS) or **sickness funds**. Legislation passed in 1928 made membership compulsory for many low-wage occupations, but coverage was still far from universal. It was not until after World War II, when the economic and social infrastructure was being rebuilt, that everyone was brought into the system. The General National Health Insurance Scheme (GNHI) covers 83 percent of French workers with the remainder covered by specific occupational funds, including agricultural workers, public employees, independent professionals, and full-time students. Spending is also a concern, and the system has consistently overspent since its inception in the 1950s. For example, the GNHI fund ran a deficit of €11.6 billion (approximately $15 billion) in 2010, creating strong dissatisfaction among patients and providers.[11] A relatively weak economy and high unemployment have resulted in chronic deficits in the public health insurance funds. Many hospitals, forced to borrow to comply with capital improvement requirements dictated by government, are now struggling to cover their debt service.

Health policy makers have found it difficult to satisfy the goal of universal access and control spending at the same time. Financing is primarily from social insurance but with a significant private, complementary insurance component. The system was originally financed almost exclusively on a payroll tax. Employers pay 13.5 percent of an employee's salary into the health insurance fund, and employees pay 0.75 percent. A social contribution tax that varies from 6.2 percent on retirement benefits to 8.25 percent on financial income reduces the reliance on payroll taxes and has taken some of the pressure off employers but has not decreased the overall cost of coverage. Employers now contribute 47 percent of the revenues that support GNHI, income-related sources provide another 37 percent, and various state taxes contribute the remainder.

French social security legislation covers all employees who must contribute to the national social security system. The system is divided into four branches: life and health insurance, occupational disability insurance, old-age pension, and family leave.

laissez faire A French term meaning literally "allow [them] to do." It depicts a situation in which individuals and firms are allowed to pursue their own self-interests without government restraint.

sickness fund A quasi-governmental group that serves as an insurance company by collecting premiums and paying providers within the national health care system of France and Germany.

---

[10]France introduced gatekeeping in 2004, requiring patients to designate a "referring" physician when consulting a specialist. Without a referral, patients pay a higher out-of-pocket cost-sharing amount.

[11]Some estimates expect the deficit to reach €66 by 2020 (Tanner, 2008).

While there are no deductibles, patients must pay a substantial copayment for both ambulatory and hospital care. The typical arrangement is for the patient to pay the entire medical fee when services are received. After paying the physician, the patient may then apply for a reimbursement of 75–80 percent of the prescribed fee. Low-income individuals who earn less than €6,600 annually are not expected to pay in advance. Hospital patients must pay 20 percent for hospital services plus a daily room charge of €10 (approximately $12) subject to a 30-day maximum. The hospital then bills the appropriate NHI fund for the balance. Patient copays for laboratory tests and dental care are 30 percent. Patients must pay 35–65 percent of the cost of covered prescription drugs and 100 percent for non-covered prescription drugs.[12] The patient is responsible for any extra billing.

To avoid copays at the point of service and balance billings, almost 90 percent of the covered population purchase complementary private insurance. The role of private insurance has expanded over the past 40 years, enabling the French to avoid most of the negative consequences associated with health care rationing. This coverage is available from mutual societies; not-for-profit insurance companies; and commercial, for-profit insurance companies. Private insurance premiums vary depending on labor force status but average about 2.5 percent of per capita income (OECD, 2016). Along with out-of-pocket spending that averages about 1 percent of income, total health care spending consumes 24 percent of the income of the typical worker.[13]

As of 2013, there were approximately 204,000 physicians in active practice nationwide, 310 per 100,000 population.[14] About one-third of all physicians are in exclusively private practice and another one-third are salaried. Those remaining have a mixed practice—they hold a salaried position with either a large public hospital or municipal health center and, at the same time, have a part-time private practice. About 53 percent of the physicians are GPs. The remainder are specialists, most with mixed practices.

Approximately 75 percent of medical practitioners are first-tier: 83 percent of all GPs and 62 percent of all specialists. First-tier physicians contract with the NHI agencies that reimburse on a fee-for-service basis according to a nationally negotiated fee schedule. The fee schedule combines a relative value scale (RVS) that assigns points to the various services and procedures with a monetary conversion factor, determining the actual fee.[15]

Before 1980, physicians considered prestigious by a commission of their peers were allowed to charge fees that exceeded the legal ceiling. In 1980, pressure from physicians' organizations forced the government to allow any physician to apply for second-tier status that carried with it the ability to balance bill at rates up to 50 percent over the approved fee schedule. By 1990, concern over high out-of-pocket costs for physicians' services led the government to suspend new entry into the second tier, effectively closing that means of resource allocation. About 25 percent of all physicians are now second tier and allowed to balance bill.

Even with the pricing flexibility enjoyed by second-tier physicians, fee schedules have had a significant effect on physicians' incomes. In 2011, physician incomes ranged from

---

[12]Certain vital drugs required for individuals with serious or debilitating conditions are reimbursed 100 percent.

[13]This is somewhat high, even by European standards. German employers pay half of the health care premiums of their workers, which ranged from 10 to 16 percent of total payroll, with an average of 15 percent. U.S. employers contributed 5.3 percent of payroll toward health insurance premiums in 2005. For the 56 percent of businesses that offered health insurance, premiums accounted for 10.3 percent of payroll.

[14]Lack of an official census of physicians makes the actual figure somewhat of a guess.

[15]The French relative value scale assigns values for each service and procedure, much like the Medicare resource-based relative value scale, but the relative weightings for procedures are not technical (i.e., they are not based on time, intensity, complexity, or training requirements as in the United States). They are based more on the political influence of the various specialties and consumer preferences. The crude nature of the RVS has created price distortions in the fee schedule that encourage inefficient medical practices (Rodwin, 1981).

⭐ **KEY CONCEPT 2**
Opportunity Cost

$97,200 for self-employed GPs to $158,100 for specialists (OECD, 2016). French physicians average less than one-third to one-half of what the typical American physician earned that same year. Not only are salaries low by U.S. standards, their relative position within the country is lower than other European countries. GPs earn about 2.4 times that of the average wage and salary worker and self-employed specialists earn 3.9 times that amount.

Most medical students study at one of 29 university-affiliated hospital centers located primarily in the regional capitals. Although first year admission at the 41 medical schools is open to all comers, entry into the second year is controlled by a quota—less than 4,000 annually (down from 8,588 in 1972). The stated goal of 250 physicians per 100,000 population has been exceeded somewhat, and the geographic distribution of physicians is uneven with shortages in the north and in rural areas (Rodwin, 2003). No policy limits physician autonomy.[16]

Hospital care is provided at one of three types of institutions: public hospitals, private nonprofit hospitals, and private for-profit clinics. In 2010, public sector hospitals contained 66 percent of the total beds, private nonprofits had 9 percent, and private for-profit clinics had 25 percent (Paris, Devaux, and Wei, 2010). The most prestigious functions are performed in public institutions: teaching, basic research, and high-tech diagnostic and surgical procedures.

Public hospitals, and the majority of the private nonprofit hospitals, are covered by prospective global budgeting with salaried physicians. Patients cannot choose their physicians in a public hospital unless they have first seen a specialist during that physician's part-time private practice. Private for-profit clinics receive the national per diem payment, and physicians treating patients in those clinics receive the standard fee. Physicians in exclusively private practice cannot treat patients in public hospitals.[17]

Public hospitals are required by law to keep occupancy rates below 95 percent of capacity. In addition, they must remain open 24 hours a day, and they must maintain a fully equipped emergency room.[18] Private clinics usually focus on more profitable services, such as elective surgeries and maternity, and avoid the high-cost procedures. Not surprisingly, the average costs of public hospitals tend to be higher than that of private clinics. Over the years, clinics have been successful in maintaining profitability by unbundling their services and thus removing certain procedures from the standard per diem rates.

The introduction of advanced technology has caused policy makers some problems in controlling health care spending. In addition to the extra investment, modern medical equipment requires more technical expertise for those who operate the equipment. This requirement translates into advanced training for physicians, nurses, and technicians and greater rates of remuneration for this new expertise.

⭐ **KEY CONCEPT 9**
Market Failure

Economic theory clearly indicates that strict budget controls will lead to lower investment in high-cost technology. Budget considerations require regulation of investment in medical equipment. The more stringent the controls the harder it will be for hospitals to adequately maintain their facilities and invest in quality-enhancing medical equipment. Theoretically, equipment standards are set to meet physician recommendations, but in actual practice, investment in medical equipment is a fiscal decision made with the approval of the Ministry of Health. The evidence suggests that the introduction of global

---

[16]Policy makers continue to explore new ways to limit spending. Ministry of Health officials even considered the extension of utilization controls and prospective budgeting to individual physicians as a means of controlling expenditures on physicians' services (U.S. General Accounting Office, 1991).

[17]A limited number can admit patients for outpatient services.

[18]In order to promote uniform quality across the hospital system, air conditioning is not allowed. This restriction played a role in the high death toll, estimated at 15,000, resulting from the record heat wave experienced in central Europe in the summer of 2003.

POLICY ISSUE

Is it possible to establish a tightly controlled national health care budget without creating shortages of medical technology?

budgeting in 1984 adversely affected innovation. The National Health Authority has created a mechanism to judge the effectiveness of medical procedures and technology, using the concept of medical service rendered (MSR). If MSR is determined to be insufficient, the product or procedure is no longer eligible for reimbursement, effectively removing it from use.

The introduction and diffusion of new technology, especially when it requires costly equipment, have been much slower in France than in the United States. As we saw in Table 14.1, the adoption levels for costly diagnostic and treatment services are far different in France from their counterparts in the developed world. The French have 1 MRI for every 106,500 residents, compared to 1 per 28,200 in the United States; and there is 1 CT scanner for every 69,000, compared to 1 per 23,000 in the United States.

Imposition of a single public insurance plan does not guarantee equal health outcomes. Occupational and geographic disparities in life expectancy exist despite universal access. Male life expectancy at age 35 varies by as much as seven years between professional workers and laborers. Life expectancy at birth in Midi-Pyrénées in the south is over four years greater than in Nord-Pas-de-Calais in the north. Access to resources differs by region. Ile-de-France has 423 physicians per 100,000 compared to 249 in Picardie (Petkantchin, 2007).

The NHI system in France covers virtually 100 percent of the country's population. In their quest for social solidarity and equality, however, the French have given up a lot. Practitioners have suffered erosion in their real incomes relative to the rest of the population. The system imposes global budgets on public hospitals, limits the availability of medical technology, and requires high out-of-pocket spending in the name of cost control. Physician autonomy remains intact, at least in the private sector. The French have avoided the outright waiting lists so prevalent in many public systems because of their relatively high copays and large reliance on complementary insurance. The system is at a crossroads. Fully, 60 percent of the population surveyed believes that the system needs to undergo fundamental change or be completely rebuilt (Schoen et al., 2013). The unique social character of the French people is apparent. By a 3 to 1 margin, they support equal access to care for everyone over quality care for himself or herself. Fundamental change is needed because of chronic operating deficits. Nevertheless, the change needed is a change in philosophy, something the French people are ill prepared for (LePen, 2003).

Germany: Sickness Funds[19]

After World War II, the Allies divided Germany into two separate entities. The German Democratic Republic (East Germany) was under the influence of the former Soviet Union and adopted the Socialist form of government. The Federal Republic of Germany (West Germany) maintained its connections with the West and continued to utilize the prewar economic system, including the health care delivery system. Since the unification of East and West Germany in 1990, East Germany has been subjected to most West German laws, including legislation relating to the medical insurance system. With a combined population of 80.6 million, Germany is divided into 16 provinces or Laenders, each with a great deal of independence in determining matters related to health and education.

The overall provision of health insurance, from organization to financing, is a provincial responsibility. Administrative control was the responsibility of approximately 132 sickness funds in 2014, financed by the social insurance scheme established by federal law.

---

[19]Thanks to Klaus Geldsetzer for his insightful comments on this section. Of course, any remaining errors and omissions are my responsibility.

Germany's health care system has its origins in the "mutual aid societies" created in the early nineteenth century. The German system of social benefits is based on the concept of statutory health insurance (SHI) as embodied in three founding principles: social solidarity, subsidiarity, and corporatism. Social solidarity refers to government's obligation to provide access to a wide range of social benefits to all citizens, including medical care, old-age pensions, unemployment insurance, disability payments, maternity benefits, and other forms of social welfare, and that everybody contributes according to their ability to pay. Subsidiarity is embodied in a decentralized system in which policy is implemented by the smallest possible administrative unit. Corporatism is manifested in the governing boards of sickness funds, which have widespread participation from business, medical providers, and insurers.

By the time Otto von Bismarck became Germany's chancellor in 1871, hundreds of sickness insurance funds were already in operation. Bismarck, a member of the Prussian aristocracy, saw the working class movement represented by socialist-oriented political parties as a threat. This concern led him to advocate the expansion of the existing sickness benefit societies to cover workers in all low-wage occupations. Passed in 1883, the Sickness Insurance Act represented the first social insurance program organized on a national level.

In the past 130 years, the system has grown to the point that virtually all of the population has access to medical care. All individuals are required by law to have health insurance. Those earning less than €53,550 (in 2014, about $60,000) must join one of the sickness funds for their health care coverage. Those earning more than the "opt-out" threshold may choose private health insurance instead.[20] Approximately 85 percent of the population participates in the SHI system, including 9 percent who are members voluntarily, even though their income exceeds the statutory cutoff.[21] The remaining 15 percent, the majority of which are civil servants, have comprehensive private insurance paid by their employers that provides them better access to care (Britnell, 2015). The switch from public to private insurance is a switch from income-dependent-health contributions to health-dependent contributions. Private health insurance premiums are risk rated. However, enrollees receive lifetime contracts where premiums do not increase with age.

Approximately one of every ten Germans covered by sickness fund insurance also purchased private supplementary insurance used primarily to cover other amenities, including overseas treatment, greater privacy during treatment, and private-room supplements. Individuals may tailor private insurance to meet their needs; they may choose policies that offer full coverage with no deductibles or coinsurance requirements, or they may instead choose policies with those cost-sharing features (Green and Irvine, 2001).

Individual health insurance premiums for workers enrolled in sickness funds are calculated based on income and not age or the number of dependents. Premiums are collected through a payroll deduction averaging 15.5 percent of a worker's gross salary in 2011.[22] An additional contribution for long-term care insurance of 1.95 percent of income has been required since 1996, bringing the average contribution for health insurance plus long-term care insurance to over 17 percent of payroll. The average payroll tax has risen sharply over the past 40 years. It was 8.2 percent in 1970 and rose to 13.5 percent by 1996 and 14.9 percent in 2010. Employers pay 47 percent of the tax directly for their workers. The Federal

---

[20]Regardless of salary, government employees and the self-employed can choose private insurance.

[21]An unemployed spouse receives public insurance at no additional cost. Those wishing private insurance would be required to pay a premium.

[22]The income threshold caps premiums. Workers earning more than the opt-out threshold and choosing a public sickness fund pay a premium equal to about 14 percent of the first €53,550 of their income or €7,500. This premium also covers nonworking family members.

Labor Administration or local welfare agencies pay the premiums of those who are unemployed.[23] Retirees pay a percentage of their pensions equal to the average contribution paid by workers. Private insurance premiums vary, depending on the type of policy chosen. Even though private policies holders receive better benefits, private premiums average 20 percent less than the average payroll tax because they do not provide subsidies for the public health insurance system. Private benefits are better, and per capita administrative costs are half those of the public system (Prewo, 2006).

Private insurance creates a highly effective competitive fringe. Even though only half of those who qualify actually opt out of the public system, the threat of the loss of its most profitable enrollees ensures that the service gap between the public and private systems does not grow. For example, as recently as the late 1990s, CT scanners were not covered by public insurance. In contrast, private insurance covered the service as part of routine diagnostics. Competitive pressure forces the public system to provide coverage. The overall result is faster adoption and increased use of medical innovation.

Membership in a sickness fund entitles a person to a comprehensive package of medical and dental benefits. Germans can expect to receive high-quality care that includes hospital care, ambulatory care, prescription drugs, dental care, disability income benefits, and even visits to health spas. The system is weak in several areas. In particular, public health services and psychiatric services are minimal.

The German health care system experienced the same problems as the rest of the developed world in controlling health care costs during the decades of the 1960s and 1970s. Economic recession in the mid-1970s forced government policy makers to address the issue of the growth in medical expenditures. In 1977, the first of over 40 health care acts was passed to control rising health care spending and avoid the financial collapse of the system. The stated goal was to limit the growth of health care expenditures to the growth of wages and salaries while maintaining open access to the system.

Health care spending grew more rapidly than GDP, and government initiated five major reforms during the 1990s to slow spending growth. The 2004 reform added copayments for physicians' visits and increased them for prescription drugs.

Copayments are still low by U.S. standards. The first office visit to a physician during a calendar quarter has a patient copay of €10 (approximately $12) with an annual cap on out-of-pocket spending of 2 percent of income. There are no copays for preventive care visits, including physicals, dental exams, and cancer screenings. Fees for prescription drugs are 10 percent of the drug's price and range from €5 to €10 based on package size. Hospital charges are about €10 per day for the first 28 days, and inpatient preventive and rehabilitative care is €10 per day. Copays for dental services are another matter, and many procedures have copays as high as 50–100 percent of the cost. Children and low-income individuals are exempt from most copays, and the chronically ill have an annual cap of 1 percent of income.

The strict division between ambulatory care and hospital care may explain Germany's success in controlling costs. A third care setting, integrated ambulatory specialist care (IASC) was created in 2012. This new approach to care delivery separates the specialized treatment of rare and severe diseases from traditional ambulatory care. Five rare diseases and four with severe trajectories are included in this new care model. An interdisciplinary team of clinicians from both the ambulatory and hospital sectors provides care. The IASC faces many challenges. Care delivery and cooperative care across settings are difficult due to information sharing across sectors (Stock, 2015).

---

[23]Low-income individuals are also exempted from paying into the health insurance fund. For individuals earning less than €5,400 per annum do not pay directly for their health insurance; employers pay 13 percent of their income.

Ambulatory care physicians are paid on a fee-for-service basis and, for the most part, are prohibited from treating patients in a hospital setting. Primary care physicians operate with over 100 separate quarterly budgets for categories ranging from office visits, laboratory tests, prescription drugs, referrals, and hospital admissions. No payments exceeding the budget are allowed with predictable results—GPs who exceed key budget limits close their practices until the next billing period. Hospital physicians are paid a salary and are not allowed to treat patients on an outpatient basis. The fees that physicians charge are determined through negotiations between the sickness funds and regional physicians' organizations.

Hospitals are paid under a dual financing scheme with operating expenses covered by the sickness funds and capital investments covered by the state. With the introduction of diagnosis-related groups (DRGs) into the hospital sector, the health authorities hope to reduce the average length of stay by 30 percent, now among the highest in Europe.[24]

More than 100,000 students attend one of the 29 medical schools run by the state. After completing the six-year curriculum, physicians must first practice in a hospital setting for six years before they are allowed to enter private practice. Approximately 9,500 graduate each year and enter hospital practice.

KEY CONCEPT 2
Opportunity Cost

By linking medical expenditures to the income of sickness fund members, the success of the policy depends upon the continued growth in wages and salaries and the success of the negotiations between sickness funds and medical practitioners. The cost-containment measures have resulted in a dramatic decrease in the relative salaries of primary care physicians, falling from 5.1 times the average for wage and salary workers in 1975 to 2.4 times that average by 2011. That same year, the average self-employed GP earned $176,000 and the average self-employed specialist earned $230,800. Hospital-based physicians earned an average income of $160,000 (OECD, 2016).

In 2012, there were over 2,000 general hospitals with 501,000 acute care beds. Hospitals also have less high-technology diagnostic, therapeutic, and surgical equipment than is available in the typical urban hospital in the United States. Germany has one-third the number of MRI units and less than half the number of CT scanners per million compared to the United States.

Although the negotiated fee schedule controls the unit price of medical care, it does nothing to limit the volume of services provided. Individual physicians can increase their income by treating more patients, but if every physician tries this strategy, global budget limits reduce unit fees proportionately. Thus, physicians who treat sickness fund patients never know in advance exactly how much they will be paid for a certain procedure. Physicians who treat privately insured patients may charge fees that are over two times higher than fees charged to sickness fund patients. As a result, privately insured patients tend to get better service. Privately insured patients receive better treatment (Jürges, 2009), spend more time with their physicians (Deveugele et al., 2002), and overall have better access to medical care (Lungen et al., 2008).

The ability of the system to control costs depends primarily on the relative bargaining power between sickness funds and medical providers. Because expenditures are determined by negotiations between these two groups, the recent success in controlling the growth in spending is the result of legislative reform that has shifted the relative bargaining strength to the sickness funds. Continued success depends on the willingness of physicians' organizations to accept the burden of the responsibility in controlling spending, which translates into falling relative incomes.

---

[24]By 2004, the new compulsory system contained over 600 DRGs.

Recent reform has introduced a warning system, a budget-capping mechanism that directly challenges the independence of physicians. Those physicians whose per-patient spending exceeds the average are subject to a medical practice review. Physicians who exceed the average spending by 5–15 percent must submit a letter of explanation. Those who exceed their budgets by 15–25 percent must convince a panel of physicians and sickness fund representatives that the spending was justified based on medical factors. Physicians exceeding their budgets by more than 25 percent are subject to fines in the form of reduced fees. About 7 percent of German physicians receive notice of overspending each year, and about half of those have their fees reduced. These fines amount to 100 percent of the amount in excess of 1.25 times their budgets.

The incentive structure created by the budget-capping mechanism has changed the way physicians relate to their patients. Anecdotal evidence indicates that physicians treat less-demanding patients less aggressively, which is cheaper, and that they use more expensive therapies and procedures that are not part of their budgets when less-expensive means are available that are part of their budgets. Studies also indicate that private patients are up to four times more likely to receive the newest drugs than are sickness fund patients (Green and Irvine, 2001).

Another problem with the system is its tendency to use resources inefficiently. Incentives promote the provision of invasive acute care procedures and discourage the provision of personal services. Based on the latest available OECD figures, Germans see their doctors more often, are provided more prescription drugs, have higher hospital admission rates, and stay in the hospital longer than citizens of the major developed countries in the OECD. The average length of stay in the hospital was 45 percent higher in Germany than in the United States in 2011 (7.7 days compared to 5.4 days). Excess capacity in terms of the number of hospital beds relative to the population exists in Germany, where there are 1.1 excess beds per 1,000 population, compared to 1.9 in Japan. Even with strict cost-containment measures for prescription drugs (reference pricing and budget limits), average drug prices are higher in Germany than in any other member country of the European Union.

What lessons can we learn from the German system of medical care delivery? First, a system that provides comprehensive coverage and mandates universal participation is expensive. Germans paid an average of 17.2 percent of their gross income in premiums and over 13.2 percent of total medical expenditures are unreimbursed out-of-pocket charges. Secondly, cost control in a government-run system is usually accomplished through a system of global budgets and caps on expenditures for physicians' services. Germany has managed to keep spending within targeted amounts by establishing an explicit trade-off between volume and price. In other words, when utilization is higher than anticipated, fees are lowered proportionately. Thirdly, spending caps instituted in 1985 as a temporary cost-containment measure have become permanent. Legislation adopted in 1993 and 1997, designed to increase competition among sickness funds, lowered pharmaceutical prices and physicians' fees, increased required copayments, and placed more regulations on hospital billing practices—all to reach desired spending targets. Even with all these changes, the system will be tested. The ruling Free Democratic Party faced a 2010 budget shortfall of €7.5 billion ($11.1 billion). Radical reform was initiated in 2009 when sickness funds were allowed to collect for the first time an annual flat-rate premium of €96 per person ($105 in 2015 and scheduled to increase in 2016). Another controversial change is to define a basic benefit package for sickness fund participants with a supplementary private option for additional benefits. For now, support for the system is mixed. Only 17 percent of those surveyed give the overall system a grade of A or B (Kleckley and Arnold, 2010), and almost 60 percent think that the system is in need of fundamental change or should be completely rebuilt (Schoen et al., 2013).

KEY CONCEPT 5
Markets and Pricing

POLICY ISSUE
How important is the private insurance safety valve in maintaining public support for a government-run health care system?

Japan: The Company Is People

One of the most notable accomplishments of Japanese postwar development has been the exceptionally good record of health and longevity of the population. Life expectancy at birth for both males and females ranks at the top of the industrialized countries (in 2013, 80.2 years for males and 86.6 years for females). Likewise, infant mortality rates are among the lowest of the countries charted by the OECD (2.2 in 2013). Undoubtedly, the medical care system has contributed to this record, but the extent of the contribution is hard to define.[25]

The Japanese enjoy an environment that is relatively free of crime, pollution, and other social problems such as divorce, teen pregnancy, obesity, drug use, and HIV. When compared to the United States, the Japanese have a much lower incidence of alcohol consumption, AIDS, drug abuse, teen pregnancy, and motor vehicle accidents.[26] The Japanese diet is relatively low in fat, resulting, at least partially, in an extremely low rate of cardiovascular disease (OECD, 2016).

Japan is a country of 127.1 million living on four major islands and 3,900 smaller islands. With most of the land mass—about the size of California—covered by mountains, the vast majority of the population is crowded into the urban areas. The population density is over 12 times that of the United States, making it the third most densely populated nation in the world, behind only Bangladesh and South Korea. Japan is divided into 47 prefectures with jurisdictional authority similar to that of states in the United States.

The medical care delivery system in Japan has evolved from the modernization efforts initiated during the Meiji Restoration dating from 1868. In the place of the primitive

---

ISSUES IN MEDICAL CARE DELIVERY

IN SEARCH OF THE PERFECT BELLY BUTTON

Japanese women are increasingly taking action to correct one of those tiny flaws of nature—the misshapen belly button. Japanese culture is belly button conscious. Japanese mothers save remnants of their baby's umbilical cords in a wooden box, much like American mothers save a lock of their newborn's hair. In Japan, a navel bent out of shape means much the same as a nose bent out of shape in America. Moreover, in Japan "your mother has an outie" is a slang expression that would translate in America as "yeah, right, give me a break."

Bare midriffs and body ornamentation require the fashion-conscious Japanese 20-something women to have the perfect belly button. Moreover, if nature did not provide one, then cosmetic surgery will. Plastic surgeons can turn an unattractive outie into a perfectly symmetrical fashion statement. Because it is not considered health care, the NHI does not cover the procedure.

Source: Norihiko Shirouzu, "Reconstruction Boom in Tokyo: Perfecting Imperfect Bellybuttons," *Wall Street Journal*, October 5, 1995, B1.

---

[25]If the health of a population is measured by disease incidence, then it is not nearly as evident whether the Japanese are healthier. Self-reported health status in surveys of Japanese citizens is among the lowest in OECD countries, with less than one-third reporting their perceived health as good. That same figure is over 88 percent in the United States (OECD, 2016).

[26]One major exception is the high percentage of the adult male population that uses tobacco products.

structure of the feudal system, the institutions and practices of the developed world were adopted. Because Germany had what many considered the most advanced medical care system at that time, it was used as the model. The formation of "mutual aid associations" in the early 1900s served as the foundation for the medical care system. Like Germany, the development of these associations among workers in Japan had as much to do with controlling a disruptive socialist movement as with promoting social welfare. The promotion and improvement of public health is a national responsibility according to the constitution. Even so, universal coverage was not fully realized until 1961.

The Ministry of Health and Welfare regulates the Universal Health Insurance system (known as *kaihoken*). The entire population is organized into over 3,500 small, independently administered health insurance societies that serve as intermediaries for its members. Individuals and their dependents are assigned with little choice to one of these organizations according to profession, trade, employer, place of residence, and age.

The Employee Health Insurance System (EHI) covers 51.5 percent of the population, divided between society-managed health insurance (SMHI) for large employers and government-managed health insurance (GMHI, sometimes called Japan Health Insurance Association) for small- and medium-sized firms. MAS provide insurance to national and local government workers and cover 8.6 percent of the population. Farmers, the self-employed, retirees, and the unemployed comprise 39.3 percent of the population and are covered through NHI. About one-fourth of NHI participants are retirees over the age of 75 covered by a separate insurance fund (Health Insurance for the Old-Old). Since 1947, over 60 laws have been passed to define the principles and policies of the national health care system. Because each plan was developed separately, they lack uniformity in terms of premiums paid and cost-sharing arrangements (Tajika and Kikuchi, 2012).

An 8.2 percent payroll tax funds GMHI premiums, divided between employer and employee.[27] GMHI premiums vary from 3 to 10 percent of income, averaging 7.4 percent. NHI enrollees are charged fixed premiums due to the monthly variation in income for many enrollees. Copayments in all plans vary between 10 and 30 percent and are capped at $800 per month for the average family.

For 10.2 percent of GDP, the Japanese receive a comprehensive package of benefits for virtually every legal resident. Medical procedures that are not associated with the onset of a disease are not included in the basic insurance package. Virtually all preventive care, physical examinations, and procedures related to normal pregnancies are not covered by NHI. In fact, out-of-pocket spending for these services is not even counted as part of national health expenditures.[28]

Private insurance plays a relatively small role in financing Japanese medical care, covering only 3.2 percent of total expenditures. Even with high copays that would seem to open up the possibility of a robust complementary private insurance market, by far the dominant type of private insurance policy is the disease-specific policy, cancer insurance in this case. Coverage is not indemnity style but pays a fixed amount, typically per diem if the enrollee is hospitalized.

Medical services are provided on a fee-for-service basis using a national fee schedule that is revised biannually. This negotiated schedule provides uniform pricing regardless of specialty of physician and service setting, and thus it offers few financial incentives to improve quality. Clinic-based physicians receive payments directly. Hospital-based physicians receive a salary.

---

[27]The employer share ranges from 50 percent to 80 percent and averages 56 percent.
[28]National expenditure data also exclude expenses for physical exams, vaccinations, prescription eyeglasses, prosthetic devices, and treatment by alternative providers such as acupuncturists. Items such as spending on public health and medical research are not classified as medical expenditures.

Inpatient reimbursement uses a diagnosis-procedure combination. Hospitals are paid a fixed amount based on diagnosis and a per diem based on length of stay. Capital funding for hospital infrastructure must come from fee revenues. The Medical Care Law, amended in 1985, restricted the establishment of private hospitals and placed a ceiling on the number of hospital beds per region, making it virtually impossible to build new hospitals in urban areas (Yoshikawa, Shirouzu, and Holt, 1991). Even prestigious hospitals in urban areas, including Tokyo, are marked by poor infrastructure, small rooms, and few support staff.

The number of clinic-based physicians has been falling for the past 30 years, and thus their political influence is waning. In 1960, they comprised 45 percent of the total number of physicians. By 1988, this percentage had fallen to 30. There are several reasons for this decline. Land prices in urban areas have priced most newcomers out of the market, and the demand for high-tech diagnostic equipment has allowed the large hospitals to siphon off much of this market share. The slowly increasing average age of clinic-based physicians has been a factor, and a growing use of outpatient facilities has increased the use of large hospitals over clinics.

In 2005, physicians earned on average $55,000 (adjusted for purchasing power parity), less than two times the income of the average wage and salary worker in Japan and only one-fourth that of U.S. physicians (www.worldsalaries.org). Clinic-based physicians earn on average about twice the income of hospital-based physicians. Physicians working in the nation's 8,500 hospitals are paid the same regardless of specialty. Waiting times are significant at the best hospitals. Many avoid them by offering "expressions of gratitude" to secure more timely services. It is common for patients to provide gifts ranging from $1,000 to $3,000 to obtain the services of a prominent specialist. These hidden charges are not officially recorded and go largely untaxed (Tanner, 2008).[29]

The typical Japanese citizen has an extreme aversion to invasive treatment. They prefer medication and bed rest to surgery. Thus, surgical rates are among the lowest in the world, one-third the U.S. rates and prescription drug use among the highest, over 20 percent of health care spending. In fact, one of the most lucrative aspects of the clinic-based practice is the sale of prescription medicine. Approximately 40 percent of all drugs are dispensed directly by physicians. Despite the popularity of prescription drug usage, the introduction of newly developed drugs takes two to three times longer in Japan as compared to the rest of the OECD (Esmail, 2013).

The point-fee system introduces a bias in the medical care delivery system, one that favors primary care. All physicians, regardless of specialty, practice like GPs: They focus on diagnostic and pharmaceutical services at the expense of technical and specialty care. Thus, no formal system of referral to specialists has emerged. Financial incentives encourage physicians to be protective of their patient volume, and expensive treatment areas tend to be ignored. Cancer treatment, neonatal pediatrics, and emergency/trauma medicine are specialties found only in the 80 tertiary care hospitals across the country (primarily teaching hospitals), called specialty function hospitals.

Direct comparison between health care spending in Japan and the United States is difficult for reasons already mentioned. Maternity expenses, the direct cost of medical education and research, grants to public hospitals, and public health promotions—all included in the United States figure—are ignored by the Japanese. Including these alone would

POLICY ISSUE

What role does culture play in the development of a national health care delivery system?

KEY CONCEPT 2

Opportunity Cost

---

[29]Interestingly enough, over half of the income of physicians is tax-free in the first place. Until recently, 72 percent of a physician's income was free from income taxes. Changes in the tax code have reduced the preferential status, so that only 52–72 percent of a physician's income escapes taxation.

increase Japanese spending by 1.5 percent of GDP. In addition, private room charges add about $100 per day to a hospital stay that already averages almost 18 days.[30]

Patients have unlimited access to primary care physicians and specialists. Japanese physicians tend to overdiagnose and overmedicate, and patient volume tends to be high. It is common for clinic-based physicians to see 30 patients an hour. Consultations per physician average over 5,600 per year, about three times the OECD average (McKinsey and Company, 2008). By U.S. standards, the total time physicians spend with patients is low. Two-thirds of the patients spend less than 10 minutes with their physicians and one in five spend less than 3 minutes. Appointments are almost nonexistent. Physicians see patients on a first-come-first-served basis. Long waits are common, with queues for ambulatory visits and waiting lists for hospitalization.

The most significant long-term problem facing the Japanese system lies in the demographics of the population, most notably the percentage elderly. Japan has the highest percentage elderly of the OECD countries with 25 percent of the population over age 65.

BACK-OF-THE-ENVELOPE
Promoting Equality

The rationale behind the public provision of medical care is easy to explain. Market failure results in a level of care that is less than optimal. Two approaches have been used with varying degrees of success to promote more equal sharing of scarce medical care resources: subsidize and ration. Subsidies for the poor increase the amount of care they receive, and rationing reduces the amount of care provided to everyone else. Both policies promote a more equal distribution of medical care consumption. Why would a group of high-income consumers agree to limit their own access to care in the name of promoting equality? Lindsay (1969) provided a theoretical justification for the simultaneous use of rationing and subsidies to promote equality in medical care consumption.

In the diagram, D_1 and D_2 represent the respective demand curves for two different segments of the population. Group 1 has less income and a lower level of demand, D_1. Assuming a perfectly elastic supply, S, they will consume Q_1 units of medical care. Those with higher incomes have a higher level of demand, D_2, and consume Q_2 units of medical care. Countries such as Great Britain and Canada have chosen to address the inequality $Q_2 - Q_1$ by providing universal coverage through taxation and subsidy and by placing limits on the availability of certain procedures.

The cost of these policies is shown in the right-hand side of the diagram. The cost of producing equality via rationing is the consumer surplus forgone by the higher income group. The vertical distance between D_2 and S represents the forgone consumer surplus. Thus, the marginal cost of promoting equality through rationing, MC_R, has a slope equal to the absolute value of the slope of D_2. Every unit of care given up by Group 2 creates a unit of equality at a marginal cost equal to the forgone consumer surplus of Group 2.

To induce the poor to consume more than Q_1 requires a subsidy. This subsidy can never be greater than P_1, the cost of care, but must be at least equal to the difference between the value of care as perceived by members of the group, represented by D_1, and the price of care, P_1. The slope of MC_S will be less than the slope of MC_R, because D_1 is more elastic than D_2. The marginal cost of promoting equality through a subsidy rises to point A and then becomes the horizontal line at P_1.

---

[30]This figure includes both chronic and acute care hospital stays. It does not include stays in TB hospitals that average 207 days or stays in psychiatric hospitals that average 536 days.

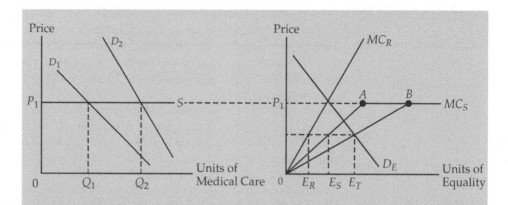

Using a combination of rationing and subsidies, more equality may be purchased at a lower overall cost. The combined marginal cost curve, *OB*, is the horizontal sum of *MC_R* and *OA*. Assuming *D_E* is the demand for equality in this case, a level of equality equal to *E_T* may be purchased using this combined strategy, *E_R* due to rationing, and *E_s* due to the subsidy. Purchasing *E_T* equality using rationing or subsidies alone would require significantly higher spending. Countries that have a well-specified demand for equality can achieve desired levels at a lower overall cost by using a combination of subsidies for the poor and limited availability of certain procedures to everyone.

Source: Cotton M. Lindsay, "Medical Care and the Economics of Sharing," *Economica* 36(144), November 1969, 351–362.

Caused by a low fertility rate, the population is expected to shrink further to around 92 million by 2055 when the proportion over 65 will top 40 percent.

Providing social services for this segment will be a growing concern. Right now everyone over 40 years of age must purchase compulsory long-term-care insurance (Kaigo Hoken), paying premiums of 1–2 percent of income. The insurance itself is quite generous and almost 20 percent of the elderly are eligible for long-term-care services.

The Japanese system of health care delivery is reflective of the basic approach business firms have toward their employees: "The Company is people." Coverage is compulsory, and participation is mandatory. The success of the system lies in its ability to control costs and to provide universal access. Criticism may be targeted at the issue of quality, which is to be expected. Service distortions usually accompany fixed fee schedules. In this regard, Japan is not immune. However, with its emphasis on equality and community, the health care system has served the Japanese well.

Switzerland: Individual Responsibility in a Federalist Framework[31]

Switzerland is divided into 26 political entities, called *cantons* and *demi-cantons*, which are sovereign in all matters not directly granted to the federal government by the constitution. Most of Switzerland's 8.1 million citizens live in the Swiss Plateau, the narrow region between the two mountain ranges that dominate the landscape, the Jura in the north and the Alps in the south. From its inception in 1911, the Swiss health insurance model has avoided the link between health insurance coverage and employment and has relied

---

[31]This section draws heavily from Grinols and Henderson (2009).

instead on personal responsibility. Insurance is sold on an individual basis; group and family plans do not exist.

The Swiss spend a lot on medical care. Second only to the United States, health care spending amounted to 11.1 percent of GDP and $6,325 per capita in 2013. The generous supply of medical resources provides unprecedented access to medical services. Whether measured in terms of physicians per 1,000, acute care bed density, or access to medical technology, resource supply is among the highest in Europe.

Permanent residents of Switzerland are subject to an individual mandate to purchase compulsory health insurance. Refusal to do so results in forcible assignment to a health insurance plan. Compulsory insurance covers a generous package of medical benefits, including inpatient and outpatient hospital care, unlimited hospital stays, and complementary and alternative medicine. Despite the generosity of the basic package, over 30 percent of the Swiss pay risk-rated premiums to purchase a supplementary policy, ensuring free choice of physician and private hospital rooms. Almost twice that number have policies covering medical services for those traveling abroad, dental services, and prescription drugs that are not covered under compulsory insurance. Complementary private insurance that covers deductibles and coinsurance is not permitted.

Sixty-seven private insurers operating on a not-for-profit basis provide compulsory insurance. Insurance funds have established a prospective risk-adjustment mechanism that subsidizes funds that have disproportionately higher costs due to adverse selection. The subsidies, calculated prospectively, are based on a fund's deviation from expected cost across 15 age brackets and 2 sex categories. An individual's health status (defined as a history of hospitalization exceeding three days) was added as an adjuster in 2012.

Physician fees are based on a uniform nationwide RVS. Negotiations between physician groups and health insurance associations within each canton determine the monetary conversion factor applied to the RVS. Physicians are paid on a fee-for-service basis and are not allowed to charge more than the negotiated fee. In over one-half of the cantons, physicians have freedom of prescription. These dispensing physicians are able to supplement their incomes by approximately one-third.

Cantons finance approximately 80 percent of all hospital investment and half of all hospital operating expenses directly through taxation. As of 2012, hospitals are paid on a DRG-based system, providing hospitals with a payment per patient based on the prospective costs of treatment.

Individuals pay age-rated premiums within a canton. There are three age brackets: 0–18, 19–25, and 26 and over. Approximately 40 percent of all households (one-third of the population) receive means-tested subsidies when premiums exceed 8–10 percent of their total income. Those earning less than 9,020 CHF ($9,335 USD) do not pay premiums. Approximately 25 percent of private health insurance premiums are paid with government funds (Esmail, 2013).

Individuals choosing the most popular health plan pay a deductible of 300 CHF ($310 USD) for the standard policy. Other plans have higher deductibles, ranging from 1,000 CHF ($1,035) up to 2,500 CHF ($2,588 USD). Policies also include coinsurance provisions of 10 percent for spending over the deductible, with an annual cap on out-of-pocket spending of 700 CHF ($725 USD). As the deductible increases, consumers receive premium discounts off the standard policy, up to 70 percent of the difference in the deductibles. In 2011, the median annual premium ranged from 3,591 CHF ($3,717 USD) in Appenzell Innerhoden to 6,070 CHF ($6,282 USD) in Basel-Stadt. Children under age 18 and students under age 25 paid lower premiums. Though the standard low-deductible plan is the most popular (35 percent of the population), the majority of the population has chosen either the higher deductibles (28 percent) or one of the managed care plans (37 percent) offered (Cheng, 2010; Herzlinger and Parsa-Parsi, 2004).

Two types of managed care plans are available to Swiss consumers: one is a plan similar to the staff-model health maintenance organization; the other is a plan based on a GP network. The second type of plan utilizes a GP-gatekeeper model in a risk-sharing arrangement between physicians and insurers. Surpluses and deficits are shared equally with an annual cap on losses absorbed by physicians of 10,000 CHF ($10,960 USD).

Three markets exist in Swiss health care: physicians compete for patients; insurers compete for customers; and, because of selective contracting, insurers compete for primary care physicians. In spite of the competitive rhetoric in the Revised Health Insurance Law, the reality of competition has fallen short of the promise. Physicians have virtually no latitude in the fees they charge or the services they provide. Competition among insurers is almost nonexistent. The generous nature of the compulsory benefits package allows little competition based on benefits offered. In fact, the appeal of supplementary insurance has been shrinking because of the expansion of the basic benefits package.

★ **KEY CONCEPT 7**
Competition

Competition among insurers is based on premiums charged and not benefits offered. The only exception to this rule is the ability to offer managed care plans that restrict access to certain providers. Enrollees are aware of the full cost of their insurance because they purchase their policies individually.

There is some empirical evidence that high-deductible plans enroll a disproportionate number of healthy individuals. In 1999, high-deductible plans transferred an average of $540 per enrollee to low-deductible plans, which in turn received an average of $175 per enrollee (Roy, 2012).

The Swiss system is a reasonable alternative to the government-run insurance plans available in most of Europe. There is an individual mandate to purchase a private insurance policy with a minimum benefits package defined by the government. Insurance coverage is automatically issued at birth and is guaranteed renewable, covering all preexisting conditions. Individuals 25 years and older pay community-rated premiums. Those individuals who want additional coverage are allowed to spend their own money to buy supplementary policies. All Swiss residents except the most destitute and incapable are expected to contribute something toward the purchase of their insurance, usually 8–10 percent of their income. Those who cannot afford to purchase a policy receive subsidies. With its heavy reliance on private payers, the Swiss system is worth careful consideration as a model for U.S. reform.

United Kingdom: National Health Service

HTTP://

The U.K. Department of Health website, with links to the NHS Executive home page, provides various information.
http://www.dh.gov.uk.

The British National Health Service (NHS) stands as a symbol of social equality and collective compassion. The Health Authorities Act of 1995 created approximately 100 Unitary Health Authorities, each serving the medical needs of about 500,000 people. With an overall budget of approximately £110 billion ($150 billion), and 1.7 million employees, the NHS is the fifth largest employer in the world.

The origins of the national health care system can be traced back to the early nineteenth century. As was the case throughout much of Europe, labor unions and other fraternal associations provided health insurance to their members. Employers encouraged their workers to join these MAS to reduce public demand for charity care.

In 1911, under the leadership of Prime Minister Lloyd George, the British Parliament passed the first National Health Insurance Act, strengthening the voluntary insurance program and providing a funding mechanism for indigent care. Although membership in a mutual aid society was not mandatory, most workers joined. Health benefits included prescription drugs and the services of a GP. Specialty care and hospitalization were not covered under the law but were provided through local government support and charity care.

The Second World War brought profound changes in the political and social attitudes toward health care in Britain. Before the end of the war, Prime Minister Winston Churchill appointed Sir William Beveridge to study the delivery of health care and make recommendations for change. The Beveridge Report of 1942 outlined a comprehensive NHI plan that would extend coverage to everyone regardless of income level. Passage of the National Health Service Act in 1948 meant that the entire population was covered under one plan that provided a comprehensive package of benefits paid out of general tax revenues, free to patients at the point of use.

The single-payer concept and limited supervision of providers kept the administrative costs of the system low, but from the beginning, the NHS was underfunded and dominated by the medical community. Budgetary constraints, especially during years of slow economic growth, politicized health care delivery and led to a series of crises, about once every three years, between government policy makers and medical practitioners. Health care reform is a regular feature of the NHS. Twelve initiatives in 26 years have been enacted, the most recent one the Five Year Forward View was implemented in 2014.

The NHS inherited a geographic distribution of resources that favored the metropolitan areas in and around London. One of the stated goals of the newly formed system was to eliminate the inequalities that existed. Targets were established to increase the availability of facilities in underserved regions and restrict the expansion of facilities in over served regions. These changes have met limited success.

Every citizen is registered with a GP and receives all primary and preventive care in this setting. The 50,000 active GPs serve as family doctors for the patient and gatekeepers to the system of specialists, or "consultants," and hospitals. Any patient that requires extensive testing or specialized treatment is referred to a specialist or is admitted directly into a hospital.

Standard practice in Britain has been to place anyone requiring an "elective" procedure on a waiting list. Procedures such as cataract surgery, hip replacement, coronary artery bypass, and breast reconstruction following a mastectomy are defined as elective procedures. In other words, if it is not life threatening, it can wait. In 2014 hospital wait lists soared to over 2.99 million, over five percent of the population. The target wait time from referral to consultant until medical treatment is 18 weeks; still over 10 percent wait more than six months. By 2013, the median wait time for hospital admission for non-emergency services reached nine weeks. In the event that any patient waits more than 52 weeks, the hospital trust must pay a mandatory fine of £5,000 ($6,500). Still 50,000 Brits travel abroad every year and spend $250 million of their own money to receive care instead of waiting.

Largely because of the waiting lists for "elective" surgery, those who can afford private supplementary health insurance have purchased it. About 12 percent of the population has private insurance coverage, concentrated among those in the professional and managerial occupations, high-income earners, and those living in London and the southeast. The majority of workers with annual earning over £50,000 purchase private health insurance. Over two-thirds of those have risk-rated group policies provided through their employers. Premiums are paid out of pretax income, and any benefit is subject to an income tax and a 5 percent premium tax. Largely, patients with private insurance still use the NHS for emergency and chronic care. The private system deals largely with quality-of-life issues such as hernia repair, gallbladder disease, and hip replacements. About 20 percent of all non-emergency surgeries are paid for privately. Thus, the private system serves as a safety valve for wait-listed patients. Critics of the private system argue that it has two main flaws: It takes the pressure off the national system, slowing improvements; and it creates a two-tiered system, undermining the perception of equality.

In 2012, the mean net earnings of self-employed GPs averaged $146,700 or 3.22 times the average wage. The pay for hospital-based physicians averaged $112,000 (OECD, 2016).

The NHS inherited nearly 3,000 hospitals at its inception. Today, the system has undergone a complete reorganization resulting in far fewer hospitals. The number of acute care hospital beds has declined markedly since the inception of the NHS, from 480,000 in 1948 to less than 146,000 in 2013. The most recent OECD figures place acute care occupancy rates at 84.3 percent for all hospitals (OECD, 2016).

The paternalistic tradition of the NHS is evident in this method of resource allocation. It is a system that is largely invisible and uniquely British. Not only are patients in the United Kingdom among the least informed in the developed world, the culture tends to leave medical decisions to the individual physician and seldom questions the medical authorities. Physicians are considered the sole authority on determining patient needs and have no real pressure to respond to patient desires, so rationing may be disguised as a clinical decision. Patient engagement in the care process is not encouraged.

The Margaret Thatcher reforms of 1993 created an internal market and GP fundholders, adding choice and competition to a system in which little of either existed. Money did not follow patients due to weak incentives, particularly in the hospital sector. As a result, competition failed to bring about the desired results. Without the ability to keep surpluses, hospital administrators sought bigger budgets. Because it was politically impossible to close a failed hospital, there was little incentive to provide services efficiently.

To be providers of health services, health organizations became NHS trusts, independent organizations competing for patients. At the same time, many GPs became fundholders with their own budgets. By 1995 all health care was provided through NHS trusts, a significant cultural shift even for the British. GPs who did not become fundholders had their budgets centrally controlled by the NHS. Patients who received treatment from fundholders often received better treatment, a source of complaints among the rest of the patient population. A two-tiered system was quickly developing.

A new government came into power with a pledge to get rid of the internal market. As a result, the NHS was reorganized in 1997 for the fifth time in 25 years. The Tony Blair reforms, based on a "third way" of running the NHS, changed GP fundholding by placing 30,000 GPs in one of 500 primary care trusts (PCTs). Each PCT receives a fully capitated budget and is responsible for providing primary care, community health services, and virtually all other medical services for a geographically defined population of 50,000–250,000. The emphasis was no longer on a market model based on choice and competition but on a government-run system based on collaboration and cooperation. Secondary care is provided through approximately 200 NHS hospital trusts, 400 small-scale community hospitals, and specialized tertiary care hospitals. In addition, PCTs are able to contract with approximately 230 private hospitals, most in one of five for-profit chains.

A major aspect of the new NHS was a 10-year plan promising more hospitals, more physicians, cleaner facilities, increased standards, and shorter waiting times. Recognizing that the biggest problem facing the NHS has always been underfunding, the NHS budget was scheduled to increase by half in nominal terms and over one-third in real terms between March 2000 and the end of 2005. Such an increase called for an average annual growth rate in NHS spending of 6.3 percent.

POLICY ISSUE

What is the appropriate role of cost-effectiveness analysis in determining the availability of medical treatment?

These reforms also created the National Institute for Health and Clinical Excellence (NICE), a special health authority accountable to the secretary of state for health. NICE was established to determine the availability of treatments, technology, and services based on cost-effectiveness analysis. Under NICE guidelines, some treatments may be available to segments of the population with certain indicators but unavailable to others. For example, expensive drug treatment for Alzheimer's patients may be available for those who score over a certain cutoff on cognitive tests but unavailable to those who score below the cutoff.

Health inequalities within the British system have widened since the inception of the NHS. Mortality rates are three times higher among unskilled workers than professionals and upper managerial staff. Prior to the NHS unskilled workers had a 20 percent higher mortality rate at any given age than professional and managerial workers. By the early 1990s, the risk of death for the unskilled worker was 2.9 times higher, and since then the gap has widened further. Life expectancy is higher for professional and managerial groups than the unskilled. Limitations from long-standing illnesses are also substantially lower for those in the higher socioeconomic class (House of Commons Health Committee, 2009).

Despite public sentiment that sees the urgent need for reform, the system continues to have strong support. Proponents point to a strong primary care system provided to everyone without regard to ability to pay. Even though 60 percent of those surveyed believe that the quality of care would be improved if individuals could spend their own money for rationed services, the public still supports equal access over personal quality of care by a two-to-one margin (Disney et al., 2004).

In 2010, a Tory-led coalition government announced its plan to reform the NHS a sixth time. "Equity in Excellence: Liberating the NHS" set out a five-year plan to completely rebuild the administrative structure of the NHS. Phasing out all strategic health authorities and PCTs by 2013, the plan set aside £80 billion ($100 billion) for primary care. The money will go straight to GP consortia, newly created GP groups designed to coordinate the purchase of care in much the same way that HMOs do in the United States. Patients will have free choice of provider in a more patient-centered approach where funding follows patients.

The plan is short on details and its implementation will require extensive legislation. The new government runs the risk of creating a tax-funded system where a relatively small number of GP consortia control one-half of the NHS budget. A similar reform in the Netherlands has resulted in a system where four health plans insure 90 percent of the population. With critical health care administration skills in relatively short supply in the United Kingdom, rather than bringing the decision-making process closer to patients, the new plan could do just the opposite.

ISSUES IN MEDICAL CARE DELIVERY

PHYSICIAN SUPPLY UNDER THE NATIONAL HEALTH SYSTEM

In labor markets where wages are determined by the market, employment levels are determined by the market-clearing wage in the short run and by expected lifetime earnings in the long run. This situation exists in the U.S. health care industry today and existed in Britain before 1948, the year the industry was nationalized.

Before National Health, British physicians were self-employed and earned over four times the income of manual workers. Today, they are employees of the government and earn less than two times the average wage. The resultant effect on physicians' supply has been remarkable. The aggregate physicians' supply curve fits that of the standard economic model—upward sloping. As the real wage spiraled downward, net emigration of trained British physicians increased, and by the early 1970s, one-third of all NHS hospital staff was foreign born and trained overseas, primarily in former Commonwealth countries. Without this infusion of foreign-trained physicians, there would be a serious shortage of trained medical practitioners in the NHS.

KEY CONCEPT 2
Opportunity Cost

The lessons are clear. The fees charged by physicians serve as market-clearing prices in the short run. Over time, physician supply will adjust to those levels based on the expected lifetime earnings potential. When the government controls the price at comparatively low levels, physicians will seek better opportunities elsewhere. To fill the gaps left by the outflow of trained physicians, the system will attract alternatives to domestically trained physicians. The foreign-trained physicians who immigrate do so because they consider the employment opportunities offered in the controlled environment superior to those in their home countries. Since 1991 almost one-fourth of all NHS consultants graduated from medical school outside the United Kingdom, and by 2002 over half of all new physicians were trained in countries outside the European Union; in 2003 the proportion was over two-thirds.

Source: Cotton M. Lindsay, *National Health Issues: The British Experience*, Nutley, NJ: Roche Laboratories, 1980.

☆ KEY CONCEPT 2
Opportunity Cost

☆ KEY CONCEPT 1
Scarcity and Choice

☆ POLICY ISSUE
What is the best way to ensure access to high-quality medical care while controlling cost at the same time? Or is it even possible to think in those terms?

ISSUES IN MEDICAL CARE DELIVERY

A MATTER OF LIFE AND DEATH

Baby boomers and their parents will remember the 1950s game show *Queen for a Day*, in which three women would tell their hard-luck stories to a studio audience. The one who received the most audience support would be crowned "Queen for a Day" and would receive a new washing machine, refrigerator, or suite of furniture. The tears would flow as the crown was put into place and the royal robes draped over the new queen's shoulders.

That was America in the 1950s. A similar game show made its way onto Dutch television in the 1990s, except this time, it was not a matter of a new washing machine or a remodeled kitchen, it was a matter of a new kidney. The show's viewers witnessed a reality-based drama of patients competing for this scarce medical resource. The show, called *The Big Donor Show*, pitted three patients in need of life-saving kidney transplant against one another. The one who received the support of the audience received the kidney. The losers remained on the waiting list. Over 1.2 million viewed the show and 23,000 voted via text message. Condemned for being in poor taste, the producers of the show justified the broadcast as an attempt to focus on the consequences of the donor shortage. Every system must make decisions on the allocation of scarce medical resources. The Dutch system simply chose a most unusual way to pick winners and losers.

Source: Inez de Beaufort and Frans Meulenberg, "The Dangers of Triage by Television," *BMJ* 334(7605), June 7, 2007, 1194–1195.

Summary and Conclusions

As we have learned, private health insurance systems operate under three guiding principles: the insurance principle, whereby premiums are risk-rated; the equivalence principle, whereby the premiums paid determine the level of coverage; and the principle of personal responsibility, whereby individuals are responsible for their own health and premiums reflect lifestyle choices. In contrast, social insurance systems operate under a different set of principles: the principle of self-administration, whereby payers and providers operate as independent entities with their rights and responsibilities determined by law; the principle of social partnership, with costs shared by members of society, typically employers and employees; and the principle of social solidarity, whereby income determines premiums.

As U.S. policy makers take the first steps in reforming the U.S. health care systems, it is important to recognize that no other country has actually solved the health care spending problem. Countries using the social insurance model have systems that deliver high-quality medical care to everyone with few financial barriers. Even though these systems meet the goal of universal access, they are not able to solve the overall spending problem. While no single health care system offers a universally applicable model, we can use their successes and failures as a guide for our own reform plans.

NHI does not guarantee public satisfaction with the system. Deloitte's 2010 Global Survey of Health Care Consumers (Kleckley and Arnold, 2010) reported an interesting dichotomy among survey respondents. In every country, the overall performance of the health care system received a less positive response than the individual's level of satisfaction with the most recent hospital stay and primary physician experience would imply. Interestingly, respondents in the two countries with an emphasis on privately provided insurance, Switzerland and the United States, have relatively higher ratings of their own health and have the highest level of confidence in the adequacy of their own insurance.

It is important to note that the European sense of reform may be quite different from that of Americans. In the European countries surveyed substantially more people feel that equal access for everyone is more important than the quality of care for the individual (Disney et al., 2004).

In a 2009 survey of OECD countries Gallup reported (see Table 14.6) that universal access does not always translate into higher levels of satisfaction. In most cases, 80–88 percent of residents are satisfied with the availability of quality health care in their countries. Only Switzerland (92 percent) and Japan (64 percent) fall outside that range. For the most part individuals are satisfied with their own health care, regardless of the level of public financing.

In contrast, confidence in the system varies considerably—from over 80 percent in Switzerland and France to levels in the mid-50 percent range in Germany, Japan, and the United States. In many countries people are happy with the quality of their own health care but a bit uneasy about the stability of the system overall.

A great deal of the public anxiety over the health care system has to do with high cost, continued access, and coverage gaps. Financial barriers to access can be eliminated, but that does not guarantee that social disparities will disappear. Universal access has done

TABLE 14.6 PUBLIC SATISFACTION WITH HEALTH CARE DELIVERY SYSTEM (IN PERCENTAGES)

	Canada	France	Germany	Japan	Switzerland	United Kingdom	United States
Satisfied with availability of quality health care	70	83	88	64	92	85	81
Satisfied with personal health care	85	85	82	68	89	85	83
Confident in national health care system	73	83	54	57	86	73	56

Source: Gallup (2009).

little to eliminate the inequalities across social classes in countries that use the social insurance model. Per capita consumption varies as much as 50 percent across income levels and as much as 100 percent between occupational categories.

Proponents of the social insurance model argue that equal access will improve health outcomes, especially for the low-income, indigent population. Opponents point out that nationalized systems do not eliminate or even substantially reduce health differences among population subgroups. Infant mortality rates and life expectancies vary considerably across socioeconomic categories. For example, England's lowest socioeconomic group has infant mortality rates that are double those of the highest socioeconomic group, a difference that has persisted since the inception of the NHS.[32] It is no different in the United States, where infant mortality rates for African Americans are roughly three to four times those of the white population.

Policy makers have a growing awareness of their inability to control utilization and thus spending, when providers are paid on a fee-for-service basis with no spending caps. However, supply-side constraints cannot control costs unless price controls and fixed budgets apply across the entire system. This inability to control expenditures for physicians' services and private hospitals leads to the extension of budget controls in these two areas. The health systems examined in this chapter all work reasonably well. Nevertheless, each has its safety valve: Canada has the United States, Britain and Germany have their private insurance sectors, Japan has its system of "gifts of appreciation" to ensure quality care, and France has, for now, maintained its commitment to the principle of "liberty" in the private sector.

The lessons are clear. There are (at least) 10 things we can learn from the preceding discussion.

1. Uncontrolled health care spending growth is a universal problem.
2. Universal access to high-quality medical care is possible without strict reliance on a single-payer system or a pure public sector approach.
3. Price-conscious behavior, with the use of deductibles and copays, can be encouraged with little impact on health.
4. Free access to health care with no out-of-pocket requirements diminishes personal responsibility, leaving no demand-side constraints often resulting in limited availability of technology and waiting lists for services.
5. People who cannot afford to purchase health insurance on their own can still have access to essential services within a system of subsidized premiums.
6. Health status and spending are closely linked to income, occupation, education, and race.
7. Universal access in a government-run system does not guarantee public satisfaction.
8. Mandatory GP gatekeeping results in waiting lists for specialized services.
9. The private sector option promotes a competitive environment and serves as a safety valve to compensate for excess demand for medical services.
10. The egalitarian culture found abroad may not easily transfer to the United States.

---

[32]Even in Scandinavia, with its relatively homogeneous population, age-standardized mortality rates vary significantly across occupational categories. Certain low-income occupations, such as restaurant workers, have mortality rates that are twice as high as some high-income occupations, such as school teachers.

⭐ **KEY CONCEPT 2**
Opportunity Cost

⭐ **KEY CONCEPT 1**
Scarcity and Choice

⭐ **POLICY ISSUE**
*What is the best way
to ensure access to
high-quality medical care
while controlling cost at
the same time? Or is it
even possible to think in
those terms?*

PROFILE   Anthony J. Culyer

Desiring to "bring intellectual cohesion to the field," Tony Culyer has spent his professional career applying economic theory to the study of social problems, particularly those associated with health care. Born in Croydon, England, Culyer spent his early years in London during the Blitz. Moving frequently as a youth, his family finally settled in Worcester when he was a teenager. He attended Exeter University and graduated with a major in economics in 1964. After spending a year at the University of California at Los Angeles as a graduate student and teaching assistant, he returned to Exeter as a tutor and lecturer. In 1969, he moved to the University of York, where he became deputy vice-chancellor and professor and head of the Department of Economics and Related Studies.

The year 1971 marked the beginning of a steady stream of contributions by Culyer to the field of health economics. Nine journal articles that year, including "The Nature of the Commodity 'Health Care' and Its Efficient Location" published in *Oxford Economic Papers* and "Medical Care and the Economics of Giving" published in *Economica*, quickly established Culyer as a major figure in health economics, not only in England but worldwide. Since that time, we can credit him with hundreds of published articles, books, and monographs in some of the leading medical and economics journals around the world. Since becoming involved in academic administration, Culyer's research output has slowed from its previous breakneck pace, but he remains productive.

In addition to a strong research agenda, Culyer has played an important public policy role, most recently in the redesign of the entire system of public funding of research and development in Britain's National Health System. As a consultant to the WHO, the Office of Economic Cooperation and Development, and government agencies in Britain, Canada, and New Zealand, his influence in public policy making is evidenced worldwide. As a teacher and mentor, Culyer has played a significant role in shaping the way a generation of British economists thinks about designing health care systems. Recognized for his work in the field of health economics, Culyer was awarded an honorary doctorate from the Stockholm School of Economics in 1999. That same year Queen Elizabeth II, in appreciation for his outstanding contribution to education, appointed him Commander of the British Empire. In 2015 he was awarded the William B. Graham Prize for Health Services Research by the Association of University Programs in Health Administration for his lasting impact on economic thinking in health care.

Culyer considers church music his "private passion." His interest in the organ dates back to his teenage years at the King's School in Worcester. In addition to his position as organist in the rural Anglican parish church he attends, Culyer also leads the choir and serves as the local chair of the Royal School of Church Music.

Keenly aware of the importance of sound analytical reasoning in the public policy arena, Culyer has spent his professional lifetime trying to expunge ad hoc reasoning and political ideology from social policy making. His heavy involvement in government planning has provided him with a sound understanding of social systems and human nature. Lasting change does not come from a top-down mechanism but rather it is driven from the bottom up.

Source: Curriculum vitae and personal correspondence.

Questions and Problems

1. Suggest several reasons why health care spending is higher in the United States than in other countries.

2. The fact that the United States spends more per capita on medical care than any other developed country is evidence of the failure of the U.S. system. Comment.

3. Some view health care systems of other developed countries as reasonable models for the reform of the U.S. health care system. Choose one of the systems discussed in this chapter and describe it in some detail. Provide reasons why you consider it workable or unworkable in the United States.

4. It takes a 13.4 percent payroll tax in Germany to finance a system that in 1993 consumed 10.6 percent of the nation's economic output. If the United States used this as a model, would you expect the average payroll tax charged to American workers to be larger or smaller than in Germany? Explain.

5. Ronald Coase in his classic October 1960 article "The Problem of Social Cost" (*Journal of Law and Economics* 3(1), pp. 1–44) discussed collective ownership of resources. Collective ownership often means that no one takes care of resources, or at minimum that resources are not cared for as well as if they were privately owned. What are some of the problems with collective ownership in the health care industry? Can you think of some examples in which collective ownership works? In what situations does it not work?

6. The Medicare system in the United States approximates the workings of a single-payer system. Using that program as evidence, critics say that expanding the program to cover all Americans "would give us all the compassion of the Internal Revenue Service and the efficiency of the postal service at Pentagon prices" (Constance Horner, HHS official under Bush, quoted in Stout, 1992). Proponents of a single-payer system point to our northern neighbors, whose Canadian version of Medicare works reasonably well. Although the Canadian system is not perfect, most citizens are satisfied with their medical care, which is available regardless of social or economic status. Does the Canadian experience translate into a successful application to a "Medicare for All" option in the United States? What is the evidence?

7. In 1989, the Chrysler Corporation released figures showing that its employee health care costs were $5,970 per employee and $700 per vehicle produced. According to the report, its foreign competitors fared much better. Health care costs for automobile companies averaged $375 in France, $337 in Germany, and $246 in Japan, placing Chrysler at a competitive disadvantage. Is there anything wrong with this conclusion? What are the microeconomic arguments and the macroeconomic arguments as they relate to this issue?

References

Armesto, Sandra Garcia, et al., "Health Care Quality Indicators Project 2006 Data Collection Update Report," *OECD Health Working Papers*, No. 29, Paris: OECD Publishing, 2007.

Baker, Lawrence, et al., "The Relationship between Technology Availability and Health Care Spending," *Health Affairs-Web Exclusive*, November 5, 2003, W3537–W3551.

Barua, Bacchus and Feluxe Ren, "The Private Cost of Public Queues for Medically Necessary Care, 2016 edition," *Fraser Alert*, Vancouver: The Fraser Institute, April 2016.

Barua, Bacchus and Feluxe Ren, "Waiting Your Turn: Wait Times for Health Care in Canada, 2016," Vancouver: The Fraser Institute, November 2016.

Britnell, Mark, *In Search of the Perfect Health System*, London: Palgrave, 2015. Barua, Bacchus and Feluxe Ren, "Waiting Your Turn: Wait Times for Health Care in Canada, 2016," Vancouver: The Fraser Institute, November 2016.

Brown, Ian T. and Christopher Khoury, "Among OECD Nations, U.S. Lags in Personal Health Care," March 31, 2009a, available at http://www.gallup.com/poll/117205/Americans-Not-Feeling-Health-Benefits-High-Spending.aspx.

Brown, Ian T. and Christopher Khoury, "In OECD Countries, Universal Health Care Gets High Marks," August 20, 2009b, available at http://www.gallup.com/poll/122393/OECD-Countries-Universal-Healthcare-Gets-High-Marks.aspx.

Chaoulli v. Quebec (Attorney General), 1 SCR 791, 2005 SCC 35, 2005.

Cheng, Tsung-Mei, "Understanding the 'Swiss Watch' Function of Switzerland's Health System," *Health Affairs* 29(8), August 2010, 1442–1451.

Deveugele, Myriam, et al., "Consultation Length in General Practice: Cross Sectional Study in Six European Countries," *British Medical Journal* 325, 2002, 472–477.

Disney, Helen, et al., *Impatient for Change: European Attitudes to Healthcare Reform*, London: Stockholm Network, 2004.

Esmail, Nadeem, "Health Care Lessons from Switzerland," Fraser Institute, August 2013.

___, "Leaving Canada for Medical Care," *Fraser Forum*, March/April 2011, 19–21.

Evans, Robert G., et al., "Controlling Health Expenditures—the Canadian Reality," *New England Journal of Medicine* 320(9), March 2, 1989, 571–577.

Fuchs, Victor, "Economics, Values, and Health Care Reform," *American Economic Review* 86(1), 1996, 1–24.

Green, David G. and Benedict Irvine, *Health Care in France and Germany: Lessons for the UK*, London: Civitas, Institute for the Study of Civil Society, 2001.

Grinols, Earl L. and James W. Henderson, *Health Care for Us All: Getting More for Our Investment*, New York: Cambridge University Press, 2009.

Henderson, James W., "Equality, Liberty, Fraternity, and the Delivery of Health Care in France," *Journal of the Medical Association of Georgia* 82(12), December 1993, 657–660.

Herzlinger, Regina E. and Ramin Parsa-Parsi, "Consumer-Driven Health Care: Lessons from Switzerland," *Journal of the American Medical Association* 292(10), September 8, 2004, 1213–1220.

House of Commons Health Committee, "Health Inequalities—Extent, Causes, and Policies to Tackle Them," 2009, available at http://www.publications.parliament.uk/pa/cm200809/cmselect/cmhealth/286/28605.htm#n10 (Accessed June 3, 2016).

Jürges, H., "Health Insurance Status and Physician Behavior in Germany," *Journal of Applied Social Science Studies* 129, 2009, 297–307.

Kleckley, Paul K. and Dean Arnold, "2010 Global Survey of Health Care Consumers," Deloitte Development LLC, 2010.

LePen, Claude, "The French Health Care System: In Search of a New Model," Presentation at the European School of Health Economics, Health Economics of Pharmaceuticals and other Medical Interventions, Sophia Antipole, France, June 11, 2003.

Lungen, Markus, et al., "Waiting Times for Elective Treatments According to Insurance Status: A Randomized Empirical Study in Germany," *International Journal for Equity in Health* 7(1), 2008, 1–7.

McKinsey and Company, *The Challenge of Reforming Japan's Health System*, Tokyo, Japan: McKinsey & Company, Inc., November 2008.

Newhouse, Joseph P., "Medical Care Costs: How Much Welfare Loss?" *Journal of Economic Perspectives* 6(3), 1992, 3–21.

OECD (Organization for Economic Cooperation and Development), *OECD Health Data*, Paris: OECD, 2016.

Paris, Valerie, Marion Devaux, and Lilian Wei, "Health Systems International Characteristics: A Survey of 29 OECD Countries," OECD Health Working Paper No. 50, April 2010.

Petkantchin, Valentin, "Pernicious Myths about Public Health Insurance in France," Economic Note, Institut Economique Molinari, January 2007, available at http://www.institutmolinari.org/IMG/pdf/note20071.pdf.

Prewo, Wilfried, "The Business of Health: How Does the U.S. Health-Care System Compare to Systems in Other Countries?" *AEI Health Policy Discussion*, October 17, 2006.

Ren, Feluxe and Bacchus Barua, "The Private Cost of Public Queues for Medically Necessary Care, 2017 Report," *Fraser Research Bulletin*, Vancouver: The Fraser Institute, May 2017.

Rodwin, Victor G., "The Health Care System under French National Health Insurance: Lessons for Health Reform in the United States," *American Journal of Public Health* 93(1), 2003, 31–37.

___, "The Marriage of National Health Insurance and La Medecine Liberale in France: A Costly Union," *Milbank Memorial Fund Quarterly* 59(1), 1981, 16–43.

Roy, Avik, "Switzerland: A Case Study in Consumer-Driven Health Care," *Forbes*, December 26, 2012.

Schoen, Cathy, Robin Osborne, David Squires, and Michelle M. Doty, "Access, Affordability, and Insurance Complexity are Often Worse in the United States Compared to Ten Other Countries," *Health Affairs* 32(12), December 2013, 2205–2215.

Schoen, Cathy, Roz Pierson, and Sandra Applebaum, "How Health Insurance Design Affects Access to Care and Costs, by Income, in Eleven Countries," *Health Affairs* 29(12), December 2010, 2323–2334.

Steinbrook, Robert, "Private Health Care in Canada," *New England Journal of Medicine* 354(16), April 20, 2006, 1661–1664.

Stock, Stephanie, "Integrated Ambulatory Specialist Care — Germany's New Health Care Sector," *New England Journal of Medicine* 372(19), May 7, 2015, 1781-1785.

Stout, Hilary, "Health Care Choices: A Bigger Federal Role or a Market Approach?" *Wall Street Journal*, January 15, 1992, A1.

Tajika, Eiji and Jun Kikuchi, "The Roles of Public and Private Insurance for the Health-Care Reform of Japan," *Public Policy Review* 8(2), July 2012, 123–144.

Tanner, Michael, "The Grass Is Not Always Greener: A Look at National Health Insurance Systems around the World," *Policy Analysis No. 613*, Washington, DC: Cato Institute, March 18, 2008.

U.S. General Accounting Office, *Canadian Health Insurance Lessons for the United States*, Pub. No. GAO/HRD 90-91, Washington, DC: United States General Accounting Office, November 1991.

Weisbrod, Burton, "The Health Care Quadrilemma: An Essay of Technological Change, Insurance, Quality of Care, and Cost Containment," *Journal of Economic Literature* 29(2), 1991, 523–552.

Wolfe, Patrice R. and Donald W. Moran, "Global Budgeting in the OECD Countries," *Health Care Financing Review* 14(3), Spring 1993, 55–71.

Yoshikawa, Aki, Norihiko Shirouzu, and Matthew Holt, "How Does Japan Do It? Doctors and Hospitals in a Universal Health Care System," *Stanford Law & Policy Review* 3, Fall 1991, 111–137.

CHAPTER 15

Medical Care Reform in the United States

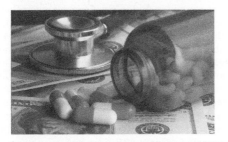

ISSUES IN MEDICAL CARE DELIVERY

LESSONS FROM CLINTONCARE

managed competition A health care reform plan first popularized by economist Alain Enthoven, whereby individuals are given a choice among competing health plans.

health alliances Called by various names, including *health insurance purchasing cooperatives (HIPC)*, these provide a way for small employers to act collectively to purchase health insurance. Often geographically based and not-for-profit, the alliance contracts with insurers and/or providers for medical coverage for its members.

⭐ **POLICY ISSUE**

Do Americans trust government enough to support the implementation of a government-run health care system?

President Bill Clinton took the oath of office in January 1993 to become the 42nd president of the United States. With both houses of Congress controlled by Democrats, most followers of politics expected that health system reform, Clinton's top domestic priority, would soon follow. Using the same "War Room" strategy that successfully catapulted him into the presidency, Clinton and his advisers (with the assistance of a 511-member task force) began drafting what many considered the most important piece of social legislation since the New Deal.

Originally conceptualized as a government-run play-or-pay system, the plan evolved into one better described as **managed competition**. Drafted primarily by Clinton's senior policy adviser and "health czar" Ira Magaziner, the plan was almost complete by the summer, except for one troubling detail—how to finance it.

Distracted by the broader tasks of running the country, the president finally presented his Health Security Act to Congress in the fall. The bill, over 1,300 pages in length, included an 800-page explanation. (A paperback summary was available in most local bookstores.) The main principles of the plan—security, simplicity, savings, choice, quality, and responsibility—were easy to support. The ensuing debate proved devastating.

The plan was comprehensive in nature, calling for universal coverage as an entitlement, mandatory participation, community-rated premiums, employer mandates, baseline (global) budgeting, uniform fee schedules, and the creation of 250 quasi-governmental agencies called **health alliances**. These health alliances would be under the supervision of a National Health Board created to issue regulations, establish requirements for state health plans, monitor compliance, and enforce budgets.

Critics emerged from all sides. Even members of the president's cabinet and key economic advisers voiced their concerns about aspects of the plan, especially its financing assumptions. Several important special interest groups voiced their opposition, including the Health Insurance Association of America and small business—represented by the Chamber of Commerce, the National Association of Manufacturers, and the National Federation of Independent Business. Some interest groups were in opposition to one another. The American Medical Association (AMA) wanted limits on awards for pain and suffering in medical malpractice cases, but the influence of the Trial Lawyers of America kept these limits out of the plan.

Congress began considering alternative plans. A single-payer group occupied the left-of-center position. Market-reform legislators represented the right-of-center alternative. As Congress debated through the summer of 1994, Republicans were convinced they could defeat the president and his bill. When first introduced, the bill received 57 percent approval from the public. As the legislative session ended in the early fall, public support was below 40 percent and congressional backing had all but vanished. In the end, the Democrat majority in Congress was never able to bring health care legislation to a vote.

Fast-forward 15 years to 2009. The situation was very similar: Democrats controlled both the presidency and Congress. Instead of direct involvement in drafting legislation, President Barack Obama remained on the sidelines, allowing Congress to do the heavy lifting. Behind the scenes, the president worked to garner support from key groups. Endorsements from the AMA, American Association of Retired Persons, and the pharmaceutical industry bolstered confidence even as public sentiment swung against the legislation. Close votes in both the House and Senate (without Republican support) led to passage. In 1994, mid-term elections swept the Republican Party to its first majority in both houses of Congress in over 40 years. In 2010, the Republicans took control of the House and recorded major gains in the Senate. Today, with Republicans in control of both houses of Congress and the presidency, efforts to repeal and replace the legislation are moving forward. Regardless, it is clear that elements of the progressive health care agenda introduced by President Clinton 25 years ago will continue to have an impact on future legislation.

Sources: Robert J. Blendon, Mollyann Brodie, and John Benson, "What Happened to Americans' Support for the Clinton Health Plan?" *Health Affairs* 14(1), Spring 1995, 24–26; Scott Gottlieb, "Clintonian Roots of the ACA," *National Affairs*, Summer 2015, 51–65; Daniel Yankelovich, "The Debate that Wasn't: The Public and the Clinton Plan," *Health Affairs* 14(1), Spring 1995, 7–23; and Walter Zelman and Larry D. Brown, "Looking Back on Health Care Reform: 'No Easy Choices,'" *Health Affairs* 17(6), November/December 1998, 61–68.

Over two decades after the failed Clinton reform plan, policymakers were finally able to pass significant health reform legislation in early 2010. Popularly known as ObamaCare, the Patient Protection and Affordable Care Act (now referred to as the Affordable Care Act or ACA) has dramatically transformed U.S. medical care delivery and finance. Proponents of the legislation expected that an additional 32 million Americans would receive coverage through a combination of Medicaid and the newly created insurance exchanges by 2020. Three years into the implementation process, the number of newly covered individuals has fallen considerably short of the predictions. Instead of 32 million, only 16.6 million received coverage and over 80 percent are newly enrolled Medicaid recipients (Haislmaier, 2017). By 2017, the premiums paid by the 9.2 million who purchase insurance through the exchanges had increased over 100 percent over 2013 levels. Moreover, health insurers are abandoning the exchanges at an alarming rate. Over 60 percent of U.S. counties, with almost 40 percent of the overall population, have only one or two insurers participating in the exchanges.

Elections have consequences. The early assessment of the Trump administration makes it clear that there will be a new emphasis on the market approach while abandoning the regulatory approach. In this chapter, we will explore medical care reform in the United States: the pressures behind the movement, the goals of reform, and an assessment of a system at the crossroads.

POLICY ISSUE

What kind of health care system does America want: government-run or market driven?

The Push for Reform

The temptation exists to view the reform debate as a struggle among competing ideologies. Admittedly, the political battle seems to overshadow the practical implications of what policymakers care trying to accomplish. However, the debate over reform of the

HTTP://

Families USA is an advocacy group dedicated to the provision of health care to all Americans. The organization issues reports, works through the media, and strives to educate the general public, opinion leaders, and policymakers on issues relevant to the health care marketplace. An extensive list of reports and other resources are available on their website. http://www.familiesusa.org.

medical sector is not new. Every congressional session since 1916 generated at least one piece of federal legislation proposing to modify the system in some way. The issues remain the same—quality, access, and affordability—the triple aim. Over the last two decades, the upward spending spiral, exacerbated by a growing number of uninsured, created an atmosphere of inevitability of reform.

For much of the past two decades, public opinion supported reform efforts. Polling results have consistently indicated that about three-fourths of all Americans are personally satisfied with the medical care that they receive (Blendon et al., 1992, 1995, 2006; Donelan et al., 1999; Robinson, 2000). Nevertheless, many are critical of the health care system and want government to enact change. Respondents want guaranteed access at lower cost. There is a policy dilemma. Our desires for guaranteed access and lower costs compete with each other and may not be simultaneously achievable, so fully satisfying these competing desires may not be possible.

The Moral Issues: Is Medical Care a "Right"?

It is essential that the issue of access to medical care be examined within a specific moral framework that clearly distinguishes between individual rights and social responsibility. While the Declaration of Independence states and the Constitution implicitly recognizes a fundamental right, a right that preexists government, to "life, liberty, and the pursuit of happiness," nowhere does it state that access to medical care is a necessary condition to the exercise of that right.

Before venturing (even briefly) into the rights debate, we must accept the fact that this is a debate that distracts from the more fundamental concern over resource allocation. No matter how you answer the rights question, you must still deal with the finite resource question. Accepting a right to health care opens us up to the tragedy of the commons dilemma. If we treat health care resources as public property devoted to communal use, we open ourselves up to the free rider problem and the need to regulate use through administrative rules.

Taking the position that health care is a right misses the distinction between a negative right and a positive right or more accurately a freedom-preserving right and a resource-extracting right. Freedom-preserving rights—those enumerated in our Constitution—protect us from others, including the government, without imposing an obligation to do anything for others, except to recognize that everyone has the same rights as we do. Your right to free speech implies that I am obligated not to interfere with your speaking; it does not mean that I am to provide you with a podium, microphone, and audience. Based on natural law, freedom-preserving (negative) rights are genuine rights, they are unchangeable, they are not man-made, and they cannot be destroyed.

In contrast, resource-extracting (positive) rights do just that, they extract resources from individuals, requiring that they act in a certain way. Legitimate only when created through voluntary agreement, these rights limit choice. When dictated to individuals, they are a threat to liberty. For Peter to exercise his right, Paul has to pay.

If people have a right to health care, it logically follows that others have a duty to provide it. What good is a right without guaranteed access? Coercion is essential to guarantee a positive right. Taken to its logical conclusion, if I have a right to health care, then I can simply enter my physician's office and demand treatment—he or she is obliged to provide care and I have no reciprocal obligation to pay. If we require that some pay for the rights of others, this act diminishes liberty.

In the United States, we have created obligations to provide medical care for the elderly and indigent based on the notion that we have a social responsibility to provide access to

☆ **POLICY ISSUE**

Do Americans consider access to medical care a right of citizenship?

care for those who cannot afford to purchase their own. Does this mean that we have a natural right to medical care access? Arguing that health care is a right is merely an argument for universal coverage through a system that requires mandatory participation, taxpayer financed. Those who advocate access to medical care as a right do not mean that individuals have the right to purchase medical care (a negative right), but that others are obligated to act in a way that guarantees access to medical care by providing the means to purchase it (positive right).

Common sense requires that we adopt a standard of medical care access that is politically acceptable, morally responsible, and economically affordable. To achieve these goals, we must come up with an acceptable definition of an appropriate level of medical care to determine the extent of our collective responsibility of providing care to those who cannot afford to purchase it. The familiar marginalist rule of thumb determines the economist's concept of "appropriate."

The optimal level of care is the amount of care where the benefit from the last unit received is just equal to its cost to society. Within this framework, the question of allocation is ultimately one of valuation of outcomes. What value do we place on life? What value do we place on reduced pain and suffering? How do these values change when we are the ones receiving medical care—when it is a relative or a friend? How do these values change when the person receiving medical care is a total stranger?

Using the economic approach as a guide to public policy requires the placement of justifiable limits on the use of certain medical options to use resources wisely. The challenge is to apply those limits uniformly across society. A national health care policy cannot provide every person with all the health care he or she may desire. Such an open-ended policy is not appropriate in an environment in which health care is not the only objective. A national policy must be able to establish reasonable priorities, and it must devise acceptable means to allocate resources sensibly.

The Goals of Reform

The economic challenge is clear: How can we satisfy our unlimited demands with limited resources. When dealing specifically with health policy, we must first recognize that health is not the only goal of society and may not be the most important goal. Individuals validate this claim daily by deciding to supersize lunch, smoke cigarettes, inject drugs, fail to wear seatbelts, and ride a motorcycle without a helmet.

Context is important. Society considers other goals important as well: strengthening national defense, improving education, increasing economic competitiveness abroad, cleaning up the environment, reducing income inequality, and balancing the federal budget. Largely, these are competing goals. The single-minded pursuit of one can lead to ever-larger expenditures in that area. In establishing spending priorities, health and medical care have a considerable advantage over other goals. It is easy to shift spending priorities by dramatizing the needs of this sector, exploiting individual cases where human welfare is involved.

Three issues stand out as critical: who is covered, what is covered, and who pays and how much? It is important to examine proposed reforms carefully, if not critically, and judge them by how they address these three criteria.

Who Is Covered?

Most participants in the reform debate agree that one of the goals of the U.S. medical care system must be expanding access to medical care. A sense of social responsibility has been one of the primary motivating factors driving the discussion. It is easy to express support

POLICY ISSUE

Are Americans willing to formally accept a multi-tiered health care system with more comprehensive coverage available to those who can afford it?

for universal coverage, but how do we get from where we are to where we want to be? Will we "just do it," or should we "first, do no harm"?

A general confusion over public opinion complicates the task. What is the American perception of fairness? Is it equal access to the providers, equal health outcomes, or something else? Does equality require that everyone participate, or should participation be voluntary?

What Is Covered?

POLICY ISSUE

What is the most politically acceptable way to ration medical care?

KEY CONCEPT 1

Scarcity and Choice

The next step is to define the basic benefits package. In the context of a normal market, the consumer decides on the appropriate composition of the basket of services purchased. When government gets involved in health care, the result is inevitably the formal design of a basic benefits package. Seldom is the basic package less generous than those available in most private insurance plans. Otherwise, policymakers are accused of promoting the rationing of services to the more vulnerable segments of the population—poor, sick, and elderly. In theory, defining a basic package of medical benefits is nothing more than an exercise in establishing priorities, determining the level of spending, and allocating the funds to provide the services according to the rank ordering. In practice, the process is much more political and often turns into a battle of special interest groups.

If collectively financed, it may be appropriate to consider a basic benefits package that is less generous than the standard insurance plan, even though a multitiered medical care system may not satisfy everyone's notion of the social ideal. Such a system, while not equal according to some definitions, is welfare enhancing. Those individuals who become eligible for the collectively provided plan are better off.

Who Pays and How Much?

KEY CONCEPT 6

Supply and Demand

One thing is certain. Expanded access will increase spending. No amount of preventive care or electronic record keeping will overcome the forces of moral hazard that will inevitably result in increased spending.

In most cases, the efficient use of scarce resources requires cost-conscious consumers or at least decision makers who behave in a responsible manner. It means that individual consumers must pay for what they consume and must benefit from any economizing behavior that they practice. In this regard, many consider medical care different. Collective financing through some combination of taxes and insurance premiums is the norm for most health care systems—whether in the United States, Canada, or Europe. Thus, it is difficult to build into any system the individual discipline that is necessary to ensure its efficient operation.

KEY CONCEPT 9

Market Failure

KEY CONCEPT 4

Self-Interest

Every reform plan must eventually face the sobering issues of affordability and overall spending. Inevitably, expanding access and providing generous benefits will drive up costs and spending. How much are we willing to pay? Who is ultimately going to pay? Individuals spending their own money will answer these questions differently than those spending someone else's money. Normally, the burden of responsibility falls on the individual to provide for his or her own care, but under certain conditions, many consider collective provision socially responsible, especially providing for those who cannot provide for themselves.

KEY CONCEPT 5

Markets and Pricing

The issue boils down to the distribution of the burden of the collectively provided portion of the medical care package. Is medical care primarily an individual or a collective responsibility? Who should pay: individuals, employers, or taxpayers? What is the appropriate distribution of costs among the payer groups? The answers to these questions will not come easily, but we must answer them before we can successfully implement any reform plan.

Policy Options

Most Americans favor the idea of expanding insurance coverage to all Americans but disagree on how to do it (Blendon et al., 2003). The more popular options include: 1) creating a single-payer system by expanding existing government programs such as Medicare, Medicaid, and SCHIP, 2) mandating insurance coverage either individually or through place of employment, and 3) expanding the use of market incentives to encourage and enable individuals to purchase insurance.

Single-Payer National Health Insurance

The all-government, single-payer option attracts its support primarily from proponents of universal insurance coverage. Under this system, everyone participates in a single health plan, administered and financed by the government or a quasi-governmental agency. A basic benefits package, defined to cover all medically necessary services, is available to the entire population. Strictly following the Canadian model requires the ban on private insurance coverage that duplicates national insurance. In contrast, the British and German models allow private insurance to compete directly with the government-run alternative.

HTTP://

The U.S. House of Representatives and the U.S. Senate have Web pages that provide access to information about the legislative process, individual members, and the various committees. Links are also provided to review schedules of activities and access information available from Congress. http://www.house.gov. http://www.senate.gov.

Physicians do not bill patients directly. Instead, they bill the single payer according to a fee schedule, determined legislatively or through negotiations between medical providers and the single payer. Hospitals submit bills to the appropriate government agency that pays them on a fee-for-service or per-diem basis. If, however, hospital payments under global budgeting eliminate the traditional bill for services, they become unnecessary, because hospitals receive a periodic appropriation. The single payer establishes global budgets annually. Hospitals are required to treat all patients who seek care. A global operating budget caps spending at the established level. The single payer must approve all capital acquisitions, including all diagnostic and high-tech surgical equipment, paying from a separate capital budget and controlling overall investment in medical technology.

The theoretical model that applies to the single-payer approach is called *monopsony*. Under a monopsonistic health care system, the government is the only health care buyer. This is not socialized medicine in its pure form unless the government also owns the delivery system and directly employs the medical care workforce. Health care delivery is often a private sector responsibility, but it requires deep involvement by the government in setting global budgets for hospitals and nursing homes, establishing a ceiling on overall spending, and setting allowable fees for providers. Many proponents of this plan even recommend that growth in health care spending be limited to the growth in the economy, usually measured by the annual percentage change in gross domestic product.

The main advantage of a single-payer system is its administrative simplicity, only one paper trail—provider to payer. The U.S. system with its labyrinth of private insurance carriers is administratively complex. Another important advantage is that everyone receives coverage regardless of employment status or financial circumstances. Proponents will argue that the single-payer system is the most equitable and efficient way to strike a balance between cost, access, and quality.

On the other hand, critics argue that within the so-called strengths of the single-payer system lay its weaknesses. It may not be socialized medicine, but it increases government involvement in a system that already has too much. A single-payer system results in a higher tax burden, even while eliminating private insurance premium. As individuals lose the direct responsibility of paying insurance premiums, they also lose the motivation to do anything about rising expenditures.

KEY CONCEPT 3
Marginal Analysis

⭐ **POLICY ISSUE**

Should health insurance be tax exempt when provided as an employer-sponsored benefit?

The argument for a single-payer system usually focuses on the duplication of services caused by a system populated by multiple insurers. Eliminate the duplication and costs will naturally come down. However, duplication is beneficial. If one source of supply is eliminated, another will spring up to take its place.

Mandated Insurance Coverage

More than 90 percent of the privately insured nonelderly population in the United States receives health insurance coverage through the workplace. In keeping with this tradition, many reformers rely on a strategy that builds on the employer-based system. The popularity of employer-sponsored insurance (ESI) is due to three important factors. First, administering insurance in a large group setting leads to economies of scale. Second, the workplace is an ideal setting to pool risk, because workers are on average healthier than non-workers, and they form groups to work, not to buy health insurance. Finally, the U.S. tax code provides favorable tax treatment for health insurance benefits when purchased by the employer.

⭐ **POLICY ISSUE**

Do state-level mandates offer the most effective-way to improve health insurance access?

Employer-Mandated Insurance

The concept of forcing employers to provide health care coverage for their workers originated from the belief that employers are better equipped to manage and finance health care delivery. The proponents of employer mandates have used this market-based principle to support their plan to provide universal insurance coverage to all working Americans and their dependents.

play-or-pay A health care reform feature whereby employers "play" by providing health care coverage to their employees, or they pay a payroll tax to fund government-provided insurance.

Many health systems across the world use employer mandates to finance health care access. One way of implementing an employer mandate is through the so-called **play-or-pay** approach. Under play-or-pay, employers would be required to purchase a basic health care package for their employees as defined by lawmakers. Employers would also have a second option. Instead of providing the basic benefits package, they could pay for a government-sponsored health plan through a new tax, most likely a payroll tax based on a certain percentage of total payroll.

HTTP://

The Office of Management and Budget (OMB) helps in formulating the president's spending plans; evaluating the effectiveness of agency programs, policies, and procedures; assessing competing funding demands among agencies; and setting funding priorities. The website provides information on the role and organization of the OMB and offers links to important budgetary documents. http://www.whitehouse. gov/omb.

Even strong proponents of play-or-pay recognize that the mechanism makes no provisions for the unemployed. In addition, play-or-pay would likely increase considerably the number of unemployed. As part of the ClintonCare debate, a study by the Joint Economic Committee of Congress estimated that play-or-pay with a 7 percent payroll tax option would increase unemployment by some 700,000 workers, over half from firms affected that employ fewer than 20 workers. In a study prepared for the Employment Policies Institute, June and David O'Neill estimate that such a mandate would lead to a loss of 3.1 million jobs (Bonilla, 1993). This mandated increase in labor costs would disproportionately impact seven low-wage industries, including restaurants, retail trade, construction, personal services, and agriculture.

Many small firms in the United States already spend 10–12 percent of payroll on medical costs. If the tax rate for participation in the government-sponsored plan were set at a lower level, many firms would be motivated to drop coverage and pay the tax. The Congressional Budget Office (CBO) estimated that half of the U.S. population would ultimately move to the government plan. With those numbers, we would soon have a system of health care delivery largely dominated by the federal government.

Individual Mandates

individual mandate A legal requirement that individuals carry their own insurance protection.

Some notable health experts have suggested that the way to minimize the free-rider problem is to require individuals to provide their own insurance coverage (Reinhardt, 1992). Instead of an employer mandate, they prefer an individual mandate. This approach to mandated coverage is similar to the way automobile liability insurance is required for drivers of all registered vehicles.

By taking the employer out of the business of providing health benefits, individuals would be more aware of the actual costs of their health insurance (Pauly, 1994). Current arrangements perpetuate the myth that employers pay health insurance premiums. Business and labor have fostered this myth, creating the impression that employers are providing free health benefits to their employees. Even the reference to a premium split between employer and employee is a veiled attempt to promote the idea that the employer pays. Business firms do not pay for health benefits. Treated as a cost of doing business, this expense is passed on to customers in the form of higher prices, absorbed by owners in the form of lower profits, or forced on employees in the form of lower wages and higher unemployment. In competitive industries where prices are market driven and profits modest, employers shift most of their health insurance costs onto workers. The shift is subtle and often unnoticed but real nevertheless. Actual wages are lower, and nonmedical benefits are less generous (Emanuel and Fuchs, 2008; Jensen and Morrisey, 1999).

Full implementation of an individual mandate (outside the ESI framework) would require that employees who currently have health benefits receive the "employer-paid" portion of the premium as gross income. To purchase insurance coverage, the individual would then use these funds. An individual mandate would expose the myth of employer-paid insurance by making the employee more aware of the cost of medical coverage.

Market-Based Alternatives[1]

At the heart of the debate between advocates of market-based alternatives and those who would give the government a bigger role in the delivery and financing of medical care is a basic ideological struggle. Can the market for medical care work like the market for other commodities? Or is medical care different, an exception to the basic laws of economics and unsuited for market delivery?

Nearly every other developed country in the world has virtually given up on the market as a primary means of delivering health care. Only the United States, Switzerland, the Netherlands and Singapore rely on market mechanisms to any extent to address the important issues of cost and access.

Critics of market-based medical care argue from the unchallenged premise that the delivery of medical care is too important to address with private markets. Highly respected health economist Uwe Reinhardt has noted, "no one can distribute Gucci loafers better than the market, but a *pure market* cannot distribute health care" (quoted in Stout, 1992).

This ideological debate allows no room for compromise. In many ways, the middle ground is the most difficult to defend. An example is the experience with President Clinton's 1994 health care reform proposal. Defenders of the market attacked the plan as a government takeover, and those who wanted a government-run system attacked it as a half-measure that did not fully address the real problems.

The Market Approach

The failures of the system prior to the passage of the ACA are evident everywhere with limited access for the uninsured and high costs for everyone, but advocates of a market

HTTP://

The CBO provides Congress with economic and budgetary information. The CBO develops forecasts and projections that serve as a baseline for measuring the effects of proposed changes in taxing and spending laws. Their site has links to reports, publications, and other information sources. http://cbo.gov.

HTTP://

The Cato Institute is a nonpartisan public policy research foundation with libertarian leanings. Their website spotlights research papers and books examining the role of government. The site provides numerous links to policy-related papers. http://www.cato.org

☆ **POLICY ISSUE**

Can market incentives be used effectively in the financing and provision of medical care in a way that also promotes fairness?

☆ **POLICY ISSUE**

Is meaningful health care reform possible given the ideological divide among the American electorate?

---

[1]Three market-oriented think tanks in Washington, DC, best typify the market approach to the health care reform debate: the American Enterprise Institute, the Heritage Foundation, and the Cato Institute. The National Center for Policy Analysis, located in Dallas, is an active think tank located outside the Beltway.

HTTP://

The Heritage Foundation is a think tank whose mission is to formulate and promote conservative public policies based on the principles of free enterprise, limited government, individual freedom, traditional American values, and a strong national defense. The site includes a library, resource bank, and links to government and other public policy organizations. http://www.heritage.org.

★ **KEY CONCEPT 3**
Marginal Analysis

HTTP://

The National Center for Policy Analysis attempts to develop and promote private alternatives to government regulation and control, solving problems by relying on the strengths of the competitive, entrepreneurial private sector. The site provides links to policy briefings, the organization's cybrary, and their publication Executive Alert. http://www.ncpa.org.

★ **POLICY ISSUE**
Do individual consumers have the ability to make their own decisions about matters concerning their own medical care?

★ **KEY CONCEPT 4**
Self-Interest

approach do not see these as market failures. Instead, the shortcomings are the government's failure to promote competitive markets as a means of addressing the problems of access and cost.

Many market advocates believe the major distortion in the health insurance market is the current tax treatment of employer-sponsored health insurance. Exempting employer-sponsored health benefits from taxation desensitizes employees to the actual cost of health insurance. Those reformers with the courage of their convictions have recommended a change in the tax exemption. A complete elimination of the tax exemption, or at least a limit on the current subsidy, would represent a big step in promoting cost-conscious behavior on the part of the consuming public.

Goodman (2014) has suggested a much simpler and more egalitarian approach, replacing the current tax deduction with a refundable tax credit equal to the approximate per capita cost of providing Medicaid to those who are under age 65. There would be no additional cost for those who currently have coverage (private insurance or Medicaid). The additional cost would be approximately $3,000 times the number of uninsured who gain coverage.

At the heart of the debate is whether a credit for any amount less than the full insurance premium would be sufficient for a family with a $30,000 annual income to purchase its own insurance. Critics argue that this is nothing more than a symbolic gesture that would have little real impact on the number of uninsured. Proponents do not expect miracles from this proposal but do feel that it would increase access for many low-income Americans. The goal of market proponents is to improve access, not by creating a vast system of government mandates, prospective budgets, price controls, and bureaucratic alliances, but by establishing a mechanism that provides incentives at the margin to encourage some to take responsibility for their own care.[2]

Furthermore, they see insurance reform as an essential element in improving access to the medical care system. A common complaint addressed by recent reform dealt with certain insurance practices that denied insurance coverage to certain vulnerable groups—job losers, job changers, and those with chronic medical conditions. Almost everyone agrees that insurance should be personal and portable. No one who maintains continuous coverage should worry about losing that coverage in the event that individual circumstances change.

Another problem that limits insurance availability in the insurance exchanges is that young, healthy individuals who purchase insurance enroll into risk pools that include a disproportionate number of older, sicker individuals. Unable to spread risk over a representative group, premiums are significantly higher because of the high costs associated with enrollees with preexisting conditions. The solution to the problem is homogeneous risk pools, or alternatively, risk-rated subsidies that make high risk enrollees as attractive to insurers as those with low risk.

The core idea of the market approach is that individual decisions are better than collective decisions. The market plan would provide more power to the individual, whereas the approach under the ACA gives more power to the government. The real debate is between those who believe that individuals can make their own decisions in matters involving medical care and those who think that medical care is too complex to rely on individual initiative.

Consumer-Directed Health Plans

Introduced in the 1990s during the managed care backlash, consumer-directed health plans (CDHP) are rapidly increasing in popularity. The consumer-directed approach links a high-deductible health plan with a personal spending account, either a health

---

[2]Many market proponents seriously consider tax credits or vouchers as a possible replacement for Medicare and Medicaid.

reimbursement account (HRA) or a health savings account (HSA). The principle behind the use of the CDHP is to encourage cost-conscious behavior on the part of the consumer of health services. When patients are required to pay for low-value, routine care, they spend their own money more wisely.

The CDHP was a fringe option until the Medicare Modernization Act of 2003 expanded access to the HSA. By the end of 2015, over 30 percent of employers offered CDHPs and 20 million of their employees chose that option. (See more detail on the CDHP option in Chapter 8.)

Managed Competition

Can choice and competition, principles that have served so well in other sectors of the economy, work in the medical care sector? To work, *choice* must mean more than whatever your employer chooses for you. Competition must be encouraged at the point where the consumer purchase decision is made, and that is either at the time the type of health insurance coverage is determined or at the point of buying the care. The original model of managed competition was Alain Enthoven's "Consumer Choice Health Plan" (Enthoven, 1978). Revised and clarified extensively since its early beginnings, managed competition emerged as a central element of President Clinton's 1994 reform package.[3] Proponents of managed competition see it as a way to increase competition in the market for health insurance. In most employer-provided plans, the employee has little choice. As members of the same group, all employees get the plan provided by the employer and rarely have the option of choosing between alternative plans.

> **POLICY ISSUE**
> *Is it possible to make medical consumers cost conscious and at the same time create a system that treats the sick and poor fairly?*

> **POLICY ISSUE**
> *How does a market-based health care delivery system attempt to control spending?*

> **KEY CONCEPT 7**
> *Competition*

> **POLICY ISSUE**
> *Can a market-based health care delivery system do a better job of controlling cost and spending?*

> **KEY CONCEPT 3**
> *Marginal Analysis*

ISSUES IN MEDICAL CARE DELIVERY

MANAGED COMPETITION IN PRACTICE: THE FEDERAL EMPLOYEES HEALTH BENEFIT PLAN

The Federal Employees Health Benefit Plan (FEHBP), enacted in 1959, covers all civilian employees of the federal government, including Congress, the executive branch, the judicial branch, civilian employees of the Pentagon, and federal retirees. Currently, FEHBP insures over 9 million civilians, making it the largest employer-sponsored health insurance program in the country.

The distinguishing feature of the plan allows recipients to choose their own health benefits package from among nearly 400 private health insurance plans. Depending on geographic location, each individual has at least 20, and in some cases as many as 40, plans from which to choose. The plans range from traditional Blue Cross-Blue Shield health insurance plans to 1 of over 300 managed care plans (HMOs). Premium costs vary depending on the type of coverage desired. The federal government pays approximately 70 percent of the average premium directly to the insurers.

Each November brings with it an "open season" in which federal employees have several weeks to decide which type of coverage to choose for the upcoming year. Health insurance companies, HMOs, local hospitals, and employee associations market these plans. Successful implementation of this model requires fully informed consumers, and federal employees get plenty of information to assist them in making their decisions. Their options are clearly spelled out in advertising, association newsletters, and independently

---

[3]After details of Clinton's plan began to surface, Enthoven penned a harsh criticism of the president's version of "managed competition" (Enthoven, 1993).

published consumer guides. When consumers perceive that they will benefit from additional information, they will demand information, and someone will provide it.

Given the number of choices available, enrollees tend to select health plans based on their own expected usage. In other words, enrollees self-select according to their likelihood of using medical care. Though the system is by no means perfect, it works reasonably well for a large number of enrollees and has emerged as a model for reforming Medicare.

Source: Robert E. Moffit, "FEHBP Controls Costs Again: More Lessons for Medicare Reformers," *The Heritage Foundation F.Y.I.* No. 64, September 25, 1995.

Under managed competition, employees choose among the competing plans, including HMOs, PPOs, and CDHPs. The employer contributes a fixed sum toward the purchase of the health plan and the employee uses the money to purchase the health plan of his or her choice. If the plan costs less than the employer contribution, the employee keeps the difference (treated for tax purposes as taxable income) or invests the surplus in an HSA. If the premium is higher than the contribution, the employee pays the difference.

For example, suppose four basic plans are available. Plan 1 costs $2,400, Plan 2 costs $3,000, Plan 3 costs $3,600, and Plan 4 costs $4,200. If the employer's contribution were set at the second lowest premium, in this case $3,000, employees choosing Plan 1 would pay nothing extra and receive $600 to contribute to their HSA. Those choosing Plan 2 would break even. Employees choosing Plan 3 pay $600 extra and those choosing Plan 4 would pay an additional $1,200.

For a market to work in medical care, cost-conscious behavior must become the rule rather than the exception. The two points of purchase in the medical marketplace are when the individual makes the decision about what type of medical plan to purchase and when the individual actually receives the service. Advocates of managed competition feel that, based on equity considerations, a system based on competition at the point of purchasing health insurance offers the best alternative for bringing competitive forces to bear in this market. Advocates of the CDHP approach disagree, viewing competition at the point of purchasing medical care as the appropriate choice.

The Patient Protection and Affordable Care Act

For too many years, the U.S. health care delivery system has performed poorly. Either directly or indirectly, the government has provided the majority of the funding, through either tax revenue or subsidies. Individual incentives are all wrong, encouraging the consumption of services whose costs outweigh their benefits. The overall cost of care is high and too many people were unable to purchase insurance at affordable premiums due to preexisting health conditions.

The ACA became law in 2010, consolidating decision-making in the federal government and initiating a 10-year process intended to expand health insurance coverage to millions of uninsured Americans. Ironically, Congress never planned that the legislation as passed would reach the president's desk. When Massachusetts voters elected Scott Brown to fill their vacant Senate seat on January 19, 2010, the dynamics of the U.S. Senate changed by denying Democrats their filibuster-proof majority. The legislative process normally takes two bills passed separately in the House and Senate through a process that results in separate votes on a single compromise bill intended for the president's signature. Because of the change in the Senate's composition, Democrats in the House of Representatives realized that their only option was to pass the Senate version of the bill or get nothing at all.

HTTP://

Project HOPE (Health Opportunities for People Everywhere) provides health education, health policy research, and humanitarian assistance in over 70 countries, including the United States. Community projects in Texas and West Virginia are featured on their website. http://www.projecthope.org.

Even with signed legislation, the reform process was not complete. A simple word search of the act finds the phrase "the secretary shall" over 1,000 times, referring to the role of the Secretary of Health and Human Services in providing the operational details that were left out of the legislation. Over 15,000 pages of regulations published in the *Federal Register* serve as a guide to the implementation process.

Key Elements of the ACA

The ACA is 2,400 pages of legislation organized into 10 sections. The act focuses on a combination of Medicaid expansion and subsidized insurance purchased in insurance exchanges, or marketplaces, throughout the country. The key provisions of the act resulted in the following:

1. Additional regulation of the private health insurance market
2. Expanded Medicaid eligibility and the creation of health insurance exchanges
3. Mandates enforced by penalties that require individuals to maintain coverage and firms to offer affordable plans
4. Reduction in Medicare spending to fund coverage expansion for non-Medicare recipients
5. New federal taxes
6. Formation of nonprofit insurance cooperatives in the insurance exchanges

Already the most regulated industry in the U.S. economy, the ACA extended federal control over what historically had been the responsibility of the states. By setting standards for qualified health plans, the act (along with the subsequent rules and regulations set out by the administration) actually defines an essential benefits package for certification.

guaranteed issue A feature of an insurance policy that requires the insurer to accept all applicants and guarantee renewal as long as premiums are paid, regardless of the health status of the applicant.

Other required features include **guaranteed issue**, guaranteed renewability, and no benefit exclusions due to preexisting conditions. Deductibles, indexed for inflation, may not exceed $6,550 for individuals and $13,100 for families for the plan year 2017. Out-of-pocket spending may not exceed $7,150 for individuals and $14,300 for families. There are no lifetime spending limits. Coverage levels are identified by the percentage of the full actuarial value of the plans' expected benefits. Bronze coverage is actuarially equivalent to 60 percent of the full actuarial value of the expected benefits, silver coverage is 70 percent, gold coverage is 80 percent, and platinum coverage is 90 percent. Individuals under age 30 may purchase high deductible, catastrophic policies.

Other insurance requirements allow risk rating by age, geographic region, tobacco use, and family size. Premiums may not vary more than 3–1 based on age and 1.5–1 based on tobacco use. Adult children may remain on their parents' insurance policy until age 26. Waiting periods for newly covered individuals may not exceed 90 days.

The act provides two primary mechanisms to increase health insurance coverage: expansion of Medicaid and creation of health insurance exchanges in the states. In an attempt to establish a uniform eligibility standard across the states, individuals qualify for Medicaid if their family income is less than 138 percent of the federal poverty level (FPL). Because of the financial implications of the expansion, the Supreme Court ruling left it up to the states to decide whether to expand Medicaid coverage. As a result, 19 states have not yet changed Medicaid eligibility standards.

Health insurance exchanges were intended to be fully functioning marketplaces where individuals shop for and purchase coverage. Established by the state or the federal government, these exchanges provide standardized information on all insurance options including benefits, premiums, and subsidies in a way that individuals can compare available plans.

Most individuals are required to purchase insurance. Failure to comply with the mandate will result in a shared responsibility payment equal to the greater of $695 ($2,085 per family) or 2.5 percent of household income.[4] Sliding scale subsidies (based on the cost of the second lowest cost silver plan) limit premiums to 2.0 percent of income for households making 100 percent of the FPL (approximately $24,300 for a family of four in 2017) to 9.5 percent of income for those making 400 percent of the FPL (approximately $97,200 for a family of four in 2017). Cost-sharing subsidies limit the percentage of out-of-pocket spending for households making less than 250 percent of the FPL.

If an employer does not offer affordable coverage and at least one employee receives a premium subsidy through an exchange, the employer pays a penalty. Large employers, those with more than 50 employees, are required to pay $2,000 per employee (in excess of 30 employees), or $3,000 per employee receiving a subsidy, whichever is less.

For the first time in program history, Medicare revenues (over $740 billion over the first decade) will be used to provide coverage for the non-elderly by expanding Medicaid eligibility and providing income-based subsidies in the insurance exchange.

Over the next decade, taxpayers will pay an additional $570 billion in new federal taxes, representing the second largest funding source for the new law. The new taxes include excise taxes on high cost plans, a tax on private insurance plans, an increase in the Medicare payroll tax on high-income taxpayers, a revenue tax on medical device manufacturers, and mandate taxes on individuals who do not purchase insurance and employers that do not provide insurance.

Another provision of the law funded start-up costs for the creation of nonprofit insurance cooperatives. The 23 co-op plans were to serve as a low-cost alternative to the for-profit insurance plans that populate the exchanges.

Major Accomplishments and Their Unintended Consequences

Claiming success often depends on how you interpret the evidence. Earlier in Chapter 1, we discussed the ACA's success through 2015 in providing additional coverage to 20 million people through the Medicaid and the exchanges (Frean, Gruber, and Sommers, 2016). Haislmaier (2017) takes a different approach to the same question using administrative data (actual enrollment figures reported by the insurers) instead of survey data (which offer approximations) and extends the analysis through the third quarter of 2016. Table 15.1 summarizes his findings.

Overall coverage for those under age 65 increased from 233.9 to 250.5 million or 16.6 million after full implementation of the program. Over 80 percent of the expansion (or 13.8 million) is due to increased enrollment in Medicaid and CHIP. Coupled with the 6.7 million increase in individual coverage (including the newly formed exchanges with average monthly enrollment of 10.4 million in 2016), the two major avenues for expanded coverage were responsible for 20.5 million additional insured. The 3.9 million decline in group enrollment lowers the overall coverage gains to 16.6 million.

Only two of the coverage groups (individuals and Medicaid/CHIP) experienced substantial gains in 2014, and all three saw small gains in 2015 and 2016. Overall, 51 percent of the increase in coverage occurred in 2014, 34 percent in 2015, and 15 percent in 2016. Exchange enrollment actually decreased during the last quarter of 2016 and by the end of the enrollment period for 2017, almost 400,000 fewer people had enrolled.

---

[4]Enforcement is weak. Failure to pay the penalties may not result in criminal prosecution or liens or levies against property.

TABLE 15.1 NUMBER OF PEOPLE WITH INSURANCE COVERAGE (IN MILLIONS)

Type of coverage	2013	2014	2015	2016	Change 2013–2016
Individual coverage	11.8	16.5	17.7	18.5	+6.7
Group coverage	161.2	156.5	157.6	157.3	−3.9
Fully insured	60.6	53.9	53.0	51.9	−8.7
Self-insured	100.6	102.6	104.6	105.4	+4.8
Total private coverage	173.0	173.0	175.3	175.8	+2.8
Medicaid/CHIP	60.9	69.3	72.7	74.7	+13.8
Total coverage	233.9	242.3	248.0	250.5	+16.8

Source: Haislmaier (2017).

Expanded insurance coverage does not necessarily translate into improved medical care access. Shortages in certain specialties, including general practitioners and surgeons, combined with low reimbursement rates to physicians have made it difficult for the newly insured to find regular sources of care. Medicaid recipients are twice as likely to visit the emergency room as are the uninsured. With over 80 percent of the newly insured covered by Medicaid, the ACA has the potential to increase emergency room visits considerably (Garcia, Bernstein, and Bush, 2010). Over time, the sustained reductions in Medicare payments to hospitals lead the chief actuary of the CMS to conclude that 15 percent of Part A providers will run operating deficits within the first decade of the program, which translates into over 800 community hospitals nationwide (Foster, 2010).

The rollout of the insurance exchanges in 2013 fell far short of expectations. Problems with the website, problems with information security, and 4.7 million insured Americans losing their plans caused disruptions and led to continued decline in the public perception of the program. Insurers are continuing to exit the exchanges. Over 60 percent of U.S. counties have only one or two insurer options in the exchanges. By 2017, cost of coverage was over 100 percent higher than the actuarially fair premium for 19–34 year olds. With 2017 premiums over 100 percent higher than 2014 premiums, young healthy people are choosing not to purchase coverage.

The penalty for refusing to purchase coverage was modest to begin with and now the Internal Revenue Service (IRS) will no longer attempt to collect it. The guaranteed issue provision has made it too easy to game the system. Weak enforcement provisions (no garnishing of wages, no attaching assets, no jail time) and liberal exemption policies have made it easy to ignore the individual mandate. At least 20 percent of enrollees take advantage of the 90-day grace period to pay delinquent premiums (which is the same number of days that you can be uninsured without facing a penalty). The game is to pay your premiums for nine months, stop paying the last three months of the year, have your coverage cancelled, and reenroll in the same plan the next year. That way you get a 25 percent discount, receive a full year's coverage, and only pay for nine months.

There are still aspects of the ACA that have the potential to create problems in the future. To slow the growth in Medicare spending, the law established the Independent Payment Advisory Board (IPAB). New target growth rates will place limits on Medicare spending and IPAB will set policy to meet those spending targets. In years when growth rates exceed the target, IPAB will set targets to reduce per capita spending. Specifically restricted in its ability to ration, raise premiums, lower benefits, or otherwise shift costs to Medicare recipients, IPAB has little power beyond reducing payments to providers. The result will likely be changes in the way providers are paid, shifting from a fee-for-service model to capitation, and further exodus of providers from participation in the program altogether. These proposals will become law unless Congress overrides them by a two-thirds majority. To date, spending has not exceeded target levels and IPAB is not active.

It is understandable that there are problems. After a close vote (220–215) in the House without a single Republican vote, the House version of the bill had to be discarded and the House had to accept the Senate version. The bill that passed is a document with glaring problems that will be its undoing if they are not fixed.

A Sustainable Market-Based Alternative

Consensus opinion is that the system is not working as intended and must either be repealed completely or repaired where it is broken. The devil is in the details and agreement on specific remedies is difficult to find. Two contrasting approaches compete for public support: a comprehensive plan focused on government decision-making, or a series of incremental changes targeted at the specific problems. There are four core problems facing the U.S. delivery system:

1. Insurance design attempts to minimize adverse selection, making it difficult for those with preexisting conditions to get coverage at affordable prices and placing those with insurance at risk of losing it should they become ill.
2. Too many Americans lack adequate insurance coverage. Either they think they do not need it, or they simply cannot afford it.
3. Too few insurance carriers offer policies in many market areas. With limited competition, premiums are too high.
4. The risk of litigation creates incentives for physicians to practice defensive medicine to avoid malpractice claims.

Successfully addressing these core problems is essential for the newly reformed system to remain viable into the future.[5]

To address the first problem it is important to establish a mechanism whereby individuals with pre-existing conditions can purchase insurance at reasonable rates. Guaranteed issue provides everyone the opportunity to purchase insurance at actuarially fair premiums. However, many in the high-risk group would find those premiums unaffordable. Too many would remain uninsured, only to receive care at hospital emergency rooms. Two reasonable policy options exist. Place everyone in the same risk pool and require low-risk to pay higher premiums to subsidize the cost of care of those with high risk (the basic approach of the ACA). Alternatively, establish separate risk pools for low and high-risk individuals, charging actuarially fair premiums to everyone while subsidizing the high-risk group through a broad-based tax (the proposed change currently being considered in Congress).

Once we reach the optimal coverage level, guaranteed renewability will solve the problem of pre-existing conditions for those who maintain continuous insurance coverage. Those who experience a change in health status will be able to renew coverage at normal rates regardless of any permanent changes in their health status. Health status insurance supports guaranteed renewability by providing separate protection against an event that would permanently place the individual in a different risk category.

The second problem stems from the fact that many people, in particular the young and healthy, do not perceive value in health insurance. The high cost discourages its purchase. Employer-sponsored insurance is offered to approximately one-third of the 10.7 million young adults (18–34 years old) who are uninsured but they refuse to enroll due to its high

---

[5]See Grinols and Henderson (2009) for a more detailed discussion of a sustainable market-based solution.

cost. Instead of mandating the purchase of insurance and penalizing its non-purchase, offering actuarially fair coverage would encourage voluntary participation.

In general, homogeneous risk pooling (rating by age, sex, region, and family size) is the answer. When pooled with older coworkers in employer-sponsored plans, young adults pay premiums that are significantly higher than they would if pooled with their own age-sex cohort. For example, prior to passage of the ACA a 30-year-old male living in central Texas could purchase a standard PPO plan in the private insurance market with a $1,500 deductible for an annual premium of about $1,500. A similarly situated 60-year-old male paid over $6,000 for a similar plan.[6] The ACA compliant plan must maintain an age band where the premiums vary by 3–1 across age cohorts. Premiums for younger cohorts exceed the actuarially fair premium to subsidize premiums for older cohorts.

Insurance markets need more competition. Allowing the purchase of insurance across state lines may provide more options for those consumers who live and work in different states and those who reside within easy commuting distance to another state.

More importantly, we must stabilize the exchanges by reducing the uncertainty inherent in these marketplaces. When risk pools are stable, insurers are reasonably certain of the composition of those pools and can accurately assess risk. Market stability requires that participants follow a clear set of rules that minimizes the ability to **game** the market. In this situation, gaming is the ability to wait until you are in need of medical care before you purchase coverage. Under the current system, a 90-day grace period before the insurance company can drop a person for nonpayment of premiums coincides with the maximum number of days a person can be without coverage and still avoid the nonparticipation penalty. Twenty percent of marketplace enrollees stop paying premiums the last three months of the year and one-half reenroll in the same plan the next year. For all practical purposes, they only pay for nine months and receive coverage for the entire year.

Another aspect of gaming is that healthy individuals have an incentive to remain uninsured as long as they are healthy and only purchase insurance when they are sick. One way to solve the problem is to create an open window for the guaranteed issue provision. Anyone failing to purchase during the open window will face higher premiums when they finally decide to participate.

Insurance companies require protection against adverse selection or they have an incentive to **shirk**—practice risk selection by encouraging the healthy to join their plans and discouraging the chronically ill. Risk adjustment eliminates the incentive for insurance companies to avoid chronically ill patients. Over the past decade both Medicare Advantage and Medicare Part D have practiced risk adjustment, as well as countries where private insurers compete with each other (Germany and Switzerland come to mind).

When individuals are free to choose their coverage, insurance providers have an incentive to market their products to healthy individuals and provide poor service to those with chronic conditions. Insurers who provide superior services to those with diabetes or heart disease will find their risk pools populated with individuals suffering from those conditions. The solution to this problem is risk adjustment. If high-risk enrollees switch plans, the insurer who accepts the enrollee will receive a payment from the prior insurer equal to the enrollee's additional expected spending.

Addressing the problem of defensive medicine will require major tort reform. The preponderance of evidence seems to support the argument that the practice of defensive medicine is a significant contributor to higher spending in the United States.

game Bending the rules of the game in order to manipulate the outcome.

shirk An action taken to avoid responsibility.

---

[6]All insurance quotes are from ehealthinsurance.com.

PricewaterhouseCoopers attributed as much as 10 percent of total health care spending to defensive medicine and its associated legal costs (PwC, 2010). Academic research is somewhat divided. Sloan and Shadle (2009) find that the different tort laws across the United States do not affect medical decision-making or patient outcomes. In contrast, Kessler and McClellan (1996) and Roberts and Hoch (2009) argue that defensive medicine may be responsible for as much as 10 percent of medical expenditures. Physician surveys indicate that the practice is widespread with 80–90 percent admitting to its practice. It is not necessary to limit damages in cases of malpractice, only that we stop punishing physicians for bad outcomes beyond their control. Changing the rule of cost to "loser pays" would eliminate frivolous lawsuits and the implementation of medical courts with expert panels of judges would minimize the emotional aspect of the adjudication process.

A System at the Crossroads

One thing that the United States has learned from its flirting with a centralized solution to the health care delivery problems is that good intentions do not always lead to good design. It may be time to tone down the ideology and consider a more practical approach.

Possibly the worst option that Congress could consider is another comprehensive government program with decision-making power centered at the federal level. Economics has a long tradition of reliance on the incremental approach to initiating major policy change in a system. Minimizing disruptions to current coverage arrangements will be politically important and may determine whether positive change is possible.

Congress will likely use budget reconciliation to bypass Senate filibuster rules and pass repeal legislation similar to the bill that President Obama vetoed in 2015. The approach will rewrite budget appropriations that support only those desired aspects of the ACA and defund those that are not. The legislation will replace as many components of the ACA as rules allow, likely focusing on stabilizing insurance markets.

What proponents are calling "Repeal Plus" seems to be the most likely replacement approach. The approach will target many of the regulation that add to uncertainty by eliminating the individual and employer mandates (or at minimum ignoring their enforcement), reducing the grace period for nonpayment of premiums to 30 days, suspending the tax on insurance plans (or at least extending the moratorium on its collection), and redefining essential benefits.

In the same or possibly separate legislation, Congress will likely tackle the challenges presented by Medicaid. The logical first step, because of the Medicaid expansion incorporated in the ACA, is to include a temporary freeze in enrollment (for those qualifying under the new eligibility standards). This change has no impact on the 19 states that did not expand Medicaid and only affects about 4.5 million who became eligible under the new eligibility standards in the expansion states.

By reducing federal control, it is essential that the states retake the leadership in regulating insurance markets. The sentiment in Congress seems to lean toward allowing states to innovate and experiment. Our federal form of government provides ample support for fighting the battle at the state level. The stakes are high for the states. Health care spending accounts for over 25 percent of most state budgets. States have a long history in trying to extend insurance coverage. Health care is not a one-size-fits-all proposition. Many argue that states are best equipped to know what their residents want and what works within their jurisdictions.

ISSUES IN MEDICAL CARE DELIVERY

OBAMACARE VERSION 1.0: THE MASSACHUSETTS PLAN

The Massachusetts legislature, overwhelmingly Democrat, joined forces with a moderate Republican Governor Mitt Romney to enact a comprehensive health insurance plan to increase coverage and improve quality of care while simultaneously creating a sustainable cost structure that rationalizes the financing of medical care. Relying on individual responsibility and social solidarity, the plan became operational in July 2007, providing a mechanism to achieve universal insurance coverage for all residents of the state.

Sharing most of the major features of the ACA, this state experiment can provide valuable lessons for policymakers across the political spectrum. Expanding access to insurance coverage is reasonably straightforward. The plan expanded Medicaid eligibility to all families making below 100 percent of the FPL and provides generous subsidies to everyone making less than 300 percent of FPL. As a result, the percentage of the state's residents who were uninsured is now less than one-half of pre-reform levels. Therein lies the problem. Subsidized insurance now increased the demand for health care, but the plan does little to increase the supply of medical services. So as coverage increases in a market that was already experiencing shortages, little is done to increase the number of providers. In fact, lawmakers have strengthened the state's certificate of need laws making it more difficult for hospitals, ambulatory surgery centers, and other outpatient treatment centers to expand (Tully, 2010).

Subsidized demand and regulated supply will lead to further price increases, making it even more difficult to control rising costs. When government is not able to control spending, the result is price controls. In April 2010, state regulators placed restrictions on the ability of insurance carriers to raise premiums, rolling back all increases determined to be excessive to 2009 levels.

Long and Masi (2009) report survey findings that indicate that expanded insurance coverage has not solved the access problem for many of the state's residents. Almost one-third of lower-income adults responding to the survey reported that the doctor was not accepting new patients with their type of insurance or not accepting new patients at all. Access barriers were the result of low payment rates and a limited panel of providers participating in the public insurance plans. Emergency department visits for non-emergency events have actually increased for this group because they are unable to get timely appointments to see participating physicians.

Sources: Sharon K. Long and Paul B. Masi, "Access and Affordability: An Update on Health Reform in Massachusetts, Fall 2008," *Health Affairs—Web Exclusive*, May 28, 2009, w578–w587; and Michael D. Tanner, "No Miracle in Massachusetts: Why Governor Romney's Health Care Reform Won't Work," *Briefing Papers No. 97*, Washington, DC: Cato Institute, June 6, 2006.

Summary and Conclusions

For now, the ACA is the law of the land, despite its shortcomings. Efforts over the next few years will focus on piecing together a plan to fix its deficiencies. Expect changes in plan design almost immediately, through either legislation or executive order. Certain elements will not change: preexisting condition exclusions will remain. There will be no lifetime maximums or annual limitations. Young adults will remain on their parents' plans until age 26.

Plan design will likely see some changes giving consumers more options to purchase a plan that better suits their needs. Many of the tax measures will remain in place, but many will be eliminated—the premium tax, the pharmaceutical tax, the medical device tax, to name a few. Expect removal of the cap on flexible spending plans and a rollback of the threshold for deducting medical expenses for income tax purposes (raised by the ACA from 7.5 to 10 percent).

Most of the coverage expansion that began in 2014 was due to increases in Medicaid enrollment. Therefore, to minimize immediate disruptions the Congress will likely freeze expansion enrollment until solutions that are more permanent are in place. The IRS will no longer enforce the mandates by collecting the penalties for not purchasing insurance. A ceiling on the deductibility of employer-sponsored insurance will likely replace the excise tax on high-premium plans.

The number of people who gain (or lose) coverage and whether the new plan is able to "bend the cost curve" will be the ultimate measures of success. We know that the true cost of anything is its opportunity cost. Thus, shifting cost is not reducing cost. Paying providers less is not reducing cost. Passing cost onto business and the states is not reducing cost. Higher taxes on those with higher incomes is not reducing cost. Rationing benefits is not reducing costs. The legislation as passed in 2010 was the starting point. We cannot sit back and relax now.

PROFILE Alain Enthoven

Without question, Alain Enthoven is a leading figure in the health care reform movement worldwide. His ideas have helped shape recent reforms in England and the Netherlands. Enthoven served as the intellectual backbone of the now-famous Jackson Hole Group, which has studied and discussed health care reform regularly since the mid-1970s. A respected Stanford economist, Enthoven is a strong proponent of managed competition, having developed the idea in collaboration with his long-time friend Dr. Paul Ellwood.

After completing his undergraduate work at Stanford, Enthoven won a Rhodes scholarship to study at Oxford. In 1956, he completed his Ph.D. in economics from MIT and went to work for the RAND Corporation in Santa Monica, California. His early work was on defense issues, and he soon became knowledgeable in the ways of the federal government. Well known in government circles, he went to work in the Pentagon in 1961. During his years in Washington, Enthoven became a director of Georgetown University. While on the board, he chaired the committee that built a major medical center at the school and created the university's group-practice HMO.

In 1973, Enthoven began consulting with the Kaiser-Permanente Group in California, where he developed most of his ideas for reforming medical care. That same year, Enthoven joined the Stanford faculty, where he is now the Marriner S. Eccles Professor of Public and Private Management, Emeritus, in the Graduate School of Business.

Conservative Democrats looking for an alternative to the Canadian-style single-payer approach have turned to Enthoven's plan of managed competition. Like many plans created by economists, when the politicians get through with them, they are barely recognizable. The major change that Enthoven found distasteful was the addition of budget caps or price controls. Given his work developing the theory of managed competition, it is somewhat surprising that he was not asked to participate in President Clinton's 1993 national task force on health care reform. Nevertheless, Enthoven is confident that policymakers will ultimately turn to managed competition as the only reform plan that can work within the American system.

Enthoven (1988) argued "reform should start with cost-conscious choices made by the educated middle class. In this way, the organizational cultures of the health plans are created in an environment in which they serve intelligent, relatively informed people who have choices."

Sources: John Huber, "The Abandoned Father of Health-Care Reform," *The New York Times Magazine*, July 18, 1993, 24–26, 36–37; and Alain Enthoven, *Theory and Practice of Managed Competition in Health Care Finance*, Professor Dr. F. DeVries Lectures in Economics: Theory, Institutions, Policy, Volume 9, Amsterdam: North-Holland, 1988.

Questions and Problems

1. What are the respective roles of the federal government and the state governments in providing health services?

2. Hundreds of state mandates nationwide require the provision of certain benefits or the coverage of certain providers for all plans. Do these mandates address specific failures in the private insurance market or do they reflect the political strength of certain provider groups?

3. Describe the major elements of the ACA. What problem is the legislation trying to address? How is the cost? How is it financed? What are the major objections to the legislation?

4. The U.S. health care delivery system has been criticized for its structural defects: high costs, large numbers of uninsured, and a failure to promote high-quality health in the population. What possible approaches to health care reform do you think are morally acceptable, economically effective, and politically feasible? Elaborate on the key features of your own national health care policy proposal.

5. Altman and Rodwin ("Halfway Competitive Markets and Ineffective Regulation," *Journal of Health Policy, Politics and Law* 13(2), Summer 1988, 323–339) argue that the medical care system in the United States exhibits neither effective competition nor effective government regulation. Would we be better off if we decisively adopted one approach or the other? Explain.

6. Is death an enemy that is to be fought off at all costs, or is it a condition of life that is to be accepted? How does the way we answer this question affect the kind of health care system we might embrace?

7. Should we shy away from specifying a collectively provided benefits package that is less generous than the standard package available to those who can afford to pay for it? Is the creation of a two-tiered system fair?

8. In what sense do Americans have a right to medical care? In what sense is access to medical care not a right? How have the reforms at the state level helped define the nature of the right to medical care in this country?

References

Blendon, Robert J., Jennifer N. Edwards, and Andrew L. Hyams, "Making the Critical Choices," *Journal of the American Medical Association* 267(18), May 13, 1992, 2509–2520.

Blendon, Robert J., John M. Benson, and Catherine M. DesRoches, "Americans' Views of the Uninsured: An Era for Hybrid Proposals," *Health Affairs—Web Exclusive* (W3), August 27, 2003, 405–414.

Blendon, Robert J., John M. Benson, and Catherine M. DesRoches, "Understanding the American Public's Health Priorities: A 2006 Perspective," *Health Affairs—Web Exclusive*, 17 October 2006, w508–w515.

Bonilla, Carlos, "The Price of a Health Care Mandate," *Wall Street Journal*, August 20, 1993, A10.

Donelan, Karen, et al., "The Cost of Health System Change: Public Discontent in Five Countries," *Health Affairs* 18(3), May/June 1999, 206–216.

Emanuel, Ezekiel J. and Victor R. Fuchs, "The Perfect Storm of Overutilization," *Journal of the American Medical Association* 299(33), June 18, 2008, 2789–2791.

Enthoven, Alain C., "A Good Health Care Idea Gone Bad," *Wall Street Journal*, October 7, 1993, A18.

___ "Consumer Choice Health Plan," *New England Journal of Medicine* 298 (12 and 13), March 23 and March 30, 1978, 650–658 and 709–720.

___, *Theory and Practice of Managed Competition in Health Care Finance*, Professor Dr. F. DeVries Lectures in Economics: Theory, Institutions, Policy, Volume 9, Amsterdam: North-Holland, 1988.

Foster, Richard S., Chief Actuary, Centers for Medicare and Medicaid Services, "Estimated Financial Effects of the 'Patient Protection and Affordable Care Act,' As Amended," April 22, 2010, www.cms.gov/ActuarialStudies/Downloads/PPACA_2010-04-22.pdf (accessed February 17, 2011).

Frean, Molly, Jonathan Gruber, and Benjamin D. Sommers, "Disentangling the ACA's Coverage Effects—Lessons for Policymakers," *New England Journal of Medicine* 375(17), October 27, 2016, 1605–1608.

Garcia, Tamyra Carroll, Amy B. Bernstein, and Mary Ann Bush, "Emergency Department Visitors and Visits: Who Used the Emergency Room in 2007?" NCHS Data Brief No. 38, May 2010, www.cdc.gov/nchs/data/databriefs/db38.pdf (accessed April 13, 2011).

Goodman, John C., "Health Solutions for Post-Obamacare America," Oakland, CA: The Independent Institute, November 17, 2014, available at http://www.independent.org/publications/policy_reports/detail.asp?id=44.

Haislmaier, Edmund F., "The Real Changes in Health Insurance Enrollment under the Affordable Care Act," Testimony before Committee on the Budget, U.S. House of Representatives, January 24, 2017, http://budget.house.gov/uploadedfiles/house_budget_testimony-haislmaier.pdf (accessed February 16, 2017).

___, "The Significance of Massachusetts Health Reform," *Web Memo #1035*, Washington, DC: The Heritage Foundation, April 11, 2006.

Jensen, Gail A. and Michael A. Morrisey, *Mandated Benefit Laws and Employer-Sponsored Health Insurance*, Washington, DC: Health Insurance Association of America, 1999.

Kessler, Daniel and Mark McClellan, "Do Doctors Practice Defensive Medicine?" *The Quarterly Journal of Economics* 111(2), May 1996, 353–390.

Pauly, Mark V., "Making a Case for Employer-Enforced Individual Mandates," *Health Affairs* 13(2), Spring (II) 1994, 21–33.

PwC (PricewaterhouseCoopers), "The Price of Excess: Identifying Waste in Healthcare Spending," 2010, pwchealth.com/cgi-local/hregister.cgi?link=reg/waste.pdf (accessed April 13, 2011).

Reinhardt, Uwe, "You Pay When Business Bankrolls Health Care," *Wall Street Journal*, December 2, 1992, A10.

Roberts, Brandon and Irving Hoch, "Malpractice Litigation and Medical Costs in the United States," *Health Economics* 18, 2009, 1394–1419.

Robinson, Ray, "Managed Care in the United States: A Dilemma for Evidence-Based Policy?" *Health Economics* 9(1), January 2000, 1–7.

Sloan, Frank A. and John H. Shadle, "Is There Empirical Evidence for 'Defensive Medicine'? A Reassessment," *Journal of Health Economics* 28, 2009, 481–491.

Stout, Hilary, "Health Care Choices: A Bigger Federal Role of a Market Approach?" *Wall Street Journal*, January 15, 1992, A1.

Tully, Shawn, "5 Painful Health-Care Lessons from Massachusetts," *CNNMoney.com*, June 16, 2010, money.cnn.com/2010/06/15/news/economy/massachusetts_healthcare_reform.fortune/index.htm (accessed February 17, 2011).

CHAPTER 16

Lessons for Public Policy

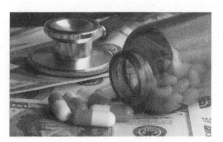

Throughout the book, we have attempted to use the 10 key economic concepts as guiding principles to organize our approach to the study of health economics. Some of the lessons are obvious, some not quite so obvious. Because they are not all based on positive analysis, many of the following propositions are likely to prompt some disagreement. By their very nature, public policy discussions are normative. Now you are armed with many of the economic tools that will help you analyze the issues more carefully. The bracketed number notes the chapter where the principle is discussed.

Scarcity and Choice

Economics recognizes the problem of limited resources and unlimited wants and desires. Without enough resources to satisfy all the desires of all the people, allocating those resources among competing objectives becomes essential.

- *We must face the fact that resources used in the delivery of medical care have alternative uses that are also beneficial. To strike a balance between scarce resources and unlimited wants involves making choices. We cannot have everything we want. In the world where most of us live, trade-offs are inevitable. [2]*

Opportunity Cost

Everything and everyone has alternatives. Time and resources used to satisfy one set of desires cannot be used to satisfy another set. The cost of any decision or action is measured in terms of the value placed on the opportunity forgone.

- *Medical care decisions involve costs as well as benefits. For many clinicians, allowing cost considerations into treatment decisions is morally repugnant. To counter this feeling, it is essential that practitioners have knowledge of the fundamentals of economics to provide a foundation for understanding the issues that affect medical care delivery and policy. [2]*
- *Long-run savings is not the sole determinant of wise resource use. A more relevant factor in decision-making is what other beneficial use of the same resources is foregone. [4]*

■ *Resources taken from Medicare and used to fund the expansion of Medicaid cannot be used simultaneously to extend the solvency of the Medicare Trust Fund. [12]*

■ *Universal coverage is expensive and state-financed programs will crowd out private programs, making coverage costlier than originally estimated. [15]*

Marginal Analysis

The economic way of thinking about the optimal resource allocation may be classified as marginal decision-making. Choices are seldom made on an all-or-nothing basis—they are made "at the margin." Decision makers weigh the trade-offs considering the incremental benefits and incremental costs of decisions they are about to make. This principle manifests itself in medical markets in several ways.

■ *When the marginal cost to the consumer is held at artificially low levels, resources are treated as if they have little or no value—a prescription for overconsumption. [2]*

■ *Balancing incremental benefits and incremental costs is essential for optimal resource allocation. Most choices in medical care involve determining the level of an activity, not its very existence. Decision-making is seldom an all-or-nothing proposition. It usually involves a trade-off. If we are to spend a little more on one thing, we must spend a little less on something else. [2]*

■ *In an economy in which productivity is growing in most sectors and declining in none, consumers can have more of everything. True of many service industries, including education, the arts, and medical care, the benefits of economy-wide productivity gains may be transferred to enable greater consumption of these superior goods. [3]*

■ *Wise resource use is determined by comparing one alternative use to the next best option. [4]*

■ *The relevant issues deal with marginal changes in utilization and spending, not overall utilization and spending. [5]*

■ *Medical care spending is not the only way to improve the health status of an individual or population. Other factors, including lifestyle choices and genetics, play important roles. [5]*

■ *The apparent relationship between health care spending and the proximity to death is due primarily to the relationship between age and mortality. [6]*

■ *Risk-averse individuals will insure against low-probability, high-cost events, such as hospitalizations. Insurance covering routine care, such as primary and preventive care, physical examinations, and teeth cleaning, is not as common. [7]*

■ *People often engage in opportunistic behavior after they enter into an insurance contract because their behavior cannot be monitored. The fact that a person has insurance coverage increases expected medical care spending. Having insurance increases the likelihood of purchasing medical services and induces higher spending in the event of an illness. In other words, lowering the cost of medical care to the individual through the availability of insurance increases usage. [7]*

■ *A one-size-fits-all benefits package is expensive and pressures to expand coverage are enormous. [15]*

Self-Interest

Economic decision makers are motivated to pursue their own self-interest. People respond to incentives and practice economizing behavior only when they individually benefit from such behavior. According to Adam Smith, this pursuit of self-interest leads each individual to a course of action that promotes the general welfare of everyone in society.

■ *The pursuit of self-interest dominates decision making. [1]*

■ *Human behavior is responsive to incentives and constraints. If you want people to practice economizing behavior, they must benefit individually from their own economizing. People spending other people's money show little concern for how it is spent. People spending their own money tend to spend more wisely. [2]*

■ *Decisions must be made by well-informed, cost-conscious consumers. Motivated by self-interest and adequately informed about treatment alternatives, cost-conscious consumers will economize because they will personally benefit from their own economizing behavior. [3]*

■ *The patient/buyer must be an active participant in the decision-making process if cost containment is to be achieved without artificial controls such as mandatory fee schedules, fixed budgets, and resource rationing. [3]*

■ *Patients and providers fail to practice economizing behavior because there is very little direct benefit to the individual who economizes. [3]*

■ *Good health is not always the primary goal in life for most people. Individual behavior proves this daily. Motorists fail to buckle their seat belts, cyclists refuse to wear helmets, millions engage in risky sexual practices, and others use drugs, smoke cigarettes, and consume unhealthy quantities of alcohol. [5]*

■ *The best way to control overall spending is to require more personal responsibility in financing medical care consumption. [5]*

■ *Economic incentives matter in determining the demand for medical care. [5]*

■ *Evidence that medical decisions are affected by a patient's insurance coverage supports the notion that physicians respond to economic incentives. [9]*

■ *The differences between the for-profit and not-for-profit organizational form may be classified as differences in property rights. The differences affect the incentive structure facing decision makers. [10]*

■ *When consumers perceive that they will benefit from additional information, they will demand information, and it will be provided. [15]*

Markets and Pricing

The market has proven to be the most efficient way to allocate scarce resources. The market accomplishes its tasks through a system of prices, Smith's "invisible hand." Resources can be allocated by the market because everyone and everything has a price. The price mechanism becomes a way to bring a firm's output decisions into balance with consumer desires—something that we refer to as *equilibrium*.

■ *Providing all necessary care for a fixed fee changes the nature of the physician–patient relationship. [9]*

■ *With Medicare and Medicaid paying such a large percentage of the total hospital bill, government reimbursement rules play a big role in determining the financial stability of the hospital sector. [10]*

■ *As the inefficiencies in the hospital system are eliminated, so too is the ability to subsidize charity care for the uninsured and medical education, increasing the pressure on public policy makers to improve the social safety net for the more vulnerable population groups, including pregnant women, children, and the poor. [10]*

- *The availability of reliable transportation and Internet communication eliminates the boundaries of the medical marketplace. For all practical purposes, the market for elective procedures is worldwide. [14]*
- *It is relatively simple to expand coverage to those who will receive free or heavily subsidized care. Policy makers must be ready to respond to the inevitable cost pressures that have the potential to undermine any early access. [15]*
- *Expanding insurance coverage beyond a delivery system's ability to provide care results in shortages and a call to ration care. [15]*

Supply and Demand

The forces of supply and demand determine pricing and output decisions. Goods and services are allocated among competing uses by equating the consumers' willingness to pay and the suppliers' willingness to provide—rationing via prices.

- *The quantity of medical care demanded increases as the cost to the individual declines. [1]*
- *Price controls create shortages. [2, 13]*
- *The favorable tax treatment for employer-based health insurance distorts the composition of the typical employee compensation package. [7]*
- *Information costs are a central factor in economic decision-making. [7]*
- *Managed care can control utilization when patient choice is restricted and clinical decision making is controlled. [7]*
- *The problems inherent in any system emphasize cost containment over quality and access. Patient desires for expensive treatments will be sacrificed to the demand to control costs and spending. [8]*
- *When the physician faces a zero price for other medical inputs, too many other inputs will be used relative to physician inputs, resulting in inefficiencies. [10]*
- *When government attempts to micromanage medical care delivery and provide "free" care to a well-organized constituency, shortages develop in the form of long waits, and the quality of specialized care deteriorates. [12]*
- *After the initial cost efficiencies are realized, the lower prices associated with the mandatory fee schedules lead to fixed budgets and eventually to limits on services. [13]*

Competition

Competition forces resource owners to use their resources to promote the highest possible satisfaction of society: consumers, producers, and investors. If resource owners do this well, they are rewarded. If they are inept or inefficient, they are penalized. Competition takes production out of the hands of the less competent and puts it into the hands of the more efficient, constantly promoting more efficient methods of production.

- *Competition among providers is essential for well-functioning markets. Competition guards against undue concentration because substitutes are readily available. Consumer demand becomes more sensitive to price changes. [3]*
- *Competition in markets forces suppliers to improve efficiency resulting in lower prices for consumers. [7]*
- *Competition forces providers to charge prices reflecting their costs. Consolidations leading to the concentration of market power will allow providers to act more like monopolists and price their services above costs. [9]*

■ *Competition on the demand side of the market serves to reduce inefficiencies. Inefficient hospitals become prime targets for acquisition. [10]*

■ *The nature of competition in a market dominated by nonprofit providers does not promote cost efficiency but instead promotes quality enhancement. Providers have little incentive to increase productivity, consumers have no incentive to limit their demand, and providers have no incentive to limit their supply. This is a prescription for increased spending. [10]*

Efficiency

Economic efficiency measures how well resources are being used to promote social welfare. Inefficient outcomes waste resources, but the efficient use of scarce resources enhances social welfare.

■ *In making medical care decisions, the ethical use of resources may be just as important as their efficient use. [4]*

■ *Specialization leads to cost savings through a more efficient allocation of resources. [8]*

■ *Given the wide range of managed care arrangements, we must be cautious about forming conclusions about the overall effectiveness of the new forms of controlling costs. [8]*

■ *Physician ownership improves hospital efficiency by allowing physicians to benefit from the shared savings. [9, 10]*

■ *Efficiency is not rewarded in a cost-plus environment. Thus, finding little difference in efficiency between for-profit and not-for-profit hospitals is not surprising, or at least it should not be. With the increasing use of managed care and prospective payment, only recently have hospitals been given an incentive to be efficient. [10]*

■ *The fiscal realities of expanding coverage to the uninsured may eventually require a scaling back of the basic benefits package to one that covers much less than the standard policy that those with private insurance expect. [15]*

Market Failure

Free markets sometimes fail to promote the efficient use of resources by producing either more or less than the optimal level of output. Sources of market failure include natural monopolies, externalities in production and consumption, and public goods. Other market imperfections, such as incomplete information and immobile resources, also contribute to this problem.

■ *Policymaking based on sound economics is better than policymaking in an economic vacuum. [2]*

■ *Various imperfections in medical markets make the dual task of delivering a product equitably and efficiently more difficult. [3]*

■ *Market power insulates a firm from the competitive forces that insure optimal resource allocation, resulting in a loss to society. [3]*

■ *To use taxes to address market failure, policy makers must first make sure they are taxing the right behavior. Taxing the wrong behavior can actually reduce welfare and result in government failure, which is far more difficult to eliminate. [6]*

■ *The purpose of insurance is to share risk, not wealth. Policy makers, even those not interested in wealth redistribution, have used market failure to justify the provision of social insurance as a safety net. [7]*

- *Because the private insurance market cannot provide adequate insurance for those with preexisting conditions, it becomes a collective responsibility if this group is to have access to medical care. [7]*
- *Cream skimming is the result of regulation in the insurance industry, not competition. [7]*
- *The market has found it increasingly difficult to subsidize care for the elderly, the indigent, and the uninsured, providing justification for collective action through government to ensure access for these groups. [7]*
- *Hospital markets may not fit the competitive model very well, because so many of the structural characteristics of perfect competition are violated. [10]*
- *Legislating the definition of a full-time worker (for employer-mandated coverage) will create an abundance of part-time workers. [15]*
- *Tax-financed government spending often crowds out private spending. [15]*

Comparative Advantage

Markets promote economic efficiency and ensure that all mutually beneficial transactions occur when individuals are free to engage in exchange based on opportunity cost. Every transaction that will benefit both a consumer and a provider takes place. The market system is grounded in the concept of consumer sovereignty: What is produced is determined by what people want and are able to buy. No one individual or group dictates what is produced or purchased. No one limits the range of choice. Individuals specialize in the activity they do best—the one with the lowest opportunity cost.

- *Transferring decision making from the private sector to the public sector substitutes bureaucratic discipline for economic discipline. [3]*
- *Cost-conscious decisions are possible only if consumers who desire to enter the market have money to spend. Often phrased in terms of equity, the real issue is economic self-sufficiency. For medical care markets, this requires either universal insurance coverage or universal access to insurance. The choice depends on whether the majority of the populace is concerned with equal outcomes or equal opportunities. Satisfying this condition ensures that the system is morally acceptable to a majority of the people. [3]*

Final Reflections

By now you should be aware of the issues that can make the study of health economics both fascinating and frustrating. Those of you with little background in economics are likely fascinated with the wide range of issues for which economics has relevance. If you were expecting answers to many of the questions that confront policy makers, you are likely frustrated. Economics does not promise answers, only a systematic way to study the alternatives.

Whether this ends your formal training in health economics, or it is merely the first of many courses you will take, let this be the beginning of a lifetime of inquiry into health care issues using the tools of analysis introduced in this text. Remember, taking one course or reading one book cannot possibly make you an expert. Fortunately, health economics is rich with opportunities for further research and study.

Glossary

A

actuarially fair premium   Insurance premium based on the actuarial probability that an event will occur.

allocative efficiency   The situation in which producers make the goods and services that consumers desire. For every item, the marginal cost of production is less than or equal to the marginal benefit received by consumers.

any willing provider   A situation in which a managed care organization allows any medical provider to become part of the network of providers for the covered group.

applied research   Research whose purpose is typically the commercialization of a product.

arbitrage   The practice of simultaneously buying a commodity at one price and selling it at a higher price.

assignment   A Medicare policy providing physicians with a guaranteed payment of 80 percent of the allowable fee. By accepting assignment, physicians agree to accept the allowable fee as full payment and forgo the practice of balance billing.

asymmetric information   A situation in which information is unequally distributed between the individuals in a transaction. The person with more information will have an unfair advantage in determining the terms of any agreement.

average product   Output per unit of input.

B

balance billing   Billing a patient for the difference between the physician's usual charge for a service and the maximum charge allowed by the patient's health plan.

basic research   Research whose purpose is to advance fundamental knowledge.

bilateral monopoly   When there is monopoly on the seller's side of the market and monopsony on the buyer's side.

C

capitation   A payment method providing a fixed, per capita payment to providers for a specified medical benefits package. Providers are required to treat a well-defined population for a fixed sum of money, paid in advance, without regard to the number or nature of the services provided to each person.

case management   A method of coordinating the provision of medical care for patients with specific high-cost diagnoses such as cancer and heart disease.

certificate-of-need (CON)   Regulations that attempt to avoid the costly duplication of services in the hospital industry. Providers are required to secure a certificate of need before undertaking a major expansion of facilities or services.

clinical rule   Is a specific practice required of all participating physicians, such as a policy to refer patients only to a specific panel of specialists.

closed panel   A designated network of providers that serves the recipients of a health care plan. Patients are not allowed to choose a provider outside the network.

coinsurance   A standard feature of health insurance policies that requires the insured person to pay a certain percentage of a medical bill, usually 10 to 30 percent, per physician visit or hospital stay.

collective bargaining   The negotiation process whereby representatives of employers and employees agree upon the terms of a labor contract, including wages and benefits.

community rated   Basing health insurance premiums on the health care utilization experience of the entire population of a specific geographic area. Premiums are the same for all individuals regardless of age, gender, risk, or prior use of health care services.

consumer-directed health plan   A health plan that combines an HSA with a high-deductible insurance policy.

coordinates   A system of uniquely determining the position of a point in a number space.

copayment   A standard feature of many managed care plans that requires the insured person to pay a fixed sum for each office visit, hospital stay, or prescription drug.

correlation coefficient   A measure of the linear association between two variables.

cost containment   Strategies used to control the total spending on health care services.

cost shifting   The practice of charging higher prices to one group of patients, usually those with health insurance, in order to provide free care to the uninsured or discounted care to those served by Medicare and Medicaid.

cost-plus pricing   A pricing scheme in which a percentage profit is added to the average cost.

cream skimming   A practice of pricing insurance policies so that healthy (low-risk) individuals will purchase coverage and those with a history of costly medical problems (high-risk) will not.

cross-price elasticity   The sensitivity of consumer demand for good A as the price of good B changes.

D

deductible   The amount of money that an insured person must pay before a health plan begins paying for all or part of the covered expenses.

defensive medicine   Medical services that have little or no medical benefit; their provision is simply to reduce the risk of being sued.

dependent variable   Response variable.

diagnosis-related group   A patient classification scheme based on certain demographic, diagnostic, and therapeutic characteristics developed by Medicare and used to compensate hospitals.

disproportionate share   A payment adjustment under Medicare and Medicaid that pays hospitals that serve a large number of indigent patients.

E

economic efficiency   Producing at a point at which average product is maximized and average variable cost is minimized.

economies of scale   A situation in a production process where long run average costs decline as output expands.

economizing behavior   When individuals choose to limit their demand for goods and services voluntarily to save money.

Employee Retirement Income Security Act (ERISA) Federal legislation passed in 1974 that sets minimum standards on employee benefit plans, such as pension, health insurance, and disability. The statute protects the interests of employees in matters concerning eligibility for benefits. The law also protects employers from certain state regulations. For example, states are not allowed to regulate self-insured plans and cannot mandate that employers provide health insurance to their employees.

employer mandate   A requirement that employers must offer a qualified health plan to every employee or pay a penalty (usually in the form of a payroll tax).

entitlement programs   Government assistance programs where eligibility is determined by a specified criteria, such as age, health status, and level of income. These programs include Social Security, Medicare, Medicaid, and Temporary Assistance for Needy Families (TANF), and many more.

equilibrium   The market-clearing price at which every consumer wanting to purchase the good finds a willing seller.

expected value of an outcome   The weighted average of all possible outcomes, with the probabilities of those outcomes used as weights.

experience rated   Basing health insurance premiums on the utilization experience of a specific insured group. Premiums may vary by age, gender, or other risk factors.

externality   A cost or benefit that spills over to parties not directly involved in the actual transaction and is thus ignored by the buyer and seller.

F

fee-for-service   The traditional payment method for medical care in which a provider bills for each service provided.

financial risk   The risk associated with contractual obligations that require fixed monetary outlays.

fixed cost   The total cost of the fixed inputs.

fixed inputs   Inputs in a production process that are difficult to increment.

Flexner Report   A 1910 report published as part of a critical review of medical education in the United States. The response of the medical establishment led to significant changes in the accreditation procedures of medical schools and an improvement in the quality of medical care.

Food and Drug Administration (FDA)   A public health agency charged with protecting American consumers by enforcing federal public health laws. Food, medicine, medical devices, and cosmetics are under the jurisdiction of the FDA.

free rider   An individual who does not buy insurance, knowing that in the event of a serious illness, medical care will be provided free of charge.

G

game   Bending the rules of the game in order to manipulate the outcome.

gatekeeper   A primary care physician who directs health care delivery and determines whether patients are allowed access to specialty care.

global budget   A limit on the amount of money available to a health care system during a specified time. All medically necessary care must be provided to all eligible patients within the limits of a fixed budget.

graph   Chart or diagram depicting the relationship between two or more variables.

gross domestic product (GDP)   The monetary value of the goods and services produced in a country during a given time period, usually a year.

group insurance   A plan whereby an entire group receives insurance under a single policy. The insurance is actually issued to the plan holder, usually an employer or association.

group-model HMO   A group of physicians—often a large, multispecialty group practice—that agree to provide medical care to a defined patient group, usually the employees of the corporation, in return for a fixed per capita fee or for discounted fees.

guaranteed issue   A requirement that insurers must issue a policy to anyone who applies for one with no consideration of health status.

guaranteed renewability   A feature of an insurance policy that requires the insurer to guarantee renewal of the policy as long a premiums are paid, regardless of any changes in the health status of the policy holder.

H

health alliances   Called by various names, including *health insurance purchasing cooperatives (HIPC)*, these provide a way for small employers to act collectively to purchase health insurance. Often geographically based and not-for-profit, the alliance contracts with insurers and/or providers for medical coverage for its members.

health maintenance organization (HMO)   A type of managed care organization that functions like an insurer and also arranges for the provision of care.

histogram   Graphical presentation in the form of a bar graph of the probability distribution of a continuous variable.

horizontal integration   The merger of two or more firms that produce the same good or service.

I

iatrogenic disease   An injury or illness resulting from medical treatment.

income elasticity of demand   The sensitivity of demand to changes in consumer income, determined by the percentage change in quantity demanded relative to the percentage change in consumer income.

indemnity insurance   Insurance based on the principle that someone suffering an economic loss receives a payment approximately equal to the size of the loss.

independent practice association (IPA)   An organized group of health care providers that offers medical services to a specified group of enrollees of a health plan.

independent variable   Causal variable.

individual mandate   A legal requirement that individuals carry their own insurance protection.

in-kind transfer   Welfare subsidies provided in the form of vouchers for specific goods and services, such as food stamps and Medicaid.

isocost curve   A locus of points that shows the various combinations of inputs that have the same cost.

isoquants   Literally "equal quantity." A contour line that shows the different combinations of two inputs that produce the same level of output.

L

laissez faire   A French term meaning literally "allow [them] to do." It depicts a situation in which individuals and firms are allowed to pursue their own self-interests without government restraint.

law of diminishing returns   The empirical observation that expanding the use of one input (holding all others constant) will eventually result in a decreasing rate of change in productivity.

long run   The period of time where all inputs are variable.

luxury or superior goods   Goods are considered superior if an increase in consumer income causes the percentage of the consumer's income spent on the good to increase and vice versa.

M

major medical   Health insurance to provide coverage for major illnesses requiring large financial outlays, characterized by payment for all expenses above a specified maximum out-of-pocket amount paid by the insured (often $2,000–$5,000).

managed care   A delivery system that originally integrated the financing and provision of medical care in one organization. Now the term encompasses different arrangements designed to coordinate services and control costs.

managed competition   A health care reform plan first popularized by economist Alain Enthoven, whereby individuals are given a choice among competing health plans.

marginal benefit   The change in total benefits resulting from a one-unit change in the level of output.

marginal cost   The change in total cost resulting from a one-unit change in the level of output.

marginal product   The change in total product resulting from a unit change in input.

marginal rate of technical substitution (MRTS)   As the amount of one input in a production process increases, the amount in the other input can be decreased without changing the level of output.

marginal revenue product   The change in total revenue resulting from the sale of the output produced by an additional unit of a resource.

market failure   A situation in which a market fails to produce the socially optimal level of output.

mean   The average of a set of numbers.

median   The middle value of a finite set of numbers arranged from lowest to highest.

Medicaid   Health insurance for the poor financed jointly by the federal government and the states.

medical savings account   A tax-exempt savings account used in conjunction with high-deductible health insurance. Individuals pay their own medical expenses using funds from the savings account up to the amount of the deductible. Once the deductible is met, the insurance policy pays all or most of the covered expenses.

Medicare   Health insurance for the elderly provided under an amendment to the Social Security Act.

Medigap insurance   A supplemental insurance policy sold to Medicare-eligible individuals to pay the deductibles and coinsurance that are not covered by Medicare.

merit good   A good whose benefits are not fully appreciated by the average consumer and thus should be provided collectively.

microeconomics   The study of individual decision making, pricing behavior, and market organization.

mode   The most frequently occurring number in a set of numbers.

monetary conversion factor   A monetary value used to translate relative value units into dollar amounts to determine a fee schedule.

moral hazard   Insurance coverage increases both the likelihood of making a claim and the actual size of the claim. Insurance reduces the net out-of-pocket price of medical services and thus increases the quantity demanded.

morbidity   The incidence and probability of illness or disability.

mortality   The probability of death at different ages, usually expressed as the number of deaths for a given population, either 1,000 or 100,000, or the expected number of years of life remaining at a given age.

N

national health insurance   A government-run health insurance system covering the entire population for a well-defined medical benefits package. Usually administered by a government or quasi-government agency and financed through some form of taxation.

natural monopoly   A firm becomes a natural monopoly based on its ability to provide a good or service at a lower cost than anyone else and satisfy consumer demand completely.

necessity   A good or service with an income elasticity between zero and one.

neoclassical economics   A branch of economic thought that uses microeconomic principles to defend the efficacy of perfectly competitive markets in resource allocation.

network-model HMO   A managed care organization that contracts with several different providers, including physicians' practices and hospitals, to make a full range of medical services available to its enrollees.

nonexcludable good   A good or service that is difficult to limit to a specific group of consumers. In other words, if the item is available to anyone, it becomes available to everyone.

nonrival good   A good or service that does not, when consumed by one individual, limit the amount available to anyone else.

normal distribution   The distribution of a set of numbers around the mean that takes on a symmetrical bell shape.

normative analysis   An economic statement based on opinion or ideology.

not-for-profit   A business classification that is exempt from paying most taxes. In return for this tax-exempt status, the firm is restricted in how any operating surplus may be distributed among its stakeholders.

O

opportunity cost   The cost of a decision based on the value of the foregone opportunity.

optimal output level   A market equilibrium in which the marginal benefit received from every unit of output is greater than or equal to the marginal cost of producing each unit. The social optimum is that output level at which the marginal benefit of the last unit produced is equal to its marginal cost.

optimizing behavior, or **optimization**   A technique used to determine the best or most favorable outcome in a particular situation.

P

participating physician   A physician who agrees to accept Medicare assignment.

patent   An exclusive right to supply a good for a specific time period, usually 20 years. It serves as a barrier to entry, virtually eliminating all competition for the life of the patent.

physician-induced demand   A situation in which providers take advantage of uninformed consumers to purchase services that are largely unnecessary.

play-or-pay A health care reform feature whereby employers "play" by providing health care coverage to their employees, or they pay a payroll tax to fund government-provided insurance.

point-of-service plan (POS) A hybrid managed care plan that combines the features of a prepaid plan and a fee-for-service plan. Enrollees use network physicians with minimal out-of-pocket expenses and may choose to go out of the network by paying a higher coinsurance rate.

portability The ability to easily transfer insurance coverage from one plan to another as a covered employee changes jobs.

positive analysis A factually based statement whose validity can be tested empirically.

practice guidelines A specific statement about the appropriate course of treatment that should be taken for patients with given medical conditions.

preexisting condition A medical condition caused by an injury or disease that existed prior to the application for health insurance.

preferred provider organization (PPO) A group of medical providers that has contracted with an insurance company or employer to provide health care services to a well-defined group according to a well-defined fee schedule. By accepting discount fees, providers are included on the list of preferred providers.

premium A periodic payment required to purchase an insurance policy.

prepaid group practice An arrangement through which a group contracts with a number of providers who agree to provide medical services to members of the group for a fixed, capitated payment.

price ceiling A maximum price established by law, contract, or agreement.

price discrimination The practice of selling the same good or service to two different consumers for different prices. The price differential is not based on differences in cost.

price floor A minimum price.

primary and preventive care Routine medical care and screening generally provided by physicians specializing in family practice, general internal medicine, and pediatrics.

principal-agent relationship A relationship in which one person (the principal) gives another person (the agent) authority to make decisions on his or her behalf.

probability The likelihood or chance that an event will occur. Probability is measured as a ratio that ranges in value from zero to one.

production function A way to depict the relationship between the inputs in a production process and the resulting output.

prospective payment Payment determined prior to the provision of services. A feature of many managed care organizations that base payment on capitation.

public good A good that is nonrival in distribution and nonexclusive in consumption.

public health Collective action undertaken by government agencies to ensure the health of the community. These efforts include the prevention of disease, identification of health problems, and the assurance of sanitary conditions, especially in the areas of water treatment and waste disposal.

Q

quality-adjusted life years (QALY) A measure of the effectiveness of a medical treatment that captures improvements in the quality of life, as well as extensions in the length of life.

R

rate of return The amount earned on an investment translated into an annual interest rate.

rational behavior A key behavioral assumption in neoclassical economics that decision makers act in a purposeful manner. In other words, their actions are directed toward achieving an objective.

rational ignorance A state in which consumers stop seeking information on a prospective purchase because the expected cost of the additional search exceeds the expected benefits.

reinsurance Stop-loss insurance purchased by a health plan to protect itself against losses that exceed a specific dollar amount per claim, per individual, or per year.

relative-value scale An index that assigns weights to various medical services used to determine the relative fees assigned to them.

resource-based relative value scale (RBRVS) A classification system for physicians' services, using a weighting scheme that reflects the relative value of the various services performed. Developed for Medicare by a group of Harvard researchers, the RBRVS considers time, skill, and overhead cost required for each service. When used in conjunction with a monetary conversion factor, medical fees are determined.

retrospective payment Payment determined after delivery of the good or service. Traditional fee-for-service medicine determines payment retrospectively.

return on sales A financial measure of a firm's ability to generate after-tax profit out of its total sales. Calculated by dividing after-tax profit by total sales.

risk A state in which multiple outcomes are possible, and the likelihood of each possible outcome is known or can be estimated.

S

scarcity A situation that exists when the amount of a good or service demanded in the aggregate exceeds the amount available at a zero price.

self-insurance A group practice of not buying health insurance but setting aside funds to cover the projected losses incurred by members of the group.

self-interest A behavioral assumption of neoclassical economics that individuals are motivated to promote their own interests.

shirk An action taken to avoid responsibility.

short run The increment of time where at least one input is fixed.

sickness fund A quasi-governmental group that serves as an insurance company by collecting premiums and paying providers within the national health care system of France and Germany.

"single-payer" system Usually associated with Canada, a system of financing medical care in which payment comes from a single source, typically the government.

skewed distribution An asymmetric distribution with a majority of the data points lying on one side of the mean, resulting in a tail on the other.

social insurance Serves as the basis of all government redistribution programs. An insurance plan supported by tax revenues and available to everyone regardless of age, health status, and ability to pay.

spending cap A limit on total spending for a given time period.

staff-model HMO A managed care organization that serves as both payer and provider, owns its own facilities, and employs its own physicians.

standard deviation A measure of dispersion equal to the square root of the variance.

statistical relationship Association between two or more random variables indicating correlation or association.

T

technical efficiency Efficiency in production, or cost efficiency.

third-party payers A health insurance arrangement where the individual, or an agent of the individual, pays a set premium to a third party (an insurance company, managed care organization, or the government), which in turn pays for health care services.

total product Total output that results from using different levels of an input.

Type I error Rejecting a hypothesis that is actually true.

Type II error Accepting a hypothesis that is actually false.

U

unbundling Separating a number of related procedures and treating them as individual services for payment purposes.

uncertainty A state in which multiple outcomes are possible but the likelihood of any one outcome is not known.

underwriting The insurance practice of determining whether or not an application for insurance will be accepted. In the process, premiums are also determined.

universal access A guarantee that all citizens who desire health insurance will have access to health insurance regardless of income or health status. Those who cannot afford insurance are usually subsidized, and participation is voluntary.

universal coverage   A guarantee that all citizens will have health insurance coverage regardless of income or health status. Coverage usually requires mandatory participation.

usual, customary, and reasonable (UCR) charges A price ceiling set to limit fees to the minimum of the billed charge, the price customarily charged by the provider, and the prevailing charge in the geographic region.

utilization review   An evaluation of the appropriateness and efficiency of prescribed medical services.

V

variable cost   The total cost of the variable inputs.

variable inputs   Inputs in the production process that are easily incremented.

variance   A measure of dispersion of a set of numbers around their mean.

Index